FOOD & WINE
ANNUAL COOKBOOK 2018

Copyright © 2018 Time Inc. Books

Published by Oxmoor House,
an imprint of Time Inc. Books
225 Liberty Street
New York, NY 10281

FOOD & WINE is a trademark of Time
Inc. Affluent Media Group, registered in
the U.S. and other countries.

SENIOR EDITOR **Betty Wong**
BOOKS EDITOR **Anne Cain**
ART DIRECTOR **James Maikowski**
DESIGNER **Alisha Petro**
PRODUCTION MANAGER
Stephanie Thompson
ASSISTANT PRODUCTION DIRECTOR
Sue Chodakiewicz
ASSISTANT PRODUCTION MANAGER
Diane Rose Keener
PROJECT EDITOR **Tara Stewart Hardee**
COPY EDITOR **Lisa Leventer**
PROOFREADER **Donna Baldone**
INDEXER **Mary Ann Laurens**

ISBN 13: 978-0-8487-5611-6

ISSN: 1097-1564

Printed in the United States of America

10 9 8 7 6 5 4 3 2 1

First Edition 2018

FOOD & WINE MAGAZINE

EDITOR IN CHIEF **Hunter Lewis; Nilou Motamed**
EXECUTIVE EDITOR **Dana Bowen**
DEPUTY EDITOR **Christine Quinlan**
MANAGING EDITOR **Caitlin Miller**
VISUAL DIRECTOR **David Cicconi**
EXECUTIVE FOOD EDITOR **Kate Heddings**
SENIOR FOOD EDITOR **Mary-Frances Heck**
EXECUTIVE WINE EDITOR **Ray Isle**
DIGITAL DIRECTOR **Danica Lo**

FOOD

TEST KITCHEN DEPUTY EDITOR **Justin Chapple**
TEST KITCHEN SENIOR EDITOR **Laura Rege**
TEST KITCHEN ASSOCIATE EDITORS
Anna Painter, Paige McCurdy-Flynn
ASSISTANT EDITOR **Julia Heffelfinger**
TEST KITCHEN ASSISTANT **Kelsey Youngman**

FEATURES

RESTAURANT EDITOR **Jordana Rothman**
DEPUTY DIGITAL EDITORS
Noah Kaufman, Lawrence Marcus
STYLE EDITOR **Suzie Myers**
SENIOR AUDIENCE ENGAGEMENT EDITOR **Meg Clark**
ASSOCIATE RESTAURANT EDITORS **Elyse Inamine,
Marla Yagoda**
ASSISTANT EDITOR **Brianna Wippman**
ASSOCIATE NEWS EDITOR
Adam Campbell-Schmitt
DIGITAL REPORTER **Elisabeth Sherman**
EDITORIAL ASSISTANTS
Morgan Goldberg, Hannah Walhout
WINE INTERNS **Brittany Berkey, Cyle Cucinotta,
Deanna Gonnella**

ART

ART DIRECTOR **James Maikowski**
ASSOCIATE ART DIRECTOR **Kelly McGuire**
DESIGNER **Mark Romero**

PHOTO

PHOTO EDITORS **Mackenzie Craig, Sara Parks**
ASSOCIATE PHOTO EDITOR **Dan Bailey**
PHOTO ASSISTANT **Rebecca Delman**
DIGITAL PHOTO EDITOR **Abby Hocking**

COPY & RESEARCH

COPY CHIEF **Elizabeth Herr**
SENIOR EDITOR **Amanda Woytus**
ASSOCIATE RESEARCH EDITOR **Erin Laverty Healy**

PRODUCTION

DIRECTOR **Joseph Colucci**
MANAGERS **Nestor Cervantes, John Markic**
DIGITAL OPERATIONS EDITOR **Elsa Säätelä**
DIGITAL PRODUCER **Megal Soll**
DIGITAL CONTENT DIRECTOR, FOOD@TIME INC.
Stacey C. Rivera

FRONT COVER

CHICKEN WITH CHARRED-ROSEMARY VINAIGRETTE
PHOTOGRAPHER **Con Poulos**
FOOD STYLIST **Simon Andrews**
STYLE EDITOR **Suzie Myers**

BACK COVER

MOODY TONGUE'S CHOCOLATE CAKE AND GRILLED
STRAWBERRY-AVOCADO TOASTS
PHOTOGRAPHER **Con Poulos**

FRAGRANT RICE WITH PEPITAS AND DATES
PHOTOGRAPHER **Eva Kolenko**

ADDITIONAL PHOTO CREDITS

Julian Broad 317, 377
David Cicconi 159, 194, 228
John Cullen 6 (TOP LEFT, MIDDLE RIGHT), 164,
233, 254
Bobby Fisher 193
Douglas Friedman 261
Ingalls Photography 6 (TOP RIGHT)
Dittie Isager 157, 241
John Kernick 5, 6 (MIDDLE LEFT, BOTTOM
CENTER), 23, 29, 35, 66, 67, 77, 83, 84, 87, 91, 98,
134, 135, 144, 145, 167, 172, 175, 212, 216, 225, 237,
244, 250, 258, 283, 292, 298, 306, 312, 323, 327, 328,
335, 339, 343, 347, 350, 370, 378
Eva Kolenko 17, 33, 39, 55, 65, 101, 153, 178, 210,
213, 245, 252, 289, 302, 311, 325, 336, 361, 366
David Malosh 9, 26, 27
Charles Masters 74, 230
Marcus Nilsson 6 (BOTTOM LEFT) 21, 44, 54, 62,
70, 73, 137, 189, 202, 215, 249, 269, 280, 305, 340,
360, 367, 384
Con Poulos 6 (TOP CENTER, MIDDLE CENTER,
BOTTOM RIGHT), 8, 14, 20, 32, 36, 43, 47, 50, 53,
58, 61, 71, 80, 88, 95, 102, 107, 108, 112, 115, 118,
119, 121, 122, 128, 132, 141, 148, 150, 154, 158, 161,
168, 171, 176, 180, 183, 184, 190, 198, 201, 209, 219,
222, 246, 260, 263, 264, 265, 270, 273, 276, 279, 288,
291, 308, 318, 321, 324, 353, 354, 359, 363, 364,
369, 376, 383
Javier Salas 89
Fredrika Stjärne 180
Christopher Testani 11, 30, 57, 116, 125, 131, 142,
206, 226, 234, 238, 284, 287, 297, 373, 332, 357
Michael Turek 380
Joanna Van Mulder 309

FOOD&**WINE**

ANNUAL
COOKBOOK
2018

AN ENTIRE YEAR
OF COOKING

FOOD&**WINE**
BOOKS

Contents

7 FOREWORD

8 STARTERS

32 SALADS

54 SOUPS & STEWS

70 PASTA & NOODLES

88 FISH & SHELLFISH

118 POULTRY

158 PORK & VEAL

180 BEEF & LAMB

212 VEGETABLES & TOFU

238 POTATOES, GRAINS & BEANS

260 BREADS, PIZZAS & SANDWICHES

288 BREAKFAST & BRUNCH

308 PIES, TARTS & FRUIT DESSERTS

324 CAKES, COOKIES & MORE

360 SNACKS, CONDIMENTS & SAUCES

376 DRINKS

386 RECIPE INDEX

398 CONTRIBUTORS

400 MEASUREMENT GUIDE

Foreword

THIS YEAR HAS SEEN SOME EXCITING changes at Food & Wine with a new hybrid team of talented editors, designers, and test kitchen pros based in both New York City and Birmingham, Alabama. We're honored to be stewards of this 40-year-old brand, and we aim to make the publication even more fun and easier to use in the coming year.

In keeping with that spirit of change, the recipes in this year's *Annual Cookbook* reflect today's ever-evolving culinary landscape and the food trends we're seeing on the horizon. Recipes such as Charred Shishito Peppers with Furikake (p. 231) and Spicy Eggplant Gratin (p. 236) represent the "vegetable forward" movement led by the world's best chefs, but there are also plenty of options for meat lovers such as a stunning Prime Rib with Sour Cherry Conserva, Truffle and Chocolate (p. 192). Alternative flours and sugars that add depth of flavor to desserts like Chocolate, Cinnamon and Almond Loaf Cake (p. 326), and aromatics spices add intrigue to frozen treats like Rosewater-and-Saffron Ice Cream (p. 359) and refreshing drinks like Layered Blackberry-and-Turmeric Lemonade (p. 385).

One thing that has not changed this year is our love of the classics. Recently, our editors traveled to Spain with Chef José Andrés and fell in love (again) with Chicken and Pork Paella (p. 130) and Empanada Gallega with Tuna (p. 286), all washed down with glasses of Rioja and sherry.

And we raise a glass to you. We are proud to share these dynamic flavors from the Food & Wine kitchen, and we hope that you'll use these recipes to celebrate at the table with your friends and family.

—Editors of
FOOD & WINE

STARTERS

The Stinker Cheese
Fondue (p. 27)
OPPOSITE Crab
Summer Rolls with
Nuoc Cham Sauce
(p. 24)

Summer Vegetable Tower
Total **45 min**; Serves **8 to 10**

The key to this impressive tower is seasoning the vegetables before they go on the platter. "We want all the vegetables to be delicious on their own before they take a dunk in any dip or sauce," says Emily Fiffer, co-owner of L.A.'s Botanica. Try tossing some of the veggies with olive oil and seasoning with salt, za'atar, lemon zest or smoked paprika, as we do here.

1 **lb. small potatoes**
  Kosher salt and pepper
1 **Tbsp. plus 2 tsp. extra-virgin olive oil, plus more for brushing**
¼ **tsp. smoked paprika**
8 **oz. multicolored carrots, sliced ½ inch thick on the bias**
  Beet Muhammara (recipe follows), for serving
  Green Tahini (recipe follows), for serving
  Grilled ciabatta bread, sliced vegetables—such as radishes with greens, pattypan squash, thinly sliced fennel, sliced Persian cucumbers, endive spears, Romanesco and/or cauliflower florets, blanched Broccolini and blanched green and/or wax beans— for serving
  Edible flowers and herb sprigs (optional), for garnish

1. In a large pot, cover the potatoes with cold water and bring to a boil. Add a generous pinch of salt and simmer until tender, 15 to 20 minutes. Drain and let cool, then halve the potatoes.

2. Light a grill and oil the grate. In a medium bowl, toss the potatoes with 1 tablespoon of the olive oil and ⅛ teaspoon of the paprika. Season with salt and pepper. Grill the potatoes, turning, until lightly charred, about 6 minutes. Transfer to a plate and let cool completely. Keep the grill on.

3. Meanwhile, in a medium bowl, toss the carrots with the remaining 2 teaspoons of olive oil and ⅛ teaspoon of paprika. Season with salt and pepper. Grill the carrots, turning once, until tender and lightly charred, about 6 minutes. Transfer to a plate and let cool completely.

4. Set the muhammara and tahini on a large platter or tiered stand. Arrange the grilled bread and the blanched, grilled and raw vegetables in bunches around the dips. Garnish with edible flowers and herb sprigs; serve. —*Emily Fiffer and Heather Sperling*

BEET MUHAMMARA
Total **5 min**; Makes **about 1⅓ cups**

This vibrant purple dip, a take on the Middle Eastern red pepper spread, gets great flavor from beet, cumin and walnuts. "I love the texture and sweet earthiness that come from the raw beet," says Fiffer.

1½ **tsp. ground cumin**
1 **large red beet, peeled and chopped**
¾ **cup chopped toasted walnuts, plus more for garnish**
3 **Tbsp. fresh lemon juice**
1 **Tbsp. pomegranate molasses**
1 **garlic clove**
1¼ **tsp. Urfa biber (see Note), plus more for garnish**
¼ **cup extra-virgin olive oil**
  Kosher salt

In a small skillet, toast the cumin over moderately high heat until fragrant, 1 minute. Transfer to a food processor. Add the beet, ¾ cup of walnuts, lemon juice, pomegranate molasses, garlic and the 1¼ teaspoons of Urfa. Pulse to finely chop. With the machine on, drizzle in the olive oil until the dip is almost smooth. Season with salt. Transfer to a small bowl and garnish with more walnuts and Urfa. —*EF and HS*

NOTE Urfa biber, or Urfa pepper, is a smoky, sour Turkish chile. It's available at laboiteny.com or amazon.com.

MAKE AHEAD The muhammara can be refrigerated for up to 1 week.

GREEN TAHINI
Total **10 min**; Makes **about 1⅓ cups**

¾ **cup chopped dill sprigs**
½ **cup tahini**
½ **cup fresh lime juice (from 4 limes)**
2 **Tbsp. extra-virgin olive oil**
1 **tsp. finely chopped garlic**
1 **tsp. vadouvan (see Note)**
  Kosher salt

In a blender, combine the first 6 ingredients until smooth. With the machine on, drizzle in ⅓ cup of warm water until incorporated. If the dip is too thick, add more water, 1 tablespoon at a time. Season generously with salt. Transfer to a small bowl. —*EF and HS*

NOTE Vadouvan, a French spice blend inspired by Indian curry, is available at Whole Foods and from amazon.com.

MAKE AHEAD The tahini can be refrigerated for up to 1 week.

Crudité Upgrade

Best New Chef alum Grant Achatz shares his secrets to making a majestic crudité platter.

SEASON THE VEGETABLES LIKE MEAT Achatz dresses carrots and blanched green beans in a basic vinaigrette to add dimension.

BREAK OUT YOUR MANDOLINE Vary the chopping style—wedges, matchsticks, slices—to add visual and textural interest.

EMBRACE THE FRUDITÉ "There's only so much raw broccoli you can eat," says the chef, who advocates for fruit on every crudité platter.

TURN UP THE PLUMAGE "It's cliché, but you eat with your eyes first," Achatz says. Garnish your platter with bushy bouquets of herbs, like tarragon, chive and chervil bundled up with lettuce.

Summer Vegetable Tower

Grilled Rockamole

Active **30 min**; Total **1 hr 30 min**; Serves **8**

Marfa, Texas, chef Rocky Barnette calls his eponymous grilled-avocado guacamole "vegan foie gras" because of its creamy texture. Chargrilling the avocados gives the guac a smoky dimension.

- ½ **large red onion, cut into ¼-inch dice**
- ½ **cup finely chopped cilantro**
- 4 **small jalapeños, seeded and finely chopped**
- ⅓ **cup fresh lime juice, plus more for brushing**
- 3 **Tbsp. avocado oil, plus more for brushing**

  Kosher salt and pepper
- 5 **firm, ripe Hass avocados, halved and pitted**

  Pinch of ground cumin

  Tostones (recipe follows) or plantain chips, for serving

1. In a medium bowl, combine the onion with the cilantro, jalapeños, the ⅓ cup of lime juice and 1 tablespoon of the oil. Season with salt. Cover the pico de gallo and refrigerate for 1 hour.

2. Light a grill and oil the grate. Lightly brush the cut sides of the avocados with oil and lime juice; season with salt. Grill cut side down over high heat until charred, about 2 minutes. Transfer to a plate and let cool.

3. Scoop the avocado flesh into a large bowl and coarsely mash with a fork. Gently fold in 1 cup of the pico de gallo, the remaining 2 tablespoons of oil and the cumin and season generously with salt and pepper. Garnish with the remaining ⅓ cup of pico de gallo. Serve with tostones. —*Rocky Barnette*

MAKE AHEAD The guacamole can be covered with plastic wrap and refrigerated overnight.

TOSTONES

Total **1 hr**; Serves **8**

These twice-fried plantains make crispy yet chewy scoopers for guacamole.

- 4 **large green plantains**

  Vegetable oil, for frying

  Sea salt, preferably sal de gusano (see Note) or Himalayan

1. Cut off the ends of the plantains. Using a knife, score each one lengthwise 3 times and pry off the peel. Slice the plantains crosswise into 2-inch pieces.

2. In a deep skillet, heat 1½ inches of oil to 350°. Fry the plantains in batches, turning occasionally, until light golden, about 5 minutes per batch. Using a slotted spoon, transfer the plantains to a paper towel–lined baking sheet to cool. Using a small skillet, flatten each plantain ⅛ inch thick between 2 sheets of parchment paper.

3. Reheat the oil to 350°. Fry the flattened plantains in batches, turning once, until golden and crispy, 4 to 6 minutes per batch. Transfer to a paper towel–lined baking sheet as they're done and season generously with sea salt. Serve right away. —*RB*

NOTE Sal de gusano, or worm salt, is Oaxacan sea salt flavored with dried worms and chiles.

Deviled Crab Dip

Active **20 min**; Total **40 min** Serves **8 to 10**

Make this creamy crab dip in a large baking dish for a crowd, or divide into 6-ounce ramekins for individual servings.

- 8 **oz. cream cheese, softened**
- ⅓ **cup crème fraîche**
- ¼ **cup packed tarragon leaves, chopped**
- ½ **cup packed parsley leaves, chopped**
- 1 **Tbsp. toasted benne or sesame seeds, plus more for garnish**
- 2 **tsp. finely grated lemon zest plus 4 tsp. fresh lemon juice**
- 2 **tsp. kosher salt**
- ½ **tsp. smoked paprika**
- ¼ **tsp. pepper**
- 1 **lb. lump crabmeat, picked over**

  Saltine crackers and crudités, for serving

Preheat the oven to 350°. In a stand mixer fitted with the paddle, beat all of the ingredients through the pepper on low speed until smooth. Using a spatula, gently fold in the crab. Transfer to a 1-quart baking dish and bake until heated through and the edges are bubbling, 20 minutes. Garnish with more benne seeds and serve with crackers and crudités. —*Joe Kindred*

MAKE AHEAD The unbaked crab dip can be refrigerated overnight. Bring to room temperature before baking.

WINE Flinty Sauvignon Blanc: 2016 Domaine Vacheron Sancerre.

Brock Eggs

Active **1 hr**; Total **3 hr 30 min**; Serves **4**

At The Pig Brockenhurst in Hampshire, England, chef James Golding plays on classic Scotch eggs with these deep-fried ham-encased quail eggs. Bubbly is the perfect thing to drink with them.

- 8 **ham hocks (6 lbs.)**
- 1 **onion, coarsely chopped**
- 1 **leek, white and light green parts only, coarsely chopped**
- 1 **celery rib, coarsely chopped**
- 1 **carrot, coarsely chopped**
- 1 **tsp. black peppercorns**
- 1 **bay leaf**
- 1 **Tbsp. coarsely chopped thyme leaves**

  Fine sea salt and pepper
- 3 **Tbsp. chopped flat-leaf parsley**
- 1 **large egg yolk**
- 1 **Tbsp. white wine vinegar**
- ½ **Tbsp. Dijon mustard**
- 4½ **cups canola oil**
- 8 **quail eggs**
- ½ **cup all-purpose flour**
- ½ **cup fine dry breadcrumbs**
- 2 **large eggs, beaten**

  Celery salt, for serving

  Baby beet greens, for garnish (optional)

1. In a large pot, combine the ham hocks with the onion, leek, celery, carrot, peppercorns, bay leaf, thyme and 1 teaspoon of salt. Cover with 1 inch of cold water and simmer over moderately low heat, partially covered, until the meat is tender, about 2½ hours. Strain the stock into a medium bowl. Transfer the ham hocks to a work surface to cool, then remove the meat from the bones and finely shred (discard the other solids). Transfer the ham to a medium bowl, stir in the parsley and season with pepper. Moisten with about 2 tablespoons of stock, stirring until the mixture comes together. Save the remaining stock for another use.

2. Meanwhile, in a blender, combine the egg yolk, vinegar and mustard. With the machine running, slowly add ½ cup of the oil until the dressing is emulsified. Transfer to a small bowl and season with salt and pepper. Cover and keep chilled.

3. In a saucepan, cover the quail eggs with 1 inch of cold water. Bring to a simmer, then cook over moderate heat for 2½ minutes. Immediately transfer to a bowl of ice water. Let stand for 3 minutes, then peel carefully.

4. Divide the meat mixture into 8 portions, about 3 tablespoons each. Place the meat in the palm of your hand, top with a quail egg, then enclose the egg in the meat. Transfer to a plate and refrigerate for 30 minutes.

5. In a saucepan, heat the remaining oil to 350°. Arrange the flour, breadcrumbs and beaten eggs in separate bowls; season each with salt and pepper. Dip each egg patty in the flour, then the eggs, then the breadcrumbs, shaking off any excess. Working in 2 batches, fry over moderate heat, turning once, until golden brown, 2 to 3 minutes. With a slotted spoon, transfer to paper towels to drain. Spoon some mustard dressing onto plates. Halve the eggs and place on the plates. Sprinkle with celery salt and garnish with beet greens, if desired. —*James Golding*

MAKE AHEAD The recipe can be prepared through Step 4 and refrigerated overnight.

WINE English sparkling wine with lemon-blossom notes and fine, zesty acidity: 2013 Hattingley Valley Classic Reserve.

Pickled Onions with Trout Roe and Verbena

Active **1 hr**; Total **1 hr 40 min** plus overnight pickling and sitting; Serves **4**

This smart and delicious starter from chef Jordan Kahn of L.A.'s Destroyer is a perfect dish for aspiring chefs to make. It begins with pickled onion petals that are filled with trout roe, tiny peas and lemon curd, then finishes with a dusting of lemon verbena powder and a spoonful of verbena oil.

PICKLED ONIONS

- **2 large spring onions—bulbs halved, cored and separated into petals (stems reserved for another use)**
- **10 fresh lemon verbena leaves**
- **1 cup apple cider vinegar**
- **3 Tbsp. sugar**
  Kosher salt

LEMON CURD

- **3 Tbsp. fresh lemon juice**
- **1 large egg**
- **1½ tsp. light corn syrup**
- **¼ tsp. kosher salt**
- **4 Tbsp. softened unsalted butter, cut into pieces**

VERBENA OIL AND POWDER

- **1 cup packed fresh lemon verbena leaves**
- **⅓ cup grapeseed oil**

SNAP PEA SALAD

- **¾ lb. sugar snap peas, shelled (⅓ cup peas)**
- **¾ tsp. fresh lime juice**
- **½ tsp. virgin sunflower seed oil**
  Sea salt
- **4 tsp. trout roe**
  Watercress, for garnish

1. **Pickle the onions** Pack the onion petals into a clean 2-cup glass jar. In a small saucepan, combine the lemon verbena with the vinegar, sugar, 1 teaspoon of salt and ¼ cup of water; bring to a boil. Pour the brine over the onions; add additional warm water if the onions are not fully submerged. Close the jar and refrigerate the onions overnight.

2. **Make the lemon curd** In a small saucepan, whisk the lemon juice with the egg, corn syrup and salt. Bring to a simmer over moderately low heat, whisking constantly, about 3 minutes. As soon as the mixture comes to a simmer, transfer it to a blender. With the machine on, gradually blend in the butter until smooth, about 45 seconds. Transfer to an airtight container and refrigerate the lemon curd overnight.

3. **Make the verbena oil and powder** In a small saucepan of boiling water, blanch ⅓ cup of the lemon verbena for 10 seconds. Transfer to a small bowl of ice water to cool completely. Drain and squeeze the lemon verbena dry, then transfer to a blender. Add the grapeseed oil and puree at high speed for 4 minutes. Cover and refrigerate overnight. Strain the oil through a cheesecloth-lined fine sieve before using.

4. Preheat the oven to 225°. Spread the remaining ⅔ cup of lemon verbena in an even layer on a small rimmed baking sheet. Bake for about 10 minutes, until the leaves are dry and crisp. Transfer to a spice grinder and let cool, then grind the leaves to a powder.

5. **Make the snap pea salad** In a small bowl, combine the shelled peas with the lime juice and sunflower oil; season with sea salt. Remove 8 of the onion cups from the pickling liquid and blot dry with paper towels; reserve the remaining pickled onions for another use. Spoon ½ teaspoon of trout roe into each onion cup and top with the pea salad and lemon curd, so that the filling is flush with the top of the onion cup. Carefully flip the onion cups over. Using a small fine sieve, dust the top of the onions with the verbena powder. Use a spatula to transfer the onion cups one by one to clean plates. Place a spoonful of verbena oil on the plate. Garnish with watercress and serve. —*Jordan Kahn*

WINE Citrusy Loire sparkling wine: NV Domaine de la Taille aux Loups Brut Tradition.

Chilled Tofu with
Apple Soy Sauce

Green Zebra Tomatoes with Tomato-Dashi Sorbet

Active **40 min**; Total **3 hr 15 min**; Serves **4**

Chef Noah Sandoval of Chicago's Oriole highlights summer's sweetest tomatoes by serving them alongside a savory dashi- and-tomato-water-based sorbet. The dish is cold and refreshing—ideal for a hot summer day.

- **4** lbs. vine-ripe red tomatoes, quartered
- **3** Tbsp. unseasoned rice vinegar
- **2** Tbsp. sugar
- **1½** tsp. kosher salt
  One 5-gram bag bonito flakes (¼ cup plus 2 Tbsp.)
  Three 4-inch pieces of kombu (½ oz.)
- **8** small green zebra or heirloom tomatoes, cut into wedges
  Flaky sea salt and freshly ground black pepper
  Cilantro and mint leaves, for garnish

1. Juice the red tomatoes in an electric juicer (you should have 4 cups of juice). In a medium saucepan, combine the tomato juice with the rice vinegar, sugar and kosher salt and bring just to a boil. Remove from the heat and add the bonito flakes and kombu. Let steep for 20 min- utes, then discard the kombu. Transfer the mixture to a blender and puree until very smooth, then strain through cheesecloth into a medium bowl. Refrigerate the sorbet base until it is well chilled, about 2 hours.

2. Transfer the chilled sorbet base to an ice cream maker and freeze according to the manufacturer's directions.

3. Meanwhile, arrange the green tomato wedges in 4 shallow bowls and season with sea salt and pepper. Garnish with cilantro and mint. Add 2 small scoops of the sorbet to each bowl and serve right away. —*Noah Sandoval*

MAKE AHEAD The sorbet is best eaten right away but can be frozen for up to 2 days.

WINE Flinty, tart Pouilly-Fumé: 2015 de Ladoucette.

Chilled Tofu with Apple Soy Sauce

Total **30 min**; Serves **6**

- **¼** cup Fuji apple juice
- **1** Tbsp. soy sauce
- **1** Tbsp. unseasoned rice vinegar
- **4** mixed radishes, very thinly sliced
- **1** large scallion, cut into 2-inch lengths and julienned
- **¼** cup cilantro stems, very thinly sliced on the bias
- **1** lb. cold silken tofu, cut into 6 pieces
- **1½** tsp. hot sesame oil
  Toasted sesame seeds, for garnish

1. In a small bowl, whisk the apple juice with the soy sauce and vinegar. In another small bowl, toss the radishes with the scallion and cilantro. Refrigerate the sauce and slaw separately until they are nicely chilled, about 15 minutes.

2. Divide the tofu among 6 bowls. Spoon the apple soy sauce on top. Pile the slaw on top of the tofu and drizzle each with ¼ teaspoon of the hot sesame oil. Garnish with toasted sesame seeds and serve cold. —*Justin Chapple*

Herbed Ricotta with Grilled Bread

Total **30 min**; Serves **8**

- **1** lb. fresh ricotta cheese
- **1** tsp. finely grated lemon zest plus 3 Tbsp. fresh lemon juice
- **1** garlic clove, finely grated
- **¼** cup extra-virgin olive oil, plus more for brushing and drizzling
- **1** cup finely chopped mixed chives, parsley, mint and tarragon, plus more for garnish
  Kosher salt and pepper
- **2** baguettes, split lengthwise
  Fresh cracked black pepper, for garnish

1. In a food processor, puree the ricotta, lemon zest, lemon juice, garlic and the ¼ cup of olive oil until smooth. Scrape into a medium bowl, stir in the herbs and season generously with salt and pepper.

2. Light a grill. Brush the baguettes with olive oil. Grill over moderately high heat, turning once, until lightly charred, 3 min- utes. Drizzle the herbed ricotta with olive oil and garnish with herbs and cracked pepper. Serve with the bread. —*Justin Chapple*

Tomatillo Toasts with Prosciutto and Manchego

Total **20 min**; Serves **4**

Inspired by classic *pan con tomate*, a Catalan dish of bread rubbed with fresh tomato, F&W's Justin Chapple tops grilled rustic bread with grated tomatillos, thin slices of prosciutto and shaved Manchego cheese. Serve these savory toasts with wine or cocktails.

  Four 1-inch-thick slices of rustic bread
- **2** Tbsp. extra-virgin olive oil, plus more for brushing
- **1** lb. tomatillos—husked, rinsed and halved
- **½** tsp. crushed red pepper
  Kosher salt and black pepper
- **4** oz. thinly sliced prosciutto
  Shaved Manchego cheese, for topping

1. Light a grill or preheat a grill pan. Brush the bread with olive oil and grill over high heat, turning once, until lightly charred, about 2 minutes. Transfer to a work surface.

2. Working over a medium bowl, grate the tomatillo halves on the large holes of a box grater until only the skins remain; discard the skins. Stir in the 2 tablespoons of olive oil and the crushed red pepper. Season generously with salt and black pepper.

3. Spoon the tomatillo mixture evenly on the toasts and top with the prosciutto. Top generously with shaved Manchego and serve right away. —*Justin Chapple*

MAKE AHEAD The grated tomatillo mixture can be refrigerated for up to 3 days.

WINE Bright, fruity Rioja: 2011 Marqués de Riscal Reserva.

Spinach-and-Arugula Bruschetta with Dukka

Total **45 min**; Makes **20**

These vegetable-heavy toasts get a flavor hit from dukka, the Middle East's seriously addictive nut-and-spice blend. (You'll want to eat it like a snack.)

- **2 Tbsp.** walnut pieces
- **3 Tbsp.** coriander seeds
- **2 Tbsp.** toasted sesame seeds
- **½ tsp.** freshly grated nutmeg
  Kosher salt and pepper
- **3 Tbsp.** extra-virgin olive oil, plus more for brushing
- **1** large onion, thinly sliced
- **2¼ lbs.** leaf spinach, stemmed
- **20** baguette slices
- **2 cups** baby arugula
- **1 Tbsp.** fresh lemon juice

1. In a mortar, using a pestle, finely grind the walnuts with the coriander, sesame and nutmeg. Season the dukka with salt.

2. In a large saucepan, heat the 3 tablespoons of olive oil. Add the onion and cook over moderate heat, stirring, until lightly browned, about 10 minutes. Stir in the spinach in large handfuls, letting each wilt slightly before adding more, 5 to 7 minutes. Season with salt and pepper.

3. Meanwhile, light a grill or preheat a grill pan. Brush the baguette slices with olive oil and grill over high heat, turning, until lightly charred, 2 to 4 minutes. Transfer to a platter.

4. In a medium bowl, toss the arugula with the lemon juice and season with salt and pepper. Top the baguette slices with the spinach and arugula, sprinkle with the dukka and serve. —*Dan Zoaretz*

Smoked-Trout Crackers with Broken Tapenade

Total **30 min**; Serves **8**

Chef Eli Dahlin heats this two-ingredient olive tapenade to draw out the oil. The result is a quick, briny sauce that's fantastic drizzled on smoked fish, roasted vegetables or a sandwich with spicy cured meats.

- **¼ cup** pitted kalamata olives
- **3 Tbsp.** extra-virgin olive oil
- **8 oz.** feta cheese, crumbled
  Seeded crackers
- **12 oz.** smoked-trout fillets, skin and bones discarded and flesh flaked
  Baby arugula, for garnish

1. In a food processor, pulse the olives with the olive oil until finely chopped. Scrape into a small saucepan and cook over moderately low heat, stirring occasionally, until the oil separates and the mixture looks broken, 2 to 3 minutes. Transfer the tapenade to a small bowl. Clean the food processor.

2. In the food processor, puree the feta until smooth. Transfer to a small bowl. To serve, spread the feta on crackers and top with the smoked trout, broken tapenade and arugula. —*Eli Dahlin*

Amp Up Hors d'oeuvres

Pop open a tin of salty sardines, smoky smelt or spicy octopus suggests chef Zoi Antonitsas of Seattle's Little Fish. "Just because it comes out of a tin doesn't mean it's a lesser ingredient—sometimes, it's a better one."

KEEP IT SIMPLE Antonitsas likes to serve fatty sardines on thin crackers with flecks of parsley.

UP THE FLAVOR Add canned squid or sardines to puttanesca sauce for a savory heft.

USE THE OIL Hang on to leftover sardine oil for homemade aioli or a great Caesar salad base.

Potato, Tuna and Pepper Confetti Pintxos

Active **20 min**; Total **1 hr 20 min**
Makes **12**

Pintxos are bite-size bar snacks served in the Basque region of Spain. This one is an authentic combination of potato, flaked tuna and vinegary peppers and onion piled on crisp toast. It's spectacular served with Spanish wine.

- **¼ cup** minced red bell pepper
- **¼ cup** minced green bell pepper
- **¼ cup** minced white onion
- **3 Tbsp.** canola oil
- **3 Tbsp.** white wine vinegar
  Kosher salt and pepper
- **1** medium Yukon Gold potato
  Twelve ½-inch-thick baguette slices, toasted
  Mayonnaise, for spreading
  Two 6-oz. jars oil-packed tuna, preferably ventresca (from the belly), drained and flaked
- **6** cornichons, halved lengthwise

1. In a medium bowl, mix the bell peppers with the onion, canola oil, vinegar and a generous pinch each of salt and pepper. Let stand at room temperature for 1 hour.

2. Meanwhile, in a saucepan, cover the potato with water and bring to a boil. Add a generous pinch of salt and simmer over moderate heat until tender, 20 to 25 minutes. Drain and cool; peel and thinly slice.

3. Spread each toast with mayonnaise. Top the toasts with the potato, flaked tuna, pepper confetti and cornichons. Serve. —*Anya von Bremzen*

WINE Crisp, peach-scented Godello: 2015 Bodegas Godeval.

Smoked-Trout Crackers
with Broken Tapenade

Crab and Smoked Salmon Pintxos with Vanilla Oil

⏱ Active **20 min**; Total **40 min**; Makes **12**

These delightful little bites combine a lemony fresh crab salad with smoked salmon and salty pops of salmon roe. A drizzle of fragrant vanilla oil is a surprise complement to the seafood, but it can be optional.

¼ cup grapeseed oil

½ vanilla bean, split lengthwise and seeds scraped

6 oz. jumbo lump crabmeat, picked over

2 Tbsp. mayonnaise

2 Tbsp. minced chives, plus snipped chives for garnish

1 Tbsp. fresh lemon juice

Kosher salt and pepper

Twelve ½-inch-thick baguette slices, toasted

3 oz. smoked salmon, cut into 12 pieces

2 Tbsp. salmon roe

1. In a microwave-safe bowl, heat the oil at high power until warm, 15 to 25 seconds. Whisk in the vanilla seeds and let cool completely, about 20 minutes.

2. In a medium bowl, gently mix the crab with the mayonnaise, 2 Tbsp. minced chives and lemon juice. Season with salt and pepper. To serve, spoon the crab salad on the toasts and top with the smoked salmon, salmon roe, a drizzle of the vanilla oil and snipped chives. —*Anya von Bremzen*

MAKE AHEAD The crab salad can be refrigerated overnight.

WINE Citrusy, mineral-tinged Albariño: 2015 Do Ferreiro.

Herbed Salmon Tartare with Chips

⏱ Active **15 min**; Total **45 min**
Serves **8**

This is a great tartare for people who aren't sure if they like raw fish, since it combines both raw and hot-smoked salmon, which, along with cucumber, cornichons and crème fraîche, give this dish an appealing range of texture and flavor.

1 English cucumber—peeled, seeded and cut into ¼-inch pieces
Fine sea salt and pepper

8 oz. skinless salmon fillet, finely chopped

8 oz. skinless hot-smoked salmon fillet, finely chopped

½ cup finely chopped chives

½ cup finely chopped dill sprigs

12 cornichons, finely chopped

1 small shallot, finely chopped

1 Tbsp. fresh lemon juice

¾ cup crème fraîche

Potato chips or crostini, for serving

1. In a colander set over a bowl, toss the cucumber with 2 teaspoons of sea salt and let stand for 30 minutes. Rinse the cucumber well and pat dry with paper towels.

2. Transfer the cucumber to a medium bowl and stir in the fresh salmon, hot-smoked salmon, chives, dill, cornichons, shallot and lemon juice. Gently fold in the crème fraîche until just incorporated. Season with salt and pepper and serve with potato chips or crostini.
—*Nadine Levy Redzepi*

WINE Complex rosé Champagne: NV Fleury Rosé de Saignée Brut.

Beet-and-Vodka-Cured Gravlax

Total **45 min** plus 2 to 3 days curing
Serves **6**

⅓ cup turbinado sugar

½ cup fine sea salt, plus more for seasoning

3 Tbsp. vodka

2 Tbsp. orange zest plus 6 Tbsp. fresh orange juice (from 2 large oranges)

1 Tbsp. lemon zest plus 3 Tbsp. fresh lemon juice (from 1 large lemon)

2 lbs. center-cut skin-on salmon fillet, pinbones removed

2 large beets, coarsely shredded

¼ cup mayonnaise

3 Tbsp. Dijon mustard

2 Tbsp. chopped fresh dill

1 Tbsp. finely grated fresh peeled horseradish

1 lb. celery root, peeled and coarsely shredded (4 cups)

Sliced cocktail rye bread or rye crackers, for serving

1. In a medium bowl, whisk the sugar and ½ cup of salt with the vodka and the citrus zest and juice until the sugar dissolves. Place the salmon, skin side down, in a glass or ceramic dish lined with a large sheet of plastic wrap. Spread the sugar-citrus mixture evenly on the fish, then pat the beets on top. Wrap tightly in the plastic. Top with a plate and a few heavy cans to weigh it down. Refrigerate until the fish feels firm and looks cured in the center, 2 to 3 days. The sides of the fillet will have the strongest flavor and driest texture.

2. In a medium bowl, whisk the mayonnaise with the Dijon, dill and horseradish until smooth. Stir in the celery root and season the remoulade with salt.

3. Rinse the cured salmon and pat dry. Slice very thinly across the grain and serve with the remoulade and rye bread.
—*Dane Allchorne*

MAKE AHEAD The cured and rinsed gravlax can be wrapped tightly in plastic and refrigerated for up to 1 week. The remoulade can be refrigerated for up to 2 days.

Striped Bass Crudo with Popcorn Crema and Shishito Vinaigrette

📷 PAGE 20

⏱ Total **45 min**; Serves **4**

¼ cup extra-virgin olive oil

2 oz. shishito peppers, stemmed and thinly sliced crosswise (1 cup)

2 large garlic cloves, finely chopped

⅓ cup seasoned rice vinegar

2 Tbsp. fresh lime juice

2 Tbsp. finely chopped tarragon

1 Tbsp. finely chopped parsley, plus small leaves for garnish

1 Tbsp. finely chopped chives, plus snipped chives for garnish

½ tsp. crushed red pepper

Kosher salt

1 Tbsp. unsalted butter

1 large shallot, finely chopped

1½ cups heavy cream

4 cups plain popped popcorn, plus more for garnish

½ lb. skinless striped bass fillet, sliced on the bias ⅛ inch thick

Flaky sea salt and freshly cracked black pepper, for sprinkling

1. In a small saucepan, heat the olive oil. Add the peppers and garlic and cook over moderately low heat, stirring occasionally, until just softened, about 3 minutes. Scrape the mixture into a small bowl and whisk in the vinegar, lime juice, herbs and crushed red pepper. Season the vinaigrette with salt.

2. In a medium saucepan, melt the butter. Add the shallot and cook over moderately low heat, stirring frequently, until softened, about 3 minutes. Add the cream and the 4 cups of popcorn and cook, stirring occasionally, until the popcorn breaks down and the mixture is creamy, about 10 minutes. Scrape the mixture into a high-speed blender and puree until smooth. Strain the crema through a fine sieve set over a medium bowl and season with salt.

3. Spread some of the crema onto 4 small plates. Arrange the fish over it and drizzle with the vinaigrette. Sprinkle with flaky salt and black pepper, garnish with parsley leaves, snipped chives and popcorn, and serve. —*Michael Scelfo*

WINE Fresh, zesty Sicilian white: 2015 Tenuta Capofaro Didyme Malvasia.

Crispy Squid with Everything Chutney

Total **1 hr**; Serves **4**

CHUTNEY

½ cup mayonnaise

¼ cup ketchup

2½ Tbsp. tomato pickle (see Note)

1½ Tbsp. chopped cilantro

1½ Tbsp. chopped mint

1½ Tbsp. finely chopped peeled fresh ginger

1½ Tbsp. chopped garlic

1 Tbsp. plus 1 tsp. tamarind paste (see Note)

1 Tbsp. fresh lime juice

1 Tbsp. finely grated jaggery (see Note)

Kosher salt and pepper

SQUID

Canola oil, for frying

1½ cups tempura flour (see Note)

1 cup ice water

1 cup white rice flour (see Note)

¾ lb. cleaned squid, bodies cut into ½-inch-thick rings and tentacles left whole

Kosher salt

Chaat masala (see Note) and thinly sliced scallions, for garnish

1. Make the chutney In a blender, puree all of the ingredients until smooth. Strain through a fine sieve set over a medium bowl; discard the solids. Season the chutney with salt and pepper.

2. Make the squid In a large enameled cast-iron casserole, heat 3 inches of oil to 350°. In a large bowl, whisk the tempura flour and ice water until smooth. Spread the rice flour in a shallow bowl. Working in 3 batches, dip the squid in the tempura batter, then dredge in the rice flour and shake off any excess. Add the squid to the hot oil and fry until golden and crisp, 1 to 2 minutes. Using a slotted spoon, transfer the squid to a paper towel–lined plate to drain; season with salt. Transfer to a platter and sprinkle with chaat masala and scallions. Serve with the chutney. —*Manish Mehrotra*

NOTE Tomato pickle, tamarind paste, jaggery and chaat masala are available at Indian groceries. Look for tempura and white rice flours at Whole Foods.

Poached Oysters with Pickled Cucumber and Caviar

⏱ Active **30 min**; Total **45 min**; Serves **4**

One 8-oz. cucumber—peeled, seeded and julienned

Fine sea salt

⅓ cup plus ¼ cup cider vinegar

2 tsp. sugar

⅓ cup dry white wine

1 medium shallot, minced

⅓ cup heavy cream

4 Tbsp. chilled unsalted butter, diced

½ tsp. fresh lime juice

2 dozen freshly shucked large oysters with their liquor, 24 shells reserved for serving

Black caviar, for serving

1. In a small bowl, toss the cucumber with ½ teaspoon of salt and let stand for 10 minutes. Rinse and drain well in a sieve. In the bowl, stir ¼ cup of the cider vinegar with the sugar and ¼ teaspoon of salt. Stir in the cucumber and refrigerate for 20 minutes. Drain.

2. Meanwhile, in a small saucepan, combine the remaining ⅓ cup of vinegar with the wine and shallot. Boil over moderately high heat until the liquid is almost completely evaporated, 6 to 8 minutes. Add the cream and simmer over moderately low heat for 5 minutes. Strain the mixture through a fine sieve into a bowl, pressing on the solids, then return to the saucepan; discard the solids. Off the heat, whisk in the butter, a couple of pieces at a time, adding more as the previous addition is incorporated. Stir in the lime juice and season with salt. Keep the beurre blanc warm.

3. Arrange the oyster shells on a platter. In a small skillet, simmer the oysters with their liquor over moderate heat until the edges begin to curl, 1 to 2 minutes. Transfer each oyster to a shell. Spoon some of the beurre blanc on each and top with pickled cucumber and caviar. Serve immediately. —*Stephen Harris*

WINE Minerally, crisp sparkling wine: 2011 Gusbourne Blanc de Blancs.

Striped Bass Crudo
with Popcorn Crema
and Shishito
Vinaigrette (p. 19)
OPPOSITE Steamed
Shrimp Dumplings with
Chinese Chives (p. 22)

Shrimp with Green Banana Cocktail Sauce

Active **1 hr**; Total **2 hr 15 min**; Serves **6**

Chefs Bryan and Michael Voltaggio serve this shrimp cocktail with pickled daikon. For a perfect bite, wrap the shrimp with the daikon and Thai basil before dipping in the cocktail sauce. You'll thank us later.

PICKLED DAIKON

- 1 **lb. daikon, peeled and very thinly sliced lengthwise, preferably on a mandoline**
- ½ **cup mirin**
- ½ **cup unseasoned rice vinegar**
- 5 **Sichuan peppercorns**
- 2 **star anise**
- 1 **Tbsp. sugar**
- 2 **tsp. kosher salt**

COCKTAIL SAUCE

- 1 **green banana, peeled and cut into ½-inch pieces**
- 1 **cup ketchup**
- ½ **cup sweet chili sauce**
- 3 **Tbsp. drained prepared horseradish**
- 2 **Tbsp. fresh lemon juice**
- 1 **Tbsp. shoyu or other soy sauce**

SHRIMP

- 4 **garlic cloves**
- 2 **lemongrass stalks, cut into 2-inch pieces**
- 1 **jalapeño, halved lengthwise**
- 1 **bay leaf**
- 1 **kaffir lime leaf**
- 3 **Tbsp. kosher salt**
- ¼ **tsp. whole allspice**
- ¼ **tsp. coriander seeds**
- ¼ **tsp. black peppercorns**
- 1 **small cinnamon stick**
- 2 **lbs. extra-jumbo shrimp (16 to 20 per lb.)**
  Shrimp chips (see Note) and Thai basil leaves, for serving

1. Make the pickles Put the daikon in a heatproof medium bowl. In a medium saucepan, bring the remaining ingredients to a simmer, stirring to dissolve the sugar. Pour the hot brine over the daikon and let cool slightly. Cover and refrigerate for at least 2 hours.

2. Meanwhile, make the sauce In a small saucepan, combine all of the ingredients and cook over moderately low heat, stirring occasionally, until thickened slightly, about 30 minutes. Let cool slightly. Transfer to a blender and puree until smooth. Transfer to a small bowl, cover and refrigerate until chilled, about 1 hour.

3. Make the shrimp Prepare an ice bath. In a large saucepan, combine the garlic, lemongrass, jalapeño, bay leaf, lime leaf, salt and spices with 8 cups of water and bring to a boil. Reduce the heat to moderately low, add the shrimp and simmer until just cooked through, about 7 minutes. Drain and transfer the shrimp to the ice bath. Let cool completely. Drain, peel and devein the shrimp, leaving the tail end intact; discard the shells and aromatics.

4. Serve the shrimp with the drained pickled daikon, cocktail sauce, shrimp chips and basil. —*Bryan Voltaggio and Michael Voltaggio*

NOTE Shrimp chips, a fried cracker, can be found at Asian groceries and amazon.com.

MAKE AHEAD The pickled daikon and the cocktail sauce can be refrigerated for up to 1 week.

Steamed Shrimp Dumplings with Chinese Chives

📷 PAGE 21

Active **45 min**; Total **1 hr 50 min**; Makes **24**

FILLING

- ½ **oz. dried shiitake mushrooms**
  Boiling water
- 8 **oz. shrimp—peeled, deveined and finely chopped**
- 1 **cup finely chopped Chinese garlic chives, chives or scallions**
- 1 **Tbsp. plus 1 tsp. canola oil**
- 2 **tsp. sugar**
- 1½ **tsp. kosher salt**
- 1 **tsp. cornstarch**

DOUGH

- 1 **cup wheat starch (see Note)**
- ½ **cup cornstarch, plus more for dusting**
- 1 **cup boiling water**
  Soy sauce, for serving

1. Make the filling In a small bowl, cover the mushrooms by 1 inch with boiling water. Let stand until tender, about 30 minutes. Drain well and finely chop (you should have ⅓ cup).

2. In a medium bowl, mix the shrimp with the mushrooms, chives, oil, sugar, salt and cornstarch. Let stand for 10 minutes.

3. Meanwhile, make the dough In a large bowl, stir the wheat starch and ½ cup of cornstarch with the boiling water until the dough comes together; let cool slightly. Lightly dust a work surface with cornstarch and turn the dough out onto it, then knead until smooth, about 2 minutes. Wrap the dough in plastic and let rest for 15 minutes at room temperature. Cut the dough into 2 equal pieces. Roll each piece into a 1-inch-thick log (12 inches long) and cut each log into twelve 1-inch-thick slices. Using a lightly cornstarch-dusted rolling pin, roll out each piece of dough to a 3½-inch round. Arrange the wrappers on a cornstarch-dusted baking sheet (it's OK if they overlap slightly) and keep covered with plastic wrap while you prepare the rest.

4. Spoon 1 tablespoon of the filling in the center of each wrapper. Fold the dough up and over the filling to form a half-moon and pleat to seal the dumpling completely. Repeat with the remaining filling and wrappers.

5. Line a large steamer basket with parchment paper and lightly grease or spray the paper with oil. Set the basket in a pot of boiling water. In 2 batches, steam the dumplings until the wrappers turn transparent and the filling is firm to the touch, 8 to 10 minutes. Serve with soy sauce for dipping. —*Mak Kwai Pui and Leung Fai Keung*

NOTE Wheat starch is a key ingredient to making the translucent wrappers for many dumplings. Look for it at Asian markets and on amazon.com.

MAKE AHEAD The filling can be refrigerated overnight.

Shrimp with Green
Banana Cocktail Sauce

Crab Summer Rolls with Nuoc Cham Sauce

📷 PAGE 8

Active **45 min**; Total **1 hr**; Makes **20**

Layering the crabmeat first in these summer rolls (often mislabeled "spring rolls") lets you see it through the translucent wrapper.

NUOC CHAM

- ¼ **cup fresh lime juice**
- 3 **Tbsp. Asian fish sauce**
- 3 **Tbsp. sugar**
- 2 **Tbsp. water**
- ½ **Thai red chile, minced**
- 1 **Tbsp. minced scallion**
- 1½ **tsp. toasted and ground sesame seeds**
- 1½ **tsp. minced cilantro**
- 1½ **tsp. minced mint**

ROLLS

- 4 **oz. rice noodles**
  Boiling water
  Twenty 8-inch round rice paper wrappers
- 1 **lb. jumbo lump crabmeat, picked over**
- ½ **English cucumber—halved lengthwise, seeded and cut into julienne**
- 2 **cups shredded iceberg lettuce**
- 2 **cups mung bean sprouts**
- 2 **cups mint leaves**
- 2 **cups cilantro leaves**
- ½ **cup crushed roasted salted peanuts, plus more for sprinkling**
- 10 **scallions, halved lengthwise, trimmed to 10 inches**
  Hoisin sauce and Sriracha, for serving

1. Make the nuoc cham In a small bowl, whisk together all of the ingredients.

2. Make the rolls In a medium, deep baking dish, cover the noodles with boiling water and let stand until softened, about 20 minutes. Drain well and pat dry with paper towels.

3. Fill a large, shallow bowl with very hot water (not boiling). Soak 1 rice paper wrapper in the water until just pliable, about 30 seconds. Spread on a work surface. Top the wrapper with some of the crab, noodles, cucumber, lettuce, bean sprouts, mint, cilantro and peanuts. Tightly fold the wrapper over the filling, tuck in the sides and roll up halfway. Lay a scallion half across the wrapper with 1 inch of overhang on both sides and tightly roll up. Transfer to a platter and cover with a damp paper towel. Repeat with the remaining wrappers and filling. Serve the rolls with the nuoc cham and a bowl of hoisin sauce sprinkled with Sriracha and peanuts. —*Andrew Zimmern*

MAKE AHEAD The summer rolls can be covered with a damp paper towel and refrigerated for up to 1 hour.

Classic Shoyu Musubi

Active **30 min**; Total **50 min**; Serves **6**

This popular Hawaiian snack of soy-and-sugar-glazed Spam wrapped in sushi rice and nori is totally addictive. Brooklyn baker turned writer Allison Robicelli admits that she had hesitations about trying it, but now it's a favorite.

- 1 **cup sushi rice, rinsed**
- 1 **Tbsp. unseasoned rice wine vinegar**
- ½ **Tbsp. granulated sugar**
- ¼ **cup soy sauce**
- 3 **Tbsp. light brown sugar**
- 1 **Tbsp. canola oil**
  One 12-oz. can Spam—cut crosswise into 6 slices, can washed and reserved (see Note)
- 3 **sheets of nori, halved crosswise**
- 1½ **tsp. furikake (Japanese seasoning mix)**

1. In a small saucepan, cover the rice with 1 cup plus 2 tablespoons of water. Bring to a boil, cover and simmer over low heat for 10 minutes. Remove from the heat and let stand, covered, for 20 minutes.

2. In a small microwavable bowl, combine the vinegar with the granulated sugar; microwave until warm, about 20 seconds. Stir to dissolve the sugar. Pour the vinegar mixture over the rice and toss to combine.

3. In another small bowl, stir the soy sauce with the brown sugar and ¼ cup of water. In a large nonstick skillet, heat the oil. Add the Spam slices and cook over high heat, turning once, until browned, about 4 minutes. Add the soy sauce mixture to the skillet and cook over moderate heat, turning the slices once, until the Spam is glazed, about 3 minutes.

4. On a work surface, arrange a half sheet of nori with the longer side facing you. Set the cleaned Spam can upright in the center of the nori sheet. Spoon 3 tablespoons of the warm sushi rice into the bottom of the can. Using the back of a spoon that's been dipped in cold water, pack the rice in an even layer. Top with 1 slice of Spam and sprinkle with ¼ teaspoon of the furikake. Spoon another 3 tablespoons of the rice over the Spam and pack in an even layer. Carefully hold down the musubi and remove the Spam can, leaving the musubi on the nori. Fold one end of the nori up over the rice. Using your fingertips, wet the other end of the nori and fold it up over the other side of the rice, pressing to adhere. Flip the musubi so it is seam side down. Repeat with the remaining nori sheets, rice, Spam and furikake.

5. Using a moistened sharp knife, cut each roll crosswise into 4 pieces, wiping the knife with a damp towel between slices. Arrange the musubi on a platter and serve. —*Allison Robicelli*

NOTE You will need the Spam can for this recipe. Using a can opener, remove both the top and the bottom of the can and remove the Spam. Use a spoon to push down any sharp edges on the side of the can. Wash and dry the can well before proceeding. You can also use a Spam musubi maker.

Pork-and-Chive Dumplings

⏱ Total **40 min**; Makes **28**

DUMPLINGS

½ cup chopped garlic chives or chives

One 1-inch piece of fresh ginger, peeled and sliced

2 garlic cloves

1 Tbsp. soy sauce

1 Tbsp. Chinese rice wine (Shaoxing)

2 tsp. light brown sugar

2 tsp. light sesame oil

1 tsp. toasted sesame oil

Kosher salt

1 lb. fatty ground pork, preferably from the shoulder

28 gyoza wrappers (3½ inch round)

Napa cabbage leaves, for steaming

DIPPING SAUCE

¾ cup chicken stock or low-sodium broth

¼ cup Chinese black vinegar

2 Tbsp. unseasoned rice wine vinegar

One 1-inch piece of fresh ginger, peeled and julienned

1. Make the dumplings In a food processor, pulse the chives, ginger, garlic, soy sauce, rice wine, brown sugar, both sesame oils and 1 teaspoon of salt until finely chopped. Transfer to a large bowl; mix in the pork.

2. Line a large baking sheet with parchment paper. Spoon about 1 tablespoon of the filling into the center of 1 gyoza wrapper and, using your finger, moisten half of the edge with water. Fold the dough up and over the filling to form a half-moon and pinch to seal the dumpling completely. Moisten the top of one end with water, bring the other end over and pinch to bring together and create a rosebud shape. Place the dumpling on the parchment-lined baking sheet and keep covered with a clean kitchen towel while you assemble the rest. Repeat the process with the remaining filling and wrappers.

3. Line 2 large steamer baskets with cabbage leaves and set the dumplings on the cabbage. Set the basket in a pot of boiling water and steam until the wrappers turn transparent and the filling is firm, 8 to 10 minutes.

4. Meanwhile, make the dipping sauce In a small saucepan, simmer the stock over moderately high heat until reduced by half, about 2 minutes. Whisk in both vinegars and the ginger. Serve the warm dipping sauce with the dumplings. —*Peter Cho*

MAKE AHEAD Uncooked dumplings can be frozen on a parchment paper–lined baking sheet, then transferred to a resealable plastic bag and frozen for up to 1 month.

WINE Tart, light-bodied red from Italy: 2015 Vietti Tre Vigne Barbera di Asti.

Crispy Potato Tarte Flambée

Active **35 min**; Total **2 hr 15 min**
Serves **4 to 6**

3 cups all-purpose flour, plus more for dusting

1 tsp. rapid-rise yeast

Kosher salt and pepper

2 Tbsp. unrefined peanut oil, plus more for drizzling

6 fingerling potatoes, very thinly sliced, preferably on a mandoline

½ small sweet potato, very thinly sliced, preferably on a mandoline

2 Tbsp. malt vinegar, plus more for drizzling

4 thick-cut slices of bacon, cut into ¼-inch pieces

4 oz. robiola cheese

½ cup crème fraîche

¼ red onion, thinly sliced

1. In a large bowl, whisk the 3 cups of flour with the yeast and 2 teaspoons of salt. Stir in 1 cup of warm water and the 2 tablespoons of peanut oil. Using your hands, knead the dough until smooth, 2 minutes. Cover with plastic wrap and let stand in a warm place until doubled in size, about 1 hour.

2. In a large bowl, toss the potatoes with the 2 tablespoons of vinegar and season with salt and pepper. Let stand for at least 30 minutes or up to 1 hour. Drain.

3. In a large nonstick skillet, cook the bacon over moderate heat until golden and crisp, about 12 minutes. Transfer to a paper towel–lined plate.

4. Set a pizza stone on the bottom of the oven; preheat the oven to 500°. Lightly flour 2 large rimless baking sheets. Divide the dough into 2 pieces. On a lightly floured work surface, roll out 1 piece to a 14-inch

round, ⅛ inch thick. Transfer to one of the baking sheets; keep the other piece covered with plastic wrap.

5. In a small bowl, stir the cheese into the crème fraîche. Spread half of the mixture over the pizza round. Top with half each of the potato and onion slices. Drizzle lightly with peanut oil. Cover with plastic wrap and let rest for 15 minutes. Repeat with the second piece of dough and the remaining toppings.

6. Carefully slide 1 tarte onto the hot pizza stone and bake for 12 to 15 minutes, until bubbling and golden in spots. Transfer to a large board, top with half of the bacon and season with salt and pepper. Repeat with the second tarte and the remaining bacon. Cut the tartes into wedges, drizzle with malt vinegar and serve. —*Laura Rege*

WINE Full-bodied, smoky Pinot Gris from Alsace: 2015 Domaine Weinbach Cuvée Ste. Catherine.

Four-Cheese Fondue

⏱ Total **30 min**; Serves **8 to 10**

2 cups dry white wine

2 tsp. cornstarch

1 garlic clove, minced

Kosher salt

6 oz. Jarlsberg cheese, shredded (1½ cups)

6 oz. Emmental cheese, shredded (1½ cups)

6 oz. Gruyère cheese, shredded (1½ cups)

½ cup finely grated Parmigiano-Reggiano cheese

1 Tbsp. kirsch

Rustic bread cubes and apple wedges, for serving

In a fondue pot or an enameled cast-iron casserole, whisk the wine with the cornstarch, garlic and a generous pinch of salt. Bring to a boil, then simmer over moderate heat until barely thickened, about 2 minutes. Add the cheese in small handfuls, whisking constantly, until very smooth and hot; let each handful melt completely before adding more. Stir in the kirsch and season with salt. Serve hot with bread and apple wedges. —*Bruce Bromberg and Eric Bromberg*

DIY Fondue

Still as cozy and crowd-pleasing as ever, a wine-spiked fondue can heat up any party. Cheese whiz Liz Thorpe updates a classic. "Fondue is flexible," she says, "and you get more complex flavors when you blend." Master the classic recipe, then mix and match cheeses and wines until you find your favorite.

Classic Cheese Fondue

⏱ Total **15 min**; Serves **4**

You'll find this old-school version, with intense, nutty Alpine cheeses, served near the fire at Swiss ski chalets. The ripe red fruitiness of the kirsch is especially good here. It's a classic for a reason.

- **1½ Tbsp. cornstarch**
- **1 Tbsp. fresh lemon juice**
- **1 cup dry white wine, such as Pinot Grigio**
- **1 garlic clove, halved**
- **1 lb. shredded mixed Alpine cheeses, such as Gruyère, Emmental, Challerhocker and Comté (5 cups)**
- **1 Tbsp. kirsch or Cognac (optional)**

1. In a small bowl, whisk the cornstarch with the lemon juice and 2 tablespoons of the wine.

2. Rub the inside of a small enameled cast-iron casserole or saucepan with the cut garlic clove. Add the remaining ¾ cup plus 2 tablespoons of wine and bring to a simmer over moderate heat.

3. Slowly whisk in the cornstarch mixture and simmer, whisking constantly, until slightly thickened, about 1 minute. Reduce the heat to moderately low and add the cheese in handfuls, whisking constantly, until the fondue is smooth, about 5 minutes; let each handful melt before adding more. Stir in the kirsch or Cognac, if using. Serve immediately in the casserole or a warm fondue pot (see Note).

SERVE WITH Pieces of crusty bread, blanched or roasted vegetables, endive spears, thinly sliced apple, dried apricots, dates, root vegetable chips, salumi, pickles like Quick-Pickled Fennel (recipe at right).

NOTE If using a fondue pot for serving, fill it with hot water and let stand, covered, for 5 minutes. Drain and dry thoroughly immediately before adding the cheese fondue.

MAKE AHEAD The fondue can be refrigerated overnight and reheated gently on the stove over very low heat.

The Crowd-Pleaser Fondue

⏱ Total **15 min**; Serves **4**

This super-buttery, creamy variation is like a grilled cheese sandwich without the bread. Made with very meltable everyday cheeses, this fondue is a good choice for game day.

- **1½ Tbsp. cornstarch**
- **1 Tbsp. fresh lemon juice**
- **1 cup dry white wine, such as Chardonnay**
- **1 garlic clove, halved**
- **1 lb. shredded mixed young cow's milk cheeses, such as young Gouda, Havarti, Asiago Fresco, Fontina, Babybel and raclette (5 cups)**
- **1 Tbsp. kirsch or Cognac (optional)**

1. In a small bowl, whisk the cornstarch with the lemon juice and 2 tablespoons of the wine.

2. Rub the inside of a small enameled cast-iron casserole or saucepan with the cut garlic clove. Add the remaining ¾ cup plus 2 tablespoons of wine and bring to a simmer over moderate heat.

3. Slowly whisk in the cornstarch mixture and simmer, whisking constantly, until slightly thickened, about 1 minute. Reduce the heat to moderately low and add the cheese in handfuls, whisking constantly, until the fondue is smooth, about 5 minutes; let each handful melt before adding more. Stir in the kirsch or Cognac, if using. Serve immediately in the casserole or a warm fondue pot (see Note).

NOTE If using a fondue pot for serving, fill it with hot water and let stand, covered, for 5 minutes. Drain and dry thoroughly immediately before adding the cheese fondue.

MAKE AHEAD The fondue can be refrigerated overnight and reheated gently on the stove over very low heat.

STEP-BY-STEP CHEESE FONDUE

ADD SUBTLE FLAVOR Rub the inside of the pot with cut garlic. .

SIMMER THE WINE An acid is essential for smooth melting. Add the white wine and bring to a simmer over moderate heat.

ADD STARCH Whisk in a mixture of cornstarch, lemon juice and wine. Simmer, whisking, until slightly thickened.

ADD CHEESE Reduce the heat and add cheese in handfuls, whisking constantly, until smooth. Stir in kirsch.

The Stinker Cheese Fondue

📷 PAGE 9

⏱ Total **15 min**; Serves **4**

Thorpe's favorite fondue is made with Taleggio, a melty, brine-washed Italian cheese. Including its rind enhances the funkiness and adds an almost bacony flavor. Scoop soft Époisses right out of the rind and into the pot.

- 1½ **Tbsp. cornstarch**
- 1 **Tbsp. fresh lemon juice**
- 1 **cup dry white wine, such as Riesling**
- 1 **garlic clove, halved**
- ½ **lb. Taleggio cheese, cut into ½-inch cubes with the rind left on**
- ½ **lb. Époisses cheese**
- 1 **Tbsp. kirsch or Cognac (optional)**

1. In a small bowl, whisk the cornstarch with the lemon juice and 2 tablespoons of the wine.

2. Rub the inside of a small enameled cast-iron casserole or saucepan with the cut garlic clove. Add the remaining ¾ cup plus 2 tablespoons of wine and bring to a simmer over moderate heat.

3. Slowly whisk in the cornstarch mixture and simmer, whisking constantly, until slightly thickened, about 1 minute. Reduce the heat to moderately low and add the cheese in batches, spooning the Époisses directly into the pot and whisking constantly, until the fondue is smooth, about 5 minutes; let each addition melt before adding more. Some small, edible pieces of rind will remain. Stir in the kirsch or Cognac, if using. Serve immediately in the casserole or a warm fondue pot (see Note).

SERVE WITH Pieces of crusty bread, blanched or roasted vegetables, endive spears, thinly sliced apple, dried apricots, dates, root vegetable chips, salumi, pickles like Quick-Pickled Fennel (recipe at right).

NOTE If using a fondue pot for serving, fill it with hot water and let stand, covered, for 5 minutes. Drain and dry thoroughly immediately before adding the cheese fondue.

MAKE AHEAD The fondue can be refrigerated overnight and reheated gently on the stove over very low heat.

Pick sturdy dippers that contrast yet complement the cheese.

QUICK-PICKLED FENNEL

⏱ Active **15 min**; Total **40 min** Makes **about 1 qt**

This super-easy recipe has just 1 easy step.

- 1 **large fennel bulb (1 lb.), trimmed and thinly sliced**
- 1 **cup white wine vinegar**
- ¼ **cup sugar**
- 2 **Tbsp. kosher salt**

Pack the fennel into a heatproof 1-quart jar. In a small saucepan, bring the vinegar, sugar, salt and 1 cup of water to a boil, stirring to dissolve the sugar. Pour the hot brine over the fennel and let cool slightly at room temperature. Cover and refrigerate until almost chilled, about 20 minutes. Drain before serving.

MAKE AHEAD The pickles in their brine can be refrigerated for up to 2 weeks.

Pigs in a Blanket with Black Pepper Pastry

Active **15 min**; Total **1 hr**; Makes **12**

    Canola oil, for greasing

1½ **Tbsp. unsalted butter**

1½ **Tbsp. packed light brown sugar**

1 **Tbsp. honey**

¼ **cup Dijon mustard**

    One 12- to 14-oz. sheet of thawed frozen all-butter puff pastry

    Flaky sea salt and coarsely ground black pepper

4 **long (about 8 inches) hot dogs, cut into thirds**

1 **egg beaten with 1 Tbsp. milk**

1. Preheat the oven to 375°. Lightly oil a large baking sheet. In a small saucepan, melt the butter with the sugar and honey over moderate heat. Remove from the heat and whisk in the Dijon until smooth. Let the glaze cool completely.

2. On a lightly floured work surface, unfold the puff pastry and roll out to a 12-inch square. Cut the dough in half, then cut each half into 6 triangles. Brush 1 triangle with the glaze and season with coarsely ground black pepper. Put 1 piece of hot dog on the wide end of the triangle, then loosely roll up. Put the pig in a blanket seam side down on the prepared baking sheet. Repeat with the remaining triangles, glaze and hot dogs. Brush the pigs in a blanket with the egg wash and sprinkle with flaky sea salt and coarsely ground black pepper. Refrigerate for 15 minutes.

3. Bake the pigs in a blanket for 30 to 35 minutes, until puffed and golden; rotate the baking sheet halfway through baking. Serve hot. —*Jen Pelka*

MAKE AHEAD The unbaked pigs in a blanket can be refrigerated overnight.

Winter Galette

Active **1 hr**; Total **2 hr 30 min** plus cooling
Serves **6 to 8**

Top Chef judge Gail Simmons varies this tart with the seasons. In colder months, she prepares it with root vegetables, layering paper-thin slices of whatever's on hand, from potatoes to celery root. The versatile dough is easy to shape into a free-form crust, and fresh ricotta, infused with herbs and lemon zest, forms a creamy base.

DOUGH

¾ **cup all-purpose flour, plus more for dusting**

¾ **cup whole-wheat flour**

½ **tsp. kosher salt**

1 **stick unsalted butter, cubed and chilled**

¼ **cup sour cream**

2 **Tbsp. ice water**

1 **Tbsp. fresh lemon juice**

FILLING

2 **Tbsp. extra-virgin olive oil**

1 **large shallot, thinly sliced**

    Kosher salt and pepper

1 **cup whole-milk ricotta cheese**

1½ **tsp. finely grated lemon zest plus 1 tsp. fresh lemon juice**

1 **large garlic clove, finely grated**

1 **tsp. thyme leaves, plus more for sprinkling**

1 **tsp. minced oregano, plus leaves for sprinkling**

½ **tsp. minced rosemary, plus leaves for sprinkling**

½ **lb. acorn squash—seeded, peeled and shaved into ribbons**

½ **lb. celery root, peeled and shaved into ribbons**

1 **small baking potato, peeled and shaved into ribbons**

1 **large egg beaten with 1 Tbsp. water**

¼ **cup freshly grated Parmigiano-Reggiano cheese**

2 **tsp. honey, warmed**

1. Make the dough In a food processor, combine both flours with the salt and pulse to mix. Add the butter and pulse until pea-size pieces form. Add the sour cream, ice water and lemon juice and pulse until the dough starts to come together. Transfer to a lightly floured work surface and pat into a disk. Wrap in plastic and refrigerate until chilled, about 1 hour.

2. Make the filling Preheat the oven to 400°. Line a baking sheet with parchment paper. In a small skillet, heat 1 tablespoon of the olive oil. Add the shallot, season with salt and cook over moderately low heat, stirring, until softened, about 5 minutes. Let cool.

3. In a small bowl, mix the ricotta with the lemon zest, garlic, the 1 teaspoon of thyme and the minced oregano and rosemary. Season with salt and pepper. In a large bowl, toss the squash with the celery root, potato and remaining 1 tablespoon of olive oil. Season with salt and pepper.

4. On a lightly floured work surface, roll out the dough to a 13-inch round. Transfer to the prepared baking sheet. Spread the ricotta on the dough, leaving a 1-inch border. Pile the squash mixture on the ricotta and scatter the shallot on top. Fold 1½ inches of the dough edge over the vegetables. Sprinkle with thyme, oregano and rosemary leaves. Brush the dough edge with the egg wash.

5. Bake the galette for 15 minutes, until starting to brown. Sprinkle the Parmigiano over the filling and bake for 15 to 20 minutes, until the vegetables are tender and the crust is golden.

6. In a small bowl, mix the honey with the lemon juice. Drizzle the lemon honey over the galette. Serve warm or at room temperature. —*Gail Simmons*

MAKE AHEAD The galette can be baked up to 3 hours ahead and rewarmed before serving.

WINE Full-bodied California Chardonnay: 2015 Cambria Fog Tide.

Baked Kabocha Falafel with Almond Milk Yogurt

Active **30 min**; Total **1 hr**;
Makes **about 16 falafel**

- 2 Tbsp. coconut oil, melted and cooled, plus more for brushing
- ¾ lb. kabocha squash—peeled, seeded and cut into ½-inch-thick wedges
- 1 cup chickpea flour (see Note)
- 2 Tbsp. chopped parsley leaves
- 1 Tbsp. chopped cilantro leaves
- 2 garlic cloves, minced
- 1 tsp. ground coriander
- ½ tsp. ground cumin
  Pinch of cayenne
- ¼ cup plus 1 tsp. fresh lemon juice
  Kosher salt
- 2 Tbsp. white sesame seeds
- 2 Tbsp. black sesame seeds
- 1 cup almond milk yogurt
- 1 Tbsp. chopped mint

1. Preheat the oven to 350°. Brush a large rimmed baking sheet with coconut oil and arrange the squash in a single layer. Roast until tender, about 30 minutes.

2. Transfer the squash to a large bowl and mash with a fork until smooth. Stir in the chickpea flour, parsley, cilantro, garlic, coriander, cumin, cayenne, ¼ cup of the lemon juice and 6 tablespoons of water. Season the falafel mixture with salt.

3. In a shallow bowl, mix the sesame seeds. Shape the falafel mixture into 16 heaping-tablespoon-size balls and roll them in the sesame seeds, pressing to adhere. Transfer to a large rimmed baking sheet.

4. Gently toss the falafel with the 2 table-spoons of coconut oil and space them at least 1 inch apart on the baking sheet. Bake for 20 minutes, until crisp and starting to brown in spots; turn the falafel halfway through baking.

5. Meanwhile, in a small bowl, whisk the yogurt with the mint and the remaining 1 teaspoon of lemon juice. Season with salt. Serve the falafel warm with the yogurt sauce. —*José Catrimán*

NOTE Chickpea flour is available at Indian and Mediterranean markets, as well as at Whole Foods.

WINE Crisp Cava: NV Castellroig Brut.

Albóndigas with Mushrooms

Active **1 hr 25 min**; Total **3 hr 40 min**
Serves **6**

A quick béchamel makes these Spanish-style meatballs wonderfully moist and tender. They're cooked in a deeply flavorful tomato-based sauce made with wine and brandy, then topped with crisp mushrooms.

MEATBALLS

- 2 Tbsp. unsalted butter
- 2 Tbsp. all-purpose flour, plus more for dredging
- ½ cup milk
- 1 lb. ground chuck
- ½ lb. ground pork
- 2 large eggs, lightly beaten
- 3 Tbsp. minced parsley
- 1 Tbsp. white Rioja or other dry white wine
- 1 large garlic clove, grated
- 1 tsp. sweet paprika
  Kosher salt and pepper
- ¼ cup extra-virgin olive oil

SAUCE

- 2 medium tomatoes, halved crosswise
- ½ cup minced onion
- ½ cup finely chopped carrot
- 5 garlic cloves, minced
  Kosher salt and pepper
- ½ tsp. sweet paprika
- 1 Tbsp. all-purpose flour
- ½ cup white Rioja or other dry white wine
- 3 Tbsp. brandy or dry sherry
- 2 cups chicken stock or low-sodium broth
- ¼ cup finely chopped parsley

MUSHROOMS

- ¼ cup extra-virgin olive oil
- 1 lb. mixed wild mushrooms, such as cremini, oyster and chanterelle, cut into 1-inch pieces
  Kosher salt and pepper

1. Make the meatballs In a small saucepan, melt the butter. Add the flour; cook over moderate heat, whisking, until a thick paste forms, 1 minute. Gradually whisk in the milk and cook until thick, 2 to 3 minutes. Scrape into a large bowl and let cool slightly. Add the chuck, pork, eggs, parsley, wine, garlic, paprika, 2 teaspoons of salt and 1 teaspoon of pepper; mix well. Cover and refrigerate for about 2 hours.

2. Form the meat mixture into 1½-inch balls. In a large saucepan, heat 2 tablespoons of the oil. Dredge half the meatballs in flour. Cook over moderately high heat, turning, until browned all over, about 8 minutes. Transfer to a plate. Repeat with the remaining 2 tablespoons of oil and meatballs; don't wipe out the pan.

3. Make the sauce Grate the tomato halves on the large holes of a box grater set in a bowl until only the skins remain; discard the skins.

4. Add the onion, carrot, garlic and a generous pinch of salt to the saucepan and cook over moderate heat, stirring occasionally, until just starting to brown, about 8 minutes. Add the tomatoes and paprika and simmer over moderate heat until slightly reduced, 3 to 5 minutes. Stir in the flour, then stir in the wine and brandy and simmer until barely thickened, 5 minutes. Transfer to a blender and puree until very smooth. Return to the saucepan, whisk in the stock and bring to a boil. Season with salt and pepper.

5. Add the meatballs to the sauce, cover and simmer over moderately low heat until cooked through, about 15 minutes. Uncover and simmer until the sauce is slightly thickened, about 5 minutes. Stir in the parsley, cover and keep warm over very low heat.

6. Meanwhile, make the mushrooms In a large skillet, heat 2 tablespoons of the oil until shimmering. Add half the mushrooms; season with salt and pepper and cook over moderately high heat, stirring occasionally, until browned, 8 minutes. Transfer to a bowl. Repeat with the remaining oil and mushrooms.

7. Spoon the meatballs and sauce into bowls, top with the mushrooms and serve. —*Anya von Bremzen*

WINE Earthy, complex Ribera del Duero: 2014 Finca El Encinal Crianza.

SALADS

SingleThread farm,
restaurant and inn,
Sonoma, California
OPPOSITE
Persimmon-and-Endive
Salad with Honey
Vinegar and Avocado
Oil Vinaigrette (p. 42)

Lettuces with Parmigiano, Radish and Dill Pickle Vinaigrette

Total **20 min**; Serves **4**

- **1** lb. small lettuces, such as Little Gem or baby romaine, leaves torn into bite-size pieces
- **12** radishes (about 6 oz.), thinly sliced

  One ¼-lb. piece of Parmigiano-Reggiano, thinly shaved with a vegetable peeler

  Kosher salt
- **½** cup Dill Pickle Vinaigrette (recipe follows)

In a large bowl, combine the lettuces, radishes and cheese and season with salt. Gently toss with the vinaigrette and serve. —*Hugh Acheson*

BASIC VINAIGRETTE

Total **5 min**; Makes **1 cup**

- **3** Tbsp. red wine vinegar
- **1** garlic clove, minced
- **1** tsp. Dijon mustard

  Kosher salt and pepper
- **¾** cup extra-virgin olive oil

In a pint-size jar, combine red wine vinegar, garlic, Dijon mustard, ¾ teaspoon salt and ½ teaspoon pepper. Cover and shake to dissolve the salt. Add olive oil and shake to blend.

MAKE AHEAD Vinaigrette can be refrigerated in an airtight container for 2 weeks.

GREEK VARIATION Add 1 teaspoon chopped oregano and ½ teaspoon finely grated lemon zest

DILL PICKLE VARIATION Puree with 1 chopped large kosher dill pickle

MISO VARIATION Add 1 tablespoon white miso paste

FRENCH-STYLE VARIATION Add 1 teaspoon chopped tarragon

SPICY SESAME VARIATION Add 1 tablespoon toasted sesame seeds, 1 tablespoon toasted sesame oil and 1 teaspoon crushed red pepper

KIMCHI VARIATION Add 2 tablespoons finely chopped cabbage kimchi

GINGER VARIATION Add 2 tablespoons minced peeled fresh ginger

Little Gems with Warm Garlic Dressing

Total **15 min**; Serves **4**

- **4** heads of Little Gem lettuce, halved lengthwise
- **¼** cup extra-virgin olive oil
- **2** large garlic cloves, thinly sliced
- **4** tsp. sherry vinegar
- **2** oil-packed anchovies, finely chopped

  Flaky sea salt and smoked paprika, for garnish

1. Fill a large bowl with cold water. Holding the lettuce halves by the roots, submerge them in the water and shake gently to release the grit. Shake out the excess water, then pat the leaves dry with paper towels. Divide the lettuce halves among 4 plates.

2. In a small skillet, heat the olive oil and the garlic over moderate heat, stirring occasionally, until the garlic is light brown, about 3 minutes. Remove the skillet from the heat and spoon the oil over the lettuce. Drizzle with the sherry vinegar. Garnish with the anchovies, sea salt and a sprinkle of smoked paprika and serve. —*José Andrés*

Caesar Salad with Anchovy Fritters

Active **1 hr**; Total **1 hr 30 min**; Serves **6**

FRITTERS

- **½** cup all-purpose flour
- **½** cup stone-ground cornmeal
- **1** tsp. baking powder
- **½** tsp. baking soda
- **¼** cup finely grated Parmigiano-Reggiano cheese

  Kosher salt and pepper
- **¼** cup whole milk
- **¼** cup buttermilk
- **1** large egg
- **2** Tbsp. minced chives
- **10** oil-packed anchovy fillets, chopped, plus 1 Tbsp. oil from the jar

  Canola oil, for frying

SALAD

- **2** oil-packed anchovy fillets
- **1** large egg yolk
- **1** small shallot, coarsely chopped
- **1** garlic clove
- **1** Tbsp. Dijon mustard
- **1** Tbsp. sherry vinegar
- **1** Tbsp. fresh lemon juice
- **½** tsp. piment d'Espelette

  Kosher salt
- **1** cup extra-virgin olive oil, plus more for drizzling
- **⅓** cup finely grated Parmigiano-Reggiano, plus shaved cheese for garnish
- **6** heads of Little Gem lettuce, trimmed and halved lengthwise

1. Make the fritters In a medium bowl, whisk the flour with the cornmeal, baking powder, baking soda, cheese, ½ teaspoon of salt and ¾ teaspoon of pepper. In another medium bowl, whisk the milk with the buttermilk, egg, chives, anchovies and anchovy oil. Stir the wet ingredients into the dry ingredients until just combined. Cover and refrigerate the batter for 1 hour.

2. Meanwhile, make the salad In a blender, puree the anchovies with the egg yolk, shallot, garlic, mustard, vinegar, lemon juice, piment d'Espelette and 1 teaspoon of salt until smooth. With the machine on, drizzle in the 1 cup of olive oil until incorporated. Transfer the dressing to a small bowl and stir in the finely grated Parmesan.

3. In a medium saucepan, heat 2 inches of canola oil to 360°. Drop 8 rounded tablespoonfuls of batter into the oil and fry, turning once, until the fritters are golden brown and crisp, 1 to 2 minutes. Using a slotted spoon, transfer to a paper towel–lined plate to drain. Repeat with the remaining batter.

4. Arrange the lettuce and anchovy fritters on 6 plates or a large platter. Drizzle the salad with the dressing. Garnish with Parmesan shavings and a drizzle of olive oil; serve immediately. —*Bryan Voltaggio and Michael Voltaggio*

MAKE AHEAD The anchovy fritter batter and the dressing can be refrigerated separately overnight.

WINE Tart, grapefruity Sauvignon Blanc: 2015 Honig Napa Valley.

Caesar Salad with
Anchovy Fritters

Grilled Romanesco Salad
with Charred-Herb Dressing

Smoked Salmon Salad with Dill Sauce

Active **40 min**; Total **1 hr**; Serves **4**

This dish is inspired by the fantastic hot-smoked fish in Stockholm's markets. Flaked over vegetables and lettuce, it's an ideal summer lunch.

DILL SAUCE

- 6 Tbsp. crème fraîche
- ¼ cup chopped dill
- 2 Tbsp. fresh lemon juice
  Kosher salt and pepper

DRESSING

- 6 Tbsp. unsalted butter, diced
- ¼ cup capers
- ¼ cup sherry vinegar
- ½ tsp. Dijon mustard
- 2 Tbsp. extra-virgin olive oil
  Kosher salt and pepper

SALAD

- 5 oz. haricots verts, trimmed
  One 12-oz. head of Little Gem lettuce, leaves separated (3 cups)
  One 12-oz. head of red butter lettuce, leaves separated (3 cups)
- 2 cups baby arugula
- 1 cup young watercress, trimmed
- 4 radishes, very thinly sliced, preferably on a mandoline
- 4 scallions, thinly sliced
- ¼ cup plus 1 Tbsp. chopped dill
- ⅔ cup cherry tomatoes, halved
- 12 oz. hot-smoked salmon, torn into large flakes

1. Make the sauce In a small bowl, stir the crème fraîche with the dill and lemon juice. Season with salt and pepper. Refrigerate until ready to serve.

2. Make the dressing In a medium saucepan, cook the butter over moderate heat, swirling the pan occasionally, until browned, about 4 minutes. Add the capers and fry until crisp, about 1 minute. Using a slotted spoon, transfer to a paper towel–lined plate and reserve. Strain the browned butter into a small bowl. Whisk in the vinegar and mustard, then slowly whisk in the olive oil until emulsified. Season with salt and pepper. Keep warm.

3. Make the salad Fill a medium bowl with ice water. In a medium saucepan of salted boiling water, cook the haricots verts until crisp-tender, about 4 minutes. Drain and transfer to the ice water. Drain and pat dry; halve the beans crosswise. In a large bowl, combine the haricots verts and reserved capers with both lettuces, the arugula, watercress, radishes, scallions, dill and tomatoes. Gently toss with the dressing. Spread the dill sauce on plates. Mound the salad and salmon on top; serve.
—*Andrew Zimmern*

MAKE AHEAD The dill sauce can be refrigerated overnight.

Buttermilk-Dressed Spring Greens

Total **30 min**; Serves **8**

"I have a cordial dislike for dressings made with mayonnaise," says chef Eli Dahlin. To achieve the same lush, creamy texture, he blends cottage cheese into his buttermilk dressing until it is thick and smooth.

- 1 cup buttermilk
- ½ cup cottage cheese (4% milk fat)
- 2 Tbsp. red wine vinegar
- 1 tsp. Dijon mustard
- 1 tsp. minced shallot
- 3 Tbsp. finely chopped tarragon
  Kosher salt and pepper
- 1 medium head of red leaf lettuce, torn
- 2 heads of Boston lettuce, torn
- 1 cup smoked almonds (5 oz.), chopped

1. In a blender, puree the buttermilk with the cottage cheese, vinegar, Dijon and shallot until smooth. Scrape the dressing into a small bowl and stir in the tarragon; season with salt and pepper.

2. In a serving bowl, toss the lettuces with some of the dressing. Garnish with the almonds and serve, passing the remaining dressing at the table. —*Eli Dahlin*

MAKE AHEAD The dressing can be refrigerated overnight.

Grilled Romanesco Salad with Charred-Herb Dressing

Total **40 min**; Serves **6**

Grilling is the best way to go with Romanesco and other brassicas, like broccoli and cauliflower. Char adds critical flavor, boosted by parsley and basil, which also get toasted on the grill.

- 3 cups loosely packed parsley sprigs
- 1 cup loosely packed basil sprigs
- ½ cup plus 2 Tbsp. extra-virgin olive oil
  Kosher salt and pepper
- 2 cups 1½-inch Romanesco florets (10 oz.)
- 1 garlic clove, minced
- 2 tsp. finely grated lemon zest plus 3 Tbsp. fresh lemon juice
  One 7-oz. head of butter lettuce, leaves torn (4 cups)
  One 8-oz. bunch of curly kale, stemmed, cut into 2-inch pieces (4 cups)
- ½ cup cherry tomatoes, halved
- 1 medium, firm-ripe Hass avocado—pitted, peeled and cut into ¼-inch-thick wedges

1. Light a grill or preheat a grill pan. Tie the parsley and basil together with kitchen string to make a bouquet. Drizzle with 1 tablespoon of the olive oil and season with salt and pepper.

2. In a medium bowl, toss the Romanesco with 1 tablespoon of the olive oil and season with salt and pepper. Grill the Romanesco over moderately high heat, turning occasionally, until crisp-tender and charred in spots, 8 to 10 minutes; return to the bowl.

3. Grill the herb bouquet, turning often, until charred in spots, about 2 minutes. Transfer the bouquet to a work surface, discard the string and stems and chop the charred leaves.

4. In a large bowl, combine the chopped herbs with the garlic, lemon zest and lemon juice. Whisk in the remaining ½ cup of olive oil and season with salt and pepper. Add the Romanesco, lettuce, kale, tomatoes and avocado to the bowl and toss to coat; serve. —*Daniele Uditi*

Kale Salad with Bacon–Brown Sugar Vinaigrette

Total **35 min**; Serves **10 to 12**

Cookbook author and TV cook Ayesha Curry dresses her tasty kale, apple and cranberry salad with a deliciously warm dressing made with rendered bacon fat, brown sugar and apple cider vinegar.

- 1 cup pecans
- ½ lb. bacon, finely chopped
- 2 Tbsp. light brown sugar
- ⅓ cup apple cider vinegar
- 1 Tbsp. Dijon mustard
  Kosher salt and pepper
- 1 lb. mixed Tuscan and curly kale, stemmed, leaves torn
- 2 Granny Smith apples—cored, quartered and thinly sliced
- 1 cup unsweetened dried cranberries
- 8 radishes, thinly sliced

1. Preheat the oven to 375°. Spread the pecans in a pie plate. Toast in the oven for about 6 minutes, until fragrant. Let cool, then coarsely chop.

2. Meanwhile, in a large skillet, cook the bacon over moderate heat, stirring occasionally, until rendered and crisp, about 8 minutes. Using a slotted spoon, transfer to paper towels to drain; reserve the bacon for another use.

3. In a small heatproof bowl, whisk the hot bacon fat with the brown sugar until dissolved. Whisk in the vinegar and Dijon and season the dressing with salt and pepper. Keep warm.

4. In a large serving bowl, toss the kale with the toasted pecans, the apples, dried cranberries, radishes and warm dressing. Season with salt and pepper and toss again. Serve. —*Ayesha Curry*

MAKE AHEAD The dressing can be refrigerated for up to 3 days. Warm gently in a microwave before using.

WINE Fruity, dry California rosé: 2016 Balletto Winery Rosé or Pinot Noir.

Savory Kale Salad

Active **30 min**; Total **1 hr 30 min**
Serves **10**

At Dovecote Café in Baltimore, chef Amanda Mack looks to superlocal farms to create her seasonal salads.

- One 3½-lb. sugar pumpkin or butternut squash, peeled and cut into 1-inch pieces
- ½ cup plus 1 tsp. extra-virgin olive oil
- 1 tsp. ground cumin
  Kosher salt and pepper
- ½ cup pepitas
- 1½ cups whole-milk yogurt
- 2 Tbsp. fresh lemon juice
- 1 Tbsp. almond butter
- 1 Tbsp. minced chipotle chile in adobo sauce
- 1 small garlic clove, finely grated
- 1 tsp. sweet paprika
- 15 oz. baby kale
- 1 small red onion, very thinly sliced
- 4 oz. blue cheese, crumbled

1. Preheat the oven to 425°. On a large rimmed baking sheet, toss the pumpkin with ½ cup of the oil and the cumin and season with salt and pepper. Bake for about 30 minutes, stirring halfway through, until tender and just browned in spots. Let cool. Leave the oven on.

2. On another baking sheet, toss the pepitas with the remaining 1 teaspoon of olive oil. Toast for about 7 minutes, until puffed and lightly browned. Let cool.

3. Meanwhile, in a medium bowl, whisk the yogurt with the lemon juice, almond butter, chipotle, garlic and paprika. Season the dressing with salt and pepper.

4. In a large bowl, toss the kale with half the dressing and season with salt and pepper. Fold in the pumpkin and onion. Top with the pepitas and blue cheese and serve, passing the remaining dressing at the table. —*Amanda Mack*

Chile-Kale Salad with Fennel

Total **40 min**; Serves **4**

Chef Jehangir Mehta of NYC's Graffiti Earth rethinks the ubiquitous kale salad with lots of hot chiles, fresh herbs and crunchy chickpea croutons.

- 1½ Tbsp. Dijon mustard
- 1 Tbsp. mirin
- 2 tsp. fresh lemon juice
- 3 Thai bird chiles—1 stemmed, seeded and minced, 2 halved and seeded
- 4½ Tbsp. extra-virgin olive oil
- 1 cup small cilantro sprigs plus 1 Tbsp. chopped cilantro
  Kosher salt and pepper
- 2 large fennel bulbs, halved lengthwise and cut through the core into ¼-inch wedges
- 3 garlic cloves, crushed
- 8 oz. curly kale, stemmed and chopped
- ½ cup thinly sliced red onion
- ⅔ cup store-bought crispy chickpeas

1. Preheat the oven to 400°. In a small bowl, whisk the mustard with the mirin, lemon juice and minced chile. While whisking constantly, drizzle in 2½ tablespoons of the olive oil until incorporated. Stir in the chopped cilantro and season the dressing with salt and pepper.

2. In a large ovenproof skillet, heat 1 tablespoon of the olive oil until shimmering. Add half of the fennel and season with salt and pepper. Cook over moderate heat, turning once, until the fennel is lightly browned on both sides, about 5 minutes. Transfer to a plate. Add the remaining 1 tablespoon of olive oil, the halved chiles, crushed garlic and the remaining fennel to the skillet and cook over moderate heat until the fennel is lightly browned on both sides, 5 minutes. Return all of the fennel to the skillet and roast in the oven until tender, 15 minutes; discard the garlic and chiles.

3. In a large serving bowl, toss the kale, red onion and cilantro sprigs with the dressing; season with salt and pepper. Gently fold in the fennel and crispy chickpeas; serve. —*Jehangir Mehta*

Kale Salad with Bacon–
Brown Sugar Vinaigrette

Kale-and-Brussels Sprout Caesar Salad

Total **1 hr**; Serves **8**

Instead of Parmesan cheese, Whitney Tingle and Danielle DuBoise, creators of the plant-based meal-delivery service Sakara Life, toss their vegan Caesar salad with a savory, nutty crumble of almonds, hemp seeds and nutritional yeast. Use leftover crumble on roasted vegetables, fried eggs or a grain bowl.

CRUMBLE

- ½ cup raw almonds
- ¼ cup hulled hemp seeds
- 2 Tbsp. nutritional yeast (see Note)
- 2 tsp. sweet paprika
- Fine Himalayan pink salt

DRESSING

- ½ small Hass avocado, pitted and peeled
- 1 small garlic clove
- 2 Tbsp. extra-virgin olive oil
- 2 Tbsp. fresh lemon juice
- 1½ Tbsp. Dijon mustard
- 1 Tbsp. nutritional yeast
- 1½ tsp. hulled hemp seeds
- 1½ tsp. chia seeds
- ½ tsp. dulse granules (see Note)
- Fine Himalayan pink salt and pepper

SALAD

- 2 lbs. brussels sprouts, trimmed and thinly sliced
- ⅓ cup extra-virgin olive oil
- Fine Himalayan pink salt and pepper
- One 5-oz. container baby kale (12 cups)
- Lemon wedges, for serving

1. Make the crumble In a food processor, pulse all of the ingredients, until the mixture resembles fine crumbs. Transfer the crumble to a small bowl and season with salt. Wipe out the food processor.

2. Make the dressing In the food processor, puree all of the ingredients, with 2 tablespoons of water until smooth. Season with salt and pepper.

3. Make the salad Preheat the oven to 450°. In a large bowl, toss the brussels sprouts with the olive oil and season with salt and pepper; spread on 2 large rimmed baking sheets. Roast the sprouts, rotating the pans from top to bottom halfway through baking, until crisp-tender and lightly browned in spots, about 10 minutes. Let cool slightly.

4. In a large bowl, toss the brussels sprouts with the kale, half of the dressing and 2 tablespoons of the crumble. Serve with lemon wedges, passing the remaining dressing and crumble at the table.
—*Whitney Tingle and Danielle DuBoise*

NOTE Nutritional yeast is a nutty-tasting vegan seasoning. Dulse is a red seaweed that has a faint bacon-like flavor when dried. Both ingredients can be found at Whole Foods and on amazon.com.

MAKE AHEAD The crumble can be refrigerated for up to 2 weeks and the dressing can be refrigerated overnight.

Caesar Brussels Salad

Active **25 min**; Total **1 hr 25 min**; Serves **10**

This recipe from Julia Sherman, of the blog Salad for President, is ideal for a party because it can be prepared ahead, doesn't wilt or get soggy and makes great leftovers.

DRESSING

- 2 large egg yolks
- 2 Tbsp. fresh lemon juice
- 5 oil-packed anchovy fillets, drained
- 3 Tbsp. chopped parsley leaves, plus more leaves for garnish
- 2 Tbsp. chopped chives
- 1 tsp. Dijon mustard
- 1 tsp. white wine vinegar
- ¼ cup extra-virgin olive oil
- ¼ cup grapeseed oil

BRUSSELS SPROUTS

- 2 lbs. brussels sprouts
- ¼ cup extra-virgin olive oil
- 3 Tbsp. white wine vinegar
- 1 garlic clove, finely grated
- Kosher salt and pepper
- ½ cup freshly grated Parmigiano-Reggiano cheese

1. Make the dressing In a food processor, pulse the egg yolks, lemon juice, anchovies, chopped parsley, chives, mustard and vinegar until smooth. With the machine on, drizzle in both oils until smooth. Transfer to a bowl, cover with plastic and refrigerate. Clean out the processor.

2. Make the brussels sprouts Thinly slice 2 cups of the smallest brussels sprouts and transfer to a large bowl. In a food processor fitted with the slicing blade, shred the remaining brussels sprouts; transfer to the bowl. Toss with the olive oil, vinegar and garlic and season with salt and pepper. Cover and let stand for 1 hour. Toss in the Caesar dressing and cheese. Garnish with parsley and serve. —*Julia Sherman*

MAKE AHEAD The dressing can be refrigerated in an airtight container for up to 2 days.

Supersimple Green Salad

Total **10 min**; Serves **8**

This very easy salad is a staple on cookbook author Nadine Redzepi's table because it's fresh, tasty and completely versatile.

- 1 Tbsp. Dijon mustard
- 1 Tbsp. whole-grain mustard
- 1½ tsp. balsamic vinegar
- ¼ cup extra-virgin olive oil
- 1 head of red leaf lettuce, leaves separated and torn if large
- 1 large head of romaine lettuce, leaves separated and torn
- Kosher salt and pepper

In a large bowl, whisk the mustards and vinegar. While whisking constantly, slowly drizzle in the oil until incorporated. Gently toss the lettuces in the dressing. Season with salt and pepper and serve immediately. —*Nadine Levy Redzepi*

Winter Salad with Walnut Milk Vinaigrette

Total **25 min**; Serves **4**

NYC chef George Mendes of Aldea and Lupulo restaurants likes using nut milks to flavor all sorts of things, including this creamy and rich-tasting vinaigrette.

½ cup walnut halves

1½ Tbsp. sherry vinegar

1 Tbsp. extra-virgin olive oil

1 tsp. walnut oil

Kosher salt and pepper

1 small head of red leaf lettuce, torn into bite-size pieces

One 8-oz. head of escarole, white and light green leaves only, torn into bite-size pieces

Thinly sliced candy-striped beets, for serving

1. Preheat the oven to 350°. Spread the walnuts in a pie plate and toast for 8 to 10 minutes, until fragrant. Let cool.

2. In a blender, puree the cooled walnuts with ½ cup of water until smooth. Add the vinegar and pulse to combine. Using a fine-mesh sieve set over a small bowl, strain the walnuts, pressing on the solids; discard the solids. Whisk in the olive and walnut oils and season the dressing with salt and pepper.

3. In a serving bowl, combine the lettuce, escarole and beets. Add the vinaigrette and toss well; serve. —*George Mendes*

MAKE AHEAD The dressing can be refrigerated overnight.

Sunflower Sprout and Herb Salad with Pomegranate Dressing

Total **20 min**; Serves **6**

Tel Aviv chef Osama Dalal's sweet, tangy, salad gets a stealth buzz from jalapeño.

2 Tbsp. pure pomegranate syrup (see Note)

2 Tbsp. extra-virgin olive oil

1 Tbsp. fresh lemon juice

Kosher salt and pepper

8 oz. sunflower sprouts, watercress or purslane, thick stems trimmed (10 cups)

3 cups mint leaves (2 oz.)

3 cups cilantro leaves (2 oz.)

1 jalapeño, very thinly sliced

In a large serving bowl, whisk the pomegranate syrup with the olive oil and lemon juice. Season with salt and pepper. Add the sunflower sprouts, mint, cilantro and jalapeño and toss to coat. Season with salt and pepper and toss again. Serve right away. —*Osama Dalal*

NOTE Pomegranate syrup, which is sweeter than pomegranate molasses, is available at Mediterranean markets and kalustyans.com.

Spinach-Sprout Salad with Coconut Ranch

Total **30 min**; Serves **4**

F&W's Justin Chapple uses vegan coconut yogurt as the base for a healthy version of ranch dressing. It's wildly versatile but also especially tasty on this supercrunchy sprout-packed salad.

½ cup plain vegan coconut yogurt (not coconut-flavored)

1 Tbsp. Champagne vinegar

¾ tsp. onion powder

¾ tsp. garlic powder

Kosher salt and pepper

4 oz. baby spinach

4 oz. sunflower sprouts

1 cup mixed crunchy sprouts (sprouted beans)

1 cup cherry or grape tomatoes, halved

1 large Hass avocado—peeled, pitted and cut into 2-inch pieces

6 radishes, thinly sliced

¼ cup roasted salted sunflower seeds

1. In a small bowl, mix the yogurt with the vinegar and onion and garlic powders. Season generously with salt and pepper.

2. In a large serving bowl or on a platter, toss the spinach with the sunflower sprouts, crunchy sprouts, tomatoes, avocado and radishes. Scatter the sunflower seeds on top and serve with the coconut ranch. —*Justin Chapple*

MAKE AHEAD The coconut ranch dressing can be refrigerated for up to 3 days.

WINE Crisp Sauvignon Blanc: 2016 Honig Napa Valley.

Warm Spinach and Sunchoke Salad

Active **25 min;** Total **50 min**
Serves **4 to 6**

This next-level wilted spinach salad gets sweetness and bite from sliced apples and crumbled cheddar.

- ¼ cup extra-virgin olive oil
- 1 lb. sunchokes, scrubbed and cut into 1-inch pieces
- 15 garlic cloves, peeled
  Pinch of crushed red pepper
  Kosher salt and black pepper
- 1 lb. leaf or curly spinach, stemmed, large leaves torn
- ¼ cup apple cider vinegar
- 1 Honeycrisp apple, sliced
- 4 oz. clothbound cheddar cheese, crumbled (1 cup)

1. Preheat the oven to 400°. In a large cast-iron skillet, heat 2 tablespoons of the olive oil until nearly smoking. Add the sunchokes, garlic and crushed red pepper and season with salt and black pepper. Transfer the skillet to the oven and roast for 25 to 30 minutes, until the sunchokes are just tender.

2. Put the spinach in a large bowl. Remove the skillet from the oven and add the vinegar and remaining 2 tablespoons of olive oil; immediately scrape the sunchoke mixture and any liquid over the spinach and toss until gently wilted. Add the apple and half of the cheese, season with salt and black pepper and toss to mix; transfer to a serving bowl. Top with the remaining cheese; serve. —*Justin Chapple*

WINE Floral, delicate white: 2016 Idlewild Arneis.

Shaved Artichoke Salad

Active **25 min;** Total **55 min;** Serves **4**

Thinly sliced raw artichokes are the star of this salad from chef Chris Behr of the Rome Sustainable Food Project. Buy the freshest ones you can get your hands on. A true test: The leaves should squeak when you squeeze them.

- ¼ cup plus 2 Tbsp. fresh lemon juice
- 2 lbs. baby artichokes (about 8)
  Kosher salt and pepper
  One 8-oz. bunch of arugula, stemmed and chopped, or 4 packed cups of baby arugula
- 1 head of radicchio (6 oz.)—halved, cored and sliced
- ½ cup parsley leaves
- ¼ cup small dill sprigs
- 5 Tbsp. extra-virgin olive oil

1. Pour the lemon juice into a large bowl. Working with 1 artichoke at a time, pull off the tough outer leaves. Using a small knife, slice ¼ inch off the top of each artichoke, then trim and peel the stems. Very thinly slice each artichoke lengthwise and add to the bowl. Toss with the lemon juice and ½ teaspoon of salt. Let stand for 30 minutes, tossing occasionally.

2. Spread the arugula and radicchio on a platter. Using a slotted spoon, lift the artichokes from the lemon juice and scatter over the greens. Sprinkle with the herbs.

3. Whisk the olive oil with the remaining lemon juice in the large bowl and season with salt and pepper. Drizzle the dressing over the salad; serve. —*Chris Behr*

Persimmon-and-Endive Salad with Honey Vinegar and Avocado Oil Vinaigrette

📷 PAGE 33

Total **15 min;** Serves **4**

The combination of buttery avocado oil and bracing honey vinegar (made from mead) makes a fantastic vinaigrette in this crunchy, colorful and delicious salad.

- ¼ cup honey vinegar
- ½ tsp. Dijon mustard
- ¼ cup unrefined avocado oil
  Kosher salt and pepper
- 4 heads of Belgian endive, leaves separated
- 2 persimmons, very thinly sliced crosswise on a mandoline
- 1 Hass avocado—peeled, pitted and cut into thin wedges
- ½ cup toasted almonds, chopped, plus more for garnish
- ¼ cup pomegranate seeds, plus more for garnish

In a large bowl, whisk the vinegar with the Dijon. While whisking constantly, slowly drizzle in the avocado oil until incorporated; season with salt and pepper. Gently fold in the remaining ingredients and season with salt and pepper. Garnish with additional almonds and pomegranate seeds and serve. —*Laura Rege*

Roasted Eggplant and
Cauliflower Salad with Tahini
Green Goddess Dressing

Roasted Eggplant and Cauliflower Salad with Tahini Green Goddess Dressing

Total **1 hr**; Serves **6 to 8**

- 1½ lbs. cauliflower, cored and cut into 1-inch florets
- ½ cup plus 1 Tbsp. extra-virgin olive oil

  Kosher salt and pepper
- 1 lb. Japanese eggplant, sliced ¼ inch thick
- 1 cup Greek yogurt, preferably 2%
- ¼ cup tahini
- 5 oil-packed anchovy fillets, drained
- 2 garlic cloves
- 1 Tbsp. fresh lemon juice
- 2 Tbsp. chopped dill
- 2 Tbsp. chopped parsley
- 8 oz. Persian or Kirby cucumbers, thinly sliced
- 2 Hass avocados, peeled and cut into wedges
- 6 cups watercress (4 oz.), stemmed

1. Preheat the oven to 450°. On a rimmed baking sheet, toss the cauliflower with 2 tablespoons of the olive oil and season with salt and pepper; spread in an even layer. On a second rimmed baking sheet, toss the eggplant with ¼ cup of the olive oil and season with salt and pepper; spread in an even layer. Roast the vegetables, stirring occasionally, until golden and tender, 20 to 25 minutes. Transfer the vegetables to racks to cool.

2. Meanwhile, in a food processor, puree the yogurt, tahini, anchovies, garlic and lemon juice until smooth. With the machine on, drizzle in 3 tablespoons of water and the remaining 3 tablespoons of olive oil until smooth; season with salt and pepper. Stir in the dill and parsley.

3. In a 3- to 4-quart glass trifle dish or bowl, spread the cucumbers in an even layer; season with salt and pepper. Top with the cooled eggplant and cauliflower and the avocados and season with salt and pepper. Finish with the watercress and serve the salad with the tahini dressing. —*Kay Chun*

MAKE AHEAD The roasted vegetables and the dressing can be refrigerated separately overnight.

Hmong Papaya Salad

⏱ Total **20 min**; Serves **4**

Globe-trotting TV chef and Twin Cities native Andrew Zimmern pays tribute to the large Hmong population in Minneapolis–St. Paul with this tangy, crunchy salad. It's inspired by a favorite dish at Hmong Village market in St. Paul.

- 2 Thai chiles, thinly sliced
- 1 garlic clove
- 2 Tbsp. fresh lime juice
- 1 Tbsp. fish sauce
- 1 Tbsp. light brown sugar
- 1 Tbsp. tamarind paste
- ¼ tsp. fermented crab paste (see Note)
- 1 small green papaya (1¼ lbs.)
- ½ lb. Chinese long beans, cut into 1-inch pieces
- 8 cherry tomatoes, halved
- 3 small Thai eggplants, halved and thinly sliced
- ¼ cup toasted peanuts, chopped

  Tiny dried shrimp (optional)

  Kosher salt

  Sticky rice, for serving

1. In a mini food processor, pulse the chiles and garlic until finely chopped. Add the lime juice, fish sauce, brown sugar, tamarind paste and crab paste and pulse until combined. Scrape into a large bowl.

2. Peel the papaya. Using a serrated knife, halve it crosswise and scrape out the seeds. Using a mandoline, cut the flesh into matchstick strips. In the large bowl, toss the papaya with the chile dressing, the long beans, tomatoes, eggplant, peanuts and dried shrimp, if desired. Season with salt. Using your fingers, massage the dressing into the vegetables. Serve with sticky rice. —*Andrew Zimmern*

NOTE Shrimp or anchovy paste can be substituted for the crab paste.

Sirloin, Celery and Cherry Salad

⏱ Total **30 min**; Serves **4**

Chef Asaf Doktor of the Tel Aviv restaurant Dok tosses his chargrilled steak with a tart-sweet, jalapeño-inflected mix of celery and red cherries.

- One 1-lb. sirloin steak, cut into 4 individual steaks
- ½ cup extra-virgin olive oil, plus more for brushing

  Kosher salt and pepper
- ⅓ cup fresh lime juice
- 3 small shallots, thinly sliced
- 1 jalapeño—stemmed, seeded and minced
- 1 garlic clove, minced
- 6 celery ribs, thinly sliced, plus leaves for garnish
- 2 cups sweet cherries, pitted and halved (10 oz.)

1. Light a grill or preheat a grill pan. Brush the steaks with olive oil and season with salt and pepper. Grill over high heat, turning, until browned outside and rare within, about 3 minutes total. Transfer to a carving board and let rest for 5 minutes, then thinly slice against the grain.

2. Meanwhile, in a small bowl, whisk the ½ cup of olive oil with the lime juice, shallots, jalapeño and garlic. Season the dressing with salt and pepper.

3. In a large bowl, toss the steak with the sliced celery, cherries and half of the dressing. Season with salt and pepper. Garnish with celery leaves. Serve; pass more dressing at the table. —*Asaf Doktor*

WINE Smoky Israeli Cabernet: 2014 Carmel Appellation.

Greek Salad of Sorts

Total **30 min**; Serves **4 to 6**

Of his delicious and crowd-pleasing Greek salad, Athens, Georgia, chef Hugh Acheson says, "It feeds four people like champions, six like semifinalists."

- **1 lb. ripe red tomatoes (about 2 large), cored and cut into ½-inch pieces**
- **½ red onion, cut into ¼-inch dice**
- **½ English cucumber, cut into ½-inch pieces**
- **1 red bell pepper, cored and cut into ½-inch pieces**
- **½ cup parsley, finely chopped**
- **¼ cup mint leaves, chopped**
- **¼ cup pitted kalamata olives, chopped**
- **2½ oz. feta, crumbled (about ½ cup)**
- **4 medium peperoncini, stemmed and chopped**
- **2 cups salted pita chips, broken into pieces**
- **½ cup Greek Vinaigrette (p. 34)**

In a large bowl, combine all the ingredients and toss to coat with the vinaigrette. Serve. —*Hugh Acheson*

Caprese Salad

Total **15 min**; Serves **4**

This is a simple, seasonal salad that can be thrown together as part of a carefree meal.

- **½ lb. cherry or grape tomatoes, halved**
- **One 8-oz. ball of buffalo mozzarella cheese, sliced**
- **½ cup packed basil leaves**
- **1½ Tbsp. extra-virgin olive oil**
- **Flaky sea salt and freshly ground black pepper**

Arrange the tomatoes and mozzarella in a shallow serving bowl. Scatter the basil over the top and drizzle with the olive oil. Sprinkle with flaky sea salt and garnish with freshly ground black pepper; serve. —*Chantal Dussouchaud*

Beefsteak Tomato and Burrata Salad with Olive Streusel

Total **1 hr**; Serves **4 to 6**

- **½ cup extra-virgin olive oil, plus more for drizzling**
- **½ oz. dried shiitake mushrooms, chopped**
- **8 garlic cloves, thinly sliced**
- **One 28-oz. can crushed tomatoes**
- **One 8-inch piece kombu (see Note), broken into pieces**
- **2 tsp. sugar**
- **Kosher salt**
- **1 cup panko**
- **¼ cup all-purpose flour**
- **½ tsp. unsweetened cocoa powder**
- **¼ cup pitted kalamata olives**
- **4 Tbsp. cold unsalted butter, cubed**
- **4 large, ripe beefsteak tomatoes, cut into 1-inch-thick slices**
- **Two 4-oz. balls of burrata, patted dry and halved**
- **Basil leaves and small fennel fronds, for garnish (optional)**
- **Flaky sea salt, for serving**

1. In a medium saucepan, heat the ½ cup of olive oil. Add the dried shiitake and garlic and cook over moderately low heat, stirring, until softened, about 3 minutes. Add the crushed tomatoes, kombu and sugar and simmer until thickened slightly, about 30 minutes. Strain the pomodoro sauce through a fine sieve set over a medium bowl, pressing on the solids; season with kosher salt. Let cool to room temperature.

2. Meanwhile, preheat the oven to 350° and line a large rimmed baking sheet with parchment paper. In a food processor, pulse the panko, flour and cocoa powder until combined. Add the olives and pulse until finely chopped. Add the butter and pulse until the mixture resembles coarse crumbs. Spread the streusel on the prepared baking sheet. Bake for about 15 minutes, until toasted and golden brown. Transfer to a rack and let cool completely.

3. Spoon some of the pomodoro sauce onto a platter or plates. Arrange the tomato slices over the sauce and top with the burrata. Generously sprinkle with the olive streusel and garnish with basil leaves and fennel fronds, if using. Drizzle the salad with olive oil and sprinkle with sea salt before serving. —*Bryan Voltaggio and Michael Voltaggio*

NOTE Kombu (dried seaweed) is available at Whole Foods and from amazon.com.

MAKE AHEAD The pomodoro sauce can be refrigerated for up to 5 days. The olive streusel can be stored at room temperature in an airtight container overnight.

WINE Fragrant, berry-scented rosé: 2016 Crios de Susana Balbo Rosé of Malbec.

Grilled Eggplant, Apricot and Tomato Salad

Active **40 min**; Total **1 hr 40 min**
Serves **4 to 6**

This colorful salad showcases summer produce at its peak. When corn season is in full swing, cut the sweet, raw kernels off the cob and toss them into this dish.

- **4 Japanese eggplants (1½ lbs.), trimmed and halved lengthwise**
- **Kosher salt and pepper**
- **½ cup extra-virgin olive oil, plus more for brushing**
- **½ lb. mixed heirloom tomatoes, cut into bite-size pieces**
- **½ lb. apricots—halved, pitted and cut into wedges**
- **6 scallions, thinly sliced on the bias and soaked in ice water for 20 minutes**
- **¼ cup red wine vinegar**
- **½ cup lightly packed mint leaves**
- **½ cup lightly packed parsley leaves**
- **¼ cup snipped chives**

1. Season the eggplant with salt and let stand in a colander for 1 hour; pat dry.

2. Light a grill. Brush the eggplant with olive oil and season lightly with pepper. Grill over moderately high heat, turning occasionally, until lightly charred and tender, 10 to 12 minutes. Transfer to a work surface and let cool slightly. Cut into 1½-inch pieces.

3. In a serving bowl, toss the eggplant with the tomatoes, apricots, scallions, vinegar and the ½ cup of olive oil. Fold in the mint, parsley and chives. Season the salad with salt and pepper and serve. —*Joshua McFadden*

Grilled Eggplant, Apricot
and Tomato Salad

Tomatoes with Bagna Cauda and Chinese Sausage

Total **1 hr 15 min**; Serves **8**

The killer garlic-anchovy sauce is as tasty on pasta as it is as a dip for vegetables.

- 1 cup extra-virgin olive oil
- 1 cup minced garlic
- 4 Tbsp. unsalted butter
- 2 anchovy fillets, minced
- 1 Tbsp. crushed red pepper
  Kosher salt
- 6 Chinese sausages (10 oz.), cut into ½-inch pieces (see Note)
- ½ cup canola oil
- ¼ cup finely chopped chives
- ¼ cup finely chopped parsley
- ¼ cup finely chopped dill
- ¼ cup finely chopped mint
- ½ cup Kewpie mayonnaise (see Note)
- ½ cup crème fraîche
- 2 Tbsp. fresh lemon juice
  Eight 4-oz. tomatoes, preferably Momotaro, cut into wedges
  Fleur de sel, for sprinkling

1. In a medium saucepan, cook the olive oil, garlic and butter over moderate heat, whisking frequently, until the garlic just starts to color, about 7 minutes. Whisk in the anchovies and cook, whisking, until the garlic is golden, 5 to 7 minutes more. Transfer the bagna cauda to a heatproof medium bowl and let cool slightly. Whisk in the crushed red pepper and let the bagna cauda cool completely, stirring occasionally. Season with kosher salt.

2. Meanwhile, in a food processor, pulse the sausages until finely ground. In a large skillet, combine the ground sausage with ½ cup of water and cook over high heat, stirring frequently, until the water evaporates and the sausage is rendered, about 5 minutes. Add the canola oil and cook over moderately high heat, stirring constantly, until the sausage bits are browned and crisp, about 7 minutes more. Using a slotted spoon, transfer the crispy sausage to paper towels to drain.

3. In a small bowl, mix the chives with the parsley, dill and mint. In a medium bowl, whisk the Kewpie mayo with the crème fraîche, lemon juice and ¼ cup of the mixed herbs. Season the herbed dressing with kosher salt.

4. Spread the herbed dressing in 8 very shallow bowls or on a platter. Arrange the tomatoes on top. Spoon some of the bagna cauda on top, then sprinkle with the crispy sausage, remaining mixed herbs and fleur de sel. Serve right away. —Jonathan Whitener

NOTE Look for Chinese sausage and Kewpie mayonnaise at Asian markets.

WINE Light-bodied Provençal rosé: 2016 Domaine Houchart Côtes de Provence.

Spring Asparagus Salad with Feta

Active **40 min**; Total **1 hr 15 min**; Serves **6**

- 1 lb. medium asparagus, trimmed
- ½ cup fresh or thawed frozen peas
- ½ cup shelled edamame
- ½ cup mayonnaise
- 1 tsp. finely grated lemon zest plus 1 Tbsp. fresh lemon juice
- 2 tsp. chopped lemon thyme or thyme leaves
- 1 small garlic clove, mashed to a paste
  Fine sea salt and pepper
- 2 cups pea shoots (3 oz.)
- 4 oz. feta cheese, crumbled (¾ cup)

1. Fill a medium bowl with ice water. Using a sharp vegetable peeler, peel half of the asparagus lengthwise into ribbons. Transfer to the ice bath to chill until the asparagus curls, about 1 hour. Drain and gently pat dry.

2. Meanwhile, fill a large bowl with ice water. In a medium saucepan of salted boiling water, blanch the remaining asparagus with the peas and edamame for 3 minutes; transfer to the ice bath to cool, then drain and pat dry.

3. In a large bowl, whisk the mayonnaise with the lemon zest, lemon juice, thyme and garlic and season with salt and pepper. Add the asparagus ribbons, blanched vegetables and pea shoots, season with salt and pepper and gently toss to combine. Mound the salad on plates, sprinkle with feta and serve. —Dane Allchorne

MAKE AHEAD The dressing can be refrigerated for up to 2 days.

Grilled Pepper Salad with Cucumbers

Total **45 min**; Serves **4**

Chefs Sara Kramer and Sarah Hymanson, of Kismet in Los Angeles, grill all kinds of peppers before tossing them in this delicious and compelling salad that includes grapes, cucumbers, purslane and a lemon and Urfa pepper dressing.

- ¼ cup plus 1 Tbsp. extra-virgin olive oil, plus more for brushing
- 1 poblano chile, halved and seeded
- 1 Cubanelle pepper, halved and seeded
- 1 lb. mini sweet peppers (about 16), halved and seeded
  Kosher salt
- 4½ tsp. finely grated lemon zest plus ¼ cup fresh lemon juice
- 1 garlic clove, finely grated
- 1 Tbsp. Urfa biber (see Note)
- 1 tsp. dried thyme
- 3 Persian cucumbers, cut on the bias into bite-size pieces
- 1 cup seedless green grapes, halved
- 2 cups purslane or parsley leaves

1. Light a grill and oil the grate. Toss the poblano, Cubanelle and sweet peppers with 1 tablespoon of the olive oil and season generously with salt. Grill over moderately high heat, turning occasionally, until the peppers are crisp-tender, about 4 to 8 minutes, depending on the pepper size. Let cool completely.

2. Meanwhile, in a large bowl, whisk the remaining ¼ cup of olive oil with the lemon zest, lemon juice, garlic, Urfa biber and thyme. Season with salt.

3. Cut the cooled peppers into bite-size pieces. Add to the dressing along with the cucumbers, grapes and purslane. Season with salt and toss well. Transfer to plates and serve. —Sara Kramer and Sarah Hymanson

NOTE Urfa biber, also known as Urfa pepper, is a Turkish chile that's distinctive for its dark-burgundy color, irregularly sized flakes and intriguing salty-sweet-smoky-sour flavor. Look for it on amazon.com.

Marinated Watermelon with Whipped Feta

Active **30 min**; Total **55 min**; Serves **8 to 10**

Steeping watermelon in a savory, acidic marinade draws out the juices from the fruit and intensifies its flavor.

- **2** Tbsp. Champagne vinegar
- **1** small shallot, minced
- One 2-inch piece of ginger, peeled and finely grated
- **¼** cup plus 3 Tbsp. extra-virgin olive oil
- Kosher salt
- One 5-lb. seedless watermelon, peeled and cut into 4-by-1-inch rectangles
- **1** Tbsp. pink peppercorns
- **1½** tsp. black peppercorns
- **1** tsp. sumac
- **½** tsp. cayenne
- **1** lb. feta cheese, preferably Greek
- **⅓** cup lightly packed basil leaves, torn
- **⅓** cup lightly packed mint leaves, torn
- **⅓** cup lightly packed tarragon leaves, chopped
- Flaky sea salt

1. In a medium bowl, whisk the vinegar with the shallot, ginger and 3 tablespoons of the olive oil. Season the marinade with kosher salt. Place the watermelon in a large resealable bag and pour in the marinade. Refrigerate for 30 minutes.

2. Meanwhile, in a small skillet, toast the pink and black peppercorns over moderately high heat until fragrant, 2 minutes. Transfer to a spice grinder and let cool, then grind to a powder. Transfer to a small bowl and mix with the sumac and cayenne.

3. In a food processor, puree the feta until smooth. With the machine on, drizzle in the remaining ¼ cup of olive oil.

4. Spread the whipped feta on a platter. Using a slotted spoon, remove the watermelon from the marinade and arrange on the feta. Drizzle with some of the marinade and generously sprinkle with the spices. Garnish with the herbs and sea salt; serve. —*Joe Kindred*

Watermelon Slabs with Jicama

Total **30 min**; Serves **4**

- **¼** cup fresh lime juice
- **¼** cup extra-virgin olive oil
- **2** Tbsp. minced cilantro, plus chopped leaves for garnish
- Flaky sea salt and pepper
- **1½** lbs. jicama, peeled and shaved into ribbons
- One 3-lb. piece of seedless watermelon, peeled and cut into ¾-inch-thick wedges
- Ancho chile or ají amarillo powder, for dusting

1. In a medium bowl, whisk the lime juice, oil and minced cilantro and season with sea salt and pepper. Gently toss in the jicama.

2. Arrange the watermelon on 4 plates and season with sea salt and pepper. Pile the jicama on top and garnish with chopped cilantro. Dust with chile powder and serve. —*Justin Chapple*

Grilled Cobia Salad with Corn and Watermelon

Active **30 min**; Total **2 hr 15 min**; Serves **4**

When fishing in the Northern Gulf, Kevin Willmann of Farmhaus in St. Louis catches cobia, a flaky white fish for this refreshing salad. Mahimahi and farm-raised cobia are also sustainable choices for this dish.

- **2** Tbsp. extra-virgin olive oil, plus more for brushing
- One ¾-lb. skinless cobia fillet (about 1 inch thick)
- Kosher salt and pepper
- **1** small poblano chile
- **2** ears of corn, in the husk, soaked in water for 1 hour
- **2** Tbsp. fresh lime juice
- **½** lb. seedless watermelon—rind removed, flesh cut into ¾-inch pieces (2 cups)
- **¼** cup small cilantro sprigs
- Plantain chips, for garnish

1. Light a grill and set it up for direct and indirect grilling. Oil the grate. Brush the fish with olive oil and season with salt and pepper. Grill the fish over moderately high direct heat, turning once, until cooked through and lightly charred, 10 minutes.

Transfer to a plate and let cool. Refrigerate for 30 minutes. Keep the grill on.

2. Meanwhile, grill the poblano over moderately high direct heat and the corn over indirect heat, turning, until both vegetables are tender and the chile is charred, 8 minutes for the poblano and 12 to 15 minutes for the corn. Transfer to a cutting board and let cool slightly. Peel, stem and seed the poblano, then chop finely. Shuck the corn; cut the kernels from the cob. Let cool.

3. In a serving bowl, whisk the 2 tablespoons of olive oil with the lime juice. Flake the fish with a fork and add to the bowl with the poblano, corn, watermelon and cilantro. Gently toss the salad and season with salt and pepper. Let stand for 10 minutes, then garnish with plantain chips and serve. —*Kevin Willmann*

WINE Nectarine-inflected Oregon Pinot Gris: 2015 Bethel Heights Vineyard.

Radish-and-Avocado Salad

Total **15 min**; Serves **8**

Ripe avocados balance the bite of peppery radishes and chiles in this salad.

- **20** radishes, thinly sliced
- **1** small red onion, thinly sliced (1 cup)
- **1** jalapeño, thinly sliced
- **¼** cup fresh lime juice
- **1** Tbsp. extra-virgin olive oil, plus more for drizzling
- Flaky sea salt
- **3** ripe Hass avocados—peeled, pitted and sliced
- **1** cup cilantro leaves
- **½** cup torn basil leaves

In a medium bowl, combine the radishes with the onion, jalapeño, lime juice and the 1 tablespoon of olive oil and toss to coat. Season with salt. Arrange the avocados on a platter, drizzle with olive oil and season with salt. Spoon the radish salad on top, strew with the cilantro and basil and serve as soon as possible. —*Lorena Herrera*

MAKE AHEAD The ingredients can all be prepped up to 4 hours ahead, but toss the radish mixture with the lime juice and olive oil and then assemble the salad just before serving or the radishes will get soggy.

Chorizo-and-Fig Salad

Chorizo-and-Fig Salad

Active **20 min**; Total **45 min**; Serves **4**

The nutty flavor of sherry vinegar is delicious in this ultimate fall salad, which combines crisp roasted fingerlings and chorizo with fresh, sweet figs, crunchy fennel and sharp arugula.

- 1 **lb. fingerling potatoes, halved lengthwise**
- 1 **Tbsp. extra-virgin olive oil**
  Kosher salt and pepper
- 1 **lb. Spanish chorizo, thinly sliced**
- ¼ **cup sherry vinegar**
- 1 **Tbsp. honey Dijon mustard**
- ¼ **cup unrefined sunflower oil**
- ¾ **lb. fresh green and purple figs, each cut into 4 wedges**
- ½ **small fennel bulb—halved, cored and thinly sliced**
- 2 **bunches of arugula (¼ lb. each), tough stems discarded**

1. Preheat the oven to 425°. On a rimmed baking sheet, toss the potatoes with the olive oil and season with salt and pepper. Roast for 10 minutes, then flip the potatoes and add the chorizo. Continue to roast for 15 minutes longer, until the potatoes and chorizo are golden and tender. Carefully toss with 2 tablespoons of the vinegar and roast for 5 minutes longer, until the vinegar is reduced and the potatoes are crisp. Let cool slightly.

2. Meanwhile, in a small bowl, whisk the remaining 2 tablespoons of vinegar with the mustard. While whisking constantly, slowly drizzle in the sunflower oil and whisk until incorporated. Season with salt and pepper.

3. Arrange the potatoes, chorizo, figs, fennel and arugula on plates. Drizzle the dressing over the top. Season with salt and pepper and serve with the remaining dressing. —*Laura Rege*

WINE Dry, nutty amontillado sherry: Emilio Lustau Los Arcos.

Snap Pea–Radish Salad with Herbed Yogurt

Total **30 min**; Serves **6**

Mix up the herbs (tarragon, dill, cilantro) or throw in chopped pickled ramps from spring. After snap peas pass their peak, swap in crisp cucumbers.

- 1½ **cups whole-milk yogurt**
- 3 **scallions, thinly sliced**
- 1 **cup lightly packed mint leaves, torn**
- 1 **cup lightly packed basil leaves, torn**
- ½ **tsp. finely grated lemon zest plus 2 Tbsp. fresh lemon juice**
- ½ **tsp. crushed red pepper**
  Kosher salt and black pepper
- 1 **lb. sugar snap peas, strings removed and peas halved on the bias**
- 10 **radishes, thinly sliced**
- ¼ **cup extra-virgin olive oil**
- 2 **Tbsp. sweet red wine vinegar, preferably Katz**
  Poppy seeds, for sprinkling

1. In a medium bowl, mix the yogurt with the scallions, mint, basil, lemon zest and juice and the crushed red pepper. Season with salt and black pepper.

2. In a large bowl, toss the snap peas with the radishes, olive oil and vinegar. Season with salt and black pepper.

3. Spread the herbed yogurt in a shallow serving bowl. Pile the vegetables on top and sprinkle with poppy seeds; serve. —*Joshua McFadden*

Beet-and-Onion Salad

Active **15 min**; Total **1 hr**; Serves **8**

Sweet beets, crisp onion, and great olive oil and vinegar are all you need to make this crowd-pleasing salad from Spanish winemaker Álvaro Palacios.

- 2 **lbs. medium beets, peeled**
  Kosher salt and pepper
- 1 **small red or white onion, halved and thinly sliced lengthwise**
- ¼ **cup extra-virgin olive oil**
- 2 **Tbsp. red wine vinegar**

1. In a saucepan, cover the beets with water and bring to a boil. Add a generous pinch of salt and simmer over moderate heat until tender, about 20 minutes. Drain well and let cool, then cut into bite-size pieces.

2. In a bowl, cover the onion with ice water. Add a generous pinch of salt and let stand until crisp, 20 minutes. Drain well; pat dry.

3. In a bowl, toss the beets and onion with the olive oil and vinegar. Season with salt and pepper and toss again. Serve. —*Álvaro Palacios*

MAKE AHEAD The boiled beets can be refrigerated in an airtight container for up to 2 days. Bring to room temperature before using.

WINE Complex, oak-aged white Rioja: 2014 Palacios Remondo Plácet Valtomelloso.

Beet Salad with Shiso

Total **30 min**; Serves **4 to 6**

Chef Greg Baxtrom makes a very special beet and snow pea salad at Olmsted in Brooklyn, thinly shaving beets and tossing them with fragrant shiso leaves, nutty sesame seeds and a warming chile oil spiked with coriander, fish sauce and citrus.

- ¼ **lb. snow peas**
- ¼ **cup grapeseed or canola oil**
- 1 **Tbsp. crushed coriander seeds**
- 1 **Tbsp. Asian fish sauce**
- 1 **Tbsp. hot chile oil**
- 1 **Tbsp. fresh lemon juice**
- 1 **Tbsp. fresh lime juice**
- 1½ **lbs. small mixed colored beets, peeled and shaved into ribbons**
- 8 **shiso leaves, thinly sliced**
- 1 **Tbsp. toasted sesame seeds, plus more for garnish**
  Kosher salt

1. In a medium saucepan of salted boiling water, blanch the snow peas until crisp-tender, 1 to 2 minutes. Drain well and transfer to a bowl of ice water to cool. Drain well and pat dry.

2. In a small bowl, whisk the grapeseed oil with the coriander, fish sauce, chile oil, lemon juice and lime juice.

3. In a serving bowl, toss the beets and snow peas with the dressing, shiso and the 1 tablespoon of sesame seeds. Season with salt; toss. Garnish with more sesame seeds and serve. —*Greg Baxtrom*

Beet-and-Quinoa Salad

Active **20 min;** Total **1 hr 25 min;** Serves **4**

This insanely easy salad is all about the beets. Double the recipe and make it for the week—the beets hold up nicely and the plump raisins absorb the olive oil, making a delicious, no-fuss work lunch.

- **2 medium beets, scrubbed**
- **1 cup cooked quinoa**
- **2 large carrots, shredded**
- **½ cup golden raisins**
- **3 Tbsp. extra-virgin olive oil**
- **Flaky sea salt and pepper**

In a medium saucepan, cover the beets with water. Simmer over moderate heat, partially covered, until tender, 1 hour. Let cool, then peel and cut into ½-inch pieces. In a large bowl, toss the beets with the quinoa, carrots, raisins and olive oil. Season with salt and pepper; serve.
—*Chantal Dussouchaud*

Kimchi Thousand Island Dressing

Total **10 min;** Makes **1 cup**

Portland, Oregon, chef Johanna Ware tosses her salmon salad with this spicy-sweet dressing, which is also irresistible as a dip for crudités, smeared on a sandwich or drizzled over Little Gem lettuce. Trust us, you'll be putting it on everything.

- **5 garlic cloves, chopped**
- **6 Tbsp. mayonnaise**
- **¼ cup sugar**
- **2 Tbsp. gochugaru (Korean red pepper flakes)**
- **2 Tbsp. fish sauce**
- **2 Tbsp. chopped scallions**
- **2 Tbsp. shredded carrot**
- **4 tsp. soy sauce, plus more for seasoning (optional)**
- **1 Tbsp. fresh lemon juice**
- **½ tsp. peeled chopped fresh ginger**

In a blender, puree all of the ingredients with 1 tablespoon of water until smooth. Season with more soy sauce, if desired.
—*Johanna Ware*

MAKE AHEAD The dressing can be refrigerated for up to 1 week.

Arugula-and-Squash Salad

Active **25 min;** Total **1 hr**
Serves **6 to 8**

- **2 Tbsp. fresh marjoram leaves**
- **2 garlic cloves**
- **1 tsp. ground coriander**
- **¼ tsp. ground cinnamon**
- **Kosher salt**
- **¼ cup extra-virgin olive oil, plus more for drizzling**
- **One 2½-lb. kabocha squash—peeled, seeded and cut into 1½-inch pieces**
- **¼ cup pine nuts**
- **3 Tbsp. fresh lemon juice**
- **¼ cup pomegranate seeds**
- **Pinch of cayenne**
- **2 small bunches of arugula, trimmed**
- **1 oz. pecorino cheese, shaved**
- **Aged balsamic vinegar, for drizzling**

1. Preheat the oven to 350°. Line a rimmed baking sheet with parchment paper. In a mini food processor, pulse the marjoram with the garlic, coriander, cinnamon and 1½ teaspoons of salt until finely chopped. Scrape the mixture into a large bowl and stir in 2 tablespoons of the olive oil. Add the squash and toss to coat, then scrape onto the prepared baking sheet. Roast for about 40 minutes, tossing once, until tender and golden. Let cool.

2. Meanwhile, place the pine nuts in a pie plate and toast for about 6 minutes, until golden and fragrant. Let cool.

3. Scrape the squash back into the large bowl and drizzle with 2 tablespoons of the lemon juice and 1 tablespoon of the olive oil. Add the toasted pine nuts, the pomegranate seeds and cayenne and gently toss to combine. Add the arugula and the remaining 1 tablespoon each of olive oil and lemon juice. Season with salt and toss to combine. Arrange the salad on a platter. Top with the pecorino, drizzle with olive oil and balsamic vinegar and serve.
—*April Bloomfield*

Acorn Squash and Escarole Salad

Active **30 min;** Total **1 hr 15 min**
Serves **10**

This lovely knife-and-fork salad gets fantastic texture from crunchy hazelnuts and pomegranate seeds, and the creamy buttermilk drizzle does the perfect job of tying all the components together.

- **1 cup raw hazelnuts**
- **1½ lbs. acorn squash—quartered lengthwise, seeded and cut crosswise into ¼-inch wedges (9 oz.)**
- **2 Tbsp. extra-virgin olive oil**
- **1 Tbsp. coriander seeds, crushed**
- **Kosher salt and pepper**
- **¾ cup buttermilk**
- **¼ cup mayonnaise**
- **1 garlic clove, finely grated**
- **1 lb. escarole, white and light green parts only, leaves torn**
- **1 lb. arugula (not baby), stemmed and leaves torn**
- **1 cup pomegranate seeds**

1. Preheat the oven to 400°. Spread the hazelnuts on a large rimmed baking sheet. Bake for 8 to 10 minutes, until fragrant and lightly browned. Transfer the hazelnuts to a kitchen towel and rub together in the towel to remove the skins. Let the hazelnuts cool, then coarsely chop. Leave the oven on.

2. On the large rimmed baking sheet, toss the squash with the olive oil and coriander and season with salt and pepper. Roast for about 20 minutes, turning once, until tender and browned in spots. Let cool.

3. Meanwhile, in a small bowl, whisk the buttermilk with the mayonnaise, garlic and 2 teaspoons of pepper. Season generously with salt.

4. On a large platter, toss half of the escarole with half of the arugula. Scatter half each of the squash, hazelnuts and pomegranate seeds on top. Repeat the layering one more time. Serve, passing the buttermilk drizzle at the table. —*Justin Chapple*

MAKE AHEAD The buttermilk drizzle can be refrigerated for up to 3 days. The layered salad can be covered with damp paper towels and refrigerated for up to 3 hours.

Acorn Squash and
Escarole Salad

SOUPS
& STEWS

Frogmore Stew (p. 64)
OPPOSITE Whitefish,
Leek and Celery
Chowder with White
Beans (p. 64)

Cherry Gazpacho

Active **30 min**; Total **5 hr 30 min**
Serves **6**

This gazpacho is inspired by Spanish chef Dani García, who uses sweet cherries.

- **2 lbs.** ripe tomatoes, cored and chopped
- **½ lb.** sweet cherries, pitted
- **1** small Italian frying pepper or Cubanelle pepper—stemmed, seeded and chopped
- **1½ cups** day-old cubed crustless rustic white bread (2 oz.)
- **⅓ cup** chopped red onion
- **¼ cup** sherry vinegar
- **1** garlic clove, finely chopped
- **½ cup** plus ⅓ cup extra-virgin olive oil
  Kosher salt and pepper
- **1 cup** packed basil leaves
  Slivered anchovy fillets, chopped pistachios and grated frozen goat cheese, for garnish

1. In a large bowl, toss the tomatoes with the cherries, Italian pepper, bread, red onion, vinegar, garlic, ½ cup of the olive oil and a very generous pinch each of salt and pepper. Let the gazpacho base stand at room temperature for 2 hours.

2. In batches, puree the gazpacho base until very smooth, about 2 minutes. Transfer to another large bowl. Cover and refrigerate for at least 3 hours or overnight.

3. Meanwhile, in a small saucepan of simmering water, blanch the basil until tender, about 1 minute. Drain well and cool under running water. Squeeze out the excess moisture and transfer to a blender. With the machine on, gradually add the remaining ⅓ cup of olive oil until the mixture is bright green and very smooth. Strain through a fine sieve into a small bowl, then season the basil oil with salt.

4. Season the gazpacho with salt, adding tablespoons of water if too thick. To serve, spoon the soup into bowls and garnish with slivered anchovy fillets, chopped pistachios, grated frozen goat cheese and the basil oil. —*Anya von Bremzen*

MAKE AHEAD The gazpacho can be refrigerated for up to 3 days. Add a bit of water if it's too thick.

WINE Fino sherry: NV Valdespino Inocente.

Chilled Tomato Soup with Parsley-Olive Salsa

Active **30 min**; Total **2 hr 30 min**
Serves **6 to 8**

Pizzana chef Daniele Uditi's ultrasilky, gazpacho-like soup (fresh vegetables pureed with bread and ice) is ideal for a summer party—it's refreshingly cool and can be made in big batches ahead of time.

SOUP
- **One ½-inch-thick** slice of rustic bread, crust removed and bread chopped (¾ cup)
- **½** large red bell pepper, chopped
- **2** medium celery ribs, coarsely chopped
- **¼ cup** finely chopped onion
- **1½ lbs.** heirloom tomatoes, cored and chopped
- **2** plum tomatoes, cored and chopped
- **1 cup** ice
- **2 Tbsp.** fresh lemon juice
- **1 Tbsp.** honey
- **1 tsp.** crushed red pepper
- **¼ cup** extra-virgin olive oil
  Kosher salt and black pepper

SALSA
- **⅓ cup** pine nuts
- **1 cup** lightly packed parsley, finely chopped
- **⅓ cup** extra-virgin olive oil
- **¼ cup** kalamata olives, coarsely chopped
- **1** small garlic clove, minced
  Kosher salt and pepper

1. Make the soup In a small bowl, cover the bread with water and let stand for 2 minutes; drain. In a blender, finely chop the bread with the bell pepper, celery and onion. Add all of the tomatoes, the ice, lemon juice, honey, crushed red pepper and olive oil and puree until smooth. Season generously with salt and black pepper. Transfer to a bowl, cover and refrigerate until well chilled, about 2 hours.

2. Make the salsa In a small skillet, toast the pine nuts over low heat, stirring, until golden, 6 to 8 minutes. Transfer to a small plate and let cool.

3. In a medium bowl, mix the parsley with the toasted pine nuts, olive oil, olives and garlic. Season with salt and pepper. Ladle the soup into chilled bowls, top with the salsa and serve. —*Daniele Uditi*

MAKE AHEAD The tomato soup can be prepared through Step 1 and refrigerated for up to 3 days.

WINE Crisp, pineappley Albariño from Rías Baixas: 2015 Martin Codax Burgáns.

Salmorejo

Active **15 min**; Total **45 min**; Serves **4**

Salmorejo is a classic Spanish soup made primarily of tomatoes and bread. It's best with a splash of sherry vinegar, but Andalusian tomatoes pack such a great hit of acidity that cooks in Spain often omit the vinegar. The soup is also frequently thickened with *pan de telera*, a type of hard roll, but anything from a ciabatta to a rustic white loaf will be a good substitute.

- **2½ lbs.** vine-ripened tomatoes, cored and chopped
- **½ lb.** rustic white bread, crust removed, bread cubed (2½ cups)
- **2** garlic cloves
- **1 tsp.** sherry vinegar
- **¼ cup** extra-virgin olive oil, plus more for serving
  Kosher salt
- **2** hard-boiled eggs, peeled and chopped
- **½ cup** chopped serrano ham

1. In a blender, puree the chopped tomatoes with the bread, garlic, sherry vinegar and ½ cup of water at high speed until very smooth, about 1 minute. With the blender on, drizzle in the ¼ cup of olive oil until incorporated. Season with salt. Cover and refrigerate until the soup is cold, at least 30 minutes.

2. Divide the soup among 4 bowls. Garnish with the chopped eggs and ham, drizzle with olive oil and serve. —*José Andrés*

MAKE AHEAD The soup can be refrigerated for up to 2 days.

WINE Brisk fino sherry: NV González Byass Tio Pepe.

Cherry
Gazpacho

Green Corn Soup

Green Corn Soup

Active **30 min**; Total **2 hr 30 min**; Serves **4**

This silky, cool corn soup gets its great flavor and fun color from spinach and jalapeños.

- **8** ears of corn, shucked
- **¼** cup extra-virgin olive oil, plus more for drizzling
- **1** medium onion, chopped
- **3** garlic cloves, thinly sliced
  Kosher salt and pepper
- **¾** cup packed baby spinach leaves
- **4** jalapeños—2 stemmed, seeded and roughly chopped; 2 stemmed and thinly sliced
- **1** Tbsp. plus 1 tsp. fresh lime juice

1. Using a thin knife and working in a bowl, cut the kernels from the cobs; you should have 6 cups. Working over another bowl, scrape the cobs with the back of a knife to release the corn milk; discard the cobs.

2. In a large skillet, heat 3 tablespoons of the olive oil over moderately high heat. Add the onion and garlic and cook, stirring occasionally, until softened, about 4 minutes. Add 4½ cups of the corn kernels and the corn milk and cook, stirring occasionally, until the corn is crisp-tender, about 6 minutes. Season with salt and pepper. Transfer to a blender and let cool slightly. Wipe out the skillet.

3. Add 1½ cups of water to the blender with the corn and puree at high speed until very smooth, about 5 minutes. Strain the puree through a fine sieve set over a large bowl, pressing on the solids. Discard the solids. Return the corn puree to the blender and add the spinach, chopped jalapeños and 1 tablespoon of the lime juice and puree until the spinach is finely chopped and the soup is green. Transfer to a large bowl and stir in 1½ cups of water. Cover and refrigerate the soup until cold, at least 2 hours.

4. Meanwhile, in the same skillet, heat the remaining 1 tablespoon of olive oil. Add the remaining 1½ cups of corn kernels and cook over moderately high heat, stirring occasionally, until crisp and golden, 1 minute. Transfer the corn to a small bowl and refrigerate until cold.

5. Add the sliced jalapeños and the remaining 1 teaspoon of lime juice to the chilled corn kernels and season with salt and pepper. Ladel the soup into bowls and top with the corn. Drizzle with olive oil and serve.
—*Laura Rege*

MAKE AHEAD The soup can be refrigerated for up to 2 days.

WINE Lime-scented dry Australian Riesling: 2016 Penfolds Bin 51 Eden Valley.

Chilled Watercress Soup with Crème Fraîche and Za'atar

Active **15 min**; Total **2 hr 45 min** Serves **8**

- **1½** lbs. Yukon Gold potatoes (about 3 large), peeled and cut into 1-inch pieces
- **1** large garlic clove, halved
- **½** lb. watercress with stems
- **½** cup extra-virgin olive oil
- **1** cup cold buttermilk
- **1** cup cold whole milk
  Kosher salt
- **½** cup crème fraîche
- **8** tsp. za'atar (see Note)

1. In a medium saucepan, combine the potatoes and garlic with 4 cups of water and bring to a boil. Cover and simmer over moderately low heat until the potatoes are tender, about 20 minutes. Add the watercress and cook until the greens are just tender, 2 to 3 minutes. Let cool slightly, then refrigerate until cold.

2. Transfer the cold potato-watercress mixture to a blender and puree until smooth. With the machine on, drizzle in the olive oil until incorporated. Pour the soup into a large bowl and stir in the buttermilk, whole milk and ½ cup of cold water; stir in more water if the soup is too thick. Cover and refrigerate until cold, about 1 hour. Season with salt.

3. Pour the chilled soup into 8 bowls. Top each with a tablespoon of crème fraîche and 1 teaspoon of za'atar and serve.
—*Jenn Louis*

NOTE Za'atar is a Middle Eastern blend of sesame seeds, herbs and sumac. It's available at Middle Eastern markets and penzeys.com.

Chilled Avocado Soup with Crab

Active **30 min**; Total **1 hr 30 min**; Serves **4**

At Mixtli, in San Antonio, Texas, this zesty, creamy soup is served as a refreshing beginning course to the Michoacán menu. That region is the largest and most important avocado producer in Mexico, so this dish is a fitting start to the meal.

- **3** large Hass avocados—halved, pitted and peeled
- **2** cups cold vegetable stock, preferably homemade
- **¼** cup plus 1 Tbsp. fresh lime juice
- **½** cup heavy cream
  Kosher salt
  Canola oil, for frying
- **4** medium serrano chiles, thinly sliced crosswise with seeds
- **½** lb. jumbo lump crabmeat, picked over
  Mexican crema and micro cilantro, for garnish

1. In a food processor, combine the avocados, stock, 1 cup of water and ¼ cup of the lime juice and puree until very smooth. With the machine on, gradually add the heavy cream. Strain through a fine sieve into a large bowl, then season with salt. Cover and refrigerate until well chilled, about 1 hour.

2. Meanwhile, in a medium saucepan, heat ¼ inch of canola oil until shimmering. Add the serranos and fry over moderately high heat, stirring, until lightly browned and crisp, 1 to 2 minutes. Using a slotted spoon, transfer to paper towels to drain.

3. In a medium bowl, gently toss the crab with the remaining 1 tablespoon of lime juice. Ladle the chilled soup into bowls and top with the crab and crispy serranos. Garnish with crema and cilantro and serve.
—*Rico Torres and Diego Galicia*

MAKE AHEAD The avocado soup can be refrigerated overnight.

Summer Vegetable Soup

Active **30 min**; Total **1 hr**; Serves **4 to 6**

- 3 Tbsp. extra-virgin olive oil or schmaltz
- 2 Tbsp. minced garlic
- 1 large onion, finely chopped
  Kosher salt and pepper
- 2 qts. chicken stock, preferably homemade
- 1 Tbsp. finely grated peeled fresh turmeric
- ¼ lb. green beans, trimmed and cut into 1-inch lengths
- ½ cup peas, thawed if frozen
- ½ cup lima beans, thawed if frozen, peeled
- ½ cup fresh corn kernels (from 1 ear)
- 1 cup cherry tomatoes, halved
- 1 Tbsp. fresh lime juice
- ¾ cup mixed finely chopped dill, parsley and chives

1. In a large saucepan, heat 2 tablespoons of the olive oil. Add the garlic and cook over moderate heat, stirring, until lightly browned, about 2 minutes. Add the onion and a generous pinch of salt and cook, stirring occasionally, until softened, about 5 minutes. Add the chicken stock and turmeric and bring to a boil. Simmer over moderately low heat until reduced to 6 cups, 25 to 30 minutes.

2. Meanwhile, set up an ice bath. In a medium saucepan of salted boiling water, blanch the green beans until crisp-tender, about 3 minutes. Using a slotted spoon, transfer to the ice bath to cool. Add the peas and lima beans to the saucepan and blanch until crisp-tender, about 1 minute. Drain well and transfer to the ice bath to cool. Drain all of the beans and peas well.

3. Wipe out the medium saucepan and heat the remaining 1 tablespoon of oil in it. Add the corn and cook over moderate heat, stirring, until crisp-tender, about 3 minutes.

4. Stir the green beans, peas, lima beans, corn, tomatoes and lime juice into the broth and season with salt and pepper. Stir in the mixed herbs and serve right away. —*Erin O'Shea*

Supergreen Gumbo

Active **45 min**; Total **2 hr**; Serves **6 to 8**

- 4 thick-cut slices of bacon, chopped
- 1 medium white onion, finely chopped
- 1 medium carrot, finely chopped
- 1 celery rib, finely chopped
- 3 dried chiles de árbol, finely crushed
  Kosher salt and pepper
- 4 oz. smoked ham, finely chopped
- 1 medium leek, white and light green parts only, halved lengthwise and thinly sliced crosswise
- 3 large garlic cloves, minced
- ½ cup dry white wine
- 2 qts. chicken stock or low-sodium broth
- 3 bay leaves
- 10 oz. leaf spinach, thick stems trimmed
- 1 lb. mustard greens, stems discarded
  One 15-oz. can navy beans, rinsed and drained
  Steamed jasmine rice and chile vinegar (see Note), for serving

1. In a large saucepan, cook the bacon over moderate heat, stirring occasionally, until rendered but not crisp, about 5 minutes. Add the onion, carrot, celery, chiles and a generous pinch of salt. Cook, stirring occasionally, until the vegetables are softened and just starting to brown, about 10 minutes. Add the ham, leek and garlic and cook, stirring occasionally, until fragrant, about 3 minutes. Stir in the wine and simmer until reduced by half, 2 to 3 minutes.

2. Add the stock and bay leaves to the saucepan and bring to a boil over high heat, then simmer over moderately low heat until the vegetables and ham are very tender, about 20 minutes. Remove from the heat and let cool to room temperature; discard the bay leaves.

3. Add the spinach and mustard greens to the saucepan and stir well until wilted slightly. In batches, puree the mixture in a blender until a chunky puree forms. Return all of the gumbo to the saucepan and bring to a simmer. Cook, stirring occasionally, until the greens are tender, about 5 minutes. Stir in the beans and season with salt and pepper. Ladle the gumbo into bowls and serve with steamed rice and chile vinegar. —*Andrea Reusing*

NOTE Chile vinegar (also called hot pepper vinegar or pepper sauce) is a staple on Southern tables. Look for it at markets and on amazon.com.

MAKE AHEAD The gumbo can be refrigerated for up to 3 days. Reheat gently before serving.

WINE Citrusy Albariño from Spain's Rías Baixas region: 2015 Bodegas Fillaboa.

Seaweed Soup

Active **40 min**; Total **2 hr**; Serves **8 to 10**

- 1 oz. dried wakame seaweed
- 2 Tbsp. extra-virgin olive oil
- 1 lb. trimmed beef chuck, cut into ½-inch pieces
  Kosher salt and pepper
- 10 garlic cloves, minced
- 2 Tbsp. toasted sesame oil
- 2 Tbsp. Asian fish sauce
- 2 Tbsp. soy sauce
- 1 tsp. mirin
  Thinly sliced scallions and toasted sesame seeds, for garnish

1. In a medium bowl, cover the seaweed with 2 cups of warm water and let stand at room temperature until softened, about 20 minutes; drain.

2. In a large saucepan, heat the olive oil over high heat until shimmering. Add the beef and season with salt and pepper. Cook, stirring occasionally, until lightly browned all over, 5 to 7 minutes. Add the garlic and cook, stirring, until very fragrant, 1 to 2 minutes. Add the drained seaweed and the sesame oil and cook over moderately high heat, stirring, until sizzling, about 3 minutes.

3. Add 3 quarts of water to the saucepan and bring to a boil over high heat. Stir in the fish sauce, soy sauce, mirin, 2 teaspoons of salt and 1 teaspoon of pepper. Simmer over low heat, stirring occasionally, until the beef is very tender, about 1 hour and 30 minutes. Season with salt and pepper. Ladle into bowls. Garnish with sliced scallions and toasted sesame seeds and serve. —*Sohui Kim*

MAKE AHEAD The seaweed soup can be refrigerated for up to 3 days. Reheat gently before serving.

Summer Vegetable Soup

Harissa White
Bean Stew with
Turmeric Yogurt

Million Dollar Stew

Active **40 min**; Total **2 hr 5 min**
Serves **10 to 12**

It's said that eating collards and black-eyed peas on New Year's is good luck, so F&W's Justin Chapple includes both in his hearty, rich pork stew.

- 3 **lbs. boneless pork shoulder, cut into 1-inch pieces**
  Kosher salt and pepper
- 2 **Tbsp. canola oil**
- 2 **large onions, 1 finely chopped and 1 quartered**
- 16 **garlic cloves, 8 finely chopped and 8 whole**
  One 15-oz. can whole peeled tomatoes, crushed by hand
- 2 **chipotle chiles in adobo sauce, seeded and minced**
- 1 **Tbsp. chili powder**
- 2 **tsp. ground cumin**
- 1 **tsp. dried oregano**
- 3 **qts. chicken stock or low-sodium broth**
- ½ **lb. black-eyed peas, picked over**
- 2 **lbs. collard greens, stemmed and chopped**

1. Season the pork with salt and pepper. In a large enameled cast-iron casserole, heat the oil until shimmering. Add half the pork and cook over moderately high heat, turning occasionally, until browned all over, about 8 minutes. Using a slotted spoon, transfer to a plate. Repeat with the remaining pork.

2. Add the chopped onion, chopped garlic and a generous pinch of salt to the casserole. Cook over moderate heat, stirring occasionally, until softened and lightly browned, 5 to 7 minutes. Stir in the tomatoes, chipotles, chili powder, cumin and oregano and cook until bubbling. Stir in the stock and bring to a boil over high heat. Stir in the pork, cover and simmer over low heat until tender, about 1 hour.

3. Meanwhile, in a large saucepan, combine the black-eyed peas with the quartered onion, whole garlic cloves and 12 cups of water. Bring to a boil, then simmer over low heat until the peas are tender, about 45 minutes. Remove from the heat, add 1 tablespoon of salt and let stand for 5 minutes. Drain well and discard the onion and garlic.

4. Stir the collard greens into the stew in large handfuls, letting each handful wilt slightly before adding more. Cover and simmer over low until the pork is very tender and the collards are just softened, about 20 minutes. Stir in the peas, cover and simmer until hot, about 5 minutes. Ladle into bowls and serve. —*Justin Chapple*

MAKE AHEAD The stew and black-eyed peas can be refrigerated overnight. Reheat the stew before adding the peas.

WINE Robust California Syrah: 2014 Martinelli Terra Felice.

Harissa White Bean Stew with Turmeric Yogurt

Active **30 min**; Total **6 hr 45 min**
Serves **4 to 6**

- 3 **Tbsp. unsalted butter**
- 1 **large red onion, finely chopped**
- 5 **garlic cloves, finely chopped**
  Kosher salt
- ¼ **cup plus 3 Tbsp. harissa**
- 3 **Tbsp. tomato paste**
- 1 **tsp. ground cumin**
- 1 **tsp. sweet paprika**
- 1 **lb. dried cannellini beans**
- 2 **large carrots, sliced ½ inch thick**
- 3 **thyme sprigs plus 1½ tsp. fresh thyme leaves**
- 2 **fresh bay leaves**
  One 3-inch strip of lemon zest plus 3 Tbsp. fresh lemon juice
- 2 **tsp. ground turmeric**
- 1½ **cups full-fat Greek yogurt**
- ½ **cup finely chopped parsley, plus leaves for garnish**
- ½ **preserved lemon, pulp discarded and rind thinly sliced**

1. In a large skillet, melt 2 tablespoons of the butter. Add the onion and garlic, season generously with salt and cook over moderately high heat, stirring occasionally, until the onion has softened and is starting to brown, about 8 minutes. Stir in ¼ cup of the harissa and the tomato paste and cook, stirring, until fragrant, about 1 minute. Stir in the cumin and paprika, then add 2½ cups of water and bring to a simmer, scraping up any browned bits on the bottom of the pan. Transfer to a 6-quart slow cooker along with the dried beans, carrots, thyme sprigs, bay leaves, lemon zest and lemon juice. Add 1 tablespoon of salt and 3½ cups of water. Cover and cook on high until the beans are tender, about 6 hours.

2. Meanwhile, in a small nonstick skillet, melt the remaining 1 tablespoon of butter. Add the turmeric and cook over moderately low heat, stirring constantly, until it dissolves, about 30 seconds. Transfer to a medium bowl and let cool slightly, about 5 minutes. Slowly whisk in the yogurt until smooth. Season with salt.

3. Discard the bay leaves and thyme sprigs from the stew. Just before serving, stir in the thyme leaves, chopped parsley and the remaining 3 tablespoons of harissa; season with salt. Ladle into bowls and garnish with the preserved lemon and parsley leaves. Serve, passing the turmeric yogurt at the table. —*Sarah DiGregorio*

MAKE AHEAD The turmeric yogurt can be refrigerated for 2 days. The stew can be refrigerated for 4 days; reheat gently before serving.

WINE Peppery Mediterranean Monastrell: 2015 Bodegas Volver Tarima Hill.

Whitefish, Leek and Celery Chowder with White Beans

📷 PAGE 54

⏱ Total **45 min; Serves 4**

- 3 **Tbsp. extra-virgin olive oil, plus more for drizzling**
- 2 **large leeks, halved lengthwise and cut into 1-inch lengths**
- 4 **celery ribs, cut into ½-inch pieces, plus leaves for garnish**
- 1 **white onion, finely chopped**
- 3 **garlic cloves, minced**
   Kosher salt and pepper
- 3 **Tbsp. all-purpose flour**
   Three 8-oz. bottles clam juice
- 3 **cups chicken stock or low-sodium broth**
- ½ **cup heavy cream**
- 1 **bay leaf**
- 1 **lb. skinless hake or cod, cut into 1-inch pieces**
- ½ **lb. smoked whitefish, flaked**
   One 15-oz. can cannellini beans, rinsed and drained
   Snipped chives, for garnish
   Crusty bread, for serving

1. In a large saucepan, heat the 3 table-spoons of olive oil. Add the leeks, celery, onion, garlic and a generous pinch of salt. Cook over moderately high heat, stirring occasionally, until the vegetables are just softened but not browned, about 10 minutes. Stir in the flour and cook for 1 minute. Add the clam juice, stock, cream and bay leaf and bring just to a boil. Simmer over moderately low heat, stirring occasionally, until the vegetables are tender and the chowder is slightly thickened, about 7 minutes.

2. Stir the fresh and smoked fish and the beans into the soup and simmer over moderately low heat until the fresh fish is just cooked through, 5 to 7 minutes. Discard the bay leaf and season the chowder with salt and pepper. Ladle the chowder into bowls and garnish with celery leaves, chives, pepper and a drizzle of olive oil. Serve with crusty bread. —*Justin Chapple*

MAKE AHEAD The soup can be refrigerated for up to 3 days. Reheat gently.

WINE Fresh, light Spanish white: 2015 CVNE Monopole.

Frogmore Stew with Old Bay Aioli

📷 PAGE 55

Active **2 hr**; Total **2 hr 30 min**
Serves **8 to 10**

- 1 **cup extra-virgin olive oil**
- 6 **celery ribs, coarsely chopped, plus light green leaves for garnish**
- 2 **large carrots, coarsely chopped**
- 1½ **heads of garlic (26 cloves), crushed**
- 1 **large fennel bulb, chopped**
- 1 **large white onion, chopped**
   Kosher salt and pepper
- 1 **small bunch of thyme**
- 2 **Tbsp. fennel seeds**
   One 28-oz. can whole peeled San Marzano tomatoes
- 4 **qts. chicken stock or low-sodium broth**
   Two 12-oz. bottles lager or pilsner
   One 5-lb. whole tilefish or snapper—filleted and skinned, fillets cut into thirds and head and bones reserved (ask your fishmonger to do this; see Note)
- 2 **Tbsp. Old Bay Seasoning**
- 1¾ **lbs. small new potatoes**
- 40 **littleneck clams (3½ lbs.)**
- 1 **lb. Spanish chorizo, sliced ¼ inch thick**
- 4 **ears of corn, shucked and cut into thirds**
- 8 **live large blue crabs (see Note)**
- 40 **extra-large shell-on shrimp (2 lbs.)**
   Cilantro and parsley leaves, for garnish
   Old Bay Aioli (recipe follows), lemon wedges, hot sauce and melted salted butter, for serving

1. In a large pot, heat the olive oil. Add the celery, carrots, garlic, chopped fennel and onion, season with salt and cook over moderately high heat, stirring occasionally, until very tender, 20 minutes. Add the thyme and fennel seeds and cook, stirring, until fragrant, 2 minutes. Add the tomatoes and their juices and cook over moderately high heat, breaking them up with a wooden spoon and stirring occasionally, until the tomato liquid is reduced, about 10 minutes. Stir in the stock, beer, fish head and bones, Old Bay and 8 cups of water. Bring to a boil, then reduce the heat to moderate and simmer for 30 minutes.

2. Strain the fish stock through a fine sieve set over a very large pot, pressing on the solids; discard the solids. Season generously with salt. Bring the stock to a boil over high heat, add the potatoes and cook until barely tender, 15 to 17 minutes. Add the clams and chorizo, cover and cook for 2 minutes. Add the corn, cover and cook for 4 minutes. Season the fish fillets with salt and pepper and add to the stew. Cover and cook for 2 minutes. Add the crabs, cover and cook for 3 minutes. Finally, add the shrimp, cover and cook until all of the seafood is cooked through and the potatoes and corn are tender, about 5 minutes more. Using a slotted spoon, transfer the seafood, potatoes and corn to 2 large platters. Alternatively, spread the seafood on a paper-lined table. Garnish with celery leaves, cilantro leaves and parsley leaves and serve immediately with the Old Bay Aioli, lemon wedges, hot sauce and melted butter. Reserve the fish stock for another use. —*Joe Kindred*

NOTE If you can't get a 5-pound snapper, use 2 smaller snappers. As an alternative to live blue crabs, use 2 pounds of frozen cooked king crab legs and add with the shrimp in Step 2. Also, if making this recipe in a large turkey fryer pot, add the perforated insert after your fish stock has finished simmering and skip the straining process.

BEER Malty, full-flavored ale: The Duck-Rabbit Amber Ale.

OLD BAY AIOLI

⏱ Total **5 min**; Makes **1½ cups**

- 2 **Tbsp. fresh lemon juice**
- 1 **large egg yolk**
- 1 **garlic clove**
- 1¼ **tsp. Old Bay Seasoning**
- 1 **cup canola oil**
   Kosher salt

In a food processor, pulse the lemon juice, egg yolk, garlic, Old Bay and ¼ cup of cold water until the garlic is finely chopped. With the machine on, slowly drizzle in the oil until the aioli is emulsified, about 2 minutes. Season the Old Bay aioli with salt. Transfer to a medium bowl and serve. —*JK*

MAKE AHEAD The aioli can be refrigerated for up to 1 week.

Frogmore Stew
with Old Bay Aioli

Chicken-Orzo Soup
with 10 Vegetables
(p. 68)
OPPOSITE Basic
Chicken Stock
(p. 68)

Basic Chicken Stock

📷 PAGE 66

Active **30 min**; Total **8 hr 30 min**
Makes **3 qts**

Top Chef star, chef Hugh Acheson says, "We use a lot of chicken stock in my house. It is a beautiful thing when created from scratch, and who knew it would be so easy? Throw all of the ingredients in and walk away. It's like a culinary mic drop."

- **One 3½- to 4-lb. chicken, quartered**
- 2 **medium white onions, quartered**
- 3 **large carrots, scrubbed and cut into 2-inch pieces**
- 3 **celery ribs with leaves, cut into 2-inch pieces**
- 2 **garlic cloves**
- 2 **parsley sprigs**
- 2 **thyme sprigs**
- 2 **bay leaves**
- 1 **tsp. coriander seeds**
- 6 **black peppercorns**
  Kosher salt

1. In a large stockpot, combine 4 quarts of water with all of the ingredients except the salt. Simmer over very low heat, partially covered, for 8 hours; skim the surface of the stock as necessary.

2. Strain the stock into a large bowl and season with salt; discard the solids. Let the stock cool, then refrigerate. Skim the fat from the surface before using.
—Hugh Acheson

MAKE AHEAD The stock can be refrigerated for up to 5 days or frozen for up to 1 month.

Stracciatella

📷 Total **30 min**; Serves **4**

Stracciatella is the Italian version of egg drop soup. This tasty one from Georgia chef Hugh Acheson includes shredded chicken, spinach, basil, peas, grated Parmigiano-Reggiano cheese and eggs.

- 6 **cups Basic Chicken Stock (recipe at left) or good-quality store-bought stock**
- 2 **large eggs**
- ¼ **cup finely grated Parmigiano-Reggiano cheese**
- 2 **cups shredded Best-Ever Roast Chicken (p. 146) or rotisserie chicken**
- 1 **cup frozen peas**
- 2 **cups leaf spinach (about 2 oz.), thinly sliced**
- 1 **cup basil leaves, thinly sliced**
  Kosher salt and pepper

In a medium pot, bring the chicken stock to a simmer over moderate heat. In a small bowl, whisk together the eggs and cheese. Slowly add the egg mixture into the hot stock, stirring constantly, until the eggs are just set, about 1 minute. Stir in the chicken and peas and simmer until heated through, about 2 minutes. Add the spinach and basil and cook until just wilted, about 1 minute. Season with salt and pepper and serve.
—Hugh Acheson

Chicken-Orzo Soup with 10 Vegetables

📷 PAGE 67

⏱ Total **45 min**; Serves **4**

Any combination of vegetables will work in this nutritious soup. If including 10 vegetables isn't a priority, you can also cut some and double up on others.

- 2 **Tbsp. extra-virgin olive oil**
- 1 **medium carrot, halved lengthwise and thinly sliced crosswise**
- 1 **small turnip, finely diced**
- ½ **small sweet onion, finely chopped**
- ½ **small fennel bulb, cored and finely diced**
- 1 **celery rib, thinly sliced**
- 2 **garlic cloves, minced**
  Kosher salt and pepper
- ¼ **lb. green or yellow beans, cut into ¼-inch pieces**
- 6 **cups Basic Chicken Stock (recipe at left) or good-quality store-bought stock**
- ¼ **cup cherry tomatoes, quartered**
- ½ **cup frozen peas**
- ¾ **cup orzo, boiled and drained**
- 2 **oz. arugula (about 2 cups packed), thinly sliced**
- ½ **cup basil leaves, thinly sliced**

In a heavy medium saucepan or enameled cast-iron pot, heat the olive oil over moderate heat. Add the carrot and turnip, then add the onion, fennel, celery, garlic and a generous pinch of salt and cook, stirring occasionally, until the vegetables begin to soften, about 6 minutes. Stir in the green beans and cook for 1 minute. Add the chicken stock and bring to a simmer, then add the cherry tomatoes and peas. Simmer the soup over moderately low heat, partially covered, until the vegetables are tender, about 15 minutes. Season with salt and pepper. Divide the orzo, arugula and basil among 4 bowls and ladle the hot soup on top. Serve hot. *—Hugh Acheson*

MAKE AHEAD The soup can be refrigerated overnight. Stir in the orzo, arugula and basil before serving.

Chicken-Barley Soup with Herbs and Egg Noodles

Active **45 min**; Total **2 hr 30 min**; Serves **8**

- 2 Tbsp. extra-virgin olive oil
- 3 lbs. skin-on, bone-in chicken legs
   Kosher salt and pepper
- 2 leeks, white and light green parts only, thinly sliced
- 2 celery ribs, thinly sliced, plus chopped light green leaves for garnish
- 8 oz. mixed mushrooms, such as small white button and oyster, halved
- 3 garlic cloves, finely chopped
- 3 thyme sprigs
- 4 qts. chicken stock or low-sodium broth
- 1¼ cups pearled barley
- 8 oz. egg noodles
- 1 Tbsp. fresh lemon juice
   Chopped parsley and tarragon, for garnish

1. In a large enameled cast-iron casserole, heat the olive oil. Season the chicken with salt and pepper and cook over moderate heat, turning, until golden, about 8 minutes. Transfer to a large plate. Add the leeks and sliced celery to the casserole and cook, stirring occasionally, until softened, about 5 minutes. Add the mushrooms and garlic and cook, stirring occasionally, until the garlic is fragrant, 2 minutes. Add the thyme sprigs, stock, chicken and 2 quarts of water and bring to a simmer. Partially cover and simmer for 30 minutes; stir in the barley and cook until tender and the chicken is cooked through, about 1 hour longer. Transfer the chicken to a baking sheet; when cool enough to handle, discard the skin and shred the meat.

2. Discard the thyme sprigs. Add the egg noodles to the casserole and cook until al dente, then stir in the shredded chicken and the lemon juice and season with salt and pepper. Serve the soup garnished with chopped parsley, tarragon and celery leaves. —*Kay Chun*

MAKE AHEAD The soup can be refrigerated for up to 2 days.

Spicy Green Posole

Active **45 min**; Total **1 hr 20 min**
Serves **4 to 6**

This pozole from star chef Richard Blais gets amazing flavor from tomatillos, poblanos and jalapeños. Be sure to serve the fragrant chicken stew with all of the delicious garnishes suggested.

- 1 lb. tomatillos, husked
- 2 medium poblano chiles
- 2 jalapeños
- 2 Tbsp. extra-virgin olive oil
- 4 chicken thighs (1 lb.)
- 1 small onion, diced
- 4 garlic cloves, minced
   Two 15-oz. cans hominy, drained and rinsed
- 5 cups chicken stock
   Kosher salt and pepper
   Sliced cabbage, radishes and scallions, cilantro, watercress or purslane, Mexican crema and lime wedges, for serving

1. Preheat the broiler and position a rack 4 to 6 inches from the heat. Spread the tomatillos, poblanos and jalapeños on a rimmed baking sheet. Broil for about 10 minutes, turning occasionally, until charred. Transfer to a work surface, then peel and seed the chiles. Finely chop the chiles and tomatillos.

2. Meanwhile, in a large saucepan, heat the oil over moderately high heat. Add the chicken and cook, turning once, until browned, about 10 minutes. Add the onion and garlic and cook, stirring, until translucent, about 3 minutes. Add the tomatillos, chiles, hominy and stock. Bring to a boil, then reduce the heat and simmer for 45 minutes, until the chicken is tender. Season with salt and pepper.

3. Transfer the chicken to a work surface and shred the meat with a fork; discard the skin and bones. Return the chicken to the soup and simmer until heated through. Serve the posole with cabbage, radishes, scallions, cilantro, watercress, crema and lime wedges. —*Richard Blais*

WINE Crisp Spanish white: 2016 CVNE Monopole Blanco.

Hot-and-Sour Meatball Soup

Total **40 min**; Serves **4**

- ¾ oz. dried wood ear mushrooms
   Three 1-inch pieces peeled ginger, 2 pieces cut into thin matchsticks
- 2 scallions, chopped, plus thinly sliced scallions for garnish
- 1 garlic clove
- ½ lb. large shrimp, peeled and deveined
- ½ lb. fatty ground pork
- 6 Tbsp. black vinegar
   Kosher salt and white pepper
- 6 cups chicken stock or low-sodium broth
- 1 large egg, beaten with a pinch of salt
- ½ lb. firm tofu, cut into ½-inch pieces
   One 8-oz. can sliced bamboo shoots, drained
- 2 tsp. toasted sesame oil

1. In a small heatproof bowl, cover the mushrooms with boiling water and let stand until softened, about 20 minutes. Drain.

2. Meanwhile, in a food processor, pulse the uncut piece of ginger with the chopped scallions and garlic. Add the shrimp and pulse to chop. Scrape the mixture into a bowl; fold in the pork, 1 tablespoon of the black vinegar and 1 teaspoon of salt. Roll into twenty 1-inch balls; transfer to a baking sheet.

3. In a large pot, bring the stock and half of the ginger matchsticks to a simmer over moderately high heat. Using a circular motion, pour the beaten egg into the broth. Wait 5 seconds, then stir the broth to distribute the egg throughout. Add the meatballs, drained mushrooms, tofu and bamboo shoots and simmer over moderate heat until the meatballs are just cooked through, about 5 minutes. Remove the pot from the heat. Stir in 3 tablespoons of the vinegar, the sesame oil and a pinch of pepper. Season with salt.

4. IN a small bowl, stir the remaining ginger matchsticks into the remaining 2 tablespoons of black vinegar. Ladle the soup into bowls, garnish with sliced scallions and serve hot with the ginger-vinegar mixture. —*Laura Rege*

MAKE AHEAD The recipe can be prepared through Step 3 and refrigerated overnight.

PASTA
& NOODLES

Smoked Gouda
Carbonara (p. 79)
OPPOSITE Pork-and-
Ricotta-Stuffed Jumbo
Shells (p. 82)

Garlicky Spaghetti with Mixed Greens

Total **1 hr**; Serves **6**

Packed with intensely flavorful ingredients, this garlicky pasta is fiery, fun and loaded with greens so that each bite is equal parts of both.

- ¾ cup extra-virgin olive oil
- 1 cup panko
- 2 Tbsp. finely chopped parsley
  Kosher salt and pepper
- 1 lb. spaghetti
- ⅔ cup thinly sliced garlic (about 18 cloves)
- 2 lbs. mustard greens and kale, stemmed and leaves coarsely torn (24 cups)
- 2 Tbsp. fresh lemon juice

1. In a small skillet, heat ¼ cup of the olive oil. Add the panko and toast over moderate heat, stirring, until golden, about 5 minutes. Stir in the parsley and season with salt and pepper. Transfer to a paper towel–lined plate to drain; let cool.

2. Meanwhile, in a pot of salted boiling water, cook the spaghetti until al dente. Drain well, reserving 1 cup of the pasta water.

3. In a large pot, combine the remaining ½ cup of oil with the garlic and cook over low heat, stirring occasionally, until the garlic is fragrant and light golden, 7 to 8 minutes. In batches, add the greens and cook, tossing, until wilted, about 3 minutes. Season with salt and pepper. Add the pasta, ½ cup of the reserved pasta water and the lemon juice; cook, stirring, until a sauce forms, 2 minutes. Divide the pasta among bowls, top with the panko, and serve. —*Kay Chun*

MAKE AHEAD The toasted panko (without the parsley) can be stored in an airtight container at room temperature overnight. Stir in the parsley before serving.

WINE Herbal Sardinian white: 2015 Argiolas Costamolino.

Greens Pasta Salad

Active **40 min**; Total **1 hr 15 min**; Serves **8**

F&W's Justin Chapple set out to improve pasta salad, which is often bland and laden with mayonnaise. Here, the pasta is dressed with a tangy and creamy mix of buttermilk, vinegar and mayo. The greens add a fresh, bright note.

- Ice
  Kosher salt and pepper
- 1 lb. asparagus, trimmed and cut into 1-inch lengths
- 2 cups peas, fresh or frozen
- 1 lb. campanelle pasta
- 1 cup buttermilk
- ½ cup mayonnaise
- 3 Tbsp. Champagne vinegar
- 1 large garlic clove, grated
- ½ lb. arugula (not baby), thick stems discarded, leaves coarsely chopped

1. Set up an ice bath. In a large saucepan of salted boiling water, cook the asparagus and peas until crisp-tender, about 2 minutes. Drain and transfer the vegetables to the ice bath to cool completely; drain well.

2. Fill the saucepan with water and return to a boil; season generously with salt. Add the pasta and cook until al dente. Drain well and transfer to a large bowl.

3. In a medium bowl, whisk the buttermilk with the mayonnaise, vinegar and garlic. Season with salt and pepper.

4. Toss half of the dressing with the warm pasta; let cool for 30 minutes. Stir in the asparagus, peas and remaining dressing. Season with salt and pepper, then fold in the arugula and serve. —*Justin Chapple*

MAKE AHEAD The pasta salad can be refrigerated for a few hours. Fold in the arugula before serving.

Vinegar-Glazed Butternut Squash Pasta Salad

Active **20 min**; Total **55 min**; Serves **4**

This rustic whole-wheat pasta dish combines some fall classic flavors. For best results, seek out a great-quality unrefined hazelnut oil, which imbues the whole dish with a lovely nuttiness.

- One 2-lb. butternut squash—peeled, seeded and cut into ¾-inch pieces (6 cups)
- ¼ cup plus 2 Tbsp. red wine vinegar
- 2 Tbsp. extra-virgin olive oil
- 1 Tbsp. honey
  Kosher salt and pepper
- ¾ lb. whole-wheat fusilli
- ¼ cup plus 1 Tbsp. unrefined hazelnut oil
- 1 head of Treviso or ½ small head of radicchio, thinly sliced
- ½ cup packed parsley leaves
  Shaved Pecorino Toscano or Romano, for serving

1. Preheat the oven to 425°. On a rimmed baking sheet, toss the squash with ¼ cup of the vinegar, the olive oil and honey and spread evenly on the baking sheet. Season with salt and pepper. Roast for about 35 minutes, tossing halfway through, until browned and glazed.

2. Meanwhile, in a large pot of salted boiling water, cook the pasta until al dente. Drain. Toss with 3 tablespoons of the hazelnut oil.

3. In a large bowl, whisk the remaining 2 tablespoons each of vinegar and hazelnut oil. Stir in the squash, Treviso and parsley, then fold in the pasta. Season with salt and pepper. Serve warm or at room temperature with shaved pecorino. —*Laura Rege*

MAKE AHEAD The pasta salad can be refrigerated overnight. Stir in the Treviso and parsely before serving.

WINE California rosé: 2016 Grgich Hills.

Garlicky Spaghetti
with Mixed Greens

Spaghetti with Squash
Blossom Butter and
Summer Beans

Spaghetti with Squash Blossom Butter and Summer Beans

⏱ Total **35 min**; Serves **4**

The generous amount of crisp beans in Colorado chef Lachlan Mackinnon-Patterson's light summer pasta gives it crunch and body, so you can use fewer noodles.

Ice

- **4** **Tbsp. unsalted butter, at room temperature**
- **9** **squash blossoms, stems and pistils removed and petals finely chopped (½ cup), plus whole petals for garnish**
- **8** **oz. green beans, trimmed**
- **6** **oz. wax beans, trimmed**
- **½** **lb. spaghetti**
- **¼** **cup snipped chives**
- **2** **Tbsp. chopped basil leaves, plus small leaves for garnish**
- **2** **Tbsp. finely grated Pecorino Toscano or Romano cheese, plus more for serving**
- **½** **tsp. finely grated lemon zest, plus 1 Tbsp. fresh lemon juice**
- **Kosher salt and pepper**

1. In a small bowl, mix the butter with the chopped squash blossom petals.

2. Set up an ice bath. In a large pot of salted boiling water, blanch the green and wax beans until crisp-tender, about 3 minutes. Using a slotted spoon, transfer the beans to the ice bath to cool completely. Drain, pat dry and halve the beans lengthwise.

3. Meanwhile, return the water to a boil. Cook the pasta until al dente. Drain, reserving 1½ cups of the cooking water.

4. In a large skillet, melt the squash blossom butter. Add the pasta and pasta water and bring to a boil over moderately high heat. Add the beans and cook, stirring, until the sauce is thickened and the beans are heated through, about 2 minutes. Add the chives, the chopped basil, the 2 tablespoons of cheese, and the lemon zest and lemon juice; season with salt and pepper. Transfer the pasta to shallow bowls and garnish with more cheese, squash blossom petals and basil leaves; serve. —*Lachlan Mackinnon-Patterson*

WINE Vibrant northern Italian white: 2015 Livio Felluga Pinot Grigio.

Rye Capellini with Yeast Butter and Truffles

Active **1 hr 30 min**; Total **3 hr 30 min** Serves **6**

Chef Noah Sandoval of Chicago's Oriole, has created one of the most delicious pastas we've ever eaten. The fresh capellini is redolent with caraway and rye, and gets tossed with an umami-rich truffle butter sauce and just a whisper of citrus. Making the pasta takes a bit of effort, but the results are well worth it.

- **2** **cups 00 flour (see Note), plus more for dusting**
- **¾** **cup rye flour**
- **2** **Tbsp. caraway seeds, ground to a powder in a spice grinder**
- **Kosher salt and pepper**
- **14** **large egg yolks**
- **1** **large egg**
- **1** **Tbsp. extra-virgin olive oil**
- **¼** **cup heavy cream**
- **1** **Tbsp. active dry yeast**
- **2** **sticks unsalted butter, cut into tablespoons**
- **¼** **cup black truffle butter**
- **¼** **tsp. finely grated orange zest**
- **¼** **cup finely grated Parmigiano-Reggiano cheese, plus more for serving**
- **Shaved black truffle (optional) and snipped chives, for garnish**

1. Sift both flours with the caraway and 1½ tablespoons of salt into a large bowl. Make a well in the center and add the egg yolks, whole egg, olive oil and 1 tablespoon of water. Using a fork, gradually whisk the flour mixture into the wet ingredients until a shaggy dough forms. Scrape the dough out onto a work surface and knead until very stiff but smooth, about 15 minutes. Wrap in plastic and let rest at room temperature until softened and relaxed, about 2 hours.

2. Divide the dough into 12 pieces and work with 1 piece at a time; keep the rest covered. Press the dough to flatten. Set up a pasta machine to roll flat pasta. Starting at the widest setting, run the dough through successively narrower settings until it's a scant ⅛ inch thick. Transfer the sheet to a lightly floured work surface and dust with 00 flour. Repeat with the remaining pieces of dough.

3. Set up a pasta machine with a capellini cutter. Working with 1 sheet of dough at a time, gradually feed the dough through the cutter. Gently toss with 00 flour and transfer the capellini pile to a lightly floured baking sheet. Repeat with the remaining sheets of pasta to form 12 piles.

4. In a small saucepan, whisk the cream with 2 tablespoons of water and the yeast and cook over moderately low heat, stirring, until the yeast is dissolved and the mixture is very thick, 3 to 5 minutes. Whisk in the unsalted butter 1 tablespoon at a time until emulsified, then season with salt and pepper.

5. In a large saucepan of salted boiling water, cook the pasta until al dente, about 1 minute. Drain, reserving 1 cup of the cooking water. Wipe out the saucepan.

6. In the large saucepan, melt the yeast butter with the truffle butter and orange zest over moderately high heat. Add the pasta, the ¼ cup of Parmigiano and ½ cup of the reserved cooking water and toss until hot and evenly coated with the butter, about 2 minutes. Add a little more of the cooking water if necessary. Transfer the capellini to shallow bowls. Top with grated Parmigiano and garnish with shaved black truffle, if desired, and snipped chives. Serve right away. —*Noah Sandoval*

NOTE Doppio zero ("double zero," or 00) is a fine Italian flour available at specialty food shops and amazon.com.

WINE Earthy red Burgundy: 2014 Albert Bichot Fixin.

Pappardelle with Chicken and Pistachio-Mint Pesto

Total **30 min**; Serves **4 to 6**

A mint-and-pistachio pesto brightens this summery pasta dish.

- **1½ cups lightly packed mint leaves, plus more for garnish**
- **½ cup shelled unsalted pistachios**
- **¼ cup fresh lemon juice**
- **½ cup extra-virgin olive oil**
  Kosher salt and pepper
- **8 oz. pappardelle pasta**
- **12 oz. shredded rotisserie chicken (3 cups)**
- **1 small zucchini, very thinly sliced or shaved**
- **1 small yellow squash, very thinly sliced or shaved**
- **1½ cups mixed cherry tomatoes, halved, or quartered if large**

1. In a food processor, combine the 1½ cups of mint with the pistachios and lemon juice and pulse until finely chopped. With the machine on, gradually add the olive oil until incorporated and the pesto is nearly smooth. Scrape into a large bowl and season generously with salt and pepper.

2. Meanwhile, in a large saucepan of salted boiling water, cook the pasta until al dente. Drain well, reserving 1 cup of the cooking water. Add the pasta, chicken, zucchini, yellow squash, tomatoes and reserved cooking water to the pesto and toss well. Season generously with salt and pepper and toss again. Garnish with mint leaves and serve right away. —*Justin Chapple*

MAKE AHEAD The pistachio-mint pesto can be refrigerated overnight. Bring it to room temperature before using.

WINE Floral, medium-bodied Italian white: 2015 Feudi di San Gregorio Falanghina.

Caviar Carbonara

Active **1 hr**; Total **2 hr 30 min**; Serves **4**

For special occasions, F&W's Justin Chapple makes this beautiful, fresh pappardelle pasta, then tosses it with a quick and decadent carbonara sauce laced with briny pops of caviar and lemon zest. When he doesn't feel like making the pasta from scratch, he buys the noodles fresh at his local Italian market.

PASTA

- **1¾ cups 00 flour (see note on p. 75), plus more for dusting**
- **2 tsp. kosher salt**
- **4 large egg yolks**
- **1 large egg**
- **1½ Tbsp. extra-virgin olive oil**

CARBONARA

- **3 large egg yolks**
- **1 large egg**
- **½ cup finely grated Parmigiano-Reggiano cheese**
- **1 Tbsp. finely grated lemon zest**
  Kosher salt and pepper
- **60 grams caviar**
  Snipped dill, for garnish

1. Make the pasta In a food processor, pulse the 1¾ cups of flour with the salt. In a medium bowl, beat the egg yolks with the whole egg and olive oil. Add to the flour in the food processor and pulse until the dough just comes together. Transfer to a lightly floured work surface and knead until very smooth but stiff, 5 to 10 minutes. Cover with plastic wrap and let stand at room temperature for 1 hour.

2. Divide the dough into 4 pieces and work with 1 piece at a time, keeping the rest covered. Press the dough to flatten it. Using a pasta machine set at the widest setting, run the dough through successively narrower settings until you reach the sixth one. Cut the pasta sheet into a 10-inch length, lay it on a lightly floured work surface and generously dust with flour. Repeat with the remaining dough.

3. Loosely roll up the pasta sheets and then, using a very sharp knife, cut them into scant ¾-inch-wide ribbons. Transfer the pappardelle to a large baking sheet and gently toss with more flour. Let stand at room temperature for 30 minutes.

4. In a large pot of salted boiling water, cook the pasta until al dente, 2 to 3 minutes. Drain, reserving 1 cup of the cooking water.

5. Meanwhile, make the carbonara In a large bowl, beat the egg yolks with the whole egg, the cheese, lemon zest, ½ teaspoon of salt and 1 teaspoon of pepper. Very gradually whisk in ½ cup of the reserved hot pasta water to temper the eggs. Add the pasta and half of the caviar and toss vigorously until hot and creamy, 1 to 2 minutes. Transfer to bowls and top with snipped dill and dollops of the remaining caviar. —*Justin Chapple*

MAKE AHEAD The uncooked pappardelle can be covered with plastic wrap and refrigerated overnight.

WINE Elegant, brioche-scented Champagne: NV Pol Roger Brut Réserve.

Caviar Dreams

Here are other easy ways to upgrade anything with caviar.

PASTA Another elegant pasta dish: plump clams, chilled, delicate capellini and a big spoonful of caviar.

EGGS Start your day like a real high roller with creamy, custardy scrambled eggs, caviar and toasted challah, or add a salad and Champagne for a perfect dinner.

PIZZA Try a luxe pizza topped with smoked salmon, crème fraîche and chives.

POTATO CHIPS A simple snack of crispy, salty potato chips and briny, bursting caviar is hard to beat, but if you want to take things to the next level, try layering potato chips with caviar, crème fraîche and thinly sliced scallops.

A SPOON For a truly indulgent caviar-eating experience, all you need is a spoon—preferably a small one made out of mother-of-pearl. Eat it straight out of the tin and enjoy every bite in its purest form.

Caviar Carbonara

Thin Spaghetti with Crab and Asparagus

⏲ Total **30 min**; Serves **4 to 6**

At Josephine Estelle in New Orleans, chefs Andy Ticer and Michael Hudman serve this sublime buttery crab pasta with home-made tajarin, a ribbon-type noodle. Thin spaghetti works nicely, too.

- **1 lb. thin spaghetti**
- **1 lb. asparagus, trimmed and cut into 1-inch pieces**
- **1 stick unsalted butter**
- **2 basil sprigs, plus leaves for garnish**
- **¼ cup freshly grated Parmigiano-Reggiano cheese, plus more for serving**
- **Kosher salt and pepper**
- **1 lb. jumbo lump crabmeat**

1. In a large saucepan of salted boiling water, cook the pasta until almost al dente, 5 to 7 minutes. Add the asparagus and cook until the pasta is al dente and the asparagus is crisp-tender, about 2 minutes longer. Reserve 1 cup of the cooking water, then drain well.

2. Meanwhile, in a very large skillet, melt the butter with the basil sprigs over moderate heat. Add the pasta and asparagus, the ¼ cup of cheese and ½ cup of the cooking water. Cook over moderate heat, tossing, until the pasta is coated in a light sauce, 3 to 5 minutes; add more of the cooking water if needed. Season the pasta generously with salt and pepper. Gently fold in the crab and cook until hot, 1 to 2 minutes. Discard the basil sprigs. Garnish with basil leaves and serve, passing more cheese at the table. —*Michael Hudman and Andy Ticer*

WINE Minerally Italian white: 2016 Antinori Tenuta Guado al Tasso Vermentino.

Buttered Pasta with Clams and Green Chiles

Active **1 hr**; Total **1 hr 20 min**; Serves **4 to 6**

Chef Andrew Brochu of Chicago's Roister restaurant puts a delicious spin on classic pasta with clam sauce, adding a spicy green chile ragout, fresh herbs, crème fraîche and lime juice.

- **½ cup plus 1 Tbsp. extra-virgin olive oil**
- **¾ cup lightly packed mint leaves, plus more for garnish**
- **½ cup lightly packed parsley leaves**
- **¼ cup snipped chives**
- **2 small poblano chiles—stemmed, seeded and diced**
- **1 Cubanelle pepper—stemmed, seeded and diced**
- **2 oz. shishito peppers, stemmed and thinly sliced**
- **Kosher salt and pepper**
- **3 shallots—2 thinly sliced and 1 minced**
- **4 garlic cloves—2 minced and 2 crushed**
- **2 Tbsp. drained capers**
- **2 tsp. each black peppercorns, coriander seeds, fennel seeds and mustard seeds**
- **1 cup dry white wine**
- **2 cups bottled clam juice**
- **3½ dozen mixed clams, such as Manila, razor and littleneck, scrubbed**
- **12 oz. pipe rigate or mezze rigatoni pasta**
- **4 Tbsp. unsalted butter**
- **4 Tbsp. crème fraîche**
- **2 Tbsp. fresh lime juice**
- **Wasabi masago (wasabi caviar), for garnish**

1. In a blender, combine ½ cup of the olive oil with ¼ cup of the mint and the parsley and chives and puree until smooth. Strain the herb oil through a fine sieve into a small bowl, pressing on the solids; discard the solids in the sieve.

2. In a large cast-iron skillet, heat the remaining 1 tablespoon of olive oil until nearly smoking. Add the poblanos, Cubanelle, shishitos and a generous pinch each of salt and pepper. Cook over high heat, stirring occasionally, until blistered in spots and just softened, about 3 minutes. Add the minced shallot, minced garlic and capers and cook over moderate heat, stirring, until just softened, 1 to 2 minutes. Let cool slightly, then stir in the herb oil.

3. In a large pot, toast the mixed spices over moderate heat until fragrant, about 2 minutes. Add the sliced shallots and crushed garlic, then carefully add the wine and simmer until reduced by half, 3 to 5 minutes. Add the clam juice and bring to a boil. Add the clams, cover and steam over high heat, stirring occasionally, until the clams open, about 10 minutes. Using tongs, transfer the clams to a large rimmed baking sheet to cool slightly, then remove the meat from the shells; discard the shells and any clams that do not open. Strain the clam cooking liquid through a fine sieve into a bowl; discard the solids.

4. Meanwhile, in a large pot of salted boiling water, cook the pasta until al dente. Drain well.

5. Wipe out the pot. Add the butter and cook until melted. Add the clams, chile mixture, pasta, crème fraîche and ½ cup of the strained clam cooking liquid and cook over moderately high heat, tossing, until hot, about 3 minutes. Stir in the lime juice and the remaining ½ cup of mint and season generously with salt and pepper. Transfer to bowls, garnish with more mint and the wasabi masago and serve right away. —*Andrew Brochu*

MAKE AHEAD The prepared chile mixture can be refrigerated overnight. Bring to room temperature before using.

WINE Lemony California Chardonnay: 2015 Charles Krug Carneros.

Chorizo-Poached Shrimp Pasta

⏱ Total **45 min;** Serves **4**

Cooking the chorizo in oil, then using that oil to cook the shrimp and garlic, infuses this entire dish with excellent smoky flavor.

- 1 cup extra-virgin olive oil
- 4 oz. Spanish chorizo, cut into ½-inch pieces
- 1 lb. shelled and deveined large shrimp
- 4 large garlic cloves, thinly sliced
  Kosher salt and pepper
- 12 oz. strozzapreti pasta
- 1 pint cherry or grape tomatoes, halved if large
- 1 cup torn basil, plus more for garnish

1. In a medium saucepan, cook the olive oil and chorizo over moderate heat, stirring occasionally, until the chorizo is tender, about 10 minutes. Using a slotted spoon, transfer to a small bowl. Add the shrimp, garlic and a generous pinch of salt to the saucepan and cook over low heat, stirring occasionally, until the shrimp are cooked through, 8 to 10 minutes. Using a slotted spoon, transfer the shrimp and garlic to the bowl with the chorizo. Reserve the oil.

2. Meanwhile, in a large pot of salted boiling water, cook the pasta until al dente. Drain well.

3. In the pot, combine the tomatoes and ½ cup of the reserved chorizo oil; discard the remaining oil. Cook over moderately high heat, stirring occasionally, until the tomatoes just start to soften, about 3 minutes. Add the shrimp mixture and the pasta and cook, tossing, until hot and the pasta is coated in a light sauce, about 2 minutes. Season generously with salt and pepper, then stir in the torn basil. Transfer to bowls, garnish with more basil and serve right away. —*Justin Chapple*

WINE Full-bodied Rhône-style white: 2014 Anaba Turbine White.

Clams Carbonara

⏱ Total **40 min;** Serves **6**

Boston chef Matt Jennings's briny pasta combines two beautiful things: rich carbonara and spaghetti alle vongole, prepared with New England clams.

- 2 lbs. razor or littleneck clams, scrubbed
  Kosher salt and pepper
- 1 lb. spaghetti
- 1 large egg, plus 4 large egg yolks
- ¾ cup freshly grated Parmigiano-Reggiano cheese, plus more for serving
  Pinch of freshly grated nutmeg
- 8 oz. pancetta, cut into ¼-inch dice
- 1 medium yellow onion, halved and thinly sliced
- 4 garlic cloves, thinly sliced
- ½ cup finely chopped parsley leaves
- 1 Tbsp. unsalted butter

1. In a large pot, bring ½ inch of water to a boil. Add the clams, cover and steam over moderately high heat until just opened, 5 to 7 minutes. Remove the pot from the heat. Using a slotted spoon, transfer the clams to a rimmed baking sheet; discard any that don't open.

2. Strain the cooking liquid through a cheesecloth-lined sieve into a large bowl. Wipe out the pot and return the cooking liquid to it. Add enough water to the pot until three-fourths full and bring to a boil. Generously salt the water, add the spaghetti and cook until al dente. Drain, reserving 1 cup of the pasta water.

3. Meanwhile, remove the clams from their shells; discard the shells. Thickly slice the clams. In a small bowl, whisk the egg with the egg yolks, the ¾ cup of cheese and the nutmeg.

4. Heat a large skillet over moderate heat. Add the pancetta and cook, stirring occasionally, until lightly browned and most of the fat is rendered, about 10 minutes. Using a slotted spoon, transfer the pancetta to a plate; leave the fat in the skillet.

5. Add the onion and garlic to the skillet and cook over moderate heat, stirring occasionally, until softened, about 5 minutes. Add the pancetta, clams and spaghetti and stir to coat, about 1 minute. Remove the skillet

from the heat and slowly drizzle in the egg mixture, tossing, until incorporated. Add the reserved pasta water, the chopped parsley and butter and toss to coat; season with salt and pepper. Divide the pasta among bowls and serve, passing more cheese at the table. —*Matt Jennings*

WINE White: floral, lightly honeyed 2015 Feudi di San Gregorio Fiano. Red: fresh, juicy 2015 Massolino Barbera d'Alba.

Smoked Gouda Carbonara

📷 PAGE 71

⏱ Total **30 min;** Serves **6**

- 1 lb. spaghetti
- 5 large egg yolks
- 1 large egg
- 1 cup (4 oz.) finely shredded smoked Gouda, plus more for serving
  Kosher salt and black pepper
- 1 Tbsp. extra-virgin olive oil
- 6 oz. slab bacon, finely diced
- ¾ tsp. crushed red pepper

1. In a large pot of salted boiling water, cook the pasta until al dente. Drain, reserving 1 cup of the cooking water.

2. In a large bowl, beat the egg yolks with the whole egg, the 1 cup of Gouda, ½ teaspoon of salt and 2 teaspoons of black pepper. Very gradually whisk in ½ cup of the reserved cooking water to temper the eggs.

3. Meanwhile, in the large pot, heat the olive oil. Add the bacon and cook over moderate heat until rendered but not crisp, 5 to 7 minutes. Add the pasta, crushed red pepper and ¼ cup of the reserved pasta cooking water. Cook, tossing, until the pasta is coated, 1 to 2 minutes. Scrape the pasta mixture into the large bowl and toss vigorously until creamy, 1 to 2 minutes; add more cooking water if needed. Season with salt and pepper. Transfer the pasta to bowls and serve, passing more Gouda at the table. —*Justin Chapple*

WINE Smoky, intense Pinot Noir: 2015 J. Hofstatter Meczan.

Pasta with Sausage
and Mustard Greens

Pasta with Sausage and Mustard Greens

⏱ Total **45 min**; Serves **4 to 6**

The genius of this pasta recipe is the contrast of flavors—creamy, meaty, tangy and nicely bitter.

- **12 oz. mezzi rigatoni**
- **¼ cup extra-virgin olive oil**
- **1 lb. Bilbro Family Sausage (p. 177) or bulk Italian sweet sausage, crumbled**
- **2 leeks, white and light green parts only, halved lengthwise and sliced ½ inch thick**
- **6 garlic cloves, thinly sliced**
  Kosher salt and pepper
- **½ lb. mustard greens, stemmed, leaves chopped**
- **1 pint cherry tomatoes**
- **½ cup crème fraîche**

1. In a large pot of salted boiling water, cook the pasta until al dente. Reserve 1 cup of the pasta water, then drain.

2. In the same pot, heat the olive oil until shimmering. Add the sausage and cook over moderately high heat, stirring occasionally, until just cooked through, about 8 minutes. Using a slotted spoon, transfer to a bowl. Add the leeks, garlic and a generous pinch of salt to the pot and cook over moderate heat, stirring occasionally, until the leeks are softened, about 5 minutes.

3. Return the sausage to the pot. Add the mustard greens and tomatoes and cook over moderately high heat, stirring, until the greens are just wilted and the tomatoes start to burst, 5 to 7 minutes. Add the pasta, crème fraîche and reserved pasta water and cook, tossing, until the pasta is hot and coated in a light sauce, about 2 minutes. Season the pasta with salt and pepper and serve right away. —*Justin Chapple*

WINE Plummy red blend: Marietta Old Vine Red Lot Number 66.

Bucatini Amatriciana

Active **15 min**; Total **1 hr**; Serves **4**

Georgia chef Hugh Acheson's amatriciana sauce strikes the perfect balance of porky (from the pancetta) and spicy.

- **5 oz. pancetta, finely chopped**
- **1 small white onion, finely chopped**
- **1 Tbsp. chopped marjoram**
- **½ tsp. crushed red pepper**
- **1 medium carrot, grated**
  One 28-oz. can whole plum tomatoes in juice, coarsely pureed
  Kosher salt
- **1 lb. bucatini**
- **1 Tbsp. unsalted butter**

1. In a medium saucepan, cook the pancetta over moderate heat until browned and crisp, about 6 minutes. Add the onion, marjoram and crushed red pepper and cook until the onion is softened, about 8 minutes. Add the carrot and tomatoes, season with salt and simmer over moderately low heat, stirring occasionally, until the sauce has thickened, about 40 minutes.

2. Meanwhile, in a large pot of salted boiling water, cook the bucatini until al dente. Drain and return the pasta to the pot. Stir the butter into the tomato sauce and add to the bucatini. Toss to coat, season with salt and serve. —*Hugh Acheson*

WINE Intense Italian red: 2013 Aia Vecchia Sor Ugo.

Sweet Potato Gnocchi with Mint–Pine Nut Pesto

Active **30 min**; Total **50 min**; Serves **6**

This vegan and gluten-free gnocchi is suprisingly light and pillowy.

- **½ cup pine nuts**
- **¼ cup packed mint leaves, chopped**
- **1 tsp. finely grated lemon zest plus 2 Tbsp. fresh lemon juice**
- **¼ cup plus 2 Tbsp. extra-virgin olive oil**
  Gray sea salt
- **2 large sweet potatoes (1¾ lbs.), peeled and sliced ½ inch thick**
- **1 cup gluten-free flour, such as Cup4Cup or King Arthur brand, plus more for dusting**
- **5 Tbsp. cornstarch**
  Thyme leaves, for sprinkling

1. Preheat the oven to 425°. Spread the pine nuts on a rimmed baking sheet and toast until golden brown, about 3 minutes. Transfer the nuts to a work surface and let cool, then chop and transfer to a small bowl. Stir in the mint, lemon zest and juice and ¼ cup of the olive oil. Season the pesto with salt.

2. On a large rimmed baking sheet, spread the sweet potatoes in a single layer. Bake until tender, about 20 minutes. Transfer to a food processor and let cool, then pulse until smooth. Scrape the pureed sweet potatoes into a large bowl and stir in the 1 cup of flour, the cornstarch and 1 teaspoon of salt.

3. Lightly dust a rimmed baking sheet with flour. On a lightly floured work surface, cut the dough into 8 pieces and roll each piece into a ½-inch-thick rope, about 15 inches long. Using a knife, cut the ropes into 1-inch pieces. Roll each piece against the tines of a fork to make ridges and transfer to the prepared baking sheet.

4. In a large pot of salted boiling water, cook the gnocchi until they rise to the surface, then cook for 1 minute longer. Drain well and transfer to a serving bowl. Toss with the remaining 2 tablespoons of olive oil, then spoon the pesto on top. Sprinkle with thyme leaves and more salt; serve. —*Angèle Ferreux-Maeght*

MAKE AHEAD The uncooked gnocchi can be covered and refrigerated overnight.

Pork-and-Ricotta-Stuffed Jumbo Shells

📷 PAGE 70

Active **45 min**; Total **2 hr**; Serves **6 to 8**

These best-ever stuffed shells have a filling that's both meaty and cheesy.

- **12 oz. jumbo pasta shells**
- **1¼ lbs. ground pork**
- **1¼ cups fresh ricotta cheese**
- **¾ cup panko**
- **3 garlic cloves, minced**
- **1 large egg, beaten**
- **½ cup finely grated Parmigiano-Reggiano cheese**
- **½ cup finely chopped parsley, plus more for garnish**
- **½ cup heavy cream**
- **Kosher salt and pepper**
- **4½ cups prepared marinara sauce**
- **½ lb. fresh, lightly salted mozzarella, torn**

1. Preheat the oven to 375°. In a large pot of salted boiling water, cook the shells until they are al dente, about 9 minutes. Drain well and transfer to a baking sheet to cool slightly.

2. Meanwhile, in a large bowl, combine the pork, ricotta, panko, garlic, egg, Parmigiano, the ½ cup of parsley, ¼ cup of the cream, 2 teaspoons of salt and 1 teaspoon of pepper; mix well.

3. In a medium bowl, mix the marinara sauce with the remaining ¼ cup of cream. Spoon half of the sauce into a 9-by-13-inch baking dish. Stuff each shell with a heaping tablespoon of the filling and nestle in the sauce. Spoon the remaining sauce over the shells and scatter the mozzarella on top.

4. Cover the baking dish and bake for about 45 minutes, then uncover and bake for 15 minutes longer, until bubbling and the pork is cooked through. Let stand for 10 minutes, then garnish with parsley and serve. —*Justin Chapple*

MAKE AHEAD The recipe can be prepared through Step 3 and refrigerated overnight. Bring the pasta to room temperature before baking.

WINE Medium-bodied Italian red: 2014 Cecchi Sangiovese Tosca.

Spaghetti Pie with Wild Mushrooms and Spinach

Active **45 min**; Total **1 hr 35 min**
Serves **8 to 10**

Top Chef judge Gail Simmons's spaghetti pie gets a flavor boost from mushrooms, spinach and three kinds of cheese. Bonus: If you don't finish it all in one sitting, leftovers make possibly the best next-day treat of all time.

- **Unsalted butter, softened, for brushing**
- **1 lb. spaghetti**
- **3 Tbsp. extra-virgin olive oil**
- **1 medium yellow onion, minced**
- **2 garlic cloves, minced**
- **1 lb. mixed wild mushrooms, such as cremini, porcini and stemmed shiitake, cut into 1-inch pieces**
- **Kosher salt and pepper**
- **5 oz. baby spinach**
- **3 large eggs**
- **1½ cups whole milk**
- **3 cups shredded Fontina cheese (10 oz.)**
- **1 cup fresh ricotta cheese**
- **1 cup finely grated Parmigiano-Reggiano cheese**
- **1 Tbsp. finely chopped sage**
- **1 Tbsp. thyme leaves**

1. Preheat the oven to 425°. Tightly wrap the outside of a 9-inch springform pan with foil and brush the inside with butter. In a pot of salted boiling water, cook the spaghetti until barely al dente; drain.

2. In a large skillet, heat 2 tablespoons of the olive oil. Add the onion and garlic and cook over moderately high heat, stirring, until sizzling, about 1 minute. Add the mushrooms, season with salt and pepper and cook, stirring occasionally, until browned, 10 to 12 minutes. Scrape into a bowl.

3. In the same skillet, heat the remaining 1 tablespoon of olive oil. Add the spinach, season with salt and pepper and cook over moderate heat, stirring, until just wilted, about 2 minutes. Scrape into the mushrooms and let cool slightly.

4. In a large bowl, beat the eggs with the milk. Add the spaghetti, mushroom mixture, 3 cheeses, sage, thyme, 1½ teaspoons of salt and 1 teaspoon of pepper; mix well. Scrape into the prepared pan and smooth the top. Set the pan on a baking sheet and bake for about 35 minutes, until bubbling and the top is golden. Let stand for 15 minutes. Remove the ring, cut the pie into wedges and serve. —*Gail Simmons*

MAKE AHEAD The pie can be baked up to 2 hours ahead and eaten warm or at room temperature.

WINE Juicy Russian River Valley Pinot Noir: 2015 Hartford Court.

Fork It Over

We tasted 21 brands of spaghetti to find six standouts.

BARILLA The spaghetti is a stellar supermarket find. It's chewy and has a robust flavor that works nicely with all kinds of sauces. barilla.com

DE CECCO This iconic brand is our go-to for whole-wheat spaghetti. dececco.it

FILOTEA These eggy strands of spaghetti alla chitarra soak up arrabbiata like a charm. amazon.com

GIOVANNI RANA This pasta–slow-dried at a low temperature to preserve its hearty flavor–is now available all over America. giovanniranausa.com

MASCIARELLI Extruded through bronze dies, which impart a rough-hewn texture, these noodles elevate any dish. marcelliformaggi.com

RUSTICHELLA D'ABRUZZO Their remarkably delicious Rapida spaghetti cooks in just 90 seconds. markethallfoods.com

Spaghetti Pie with Wild
Mushrooms and Spinach

Mac and Cheese with
Cracker Crumble

Mac and Cheese with Cracker Crumble

Active **30 min**; Total **1 hr**; Serves **6 to 8**

To create a mac and cheese with the silky consistency of Velveeta, but using a rich, aged cheddar, chefs and brothers Michael and Bryan Voltaggio add sodium citrate to bind their sauce. "Sodium citrate, a flavorless powdered emulsifier, will be your new best friend for sauces," says Bryan. "It gives you that dreamy, gooey texture, but with nutty, sharp cheeses that don't typically melt smoothly." Think of the nacho cheese possibilities!

- **1 lb. radiatore pasta**
- **3 cups whole milk**
- **1 Tbsp. sodium citrate (see Note)**
- **1 lb. aged extra-sharp cheddar, preferably Tillamook, shredded**
- **1 Tbsp. Worcestershire sauce**
- **¾ tsp. kosher salt**
- **4 cups crumbled buttery crackers, preferably Ritz**
- **1 stick unsalted butter, melted**
- **½ cup finely grated Parmigiano-Reggiano cheese**
- **¾ tsp. pepper**

1. Preheat the oven to 375°. In a large pot of salted boiling water, cook the pasta until al dente. Drain and transfer to a 9-by-13-inch baking dish.

2. In a medium saucepan, bring the milk and sodium citrate to a simmer. Whisk in the cheddar, ½ cup at a time, until smooth. Whisk in the Worcestershire and the salt. Pour the sauce over the pasta.

3. In a bowl, mix the crackers with the butter, Parmesan and pepper; sprinkle over the pasta. Bake the mac and cheese for 20 minutes, until bubbling and the top is browned. Let stand for 5 minutes; serve. *—Bryan Voltaggio and Michael Voltaggio*

NOTE Sodium citrate is available at amazon.com. To make this recipe in eight 1-cup ramekins, halve the crumble and bake the mac and cheese at 375° for 8 to 10 minutes.

Buckwheat Soba Tiger Salad

Total **35 min**; Serves **4**

Chef Peter Cho of Han Oak in Portland, Oregon, is a master at riffing on Asian classics. He says that he created this dish to curb his wife's cravings for one of their favorite places in New York City, Xi'an Famous Foods. "When we lived in New York, we went there pretty regularly, and we always ate the tiger vegetable salad, warm spicy tofu and the pork *zha jjang* hand-pulled noodles," he says. "This is my version of a combination of those dishes."

- **1 Tbsp. sesame seeds**
- **8 oz. soba noodles**
- **3 Tbsp. rice wine vinegar**
- **1 Tbsp. fresh lime juice plus 1 tsp. finely grated zest**
- **1 Tbsp. kombu tsuyu (see Note)**
- **1 Tbsp. tamarind concentrate**
- **1 Tbsp. light brown sugar**
- **1 tsp. minced garlic**
- **½ tsp. gochugaru or crushed red pepper**
- **3 Tbsp. sesame oil**
  Kosher salt
- **1 small English cucumber, halved lengthwise and thinly sliced on the bias**
- **2 celery ribs, thinly sliced**
- **½ cup chopped cilantro leaves and thin stems**
- **2 scallions, thinly sliced**
- **1 small red chile—halved lengthwise, seeded and thinly sliced**

1. Preheat the oven to 350°. Spread the sesame seeds on a small rimmed baking sheet and toast until browned, tossing once, about 6 minutes. Transfer the seeds to a spice grinder and let cool completely. Process until finely ground.

2. In a large pot of boiling water, cook the soba noodles until just tender. Drain and cool under cold running water. Transfer the noodles to a bowl of ice water to chill. Drain well.

3. Meanwhile, in a large bowl, combine the toasted sesame seeds with the vinegar, lime juice, lime zest, kombu tsuyu, tamarind, brown sugar, garlic and gochugaru. While whisking constantly, slowly drizzle in the sesame oil until incorporated. Season with salt. Add the cold noodles along with the cucumber, celery, cilantro, scallions and chile. Season with salt and toss. Transfer to bowls and serve. *—Peter Cho*

NOTE Kombu tsuyu is a Japanese condiment made from dashi soup stock, soy sauce, mirin and sugar. It's available at Japanese markets and amazon.com.

WINE Lime-scented Washington Riesling: 2015 Poet's Leap.

Soba Noodles with Poached Egg

Active **15 min**; Total **45 min**; Serves **4**

For a light but nourishing breakfast, NYC recipe developer Kay Chun likes making a savory dashi broth, which she eats with soba noodles and Japanese soft-cooked eggs called *onsen*.

- **1½ oz. kombu (two 12-by-1-inch pieces)**
- **1 Tbsp. instant dashi**
  Kosher salt
- **8 oz. soba noodles**
- **4 large eggs**
- **6 oz. daikon, peeled and finely grated**
  Thinly sliced roasted, salted nori, for garnish

1. In a medium saucepan, combine the kombu with 8 cups of water and bring to a simmer. Stir in the instant dashi and remove the pan from the heat; let stand for 30 minutes. Strain the broth through a fine sieve set over a large bowl; discard the solids or reserve for another use. Return the broth to the saucepan, season with salt and bring to a simmer. Add the noodles and cook until al dente. Divide the noodles and broth among 4 bowls.

2. Meanwhile bring a medium saucepan of water to a simmer. Break each egg into a small bowl and gently pour into the simmering water. Cook until the whites are just firm and the yolks are still runny, 2 to 3 minutes. Using a slotted spoon, transfer the eggs to a paper towel–lined plate and let drain briefly. Top each bowl of noodles with an egg. Spoon a tablespoon of daikon next to each egg, then garnish with nori. Serve with the remaining daikon on the side. *—Kay Chun*

MAKE AHEAD The broth can be refrigerated for up to 2 days.

Curried Noodles with Shrimp

Active **30 min;** Total **50 min;** Serves **4**

F&W's Justin Chapple dissolves curry powder in boiling water to soak rice noodles and infuse them with excellent flavor. He then stir-fries the noodles with shrimp, garlic, ginger and plenty of fresh herbs.

- **6** cups boiling water
- **2** Tbsp. Madras curry powder
  Kosher salt and pepper
- **8** oz. stir-fry rice noodles
- **¾** lb. shelled and deveined large shrimp
- **¼** cup canola oil
- **¼** cup minced garlic
- **¼** cup minced peeled fresh ginger
- **3** Tbsp. fresh lime juice, plus wedges for serving
- **2** Tbsp. low-sodium soy sauce
- **1** cup each chopped basil and cilantro, plus more for garnish
- **½** cup thinly sliced scallions
- **1** serrano chile, thinly sliced

1. In a 9-by-9-inch baking dish, mix the boiling water, curry powder and a pinch of salt. Add the noodles and let stand until softened, about 20 minutes. Drain.

2. Season the shrimp with salt and pepper. In a large saucepan, heat 1 tablespoon of the oil until shimmering. Add the shrimp and cook over moderately high heat, turning once, until just cooked through, 3 to 5 minutes. Transfer to a plate.

3. Wipe out the saucepan. Heat the remaining 3 tablespoons of oil in it. Add the garlic and ginger and stir-fry over moderately high heat until softened, 2 minutes. Add the noodles, shrimp, lime juice and soy sauce and stir-fry until hot, about 3 minutes. Fold in the herbs, scallions and serrano. Season with salt and pepper. Garnish with herbs and serve with lime wedges. —*Justin Chapple*

WINE Lime-scented dry Riesling: 2015 Fritz Haag Estate Trocken.

Icy-Cold Kimchi Ramen

Active **25 min;** Total **2 hr;** Serves **4**

These noodles stay cool thanks to the slushy broth, which is seasoned with kimchi juice.

- **1** cup chopped kimchi, plus ⅓ cup kimchi juice from the jar
- **3** Tbsp. plus 1 tsp. seasoned rice wine vinegar
- **2** tsp. Asian fish sauce
  Kosher salt
- **2** ears of corn, husked
- **1** lb. ramen noodles, preferably fresh
- **1** tsp. toasted sesame oil
- **2** scallions, thinly sliced
- **2** white button mushrooms, very thinly sliced
- **1** small cucumber, thinly sliced lengthwise

1. In a medium bowl, whisk the kimchi juice with 3 tablespoons of the rice wine vinegar, the Asian fish sauce and 1½ cups of water. Season with salt. Cover and freeze, stirring with a fork and scraping the frozen edges into the center a few times, until slushy, about 1 hour and 30 minutes.

2. Meanwhile, in a pot of boiling water, blanch the corn until crisp-tender and bright yellow, about 2 minutes. Using tongs, transfer the corn to a colander and cool under cold running water, then cut the kernels off the cobs and transfer to a small bowl. Season the corn with salt, cover and refrigerate.

3. Return the water to a boil. Add the ramen and cook until al dente. Drain and cool under cold running water, then drain again and transfer to a large bowl. Add the remaining 1 teaspoon of vinegar and the toasted sesame oil. Season with salt and toss to coat.

4. Stir the partially frozen broth, then transfer to bowls. Top with the ramen, corn, chopped kimchi, scallions, mushrooms and cucumber and serve. —*Laura Rege*

WINE Unoaked, melony Italian white: 2016 Donnafugata SurSur Grillo.

Miso Chicken Ramen

Total **30 min;** Serves **2**

Sometimes a ramen fix is just the right thing, and this quick and easy version hits the spot. The addition of white miso and runny eggs are key to making it feel more special than standard chicken noodle soup

- **1** qt. chicken stock or low-sodium broth
- **3** Tbsp. white miso
- **1** Tbsp. soy sauce
- **½** lb. shredded cooked chicken (about 2 cups)
- **2** large eggs
  Two 3-oz. packages ramen noodles, seasoning packets discarded
  Shredded carrot, thinly sliced scallion and Sriracha, for serving

1. In a medium saucepan, combine the stock, miso and soy sauce; bring to a boil over high heat, whisking to dissolve the miso. Add the chicken and simmer over moderate heat for 2 minutes. Keep hot over low heat.

2. Set up a small ice bath. Fill another medium saucepan with water and bring to a boil. Add the eggs and simmer over moderate heat for exactly 7 minutes. Using a slotted spoon, transfer the eggs to the ice bath to cool. Carefully peel the eggs and cut them in half lengthwise.

3. Meanwhile, return the saucepan of water to a boil. Add the ramen and cook until just softened, about 3 minutes. Drain well and transfer to 2 large bowls. Ladle the broth and chicken over the noodles and top with the eggs. Serve with shredded carrot, thinly sliced scallion and Sriracha. —*Justin Chapple*

FISH & SHELLFISH

Salt-Baked Fish
(p. 103)
OPPOSITE Steamed
Grouper with Martini
Relish and Sour
Orange Sauce (p. 105)

Arctic Char with Soba and Green Beans

Active **35 min**; Total **50 min**; Serves **4**

Brooklyn chef Sohui Kim serves this excellent meal to her family on nights when she isn't working at one of her restaurants, The Good Fork or Insa. She makes a bright, refreshing soba noodle salad with green beans, radishes, romaine and fresh basil, and serves it with perfectly crisped arctic char fillets.

- 1 cup chicken stock or low-sodium broth
- ⅓ cup soy sauce
- ¼ cup honey
- 2 Tbsp. mirin
- ½ lb. green beans, halved crosswise on the bias
- 8 oz. buckwheat soba noodles
- 2 Tbsp. fresh lime juice
- 2 Tbsp. toasted sesame oil
- 5 radishes, thinly sliced
- 2 cups thinly sliced inner romaine lettuce leaves
- ½ cup torn basil leaves, plus small leaves for garnish
- 1 scallion, thinly sliced on the bias

  Kosher salt and pepper

  Four 4- to 5-oz. arctic char fillets
- 1 Tbsp. grapeseed oil

1. In a small saucepan, combine the chicken stock, soy sauce, honey and mirin and bring to a boil. Simmer over moderate heat, stirring occasionally, until reduced to a glaze, about 12 minutes. Let the glaze cool slightly.

2. Set up an ice bath. In a large saucepan of salted boiling water, blanch the green beans until crisp-tender, 2 to 3 minutes. Using a slotted spoon, transfer to the ice bath to cool. Drain the greens beans well and pat them dry.

3. In the saucepan of salted boiling water, cook the soba until al dente, 3 to 4 minutes. Drain and cool under cold running water, then pat dry with paper towels. In a large bowl, toss the soba with the lime juice, sesame oil and 3 tablespoons of the glaze. Fold in the green beans, radishes, romaine, the ½ cup of basil and the sliced scallion and season with salt and pepper.

4. Season the arctic char with salt and pepper. In a large nonstick skillet, heat the grapeseed oil until shimmering. Add the fish, skin side down, and press gently with a spatula to flatten. Cook over moderately high heat until the skin is browned and crisp, about 4 minutes. Flip the fish and cook until medium within, about 1 minute longer. Transfer to plates. Spoon the soba salad alongside, garnish with basil and serve, passing the glaze at the table. —*Sohui Kim*

WINE Crisp, citrusy Sauvignon Blanc: 2016 Honig Napa Valley.

Pecan-and-Maple-Glazed Salmon

Active **15 min**; Total **1 hr 5 min**
Serves **10 to 12**

-   One 3-lb. side of salmon

    Kosher salt and pepper
- ½ cup pure maple syrup
- 1 Tbsp. unsalted butter, melted
- 1 Tbsp. Dijon mustard
- ½ cup pecans, coarsely chopped

1. Preheat the oven to 400°. Line a large rimmed baking sheet with parchment and set the salmon on it, skin side down. Season with salt and pepper.

2. In a small bowl, mix the maple syrup with the butter and mustard. Drizzle the maple mixture on the salmon and sprinkle the pecans evenly on top, pressing to help them adhere. Bake the salmon for about 40 minutes, until medium within and lightly caramelized on top. Let stand for 10 minutes before serving. —*Ayesha Curry*

WINE Cherry-inflected Anderson Valley Pinot Noir: 2015 Migration.

Crispy Salmon and Wilted Chard

Total **30 min**; Serves **4**

Earthy, tarragon-infused chard is a perfect accompaniment to the buttery, pan-seared salmon here.

- 2 Tbsp. Champagne vinegar
- 2 Tbsp. finely chopped tarragon, plus leaves for garnish
- 2 tsp. Dijon mustard
- 1 tsp. honey
- ¼ cup plus 2 Tbsp. extra-virgin olive oil

  Kosher salt and pepper
- 1 lb. rainbow Swiss chard, stems cut into 2-inch lengths and leaves coarsely torn
- 1 large shallot, minced
- 2 garlic cloves, minced

  Four 5- to 6-oz. salmon fillets

1. In a small bowl, whisk the vinegar with the chopped tarragon, mustard, honey and ¼ cup of the olive oil. Season the vinaigrette with salt and pepper.

2. In a large saucepan, heat 1 tablespoon of the olive oil. Add the chard stems, shallot and garlic and cook over moderate heat, stirring occasionally, until the stems are softened, about 5 minutes. Stir in the chard leaves in large handfuls and cook until just wilted, about 5 minutes. Stir in half of the vinaigrette and season with salt and pepper.

3. Meanwhile, season the salmon with salt and pepper. In a large nonstick skillet, heat the remaining 1 tablespoon of olive oil until shimmering. Add the salmon, skin side down, and cook over moderately high heat, pressing gently with a spatula to flatten, until the skin is browned and crisp, about 3 minutes. Flip the salmon and cook until medium within, about 3 minutes. Transfer the salmon and wilted chard to plates. Garnish with tarragon leaves and serve, passing the remaining vinaigrette at the table. —*Justin Chapple*

WINE Rich, substantial rosé: 2016 Flower, Flora & Fauna Rosé.

Arctic Char with Soba
and Green Beans

Charmoula-Spiced Salmon with Za'atar Vegetables

Active **40 min**; Total **1 hr**; Serves **4**

VEGETABLES

- ½ lb. baby golden beets, scrubbed and quartered
- ½ lb. baby carrots, halved lengthwise
- ¼ lb. shiitake mushrooms, stemmed and sliced
- 2 Tbsp. extra-virgin olive oil
- 2 Tbsp. za'atar (see Note)
  Kosher salt and pepper
- ¾ lb. baby bok choy, chopped
- 2 Tbsp. fresh lemon juice

CHARMOULA

- 1 cup lightly packed parsley leaves
- 1 cup lightly packed cilantro leaves
- 2 large garlic cloves, crushed
- 2 tsp. ground coriander
- 2 tsp. ground cumin
- 1 tsp. smoked paprika
- 1 tsp. crushed red pepper
- ½ cup extra-virgin olive oil
- ¼ cup fresh lemon juice
  Kosher salt and black pepper

SALMON

- Four 5- to 6-oz. salmon fillets
  Kosher salt and black pepper
- 1 tsp. each ground coriander and cumin
- ½ tsp. smoked paprika
- ½ tsp. crushed red pepper
- 1 Tbsp. extra-virgin olive oil

1. Make the vegetables Preheat the oven to 375°. On a large rimmed baking sheet, toss the beets, carrots and mushrooms with the olive oil and za'atar and season with salt and pepper. Roast for about 30 minutes, until the vegetables are tender. Immediately transfer the vegetables to a large bowl and fold in the bok choy until just wilted. Stir in the lemon juice and season with salt and pepper.

2. Meanwhile, make the charmoula In a food processor, combine everything except the salt and pepper and puree until nearly smooth. Scrape into a medium bowl and season with salt and pepper.

3. Make the salmon Season the fish with salt and black pepper. In a small bowl, whisk the ground coriander and cumin with the paprika and crushed red pepper. Season the salmon with the spice mixture.

4. In a large nonstick skillet, heat the olive oil until shimmering. Add the fish to the skillet skin side down and press gently with a spatula to flatten. Cook the fish over moderate heat until the skin is golden, about 4 minutes. Flip the fish and cook until medium within, about 3 minutes longer. Drain briefly on paper towels. Serve the fish with the vegetables and charmoula. —*Jared Wentworth*

NOTE Za'atar, a Middle Eastern spice blend made with sesame seeds, sumac and herbs, is available at specialty food stores and Middle Eastern markets and on amazon.com.

MAKE AHEAD The charmoula can be refrigerated overnight. Bring to room temperature before serving.

WINE Crisp, spicy Moroccan rosé: 2015 Ouled Thaleb.

Salmon Skewers with Almond Charmoula

Active **25 min**; Total **1 hr**; Serves **4**

For these skewers, TV chef Andrew Zimmern pairs rich salmon with North African charmoula, a brightly acidic herb paste tempered with sweet fruit and—his personal twist—crunchy nuts.

- ½ cup sliced almonds
- 3 medium sweet onions—1 minced, 2 cut into 1-inch pieces
- ½ cup raisins or dried currants
- ½ tsp. saffron, soaked in 2 Tbsp. warm water
- 3 garlic cloves
- 3 cups loosely packed cilantro leaves
- 1 cup loosely packed mint leaves
- 1 small jalapeño, minced
- ⅔ cup extra-virgin olive oil
- ¼ cup fresh lime juice
  Kosher salt and pepper
  Twelve 8-inch wooden skewers, soaked in water for 30 minutes
- 1½ lbs. skinless center-cut salmon fillets, cut into 1½-inch cubes
- 1 lb. small cremini mushrooms
- 12 oz. cherry tomatoes
- 2 yellow bell peppers, cut into 1-inch squares

1. Preheat the oven to 350°. Spread the almonds on a rimmed baking sheet and bake for 15 minutes, until lightly browned.

2. In a medium bowl, combine the minced onion with the raisins, soaked saffron and ¼ cup of the toasted almonds.

3. In a food processor, pulse the garlic with the remaining ¼ cup of almonds until chopped. Add the cilantro, mint and jalapeño and pulse until finely chopped. Add the olive oil and lime juice and process until smooth. Season with salt and pepper. Stir ⅔ cup of the herb mixture into the onion-saffron mixture to make charmoula. Reserve the remaining herb mixture for grilling.

4. Light a grill or preheat the broiler. On the skewers, thread the fish cubes alternately with the mushrooms, cherry tomatoes, bell peppers and onion pieces. Season with salt and pepper and brush all over with the reserved herb mixture.

5. Grill the skewers over moderate heat or broil them, turning occasionally, until the fish is medium within, 5 to 7 minutes. Transfer the skewers to a platter and serve with the charmoula. —*Andrew Zimmern*

MAKE AHEAD The charmoula can be refrigerated overnight.

WINE Creamy, lightly nutty Rhône-style white: 2015 Qupé Marsanne.

Quick-Brined Roast Salmon with Lemon-Garlic Oil

Active **15 min**; Total **1 hr**; Serves **4**

A quick mix of miso, lemon juice, garlic and butter creates a fantastic glaze for roast salmon as well as hake and cod.

1 **Tbsp. kosher salt, plus more for seasoning**

Four 5-oz. skinless salmon or hake fillets

2 **Tbsp. canola oil**

2 **Tbsp. melted butter, cooled**

1 **Tbsp. fresh lemon juice**

1 **Tbsp. shiro miso (white)**

½ **tsp. grated garlic**

Sesame seeds, for garnish

Lemon wedges, for serving

1. In a medium bowl, combine the 1 tablespoon of salt with 2 cups of hot water and stir to dissolve the salt. Let cool to room temperature, then add the fish to the bowl and let brine at room temperature for 30 minutes.

2. Meanwhile, in a small bowl, whisk the oil with the butter, lemon juice, miso and garlic until smooth; season with salt.

3. Preheat the oven to 450°. Line a baking sheet with parchment paper. Drain the fish and transfer to the prepared baking sheet; brush all over with the lemon-garlic butter. Roast until golden and just cooked through, about 10 minutes for salmon and 15 minutes for hake. Transfer to plates, garnish with sesame seeds and serve with lemon wedges. —*Kay Chun*

MAKE AHEAD The lemon-miso butter can be refrigerated overnight. Bring to room temperature before using.

Amberjack Crudo "Tacos"

Total **30 min**; Serves **4 as a starter**

Sometimes the simplest dishes speak the loudest, like these delightful "tacos" from chef Yoshi Okai of Austin's Otoko. He wraps superfresh amberjack fish (or char, salmon or yellowtail) in thin slices of crisp chayote, then lays the tacos in a mix of rice vinegar and soy. The garnish—mint, Meyer lemon zest and flaky salt—is key.

¼ **cup unseasoned rice vinegar**

2 **Tbsp. soy sauce**

Kosher salt

2 **medium chayote, very thinly sliced lengthwise, preferably on a mandoline**

6 **oz. superfresh amberjack, salmon, yellowtail or char fillets, cut into ½-inch strips**

4 **tsp. extra-virgin olive oil**

Mint, finely grated Meyer lemon zest and flaky sea salt, for garnish

1. In a small bowl, mix the unseasoned rice vinegar with the soy sauce and a pinch of kosher salt. Spoon the sauce into 4 small, shallow bowls or rimmed plates.

2. Arrange 12 of the chayote slices on a work surface and divide the fish strips among them. Fold the chayote over the fish and transfer the "tacos" to the bowls. Drizzle the olive oil evenly on top and garnish with mint, grated Meyer lemon zest and flaky sea salt. Serve right away. —*Yoshi Okai*

WINE Crisp Italian white from the Puglia region: 2016 Masseria Li Veli Askos Verdeca.

Grilled Fish Tacos with Cantaloupe Pico de Gallo

Total **30 min**; Serves **4**

Make these simple fish tacos when cantaloupe is at its peak. The floral, fruity melon in the pico de gallo is the perfect complement to the sweet, flaky grilled fish.

¼ **cup extra-virgin olive oil, plus more for brushing**

One 3-lb. whole fish, such as snapper, black sea bass or branzino, cleaned and scored on both sides

Flaky sea salt and pepper

Small cilantro sprigs, thinly sliced scallions and thinly sliced jalapeños, for garnish

Lime wedges, warm small corn tortillas and Cantaloupe Pico de Gallo (recipe follows), for serving

Preheat a grill or grill pan and oil the grate. Rub the fish with the olive oil and season inside and out with salt and pepper. Grill the fish over moderately high heat, turning once, until the skin is crisp and charred and the flesh is flaky and just opaque, about 15 minutes. Transfer to a platter, sprinkle with salt and garnish with cilantro, scallions and jalapeños. Flake the fish with a fork and serve with lime wedges, corn tortillas and Cantaloupe Pico de Gallo. —*Harold Moore*

CANTALOUPE PICO DE GALLO

Total **30 min**; Serves **4**

1 **cup finely chopped cantaloupe**

¾ **cup finely chopped English cucumber**

¾ **cup finely chopped tomato**

½ **cup minced red onion**

½ **cup chopped cilantro leaves**

2 **Tbsp. fresh lime juice**

1 **Tbsp. finely grated jalapeño**

Kosher salt and pepper

In a large bowl, combine the first 7 ingredients and season with salt and pepper. Let sit for 15 minutes before serving. —*HM*

Atún Encebollado (Tuna Smothered in Onions)

⏱ Total **45 min**; Serves **4**

Despite Spain's 3,000-year history of catching wild bluefin tuna, the country's tuna culture has largely been limited to canned and salted tuna products. This luscious dish, a staple of southern Spain, is one of the exceptions.

- ¼ cup extra-virgin olive oil
- 2 garlic cloves, thinly sliced
- 1 large yellow onion, halved and thinly sliced
- 2 bay leaves
- ½ tsp. dried oregano
- ½ tsp. smoked paprika
  Kosher salt
- 2 Tbsp. sherry vinegar
- 1 lb. fresh tuna belly (fatty tuna), cut into 1-inch pieces
  Fresh oregano leaves, for garnish (optional)

1. In a large skillet, heat the olive oil over moderately low heat. Add the garlic, onion, bay leaves, dried oregano and paprika and cook, stirring occasionally, until the onion is very soft but not browned, about 25 minutes. Season with salt.

2. Stir in the vinegar and 3 tablespoons of water and bring to a simmer. Add the tuna in a single layer over the onions, cover and simmer until the fish is just cooked through, about 5 minutes. Spoon the sauce over the tuna, garnish with fresh oregano, if desired, and serve. —*José Andrés*

WINE Citrusy white from La Mancha: 2015 Paso a Paso.

Japanese-Style Eel and Rice Bowl

⏱ Total **20 min**; Serves **4**

Deceptively simple, this combination of rich eel, delicate rice, sweet sauce and tingly hot pepper is a deeply satisfying comfort dish, whether you're camping or cooking at home.

- ⅓ cup soy sauce
- ⅓ cup plus 1 Tbsp. mirin
- 2 Tbsp. sugar
  Two 6-oz. chargrilled unagi (eel; see Note)
- 2 cups steamed sushi rice
  Sansho pepper or Sichuan peppercorns, for garnish (optional)

1. Preheat the oven to 425° or prepare your grill or campfire for cooking over moderate heat. In a small saucepan, whisk the soy sauce with ⅓ cup of the mirin and the sugar and bring to a boil over high heat. Simmer over moderate heat for about 5 minutes, stirring occasionally, until the sauce is reduced by about half and lightly coats the back of a spoon.

2. Meanwhile, line a baking sheet with foil and set the unagi on it. Sprinkle with the remaining 1 tablespoon of mirin. If using a grill or campfire, sprinkle the unagi with mirin before wrapping loosely in foil. Cook for about 6 to 8 minutes, until heated through.

3. Divide the steamed rice among 4 bowls. Cut each unagi fillet in half and divide among the bowls, skin side down. Drizzle each bowl with some of the warm sauce and sprinkle with some sansho pepper or Sichuan peppercorns, if desired. Serve. —*Laurie Woolever*

NOTE Unagi can be found in Asian grocery stores. Smoked trout can be substituted.

Whole Sardines with Parsley

⏱ Total **20 min**; Serves **4 to 6**

Inspired by the southern Italian dish *sarde arraganate,* this quick dish from chef Chris Behr of the Rome Sustainable Food Project has a slightly tangy flavor from red wine vinegar. Look for fresh sardines that have clear eyes and smell like the sea.

- 12 fresh sardines (about 2 oz. each), cleaned and scaled
  Kosher salt
- ¼ cup extra-virgin olive oil, plus more for drizzling
- 6 garlic cloves, smashed
- 2 Tbsp. chopped parsley, plus more for garnish
- 1 tsp. crushed red pepper
- 2 Tbsp. red wine vinegar
  Lemon wedges and crusty bread, for serving

1. Pat the sardines dry with paper towels and season generously with salt. In a large nonstick skillet, heat 2 tablespoons of the olive oil. Add 3 of the garlic cloves and cook over moderate heat, stirring occasionally, until fragrant, about 1 minute. Add half of the sardines, 1 tablespoon of the parsley and ½ teaspoon of the crushed red pepper. Cook over moderately high heat, turning once, until the sardines are browned and just cooked through, about 5 minutes. Add 1 tablespoon of the vinegar and cook until the liquid is reduced, about 1 minute. Discard the garlic and transfer the sardines to a platter; tent with foil. Wipe out the skillet and repeat with the remaining olive oil, garlic, sardines, parsley, crushed red pepper and vinegar.

2. Drizzle the sardines with more olive oil and garnish with chopped parsley. Serve warm with lemon wedges and crusty bread. —*Chris Behr*

WINE Crisp, minerally Sicilian white: 2015 Tami' Grillo.

Whole Sardines
with Parsley

Pancetta-Wrapped Trout with Sage and Lemon

◔ Total **45 min**; Serves **4**

Globe-trotting chef Andrew Zimmern sometimes trains his roving eye on the food of his home state, Minnesota. Here he gives the Midwest's local catch the saltimbocca treatment, pairing grilled whole fish with Rome's bright and savory flavor trio: pancetta, sage and lemon.

Four ¾-lb. trout, cleaned

Kosher salt and pepper

20 **sage sprigs**

12 **thin lemon slices, plus ½ tsp. fresh lemon juice**

1 **lb. very thinly sliced pancetta**

Canola oil, for brushing

4 **Tbsp. unsalted butter**

1 **small shallot, minced**

1 **Tbsp. minced parsley**

1 **Tbsp. minced tarragon**

1 **Tbsp. minced scallion**

1 **Tbsp. minced mint**

1 **tsp. tomato paste**

2 **Tbsp. dry white wine**

¼ **cup heavy cream**

3 **Tbsp. Dijon mustard**

2 **Tbsp. apple cider vinegar**

2 **Tbsp. unrefined hazelnut oil**

2 **Tbsp. unrefined peanut oil**

8 **oz. baby watercress**

2 **Tbsp. chopped chives**

1. Season the fish all over with salt and pepper. Fill each cavity with 1 sage sprig and 1 lemon slice. Place 2 sage sprigs and 1 lemon slice on both sides of each fish.

2. Place a sheet of wax paper on a work surface. Arrange 6 to 8 slices of the pancetta in 2 overlapping rows to form a 6-by-8-inch rectangle on the wax paper. Set 1 fish on the bottom edge of the pancetta. Using the wax paper as a guide, tightly roll up the fish in the pancetta. Carefully peel off the wax paper. Brush the fish with canola oil and transfer to a rimmed baking sheet. Repeat with the remaining fish and pancetta and more oil.

3. Preheat a grill or a broiler with a rack in the top third of the oven. Grill or broil the fish, flipping halfway through, until cooked through, about 6 minutes per side. Season with pepper.

4. Meanwhile, in a small skillet, melt the butter. Cook over moderately high heat, stirring occasionally, until browned, 2 to 3 minutes. Stir in the shallot, parsley, tarragon, scallion, mint and tomato paste. Cook, stirring, for 20 seconds. Add the wine, bring the sauce to a boil and cook for 1 minute. Add 2 tablespoons of the cream and cook until the sauce thickens, about 1 minute. Scrape the sauce into a small heatproof bowl and stir in the lemon juice. Season with salt.

5. In a large bowl, combine the mustard with the vinegar. Slowly drizzle in the hazelnut and peanut oils, whisking constantly, until incorporated. Whisk in the remaining 2 tablespoons of cream. Season with salt and pepper. Add the watercress and chives and toss to coat. Serve with the fish and butter sauce. —*Andrew Zimmern*

WINE Vibrant Washington state dry Riesling: 2015 Pacific Rim.

Whole Roast Snapper with Sichuan Butter

Active **30 min**; Total **1 hr**; Serves **4**

6 **Tbsp. unsalted butter, at room temperature**

1 **tsp. hot chile oil**

1 **tsp. finely ground Sichuan peppercorns**

Kosher salt and pepper

1 **Tbsp. canola oil, plus more for greasing**

One 2½-lb. whole red snapper, cleaned

1 **leek, white and light green parts only, halved lengthwise, thinly sliced crosswise**

1 **large garlic clove, minced**

4 **small heads of baby bok choy (1½ lbs.), trimmed and cut into 2-inch pieces**

¼ **cup Chinkiang vinegar (Chinese black vinegar)**

1 **Tbsp. toasted sesame oil**

1. Preheat the oven to 375°. In a small skillet, cook 3 tablespoons of the butter over moderately high heat, stirring, until the milk solids are golden, 3 to 5 minutes. Transfer to a small bowl; let cool completely. Using a fork, mix in the chile oil, peppercorns and remaining 3 tablespoons of butter. Season the Sichuan butter with salt and refrigerate until spreadable, 10 minutes.

2. Grease a rimmed baking sheet with canola oil. Using a knife, make 4 shallow slashes on each side of the fish. Season with salt and pepper and transfer to the baking sheet. Roast for 15 minutes, then spread the Sichuan butter on top of the fish. Roast for about 20 minutes longer, basting occasionally, until the thickest part of the flesh flakes with a fork.

3. Meanwhile, in a large skillet, heat the 1 tablespoon of canola oil. Add the leek and garlic and cook over moderately high heat, stirring, until just softened, 3 minutes. Add the bok choy and a pinch of salt. Stir-fry until the bok choy is just wilted, 3 to 5 minutes. Remove from the heat and stir in the vinegar. Season with salt and pepper.

4. Using a large, thin spatula, transfer the fish to a platter and spoon any pan juices on top. Pile the bok choy around the fish and drizzle with the sesame oil. Serve right away.—*Chris Shepherd*

Baked Cod Fillet with Bouillabaisse Sauce and Green Olive Tapenade

Active **1 hr**; Total **2 hr**; Serves **4**

For a special dinner party, the highlight of this dish—the deeply rich, slightly spicy bouillabaisse sauce—is perfect to make ahead.

- 6 Tbsp. extra-virgin olive oil, plus more for drizzling
- 1 large fennel bulb (1 lb.), trimmed and finely chopped
- 1 leek, white and light green parts only, finely chopped
- 1 medium white onion, finely chopped
- 2 celery ribs, finely chopped
- 2 garlic cloves, finely chopped
- ¼ tsp. saffron threads
- 2 Tbsp. Pernod or pastis
- ¾ cup dry white wine
- ¾ cup dry vermouth
- 1 pint cherry tomatoes, halved and smashed
- ½ tsp. cayenne
- 2 lbs. white fish bones, rinsed and dried
- 2 tsp. fresh lemon juice plus more for drizzling
  Kosher salt
  Four 6-oz. cod fillets
  Green Olive Tapenade (recipe follows), for serving

1. In a large enameled cast-iron casserole, heat 2 tablespoons of the olive oil. Add the fennel, leek, onion and celery and cook over moderate heat, stirring occasionally, until the vegetables are softened, about 8 minutes. Stir in the garlic and saffron and cook until fragrant, about 2 minutes. Add the Pernod and cook over moderately high heat until the liquid is evaporated, about 2 minutes. Add the wine and vermouth and cook until the liquid is reduced by about half, about 8 minutes. Add the tomatoes and cayenne and simmer over moderate heat until the liquid is reduced by half, about 5 minutes.

2. Meanwhile, in a large skillet, heat 2 tablespoons of the olive oil. Add the fish bones to the skillet and cook over moderately high heat, turning once, until browned, about 5 minutes. Transfer the bones to the casserole along with 2 cups of water. Cover partially and simmer over moderately low heat for 30 minutes. Let the sauce cool slightly, then discard the fish bones. Using an immersion blender, puree the sauce, then strain through a fine-mesh sieve into a medium saucepan. Add the 2 teaspoons of lemon juice, season with salt and keep warm.

3. Meanwhile, preheat the oven to 375°. Season the fish with salt and refrigerate, uncovered, for 30 minutes. In a large ovenproof nonstick skillet, heat the remaining 2 tablespoons of olive oil until shimmering. Add the fish and cook until browned on the bottom, about 3 minutes. Flip the fillets and transfer the skillet to the oven. Bake for 6 to 8 minutes, until the fish is opaque and just cooked through.

4. Ladle the sauce into 4 shallow bowls and top each with a cod fillet. Spoon the tapenade over the fish and drizzle with lemon juice and olive oil. Serve immediately. —*Stephen Harris*

SERVE WITH Blanched Broccolini.

MAKE AHEAD The bouillabaisse sauce can be refrigerated for up to 2 days.

WINE Full-bodied sparkling wine: 2013 Ridgeview Cavendish Brut.

GREEN OLIVE TAPENADE

Total **15 min**; Makes **¼ cup**

- ¼ cup pitted brined or oil-cured green olives, finely chopped
- 2 Tbsp. rinsed and drained capers, finely chopped
- 2 Tbsp. finely chopped parsley
- 2 Tbsp. extra-virgin olive oil
- 1½ Tbsp. fresh lemon juice
  Kosher salt and pepper

Stir everything together in a small bowl and season with salt and pepper. —*SH*

MAKE AHEAD The tapenade can be refrigerated for up to 1 week.

Steamed Fish with Spicy Broth and Cucumber

Total **30 min**; Serves **4**

Instead of discarding fish bones, F&W's Justin Chapple uses them to enrich the steaming liquid (which also includes ginger, scallions, cilantro and sambal) for this sea bass. He then strains that delicious broth and serves the fish in it.

- One 2-lb. black sea bass—filleted, bones reserved and head discarded (have your fishmonger do this)
- 1 cup cherry tomatoes, halved
  One 2-inch piece of ginger, sliced and lightly crushed
- 4 scallions
- 3 cilantro sprigs
- 2 Tbsp. tomato paste
- 1 Tbsp. sambal oelek or other Asian chile sauce
  Extra-virgin olive oil, for drizzling
  Kosher salt
- 1 English cucumber, spiralized
  Black sesame seeds, for garnish
  Steamed rice, for serving

1. In a large, deep skillet, combine the fish bones with the tomatoes, ginger, scallions, cilantro, tomato paste and sambal. Add 6 cups of water and set a bamboo steamer on top. Bring the water to a boil, then simmer over moderate heat until the tomatoes start to break down, about 5 minutes.

2. Drizzle the fish with oil and season with salt. Put the fish in the steamer basket skin side up, cover and steam over moderately low heat until just cooked through, 5 to 7 minutes.

3. Using a thin spatula, transfer the fish to shallow bowls. Strain the broth into a heatproof bowl; discard the solids. Season the broth with salt and ladle over the fish. Pile the cucumber alongside, garnish with sesame seeds and serve with steamed rice. —*Justin Chapple*

WINE Floral, dry Riesling: 2015 Fritz Haag Trocken.

**Crusted Hake with
Radishes and Turnips**

Snapper Escovitch

Total **50 min**; Serves **4**

Chef Nina Compton, of Compère Lapin in New Orleans, makes the ultimate escovitch, combining the classic crispy pan-fried fish with a sweet and spicy pepper sauce.

- **2 tsp. paprika**
- **1 tsp. ground cumin**
- **Sea salt and pepper**
- **Four 1-lb. whole red or yellowtail snappers, cleaned**
- **Canola oil, for frying**
- **2 Scotch Bonnet or habanero chiles—1 halved lengthwise and 1 stemmed, seeded and minced**
- **3 red and yellow bell peppers— stemmed, seeded and cut into ¼-inch strips**
- **1 large white onion, halved and thinly sliced**
- **1 carrot, cut into julienne**
- **1 garlic clove, crushed**
- **5 allspice berries**
- **¼ tsp. celery seeds**
- **½ cup unseasoned rice vinegar**
- **Cilantro leaves, for garnish**

1. In a small bowl, mix the paprika with the cumin, 1 tablespoon of salt and 2 teaspoons of pepper. Using a small, sharp knife, make 3 or 4 shallow slashes on both sides of each fish. Season the fish inside the cavity and all over the outside with the spice mixture, rubbing it into the slashes.

2. Line a large baking sheet with paper towels. In a very large skillet, heat ½ inch of oil until shimmering. Add half of the halved chile and 2 of the fish to the skillet. Cook over moderately high heat until browned and crisp on the bottom, 4 to 5 minutes. Using a large, thin spatula, carefully flip the fish and cook until browned and crisp on the other side, 4 to 5 minutes more. Transfer to the prepared baking sheet to drain. Repeat with the remaining halved chile and fish.

3. Pour off all but ½ cup of the oil from the skillet; discard the chile. Add the bell peppers, onion, carrot, garlic, allspice, celery seeds, the minced chile and a generous pinch of salt and pepper. Cook over moderate heat, stirring occasionally, until just softened, 5 minutes. Add the vinegar. Cook, stirring occasionally, until the vegetables are tender, 5 minutes more. Season with salt and pepper.

4. Transfer half of the pepper mixture to a blender and puree until smooth. Spread the puree on a platter and arrange the fish on top. Spoon the remaining pepper mixture over the fish, garnish with cilantro and serve right away. —*Nina Compton*

WINE Crisp, berry-scented rosé from Provence: 2016 Château Minuty M de Minuty.

Crusted Hake with Radishes and Turnips

⏱ Total **45 min**; Serves **4**

To create a crisp crust for delicate hake fillets, we use Cream of Wheat cereal, an idea inspired by NYC chef Floyd Cardoz.

- **2 Tbsp. extra-virgin olive oil, plus more for frying**
- **12 radishes with greens, halved, greens chopped**
- **4 very small turnips, cut into ¾-inch-thick wedges**
- **Kosher salt and pepper**
- **½ cup all-purpose flour**
- **2 large eggs, beaten**
- **1 cup Cream of Wheat cereal**
- **Four 5-oz. skinless hake fillets**
- **2 Tbsp. unsalted butter, cubed**
- **6 oz. (10 cups) stemmed curly spinach (not baby)**
- **1½ Tbsp. whole-grain mustard**
- **1½ Tbsp. fresh lemon juice**

1. Preheat the oven to 425°. In a large, deep ovenproof skillet, heat the 2 tablespoons of oil. Add the radishes (not the greens) and turnips and season with salt and pepper. Cook over moderately high heat, tossing occasionally, until browned in spots, 2 minutes. Transfer the skillet to the oven and roast for about 10 minutes, until tender.

2. Meanwhile, put the flour, eggs and cereal in 3 separate shallow bowls. Season the hake with salt and pepper; dust with the flour. Dip in the egg, then in the Cream of Wheat, pressing to help the cereal adhere.

3. In a large nonstick ovenproof skillet, heat ¼ inch of oil until shimmering. Add the hake and cook over moderately high heat, turning once, until browned and crisp on both sides, about 6 minutes total. Transfer the skillet to the oven and bake for 5 to 7 minutes, until the fish is cooked through.

4. Put the skillet with the radishes and turnips over moderate heat. Add the butter, spinach and radish greens and cook until just wilted. Stir in the mustard and lemon juice and season with salt and pepper. Transfer to plates with the fish and serve. —*Justin Chapple*

WINE Crisp Sauvignon Blanc: 2015 Sula Vineyards.

Halibut with Beurre Blanc and Daikon Choucroute

Active **45 min;** Total **1 hr 15 min plus 5 days fermenting;** Serves **4**

- 2 **lbs. daikon, peeled and cut lengthwise into ⅛-inch-thick ribbons, preferably on a mandoline**
- 2 **Tbsp. grey sea salt**
- 1¼ **cups dry white wine**
- ⅓ **cup distilled white vinegar**
- 1 **Tbsp. Champagne vinegar**
- ⅓ **cup finely chopped shallot**
- 2 **Tbsp. finely chopped peeled fresh ginger**
- ¾ **cup heavy cream**
- 6 **Tbsp. chilled unsalted butter, diced**
  Fine sea salt
  Four 5-oz. skinless halibut fillets, about 1 inch thick
- 4 **sorrel leaves, for garnish**
  Black pepper, for garnish

1. In a large nonreactive bowl, massage the daikon with the grey salt until wet. Pack the daikon in the bowl and press plastic wrap directly on top. Cover with a similar bowl to submerge the daikon in the brine. Let stand in a cool place for 5 days. Drain and rinse in cold water; drain. Refrigerate.

2. In a small saucepan, combine ¾ cup of the wine with both vinegars, the shallot and ginger. Boil over moderately high heat until the liquid is almost evaporated, about 15 minutes. Add the cream and simmer over moderate heat until reduced by one-third, about 5 minutes. Strain through a fine sieve into a bowl, pressing on the solids; discard the solids. Return the liquid to the pan. Off the heat, gradually whisk in the butter. Season the beurre blanc with fine sea salt and keep warm.

3. Season the fish with fine sea salt. In a steamer basket set over a medium skillet with 1 inch of simmering water, steam the fish, skin side down and covered, over moderately low heat, until just cooked through, about 8 minutes.

4. Meanwhile, in a medium saucepan, warm the drained daikon with the remaining ½ cup of wine over moderately low heat, tossing occasionally. Arrange the daikon on plates. Top with the fish and spoon the beurre blanc on top. Garnish each serving with a sorrel leaf and black pepper.
—*Daniel Rose*

WINE Creamy Rhône Valley white: 2015 E. Guigal Côtes du Rhône Blanc.

Citrus-Roasted Halibut and Braised Radishes

Total **45 min;** Serves **8**

The sliced oranges layered under the halibut do double duty here, adding a citrusy aroma to the fish while also preventing it from sticking to the pan during roasting.

- ½ **stick unsalted butter, plus more for greasing**
- 3 **bunches of radishes with greens (about 2¼ lbs.), halved if large**
  Kosher salt and pepper
- 2 **navel oranges, thinly sliced, plus wedges for serving**
  One 3-lb. halibut fillet (about 1 inch thick)
- ½ **cup dry white wine**
  Extra-virgin olive oil and flaky sea salt, for serving

1. Preheat the oven to 500°. Butter one side of a 12-inch round of parchment paper. In a large skillet, melt the ½ stick of butter. Add the radishes and greens along with 3 tablespoons of water and season with kosher salt and pepper. Top with the parchment paper, buttered side down, and cook over moderate heat, shaking the pan occasionally, until the radishes are just tender, about 15 minutes.

2. Meanwhile, butter a large rimmed baking sheet. Arrange the orange slices in a slightly overlapping layer, then top with the halibut, skin side down. Pour the wine over the fish and season with kosher salt and pepper. Roast the fish for 12 to 14 minutes, until just opaque throughout. Cut into 8 fillets and discard the skin.

3. Transfer the fish, roasted oranges and any pan juices to a platter. Drizzle with olive oil and sprinkle with sea salt. Serve with the radishes and orange wedges.
—*Eli Dahlin*

Brown Butter Sole with Herb Salad

Total **30 min;** Serves **4**

"Sole meunière was the first fish I learned to cook," recalls chef Michael Voltaggio. "I remember smelling the brown butter and thinking, I want to eat that now." This elegant dish is incredibly simple. If your fishmonger doesn't have smaller grey sole fillets, buy two larger 8- to 10-ounce fillets and halve them crosswise.

- **Four 5- to 6-oz. sole fillets, preferably grey sole**
  Kosher salt and pepper
- 4 **Tbsp. unsalted butter**
- 2 **large thyme sprigs**
- ½ **cup coarsely chopped fennel fronds**
- ½ **cup light green celery leaves**
- ½ **cup parsley leaves**
- ½ **cup cilantro leaves**
- ½ **cup Thai basil leaves**
  Extra-virgin olive oil, for drizzling
  Lemon wedges, for serving

1. Season the fish with salt and pepper. In a large skillet, melt 2 tablespoons of the butter with 1 thyme sprig and cook until starting to brown. Add 2 sole fillets and cook over moderately high heat, turning once, until golden brown, about 4 minutes. Transfer to a platter; tent with foil. Repeat with the remaining butter, thyme and fish.

2. In a medium bowl, toss the fennel fronds with the celery, parsley, cilantro and Thai basil leaves. Drizzle with olive oil, season with salt and pepper and toss to coat.

3. Transfer the sole to a platter or plates and top with the herb salad. Serve immediately, passing lemon wedges at the table.
—*Bryan Voltaggio and Michael Voltaggio*

WINE Ripe, citrusy Italian white: 2015 Nino Negri Ca'Brione.

Citrus-Roasted Halibut and
Braised Radishes

**Black Bass with Parsley
Sauce, Eggplant, Freekeh
and Chipotles**

Salt-Baked Fish

📷 PAGE 89

Active **20 min**; Total **1 hr**; Serves **4**

Famed Spanish chef José Andrés got the inspiration for this dish from Restaurante Antonio in Zahara de los Atunes, Andalusia, where he and his family spend the summer. Leaving the scales on during salt-baking ensures both incredibly moist fish and an easy time removing the skin.

- **3 lbs. kosher salt**
- **6 large rosemary sprigs**
- **10 thyme sprigs**
- **4 bay leaves**
  One 2½-lb. whole dorade or red snapper with scales, gutted
- **2 Tbsp. Spanish extra-virgin olive oil**
  Flaky sea salt, for serving

1. Preheat the oven to 400°. Line a large rimmed baking sheet with foil or parchment paper. In a large bowl, mix the kosher salt with ½ cup of water until it resembles moist sand. Strip the leaves from half of the rosemary and thyme sprigs and mix into the bowl along with 2 of the bay leaves.

2. Spread half of the salt mixture in the center of the baking sheet and place the remaining rosemary and thyme sprigs and bay leaves on top. Lay the fish on the mound, then cover with the remaining salt mixture, lightly packing it to completely cover the fish.

3. Bake the fish for 35 minutes, until an instant-read thermometer inserted into it registers 135°. Remove from the oven and let stand for 5 minutes.

4. Crack the top salt crust and discard it. Remove and discard the skin from the top of the fish and, using a fish spatula, carefully transfer the top fillet to a platter. Flip the fish over and repeat the process. Drizzle with the olive oil and sprinkle with flaky sea salt. Serve. —*José Andrés*

WINE Unoaked, light-bodied white Rioja: 2016 CVNE Monopole Blanco.

Black Bass with Parsley Sauce, Eggplant, Freekeh and Chipotles

Active **1 hr 30 min**; Total **2 hr 30 min**
Serves **4**

Moroccan-Israeli chef Meir Adoni's elegant, unconstrained crisp-skinned fish mixes the locavore (baharat spice, preserved lemon) and the far-flung (chipotles in adobo, soy sauce).

EGGPLANT CREAM

- **1 medium Italian eggplant**
- **½ cup canola oil**
- **2 garlic cloves**
- **2 tsp. fresh lemon juice**
  Kosher salt

FREEKEH

- **¼ cup extra-virgin olive oil**
- **1 small white onion, finely chopped**
  Kosher salt
- **1 cup whole freekeh**
- **1 tsp. ground cumin**
- **½ tsp. baharat spice (see Note)**
- **2½ cups boiling water**
- **3 Tbsp. fresh lemon juice**
- **1 tsp. minced preserved lemon peel (from ½ preserved lemon)**

PARSLEY SAUCE

- **2 cups lightly packed parsley leaves**
  Kosher salt

CHIPOTLE SAUCE

- **¼ cup fresh lemon juice**
- **¼ cup canola oil**
- **2 chipotle chiles in adobo, seeded**
- **1 Tbsp. finely chopped peeled fresh ginger**
- **1½ Tbsp. soy sauce**
- **1½ tsp. honey**
  Kosher salt

FISH

Four 5-oz. skin-on black bass or striped bass fillets
  Kosher salt and pepper
- **1 Tbsp. canola oil**

1. Make the eggplant cream Roast the eggplant directly over a gas flame or broil 6 inches from the heat until charred all over and very tender, 15 to 20 minutes. Transfer to a plate and let cool completely. Peel and seed the eggplant. In a blender, combine the eggplant flesh with the canola oil, garlic and lemon juice and puree until very smooth. Transfer to a small bowl and season with salt.

2. Make the freekeh In a large, deep skillet, heat the olive oil until shimmering. Add the onion and a generous pinch of salt and cook over moderate heat, stirring occasionally, until lightly browned, about 10 minutes. Stir in the freekeh, cumin and baharat and cook until fragrant, about 2 minutes. Add the boiling water, cover and cook over low heat, stirring occasionally, until the freekeh is al dente and the water is absorbed, about 1 hour. Stir in the lemon juice and preserved lemon peel and season with salt.

3. Meanwhile, make the parsley sauce In a medium saucepan of boiling water, blanch the parsley until tender, about 4 minutes. Drain well and transfer to a blender. Add ¼ cup of cold water and puree until very smooth. Season with salt.

4. Make the chipotle sauce In a blender, combine the lemon juice, canola oil, chipotles, ginger, soy sauce and honey and puree until very smooth. Season with salt.

5. Make the fish Season the fish with salt and pepper. In a large nonstick skillet, heat the canola oil until shimmering. Add the fish, skin side down, and press gently with a spatula to flatten. Cook over moderately high heat until the skin is browned and crisp, about 3 minutes. Flip the fish and cook until just opaque, about 2 minutes. Transfer to a plate.

6. Spoon 2 tablespoons of the parsley sauce into shallow bowls. Spoon the eggplant cream on top, then the freekeh. Set the fish on the freekeh skin side up and drizzle with the chipotle sauce. Serve, passing more chipotle sauce at the table. —*Meir Adoni*

NOTE Baharat spice blend commonly includes black pepper, cumin and cinnamon, and is available at kalustyans.com.

MAKE AHEAD The eggplant cream, parsley sauce and chipotle sauce can be refrigerated, separately, overnight. Bring to room temperature before using.

WINE Citrusy Chardonnay from Galilee: 2015 Yarden.

Grilled Sea Bass with Marinated Eggplant

Active **25 min**; Total **3 hr**; Serves **4**

In the summer, star chef Tom Colicchio fishes for fluke and striped bass, then grills and pairs them with produce from his garden. We used wild sea bass in this bright dish with marinated eggplant, but other thick white fish fillets like cod or sablefish will work beautifully, too.

- **3** cups loosely packed small mixed herbs, such as dill sprigs, Thai basil, cilantro and parsley leaves
- **1** cup extra-virgin olive oil
- **⅓** cup fresh lime juice, plus lime wedges for serving
- **4** Fresno chiles, thinly sliced
- **1** Tbsp. fish sauce
- **2** medium eggplants, cut crosswise into ½-inch-thick rounds
- Kosher salt and pepper
- Canola oil, for brushing
- Four 8-oz. skin-on wild sea bass fillets (about 1 to 1½ inches thick)

1. In a large bowl, mix 1½ cups of the herbs with the olive oil, half each of the lime juice and chiles and the fish sauce. Season the eggplant with salt and pepper and add to the marinade. Cover and refrigerate for 2 hours.

2. Light a grill or preheat a grill pan and oil the grate. Remove the eggplant from the marinade, brushing off any herbs and chiles, and grill over moderate heat, turning, until cooked through and lightly charred, about 10 minutes. Return the eggplant to the marinade and let cool to room temperature. Keep the grill on.

3. Season the fish with salt and pepper. Grill over moderate heat, turning once, until cooked through and lightly charred, about 15 minutes. Transfer to a cutting board.

4. Add the remaining herbs, lime juice and chiles to the bowl with the eggplant; gently toss. Arrange the eggplant on a platter with the grilled fish and serve with lime wedges. —*Tom Colicchio*

WINE Pineappley New York Chardonnay: 2013 Macari Estate from Long Island.

Walnut-Stuffed Fish with Barberries (Mahi-e Fivij)

Active **30 min**; Total **1 hr 30 min**; Serves **8**

Traditionally, this deliciously sweet-and-sour stuffed fish is cooked with its scales left on, which prevents it from sticking to the pan. For scaled fish, brush the pan with oil and line it with parchment, so the fish comes out of the pan intact.

- Canola oil, for brushing
- **1** cup walnuts
- **½** cup lightly packed cilantro
- **½** cup lightly packed parsley
- **⅓** cup plus 2 Tbsp. pomegranate syrup (not molasses)
- **½** cup dried barberries (see Note)
- Kosher salt and pepper
- One 2½-lb. whole Mediterranean sea bass or branzino, cleaned
- **¾** cup sour orange juice (or ½ cup fresh clementine juice mixed with ¼ cup fresh lemon juice)
- **3** Tbsp. unsalted butter
- **1** Tbsp. sugar
- Cilantro leaves, for garnish (optional)

1. Preheat the oven to 425°. Brush the inside of a 3- to 4-quart enameled cast-iron casserole with oil and line the bottom with parchment paper. In a food processor, pulse the walnuts until finely chopped. Add the cilantro, parsley, ⅓ cup of the pomegranate syrup and ¼ cup of the barberries and puree until a paste forms. Season the filling with salt and pepper.

2. Season the cavity of the fish with salt and pepper, then stuff it with the walnut filling. Brush the outside of the fish with oil and season with salt and pepper. Place the fish cavity side up in the casserole, curling it so it fits snugly. Drizzle the fish all over with the remaining 2 tablespoons of pomegranate syrup. Roast for about 20 minutes, until the fish starts to release juices. Add ½ cup of the sour orange juice to the casserole and roast for 25 to 30 minutes longer, basting occasionally, until it is cooked through. Let stand for 10 minutes.

3. Meanwhile, in a nonstick medium skillet, melt the butter. Add the remaining ¼ cup of barberries, the sugar and a generous pinch of salt and cook over moderate heat, stirring, until the barberries are softened and the sugar is dissolved, about 3 minutes. Add the remaining ¼ cup of sour orange juice and cook, stirring, until the barberries are coated in a light sauce, 1 to 2 minutes.

4. Using a thin metal spatula, carefully loosen the fish from the side of the casserole. Put a serving platter on top of the casserole, then invert the fish onto it. Spoon the warm barberry mixture on top, garnish with cilantro (if using) and serve. —*Mahin Gilanpour Motamed*

NOTE Small dried barberries are super tart and add a great fruity tang to dishes. They are available at Persian markets and from kalustyans.com.

WINE Light-bodied, crisp white: 2015 Fattori Danieli Soave.

Fresh-Caught Fish Tips

When it comes to cooking fresh-caught fish, it's best not to fuss with it too much, since its flavor is so full and so clean. This is not the time for complex sauces or fancy garnishes. Throw in some wild herbs, or sweet corn sliced off the cob, or bacon fat—or all three. You're cooking to please yourself and some friends on a fine summer night, so take it easy.

Fried Fish in Adobo

Active **25 min**; Total **4 hr 25 min**
Makes **4 tapas**

Spanish chef José Andrés marinates swordfish in a combination of olive oil, vinegar, garlic and paprika, coats it in flour, then fries it until crisp, creating an addictive tapas snack.

- 2 garlic cloves
  Kosher salt
- ¼ cup extra-virgin olive oil, plus more for frying
- ¼ cup white wine vinegar
- 1 Tbsp. smoked paprika
- 1½ tsp. ground cumin
- 2 bay leaves
- 1 lb. swordfish, skin discarded, fish cut into 1-inch pieces
- ¾ cup all-purpose flour

1. On a cutting board, smash the garlic with a pinch of salt and use the flat side of a chef's knife to create a smooth paste. Transfer to a large bowl and stir in the ¼ cup of olive oil, the vinegar, paprika, cumin, bay leaves, 1 teaspoon of salt and 2 tablespoons of water. Add the fish and toss to coat. Refrigerate covered for at least 4 hours or up to 10 hours.

2. In a large cast-iron skillet, heat 1 inch of olive oil to 350°. Spread the flour in a shallow bowl. Remove the fish from the marinade and coat it in the flour, using your fingers to press the flour into the fish. Working in 2 batches, fry the fish, turning a few times, until golden brown and cooked through, about 5 minutes per batch. Transfer the fish to a paper towel–lined baking sheet and season with salt. Transfer to a platter and serve immediately.
—*José Andrés*

WINE Lemony, vibrant Verdejo: 2015 José Pariente.

Steamed Grouper with Martini Relish and Sour Orange Sauce

📷 PAGE 88

Active **35 min**; Total **1 hr**; Serves **4**

Bobby Flay of NYC's Gato and Bar Americain recently rediscovered cooking in parchment, a classic technique that delicately steams fish or meat with aromatic ingredients so you don' thave to add much fat. He serves this grouper with citrus, roasted piquillos and olives for a pop of flavor.

SAUCE

- 2 cups fresh orange juice
- 1 Tbsp. honey
- ¼ tsp. finely grated lime zest plus 2 Tbsp. fresh lime juice
- ½ tsp. white wine vinegar
  Kosher salt and pepper

RELISH

- ⅓ cup pitted Picholine olives, quartered lengthwise
- 2 jarred piquillo peppers—patted dry, seeded and finely chopped
- 1 Tbsp. minced shallot
- ½ jalapeño, seeded and minced
- 1 Tbsp. extra-virgin olive oil
- 1 Tbsp. white wine vinegar
- 2 Tbsp. finely chopped dill
- 1 Tbsp. finely chopped parsley
  Kosher salt and pepper

FISH

- Four 6-oz. skinless grouper fillets
  Extra-virgin olive oil, for brushing
  Kosher salt and pepper
- 8 parsley sprigs
- 8 dill sprigs
- 2 Tbsp. dry white wine

1. Make the sauce In a small saucepan, boil the orange juice over moderately high heat until reduced to ½ cup, about 10 minutes. Transfer to a small bowl and let cool, then stir in the honey, lime zest, lime juice and vinegar. Season with salt and pepper.

2. Make the relish In a small bowl, mix everything except the dill, parsley, salt and pepper. Let stand at room temperature for 15 minutes, then fold in the dill and parsley. Season the relish with salt and pepper.

3. Meanwhile, make the fish Preheat the oven to 450°. Lay four 15-inch-long sheets of parchment paper on a work surface. Brush the fish fillets with olive oil and season with salt and pepper. Put a fillet in the center of each sheet of parchment and top with 2 sprigs each of the parsley and dill. Drizzle on ½ tablespoon of the wine. Fold the parchment over the fish, then fold the edge over itself in small pleats to seal.

4. Transfer the papillotes to a large baking sheet. Bake for about 7 minutes, until puffed. Snip the parchment open with scissors and serve the fish with the sour orange sauce and martini relish.
—*Bobby Flay*

SERVE WITH Herbed whole-wheat couscous.

WINE Grapefruity Chilean Sauvignon Blanc: 2016 Matetic EQ.

Seafood Spiedini

Active **30 min**; Total **1 hr 30 min**; Serves **6**

Fish with a firm structure like the swordfish here (but also tuna and mahimahi) holds up best when cut into pieces for these herb-lashed skewers.

- ⅓ cup finely chopped parsley
- 2 Tbsp. finely chopped oregano
- 2 garlic cloves, finely chopped
- 2 tsp. finely chopped jarred Calabrian chile
- 1 tsp. finely grated orange zest
- 1 tsp. finely grated lemon zest
- ½ cup extra-virgin olive oil
  Kosher salt and pepper
- 6 oz. swordfish (1 inch thick), skin discarded, fish cut into six 1-inch cubes
- 6 large shrimp, shelled and deveined
- 6 large sea scallops, side muscles removed

1. In a large bowl, mix the parsley with the oregano, garlic, chile, orange zest, lemon zest and olive oil. Season with salt and pepper. Add the swordfish, shrimp and scallops and toss to coat. Cover and refrigerate for 1 hour.

2. Light a grill or preheat a grill pan. On each of six 10-inch skewers, thread a piece of swordfish, a shrimp and a scallop. Grill the skewers over moderate heat, turning once, until the fish is lightly charred and cooked through, about 6 minutes. Transfer to a platter and serve. —*Daniele Uditi*

SERVE WITH Shaved fennel tossed with chopped parsley, lemon juice and extra-virgin olive oil.

WINE Minerally white from Sardinia: 2015 Jankara Vermentino di Gallura Superiore.

Turmeric-Marinated Swordfish with Dill and Rice Noodles

Active **45 min**; Total **4 hr 45 min**; Serves **4**

Hanoi restaurant Cha Ca La Vong's unequivocally delicious *cha ca*—the city's most famous fish dish—was a favorite with the French more than a century ago. The turmeric-ginger-chile–dressed fish showered with herbs created a neighborhood frenzy, and dozens of copycat eateries sprang up. The restaurant's street was even renamed as a tribute.

- Four 1-inch-long pieces of fresh turmeric, peeled and chopped
- ¼ cup minced peeled fresh ginger
- 1 Tbsp. shrimp or anchovy paste
- 2 Thai chiles, minced
- ¼ cup plus 2 Tbsp. peanut or canola oil
- 1½ lbs. skinless swordfish or monkfish fillet, cut into 2-inch pieces
  Kosher salt and pepper
- 6 oz. thin rice noodles
  Boiling water
- ⅓ cup chicken stock or low-sodium broth
- ⅓ cup fresh lime juice
- ¼ cup Asian fish sauce
- 3 Tbsp. sugar
- 2 garlic cloves, minced
- 1 medium onion, halved and thinly sliced
- 10 scallions, cut into 1-inch lengths
- 1 cup chopped dill
- ½ cup cilantro leaves
- ½ cup mint leaves
- ½ cup Thai or sweet basil leaves
- ¼ cup chopped roasted salted peanuts
  Crispy Shallots (recipe follows), for serving
  Little Gem or Bibb lettuce leaves, for serving

1. In a mini food processor, puree the turmeric, ginger, shrimp paste, 1 chile and 2 tablespoons of the oil until a paste forms. Scrape into a large bowl, add the fish and toss to coat. Season with salt and pepper and toss again. Cover; let marinate in the refrigerator for 4 hours.

2. In a large, deep baking dish, cover the rice noodles with boiling water and let stand until softened, about 20 minutes. Drain well, then transfer to 4 bowls.

3. In a small bowl, whisk the stock with the lime juice, fish sauce, sugar, 1 garlic clove and the remaining chile.

4. In a large cast-iron skillet, heat the remaining ¼ cup of oil until shimmering. Add the fish and cook over moderately high heat, turning once or twice, until browned and cooked through, about 5 minutes. Using a slotted spoon, transfer to the bowls.

5. Add the onion to the skillet and cook over moderately high heat, stirring occasionally, until browned and softened, about 5 minutes. Add the scallions and the remaining garlic and cook, stirring, until just softened, about 1 minute. Remove from the heat; stir in the herbs. Spoon over the fish and top with the peanuts and shallots. Serve right away, passing the sauce and lettuce leaves at the table. —*Andrew Zimmern*

WINE Citrusy Albariño: 2016 Lagar de Cervera.

CRISPY SHALLOTS

Total **10 min**; Makes **½ cup**

These golden, crackling shallots are an addictive garnish on soups, stews, salads, rice and beans... We could go on.

- Canola oil, for frying
- 2 large shallots, thinly sliced
  Kosher salt

In a medium skillet, heat ¼ inch of oil until shimmering. Add the shallots and fry over moderate heat, stirring, until golden and crisp, about 5 minutes. Using a slotted spoon, transfer to paper towels to drain. Season with salt and let cool. —*AZ*

MAKE AHEAD The shallot garnish can be made up to three days ahead of time.

Turmeric-Marinated
Swordfish with Dill
and Rice Noodles

Buttery Spiced
Peel-and-Eat Shrimp

Shrimp Curry with Coconut, Mustard Seeds and Chiles

Active **50 min**; Total **1 hr 50 min**; Serves **4**

This spicy shrimp and coconut curry from southern India is tomato-y, not creamy. Authentic curry recipes feature copious herbs, chiles and spices—never commercial curry powder. This variation is lighter but still deeply flavored with the region's hallmark ingredients: coconut, curry leaves, mustard seeds, red chiles, and raw rice toasted and used like a spice.

- ½ **cup finely shredded unsweetened coconut**
- 1½ **lbs. large shrimp, shelled and deveined**
- 6 **shallots, minced (1 cup)**
- 1 **tsp. mustard seeds**
- ½ **tsp. ground turmeric**
- 2 **Tbsp. coriander seeds**
- 1 **Tbsp. raw basmati rice, plus cooked rice for serving**
- 2 **tsp. cumin seeds**
- 1 **tsp. fennel seeds**
- 2 **small dried red chiles**
- 12 **fresh curry leaves (see Note)**
- 2 **cups packed cilantro leaves, plus more for garnish**
- 1 **cup packed mint leaves**
- ½ **cup tamarind puree**
- 2 **Tbsp. light brown sugar**
- 1 **Tbsp. fresh lime juice**
- 1 **jalapeño, seeded and chopped**
  Kosher salt and pepper
- ¼ **cup ghee**
  One 2-inch piece of ginger, peeled and finely grated (2 tsp.)
- 2 **garlic cloves, minced**
- 1 **large tomato—halved and shredded on the large holes of a box grater, skin discarded**

1. Preheat the oven to 375°. Spread the shredded coconut on a small rimmed baking sheet and toast, tossing halfway through, for about 4 minutes, until lightly browned. Let cool.

2. In a large bowl, toss the shrimp with the toasted coconut, ⅓ cup of the shallots, the mustard seeds and turmeric. Cover and refrigerate for 1 hour.

3. Meanwhile, in a small, dry skillet, toast the coriander seeds, raw rice, cumin seeds, fennel seeds, dried chiles and 4 of the curry leaves over moderate heat, stirring, until fragrant, about 7 minutes. Transfer to a spice grinder and let cool, then grind to a powder.

4. In a blender, pulse the 2 cups of cilantro with the mint, tamarind puree, brown sugar, lime juice and jalapeño until a finely chopped chutney forms. Season with salt.

5. In a large, deep skillet, heat the ghee until shimmering. Add the remaining ⅔ cup of shallots, the ginger and garlic and cook over moderately high heat, stirring occasionally, until lightly caramelized, about 5 minutes.

6. Season the shrimp mixture with salt and pepper, add to the skillet and cook over moderately high heat until the shrimp starts to turn pink, about 2 minutes. Add the tomato and the spice mixture and cook, stirring, for 1 minute. Stir in 1½ cups of water and the remaining 8 curry leaves, bring to a simmer and cook until the shrimp are just opaque throughout, about 4 minutes. Season with salt and pepper. Garnish with cilantro; serve with the chutney and cooked rice. —*Andrew Zimmern*

NOTE Indian cooks typically keep in the fragrant but tough whole curry leaves, but they are not to be eaten, so push them to the side of your plate.

WINE Dry, lime-scented Australian Riesling: 2016 Best's Great Western.

Buttery Spiced Peel-and-Eat Shrimp

Active **30 min**; Total **1 hr**; Serves **4**

Pass a lot of napkins with these sizzling shrimp. Everything—mouths, chins and hands—will drip with buttery juices.

- 4 **Tbsp. unsalted butter, softened**
- 1 **jalapeño—stemmed, seeded and minced**
- 1 **tsp. finely grated lime zest**
  Kosher salt and pepper
- 1½ **lbs. shell-on large shrimp (about 24 shrimp)**
  Chopped cilantro and lime wedges, for serving

1. In a small bowl, using a fork, blend the butter with the jalapeño, lime zest, 1 teaspoon of salt and ½ teaspoon of pepper.

2. Using scissors, cut along the back of each shrimp and scrape out the vein. Gently open the shell without breaking it off and, using a thin offset spatula or knife, spread some of the butter on both sides of each shrimp. Transfer the shrimp to a baking sheet and refrigerate for 30 minutes.

3. Light a grill. Season the shrimp lightly with salt and pepper. Grill over high heat, turning, until lightly charred and just cooked through, about 4 minutes. Transfer the shrimp to a platter and serve with chopped cilantro and lime wedges.
—*Justin Chapple*

MAKE AHEAD The uncooked prepared shrimp can be refrigerated overnight.

WINE Unoaked Oregon Chardonnay: 2014 Chehalem INOX.

Tortillitas de Camarones (Shrimp Fritters)

Total **30 min**; Makes **12**

Tortillitas de camarones are shrimp fritters from the province of Cádiz in Andalusia, in Spain. This version was inspired by the legendary ones made at Casa Balbino. There they're made with small, head-on shrimp, but they're equally delicious with thinly sliced raw shrimp.

1⅓ cups semolina flour

½ lb. peeled and deveined large shrimp, halved lengthwise and thinly sliced into strips

½ cup finely chopped onion

2 Tbsp. chopped fresh parsley

1 garlic clove, minced

Kosher salt

Extra-virgin olive oil, for frying

Flaky sea salt

1. In a large bowl, combine the semolina flour with 2 cups of water. Stir in the shrimp, onion, parsley and garlic. Season with kosher salt.

2. In a large cast-iron skillet, heat 1 inch of olive oil to 350°. Line a baking sheet with paper towels. Working in batches of 4, add about ¼ cup of batter at a time to the hot oil, stirring the batter in between each scoop to make sure the liquid does not settle on top. Fry the tortillitas, turning once, until golden, about 4 to 5 minutes. Transfer to the paper towels and season with sea salt. Repeat and serve. —*José Andrés*

WINE Saline, superfresh manzanilla sherry: NV Bodegas Hidalgo La Gitana.

Gambas al Ajillo (Garlic Shrimp)

Total **30 min**; Serves **4**

This dish is so simple, Spanish home cooks can make it blindfolded, but it helps to keep an eye on a few rules. Commandment numero uno is a lavish amount of olive oil that's not too heavy in texture. Equally crucial: letting the garlic slowly release its fragrance (some experts start with cold oil), so the bitterness doesn't overpower the shrimp. Finally, give the *gambas* the most gentle of baths—not a full sizzle—in that oil until just heated through.

1½ lbs. shelled and deveined large shrimp, tails intact

Kosher salt

¼ cup thinly sliced garlic

1¼ cups extra-virgin olive oil

1 small dried hot red chile, seeded and crumbled

½ cup minced parsley

2 Tbsp. dry sherry, such as manzanilla

1 tsp. finely grated lemon zest

Crusty bread, for serving

1. In a large bowl, toss the shrimp with 1 teaspoon of kosher salt and let stand for 10 minutes.

2. Meanwhile, in a 9- to 10-inch enameled cast-iron skillet, combine the garlic and olive oil and cook over moderately low heat, stirring occasionally, until the garlic is very fragrant and just starts to brown, 8 to 10 minutes. Add the chile and cook, stirring, until fragrant, 15 to 30 seconds.

3. Add the shrimp to the skillet and cook over moderately low heat, stirring and turning the shrimp occasionally, until barely pink, about 5 minutes. Stir in the parsley, sherry, lemon zest and a generous pinch of salt. Remove from the heat and let stand until the shrimp are cooked through, 3 to 5 minutes. Serve in the skillet, passing crusty bread at the table. —*Anya von Bremzen*

WINE Melony, refreshing Verdejo from Rueda: 2016 Nisia Old Vines.

Gochujang Cioppino

Total **40 min**; Serves **4**

F&W's Justin Chapple makes his zippy fish stew with shrimp, squid, mussels and cod, then, to give it a lively Korean twist, he also includes tofu and gochujang (red pepper paste).

¼ cup extra-virgin olive oil

1 onion, finely chopped

6 garlic cloves, thinly sliced

2 scallions, thinly sliced, plus more for garnish

One 15-oz. can whole peeled tomatoes, crushed by hand

½ cup dry white wine

3 Tbsp. gochujang (Korean red pepper paste)

One 8-oz. bottle clam juice

½ lb. shelled and deveined large shrimp

½ lb. cleaned squid, bodies thinly sliced and tentacles halved

½ lb. mussels, scrubbed

½ lb. cod, cut into 1-inch pieces

½ lb. firm tofu, cut into 1-inch pieces

Rice crackers or steamed rice, for serving

1. In a large cast-iron casserole, heat the oil. Add the onion, garlic and the 2 sliced scallions; cook over moderate heat, stirring occasionally, until softened, about 7 minutes. Stir in the tomatoes, wine and gochujang and cook, stirring, until the tomatoes just start to break down, about 5 minutes.

2. Add the clam juice and bring to a boil. Nestle the seafood and tofu in the broth. Cover and cook over moderate heat until the mussels open and the other seafood is opaque, about 7 minutes. Ladle the cioppino into shallow bowls and garnish with scallion. Serve with rice crackers or steamed rice. —*Justin Chapple*

WINE Off-dry Washington state Riesling: 2015 Poet's Leap.

Squid Salad with Herbed Breadcrumbs

Total **1 hr**; Serves **6**

- **1** lb. baby potatoes
  Kosher salt and pepper
- **2** cups mixed baby greens
- **1** yellow bell pepper, cored and cut into thin strips
- **2** scallions, thinly sliced
- **2** Tbsp. capers, rinsed and drained
- **1** slice of hearty white country bread (1 inch thick), torn
- **⅓** cup mixed herbs, such as parsley, marjoram, oregano and thyme
- **¾** cup extra-virgin olive oil
- **1** Tbsp. finely grated lemon zest plus ¼ cup fresh lemon juice
- **12** oz. cleaned squid, bodies cut into ½-inch-thick rings and tentacles left whole

1. In a medium saucepan, cover the potatoes with cold water and season with salt. Bring to a boil, then simmer over moderate heat until the potatoes are tender, about 15 minutes. Drain and let cool, then cut into 1-inch pieces. Transfer the potatoes to a large bowl, add the mixed baby greens, bell pepper, scallions and capers and toss to combine.

2. Meanwhile, preheat the oven to 300°. Line a small baking sheet with foil. In a food processor, pulse the torn bread with the herbs until coarse crumbs form. Transfer to a small bowl. Stir in 2 tablespoons of the olive oil and the lemon zest and season with salt and pepper. Spread the crumbs on the baking sheet and bake for about 10 minutes, stirring occasionally, until they are golden and crisp. Let cool.

3. Heat the broiler to high. On a rimmed baking sheet, toss the squid with 2 tablespoons of the olive oil and season with salt and pepper. Broil 4 inches from the heat for 3 to 5 minutes, until the squid is opaque and just cooked through.

4. In a small bowl, whisk the lemon juice with the remaining ½ cup of olive oil and season with salt and pepper. Toss the salad with some of the vinaigrette. Transfer the salad to plates and top with the squid and herbed breadcrumbs. Serve immediately with the remaining vinaigrette alongside.
—*Katie and Giancarlo Caldesi*

Pulpo a la Gallega (Grilled Octopus with Potatoes)

Active **35 min**; Total **2 hr 35 min**; Serves **4**

José Andrés prefers *pulpo* the traditional way, simply boiled and served, but here we grill the octopus to give it a nice charred flavor.

- **¼** cup kosher salt
- **1** Tbsp. black peppercorns
- **1** bay leaf
- **1** clean penny (see Note)
  One 5½-lb. octopus, cleaned
- **1¼** lbs. small Yukon Gold potatoes, peeled
- **3** Tbsp. extra-virgin olive oil, preferably Spanish, plus more for drizzling
- **1** Tbsp. fresh lemon juice
- **¼** tsp. sweet paprika
  Flaky sea salt
  Parsley leaves, for garnish

1. In a large pot, bring 8 quarts of water to a boil. Add the salt, peppercorns, bay leaf and the penny. Holding the octopus by the head, carefully and quickly dip the tentacles into the water 3 times, then lower it into the pot. Reduce the heat to moderately low and simmer until almost tender, about 1 hour and 15 minutes. If necessary, place a plate over the octopus to keep it submerged.

2. Add the potatoes and cook until the octopus and potatoes are tender, about 25 minutes more. Transfer the octopus and potatoes to a work surface; discard the braising liquid. Separate the tentacles and cut the head in half. Using a paper towel, wipe the purple skin off the tentacles, leaving the suckers intact. Thinly slice the potatoes and arrange on a platter.

3. Light a grill or preheat a grill pan. Brush the octopus with the 3 tablespoons of olive oil. Grill over moderately high heat, turning, until lightly charred, about 4 minutes. Arrange the octopus on the platter with the potatoes. Drizzle with the lemon juice and more olive oil. Sprinkle with the paprika, flaky sea salt and parsley leaves; serve.
—*José Andrés*

NOTE Andrés adds a clean penny to the saucepan to replicate the traditional technique of cooking octopus in a copper pot. Soak the penny in distilled white vinegar and salt for 10 minutes, then scrub it clean before using.

WINE Citrusy, lightly briny Albariño from Galicia: 2015 Martín Códax.

Local Scallop Sashimi

Total **20 min**; Serves **2**

Chefs Nick Kim and Jimmy Lau from Shuko in NYC share their recipe for this easy, summery scallop sashimi. Use your favorite flaky sea salt as a substitute for seaweed salt.

- **4** tsp. unsalted butter
- **2** Tbsp. panko
- **1** Tbsp. minced nori
- **5** shiso leaves, thinly sliced
- **1** Tbsp. white miso
- **2** large sea scallops, thinly sliced
  Seaweed salt
- **1** piece of Myoga ginger bud, or fresh ginger, peeled and finely chopped

1. In a small skillet, heat the butter. Add the panko and cook, stirring, until golden and crisp, 1 minute. Stir in the nori. Transfer to a plate to cool.

2. In a small bowl, combine the shiso leaves with the white miso and mash to a paste. Adjust the consistency with water until spreadable.

3. Season the scallops with seaweed salt and transfer to two plates. Garnish with the ginger and nori breadcrumbs and dollop with the shiso miso. Serve immediately.—*Nick Kim and Jimmy Lau*

Sancerre-Poached
Scallops with Soft Grits

Grilled Scallops on the Shell

Active **20 min**; Total **1 hr 20 min**
Serves **4**

NYC chefs Nick Kim and Jimmy Lau coat these scallops in a garlicky soy butter before grilling them in their shells.

- **1 head of garlic, halved crosswise**
  Extra-virgin olive oil, for drizzling
  Kosher salt and pepper
- **4 Tbsp. unsalted butter, softened**
- **1 Tbsp. soy sauce**
- **4 large sea scallops and shells (see Note)**
- **12 fresh small morels**
- **3 oz. uni**
  Parsley leaves, for garnish
- **1 lime, quartered, for serving**

1. Preheat the oven to 300°. Place the garlic cut side up on a sheet of foil and drizzle with olive oil. Season with salt and pepper and wrap in the foil. Roast the garlic for about 1 hour, until very soft. Let cool, then squeeze the garlic cloves out of the skins and mash in a small bowl with the butter and soy sauce.

2. Light a grill or preheat a grill pan. Rub the roasted garlic soy butter on the inside of the scallop shells. Place 3 morels in each buttered shell and top with a scallop. Place the scallop shells on the grill and cook over moderately high heat until the butter starts to brown and the scallops are just cooked through, 3 to 5 minutes.

3. Garnish the scallops with uni and parsley and serve with lime wedges.
—*Nick Kim and Jimmy Lau*

NOTE Ask your fishmonger for 4 single scallop shells.

Sancerre-Poached Scallops with Soft Grits

Total **35 min**; Serves **4**

F&W's Justin Chapple uses Sancerre (though any dry white wine will do) to poach delicate sea scallops.

- **1 qt. chicken stock or low-sodium broth**
- **1 cup quick-cooking grits**
- **¼ cup finely grated Parmigiano-Reggiano cheese**
- **6 Tbsp. unsalted butter**
  Kosher salt and pepper
- **1 shallot, sliced**
- **2 garlic cloves, crushed**
- **2 cups Sancerre**
- **12 jumbo sea scallops (1½ lbs.)**
- **½ cup hazelnuts—toasted, skinned and chopped**
  Snipped chives, for garnish

1. In a medium saucepan, bring the chicken stock and 1 cup of water to a boil. Gradually stir in the grits and simmer over moderately low heat, stirring frequently, until the grits are tender, about 15 minutes. Remove from the heat and stir in the cheese and 2 tablespoons of the butter. Season with salt and pepper. Keep warm over very low heat; stir in tablespoons of water if too thick.

2. Meanwhile, in another medium saucepan, melt 2 tablespoons of the butter over moderate heat. Add the shallot, garlic and a generous pinch of salt and cook until softened, about 3 minutes. Carefully add the wine and bring to a simmer. Add the scallops and simmer until cooked through, 5 to 7 minutes. Transfer the scallops to a plate and keep warm. Discard the poaching liquid.

3. In a small skillet, melt the remaining 2 tablespoons of butter. Add the hazelnuts and cook, stirring, until warmed, about 2 minutes. Serve the scallops over the grits, topped with the warm hazelnuts and snipped chives. —*Justin Chapple*

WINE Lemon-zesty Sancerre: 2015 Pascal Jolivet.

Pasta with Scallops, Capers and Grilled Scallions

Total **30 min**; Serves **4 to 6**

- **8 scallions**
- **2 Tbsp. extra-virgin olive oil, plus more for drizzling**
  Kosher salt and pepper
- **12 oz. maccheroni alla chitarra or linguine pasta**
- **½ lb. sea scallops, cut into ½-inch-thick batons**
- **½ cup capers, rinsed**
- **¼ cup Taggiasca olives, coarsely chopped**
- **2 cups drained whole peeled Italian tomatoes, chopped**
- **½ cup finely chopped parsley**

1. Light a grill or heat a cast-iron skillet. Drizzle the scallions with olive oil and season with salt and pepper. Grill over moderately high heat, turning once, until lightly charred, about 2 minutes. Let cool, then chop the scallions coarsely.

2. In a pot of salted boiling water, cook the pasta until al dente. Reserve 1 cup of the cooking water, then drain the pasta. Drizzle with olive oil and toss to coat.

3. Wipe out the pot and heat the 2 tablespoons of olive oil until shimmering. Season the scallops with salt and pepper. Add them to the pot and cook over high heat, stirring once or twice, until very lightly browned in spots and just firm, about 30 seconds. Using a slotted spoon, transfer them to a plate.

4. In the same pot, cook the charred scallions with the capers and olives over moderately high heat, stirring, until fragrant, about 30 seconds. Add the tomatoes and reserved water and cook, scraping up any browned bits from the bottom, until bubbling, about 5 minutes. Add the pasta and cook, stirring, until the sauce is slightly reduced and the pasta is coated, 3 to 5 minutes.

5. Fold the scallops and parsley into the pasta and season with salt and pepper. Transfer to shallow bowls or a platter. Drizzle with olive oil and serve. —*Chris Painter*

WINE Savory Italian white: 2014 Garofoli Verdicchio dei Castelli di Jesi Podium.

Garlicky Littleneck Clams with Fregola

Active **1 hr**; Total **3 hr 30 min**
Serves **4 to 6**

A sweet, superversatile garlic puree is the star of this satisfying dish.

GARLIC PUREE

- **3 cups garlic cloves (about 7 heads of garlic)**
- **8 fresh thyme sprigs**
- **1 fresh bay leaf**
- **1 Tbsp. kosher salt**
- **1½ tsp. black peppercorns**
- **1¼ cups canola oil**
- **1¼ cups extra-virgin olive oil**

CLAMS

- **⅔ cup dried fregola**
- **2 Tbsp. canola oil**
- **4 garlic cloves, thinly sliced**
- **5½ dozen medium littleneck clams, scrubbed**
- **1 cup dry white wine**
- **2 Tbsp. fresh lemon juice**
- **2 scallions, thinly sliced**
- **¼ cup chopped parsley leaves, plus more for garnish**
- **¼ cup chopped dill, plus small sprigs for garnish**
- **2 tsp. finely chopped mint**
- **Kosher salt and pepper**
- **Lemon wedges and crusty bread, for serving**

1. Make the garlic puree Preheat the oven to 300°. In a medium enameled cast-iron casserole, combine all of the ingredients. Cover and braise in the oven until the garlic is very tender, about 1 hour; let cool to room temperature.

2. Using a slotted spoon, transfer the garlic cloves to a mini food processor and puree until smooth. You will have about 1½ cups of garlic puree. Strain the oil from the casserole into a 1-quart heatproof jar and discard the aromatics. Let the oil cool completely, then refrigerate; reserve for another use.

3. Make the clams In a medium saucepan of salted boiling water, cook the fregola until al dente, 10 to 12 minutes; drain well.

4. Meanwhile, in a large pot, heat the oil. Add the sliced garlic and cook over moderate heat, stirring frequently, until softened, about 2 minutes. Add the clams, wine and ¼ cup plus 2 tablespoons of the garlic puree and stir to coat the clams. Cover and cook over moderately high heat, shaking the pot occasionally, until the clams open, 5 to 7 minutes. As they open, use a slotted spoon to transfer them to a serving bowl; discard any that do not open.

5. Add the fregola, lemon juice, scallions, chopped herbs and more garlic puree, if desired, to the broth; season with salt and pepper. Pour the garlic broth over the clams and garnish with chopped parsley and dill sprigs. Serve immediately with lemon wedges and crusty bread.
—Michael Psilakis

MAKE AHEAD The garlic puree can be refrigerated for up to 2 weeks or frozen for up to 1 month.

WINE Minerally Greek white: 2015 Argyros Estate Assyrtiko.

Baked Clams with Bacon and Garlic

Active **1 hr**; Total **1 hr 15 min**
Makes **24**

CLAMS

- **1 cup dry white wine**
- **3 garlic cloves, crushed**
- **1 shallot, thinly sliced**
- **2 thyme sprigs**
- **1 bay leaf**
- **24 littleneck clams, scrubbed**

FILLING

- **2 thin slices of bacon (1 oz.), finely chopped**
- **3 Tbsp. unsalted butter**
- **3 garlic cloves, minced**
- **1 medium shallot, very finely chopped**
- **½ cup dry white wine**
- **½ cup chicken stock or low-sodium broth**
- **2 shucked surf clams, mantles discarded and clams finely chopped, or 4 oz. shucked littleneck clams, finely chopped**
- **½ cup fresh brioche breadcrumbs**
- **1 Tbsp. fresh lemon juice**
- **¾ tsp. kosher salt**

TOPPING

- **¼ cup fresh brioche breadcrumbs**
- **1 Tbsp. very finely chopped parsley**
- **1 tsp. finely grated lemon zest**
- **1 Tbsp. finely grated Parmigiano-Reggiano cheese**
- **Kosher salt**
- **Lemon wedges, for serving**

1. Prepare the clams In a large saucepan, combine the wine, garlic, shallot, thyme and bay leaf. Bring to a boil over high heat. Add the clams, cover and cook, shaking the pan occasionally, until the clams open, about 5 minutes. Using tongs or a slotted spoon, transfer the clams to a large baking sheet; discard any that do not open. Discard the cooking liquid. Let the clams cool slightly, then split the shells in half and transfer the clam meat to a small bowl. Clean 24 of the shell halves and arrange on the baking sheet; discard the remaining shells.

2. Make the filling In a large skillet, cook the bacon over moderate heat, stirring occasionally, until browned and just crisp, about 5 minutes. Add the butter, garlic and shallot and cook, stirring occasionally, until softened, 3 to 5 minutes. Add the wine and cook, scraping up any browned bits, until nearly evaporated, about 5 minutes. Add the chicken stock and cook until reduced to a thin glaze, about 4 minutes. Stir in the chopped clams, breadcrumbs, lemon juice and salt. Let cool slightly.

3. Make the topping In a medium bowl, mix the breadcrumbs with the parsley, lemon zest and cheese. Season lightly with salt.

4. Preheat the oven to 350°. Put 1 clam in each half shell. Top the clams with the filling and the topping. Bake for about 15 minutes, until bubbling and the tops are golden. Serve with lemon wedges.
—Daniel Humm

WINE Savory, full-bodied white: 2014 Stolpman Vineyards L'Avion Roussanne.

Garlicky Littleneck
Clams with Fregola

Grilled Oysters with
Bacon Vinaigrette

Wu-Tang Clams

Total **30 min;** Serves **4 to 6**

Chef Richard Blais says he has an affinity for '90s hip-hop, which is why he chose to name his Chinese-style clams after the Wu-Tang Clan. Incorporating sesame oil, ginger, Chinese pork sausages and bok choy, this is the be-all, end-all of clam dishes.

- 1 Tbsp. toasted sesame oil
- 3 scallions, thinly sliced
- 2 garlic cloves, minced
- 1 Tbsp. finely chopped peeled fresh ginger
- 2 Chinese pork sausage links (3 oz.) or pork sausage, chopped
- 1 lb. baby bok choy, leaves separated
- ¼ cup Chinese cooking wine or dry sherry
  48 to 60 littleneck clams, scrubbed (5 to 6 lbs.)
- 1 stick chilled unsalted butter, cut into 8 pieces
- 2 Tbsp. chopped cilantro
- 1 Tbsp. fresh lemon juice
- 2 tsp. soy sauce
- 2 tsp. sambal oelek
  Crusty bread, for serving

1. In a large, deep pot, heat the oil. Add the scallions, garlic and ginger and cook over moderately high heat for 1 minute. Add the sausage and bok choy and stir-fry for 2 minutes. Add the wine, scraping up any browned bits, then add the clams and butter. Cover and cook until the clams open, 5 to 7 minutes; discard any clams that don't open.

2. Add the cilantro, lemon juice, soy sauce and sambal to the pot and toss to combine. Serve immediately with crusty bread. —*Richard Blais*

WINE Fruity Washington state rosé: 2016 Charles Smith Vino.

Grill-Steamed Mussels

Active **20 min;** Total **40 min** Serves **4**

These tasty steamed mussels get cooked in a foil pack right on the grill, which is ideal for summer when you want to be cooking outdoors. A chipotle chile in adobo gives the mussels a hit of smoke and spice, but if you like less heat, feel free to cut back or omit it altogether.

- ¼ cup extra-virgin olive oil
- 2 shallots, finely chopped
- 4 large garlic cloves, minced
  Kosher salt
- 1 pint cherry or grape tomatoes
- ⅓ cup dry white wine
- 1 Tbsp. thyme leaves, plus 3 sprigs
- 1 chipotle in adobo sauce, seeded and minced, plus 1 Tbsp. sauce from the can
- 3 lbs. small to medium mussels, scrubbed and debearded
  Finely chopped parsley, for garnish
  Crusty bread, for serving

1. Light a grill. In a medium saucepan, heat the olive oil until shimmering. Add the shallots, garlic and a generous pinch of salt and cook over moderate heat, stirring, until softened, about 5 minutes. Add the tomatoes, wine, thyme leaves, chipotle and sauce and cook, stirring, until just bubbling, 3 minutes. Remove from the heat.

2. Arrange a 3-foot-long double-layer sheet of heavy-duty foil on a work surface. Lay a 2-foot-long sheet of parchment paper on top. Pull up the foil on all sides to form a cup. Spoon half the tomato mixture into the packet and pile the mussels on top. Spoon the remaining tomato mixture over the mussels and add the thyme sprigs. Fold the foil up over the mussels, leaving as much space as possible for them to open, then pinch the edges to seal tightly.

3. Carefully slide the foil packet onto the grill, close the lid and cook over high heat until the mussels open, about 20 minutes; discard any mussels that don't open. Discard the thyme sprigs. Transfer the mussels and all the juices to a serving bowl and garnish with parsley. Serve with crusty bread. —*Justin Chapple*

Grilled Oysters with Bacon Vinaigrette

Active **50 min;** Total **1 hr 20 min** Serves **6**

- ¼ cup plus 1 Tbsp. apple cider vinegar
- 2 Tbsp. beet juice
- 1 Tbsp. sugar
  Kosher salt and pepper
- ¼ small red onion, very thinly sliced
- 1 slice of thick-cut bacon, finely chopped
- 1 Tbsp. plus 1½ tsp. extra-virgin olive oil
- 1 large Swiss chard leaf, stemmed
- 12 Hama Hama or Blue Point oysters

1. In a small bowl, whisk ¼ cup of the apple cider vinegar with the beet juice, sugar and ½ teaspoon of salt until the sugar and salt are dissolved. Add the red onion and refrigerate for 1 hour. Drain before using.

2. In a small skillet, cook the bacon over moderate heat, stirring, until browned but still chewy, 5 minutes. Keep warm.

3. In a small bowl, whisk 1 tablespoon of the olive oil with 1 tablespoon of the bacon fat from the skillet and the remaining 1 tablespoon of vinegar. Season the vinaigrette with salt and pepper.

4. Light a grill. Rub the chard leaf with the remaining 1½ teaspoons of olive oil and season with salt. Grill over high heat, turning, until lightly charred but still pliable, 3 minutes. Transfer to a work surface and let cool slightly, then thinly slice. Leave the grill on.

5. On a rimmed baking sheet or platter, spread an even layer of salt. Grill the oysters flat side up over high heat until the shells open slightly, 5 minutes. Using tongs, transfer the oysters to the prepared baking sheet, being careful not to spill the juices. Using a kitchen towel or mitt, remove the top shells. Spoon the vinaigrette over the oysters. Top with the chard, bacon and pickled onion; serve right away. —*Brooke Williamson*

MAKE AHEAD The pickled red onion can be refrigerated in its brine for up to 3 days.

WINE Earthy sparkling rosé: NV Anna de Cordoniu Brut Rosé.

POULTRY

Chicken with
Charred-Rosemary
Vinaigrette (p. 129)
OPPOSITE Clementine-
and-Garlic Roast
Turkey (p. 151)

Almond-Poached Chicken Salad

Active 35 min; Total 1 hr 30 min; Serves 4

In a twist on an ordinary green salad with chicken, F&W's Laura Rege poaches chicken breasts in almond milk before cooling, shredding and mixing with crunchy and colorful purple cauliflower, radishes and fresh herbs. To give the dish an extra boost of almond flavor, she finishes it with a sprinkle of salted almonds.

- 4 skinless, boneless chicken breast halves (about 1½ lbs. total)
- 3 cups unsweetened almond milk
   Kosher salt and pepper
- ¼ cup extra-virgin olive oil
- 3 Tbsp. apple cider vinegar
- ½ small head of purple cauliflower—cored, cut into florets and thinly sliced
- 4 radishes, thinly sliced
- 2 cups loosely packed watercress
- ⅔ cup packed dill fronds, chopped
- ½ cup packed basil leaves, torn if large
- ½ cup chopped salted roasted almonds, plus more for garnish

1. In a medium saucepan, cover the chicken with the almond milk. Add 1 tablespoon of salt and bring to a simmer over moderate heat. Flip the chicken and gently simmer until cooked through, about 7 minutes. Remove the chicken from the poaching liquid and transfer to a plate. Let rest for 15 minutes, then cover with plastic wrap and refrigerate until cool. Shred the meat. Discard the chicken poaching liquid.

2. In a large bowl, whisk the olive oil with the vinegar and season with salt and pepper. Add the cooled shredded chicken, the cauliflower and radishes. Season with salt and pepper and toss to coat. Gently fold in the watercress, dill, basil and the ½ cup of almonds. Transfer the salad to plates, garnish with more chopped almonds and serve. —Laura Rege

WINE Savory Rhône white: 2015 E. Guigal Saint-Joseph Blanc.

Perfect Slow Cooker Chicken Breasts

Active 30 min; Total 2 hr 30 min; Serves 4

Cookbook author Sarah DiGregorio slowly simmers chicken breasts in seasoned olive oil until they're wonderfully flavorful and juicy. She uses that delicious oil to make a silky aioli, which gets served alongside the chicken. This duo makes for a spectacular light meal with a salad, but could also be turned into a perfect sandwich.

- ¼ cup fine salt
- ¼ cup sugar
- 1 lemon, scrubbed and quartered, plus 2½ Tbsp. fresh lemon juice
   Four 7-oz. skinless, boneless chicken breast halves
- 3 cups extra-virgin olive oil
- 3 garlic cloves
- 2 fresh bay leaves
- 2 thyme sprigs
- 1 rosemary sprig
- ½ tsp. whole black peppercorns
   Kosher salt
- 2 large egg yolks
   Crusty bread and green salad, for serving

1. In a large bowl, whisk 5 cups of cold water with the fine salt and sugar until dissolved. Squeeze and add 2 of the lemon quarters to the bowl. Add the chicken, cover with plastic wrap and refrigerate for at least 1 hour or up to 6 hours.

2. Meanwhile, add the olive oil to a 6-quart slow cooker along with the garlic, bay leaves, thyme and rosemary sprigs, black peppercorns, 1½ teaspoons of kosher salt and the remaining 2 lemon quarters. Cover and cook on low until the oil registers 200° on an instant-read thermometer, about 1 hour. (The oil can be kept in the slow cooker on low for up to 6 hours.)

3. Remove the chicken from the brine and pat dry; transfer to a plate. Discard the brine. Using tongs, carefully lower the chicken into the warm oil. Cover and cook on low until the chicken registers 155° on an instant-read thermometer, about 40 minutes. Using a slotted spoon, transfer the chicken and garlic to a plate. Cover with foil and keep warm. Discard the lemon quarters and herbs. Using a ladle, transfer 1 cup of the infused oil to a measuring cup

(do not use the peppercorns) and let cool until just warm, 15 minutes. Reserve the remaining oil for another use.

4. In a blender, puree the egg yolks with the lemon juice, 1 of the cooked garlic cloves and ½ teaspoon of kosher salt until smooth, about 30 seconds. With the machine on, gradually add the 1 cup of cooled oil until creamy, about 1 minute. Season the aioli with kosher salt.

5. Slice the chicken and serve with the aioli, bread and salad. —Sarah DiGregorio

MAKE AHEAD The chicken and aioli can be refrigerated overnight.

WINE Citrusy Chilean Chardonnay: 2014 Montes Alpha.

Plugged In

Here's a crash course on the hottest kitchen appliances.

SLOW COOKER
Who it's good for Technophobes
Why it's worth it It's been around since the 1940s, so it's low-tech and easy to figure out. The large oval shape lends itself to bigger braises.

PRESSURE COOKER
Who it's good for Control freaks
Why it's worth it For quick cooking, a pressure cooker allows you to adjust the heat, so you can crank up the temperature to cook off extra liquid and intensify flavor.

MULTIPOT
Who it's good for Versatile cooks
Why it's worth it The cultish gadget combines the virtues of both slow cooking and pressure cooking—and makes rice and yogurt—which means one less appliance and more counter space for you.
—Melissa Clark, author of Dinner In an Instant

Chicken Shwarma
with Shredded-
Lettuce Salad

Smoky Chicken Cutlets with Herb-Roasted Sweet Potatoes

Active **30 min**; Total **45 min plus 2 hr marinating**; Serves **4**

George Mendes, chef at New York City's Aldea and Lupulo, loves serving his juicy chicken with sweet potatoes, but he sometimes makes it with brussels sprouts. He likes to pluck the leaves off the sprouts and sauté them in olive oil, as if they were mini cabbage leaves. They become crispy and so much fun to eat.

- ½ cup plus 2 Tbsp. extra-virgin olive oil
- ½ cup dry white wine, preferably Vinho Verde
- ½ small onion, halved lengthwise and thinly sliced crosswise
- 4 garlic cloves, thinly sliced
- 4 parsley sprigs
- 1 Tbsp. sweet smoked paprika
  Kosher salt and pepper
- 4 skinless, boneless chicken breast halves (1½ to 2 lbs.), butterflied and pounded ¼ inch thick
- 2 large sweet potatoes (3 lbs.), peeled and cut into ½-inch dice
- 1 rosemary sprig
- 1 thyme sprig
- 1 bay leaf

1. In a large resealable plastic bag, combine ½ cup of the olive oil with ¼ cup of the wine. Add the onion, garlic, parsley, paprika, 1 teaspoon of salt and ½ teaspoon of pepper. Put the chicken in the bag with the marinade and refrigerate for 2 to 3 hours.

2. Preheat the oven to 350°. On a large rimmed baking sheet, toss the sweet potatoes with 1 tablespoon of the olive oil and the rosemary, thyme and bay leaf; season with salt and pepper. Arrange in a single layer. Roast for about 30 minutes, until the potatoes are tender and golden. Discard the herb sprigs and bay leaf.

3. Meanwhile, remove the chicken from the marinade. Strain the marinade over a sieve into a bowl; discard the solids. In a large skillet, heat the remaining 1 tablespoon of olive oil over moderately high heat. Cook the chicken in 2 batches, turning once, until golden and just cooked through, about 3 minutes per side. Transfer to plates, tent with foil and keep warm.

4. Add the remaining ¼ cup of wine to the skillet and boil over moderately high heat until reduced by half, about 2 minutes. Add the reserved marinade, bring to a boil and cook until reduced by half, 2 minutes. Transfer the sweet potatoes to the plates with the chicken. Spoon the sauce over the chicken and serve. —*George Mendes*

WINE Oak-toasty Spanish Rioja: 2012 Vivanco Crianza.

Chicken Shwarma with Shredded-Lettuce Salad

Active **45 min**; Total **2 hr**; Serves **6**

Cookbook authors Giancarlo and Katie Caldesi deconstruct chicken shwarma, creating a beautiful and bountiful platter of spiced chicken, roasted onions, tangy salad, lemony crème fraîche and more.

CHICKEN

- ⅓ cup extra-virgin olive oil
- ¼ cup plus 2 Tbsp. fresh lemon juice
- 5 garlic cloves, minced
- 1 tsp. kosher salt
- 1 Tbsp. sweet paprika
- 2 tsp. ground cumin
- 1 tsp. ground coriander
- 1 tsp. ground cinnamon
- ½ tsp. crushed red pepper
- ½ tsp. ground turmeric
- ½ tsp. black pepper
- 2 lbs. skin-on, bone-in chicken thighs
- 2 medium red onions, cut into 8 wedges

SALAD

- 1 cup crème fraîche
- 1 Tbsp. finely grated lemon zest plus 2 Tbsp. plus 1 tsp. fresh lemon juice
  Kosher salt and pepper
- 2 Tbsp. extra-virgin olive oil
- ½ lb. head of romaine lettuce, thinly shredded (4 cups)
- ½ cup cilantro leaves
- 3 scallions, thinly sliced
- 2 Tbsp. finely chopped jalapeño (from ½ chile)
  Pita bread and green olives, for serving

1. Make the chicken In a large bowl, whisk the olive oil with the lemon juice, garlic, salt and spices. Add the chicken and onions and turn to coat in the marinade. Cover and refrigerate for 1 hour or overnight.

2. Preheat the oven to 450°. Line a large rimmed baking sheet with foil and arrange the chicken on it skin side up. Add the onions. Scrape any remaining marinade in the bowl over the chicken. Roast for about 40 minutes, until the chicken and onions are browned and the chicken is cooked through. Transfer the chicken to a cutting board and coarsely shred with a knife and fork.

3. Meanwhile, make the salad In a small bowl, whisk the crème fraîche with the lemon zest and 1 teaspoon of the lemon juice; season with salt. In a medium bowl, whisk the remaining 2 tablespoons of lemon juice with the olive oil; season with salt and pepper. Add the lettuce, cilantro, scallions and jalapeño and toss to coat. On a large platter, arrange the salad with the chicken, onions, pita bread and olives. Serve with the lemon crème fraîche alongside. —*Giancarlo and Katie Caldesi*

MAKE AHEAD The lemon crème fraîche can be refrigerated for up to 1 day.

WINE Spicy Mediterranean rosé: 2016 Bleu de Mer.

Hobo Pack Chicken Fajitas

⏱ Active **20 min**; Total **35 min**; Serves **4**

Instead of making fajitas on a griddle, F&W's Justin Chapple combines the essential ingredients—chicken, onion, peppers, cumin and oregano—in foil packs and cooks them on the grill. The packs are ideal for a party because they can be prepared in advance and refrigerated, then grilled to serve.

- **1 lb. chicken tenders, halved lengthwise into thin strips**
- **1 medium red onion, halved and sliced ¼ inch thick**
- **1 poblano chile, stemmed and cut lengthwise into ½-inch strips**
- **4 oz. shishito peppers, stemmed**
- **4 mini sweet peppers, stemmed and quartered lengthwise**
- **¼ cup extra-virgin olive oil**
- **1½ tsp. cumin seeds**
- **Kosher salt and pepper**
- **4 oregano sprigs**
- **1 lime, thinly sliced crosswise**
- **Warm flour tortillas, sour cream and hot sauce, for serving**

1. Light a grill. Arrange four 14-inch sheets of heavy-duty foil on a work surface.

2. In a large bowl, toss the chicken, onion and all of the peppers with the olive oil and cumin seeds. Season generously with salt and pepper and toss again. Pile the chicken and vegetables evenly on one half of each foil sheet and top with the oregano and lime. Fold the foil over the ingredients and pinch the edges to seal.

3. Place the foil packets on the grill, close the lid and cook over moderately high heat until the chicken is cooked through, about 12 minutes. Open the packets and serve with warm flour tortillas, sour cream and hot sauce. —*Justin Chapple*

MAKE AHEAD The uncooked fajita packs can be refrigerated overnight.

WINE Full-bodied, melony Chardonnay: 2014 William Hill North Coast.

Giant Chicken Parmesan

Active **50 min**; Total **1 hr 20 min**
Serves **4 to 6**

Chef Michael Schlow puts a bit of a spin on classic chicken parm at Casolare, his Italian restaurant in the Glover Park Hotel in Washington, DC. He pounds chicken breasts so they're very thin and wide, then coats them in breadcrumbs before quickly pan-frying. The result is superjuicy and extra-crisp chicken, which gets topped with homemade sauce and a combination of fresh mozzarella and Grana Padano cheese.

SAUCE

- **¼ cup extra-virgin olive oil**
- **½ red onion, finely chopped**
- **2 garlic cloves, minced**
- **One 15-oz. can whole peeled tomatoes, crushed by hand**
- **¼ tsp. crushed red pepper**
- **2 Tbsp. finely chopped basil**
- **2 tsp. chopped oregano**
- **Kosher salt and black pepper**
- **3 Tbsp. unsalted butter**

CHICKEN

- **3 large eggs**
- **1 cup all-purpose flour**
- **2½ cups panko**
- **Two 10-oz. skinless, boneless chicken breast halves, butterflied and lightly pounded until very thin (scant ¼ inch)**
- **1 Tbsp. thyme leaves, chopped**
- **1 Tbsp. finely chopped rosemary**
- **Kosher salt and pepper**
- **½ stick unsalted butter**
- **⅓ cup canola oil**
- **½ lb. fresh mozzarella, thinly sliced**
- **½ cup freshly grated Grana Padano cheese**

1. Make the sauce In a medium saucepan, heat the olive oil. Add the onion and garlic and cook over moderate heat, stirring occasionally, until softened but not browned, about 8 minutes. Add the tomatoes, crushed red pepper, 1 tablespoon of the basil, 1 teaspoon of the oregano and a generous pinch each of salt and black pepper and cook, stirring occasionally, until the tomatoes break down and the sauce is thickened, about 20 minutes.

Stir in the butter until melted, then stir in the remaining 1 tablespoon of basil and 1 teaspoon of oregano. Season the sauce with salt and black pepper.

2. Make the chicken Preheat the oven to 350°. In a large baking dish, beat the eggs. Spread the flour and panko in 2 separate large baking dishes. Sprinkle the chicken breasts all over with the thyme and rosemary and season with salt and pepper. Dust the chicken with the flour, then dip in the beaten egg and dredge in the panko, pressing to help the crumbs adhere.

3. In a very large skillet, melt the butter in the canola oil until shimmering. Add 1 piece of chicken and fry over moderate heat, turning once, until golden and cooked through, about 7 minutes. Transfer to paper towels to drain. Repeat with the remaining chicken.

4. Transfer the chicken breasts to a large rimmed baking sheet. Spread the sauce over them and top with the mozzarella and Grana Padano. Bake for about 10 minutes, until the cheese is melted and hot. Serve right away. —*Michael Schlow*

MAKE AHEAD The tomato sauce can be refrigerated for up to 3 days. Reheat gently before using.

WINE Vibrant, earthy Chianti Rufina: 2014 Selvapiana.

Hobo Pack
Chicken Fajitas

Chicken Parmesan

Active **1 hr 15 min**; Total **4 hr 45 min**
Serves **6**

Star chef Daniel Humm of Eleven Madison Park and Made Nice in New York City doesn't mess around when he makes chicken Parmesan. He tops the chicken with a silky béchamel, slow-simmered tomato sauce and lots of cheese before baking everything together.

TOMATO SAUCE

½ cup extra-virgin olive oil

1 medium onion, finely chopped

2 garlic cloves, minced

Kosher salt

Two 28-oz. cans whole peeled tomatoes, crushed by hand

2 basil sprigs

2 thyme sprigs

1 small bay leaf

BÉCHAMEL

1¼ cups whole milk

2 garlic cloves

2 thyme sprigs

2 Tbsp. unsalted butter

¼ cup all-purpose flour

Kosher salt

CHICKEN

1 cup all-purpose flour

¼ cup cornstarch

2 Tbsp. garlic powder

1½ Tbsp. dried oregano

1½ tsp. cayenne

Kosher salt and pepper

6 large eggs

2 cups plain dry breadcrumbs

2 skin-on whole chicken breasts (about 2 lbs. each)—bones cut off and discarded, breasts pounded to ½-inch thickness

Canola oil, for frying

1½ cups shredded mozzarella (6 oz.)

½ cup freshly grated Parmigiano-Reggiano cheese

Torn basil and small leaves, for garnish

1. Make the sauce In a large saucepan, heat the olive oil. Add the onion, garlic and a generous pinch of salt. Cook over moderately low heat, stirring occasionally, until soft, about 20 minutes. Add the tomatoes, basil, thyme and bay leaf and cook over low heat, stirring occasionally, until thickened and reduced by half, about 3 hours. Discard the herb sprigs and bay leaf and pass the tomato sauce through a food mill into a heatproof bowl. Season with salt.

2. Meanwhile, make the béchamel In a small saucepan, combine the milk, garlic and thyme and bring just to a simmer over moderate heat. Remove from the heat and let stand for 10 minutes, then discard the garlic and thyme sprigs. In a medium saucepan, melt the butter. Add the flour and cook over moderate heat until a thick paste forms, 3 to 5 minutes. Very gradually whisk in the warm milk until smooth. Simmer over moderate heat, stirring, until thick and no floury taste remains, 5 to 7 minutes. Season the béchamel with salt.

3. Make the chicken In a large baking dish, whisk the flour with the cornstarch, garlic powder, oregano, cayenne and 1½ teaspoons each of salt and pepper. In another large baking dish, beat the eggs. Spread the breadcrumbs in a third large baking dish. Season the chicken breasts all over with salt and pepper. Coat the chicken in the flour mixture, then dip in the beaten egg and dredge in the breadcrumbs, pressing to help them adhere. Transfer to a large baking sheet.

4. Preheat the oven to 425°. Line a large baking sheet with parchment paper. In a large saucepan, heat 3 inches of canola oil to 350°. Add 1 chicken breast and fry over moderately high heat, turning once, until an instant-read thermometer inserted in the thickest part registers 155°, about 7 minutes. Transfer to the baking sheet. Repeat with the remaining chicken breast.

5. Spread the béchamel over the chicken. Top each breast with 1 cup of the tomato sauce, ¾ cup of the shredded mozzarella and ¼ cup of the Parmigiano (reserve the remaining tomato sauce for another use). Bake for 5 minutes, until the cheese is melted. Transfer to a platter, garnish with basil and serve. —*Daniel Humm*

MAKE AHEAD The tomato sauce can be refrigerated for up to 3 days.

WINE Robust, spicy Italian red: 2012 Villa Antinori Chianti Classico Riserva.

Crispy Chicken with Champagne Vinegar Aioli

Active **30 min**; Serves **4**

Crispy pan-fried chicken tenders are hard to resist, but F&W's Laura Rege ups the ante by serving them alongside a spectacularly bright and creamy vinegar aioli for dipping.

3 Tbsp. Champagne vinegar

1 large egg yolk, plus 1 large egg

1 small garlic clove, finely grated

Pinch of cayenne

⅔ cup extra-virgin olive oil, plus more for frying

Kosher salt and pepper

¼ cup all-purpose flour

2 cups panko

1½ lbs. chicken tenders, patted dry

Crispy sweet potato fries, for serving

1. In a small bowl, whisk the vinegar, egg yolk, garlic and cayenne. Slowly whisk in the ⅔ cup of olive oil until incorporated. Season the aioli with salt.

2. Spread the flour in a shallow bowl. In a second shallow bowl, whisk the whole egg with ⅓ cup of the aioli. In a third shallow bowl, spread the panko. Season the chicken with salt and pepper, then dredge in the flour and shake off the excess. Dip the chicken in the egg mixture, then dredge in the panko, pressing to help it adhere.

3. Set a wire rack over a rimmed baking sheet. In a large, deep skillet, heat ¼ inch of olive oil until shimmering. In batches, fry the chicken over moderately high heat, turning once, until golden brown, about 3 minutes. Transfer to the rack and season with salt. Serve with the aioli and fries. —*Laura Rege*

WINE Bright, unoaked California Chardonnay: 2015 Chamisal Vineyards Stainless.

Chicken Burgers with Crispy Cheddar Cheese

⏱ Active **25 min;** Total **45 min;** Serves **4**

Louisville, Kentucky chef Edward Lee dusts these chicken patties with Old Bay before cooking to char the spices.

- **1½ lbs. ground chicken, preferably a blend of white and dark meat**
- **Kosher salt and pepper**
- **½ cup mayonnaise**
- **½ tsp. Asian fish sauce**
- **½ tsp. fresh lemon juice**
- **1 Tbsp. Old Bay Seasoning**
- **1 Tbsp. plus 2 tsp. canola oil**
- **Four ½-inch-thick slices of sharp white cheddar cheese**
- **4 potato rolls, split and toasted**
- **Boston lettuce leaves, sliced pickled jalapeños and hot pepper jelly, for serving**

1. Form the chicken into four ¾-inch-thick patties and season with salt and pepper. Transfer to a plate and refrigerate until firm, 30 minutes.

2. In a small bowl, whisk the mayonnaise with the fish sauce and lemon juice until smooth.

3. Sprinkle both sides of the patties with the Old Bay. In a large cast-iron skillet set on the grate of a preheated grill or on the stovetop, heat 1 tablespoon of the oil. Cook the burgers, covered, over moderate heat, flipping once, until browned and just cooked through, 8 to 10 minutes. Transfer to a work surface and let rest for 5 minutes.

4. In a large nonstick skillet, heat the remaining 2 teaspoons of oil. Arrange the cheese slices 2 inches apart in the skillet and cook over moderate heat until melted in the middle and browned and crisp at the edges, about 3 minutes. Remove from the heat and let the cheese rest in the skillet for 1 minute. Transfer to a paper towel–lined plate to drain.

5. Spread some of the mayo on each roll bottom and place a burger on top. Layer with a slice of crispy cheese and some lettuce and pickled jalapeños. Spread the pepper jelly on the roll tops, close the burgers and serve. —*Edward Lee*

WHISKEY Robust rye: Rittenhouse Rye.

Fried Tandoori Chicken

Total **1 hr plus 24 hr marinating;** Serves **4**

For extra-juicy—and flavorful—fried chicken, chef Rupam Bhagat of Dum in San Francisco marinates his meat using the traditional two-step tandoori process: He first lets the chicken sit in a blend of aromatic spices for 12 hours and then folds in yogurt that helps tenderize the meat and caramelize the crust when it's fried.

- **6 garlic cloves, chopped**
- **One 3-inch piece of fresh ginger, peeled and chopped**
- **⅓ cup fresh lemon juice**
- **2 Tbsp. ground coriander**
- **1½ Tbsp. ground cumin**
- **1 Tbsp. ground turmeric**
- **2 tsp. cayenne**
- **2 Tbsp. vegetable oil, plus more for frying**
- **Kosher salt and pepper**
- **6 small chicken thighs**
- **6 small chicken drumsticks**
- **1½ cups full-fat Greek yogurt**
- **1½ cups chickpea flour (see Note)**
- **Chaat masala (see box, p. 231), for sprinkling**
- **Small cilantro sprigs and lime wedges, for garnish**

1. In a food processor, puree the garlic with the ginger, lemon juice, coriander, cumin, turmeric, cayenne, the 2 tablespoons of oil, 2 teaspoons of salt and 1 teaspoon of pepper until smooth. Scrape the marinade into a large bowl, add the chicken and turn to coat. Cover and refrigerate for 12 hours.

2. Stir the yogurt into the marinade, re-cover the bowl and refrigerate for 12 more hours.

3. Preheat the oven to 250° and line a rimmed baking sheet with parchment paper. In a shallow bowl, mix the chickpea flour with 1 teaspoon of salt. Remove the chicken from the marinade, letting the excess drip back into the bowl. Dredge the chicken in the flour, then transfer to the prepared baking sheet.

4. In a large, heavy saucepan, heat 1½ inches of oil to 325°. Set a rack over a rimmed baking sheet. Working in batches, fry the chicken until golden brown and an instant-read thermometer inserted in the thickest part of each piece registers 160°, about 10 minutes. Transfer to the rack, season with salt and keep warm in the oven while you fry the remaining chicken.

5. Sprinkle the chicken with chaat masala and transfer to a platter. Garnish with cilantro leaves and lime wedges; serve. —*Rupam Bhagat*

SERVE WITH Charred Coconut Green Beans (p. 231).

NOTE Chickpea flour can be found at most health food stores and on amazon.com.

WINE Herbal Italian white: 2014 Garofoli Podium Verdicchio dei Castelli di Jesi.

Perfect Pairing

"As with any good meal, what you drink is crucial. When it comes to burgers, I will never argue against a Coke or a crisp beer, but if you want to try the perfect pairing, reach for whiskey. Whiskey is way more complex than beer and more aggressive than wine, which is exactly what an intense burger needs. The whiskey you choose depends on the flavors of the burger: Sweet goes with bourbon; spicy and funky go with Scotch; and mild goes with balanced blends like Irish whiskey.
—*Edward Lee, Whisky Dry, Louisville*

Red Wine
BBQ Chicken

Red Wine BBQ Chicken

Active **30 min**; Total **1 hr 30 min**; Serves **4**

Got some Pinot left at the bottom of a bottle? Use it to make the ultimate sticky barbecue sauce.

- 2 **Tbsp. extra-virgin olive oil, plus more for brushing**
- 2 **shallots, minced**
- 2 **garlic cloves, minced**
- 1 **cup ketchup**
- 1 **cup Pinot Noir**
- 2 **Tbsp. packed light brown sugar**
- 1 **chipotle chile in adobo sauce, seeded and minced**
- 1 **Tbsp. Dijon mustard**
  Kosher salt and pepper
- 12 **mixed chicken drumsticks and thighs**

1. In a medium saucepan, heat the 2 tablespoons of olive oil. Add the shallots and garlic and cook over moderate heat, stirring, until softened, 3 to 5 minutes. Whisk in the ketchup, wine, sugar, chipotle and mustard. Bring to a boil over moderately high heat, then simmer over moderately low heat, stirring frequently, until thickened, about 15 minutes. Let cool slightly, then puree in a blender until smooth. Season with salt and pepper.

2. Preheat the oven to 425°. Line a large rimmed baking sheet with foil and put a baking rack on it. Season the chicken with salt and pepper and put on the rack. Roast for 15 minutes, until the skin is lightly browned. Brush the chicken with some of the sauce and roast for 40 minutes longer, turning and basting every 10 minutes, until nicely glazed and an instant-read thermometer inserted in the thickest piece registers 165°. Transfer to a platter and serve. —*Justin Chapple*

MAKE AHEAD The barbecue sauce can be refrigerated for up to a week.

WINE Robust, dark-fruited California Pinot Noir: 2014 Byron Julia's Vineyard.

Crispy Chicken Thighs with Green Papaya Salad

Active **1 hr**; Total **4 hr**; Serves **4 to 6**

This fresh and crunchy Vietnamese-inspired salad gets flavor from fish sauce, lime juice, chile and more. If your unripe papaya is firm but no longer green, it will still work nicely here.

- 1½ **Tbsp. chopped cilantro, plus more for garnish**
- 5 **scallions, chopped, plus more thinly sliced for garnish**
- 6 **garlic cloves**
- 1 **jalapeño, stemmed and chopped**
- 1 **shallot, chopped**
- 1 **cup Asian fish sauce**
- ½ **cup plus 2 Tbsp. light brown sugar**
- 1 **tsp. kosher salt**
- 8 **skin-on, bone-in chicken thighs**
- 2 **Tbsp. unsalted butter**
- 2 **Tbsp. canola oil**
- 3 **Tbsp. fresh lime juice**
- 1 **Thai chile, stemmed and thinly sliced**
  One 2½-lb. unripe papaya—peeled, seeded and julienned (8 cups)
- 1 **large carrot, julienned**
- 1 **cup cherry tomatoes, halved**
  Chopped roasted salted peanuts, for garnish

1. In a blender, puree the 1½ tablespoons of cilantro, the chopped scallions, garlic, jalapeño, shallot, ½ cup of the fish sauce and ½ cup of the sugar until smooth. Season with the salt. Put the chicken in a large resealable plastic bag and pour in the marinade. Seal and refrigerate for at least 2 hours or up to 6 hours. Bring to room temperature 30 minutes before cooking.

2. Preheat the oven to 400° and line a large rimmed baking sheet with foil. In a large skillet, melt 1 tablespoon of the butter in 1 tablespoon of the oil. Add half of the chicken, skin side down, and cook over moderately high heat until the skin is brown and crispy, about 3 minutes. Reduce the heat to moderate if the chicken starts to brown too quickly. Transfer the chicken to the prepared baking sheet skin side up and repeat with the remaining butter, oil and chicken. Transfer the baking sheet to the oven and roast the chicken for about 25 minutes, until golden brown and cooked through. Let rest for 5 minutes.

3. Meanwhile, in a large bowl, whisk the lime juice with the Thai chile and the remaining ½ cup of fish sauce and 2 tablespoons of sugar. Add the papaya, carrot and tomatoes and toss to coat.

4. Transfer the papaya salad to a large platter or plates and top with the roast chicken thighs. Garnish with chopped cilantro, sliced scallions and peanuts; serve immediately. —*Chris Shepherd*

Chicken with Charred-Rosemary Vinaigrette

PAGE 119

Total **45 min**; Serves **4**

- **Four 4-inch rosemary sprigs**
- 3 **Tbsp. Champagne vinegar**
- 1 **Tbsp. Dijon mustard**
- ¼ **cup plus 1 Tbsp. extra-virgin olive oil**
  Kosher salt and pepper
- 6 **skin-on, bone-in chicken thighs**
  One 10-oz. package frozen artichoke heart quarters, thawed
- 1 **pint cherry tomatoes**
- ½ **cup drained caperberries**

1. Preheat the oven to 375°. Roast 2 of the rosemary sprigs directly on the oven rack for 5 minutes, until charred. Leave the oven on. Strip off the leaves, then finely crush them; discard the stems. In a small bowl, whisk the leaves with the vinegar, mustard and ¼ cup of the olive oil. Season with salt and pepper.

2. In a large, deep ovenproof skillet, heat the remaining 1 tablespoon of oil. Season the chicken with salt and pepper and cook skin side down over moderately high heat, turning once, until well browned, 12 minutes. Transfer to a plate.

3. Pour off all but 2 tablespoons of fat from the skillet. Stir in the artichokes, tomatoes, caperberries and the remaining rosemary sprigs. Top with the chicken and roast for 15 minutes, until an instant-read thermometer inserted in the chicken registers 165°. Drizzle with the vinaigrette and serve, passing more vinaigrette at the table. —*Justin Chapple*

WINE Herbal Grüner Veltliner: 2015 Loimer Lois.

Chicken and Pork Paella

Active **1 hr**; Total **1 hr 45 min**; Serves **6 to 8**

In this delicious version of the classic Spanish dish, chicken and pork ribs combine with rice, artichoke hearts and romano beans for a hearty and satisfying meal, laced with alluring flavors of saffron, garlic and smoky pimentón.

- 1 lb. skinless, boneless chicken thighs, cut into 1½-inch pieces
- 1 lb. boneless country-style pork ribs, cut into 1½-inch pieces
- ¼ cup plus 1 Tbsp. extra-virgin olive oil
- 2 Tbsp. finely grated garlic
- 2 tsp. pimentón de la Vera (smoked sweet Spanish paprika)

  Kosher salt and pepper

  Large pinch of saffron, finely ground in a mortar
- ¼ cup boiling water
- 2 large tomatoes, halved crosswise

  One 9-oz. package frozen artichoke hearts, thawed
- ¼ lb. romano beans, cut into 2-inch lengths
- 8 scallions, cut into 1-inch lengths
- 6 cups chicken stock or low-sodium broth
- 2 cups Bomba rice
- 1 large rosemary sprig
- 1 roasted red bell pepper—quartered lengthwise, seeded and cut crosswise into small strips
- 1 cup thawed frozen peas

1. In a large bowl, mix the chicken and pork with 1 tablespoon each of the olive oil and garlic and 1 teaspoon of the pimentón. Season generously with salt and pepper and mix again. Let stand at room temperature for 30 minutes.

2. Meanwhile, preheat the oven to 425°. In a small heatproof bowl, mix the saffron with the boiling water and let cool completely. Grate the tomato halves on the large holes of a box grater set in a bowl until only the skins remain; discard the skins.

3. In a 15-inch paella pan or large enameled cast-iron casserole, heat 2 tablespoons of the olive oil over high heat until shimmering. Add half of the chicken-pork mixture and cook, stirring occasionally, until well browned but not cooked through, about 6 minutes. Transfer to a plate. Repeat with another 1 tablespoon of the olive oil and the remaining chicken-pork mixture.

4. Add the artichokes, romano beans, the remaining 1 tablespoon of olive oil and a generous pinch each of salt and pepper to the pan and cook, stirring occasionally, until lightly browned, about 3 minutes. Push the mixture to one side of the pan and reduce the heat to medium. Add the remaining 1 tablespoon of garlic and 1 teaspoon of pimentón to the other side of the pan and cook until fragrant, about 2 minutes. Add the grated tomatoes and the scallions and cook, stirring frequently, until the vegetable mixture is deeply colored and coated in a thick sauce, about 5 minutes. Stir in the chicken-pork mixture, 4 cups of the stock and the brewed saffron. Bring to a boil over high heat, then scatter the rice evenly on top, shaking the pan to distribute it evenly. Simmer over moderately high heat, shaking the pan occasionally, until slightly reduced, about 5 minutes. Add the rosemary sprig and the remaining 2 cups of stock and season with salt and pepper.

5. Transfer the paella to the oven and bake for about 15 minutes, until the rice is tender and the liquid is absorbed. Scatter the roasted red pepper and the peas on top and bake for 3 minutes more. Serve hot. —*Anya von Bremzen*

WINE Berry-rich Monastrell from Alicante: 2014 Enrique Mendoza La Tremenda.

Sheet Pan Chicken and Mushrooms with Parsley Sauce

Active **15 min**; Total **45 min**; Serves **4**

Cookbook author Julia Turshen amps up the flavors in her simple chicken and mushroom pan roast with roasted lemons and a bright and fresh parsley sauce that takes just minutes to make.

- 1½ lbs. skinless, boneless chicken thighs

  Kosher salt and pepper
- ½ cup plus 2 Tbsp. extra-virgin olive oil
- 1 lb. mixed mushrooms, such as shiitake and cremini, stemmed and halved if large
- 1 lemon, thinly sliced, plus slices for garnish
- ½ cup finely chopped parsley, plus more for garnish
- 2 Tbsp. red wine vinegar
- 1 large garlic clove, minced

1. Preheat the oven to 450° and place a large rimmed baking sheet in the oven to heat. Season the chicken generously on both sides with salt and pepper. Drizzle 2 tablespoons of the olive oil onto the hot baking sheet. Arrange the chicken in a single layer on the hot sheet and roast for about 5 minutes, until the chicken begins to brown.

2. In a medium bowl, toss the mushrooms and lemon slices with 2 tablespoons of the olive oil, then carefully scatter evenly around the chicken in the oven. Roast for about 30 minutes, until the mushrooms and lemon are browned and the chicken is cooked through.

3. Meanwhile, in a small bowl, mix the remaining 6 tablespoons of olive oil with the ½ cup of parsley, the vinegar and garlic. Season the sauce with salt.

4. Transfer the chicken, mushrooms and lemon slices to a platter. Drizzle with some of the sauce and garnish with lemon and parsley. Serve, passing the remaining sauce at the table. —*Julia Turshen*

SERVE WITH Quinoa and a green salad.

WINE Earthy New Zealand Pinot Noir: 2014 Ata Rangi.

Chicken and Pork Paella

Sheet Pan Chicken with
Sourdough and Bacon

Sheet Pan Chicken with Sourdough and Bacon

Active **20 min**; Total **1 hr 5 min**; Serves **6**

F&W's Justin Chapple's roast chicken legs drip meaty, delicious fat onto a smoky, peppery bed of potatoes, red onion and croutons.

½ lb. sourdough boule, cut or torn into 2-inch pieces

½ lb. slab bacon, cut into 1-by-½-inch lardons

1 large baking potato—scrubbed, halved crosswise and cut into ¾-inch wedges

1 large red onion, cut into 1-inch wedges

2 Tbsp. cold unsalted butter, diced

4 oregano sprigs

½ tsp. crushed red pepper

¼ cup extra-virgin olive oil

Kosher salt and black pepper

6 whole chicken legs

1. Preheat the oven to 400°. On a large rimmed baking sheet, toss the bread, bacon, potato, onion, butter, oregano and crushed red pepper with the olive oil and season generously with salt and black pepper. Spread in an even layer. Season the chicken with salt and black pepper and arrange on the bread mixture.

2. Roast the chicken and bread mixture for about 45 minutes, until the bread is crisp and an instant-read thermometer inserted in the chicken registers 160°. Serve.—*Justin Chapple*

WINE Lucious, herb-scented Russian River Valley red: 2015 Limerick Lane Syrah-Grenache.

Sticky Baked Chicken Wings

Active **25 min**; Total **1 hr 15 min**
Serves **8 to 10**

Chef Matt Jennings of Townsman in Boston means business when it comes to his food and his beloved Patriots. For the ultimate game-day snack, he tosses chicken wings that he bakes in the oven (instead of deep-frying) in a spicy glaze made with gochujang, the Korean red pepper paste.

1 cup ketchup

1 cup unseasoned rice vinegar

½ cup soy sauce

2 Tbsp. honey

2 Tbsp. gochujang (Korean red pepper paste)

5 lbs. chicken wings, split

¼ cup canola oil

Kosher salt and pepper

Thinly sliced scallions, toasted sesame seeds and chopped cilantro, for garnish

Lime wedges, for serving

1. In a medium saucepan, whisk the ketchup with the vinegar, soy sauce, honey and gochujang and bring to a boil. Cook over moderate heat, stirring occasionally, until thickened and reduced to 1 cup, about 15 minutes.

2. Meanwhile, preheat the oven to 325°. Line 2 large rimmed baking sheets with foil. In a large bowl, toss the chicken wings with the oil; season generously with salt and pepper. Arrange in a single layer on each of the prepared baking sheets. Bake until cooked through and lightly browned, 30 minutes. Increase the oven temperature to 450°.

3. Using a slotted spoon, transfer the wings to a clean large bowl; discard any juices from the baking sheets. Toss the wings with the gochujang sauce and arrange in a single layer on each of the prepared baking sheets. Bake until glazed and lightly charred in spots, 10 to 15 minutes more. Transfer the wings to a platter and garnish with scallions, sesame seeds and cilantro. Serve with lime wedges. —*Matt Jennings*

MAKE AHEAD The prepared gochujang sauce can be refrigerated for up to 1 week.

BEER Malty, lightly hoppy beer: Samuel Adams Boston Lager.

Coconut-Curry Chicken Wings

Total **45 min plus 4 hr marinating**
Serves **4**

Marinating chicken wings in a mix of coconut milk, curry paste and lime gives them an alluring sweet-spicy flavor. They're best hot off the grill.

One 15-oz. can unsweetened coconut milk

¼ cup Thai red curry paste

1 tsp. finely grated lime zest plus ¼ cup fresh lime juice

2½ lbs. whole chicken wings

Canola oil, for brushing

Kosher salt and pepper

1. In a very large bowl, whisk the coconut milk with the curry paste, lime zest and lime juice. Add the chicken and turn to coat. Cover and refrigerate for at least 4 hours or overnight.

2. Light a grill and oil the grate. Remove the chicken from the marinade; season with salt and pepper. Grill over moderate heat, turning, until cooked through, 20 to 25 minutes. Serve hot. —*Justin Chapple*

How to Eat a Chicken Wing

Removing the bones first means you won't leave any meat behind.

STEP 1 Pull the small piece of cartilage off the wide end of the wing, exposing the ends of the bones inside.

STEP 2 Grab the small bone and twist it to release it from the wing.

STEP 3 Pull out the small bone.

STEP 4 Pull out the large bone.

DIY Potpie

"How could you eat a chicken potpie and not shed a tear?" asks **Matt Bolus**, *chef of The 404 Kitchen in Nashville. "I don't know anyone, whether you're from Knoxville or Manhattan, who didn't grow up eating it."* Each bite delivers nostalgia, and Bolus doesn't want to mess with those memories. *"It's all about enhancing that rich, roasty chicken flavor,"* he says. With that goal in mind, Bolus sets his sights on the bird: He browns then poaches the meat, and uses the stock to flavor his filling. And that impossibly flaky crust? It's all about butter and a healthy dose of schmaltz *("the real power player")*.

Chicken Potpie

Active **1 hr 20 min**; Total **3 hr 40 min**
Makes **one 9-inch pie**

CRUST

2½ cups all-purpose flour

2 Tbsp. sugar

1 tsp. kosher salt

1 stick unsalted butter, cubed and chilled

½ cup schmaltz (see Note), scooped into tablespoons and frozen

¼ cup plus 2 Tbsp. cold buttermilk

FILLING

2 lbs. skin-on, bone-in chicken parts
 Kosher salt and white pepper

¼ cup canola oil

6 cups chicken stock or low-sodium broth

½ stick unsalted butter

1 medium onion, finely chopped

1 large carrot, cut into ⅓-inch pieces

1 celery rib, cut into ⅓-inch pieces

2 garlic cloves, minced

¼ cup all-purpose flour

1¼ cups whole milk

¼ cup minced parsley

2 Tbsp. minced chives

2 tsp. minced thyme

1 Tbsp. apple cider vinegar

1 large egg beaten with 1 Tbsp. of water

MAKE THE CRUST

1. In a food processor, pulse the flour with the sugar and salt. Add the butter and schmaltz and pulse until the mixture resembles a coarse meal. Drizzle the buttermilk over the top and pulse until the dough just starts to come together. Turn out onto a work surface, gather any crumbs and gently knead the dough 2 to 3 times until smooth. Divide in half and flatten each piece into a disk. Wrap in plastic and refrigerate until firm, 1 hour.

2. Preheat the oven to 375°. On a floured work surface, roll out 1 disk of dough to a 12-inch round, about ¼ inch thick. Ease the round into a 9-inch deep-dish pie plate. Trim the overhang to ½ inch. Line the crust with parchment paper and fill with pie weights or dried beans. Bake for about 20 minutes, until the crust is just set. Remove the parchment paper and bake for 5 to 7 minutes longer, until lightly browned. Let cool completely.

MEANWHILE, MAKE THE FILLING

3. Season the chicken with salt and pepper. In a large saucepan, heat 2 tablespoons of the oil until shimmering. Add the chicken and cook over moderately high heat, turning occasionally, until browned, about 7 minutes. Add the chicken stock and bring to a boil. Simmer over moderately low heat, turning the chicken occasionally, until an instant-read thermometer inserted in the thickest piece registers 160°, about 15 minutes. Using tongs, transfer the chicken to a plate and let cool. Boil the stock over high heat until reduced to 1 cup, 15 to 20 minutes more; transfer the stock to a small heatproof bowl. Discard the chicken skin and bones, then cut the meat into 1-inch pieces. Wipe out the saucepan.

4. In the saucepan, melt the butter in the remaining 2 tablespoons of oil. Add the onion, carrot, celery, garlic and a generous pinch of salt. Cook over moderate heat, stirring occasionally, until softened, about 10 minutes. Add the chicken and flour and cook, stirring, until the vegetables and chicken are evenly coated. Gradually stir in the milk and reduced stock and bring to a boil. Simmer over moderately low heat,

STEP-BY-STEP POTPIE LESSON

MAKE THE DOUGH In a food processor, pulse the flour, sugar, salt, butter, schmaltz and buttermilk until a dough forms.

KNEAD AND DIVIDE Turn the dough out onto a work surface and knead into a ball. Divide in half and flatten into 2 disks; chill.

ROLL IT OUT Roll 1 disk into a round, ease it into a pie dish and trim the overhang. Blind-bake the crust until lightly browned.

BROWN AND SIMMER Sear the chicken, then finish cooking it in stock; remove and cut into bite-size pieces. Reduce the stock.

stirring occasionally, until thickened, 5 to 7 minutes. Stir in the parsley, chives, thyme and vinegar and season with salt and pepper. Let cool completely, about 30 minutes.

FILL AND BAKE

5. On a floured work surface, roll out the other disk of dough to a 12-inch round. Scrape the filling into the cooled pie shell and cover with the top crust. Trim the overhang to 1 inch and crimp the edge decoratively, sealing it to the bottom crust. Brush with the egg wash and cut slits in the top to vent steam. Bake the potpie for 40 minutes, until the crust is browned and the filling is bubbling. Let stand for 10 minutes before serving.

NOTE Schmaltz, rendered chicken fat, can be found in the freezer or refrigerated section of the grocery store or at your local butcher.

WINE Rich, plummy Washington state Merlot: 2013 Pepper Bridge.

CHEF'S TIP

Cook your filling just shy of that slightly loose gravy consistency. "It will continue to thicken in the oven, so pull it at that point when you think. Just a few more minutes and this will be perfect!"

"Unless peas are in season, leave them out," says Bolus. "Frozen peas add moisture and make your filling watery."

MAKE THE FILLING Sauté the vegetables, then add the chicken, flour, milk and stock. Simmer until the filling is a loose gravy.

FILL THE CRUST Scrape the cooled filling into the par-baked piecrust.

CRIMP THE EDGES Roll out the other disk of dough and cover the potpie. Trim the overhang and crimp the edges to seal.

OVEN TIME Brush the top with egg wash and cut slits to vent steam. Bake for 40 minutes, until the crust is golden brown.

Red-and-Green Chicken

Total **1 hr**; Serves **4**

This clever grilled chicken recipe from Portland, Oregon chef Joshua McFadden involves making two simple sauces— a spicy red one with 'nduja, a spreadable pork sausage, and a green one packed with herbs, capers and anchovies—that are brushed on the chicken and served alongside. Both sauces are versatile, so keep those leftovers. Try the red sauce on a grilled cheese sandwich and the green over grilled vegetables or mixed with olive oil and white wine vinegar for a vinaigrette.

RED SAUCE

- ½ cup 'nduja (see Note)
- 2 oil-packed Calabrian chiles, stemmed
- 2 Tbsp. tomato paste
- 1 Tbsp. red wine vinegar
- ¼ cup plus 2 Tbsp. extra-virgin olive oil
  Kosher salt and pepper

GREEN SAUCE

- 1 cup each lightly packed parsley, mint and basil leaves
- 4 scallions, chopped
- ¼ cup capers
- 4 anchovy fillets
- 1 cup extra-virgin olive oil
  Kosher salt and pepper

CHICKEN

- Canola oil, for brushing
- One 3½-lb. chicken, cut into 8 to 10 pieces
- Kosher salt and pepper
- Lemon wedges

1. Make the red sauce In a food processor, pulse the 'nduja with the chiles, tomato paste and vinegar until nearly smooth. With the machine on, drizzle in the olive oil until incorporated. Scrape the sauce into a medium bowl and season with salt and pepper. Clean the food processor.

2. Make the green sauce In the food processor, pulse the herbs, scallions, capers and anchovies until very finely chopped. With the machine on, drizzle in the olive oil until incorporated. Scrape the sauce into a medium bowl and season with salt and pepper.

3. Make the chicken Light a grill and oil the grate. Season the chicken with salt and pepper. Grill over moderate heat, turning occasionally, until an instant-read thermometer inserted in the thickest piece registers 155°, about 25 minutes. Brush half the chicken with some of the red sauce and half with some of the green sauce and continue to grill, turning and brushing with the sauces, until an instant-read thermometer inserted in the thickest piece registers 165°, 7 minutes longer. Transfer the chicken to a platter and serve with lemon wedges, passing the remaining sauces at the table. —*Joshua McFadden*

NOTE 'Nduja is a spicy, spreadable pork sausage. You can find it at Whole Foods.

MAKE AHEAD The sauces can be refrigerated separately overnight.

WINE Plummy southern Italian red: 2013 Cantele Salice Salentino Riserva.

Piri Piri Chicken with Crispy Potatoes

Active **30 min**; Total **1 hr 45 min** plus 30 min marinating; Serves **6 to 8**

The fiery sauce here, a combination of fresh and dried chiles, ginger, garlic, cilantro and smoky pimentón, gets used as a marinade for the chicken and also as a sauce for serving.

- 5 Fresno or red jalapeño chiles, stemmed and chopped
- 3 dried piri piri chiles or chiles de árbol, stemmed
- 3 garlic cloves, crushed
  One 2-inch piece of peeled fresh ginger, coarsely chopped
- ½ cup cilantro leaves, plus small sprigs for garnish
- 2 Tbsp. distilled white vinegar
- 1 shallot, chopped
- ½ tsp. sweet smoked paprika
- ¾ cup extra-virgin olive oil
  Kosher salt and pepper
- 3½ lbs. skin-on, bone-in chicken pieces
- 2 lbs. baking potatoes, peeled and cut into 1-inch-thick wedges
  Lemon wedges, for serving (optional)

1. In a food processor, puree the fresh and dried chiles with the garlic, ginger, ½ cup of cilantro, the vinegar, shallot, paprika and ½ cup of the olive oil until smooth. Season with salt and pepper. Reserve ½ cup of the piri piri marinade. In a large bowl, rub the chicken pieces all over with the remaining marinade and let stand at room temperature for 30 minutes.

2. Preheat the oven to 450° with the racks set in the upper and lower thirds. Set a wire rack over a large rimmed baking sheet.

3. Transfer the chicken to the prepared baking sheet; discard the marinade. Season with salt and pepper and drizzle with 2 tablespoons of the olive oil. On another rimmed baking sheet, toss the potatoes with the remaining 2 tablespoons of olive oil and season with salt and pepper; arrange in a single layer. Roast the chicken on the upper rack of the oven for 20 minutes. Add the potatoes to the bottom rack and roast the chicken and potatoes for 20 to 25 minutes longer, until the chicken is cooked through and the potatoes are golden. Transfer the chicken to a platter and garnish with cilantro sprigs. Serve with the potatoes, lemon wedges, if desired, and the reserved marinade for dipping. —*Kay Chun*

MAKE AHEAD The marinade can be refrigerated overnight.

WINE Floral, intense Portuguese red: 2015 Casa Ferreirinha Esteva Red.

Piri Piri Chicken with
Crispy Potatoes

Saffron Chicken
Tagine

Easy Braised Chicken with Kimchi

Active **30 min**; Total **1 hr**; Serves **4 to 6**

Kimchi is one of the healthiest, most versatile ingredients to have in your pantry. Cookbook author Julia Turshen pours the whole jar, juice and all, into a pot of browned chicken: The spicy liquid infuses the chicken with great flavor as it braises.

- 2 **Tbsp. vegetable or canola oil**
- 2 **lbs. skin-on, bone-in chicken pieces, breasts halved crosswise**
  Kosher salt and pepper
- 10 **scallions, trimmed and chopped, plus sliced scallions for garnish**
- 4 **garlic cloves, minced**
  One 16-oz. jar cabbage kimchi with juice (2½ cups)
  Roasted sesame seeds, for garnish (optional)

1. In a medium enameled cast-iron casserole, heat the oil over moderately high heat. Season the chicken with salt and pepper and add half of it to the casserole skin side down. Cook until browned, 6 to 8 minutes. Flip the chicken and cook until browned on the other side, 6 to 8 minutes more; reduce the heat to moderate if the chicken is getting too dark. Transfer to a plate and repeat with the remaining chicken.

2. Add the chopped scallions, garlic and kimchi with its juice to the casserole and bring to a boil over moderately high heat. Nestle the chicken in the sauce, cover and simmer over moderately low heat until an instant-read thermometer inserted into a piece of dark meat registers 165° (160° for white meat), 20 to 25 minutes. Garnish with sliced scallions and sesame seeds, if desired, and serve. —*Julia Turshen*

WINE Funky "natural" Loire red: 2015 Clos du Tue-Boeuf Touraine La Butte.

Saffron Chicken Tagine

Active **35 min**; Total **1 hr 30 min plus overnight marinating**; Serves **4**

Everyone loves North Africa's deeply flavored tagine (the stew), but no one wants to make it because they think it needs to be cooked in a tagine (the earthenware cooking vessel). Not true! This version is designed for a large enameled cast-iron casserole. Don't be intimidated by the long list of ingredients, either; it consists mostly of spices and easy-to-find staples that you will use over and over.

- **One 3½- to 4-lb. chicken, cut into 8 pieces**
  Kosher salt and black pepper
- 2 **large spring onions, halved lengthwise**
- 1 **cup chopped cilantro**
- 1 **cup chopped parsley**
- 1 **preserved lemon, quartered, seeds removed**
- 3 **garlic cloves, crushed**
  One 2-inch piece of fresh ginger, peeled and sliced ¼ inch thick
- 2 **Tbsp. sweet paprika**
- 1 **Tbsp. ghee or unsalted butter, melted**
- 1 **Tbsp. harissa**
- 1 **tsp. ground cumin**
- 1 **tsp. ground turmeric**
- ½ **tsp. ground cardamom**
- ¼ **tsp. crushed red pepper**
- ¼ **tsp. ground cinnamon**
- ¼ **tsp. saffron**
- ¼ **cup plus 2 Tbsp. extra-virgin olive oil**
- 1 **lb. multicolored carrots, peeled, halved lengthwise**
- 2 **large fennel bulbs, halved and very thinly sliced**
- 1 **cup fresh or thawed frozen peas**
- 1 **cup whole green olives**
- 3 **cups low-sodium chicken broth**
- 2 **Tbsp. fresh lemon juice**
- 1 **cup couscous**
- 1 **small yellow onion, finely chopped**

1. In a large bowl, season the chicken with salt and black pepper. Add the spring onions, ½ cup each of the cilantro and parsley, the preserved lemon, garlic, ginger, paprika, ghee, harissa, cumin, turmeric, cardamom, crushed red pepper, cinnamon and saffron and toss to coat. Cover and let marinate in the refrigerator overnight.

2. In a large enameled cast-iron casserole, heat ¼ cup of the olive oil. Scrape the marinade off the chicken and reserve. Working in batches, cook the chicken skin side down over moderate heat until browned, about 8 minutes. Add the carrots, fennel, peas, green olives, reserved marinade and 1 cup of the broth. Cover the casserole and bring the liquid to a boil, then reduce the heat to moderately low and cook until the chicken is tender, about 35 minutes. Remove from the heat and let the tagine stand, covered, for about 15 minutes. Add the lemon juice and the remaining ½ cup each of cilantro and parsley and season with salt and black pepper.

3. Meanwhile, put the couscous in a large heatproof bowl. In a medium saucepan, heat the remaining 2 tablespoons of olive oil. Add the yellow onion and cook over moderate heat, stirring occasionally, until lightly browned, about 10 minutes. Add the remaining 2 cups of broth, bring to a simmer and pour over the couscous. Cover the bowl with plastic wrap and let stand for 15 minutes. Fluff the couscous with a fork and season with salt. Serve the couscous with the tagine. —*Andrew Zimmern*

WINE Citrusy Sardinian white: 2015 Is Argiolas Vermentino.

Best-Ever Cold Fried Chicken

Active **1 hr 15 min**; Total **1 hr 45 min plus overnight refrigerating**; Serves **4 to 6**

F&W's Justin Chapple adds some of the buttermilk marinade to the dry ingredients before dredging and frying the chicken, creating extra-crispy bits that hold up well in the fridge.

- 1 qt. buttermilk
- Kosher salt and pepper
- Two 3-lb. whole chickens, cut into 8 pieces each
- 3 cups all-purpose flour
- 1 Tbsp. hot paprika
- 1½ tsp. onion powder
- 1½ tsp. garlic powder
- 48 oz. all-vegetable shortening or canola oil, for frying
- Hot sauce and assorted pickles, for serving

1. In a large bowl, whisk the buttermilk with 1½ tablespoons of salt and 2 teaspoons of pepper. Add the chicken. Cover with plastic wrap and refrigerate overnight.

2. In another large bowl, whisk the flour, paprika, onion powder and garlic powder with 1 tablespoon of salt and 2 teaspoons of pepper. Spoon ¼ cup of the buttermilk marinade into the dry ingredients and mix until the dry ingredients look slightly shaggy.

3. Remove 1 piece of chicken from the buttermilk, letting the excess drip back into the bowl. Dredge in the flour mixture, pressing to help it adhere. Transfer to a baking sheet. Repeat with the remaining chicken pieces. Let stand for 30 minutes.

4. Line a large baking sheet with paper towels and set a rack on top. In a large saucepan, heat the shortening to 325°. Fry the chicken in batches at around 320°, turning occasionally, until golden and an instant-read thermometer inserted in the thickest piece registers 160°, about 15 minutes. Transfer to the rack to drain. Let cool, then refrigerate for at least 2 hours or overnight. Serve with hot sauce and assorted pickles. —*Justin Chapple*

MAKE AHEAD The fried chicken can be refrigerated for up to 2 days.

Late-Night Fried Chicken

Total **2 hr 15 min plus overnight brining** Serves **8**

This spectacularly delicious fried chicken is a variation on the much-loved dish served at New York City's iconic Blue Ribbon Brasserie. The chicken is brined in water, salt, honey, lemon and herbs, then coated in a mix of matzo meal and flour before it's fried to crunchy perfection. To make it even more decadent, chefs Bruce and Eric Bromberg toss it in luscious foie gras fat with crispy chiles and herbs just before serving. It's the ultimate comfort food with a slightly elevated twist.

BRINE

- 4 qts. water
- ½ cup kosher salt
- ¼ cup honey
- ¼ cup fresh lemon juice, plus 2 halved lemons
- 10 thyme sprigs
- 10 sage sprigs
- 4 bay leaves
- 2 Tbsp. peppercorns
- Two 3-lb. chickens, cut into 8 pieces each

FRIED CHICKEN

- 4 oz. foie gras terrine
- 1 Tbsp. minced parsley
- 1 Tbsp. minced chives
- 2 tsp. minced sage, plus 15 large leaves
- 1 tsp. minced thyme
- ½ tsp. minced rosemary
- 6 large egg whites
- ¾ cup matzo meal
- ¾ cup all-purpose flour
- Kosher salt and pepper
- Vegetable oil, for frying
- 2 serrano chiles, sliced ¼ inch thick

1. Brine the chicken In a very large bowl, whisk the water with the salt, honey and lemon juice until the salt dissolves. Add the halved lemons along with the thyme, sage, bay leaves and peppercorns. Submerge the chicken in the brine, cover and refrigerate overnight.

2. Make the fried chicken Preheat the oven to 300°. Put the foie gras terrine in a pie plate and bake until most of the fat is rendered and the foie gras is sizzling, about 15 minutes. Scrape the foie gras and any fat into a fine sieve set over a small saucepan. Press on the solids to extract as much of the fat as possible. Discard the solids or reserve for another use. Stir the parsley, chives, minced sage, thyme and rosemary into the foie gras fat. Keep warm.

3. Lower the oven temperature to 200°. Drain the chicken and pat dry. Scrape off any herbs or peppercorns stuck to the skin.

4. In a large bowl, beat the egg whites until very frothy. In another large bowl, whisk the matzo meal with the flour and a generous pinch each of salt and pepper. Dip the chicken pieces in the egg whites, letting the excess drip back into the bowl, then dredge in the flour mixture, pressing to help it adhere. Transfer the chicken to a large rimmed baking sheet lined with wax paper.

5. Set a rack on another large rimmed baking sheet. In a large, heavy saucepan, heat 2 inches of oil to 375°. Fry the chicken in 3 or 4 batches over moderate heat, turning occasionally, until browned and an instant-read thermometer inserted in the thickest part of each piece registers 160°, about 10 minutes. Transfer the chicken to the rack to drain; keep warm in the oven. Add the sage leaves and chiles to the hot oil and fry until crisp, 30 seconds to 1 minute. Transfer to paper towels to drain.

6. Transfer all of the fried chicken to a very large bowl. Add the warm foie gras mixture and toss to coat. Transfer to a large platter and garnish with the crispy sage and serranos. Serve right away.
—*Bruce Bromberg and Eric Bromberg*

WINE Rich Rhône Valley white: 2015 Domaine Faury Saint Joseph Blanc.

Best-Ever Cold
Fried Chicken

Jerk Chicken with
Scallion Pepper Sauce

Gas Station Fried Chicken

Active **40 min**; Total **1 hr plus overnight soaking**; Serves **4**

At Nashville's Gray & Dudley restaurant in the 21c Museum Hotel, chef Levon Wallace's old-school-style fried chicken is extra-crunchy and just the right amount of salty. If you want to get really fancy, he says, drizzle the chicken with honey and your favorite spice blend, or serve it alongside some bubbly.

- 2 **cups buttermilk**
- 2 **Tbsp. Louisiana-style hot sauce**
- 2 **tsp. onion powder**
- ¼ **cup kosher salt**
  One 3½-lb. chicken, cut into 8 pieces
- 2 **cups all-purpose flour**
- ½ **cup fine cornmeal**
- 1 **Tbsp. pepper**
  Peanut or canola oil, for frying

1. In a large bowl, whisk the buttermilk with the hot sauce, onion powder and 2 tablespoons of salt. Add the chicken and stir to coat. Cover and refrigerate overnight.

2. In a large bowl, mix the flour with the cornmeal, pepper and the remaining 2 tablespoons of salt. Remove the chicken from the buttermilk, letting the excess drip back into the bowl. Dredge the chicken in the flour mixture, pressing all over so it adheres. Transfer the coated chicken to a large baking sheet and let stand for 15 minutes.

3. In a large saucepan, heat 2 inches of oil to 365°. Line another baking sheet with paper towels. In 2 batches, fry the chicken at 325°, turning occasionally, until golden and an instant-read thermometer inserted in the thickest piece registers 160°, 12 to 15 minutes per batch. Transfer the chicken to the paper towel–lined baking sheet to drain. Serve hot. —*Levon Wallace*

WINE Crisp, cherry-scented Pinot Noir: 2014 Flowers Sonoma Coast.

Jerk Chicken with Scallion-Pepper Sauce

📷 OPPOSITE PAGE

Active **1 hr 25 min**; Total **2 hr 35 min plus 24 hr marinating**; Serves **6 to 8**

Fiery jerk chicken, with its notes of warm allspice and bright vinegar, is traditionally grilled over pimento wood, available from pimentowoodproducts.com. The chicken's *sauce chien* accompaniment is like an exotic vinaigrette made with herbs, chiles, aromatic vegetables and lime juice. It's a lively, pungent and spicy topper for all kinds of grilled foods.

MARINADE

- 1 **large yellow onion, chopped**
- 10 **scallions, chopped**
- 8 **garlic cloves, crushed**
- 4 **habanero or Scotch Bonnet chiles, stemmed**
- ½ **cup tamarind paste**
- ½ **cup extra-virgin olive oil**
- ¼ **cup apple cider vinegar**
- 3 **Tbsp. thyme leaves**
- 2 **Tbsp. fresh lime juice**
- 2 **Tbsp. light brown sugar**
- 3 **bay leaves, crushed**
- 1 **Tbsp. white pepper**
- 1 **Tbsp. fine sea salt**
- 2 **tsp. ground cinnamon**
- 2 **tsp. ground allspice**
- ¾ **tsp. freshly grated nutmeg**
  Two 3½-lb. chickens, backbones removed and chickens flattened

SAUCE

- 1 **roasted red bell pepper**
- ¼ **cup minced onion**
- 6 **small scallions, minced**
- 1 **jalapeño—stemmed, seeded and minced**
- 2 **Tbsp. minced parsley**
- 2 **small garlic cloves, minced**
- ¼ **tsp. dried thyme**
- ⅔ **cup boiling water**
- ¼ **cup fresh lime juice**
- 2 **Tbsp. peanut oil**
  Kosher salt and pepper

1. Marinate the chicken In a food processor, puree all of the ingredients except the chickens. Divide the marinade between 2 very large resealable plastic bags. Add a chicken to each and seal. Refrigerate for 24 hours.

2. Meanwhile, make the sauce In a food processor, puree the roasted bell pepper until smooth. Transfer to a heatproof medium bowl and stir in the onion, scallions, jalapeño, parsley, garlic, thyme and boiling water. Let cool, then stir in the lime juice and oil. Season generously with salt and pepper.

3. Light a charcoal grill. When the coals are glowing, rake them to one side and place a large foil pan on the other side for indirect cooking. Heat the grill to 375°.

4. Remove the chickens from the marinade, scraping off some excess; reserve the remaining marinade. Set the chickens skin side up in the foil pan on the grate. Close the grill and cook until well browned, about 20 minutes. Brush the chickens generously with the reserved marinade, close the grill and cook until the marinade starts to char in spots, about 20 minutes.

5. Turn the chickens skin side down and cook, uncovered, until charred and an instant-read thermometer inserted in the thigh registers 165°, 20 to 30 minutes; use a spray bottle filled with water to stop flare-ups. Transfer to a carving board and let rest for 10 minutes, then carve and serve with the sauce. —*Andrew Zimmern*

MAKE AHEAD The sauce can be refrigerated overnight.

BEER Light-bodied Jamaican pale lager: Red Stripe.

Best-Ever Roast
Chicken (p. 146)
OPPOSITE Torn
Chicken with Crispy
Rice and Kimchi
Vinaigrette (p. 146)

Garlic Grilled Chicken

Active **45 min**; Total **2 hr 25 min**; Serves **8**

> Two 3-lb. chickens
>
> 3 heads of garlic—2 halved crosswise and 1 separated into cloves and peeled
>
> Kosher salt and pepper
>
> ¼ cup extra-virgin olive oil
>
> ¼ cup minced rosemary
>
> 4 lemons—2 zested and juiced and 2 quartered lengthwise
>
> Canola oil, for brushing

1. Set a chicken on a work surface breast side up. Using kitchen shears, cut between the breast halves to split them. Remove the breast bone with your hands, then flatten the chicken; transfer to a large rimmed baking sheet. Repeat with the remaining chicken.

2. In a mortar, using a pestle, crush the peeled garlic cloves with a generous pinch of salt until a paste forms. Scrape the paste into a small bowl and stir in the oil, rosemary and the lemon zest and juice. Spread the mixture all over the chickens and season with salt and pepper. Let stand for 1 hour.

3. Light a grill and set it up for indirect cooking. If using a charcoal grill, rake the coals to one side. Oil the grate. Grill the chickens skin side up and the halved garlic heads and lemon quarters cut side down uncovered over indirect heat until the chickens are browned on the bottom and the garlic and lemons are lightly charred, 20 to 25 minutes. Flip the chickens and place the garlic halves and lemon quarters in the cavities. Continue to grill uncovered over indirect heat until the skin is well browned and an instant-read thermometer inserted in the thickest part of each chicken registers 160°, about 20 minutes. Transfer the chickens, garlic halves and lemon quarters to a carving board and let rest for 15 minutes. Carve the chickens and serve with the grilled lemon and garlic. —*José Catrimán*

Best-Ever Roast Chicken

PAGE 144

Active **15 min**; Total **1 hr 45 min plus 5 hr drying**; Serves **4**

> One 3½- to 4-lb. chicken, rinsed and patted dry
>
> 2½ tsp. kosher salt

1. Season the chicken inside and out with the salt, then tie the legs together with kitchen string, if desired. Refrigerate uncovered for at least 5 hours or overnight. Let the chicken come to room temperature before roasting.

2. Preheat the oven to 500°. Put the chicken in a small roasting pan or large skillet. Roast for 50 minutes to 1 hour, until an instant-read thermometer inserted in the inner thigh registers 162°. Transfer to a carving board and let rest for 10 minutes. Carve the chicken and serve. —*Hugh Acheson*

Torn Chicken with Crispy Rice and Kimchi Vinaigrette

PAGE 145

Active **20 min**; Total **45 min**; Serves **4**

Mixing crispy baked rice with soft, fluffy steamed rice creates the most addictive texture. Georgia chef Hugh Acheson tops that magical rice with shredded chicken, sautéed bok choy and a spicy, tangy vinaigrette made with kimchi.

> 3 cups Jasmine Rice (p. 252) or warm cooked white rice
>
> 1½ tsp. canola oil
>
> 2 Tbsp. extra-virgin olive oil
>
> 3 small bok choy, halved lengthwise
>
> Kosher salt and pepper
>
> ¼ cup plus 2 Tbsp. Kimchi Vinaigrette (p. 34)
>
> 2 cups shredded Best-Ever Roast Chicken (recipe above) or rotisserie chicken
>
> Thai basil sprigs, for garnish

1. Preheat the oven to 375°. In a medium bowl, mix ½ cup of the rice with the canola oil. Spread on a large rimmed baking sheet. Bake for 15 to 20 minutes, until crisp.

2. Meanwhile, in a large skillet, heat the olive oil until shimmering. Add the bok choy cut side down and season with salt and pepper. Cook over moderately high heat until browned on the bottom, 2 to 3 minutes. Flip and cook until crisp-tender, 2 minutes longer. Transfer to a plate.

3. In a bowl, toss the crispy rice with the remaining 2½ cups of cooked rice and ¼ cup of the vinaigrette. Transfer to shallow bowls and top with the bok choy and chicken. Spoon the remaining vinaigrette into the bowls. Garnish with basil and sauce. —*Hugh Acheson*

WINE Fragrant Friulian Pinot Grigio: 2015 Marco Felluga Mongris.

Kewpie-Marinated Chicken

Active **30 min**; Total **1 hr plus 2 hr marinating**; Serves **4 to 6**

> 1 cup Kewpie mayonnaise
>
> 2 tsp. finely grated lime zest plus 2 Tbsp. fresh lime juice
>
> 1½ Tbsp. ground cumin
>
> 1½ Tbsp. hot paprika
>
> Kosher salt and pepper
>
> Two 3-lb. chickens
>
> Extra-virgin olive oil, for brushing

1. In a bowl, whisk the Kewpie with the lime zest and juice, cumin, paprika, 1 tablespoon of salt and 1 teaspoon of pepper.

2. Working on a large rimmed baking sheet, using scissors, cut along either side of the chicken backbones to remove them. Flatten the chickens and, using a knife, cut slashes all over the legs and breasts. Spread the marinade on both sides of the chickens. Refrigerate for 2 hours. Bring to room temperature before grilling.

3. Set up a grill for indirect grilling, then heat to 400°; oil the grate. Scrape some of the marinade off the chickens. Set the chickens skin side down on the grate over indirect heat. Close the grill and cook, turning once, until the chickens are lightly charred and an instant-read thermometer inserted in the thickest part of the breasts registers 160°, about 25 minutes. Transfer to a board and let rest for 10 minutes before serving. —*Justin Chapple*

SERVE WITH Grilled onions, such as spring onions, red onions, cipollini and scallions.

WINE Bright, berry-accented Pinot Noir: 2014 Rickshaw.

Mustard-and-Soy Roast Chicken with Carrot Top Chimichurri

Active **25 min;** Total **1 hr 45 min plus 5 hr drying;** Serves **4**

- One 3½- to 4-lb. chicken, rinsed and patted dry
- 2½ tsp. kosher salt, plus more for seasoning
- ¼ cup Dijon mustard
- ¼ cup soy sauce
- 1 cup lightly packed carrot top greens, finely chopped
- ¼ cup red wine vinegar
- 2 tsp. finely chopped oregano
- 1 tsp. finely grated lime zest
- 1 small garlic clove, minced
- ½ tsp. crushed red pepper
- ¼ cup plus 2 Tbsp. extra-virgin olive oil

1. Season the chicken inside and out with the 2½ teaspoons of salt, then tie the legs together with kitchen string, if desired. Refrigerate uncovered for at least 5 hours or overnight. Let the chicken come to room temperature before roasting.

2. Preheat the oven to 500°. Put the chicken in a small roasting pan or large skillet. Roast for 30 minutes, until lightly browned. In a small bowl, whisk the mustard with the soy sauce, then spoon the glaze all over the chicken. Roast for 20 to 30 minutes longer, until an instant-read thermometer inserted in the inner thigh registers 162°. Transfer to a carving board and let rest for 10 minutes.

3. Meanwhile, in another small bowl, mix the carrot greens with the vinegar, oregano, lime zest, garlic and crushed red pepper. Gradually whisk in the olive oil until combined. Season the chimichurri with salt.

4. Carve the chicken. Thickly slice the breast against the grain. Transfer the chicken to a platter and serve with the carrot top chimichurri. —*Hugh Acheson*

MAKE AHEAD The carrot top chimichurri can be refrigerated overnight.

WINE Spicy, berry-rich Pinot Noir: 2012 Domaine Anderson.

Buttermilk-Brined Roast Chicken

Active **30 min;** Total **1 hr 30 min plus 6 hr brining;** Serves **4**

- Kosher salt
- 11 garlic cloves—9 smashed, 2 thinly sliced
- 2 Tbsp. sugar
- 2 Tbsp. chopped rosemary or 5 Douglas fir sprigs
- 1 bay leaf
- ½ cup dried porcini mushrooms
- 1 qt. buttermilk
- One 3½-lb. chicken
- 1 tsp. unsalted butter, softened
- 2 Tbsp. extra-virgin olive oil

1. In a medium saucepan, combine ¼ cup of salt with the smashed garlic, the sugar, rosemary, bay leaf and 2 cups of water. Bring to a simmer, stirring to dissolve the salt and sugar. Transfer to a very large bowl and stir in 2 cups of cold water.

2. In a spice grinder, grind the mushrooms to a powder. (You should have about 3 tablespoons.) Whisk the porcini powder and buttermilk into the salt mixture. Place the chicken in the buttermilk brine, cover with plastic wrap and refrigerate for at least 6 hours or up to 12 hours.

3. Preheat the oven to 425°. Remove the chicken from the brine and pat dry; discard the brine. Tuck the wing tips behind the breasts, tie the legs with kitchen twine and set the chicken breast side up on a rack over a roasting pan. Season all over with salt.

4. Roast the chicken for 15 minutes. Brush the butter all over the chicken, then return it to the oven and roast for about 45 minutes longer, until an instant-read thermometer inserted in the thickest part of the thigh registers 165°. Transfer to a cutting board and let rest for 15 minutes.

5. Meanwhile, in a small skillet, simmer the olive oil with the sliced garlic over moderately high heat, stirring occasionally, until the garlic just starts to brown and the oil is hot and fragrant, about 3 minutes. Remove the skillet from the heat and let cool.

6. Carve the chicken and arrange the pieces on a platter. Brush with some of the garlic oil and serve right away, passing the remaining oil at the table. —*Sarah Rich and Evan Rich*

Slow-Roast Chicken with Green Garlic

Active **15 min;** Total **2 hr;** Serves **4**

- One 3½- to 4-lb. chicken
- Kosher salt and pepper
- 14 thyme sprigs
- 6 stalks of green garlic or 6 large scallions, trimmed and halved crosswise
- 3 Tbsp. unsalted butter, softened
- 1 Tbsp. extra-virgin olive oil
- ½ lemon, quartered, plus 1 Tbsp. fresh lemon juice
- 5 garlic cloves
- 1 large shallot, chopped

1. Preheat the oven to 325°. Pat the chicken dry with paper towels and place breast side up in a 9-by-13-inch baking dish. Starting at the top of the breast, gently separate the skin from the breast and thighs. Season the chicken cavity with salt and pepper and tuck 8 of the thyme sprigs and 4 stalks of the green garlic inside. Rub half of the butter under the skin of the breasts and thighs and rub the remaining butter all over the outside of the chicken; season with salt and pepper. Tie the legs together with kitchen string and drizzle the chicken with the olive oil and lemon juice.

2. Scatter the lemon quarters, garlic cloves, shallot and the remaining 6 thyme sprigs and 2 stalks of green garlic around the chicken. Roast for about 1½ hours, basting occasionally, until an instant-read thermometer inserted in an inner thigh registers 165°. Transfer the chicken to a carving board and let rest for 10 minutes.

3. Carve the chicken and transfer to a platter along with the green garlic, lemon wedges and garlic cloves. Spoon the pan sauce over the top and serve. —*Chantal Dussouchaud*

WINE Rich, peach-scented Rhône Valley white: 2015 Michel Gassier Nostre Païs.

Chicken with Roasted-Garlic Pan Sauce

Active **30 min**; Total **1 hr 45 min**; Serves **4**

This dish takes inspiration from the rotis-serie chicken and sauce served at El Asador de Nati in Córdoba, Spain.

> One 4½- to 5-lb. chicken, rinsed and patted dry
> Kosher salt and pepper
> 1 head of garlic, halved crosswise, plus 2 cloves, minced
> 1 Tbsp. extra-virgin olive oil
> ½ cup minced yellow onion
> ½ cup minced green bell pepper
> ½ cup dry white wine
> 1 bay leaf
> Pinch of dried thyme

1. Preheat the oven to 425°. Season the chicken all over with salt and pepper and place in a large ovenproof skillet along with the head of garlic, cut sides down. Roast for about 1 hour and 15 minutes, until an instant-read thermometer inserted in the thickest part of the chicken breast registers 160°. Transfer the chicken and garlic to a cutting board; let rest for 15 minutes. Pour the pan drippings into a heatproof bowl.

2. Meanwhile, in the skillet, heat the olive oil. Add the onion, bell pepper, minced garlic and a generous pinch of salt. Cook over moderate heat, stirring occasionally, until softened, about 10 minutes. Add the wine, bay leaf, thyme and the reserved pan drippings. Squeeze the roasted garlic into the sauce and bring to a boil over high heat, then simmer over moderately low heat until slightly reduced, about 5 minutes. Discard the bay leaf. Transfer to a blender, add 2 tablespoons of water and puree until very smooth. Season the sauce with salt and pepper.

3. Carve the chicken and transfer to a platter. Serve with the roasted-garlic pan sauce. —*José Andrés*

WINE Spicy, medium-bodied Garnacha: 2014 Bodegas Marañones Labros.

Fennel, Chicken and Potato Salad

Active **20 min**; Total **1 hr**; Serves **4 to 6**

Potato salad meets chicken salad in this bright, fresh-tasting dish that's packed with fennel and tarragon.

> 1 lb. baby red potatoes
> Kosher salt and pepper
> ⅓ cup mayonnaise
> 3 Tbsp. dry white wine, such as Pinot Grigio
> 1 Tbsp. white wine vinegar
> 1½ Tbsp. finely chopped tarragon, plus ¼ cup leaves for garnish
> 4 cups shredded cooked chicken (from a small rotisserie chicken)
> 1 fennel bulb—halved, cored and very thinly sliced, fronds reserved for garnish

1. In a medium saucepan, cover the potatoes with water and bring to a boil. Season generously with salt and simmer over moderate heat until the potatoes are tender, 15 to 20 minutes. Drain well and let cool, then cut in half.

2. In a large serving bowl, whisk the mayonnaise with the wine, vinegar and chopped tarragon. Season the dressing with salt and pepper. Add the chicken, fennel and cooled potatoes and toss well. Season generously with salt and pepper and toss again. Garnish with the tarragon leaves and fennel fronds. Serve right away. —*Justin Chapple*

MAKE AHEAD The salad can be refrigerated overnight.

WINE Nectarine-scented Pinot Grigio: 2015 Alois Lageder.

Buffalo Chicken Calzones

OPPOSITE PAGE

Active **20 min**; Total **45 min**; Serves **4**

To make the most of rotisserie chicken, F&W's Justin Chapple tosses it with a buttery Buffalo sauce, then bakes it into a calzone with Monterey Jack cheese. To stay in keeping with traditional Buffalo wings, he serves the calzone with celery sticks and blue cheese.

> ½ cup Buffalo sauce, preferably Frank's RedHot
> 2 Tbsp. unsalted butter
> 1 lb. shredded rotisserie chicken (4 cups)
> All-purpose flour, for dusting
> 1 lb. pizza dough, halved
> 1 cup shredded Monterey Jack (4 oz.)
> Extra-virgin olive oil, for brushing
> Flaky sea salt and coarse black pepper
> Blue cheese dressing and celery, for serving

1. Preheat the oven to 450°. Line a large rimmed baking sheet with parchment paper. In a small saucepan, combine the Buffalo sauce and butter and simmer over moderate heat until the butter is melted, about 3 minutes. Transfer to a bowl and stir in the chicken.

2. On a lightly floured work surface, roll out 1 piece of dough to a 10-inch round. Transfer to one side of the baking sheet. Spoon half of the chicken mixture on one half of the dough round and top with half of the cheese. Fold the dough over the filling. Moisten the edge with water, then crimp to seal. Cut 3 slits in the top, then brush the calzone with olive oil and season with flaky salt and black pepper. Repeat to make another calzone.

3. Bake the calzones for about 20 minutes, until the crust is golden. Let stand for 5 minutes, then serve with blue cheese dressing and celery. —*Justin Chapple*

Buffalo Chicken
Calzones

Clementine-and-
Garlic Roast Turkey

Lemon-Pepper Roast Turkey

Active **45 min**; Total **2 hr 40 min**; Serves **10**

One 10-to-12-pound turkey, rinsed and patted dry
1 **stick unsalted butter, softened**
2 **Tbsp. finely grated lemon zest**
Kosher salt and black pepper
Extra-virgin olive oil, for brushing
3 **heads of garlic, halved crosswise**

1. Preheat the oven to 425°. Put a baking rack on a large rimmed baking sheet. Using poultry shears, cut along each side of the turkey backbone and remove it. Flatten the turkey with your hands and put it breast side up on the prepared baking sheet.

2. In a small bowl, using a fork, blend the butter with the lemon zest, 1 tablespoon salt and 1 tablespoon pepper. Run your fingers under the breast and leg skin to loosen it, then spread the butter under the skin and over the breast and legs. Brush the turkey all over with olive oil and season generously with salt and pepper. Brush the garlic heads with olive oil and arrange cut side down around the turkey.

3. Roast the turkey and garlic for about 1 hour and 20 minutes, until an instant-read thermometer inserted in the thickest part of the turkey breast registers 160°. Transfer the turkey to a carving board and let rest for 30 minutes. Transfer the garlic to a platter. Pour any pan juice into a bowl and skim off the fat.

4. Carve the dark meat Using a large thin knife, cut through the skin that connects one breast half and one of the legs. Pull the leg away from the carcass to expose the ball joint (the joint that connects the leg to the body) and then cut through the joint to release the leg. Cut between the thigh and drumstick to separate them. Put the thigh skin side down on a work surface and, using the tip of your knife, cut around the thighbone to remove it. Flip the thigh meat skin side up and thickly slice the meat across the grain. Transfer the thigh meat and drumsticks to a platter and tent with foil. Repeat with the remaining leg.

5. Carve the breast Using a large thin knife, cut downward along one side of the breastbone, using your other hand to help pull the breast half off the bone in one piece. Transfer the breast half to a carving board and then repeat the process to remove the other breast half. Thickly slice the breast halves crosswise and transfer to the platter. Serve the turkey with the roasted garlic and pan drippings.
—*Justin Chapple*

MAKE AHEAD Arrange the carved turkey in a large baking dish. Drizzle with 1 cup of turkey or chicken stock along with any pan juices. Cover tightly with foil and refrigerate overnight. Let stand 30 minutes, then reheat for 20 to 30 minutes in a 375° oven, until hot; remove the foil the last 5 minutes.

Clementine-and-Garlic Roast Turkey

◯ PAGE 118

Active **1 hr**; Total **4 hr 30 min**; Serves **10**

1½ **sticks unsalted butter, softened**
6 **clementines, zested (1½ Tbsp.) and halved crosswise**
4 **large garlic cloves, finely grated, plus 6 whole garlic heads, halved crosswise**
2 **tsp. finely chopped thyme, plus 10 sprigs**
One 12- to 14-lb. turkey, rinsed and patted dry
Kosher salt and pepper
2 **cups chicken stock or low-sodium broth**

1. In a medium bowl, blend the butter with the clementine zest, grated garlic and chopped thyme. Run your fingers under the turkey breast and thigh skin to loosen it, then spread the butter mixture under and over the skin of the breast and thighs. Season the turkey inside and out with salt and pepper. Transfer to a rack set in a roasting pan and let come to room temperature, about 1 hour.

2. Preheat the oven to 400°. Roast the turkey for about 30 minutes, until lightly browned. Add the chicken stock to the roasting pan and roast for 30 minutes. Scatter the clementine halves, garlic heads and thyme sprigs in the pan. Roast for about 1 hour longer, rotating the pan a few times, until an instant-read thermometer inserted in the inner thigh registers 165°. Transfer the turkey to a cutting board; let rest for 30 minutes. Transfer the clementines, garlic heads and thyme to a plate, tent with foil and keep warm.

3. Meanwhile, skim the fat off the pan juices and transfer the juices to a medium saucepan. Squeeze the roasted garlic from 1 head and whisk into the pan juices. Bring to a boil over moderately high heat and cook, whisking frequently, until slightly reduced, about 5 minutes. Season the roasted garlic jus with salt and pepper. Carve the turkey and transfer to a platter. Arrange the roasted clementines, garlic heads and thyme around the carved turkey and serve with the jus. —*Justin Chapple*

SERVE WITH Roasted Cranberry-Grape Sauce (p. 368); Roasted Vegetables with Smashed-Walnut Vinaigrette (p. 218); Sourdough Stuffing (p. 267).

MAKE AHEAD The seasoned uncooked turkey can be refrigerated overnight. Bring to room temperature before roasting

WINE Citrusy, full-bodied white: 2016 Dry Creek Vineyard Dry Chenin Blanc.

Spicy Coconut Chicken Stew with Corn

◔ Total **30 min**; Serves **4**

2 **Tbsp. canola oil**
3 **shallots, thinly sliced**
2 **fresh Thai chiles, thinly sliced**
One 15-oz. can unsweetened coconut milk
½ **cup chicken stock or low-sodium broth**
¼ **cup fresh lime juice**
Kosher salt and pepper
1 **lb. shredded rotisserie chicken (4 cups)**
1½ **cups fresh corn kernels (from 2 to 3 ears)**
3 **cups spinach leaves**
1 **cup basil leaves, plus more for serving**

In a large, deep skillet, heat the oil. Add the shallots and chiles and cook over moderate heat, stirring occasionally, until tender, about 5 minutes. Add the coconut milk, stock and lime juice and bring just to a simmer. Season the broth generously with salt and pepper. Stir in the chicken and corn and cook until hot, 3 to 5 minutes. Stir in the spinach and simmer until just wilted, then stir in the 1 cup of basil. Transfer to shallow bowls, garnish with basil and serve. —*Justin Chapple*

Spatchcocked Turkey with Pink Peppercorns and Thyme

Active **30 min**; Total **2 hr 15 min**
Serves **10 to 12**

This turkey from cookbook author and TV cook Ayesha Curry is moist and juicy, with wonderful crisp skin, because it's spatchcocked (the backbone is removed and the bird is flattened before cooking), which allows it to cook evenly. Ask your butcher to spatchcock your turkey for you.

- 1 **large onion, thinly sliced into rounds**
- 2 **celery ribs, thinly sliced**
- 2 **carrots, thinly sliced**
- 2 **Tbsp. finely ground pink peppercorns**
- 2 **Tbsp. dried thyme**
- 2 **Tbsp. crushed dried rosemary**
- 2 **tsp. garlic powder**
-    **One 10- to 12-lb. turkey, spatchcocked (have your butcher do this), rinsed and patted dry**
-    **Extra-virgin olive oil, for brushing**
-    **Kosher salt and black pepper**
- ¼ **cup fresh blood orange juice**

1. Spread the onion, celery and carrots in an even layer on a large rimmed baking sheet. Put a flat baking rack on top. In a small bowl, mix the pink peppercorns with the thyme, rosemary and garlic powder.

2. Brush the turkey all over with olive oil and season generously with salt and pepper. Sprinkle the spice mixture all over the turkey. Set the bird breast side up on the rack and drizzle with the orange juice; let come to room temperature.

3. Meanwhile, preheat the oven to 450°. Roast the turkey for about 1 hour and 15 minutes, rotating the pan a few times, until an instant-read thermometer inserted in the inner thigh registers 165°; tent with foil if it browns too quickly. Transfer to a carving board and let rest for 30 minutes. Discard the onion, celery and carrots. Carve the turkey and serve. —*Ayesha Curry*

WINE Crisp, elegant Champagne: NV Taittinger Brut La Française.

Farmhouse Turkey Hot Dish

Active **1 hr**; Total **3 hr 40 min**; Serves **6 to 8**

"Hot dish" is Minnesotan for baked layers of starch, meat, vegetable and, typically, canned soup. In TV host and Twin Cities native Andrew Zimmern's version, crisp brown Tater Tots provide the starch. ("Nothing beats Tater Tots for this. Period," says the chef.) And the meat comes from freshly braised turkey legs, though 4 cups of shredded leftover meat would be excellent, too. Instead of the classic condensed mushroom soup, however, Zimmern makes a velouté sauce with the turkey braising liquid and sautéed mushrooms and aromatic vegetables.

- 2 **whole turkey legs, cut into thighs and drumsticks (4 lbs.)**
- 2 **qts. chicken stock or low-sodium broth**
- 7 **Tbsp. unsalted butter**
- 2 **small carrots, chopped**
- 1 **celery rib, thinly sliced**
- ½ **small onion, chopped**
- ¼ **fennel bulb, chopped**
- 1 **tsp. dried thyme**
-    **Pinch of freshly grated nutmeg**
- ¼ **cup all-purpose flour**
- ½ **cup heavy cream**
- ½ **cup thawed frozen peas**
- ¼ **cup minced parsley**
-    **Kosher salt and pepper**
- ½ **lb. mixed mushrooms, such as shiitake caps, cremini, white button, chanterelle and oyster, thinly sliced (3 cups)**
- 2 **leeks, white and light green parts only, halved lengthwise and thinly sliced**
- ¼ **cup chopped tarragon**
-    **One 32-oz. bag frozen Tater Tots**
-    **Flaky sea salt**
-    **Hot sauce (optional)**

1. In a large saucepan, combine the turkey legs with the chicken stock and, if necessary, water to cover. Bring to a boil, then reduce the heat to moderately low and simmer until the meat is cooked through, about 1 hour. Using tongs, transfer the turkey to a cutting board and let cool. Simmer the stock over moderately high heat until reduced to 4 cups, about 20 to 40 minutes. Shred the meat and discard the skin and bones.

2. Preheat the oven to 425°. In a large pot, melt 4 tablespoons of the butter. Add the carrots, celery, onion, fennel, thyme and nutmeg and cook over moderately high heat, stirring occasionally, until lightly browned, about 5 minutes. Add the flour and cook, stirring, for 1 minute. Add the reduced stock, bring to a boil and cook, stirring occasionally, until the sauce is thickened, about 5 minutes. Add the turkey, cream, peas and parsley, season with kosher salt and pepper and cook over moderate heat, stirring occasionally, for 5 minutes. Spread in a 9-by-13-inch baking dish.

3. In a large skillet, melt the remaining 3 tablespoons of butter. Add the mushrooms and cook over moderately high heat, stirring occasionally, until browned, about 5 minutes. Add the leeks and cook, stirring occasionally, until softened, about 5 minutes. Stir in the tarragon. Spread the mushroom mixture over the turkey in the baking dish.

4. Spread the tots over the mushroom mixture. Bake for 45 minutes, until bubbling and golden. Sprinkle with sea salt and serve with hot sauce, if desired. —*Andrew Zimmern*

MAKE AHEAD The recipe can be prepared through Step 3 and refrigerated overnight.

WINE Robust, berry-rich Zinfandel: 2015 Seghesio Sonoma County.

Turkey Shwarma with
Cabbage Salad

Turkey Shwarma with Cabbage Salad

⏱ Total **45 min**; Serves **4**

- 2 cups lightly packed cilantro, plus more for garnish
- ½ medium head of Little Gem lettuce
- 1 jalapeño, stemmed and chopped
- 2 Tbsp. fresh lemon juice
- 1 large garlic clove
- ½ tsp. ground coriander
- ½ tsp. ground cumin
- ¾ cup extra-virgin olive oil
  Kosher salt
- ½ cup finely diced green cabbage
- ¼ cup finely diced Persian cucumber
- ¼ cup finely diced celery
- 1 Tbsp. finely chopped parsley, plus more for garnish
- ½ Tbsp. finely chopped dill, plus more for garnish
- 2 Tbsp. shwarma seasoning
- 1 cup prepared hummus
- 2 large, soft lavash flatbreads, halved crosswise
- 1 lb. leftover skin-on turkey breast, thinly sliced
- 2 dill pickles, quartered lengthwise (optional)

1. In a food processor, combine the 2 cups of cilantro with the lettuce, jalapeño, 1 tablespoon of the lemon juice, the garlic, coriander and cumin and pulse until finely chopped. With the machine on, gradually add ¼ cup of the olive oil and puree until smooth. Scrape the zhug into a small bowl and season with salt.

2. In a medium bowl, toss the cabbage with the cucumber, celery, the remaining 1 tablespoon of lemon juice, 2 tablespoons of the olive oil, the 1 tablespoon of parsley and ½ tablespoon of dill. Season with salt.

3. In a small bowl, whisk the shwarma seasoning with the remaining ¼ cup plus 2 tablespoons of olive oil.

4. Spread ¼ cup of the hummus on each lavash half. Top with the turkey, some of the zhug, the cabbage salad and, if desired, pickles. Drizzle with some of the shwarma oil and garnish with cilantro, parsley and dill. Roll up the sandwiches and serve with the remaining zhug and shwarma oil.
—*Jenn Louis*

Duck B'steeya

Active **45 min**; Total **3 hr**; Serves **6**

- One 2½-inch cinnamon stick
- 2 star anise pods
- 4 dried red chiles
- One 4-inch piece of fresh turmeric, cut into 4 pieces
- 1 tsp. whole cloves
- 1 tsp. mustard seeds
- ½ tsp. allspice berries
- One 4½- to 5-lb. young duck, cut into 2 breasts, 2 legs and 2 wings
- 3 small yellow onions, minced (3 cups)
- 10 garlic cloves, smashed
  Kosher salt and pepper
- 1 cup tawny port wine
- 5 cups low-sodium chicken broth
- 1 stick unsalted butter
- 2 Tbsp. brown sugar
- 1 cup sliced almonds
- 1 Tbsp. ground cinnamon mixed with 2 Tbsp. granulated sugar
- ⅛ tsp. cayenne
- ½ cup dried currants
- 1 tsp. ground coriander
- ¼ tsp. freshly grated nutmeg
- ⅛ tsp. saffron
- 4 large eggs, lightly beaten
- 7 thin frozen phyllo sheets (No. 4), thawed
  Confectioners' sugar, for garnish

1. In a 7-inch cheesecloth square, tie the cinnamon stick with the star anise, chiles, turmeric, cloves, mustard seeds and allspice.

2. In a large enameled cast-iron casserole, cook the duck breasts skin side down over moderately low heat, spooning off the fat, until golden and crisp, about 20 minutes. Transfer the breasts to a plate. Add the legs and wings skin side down and cook until golden, about 6 minutes. Transfer to the plate.

3. Pour off all but 2 tablespoons of fat from the casserole. Add 1 cup of the onions and the garlic, season with salt and pepper and cook over moderate heat, stirring occasionally, until softened, about 5 minutes. Add the port and cook until reduced by half, about 4 minutes. Add the broth, duck pieces and spice bundle, cover and cook until the duck is tender, about 40 minutes. Using a slotted spoon, transfer the duck breasts and legs to a plate to cool; leave the wings in the pot. Increase the heat to moderately high and simmer the broth until reduced to 1 cup, about 15 minutes. Strain into a small heatproof bowl; reserve. Shred the duck meat and skin. Remove any bones and cartilage.

4. In a medium saucepan, melt 2 tablespoons of the butter with the brown sugar over moderate heat, about 1 minute. Stir in the almonds, 1 tablespoon of the cinnamon sugar and the cayenne and transfer to a plate. In the same pan, melt 2 tablespoons of the butter. Add the remaining 2 cups of onions and cook over moderate heat, stirring occasionally, until caramelized, about 15 minutes. Stir in the almond mixture, currants, coriander, nutmeg, saffron, shredded duck and eggs. Slowly add the reserved 1 cup of broth, stirring, and cook until the eggs are set and the mixture is moist, about 5 minutes. Season the filling with salt and pepper.

5. Meanwhile, preheat the oven to 400°. In a small saucepan, melt the remaining 4 tablespoons of butter. Brush a 10-inch pie plate with some of the melted butter. Unroll the phyllo sheets and cover with plastic wrap and a damp kitchen towel to keep them from drying out. Working with 1 phyllo sheet at a time, press it into the pie plate, leaving about 2 inches of overhang, and brush lightly with melted butter. Repeat with the remaining 6 sheets, layering and rotating each sheet slightly. Sprinkle the bottom with 1 tablespoon of the cinnamon sugar. Spread the duck filling in the prepared pie shell and sprinkle with the remaining 1 tablespoon of cinnamon sugar. Fold the phyllo over the filling and brush the top with the remaining melted butter. Bake for 25 to 30 minutes, until golden and crisp. Let the pie cool for 10 minutes. Dust the top with confectioners' sugar and serve.
—*Andrew Zimmern*

WINE Smoky Moroccan Cabernet blend: 2012 Ouled Thaleb Médaillon.

Saffron Butter–Basted Poussins with Apples (Joojeh ba Sib)

Active **30 min**; Total **1 hr 30 min**; Serves **8**

These tender, juicy little birds develop deliciously crisp and golden skin when brushed and basted with fragrant saffron butter. Roasting them alongside shallots and apples creates an easy, built-in side dish.

- 1 **stick unsalted butter**
- 1 **tsp. saffron, finely ground**
- **Eight 1-lb. poussins**
- **Kosher salt and pepper**
- 4 **small baking apples, such as Gala, halved and cored**
- 8 **medium shallots, halved lengthwise**
- ¼ **cup extra-virgin olive oil**

1. Preheat the oven to 425°. In a small saucepan, melt the butter. Remove from the heat, whisk in the saffron and let stand for 5 minutes.

2. Season the poussins all over and inside the cavities with salt and pepper, then tie the legs together with kitchen string. Transfer to 2 large rimmed baking sheets and brush with some of the saffron butter.

3. In a large bowl, toss the apples and shallots with the olive oil and season generously with salt and pepper. Scatter the apples and shallots around the poussins on the baking sheets. Roast for about 1 hour, basting occasionally with the saffron butter, until the juices from the cavities of the poussins run clear and the apples and shallots are tender; rotate the baking sheets halfway through roasting. Transfer the poussins, apples and shallots to plates or a platter and serve. —*Mahin Gilanpour Motamed*

WINE Rich, apple-scented Rhône white blend: 2015 Michel Gassier Nostre Païs.

Goose Stuffed with Apples and Armagnac-Soaked Prunes

Active **1 hr**; Total **4 hr 50 min**; Serves **8**

Cookbook author Nadine Levy Redzepi soaks prunes in Armagnac until they're superboozy and plump, then combines them with apples and garlic to create an elegant stuffing for roast goose. If boozy flavors aren't your thing, you can soak the prunes for as little as two hours.

- ½ **lb. pitted prunes, halved**
- 1 **cup Armagnac**
- **One 9-lb. goose—neck reserved, giblets finely chopped, goose at room temperature**
- 3 **Granny Smith apples, cored and cut into ¾-inch pieces**
- 6 **garlic cloves, peeled**
- **Canola oil**
- **Kosher salt and pepper**
- ½ **cup boiling water**
- 2 **cups chicken stock or low-sodium broth**
- 1 **cup heavy cream**
- 2 **Tbsp. sherry vinegar**
- 2 **Tbsp. currant jelly**

1. In a small bowl, combine the prunes with the Armagnac. Cover and refrigerate for at least 2 hours or for up to 1 week. Drain the prunes well and reserve the liquid for another use.

2. Preheat the oven to 325°. Using paper towels, pat the goose completely dry outside and inside. In a large bowl, toss the prunes with the apples and garlic. Stuff the goose with the fruit and tie the legs together with twine. Generously rub the goose with oil and season all over with salt. Transfer the goose breast side up to a rack set in a roasting pan. Place the neck in the bottom of the roasting pan. Roast for 40 minutes, then remove the pan from the oven. Carefully tilt the pan and spoon the fat into a small heatproof bowl.

3. Return the goose to the oven and increase the temperature to 350°. Roast for 50 minutes. Remove the pan from the oven again. Carefully tilt the pan and spoon the fat into the bowl. Remove the goose neck and reserve for snacking, if desired.

4. Return the goose to the oven and increase the temperature to 400°. Roast for about 40 minutes longer, until the skin is golden brown and an instant-read thermometer inserted in the inner thigh registers 160°. Transfer the goose to a work surface, tent with foil and keep warm. Pour the boiling water into the pan and scrape up any bits on the bottom using a wooden spoon. Pour the pan juices into a heatproof bowl.

5. In a medium saucepan, heat 2 tablespoons of the reserved goose fat over high heat. Add the giblets and cook until browned, about 1 minute. Add the chicken stock and the reserved pan juices and bring to a boil. Reduce the heat to low and simmer for 5 minutes. Add the cream and simmer for 3 minutes. Stir in the vinegar and currant jelly and season with salt and pepper. Strain the gravy into a gravy bowl or small pitcher. Carve the goose and transfer to a platter. Spoon the prunes and apples into a serving bowl and serve with the gravy.—*Nadine Levy Redzepi*

WINE Savory white Burgundy: 2015 Domaine Henri Boillot Meursault.

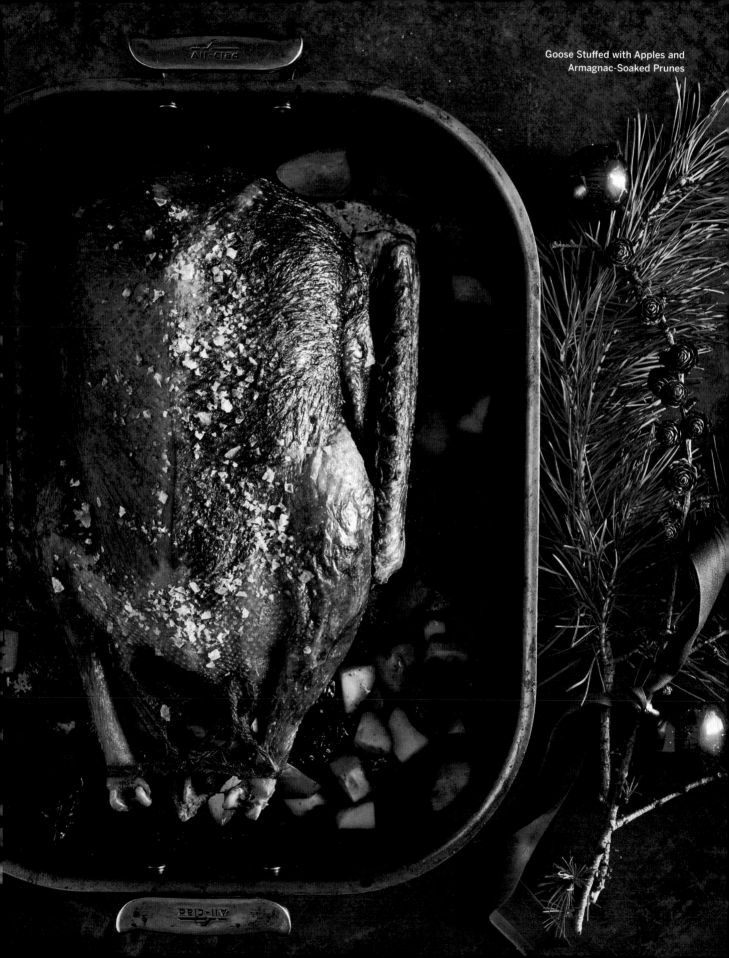

Goose Stuffed with Apples and Armagnac-Soaked Prunes

PORK & VEAL

Pork Chops with
Sunflower Seed
Gremolata (p. 160)
OPPOSITE Pork
Loin Stuffed with
Apples and Pumpkin
Seeds (p. 162).

Ham-Brined Pork Chops

Active **50 min;** Total **1 hr 15 min plus overnight brining;** Serves **4**

For incredibly juicy pork chops, chef Chris Shepherd of Underbelly in Houston soaks them overnight in a classic ham brine with honey and mustard seeds.

- **4** cups warm water
- ½ cup honey
- ⅓ cup kosher salt, plus more for seasoning
- ½ Tbsp. black peppercorns
- ½ Tbsp. yellow mustard seeds
  Four 12-oz. bone-in pork rib chops, 1-inch thick
- **1** pint cherry tomatoes
- **4** medium shallots, halved
- **3** Tbsp. extra-virgin olive oil
  Pepper
- **2** Tbsp. sherry vinegar
- 2½ Tbsp. canola oil
- ½ lb. sugar snap peas, trimmed
- ½ medium red onion, thinly sliced
- ⅓ cup chopped parsley
- **2** Tbsp. minced chives

1. In a large bowl, whisk the warm water with the honey, ⅓ cup of salt, the peppercorns and mustard seeds until the honey and salt are dissolved; let cool completely. Add the pork chops to the brine, cover and refrigerate overnight. Bring to room temperature in the brine 30 minutes before cooking.

2. Preheat the oven to 400°. On a large rimmed baking sheet, toss the tomatoes with the shallots and 1 tablespoon of the olive oil and season with salt and pepper. Roast for about 15 minutes, until the tomatoes start to wrinkle and the shallots are tender and lightly browned. Let cool completely. Increase the oven temperature to 425°.

3. In a large bowl, whisk the vinegar with 2 tablespoons of the canola oil and the remaining 2 tablespoons of olive oil. Season the vinaigrette with salt and pepper. Prepare an ice bath. In a medium saucepan of salted boiling water, cook the snap peas until crisp-tender, about 1 minute. Drain and transfer to the ice bath. Once the snap peas are cool, drain well, pat dry and transfer to the bowl with the vinaigrette. Gently fold in the tomatoes, shallots, onion, parsley and chives and season with salt.

4. Remove the pork chops from the brine and thoroughly pat dry with paper towels; discard the brine. Heat a large cast-iron skillet, then add the remaining ½ tablespoon of canola oil. Cook 2 pork chops over moderate heat, turning once, until browned, about 6 minutes. Transfer to a plate and repeat with the remaining 2 pork chops. Drain off any excess fat from the skillet. Return the pork chops to the skillet and roast in the oven for 8 to 10 minutes, until an instant-read thermometer inserted in the thickest part registers 135°. Transfer the pork chops to a work surface and let rest for 5 minutes. Serve with the snap pea salad. —*Chris Shepherd*

WINE Bright California Pinot Noir: 2013 Onward Hawkeye Ranch Pinot Noir.

Pork Chops with Sunflower Seed Gremolata

📷 PAGE 159

🕐 Total **30 min;** Serves **4**

  Four 12-oz. bone-in pork rib chops, 1½ inches thick
  Kosher salt and pepper
- **1** Tbsp. canola oil
- ½ cup finely chopped parsley
- ¼ cup roasted salted sunflower seeds
- **1** garlic clove, finely grated
- **1** lemon, zested and cut into wedges for serving

1. Heat a large cast-iron skillet. Season the pork chops all over with salt and pepper. Add the oil to the skillet and swirl to coat. Add the pork chops and cook over moderately high heat, turning occasionally, until browned and an instant-read thermometer inserted in the thickest part registers 135°, 12 to 14 minutes. Transfer to a plate and let rest for 5 minutes.

2. Meanwhile, in a medium bowl, mix the parsley with the sunflower seeds, garlic and lemon zest. Season the gremolata with salt and pepper. Serve the pork chops with lemon wedges and the gremolata. —*Justin Chapple*

WINE Spicy rosé: 2016 Tablas Creek Vineyard Patelin de Tablas.

Pork Chops with Cherry-Miso Mostarda

Active **30 min;** Total **50 min;** Serves **4**

A bit of umami-rich miso is added to a cherry mostarda to amp up the flavor, making a perfect condiment for juicy pork chops.

- **1** Tbsp. canola oil, plus more for brushing
- **1** shallot, minced
- **1** garlic clove, minced
- **1** cup dried sour cherries (5 oz.)
- ¼ cup light brown sugar
- ¼ cup unseasoned rice vinegar
- **2** Tbsp. white miso
- 1½ Tbsp. whole-grain mustard
  Kosher salt and pepper
  Four 10-oz. bone-in pork chops, about 1¼ inches thick

1. In a small saucepan, heat the 1 tablespoon of oil. Add the shallot and garlic; cook over moderate heat, stirring, until softened, about 3 minutes. Add the cherries, sugar, vinegar, miso, mustard and ½ cup of water; bring to a boil. Simmer over moderate heat, stirring occasionally, until the cherries are coated in a sauce, about 8 minutes. Season with salt and pepper. Scrape into a bowl and let cool; stir in a little water if too thick.

2. Heat a large cast-iron skillet. Brush the pork with oil and season generously with salt and pepper. Add the pork to the skillet and cook over moderate heat, turning once, until browned and an instant-read thermometer inserted in each piece near the bone registers 135°, 12 to 15 minutes. Transfer the pork chops to plates or a platter and let rest for 5 minutes. Serve with the mostarda. —*Justin Chapple*

MAKE AHEAD The cherry-miso mostarda can be refrigerated for up to 5 days. Bring to room temperature before serving.

WINE Cherry-scented, Merlot-based Bordeaux: 2015 Les Trois Croix Fronsac.

Pork Chops with
Cherry-Miso Mostarda

Citrus-Chile-Marinated Pork Tenderloin

Total **30 min** plus overnight marinating; Serves **8**

Let your pork sit in the orange juice, garlic and chile mixture overnight, then cook down the leftover marinade for the sauce.

- ¾ **cup fresh orange juice, plus 1 orange sliced into thin rounds**
- 2 **Tbsp. tomato paste**
- 2 **Tbsp. Dijon mustard**
- 3 **garlic cloves, minced**
- 1 **Fresno chile—halved, seeded and minced**
- 2 **Tbsp. muscovado or dark brown sugar**
- 1 **Tbsp. smoked paprika**
- 1 **Tbsp. Worcestershire sauce**
- 3 **pork tenderloins (about 3 lbs.)**
  Canola oil, for brushing
  Kosher salt and pepper
  Parsley, for garnish

1. In a large bowl, whisk the orange juice, tomato paste, mustard, garlic, chile, sugar, paprika and Worcestershire. Add the pork, cover and refrigerate overnight. Bring to room temperature before grilling.

2. Light a grill or preheat a grill pan and oil the grate. Remove the pork from the marinade and season with salt and pepper. Reserve the marinade. Grill the pork over moderately high heat, turning, until charred and an instant-read thermometer inserted into the thickest part registers 135°, about 20 minutes. Transfer to a work surface and let rest for 10 minutes. Keep the grill on.

3. Meanwhile, brush the orange rounds with oil and grill, turning once, until charred, about 4 minutes. Transfer to the work surface with the pork.

4. Scrape the marinade into a saucepan and bring to a boil. Cook until heated through and reduced slightly, 2 to 3 minutes.

5. Cut the pork into thick slices and arrange on a platter with the grilled orange rounds. Drizzle with the sauce and garnish with parsley; serve. —*José Catrimán*

WINE Smoky Mallorcan old-vine red: 2014 Ànima Negra ÀN/2.

Skillet Pork Tenderloin with Mustard and Smoked Paprika

Total **30 min**; Serves **4 to 6**

- 2 **Tbsp. Dijon mustard**
- 1½ **tsp. smoked paprika (hot or sweet)**
- 1 **tsp. kosher salt**
  Two 1-lb. pork tenderloins
- 2 **Tbsp. extra-virgin olive oil**

1. Preheat the oven to 425°. In a small bowl, stir the Dijon with the paprika and salt. Spread the mixture all over the pork.

2. In a large ovenproof skillet, heat the olive oil over moderately high heat. Add the tenderloins and cook until browned on the bottoms, about 5 minutes. Flip the pork and transfer the skillet to the oven. Roast for 15 to 20 minutes, until an instant-read thermometer inserted into the thickest part registers 135°. Transfer to a work surface and let rest for 10 minutes, then cut the pork into thick slices and serve. —*Julia Turshen*

WINE Smoky Ribera del Duero red: 2012 Condado de Haza Crianza.

Pork Loin Stuffed with Apples and Pumpkin Seeds

PAGE 158

Active **1 hr**; Total **3 hr**; Serves **8 to 10**

- ¼ **cup extra-virgin olive oil**
- 1 **cup finely chopped onion**
- 6 **garlic cloves, finely chopped**
- 2 **Fuji apples—peeled, cored and cut into ¼-inch dice**
- ¼ **cup plus 2 Tbsp. apple cider vinegar**
- 4 **oz. rye bread, cut into ¼-inch cubes and toasted**
- ¼ **cup pumpkin seeds, lightly toasted**
- 2 **Tbsp. chopped parsley**
  Kosher salt and pepper
  One 3½-lb. pork loin—skin removed and reserved, meat butterflied ½ inch thick (have your butcher do this)
- 8 **Lady apples, halved crosswise and seeded**
  Unrefined pumpkin seed oil, for drizzling

1. In a large skillet, heat 2 tablespoons of the olive oil. Add the onion and garlic and cook over moderately high heat, stirring, until soft and light golden, about 3 minutes. Stir in the diced apples and ¼ cup of the apple cider vinegar and boil over moderately high heat until the liquid is reduced by half, about 2 minutes. Transfer to a large bowl and stir in the toasted bread cubes along with the pumpkin seeds and parsley. Season the stuffing with salt and pepper.

2. Using a sharp knife, score the pork skin at ¼-inch intervals. Lay the pork loin butterflied side up on a work surface and season with salt and pepper. Spread the stuffing over the pork loin, then roll up the meat, leaving the seam on top. Drape the pork skin over the seam. Using kitchen twine, tightly tie the loin at 1-inch intervals. Season with salt and pepper, wrap in plastic and refrigerate for at least 1 hour or up to 24 hours.

3. Preheat the oven to 475°. In a large bowl, toss the Lady apples with the remaining 2 tablespoons each of cider vinegar and olive oil.

4. Unwrap the pork and transfer skin side up to a rimmed baking sheet. Roast for 20 minutes, until the skin is browned and bubbly. Reduce the oven temperature to 325° and roast for 25 minutes more. Scatter the Lady apples around the pork and scrape any liquid from the bowl over them. Continue to roast the pork for about 20 minutes longer, until an instant-read thermometer inserted in the center of the meat registers 140°.

5. Transfer the pork to a cutting board and set the apples on a platter. Scrape the pan drippings into a small bowl. Let the pork rest for 15 minutes, then discard the strings. Thickly slice the pork and transfer to the platter. Drizzle with the pan drippings and pumpkin seed oil and serve. —*Laura Rege*

MAKE AHEAD The pork can be prepared through Step 3 and refrigerated overnight.

WINE Dry, full-bodied Riesling from Alsace: 2015 Domaine Zind-Humbrecht.

Roast Pork with Fingerlings and Grapes

Active **20 min;** Total **50 min;** Serves **4**

An elegant dinner is easy when using tenderloin. Here, you roast the meat alongside potatoes and juicy red grapes for a super one-pan meal.

- 1 lb. fingerling potatoes, halved lengthwise
- 6 thyme sprigs
- ¼ cup extra-virgin olive oil, plus more for brushing

  Kosher salt and pepper

  One 1¼-lb. pork tenderloin
- 1 lb. red seedless grapes on the stem
- 8 large garlic cloves, halved lengthwise

1. Preheat the oven to 450°. On a large rimmed baking sheet, toss the potatoes and thyme sprigs with 3 tablespoons of the olive oil and season with salt and pepper. Roast for 10 minutes, until just starting to brown.

2. On a work surface, brush the pork all over with olive oil and season with salt and pepper. Drizzle the grapes and garlic with the remaining 1 tablespoon of olive oil and season with salt and pepper. Add the pork, grapes and garlic to the baking sheet with the potatoes. Roast for 20 to 25 minutes, until an instant-read thermometer inserted in the thickest part of the pork registers 135°.

3. Transfer the pork to a work surface and let rest for 10 minutes, then slice against the grain. Transfer the pork, fingerlings, grapes and garlic to a platter and serve. *—Justin Chapple*

WINE Bright, raspberry-fruity cru Beaujolais: 2015 Georges Duboeuf Clos des Quatres Vents Fleurie.

Pork Schnitzel with Cucumber Salad

Total **45 min;** Serves **4**

It takes only five minutes to turn lean pork tenderloin cutlets into crispy schnitzel. A bright salad of cucumber with dill and yogurt is a perfect accompaniment.

- 6 Persian cucumbers, sliced ½ inch thick

  Kosher salt and pepper
- ¼ cup finely chopped dill, plus small sprigs for garnish
- 1¾ cups whole-milk yogurt
- 1½ cups seasoned breadcrumbs

  One 1¼-lb. pork tenderloin, cut on the bias into 12 thin slices, about ¼ inch thick

  Canola oil, for frying

1. In a sieve, toss the cucumbers with 1 teaspoon of salt. Let stand for 15 minutes, then gently squeeze out the excess water. In a large bowl, mix the cucumbers with the chopped dill and ¼ cup of the yogurt and season with salt and pepper.

2. Meanwhile, put the breadcrumbs and the remaining 1½ cups of yogurt in 2 separate shallow bowls. Season the pork with salt and pepper and dip in the yogurt, letting the excess drip back into the bowl. Dredge in the breadcrumbs, pressing to flatten the pork and help the crumbs adhere.

3. In a large skillet, heat ¼ inch of oil until shimmering. In batches, add the pork in a single layer and cook over moderately high heat, turning once, until browned and crispy, about 5 minutes. Transfer to paper towels to drain. Serve the pork with the cucumber salad and garnish with small sprigs of dill. *—Justin Chapple*

WINE Lightly peppery Austrian red: 2013 Umathum Zweigelt.

Red Chile Pork and Celery Stir-Fry

Active **25 min;** Total **40 min;** Serves **4**

There's a surprise in this stir-fry: celery. F&W's Justin Chapple loves using it because he always has some in his fridge, and it gets deliciously crisp-tender in a speedy dish like this.

- One 1-lb. pork tenderloin, halved lengthwise and thinly sliced crosswise
- 3 Tbsp. soy sauce

  Kosher salt and pepper
- 3 Tbsp. canola oil
- 5 celery ribs, cut into 2-inch lengths and thinly sliced lengthwise
- 6 small dried hot red chiles

1. In a medium bowl, toss the pork with the soy sauce and season generously with pepper. Refrigerate for 15 minutes.

2. Heat a large cast-iron skillet until smoking, then add 1 tablespoon of the oil. Add the pork and cook over high heat, undisturbed, until browned on the bottom, about 2 minutes. Stir-fry until the pork is just cooked through, about 2 minutes more. Transfer to a plate.

3. In the skillet, heat the remaining 2 tablespoons of oil until shimmering. Add the celery and chiles and stir-fry over high heat until the celery is crisp-tender, 2 to 3 minutes. Return the pork to the skillet, season with salt and pepper and toss to combine. Serve immediately. *—Justin Chapple*

SERVE WITH Steamed rice.

WINE Rich, spicy Alsace white: 2014 Hugel Pinot Gris Classic.

Pork Tamales

Hawaiian Pork Bowl

Total **40 min plus 1 hr marinating; Serves 4**

Sweet tea is an ideal marinade for pork because its sugars help to caramelize the meat as it cooks. The pork stars in these satisfying rice bowls, along with grilled pineapple, red onion and a bright lime dressing.

- 1 **cup boiling water**
- ¼ **cup sugar**
- 2 **English breakfast tea bags**

  One 1-lb. pork tenderloin, butterflied and flattened

  Three ½-inch-thick slices of fresh pineapple—peeled, quartered and cored
- 1 **red onion, cut through the core into ¼-inch wedges**
- ⅓ **cup extra-virgin olive oil, plus more for brushing**

  Kosher salt and pepper
- ¼ **cup fresh lime juice**
- 2 **Tbsp. minced cilantro, plus sprigs for serving**

  Steamed rice, crisp bacon, diced avocado and thinly sliced jalapeño, for serving

1. In a large heatproof bowl, combine the boiling water, sugar and tea bags and let stand for 5 minutes. Discard the tea bags and stir the tea to dissolve the sugar. Let cool completely, then add the pork and refrigerate for 1 hour.

2. Light a grill or preheat a grill pan. Drain the pork and pat dry with paper towels. Brush the pork, pineapple and red onion with olive oil and season with salt and pepper. Grill the pork over high heat, turning once, until lightly charred and an instant-read thermometer inserted in the meat registers 135°, about 7 minutes. Transfer to a carving board and let rest for 5 minutes, then slice the pork against the grain. Meanwhile, grill the pineapple and onion, turning once, until charred, about 4 minutes.

3. In a small bowl, whisk the lime juice with the minced cilantro and the ⅓ cup of olive oil. Season the dressing with salt and pepper. Serve the pork, pineapple and onion over steamed rice with crisp bacon, diced avocado, sliced jalapeño. cilantro sprigs, and the lime dressing. —*Justin Chapple*

BEER Hoppy lager: Victory Prima Pils.

Pork Tamales

Active **1 hr 45 min** Total **4 hr 30 min;** Makes **32**

Most definitely worth it: Dried-chile salsa adds intense flavor to the braised pork so it doesn't get lost next to the supple, crumbly masa filling.

- ¼ **cup plus 2 Tbsp. extra-virgin olive oil**
- 1¼ **lbs. boneless pork shoulder, cut into 1-inch pieces**

  Kosher salt and pepper
- 2 **bay leaves**
- 32 **dried corn husks**
- 1 **medium onion, finely diced**
- 3 **garlic cloves, minced**
- 5 **dried ancho chiles—stemmed, seeded and torn into large pieces**
- 3 **dried guajillo chiles—stemmed, seeded and torn into large pieces**
- 3 **dried pasilla chiles—stemmed, seeded and torn into large pieces**
- 1 **tsp. coriander seeds**
- 1 **tsp. dried thyme**
- 1 **tsp. dried oregano**
- ½ **tsp. cumin seeds**
- 3½ **cups chicken stock or low-sodium broth**
- ½ **Tbsp. apple cider vinegar**
- 1½ **cups vegetable shortening**
- 4 **cups masa harina**
- 2 **tsp. baking powder**

1. In a large enameled cast-iron casserole, heat ¼ cup of the olive oil. Season the pork with salt and black pepper. Working in 2 batches, cook the pork over high heat until browned on all sides, 12 minutes total. Add the bay leaves and 3 cups of water, partially cover and bring to a boil. Reduce the heat to low and cook until the pork is tender, about 2½ hours. Using a slotted spoon, transfer the pork to a work surface and let cool slightly. Shred with 2 forks.

2. Meanwhile, bring a large pot of water to a boil. Add the corn husks, remove the pot from the heat and let stand, turning the husks once or twice, until softened, about 15 minutes. Drain the corn husks and shake off as much water as possible.

3. In a large skillet, heat the remaining 2 tablespoons of olive oil. Add the onion and garlic and cook, stirring occasionally, until softened, about 5 minutes. Add the ancho, guajillo and pasilla chiles, the coriander, thyme, oregano, cumin and 2 teaspoons of black pepper and cook, stirring, until fragrant and toasted, about 2 minutes. Stir in 1½ cups of the stock, season with salt and bring to a boil. Simmer over moderate heat until the liquid is nearly evaporated, about 15 minutes. Transfer the mixture to a blender. Add the vinegar and puree at high speed until smooth. Scrape the sauce into a large bowl and toss with the shredded pork. Season with salt.

4. In a stand mixer fitted with the paddle, beat the shortening until smooth, about 1 minute. Add the remaining 2 cups of stock, the masa, baking powder and ½ tablespoon of salt and beat at low speed until the masa dough is well combined.

5. Arrange 1 husk on a work surface with the narrow end pointing away from you. On the wide end, spread 2 tablespoons of the masa dough in a 4-by-3-inch rectangle, leaving a ½-inch border at the bottom. Spoon 2 tablespoons of the pork mixture in the center of the masa dough. Fold in the long sides of the husk, overlapping them to enclose the filling. Fold the narrow end over the filling. Tie closed with a strip of husk; it will be open at the wide end. Place the tamale in a large steamer insert. Repeat with the remaining corn husks, masa dough and pork.

6. Fill a steamer with 4 inches of water and bring to a boil. Set the steamer insert on top and cover with the lid; wrap foil around the edge if necessary to make a tight seal. Steam the tamales over moderately low heat for about 40 minutes. Uncover and let cool for 15 minutes before serving. —*Lorena Herrera*

MAKE AHEAD The tamales can be assembled and refrigerated for up to 5 days or frozen for up to 1 month; steam them while still frozen.

WINE Intense, mocha-scented Cabernet Sauvignon: 2013 Mi Sueño Napa Valley.

Braised Pork Shanks with Grilled Peach Salad

Active **1 hr 30 min** Total **5 hr plus overnight marinating; Serves 6**

PORK

- ¼ cup lightly packed thyme leaves, chopped, plus 6 thyme sprigs
- 2 Tbsp. packed light brown sugar
- 1½ Tbsp. kosher salt
- 1 Tbsp. ground allspice
- 1 tsp. black pepper
- 1 tsp. crushed red pepper
- 1 tsp. onion powder
- 1 tsp. garlic powder
- ¼ tsp. ground cinnamon
- ¼ tsp. ground cloves
- ¼ tsp. ground cumin
- ¼ cup plus 2 Tbsp. canola oil
- 6 pork shanks (about 1½ lbs. each)
- 4 medium yellow onions, halved and thinly sliced lengthwise
- 1 cup dry white wine
- 2 qts. chicken stock or low-sodium broth
- 2 large rosemary sprigs
- 2 bay leaves

SALAD

- 8 peaches, halved and pitted
- ½ cup extra-virgin olive oil
  Kosher salt and pepper
- 1 pint cherry tomatoes, halved
- 1 small English cucumber, diced
- 1 medium red onion, thinly sliced
- ¼ cup Champagne vinegar
- 1 cup each lightly packed mint and basil leaves

1. Make the pork In a small bowl, whisk the chopped thyme with the brown sugar, salt and spices. Stir in 2 tablespoons of the canola oil until smooth. Rub the spice mixture all over the pork, then refrigerate overnight.

2. Preheat the oven to 300°. In a large pot, heat the remaining ¼ cup of canola oil until shimmering. Add half of the pork and cook over moderately high heat, turning occasionally, until browned all over, about 10 minutes. Transfer to a large roasting pan. Repeat with the remaining pork.

3. Add the yellow onions to the pot and cook, stirring occasionally, until softened and just starting to brown, about 8 minutes. Add the wine and cook, scraping the browned bits from the bottom of the pan, until nearly evaporated, about 3 minutes. Add the chicken stock, rosemary sprigs, bay leaves and thyme sprigs. Bring to a boil over high heat, then pour the mixture over the pork. Cover with foil, braise in the oven, turning every hour, until the pork is very tender, about 3 hours and 15 minutes. Let rest for 15 minutes.

4. Meanwhile, make the salad Light a grill or preheat a grill pan. In a large bowl, toss the peaches with ¼ cup of the olive oil and season with salt and pepper. Grill over high heat, turning once, until lightly charred on both sides, about 5 minutes total. Transfer to a work surface and let cool, then cut into small wedges.

5. In a large bowl, toss the peaches with the cherry tomatoes, cucumber, red onion, vinegar and the remaining ¼ cup of olive oil. Fold in the mint and basil leaves and season generously with salt and pepper. Serve with the pork. —*Nina Compton*

WINE Robust, fruity Grenache: 2015 Bonny Doon Clos de Gilroy.

Pork-and-Potato Curry

Active **35 min;** Total **1 hr 15 min;** Serves **4 to 6**

This deeply flavorful curry is one of the many delicious staff meals prepared by chef Katianna Hong at The Charter Oak restaurant in St. Helena, California. She makes the curry with pork stock, but a rich chicken stock is nice, too.

- 2 Tbsp. vegetable oil
- ⅓ cup finely chopped shallots
- 1 jalapeño, seeded and minced
- 4 garlic cloves, finely chopped
- 1 Tbsp. finely grated fresh ginger
  Kosher salt
- 2 tsp. crushed red pepper
- 1 cup dry white wine
- 1½ cups pork or chicken stock
- 2 Tbsp. packed dark brown sugar
- 1 Tbsp. Asian fish sauce
- 1 Tbsp. ground coriander
- 2 tsp. ground cumin
- 1 tsp. ground turmeric
- 1 tsp. ground cinnamon
- 2 kaffir lime leaves
- 2 lbs. boneless pork shoulder, cut into 1-inch pieces
- 1 lb. Yukon Gold potatoes, peeled and cut into 1½-inch pieces
  One 15-oz. can unsweetened coconut milk
- 3 Tbsp. fresh lime juice
  Cilantro, mint, Thai basil and sliced scallions, for garnish
  Steamed rice, for serving

1. In a large enameled cast-iron casserole, heat the oil until shimmering. Add the shallots, jalapeño, garlic, ginger and a generous pinch of salt. Cook over moderately high heat, stirring, until softened, about 3 minutes. Stir in the crushed red pepper and cook for 30 seconds. Add the wine and simmer until reduced by half, about 5 minutes.

2. Add the stock, brown sugar, fish sauce, coriander, cumin, turmeric, cinnamon and lime leaves to the casserole and bring to a boil. Stir in the pork, cover partially and simmer over moderately low heat until the pork is nearly tender, about 25 minutes. Stir in the potatoes, cover partially and simmer until the pork and potatoes are tender, about 20 minutes.

3. Stir the coconut milk and lime juice into the curry and bring to a boil. Season with salt. Discard the lime leaves. Garnish with cilantro, mint, Thai basil and sliced scallions and serve with steamed rice. —*Katianna Hong*

MAKE AHEAD The curry can be refrigerated overnight. Reheat gently.

WINE Full-bodied, spicy Gewürztraminer: 2016 Paul Blanck.

Pork-and-Potato Curry

Standing Pork Rib
Roast with Cracklings

Pork Shoulder Skewers

Total **1 hr plus 8 hr marinating;** Serves **6**

Instead of braising pork shoulder until tender, Sam Smith of Tusk in Portland, Oregon, marinates thin slices of the meat to boost flavor, then skewers and grills it until melting and juicy within and nicely charred on the outside.

- **2 cups lightly packed cilantro, plus more for garnish**
- **1 cup lightly packed parsley**
- **1 medium onion, chopped**
- **5 garlic cloves, chopped**
- **½ cup extra-virgin olive oil**
- **1 Tbsp. ground cumin**
- **2 tsp. hot smoked paprika**
- **2 tsp. ground fennel**
- **2 tsp. ground licorice root powder (optional; see Note)**
- **Kosher salt**
- **2 lbs. well-trimmed pork shoulder, frozen for 30 minutes, then cut into ⅛-inch-thick strips**
- **Twenty-four 8-inch wooden skewers, soaked in water for 1 hour**
- **Citrus wedges, for serving**

1. In a food processor, puree the 2 cups of cilantro with the parsley, onion, garlic, olive oil, cumin, paprika, fennel, the licorice root powder, if using, and 1 tablespoon of salt until chunky. Reserve ½ cup of the marinade for basting; cover and refrigerate. In a large bowl, combine the remaining marinade with the pork and turn to coat. Cover and refrigerate for at least 8 hours or overnight.

2. Light a grill or preheat a grill pan. Thread the pork onto the skewers in a weaving motion so the meat is secure, then season lightly with salt. Grill over moderately high heat, turning occasionally and basting with the reserved marinade, until the pork is lightly charred and just cooked through, 6 to 8 minutes. Transfer the skewers to a platter, garnish with cilantro and serve with citrus wedges. —*Sam Smith*

NOTE Licorice root powder is available at health food stores and on amazon.com.

WINE Spicy Sardinian red: 2014 Argiolas Perdera.

Standing Pork Rib Roast with Cracklings

Active **20 min;** Total **7 hr plus overnight salting;** Serves **8**

- **One 8-rib pork loin roast with skin (about 5½ lbs.)—ribs frenched, skin scored at ½-inch intervals and tied**
- **½ cup kosher salt**

1. Place the pork loin on a rimmed baking sheet. Season generously all over with ¼ cup of the salt, then sprinkle the skin with the remaining ¼ cup of salt to create a thin layer of salt over it; be sure to push the salt into the crevices in the skin at each score. Refrigerate uncovered overnight.

2. Let the pork stand at room temperature for 3 hours. Preheat the oven to 275°. Set a rack in a large roasting pan. Using a damp towel, brush the excess salt off the roast, then transfer to the pan skin side up. Bake for about 1 hour and 30 minutes, until an instant-read thermometer inserted in the thickest part registers 115°.

3. Increase the heat to 450° and continue to roast for about 50 minutes longer, until the skin is crisp and an instant-read thermometer inserted in the thickest part registers 135°. Transfer the roast to a carving board and let rest for 30 minutes. Remove and discard the ties. Using a sharp serrated knife, slice the meat and serve. —*Erika Nakamura*

WINE Smoky, spicy Merlot from California: 2014 Ridge Vineyards Estate.

Pork Ribs Vindaloo

Active **1 hr;** Total **2 hr 30 min;** Serves **4 to 6**

These juicy ribs are chef Floyd Cardoz's ode to his mother's pork vindaloo. "I wanted to make something that honored the dish I grew up eating, but that is comfortable for our diners at Paowalla in NYC. There's nothing more American than ribs."

- **Two 2-lb. racks St. Louis–cut pork ribs, membranes removed and each rack halved**
- **Kosher salt and pepper**
- **2 dried New Mexico chiles, stemmed and broken into large pieces**
- **2 Tbsp. cumin seeds**
- **3 whole cloves**
- **One 1-inch cinnamon stick**
- **2 Tbsp. ancho chile powder**
- **1 tsp. ground turmeric**
- **½ tsp. cayenne**
- **⅓ cup red wine vinegar**
- **3 Tbsp. canola oil**
- **1 large red onion, finely chopped**
- **3 Tbsp. finely chopped garlic**
- **1 Tbsp. finely chopped peeled fresh ginger**
- **1 qt. chicken stock or low-sodium broth**
- **¼ cup silver tequila**
- **3 Tbsp. finely grated jaggery (see Note)**
- **Crusty bread or steamed basmati rice, for serving**

1. Season the ribs with salt and let stand at room temperature for 30 minutes.

2. Meanwhile, in a spice grinder, pulse the dried chiles with the cumin seeds, cloves and cinnamon stick until finely ground. Transfer the mixture to a small bowl and stir in the chile powder, turmeric, cayenne, 3 tablespoons of the vinegar and ½ tablespoon of pepper until a paste forms.

3. In a large enameled cast-iron casserole, heat the oil. Add the red onion and cook over moderate heat, stirring occasionally, until softened, 8 minutes. Add the garlic, ginger and the spice paste and cook over moderate heat, stirring frequently, until deep red in color, 8 to 10 minutes. Stir in the stock, tequila, jaggery, ribs and the remaining 2 tablespoons plus 1 teaspoon of vinegar and bring to a simmer. Cover and cook over moderately low heat until the ribs are very tender, about 1 hour.

4. Transfer the ribs to a work surface and let cool slightly; cut into individual ribs. Simmer the sauce until thickened and reduced by half, about 10 minutes; season with salt. Return the ribs to the sauce and stir to coat. Serve with crusty bread or steamed basmati rice. —*Floyd Cardoz*

NOTE Jaggery is an unrefined sweetener available at kalustyans.com.

MAKE AHEAD The ribs can be refrigerated in the sauce overnight.

WINE Tangy, bright Italian red: 2015 G.B. Burlotto Verduno Pelaverga.

Smoked Ribs with Blackberry-Habanero BBQ Sauce

Active **1 hr**; Total **5 hr**; Serves **4 to 6**

This recipe is a great starting point for the budding pit master. By adapting the traditional method for a gas grill, there's no worrying about replenishing coals. Plus, the gas grill maintains a steady temperature, which is essential for smoking. You will need a small spray bottle and ample propane in your tank—your grill will be on for at least three hours.

- **2 racks St. Louis–cut pork ribs (6 lbs.), membranes removed from the underside of each rack and each rack cut in half**
- **Kosher salt**
- **Pure Magic Dry Rub (recipe follows)**
- **¼ cup unseasoned rice vinegar**
- **1½ Tbsp. apple cider vinegar**
- **1½ Tbsp. Worcestershire sauce**
- **12 oz. blackberries (1 pint)**
- **3 Tbsp. dark brown sugar**
- **1 Tbsp. tomato paste**
- **1 Tbsp. seedless blackberry preserves**
- **1 tsp. minced habanero chile (from ½ chile)**
- **9 cups applewood chips, soaked in water for 1 hour and drained**
- **½ cup apple juice**

1. Pat the ribs dry with paper towels and arrange on a large rimmed baking sheet. Season with salt, then rub all over with 3 tablespoons of the dry rub. Cover and refrigerate for up to 4 hours. Bring to room temperature 30 minutes before grilling.

2. Meanwhile, in a medium saucepan, bring the rice vinegar, cider vinegar, Worcestershire, blackberries and 2 teaspoons of the dry rub to a boil over moderate heat, whisking, until the berries begin to break down, about 5 minutes. Remove from the heat. Strain the sauce through a fine-mesh sieve set over a medium bowl, pressing on the solids; discard the solids. Whisk in the brown sugar, tomato paste, blackberry preserves and habanero until smooth.

3. Set up a gas grill for indirect grilling and heat to 250°. Wrap 3 cups of the wood chips in an 18-inch-long piece of heavy-duty foil and poke several holes in the top of the packet. Repeat with the remaining wood chips and more foil, making a total of 3 packets. Pour the apple juice into a small spray bottle. Carefully set 1 wood chip packet directly on the flames; close the grill. When the chips start smoking (about 10 minutes), set the ribs on the grate, bone side down, over indirect heat. Cover and smoke for 1 hour, maintaining 250°.

4. Replace the used wood chip packet. Keeping the ribs bone side down, rotate them on the grill over the indirect heat. Sprinkle with more dry rub and spray with apple juice. Cover and grill for 2½ hours, rotating the ribs, sprinkling with the dry rub and spraying with apple juice every hour, until very tender. Replace the second wood chip packet after 1 hour.

5. Lightly brush the ribs with the blackberry-habanero sauce, cover and grill for 2 minutes. Transfer to a carving board, brush with sauce and sprinkle with more dry rub. Let rest for 15 minutes. Cut the ribs into sections and serve, passing the remaining sauce at the table. *—Amy Mills*

MAKE AHEAD The blackberry-habanero sauce can be refrigerated for up to 2 weeks.

BEER Dark, malty stout: Bent River Uncommon Stout.

PURE MAGIC DRY RUB
Total **5 min**; Makes **1 cup**

This balanced, sweet-savory dry rub is a riff on competition barbecue legend Mike Mills's top-secret "magic dust." At 17th Street Barbecue in Illinois, it's used on everything except the ice cream. Rub on smoked ribs (as we do here), braised pork shoulder and bone-in chops, or sprinkle on popcorn, french fries and deviled eggs.

- **¼ cup sweet paprika, preferably Hungarian**
- **2 Tbsp. kosher salt**
- **2 Tbsp. granulated sugar**
- **2 Tbsp. granulated garlic**
- **2 Tbsp. chili powder**
- **½ Tbsp. dry mustard powder**
- **½ Tbsp. pepper**
- **½ tsp. cayenne**

In a medium bowl, combine all of the ingredients. Store in an airtight container at room temperature for up to 2 weeks. *—AM*

Sour Cherry–Glazed Ribs

Active **1 hr**; Total **3 hr 30 min**; Serves **4 to 6**

- **Two 2-lb. racks baby back ribs, membrane removed from the underside of each rack**
- **Kosher salt and pepper**
- **2 Tbsp. extra-virgin olive oil**
- **3 small shallots, minced**
- **4 garlic cloves, minced**
- **1 lb. pitted sour cherries**
- **¼ cup sugar**
- **4½ Tbsp. red wine vinegar**
- **1 Tbsp. Sriracha**
- **1 cup cherry juice**
- **½ cup chicken stock**

1. Preheat the oven to 275°. Set a rack on a rimmed baking sheet. Season the ribs with salt and pepper and set meat side up on the rack. Bake for 1 hour and 30 minutes.

2. Meanwhile, in a medium saucepan, heat the olive oil. Add the shallots and half of the garlic and cook over moderate heat, stirring, until softened, about 5 minutes. Add the cherries, sugar and 2½ tablespoons of the vinegar and cook until the cherries burst, 5 to 7 minutes. Transfer to a blender and let cool slightly, then puree until smooth. Return to the saucepan and cook over moderately high heat, stirring often, until reduced to 1½ cups, about 7 minutes. Let the barbecue sauce cool, then stir in the Sriracha and season with salt and pepper.

3. In a medium bowl, whisk the cherry juice with the stock and the remaining garlic and 2 tablespoons of vinegar. Stack four 18-inch-long sheets of heavy-duty foil in 2 piles on a work surface. Set 1 rack of ribs meat side down in the center of each. Fold up the foil to form 4 sides and pour half of the juice mixture on each rack. Wrap the ribs tightly in the foil, then transfer the packets to the rack and bake for 1 hour and 30 minutes, until the ribs are very tender. Remove from the oven and open the packets. Let stand for 5 minutes, then discard the cooking liquid and foil. Return the ribs to the rack meat side up.

4. Increase the oven temperature to 450°. Brush the ribs liberally with the barbecue sauce and bake, turning and brushing occasionally with the sauce, for 10 to 12 minutes, until nicely glazed. Let rest for 5 minutes, then cut in between the bones and serve.

Smoked Ribs with Blackberry-Habanero BBQ Sauce

Pork-and-Apple
Bedfordshire Clangers

Pork-and-Apple Bedfordshire Clangers

Active **45 min**; Total **4 hr 45 min**
Serves **8 to 10**

PASTRY

2½ cups all-purpose flour, plus more
    for dusting

1 tsp. kosher salt

2 sticks unsalted butter, cubed
    and chilled

    Ice water

FILLINGS

½ lb. ground pork shoulder

¼ cup finely ground fresh breadcrumbs

1 Tbsp. finely chopped sage

1 small garlic clove, minced

    Kosher salt and pepper

¼ tsp. granulated sugar, plus more
    for sprinkling

½ tsp. ground ginger

¼ tsp. plus ⅛ tsp. ground allspice

    Freshly ground nutmeg

¼ cup chicken stock

2 Honeycrisp apples (1 lb. total)—
    peeled, cored and cut into ¾-inch
    pieces

2 Tbsp. dark brown sugar

1 Tbsp. cornstarch

1 tsp. fresh lemon juice

¼ tsp. ground cardamom

¼ tsp. ground cinnamon

1 large egg, lightly beaten

1. Make the pastry In a food processor, pulse the 2½ cups of flour with the salt. Add the butter and pulse until pea-size. Add ¼ cup of ice water and pulse until the dough just comes together. If needed, add up to ¼ cup of ice water. Turn out onto a work surface and knead 2 or 3 times. Quarter and press into rectangular disks. Wrap in plastic and refrigerate until firm, at least 1 hour.

2. Make the fillings In a stand mixer, combine the pork with the breadcrumbs, sage, garlic, 1 teaspoon of salt, ¼ teaspoon of pepper, ¼ teaspoon of granulated sugar, ¼ teaspoon of ginger, ⅛ teaspoon of allspice and a pinch of nutmeg. Freeze until cold but not frozen, about 30 minutes.

3. Using the paddle attachment, beat the pork mixture at low speed until just combined. Slowly beat in the stock.

4. In a medium bowl, toss the apples with the brown sugar, cornstarch, lemon juice, cardamom, cinnamon and the remaining ¼ teaspoon of ginger and ¼ teaspoon of allspice.

5. On a lightly floured work surface, roll out 1 disk of dough to a 5-by-10-inch rectangle. With a long side nearest you, spoon one-fourth of the apples along the bottom right half of the dough, leaving a 1-inch border on the bottom and side. Spoon one-fourth of the pork filling along the bottom left half of the dough to make 1 solid bar of filling, leaving a 1-inch border on the bottom and side. Fold the top half of the dough over the filling and press the edges to seal. Brush the top with the beaten egg. Sprinkle the apple half with granulated sugar and cut a few slits in the top of this side only. Transfer to a parchment-lined baking sheet. Repeat with the remaining dough and filling, spacing the pies 1 inch apart. Refrigerate until chilled, about 30 minutes.

6. Preheat the oven to 400°. Bake the pies for 50 minutes to 1 hour, rotating the baking sheet halfway through, until the apple filling is bubbling and the crust is deeply golden. Transfer the pies to a rack to cool. —*Sam Jacobson*

MAKE AHEAD The unbaked pies can be frozen for up to 1 month. Thaw slightly before baking.

BEER Malty pale ale: Cisco Brewers Whale's Tale.

Pork Belly Porchetta with Truffles

Active **25 min**; Total **2 hr**; Serves **8**

This is cookbook author Nadine Levy Redzepi's high-low approach to pork, combining a humble, fatty cut with upscale but affordable preserved truffles.

    One 2.8-oz. jar preserved truffles

    One 3-lb. skin-on, boneless
    pork belly

    Fine sea salt and pepper

10 small sage leaves, coarsely chopped

1½ lbs. small Yukon Gold potatoes,
    peeled and halved

2 Tbsp. canola oil

1. Preheat the oven to 350°. In a food processor, pulse the truffles and any liquid in the jar until finely chopped and spreadable.

2. Lay the pork on a work surface with the skin side facing down. Season with salt. Spread the truffle puree evenly over the meat and scatter the sage on top. Starting at a short edge, roll the pork belly into a log. Tie tightly at 1-inch intervals with kitchen twine. Season all over with salt.

3. Set the pork seam side down in a roasting pan and scatter the potatoes around it. Drizzle the pork and potatoes with the oil. Season the potatoes with salt and pepper and toss to coat. Arrange the potatoes cut side down.

4. Roast until the potatoes are browned and tender, about 1 hour. Transfer the potatoes to a plate and continue to roast the pork for about 20 minutes, until an instant-read thermometer inserted in the center registers 140° to 145°. If the fat is not crisp, increase the oven temperature to 450° and roast for 5 minutes longer, until crisp. Turn off the oven.

5. Transfer the pork to a work surface and let stand for 15 minutes. Put the potatoes back in the roasting pan and return to the oven to warm.

6. Remove the twine from the pork and slice the roast crosswise. Arrange the meat on a platter and pour any juices from the cutting board over it. Serve with the potatoes. —*Nadine Levy Redzepi*

WINE Spicy, aromatic red Burgundy: 2014 Domaine Mongeard-Mugneret Fixin.

Pork-and-Brisket Chili

Active **1 hr 45 min**; Total **4 hr plus overnight soaking**; Serves **10 to 12**

BEANS

- 1 **lb. small dried pink beans, such as Rancho Gordo's Pinquitos, soaked overnight and drained**
- 5 **garlic cloves**
- 1 **small yellow onion, quartered through the core**
- 1 **medium carrot, halved crosswise**
- 1 **celery rib, halved crosswise**
- 1½ **Tbsp. kosher salt**

CHILI

- 3½ **lbs. boneless pork shoulder, cut into 1½-inch pieces**
- 2 **lbs. brisket, cut into 1½-inch pieces**
  Kosher salt and pepper
- 3 **Tbsp. vegetable oil**
- 3 **medium yellow onions, chopped**
- 1 **green bell pepper—stemmed, seeded and chopped**
- 10 **garlic cloves, chopped**
- ¼ **cup tomato paste**
- ¼ **cup chili powder**
- 2 **Tbsp. light brown sugar**
- 1 **Tbsp. mustard powder**
- 1 **Tbsp. ground cumin**
  One 16-oz. jar roasted green Hatch chiles (medium heat)
  One 16-oz. can crushed tomatoes
- 5 **qts. chicken stock or low-sodium broth**
- ¼ **cup oregano leaves**
  Sour cream, shredded cheese and thinly sliced scallions, for serving

1. Make the beans In a large saucepan, cover all of the ingredients with 4 quarts of water and bring to a boil. Simmer over moderately low heat until the beans are just tender, about 1 hour. Drain well and discard the vegetables.

2. Make the chili Season the pork and brisket generously with salt and pepper. In a large pot, heat the vegetable oil until shimmering. In batches, cook the pork and brisket over moderately high heat, turning occasionally, until browned all over, about 10 minutes per batch. Using a slotted spoon, transfer the meat to a baking sheet.

3. Add the onions, bell pepper, garlic and a generous pinch of salt to the pot. Cook over moderately high heat, stirring frequently, until just starting to soften and brown, about 5 minutes. Add the tomato paste, chili powder, brown sugar, mustard powder and cumin and cook, stirring, until fragrant and the vegetables are coated, about 3 minutes. Add the Hatch chiles and tomatoes and cook, stirring, until bubbling, about 5 minutes. Add the chicken stock and bring to a boil. Add the meat and oregano and simmer over moderate heat, stirring occasionally, until the meat is barely tender, about 1 hour.

4. Stir the beans into the chili and simmer over moderate heat, stirring occasionally, until the meat and beans are tender, about 1 hour and 15 minutes longer. Serve hot with sour cream, shredded cheese and thinly sliced scallions. —*Colby Garrelts*

MAKE AHEAD The chili can be refrigerated for up to 5 days. Reheat gently before serving.

WINE Robust California Syrah: 2015 Eberle Steinbeck Vineyard.

Vietnamese Lemongrass Meatballs

Active **30 min**; Total **1 hr**; Serves **4**

- 4 **shallots, 2 thinly sliced and 2 minced**
- ¼ **cup unseasoned rice vinegar**
  Kosher salt
- 1 **lb. ground pork**
- 1 **large egg**
- 3 **Tbsp. minced lemongrass**
- 1 **Tbsp. minced cilantro, plus leaves for garnish**
- 1 **Tbsp. Asian fish sauce**
- 2 **tsp. cornstarch**
- 1 **garlic clove, minced**
- 1 **Tbsp. canola oil**
  Bibb lettuce leaves, mint and basil leaves, lime wedges, chile-garlic paste and julienned cucumber and carrot, for garnish

1. In a small bowl, mix the sliced shallots with the vinegar and a generous pinch of salt.

2. In a medium bowl, mix the pork, egg, lemongrass, minced shallots and cilantro, fish sauce, cornstarch, garlic and 1½ teaspoons of salt. Cover and refrigerate for 30 minutes. Form into 1½-inch balls.

3. In a large skillet, heat the oil. Add the meatballs and cook over moderate heat until browned and cooked through, 8 to 10 minutes. Transfer to a platter and serve in Bibb lettuce leaves with the pickled shallots and garnishes. —*Gail Simmons*

WINE Off-dry Riesling: 2016 Long Shadows Poet's Leap.

Kimchi Pork Burgers

Total **30 min**; Serves **4**

Chef Edward Lee was inspired by the classic Korean pairing of pork and kimchi when he created this pork-rind-topped burger. "The buttermilk sauce brings it all together and cools down the heat," he says.

- ½ **cup buttermilk**
- ½ **cup mayonnaise**
- 2 **Tbsp. sour cream**
- 1 **tsp. anchovy paste**
- 1 **tsp. chopped cilantro, plus sprigs for garnish**
- ½ **tsp. Asian fish sauce**
- ½ **tsp. Worcestershire sauce**
- 1 **small garlic clove, grated**
  Kosher salt and pepper
- 1½ **lbs. ground pork**
- 1 **Tbsp. canola oil**
- 4 **slices of Havarti cheese**
- 4 **pretzel rolls, split and toasted**
  Chopped kimchi and pork rinds, for garnish

1. In a small bowl, whisk together the first 8 ingredients. Season the sauce with salt and pepper. Form the pork into four ¾-inch-thick patties; season with salt and pepper. In a large cast-iron skillet set on the grate of a preheated grill or on the stovetop, heat the oil. Cook the burgers over moderate heat, 3 to 4 minutes. Flip, top each with a slice of cheese and cook, covered, until the burgers are just cooked through, about 5 minutes. Transfer to a work surface.

2. Spread the sauce on the cut sides of the rolls. Place a burger on each roll bottom and top with some of the kimchi, pork rinds and cilantro sprigs. Close the burgers and serve, passing the remaining sauce at the table. —*Edward Lee*

MAKE AHEAD The buttermilk sauce can be refrigerated for up to 2 days.

Pork-and-Brisket Chili

Brat-and-Pepper Tacos

⏱ Total **30 min**; Serves **4**

These playful brat-and-pepper tacos are inspired by classic Italian sausage-and-pepper subs.

- ¾ **lb. bratwurst, halved lengthwise and sliced crosswise into ⅓-inch-thick pieces**
- 2 **Cubanelle peppers—halved, seeded and sliced**
- 2 **poblano chiles—halved, seeded and sliced**
- 1 **red bell pepper—halved, seeded and sliced**
- 3 **Tbsp. extra-virgin olive oil**
   Kosher salt and pepper
- ½ **cup sour cream**
- ¼ **cup whole-grain mustard**
- 12 **corn tortillas, warmed**
   Pickled red cabbage and freshly grated horseradish, for serving

1. Preheat the oven to 425°. On a large rimmed baking sheet, toss the bratwurst with the peppers and olive oil and season with salt and pepper. Roast for about 20 minutes, until the sausage is browned and the peppers are tender.

2. Meanwhile, in a small bowl, mix the sour cream with the mustard. Spread the mustard cream on the tortillas and fill with the bratwurst and peppers. Top with pickled red cabbage and grated horseradish. Serve right away. —*Justin Chapple*

BEER Crisp, lightly hoppy pilsner: Victory Prima Pils.

Bilbro Family Sausage

Total **30 min plus overnight steeping**; Makes **2 lbs**

This bulk sausage recipe comes from the Sonoma-based Bilbro family of wine-makers. Red wine has been the key flavoring agent in the sausage for generations. The rich sausage meat is excellent in pasta dishes like Pasta with Sausage and Mustard Greens (p. 81), formed into patties, or used to stuff vegetables.

- ¼ **cup dry red wine**
- 6 **large garlic cloves, thinly sliced**
- 2 **pounds ground pork**
- 1 **tablespoon kosher salt**
- 2 **teaspoons black pepper**
- ½ **teaspoon ground nutmeg**
- ½ **teaspoon ground allspice**

1. In a small bowl, mix the wine and garlic. Cover and refrigerate overnight.

2. Strain the wine into a medium bowl; discard the garlic. Add the remaining ingredients and mix well.

MAKE AHEAD The sausage can be refrigerated in an airtight container for up to 5 days.

Fabada (Spanish Bean Stew with Chorizo and Blood Sausage)

Active **45 min**; Total **2 hr plus overnight soaking**; Serves **6 to 8**

Fabada asturiana is a deliciously rich and hearty stew from Asturias, Spain.

- ½ **lb. meaty pancetta**
- ½ **lb. dry Spanish chorizo**
- 1 **meaty ham hock (about 1 lb.)**
- 2 **qts. plus 2 cups chicken stock or low-sodium broth**
- 1 **lb. dried Asturian fabes beans (see Note), soaked in water overnight and drained**
   Bouquet garni: 1 small halved onion, 8 garlic cloves, 2 parsley sprigs and 1 bay leaf wrapped in cheesecloth and tied
   Large pinch of saffron, finely ground in a mortar
- ¼ **cup boiling water**
- 1 **medium tomato, halved crosswise**
- 2 **Tbsp. extra-virgin olive oil**
- 1 **medium onion, finely chopped**
   Kosher salt and pepper
- 1½ **tsp. pimentón de la Vera (smoked Spanish paprika)**
- ½ **lb. blood sausage**

1. Fill a pot halfway with water; bring to a boil over high heat. Add the pancetta, chorizo and ham hock; simmer over moderate heat for 5 minutes. Drain the meat and return to the pot. Add the stock, beans and bouquet garni and bring to a boil over high heat; skim off any foam. Cover partially and simmer over low heat until the beans are just tender, about 1 hour.

2. Meanwhile, in a small heatproof bowl, mix the saffron with the boiling water until dissolved. Grate the tomato halves on the large holes of a box grater set in a bowl until only the skins remain; discard the skins.

3. In a medium skillet, heat the olive oil until shimmering. Add the onion and a pinch of salt and cook over moderate heat, stirring occasionally, until softened, about 8 minutes. Add the pimentón and cook, stirring, until the onion is coated, about 1 minute. Add the grated tomato and simmer until reduced by half, 3 to 5 minutes. Stir the onion mixture into the pot of beans along with the brewed saffron and the blood sausage. Simmer uncovered until the beans are very tender but not falling apart, about 30 minutes.

4. Transfer the meats to a carving board and let rest for 5 minutes, then cut into bite-size pieces. Discard the ham bone and bouquet garni. Return the meats to the pot and season with salt and pepper. Transfer the fabada to bowls and serve. —*Anya von Bremzen*

NOTE Fabes are available at despanabrandfoods.com.

MAKE AHEAD The fabada can be refrigerated for up to 3 days. Reheat the stew gently before serving.

WINE Sparkling Asturian cider: NV Sidra El Gaitero.

Braised Veal Shanks

Active **45 min**; Total **3 hr 15 min**; Serves **8**

To delicately braise veal shanks, Persian cook Mahin Gilanpour Motamed simmers them on the stovetop instead of in the oven, ideally using a heat diffuser to keep the braise from getting too dark.

> **Five 1-lb. veal shanks (2 inches thick), tied (have your butcher do this) and patted dry**
>
> **Kosher salt and pepper**
>
> 1 **Tbsp. unsalted butter**
>
> 1 **Tbsp. extra-virgin olive oil**
>
> ¼ **tsp. ground turmeric**
>
> 2 **large sweet onions, quartered through the core and separated into petals**
>
> **Spice sachet: 3 garlic cloves, 1 Tbsp. coriander seeds and 1 tsp. black peppercorns, wrapped in damp cheesecloth and tied with string**

1. Season the veal shanks generously with salt and pepper. In a very large enameled cast-iron casserole set over a heat diffuser (if you have one), melt the butter in the oil. Stir in the turmeric, then add the veal shanks. Cook over moderate heat, turning once, until lightly browned on both sides, about 6 minutes total. Transfer the veal to a plate.

2. Add the onions and a generous pinch of salt to the casserole and cook over moderate heat, stirring occasionally, until barely softened, about 5 minutes. Add 4 cups of water; bring to a boil over high heat. Nestle the veal shanks and the spice sachet in the braising liquid. Cover the casserole and braise over low heat until the veal is just tender, about 1 hour and 30 minutes. Uncover the casserole and cover the shanks with a large piece of parchment. Cover the casserole and continue to braise over low heat until the veal is very tender, about 45 minutes longer.

3. Using a slotted spoon, transfer the veal shanks and onions to a platter and tent with foil. Boil the braising liquid over high heat until slightly reduced but still light in color, about 10 minutes. Discard the strings from the shanks and spoon some of the braising liquid on top. Serve.
—*Mahin Gilanpour Motamed*

WINE Delicate red Burgundy: 2014 Joseph Drouhin Chorey-les-Beaune.

Veal Roast with Green Mashed Potatoes

Active **45 min**; Total **2hr 30 min plus overnight salting**; Serves **8**

Portland, Oregon chef Eli Dahlin uses this "backwards" mashed potato technique for entertaining. Cook, cool and rice your potatoes in advance. When it's time to serve, stir them into the hot butter and cream until thickened, then finish with a chunky puree of bright green peas, mint and lemon zest.

> **Two 4-bone racks of veal (about 3 lbs. each)—chine bones removed, fat trimmed to ¼ inch and ribs frenched**
>
> **Kosher salt and pepper**
>
> 2 **lbs. Yukon Gold potatoes, peeled and cut into 1-inch pieces**
>
> 4 **cups thawed frozen peas, plus more for garnish**
>
> 1 **cup lightly packed mint leaves, plus more for garnish**
>
> 1 **Tbsp. finely grated lemon zest plus 1 Tbsp. fresh lemon juice**
>
> ¾ **cup plus 2 Tbsp. heavy cream**
>
> 1 **stick unsalted butter, cubed**
>
> 2 **cups beef stock or low-sodium broth**
>
> ½ **tsp. unflavored powdered gelatin**
>
> 1 **large shallot, thinly sliced**
>
> 1 **tsp. tomato paste**

1. Season the veal with salt and transfer to a rimmed baking sheet. Refrigerate uncovered overnight. Bring the meat to room temperature 30 minutes before roasting.

2. Preheat the oven to 250° and set a rack in a large flameproof roasting pan. Arrange the veal racks back to back in the pan, with the frenched bones crisscrossed and pointing upward. Season with salt and pepper. Roast for about 1½ hours, until an instant-read thermometer inserted in the thickest part registers 100°. Increase the oven temperature to 500° and continue to roast for about 15 minutes longer, until the outside is browned and an instant-read thermometer inserted in the thickest part registers 120°. Transfer the racks to a carving board, tent with foil and let rest for 30 minutes. Set the roasting pan aside; do not wipe out.

3. In a medium saucepan, cover the potatoes with water and bring to a boil. Add 1 tablespoon of salt and simmer over moderate heat until tender, 15 minutes; drain. Using a ricer and working over a medium bowl, rice the potatoes.

4. In a food processor, pulse the 4 cups of peas with the 1 cup of mint, the lemon zest and 2 tablespoons of the cream until finely chopped. Season with salt and pepper.

5. In a large, straight-sided skillet, melt the butter in the remaining ¾ cup of cream. Add the potatoes and cook, stirring constantly, until smooth and heated through, about 3 minutes. Fold in the pea mixture and lemon juice and season with salt and pepper. Cover and keep warm.

6. In a medium bowl, whisk the stock with the gelatin. Set the roasting pan on the stove over 2 burners. Add the shallot and cook over moderate heat, stirring occasionally, until softened, 5 minutes. Stir in the tomato paste and cook until deepened in color, 30 seconds. Add the stock mixture and bring to a boil over moderately high heat, scraping up the browned bits, until thickened slightly, 2 minutes. Strain the sauce through a fine-mesh sieve set over a heatproof medium serving bowl. Skim off any fat and season the pan sauce with salt.

7. Carve the veal into 8 chops and transfer to a platter. Drizzle the meat with some of the pan sauce. Transfer the mashed potatoes to a serving bowl and garnish with more peas and mint leaves. Serve the veal with the mashed potatoes, passing the remaining sauce at the table.
—*Eli Dahlin*

WINE Earthy Oregon Pinot Noir: 2014 Kelley Fox Momtazi Vineyard

Veal Roast with Green
Mashed Potatoes

BEEF
& LAMB

Thinly slice grilled skirt steak across the grain. OPPOSITE Beef Rib Roast (p. 195).

Steak and Brassicas with Red Wine Sauce

Total **45 min**; Serves **4 to 6**

A rich pan sauce pulls together the steak and roasted vegetables here.

- **1½ lbs. multicolored brassicas, such as baby cauliflower and Romanesco, cut into 1-inch florets**
- **4 thyme sprigs**
- **5 Tbsp. extra-virgin olive oil**
  Kosher salt and pepper
- **7 Tbsp. cold unsalted butter, diced**
  Two 1-lb. hanger steaks
- **2 small shallots, minced**
- **2 garlic cloves, minced**
- **½ cup red wine**
- **½ cup chicken stock**

1. Preheat the oven to 425°. On a large rimmed baking sheet, toss the brassicas and thyme with ¼ cup of the olive oil and season generously with salt and pepper. Spread in a layer and scatter 2 tablespoons of the butter on top. Roast for 20 to 25 minutes, until golden and tender.

2. Meanwhile, in a large cast-iron skillet, heat the remaining 1 tablespoon of olive oil. Season the steaks all over with salt and pepper. Add to the skillet and cook over moderately high heat, turning often, until an instant-read thermometer inserted in the thickest part of each one registers 120°, 12 to 15 minutes. Transfer to a carving board and let rest for 10 minutes. Do not wipe out the skillet.

3. In the same skillet, cook the shallots and garlic over moderate heat, stirring, until softened, 2 minutes. Add the wine and cook, scraping up any browned bits, until almost evaporated, 3 minutes. Add the stock and cook until slightly reduced, 2 minutes. Remove from the heat and gradually whisk in the remaining 5 tablespoons of butter until emulsified; season with salt and pepper. Carve the steaks against the grain. Serve with the brassicas and sauce. —*Justin Chapple*

WINE Firmly structured Cabernet Sauvignon 2014 Marietta Armé.

Gochujang Flank Steak and Korean Pasta Salad

Active **50 min;** Total **3 hr;** Serves **4**

STEAK

- **6 Tbsp. gochujang (Korean red pepper paste)**
- **3 Tbsp. mirin**
- **1 Tbsp. soy sauce**
- **2 tsp. toasted sesame oil**
- **4 garlic cloves**
- **1 Tbsp. chopped peeled fresh ginger**
  One 2-lb. flank steak
- **1 Tbsp. canola oil**

PASTA SALAD

- **1 lb. fusilli**
- **1 cup mayonnaise**
- **3 Tbsp. gochujang**
- **3 Tbsp. fresh lime juice**
- **1 medium zucchini, halved lengthwise**
- **1 medium yellow squash, halved lengthwise**
  One 8-inch-long slice of pineapple (from 1 peeled, quartered and cored whole pineapple)
- **1 Tbsp. canola oil**
- **1 cup thawed frozen peas**
- **3 scallions, thinly sliced**
  Kosher salt

1. Make the steak In a blender, puree the gochujang with the mirin, soy sauce, sesame oil, garlic and ginger until smooth. Put the flank steak in a large resealable plastic bag and pour in the marinade. Seal the bag and refrigerate for at least 2 hours or up to 6 hours. Bring to room temperature 30 minutes before cooking.

2. Make the pasta salad In a large pot of salted boiling water, cook the fusilli until al dente. Drain and rinse under cold water until cool; drain well. In a large bowl, whisk the mayonnaise with the gochujang and lime juice until smooth. Fold in the fusilli.

3. Heat a large cast-iron skillet. Lightly brush the zucchini, squash and pineapple with 1 tablespoon of the oil and cook over moderate heat, turning once, until charred and tender, about 8 minutes. Transfer to a work surface and let cool. Cut the vegetables and fruit into ½-inch pieces and add to the pasta. Fold in the peas and scallions and season with salt. Wipe out the skillet.

4. Heat the skillet, then add 1 tablespoon of oil. Remove the steak from the marinade, letting the excess drip off, and cook over moderate heat, turning once, until an instant-read thermometer inserted into the thickest part registers 125° for medium-rare, 5 to 6 minutes per side.

5. Transfer the steak to a work surface and let rest for 5 minutes. Thinly slice and serve with the pasta salad. —*Chris Shepherd*

Cuban Flank Steak

Total **30 min;** Serves **4 to 6**

- **1 tsp. grated fresh lime zest plus 2 Tbsp. fresh lime juice**
- **½ tsp. grated fresh orange zest plus ¼ cup fresh orange juice**
- **2 Tbsp. extra-virgin olive oil, plus more for grilling**
- **2 large garlic cloves**
- **1½ Tbsp. fresh oregano**
- **1½ tsp. ground cumin**
  Kosher salt and pepper
  One 1½-lb. flank steak
- **2 ripe, firm mangoes—peeled, pitted and sliced**
  Lime wedges, for serving

1. In a blender, combine the citrus zests and juice with the 2 tablespoons of olive oil, the garlic, oregano, cumin, 1¼ teaspoons of salt and ½ teaspoon of pepper and blend until smooth.

2. In a glass or ceramic baking dish, pour all but ¼ cup of the marinade over the steak and turn to coat. Let stand for 15 minutes, or cover with plastic wrap and refrigerate for up to 24 hours.

3. Light a grill or grill pan and oil the grate. Remove the steak from the marinade, letting the excess drip off. Season with salt and pepper and grill over moderate heat, turning once, until lightly charred and an instant-read thermometer inserted in the thickest part registers 125°, 10 to 12 minutes. Transfer the steak to a carving board and let rest for 5 minutes. Thinly slice the meat against the grain and transfer to a platter with the mango slices and lime wedges. Drizzle with the reserved marinade and serve. —*Melissa Clark*

WINE Light-bodied Loire red: 2015 Bernard Baudry Chinon.

Steak and Brassicas with
Red Wine Sauce

Vietnamese Steak au Poivre

Vietnamese Steak au Poivre

Total **1 hr 15 min;** Serves **4**

This fish sauce-spiked steak au poivre is chef Chris Shepherd's nod to the French influences in Vietnamese cooking.

- 2 Tbsp. unsalted butter
- 1 large onion, thinly sliced
- 2 garlic cloves, thinly sliced
- One 1½-inch cinnamon stick
- 1 star anise
- 2 Tbsp. Asian fish sauce
- 1 Tbsp. light brown sugar
- 2 cups beef stock or low-sodium broth
- ½ cup heavy cream
- 2 tsp. black peppercorns, crushed
- Kosher salt and pepper
- 1½ lbs. small heads of broccoli, cauliflower and/or Romanesco
- 3 Tbsp. canola oil
- 1 cup mayonnaise
- ¼ cup yellow mustard
- ¼ cup apple cider vinegar
- ¼ tsp. hot sauce, preferably Tabasco
- ½ medium red onion, thinly sliced (1 cup)
- 2 Tbsp. roasted unsalted sunflower seeds
- Four 6-oz. center-cut beef tenderloin steaks

1. In a medium saucepan, melt the butter. Add the onion and garlic and cook over moderate heat, stirring occasionally, until softened, about 8 minutes. Add the cinnamon stick and star anise and cook, stirring, until fragrant, about 1 minute. Stir in the fish sauce and sugar and cook for 1 minute. Add the stock and simmer over moderately high heat until reduced to 1 cup, about 15 minutes. Add the cream and simmer until the sauce is thickened and reduced by half, about 10 minutes longer. Strain the sauce through a fine sieve set over a medium bowl; discard the solids. Return the sauce to the saucepan and stir in the crushed peppercorns. Season with salt and keep warm.

2. Heat a large cast-iron skillet. In a large bowl, toss the broccoli, cauliflower and Romanesco with 1 tablespoon of the oil. Working in batches, cook over moderately high heat, turning occasionally, until lightly charred all over and crisp-tender, about 15 minutes. Transfer to a work surface and let cool. Cut into bite-size pieces and wipe out the bowl. In the bowl, whisk the mayonnaise with the mustard, vinegar and hot sauce until smooth. Fold in the charred vegetables, the red onion and sunflower seeds and season the salad with salt. Wipe out the skillet.

3. In the skillet, heat the remaining 2 tablespoons of oil. Season the steaks with salt and pepper and cook over moderate heat, turning once, until an instant-read thermometer inserted in the thickest part registers 125° for medium-rare, 6 minutes per side. Transfer to a work surface and let rest for 5 minutes. Serve with the peppercorn sauce and the charred-vegetable salad. —*Chris Shepherd*

WINE Peppery Crozes-Hermitage from France's Rhône Valley: 2013 Emmanuel Darnaud Les Trois Chênes.

Grilled and Chilled Beef with Buttermilk-Horseradish Sauce

Active **45 min;** Total **2 hr 30 min plus overnight chilling;** Serves **8**

- 2 Tbsp. extra-virgin olive oil
- 3 garlic cloves, minced
- 1 Tbsp. ground fennel
- 1 Tbsp. minced thyme leaves
- Kosher salt and pepper
- One 3½-lb. center-cut beef tenderloin roast, tied
- 1 cup buttermilk
- ½ cup mayonnaise
- 2 Tbsp. freshly grated horseradish, plus more for serving

1. In a small bowl, whisk the oil, garlic, fennel, thyme, 1 tablespoon of salt and 2 teaspoons of pepper. Rub the paste over the beef and bring to room temperature, 1 hour.

2. Light a grill. Grill the roast over moderate heat, turning often, until charred and an instant-read thermometer inserted in the thickest part registers 118°, 35 to 40 minutes. Transfer to a carving board,

tent with foil and let cool for 30 minutes. Wrap the roast tightly in foil and let cool completely, then refrigerate overnight.

3. In a bowl, whisk the buttermilk, mayonnaise and the 2 tablespoons of horseradish. Season with salt and pepper. Carve the roast into ¼-inch-thick slices and serve cold with the buttermilk sauce and more freshly grated horseradish. —*Justin Chapple*

WINE Aromatic Italian red: 2014 Russiz Superiore Collio Cabernet Franc.

Juicy Steak-and-Tomato Salad

Total **30 min;** Serves **4 to 6**

You can use any type of leftover beef in this salad, but for the tastiest results, try our Grilled and Chilled Beef (at left), a perfectly cooked tenderloin roast seasoned with garlic, ground fennel and thyme.

- ¼ cup very finely chopped red onion
- ¼ cup Champagne vinegar
- ⅓ cup extra-virgin olive oil
- 1 Tbsp. Dijon mustard
- Kosher salt and pepper
- 1½ lbs. cherry and medium-size heirloom tomatoes—cherry tomatoes halved, heirloom tomatoes cut into chunks
- 1 lb. leftover Grilled and Chilled Beef (recipe at left) or other chilled steak, cut into strips
- 2 medium avocados—peeled, pitted and cut into 1½-inch pieces
- ½ cup snipped dill
- ⅓ cup tarragon leaves

In a large bowl, whisk the red onion with the Champagne vinegar and let stand for 10 minutes. Whisk in the olive oil and Dijon mustard and season with salt and pepper. Add the tomatoes, beef and avocados and toss to coat. Season with salt and pepper and toss again. Fold in the dill and tarragon and serve right away. —*Justin Chapple*

WINE Full-bodied, fruity California rosé: 2016 Donelan Family.

Creamed Spinach–Stuffed Filet Roast

Active **45 min**; Total **1 hr 30 min**
Serves **6 to 8**

- 3 Tbsp. unsalted butter
- 1 small shallot, minced
- 1 garlic clove, minced
- ¼ cup all-purpose flour
- 1½ cups heavy cream
  - Three 10-oz. packages thawed frozen chopped spinach, excess water squeezed out
- ¼ cup freshly grated Parmigiano-Reggiano cheese
- ¼ tsp. freshly grated nutmeg
- 2 tsp. fresh lemon juice
  - Kosher salt and pepper
  - One 3-lb. center-cut filet mignon, butterflied ¼ inch thick (have your butcher do this)
- 2 Tbsp. extra-virgin olive oil

1. In a medium saucepan, melt the butter. Add the shallot and garlic and cook over moderate heat, stirring occasionally, until softened, about 2 minutes. Add the flour and cook, stirring, until the flour is golden, about 3 minutes. Whisk in the cream until smooth, then add the spinach. Cook, stirring occasionally, until the mixture is very thick, about 5 minutes. Stir in the cheese, nutmeg and lemon juice and season with salt and pepper. Let cool slightly.

2. Preheat the oven to 450°. Set a rack over a large rimmed baking sheet. Arrange the filet on the rack and season the top with salt and pepper. Spread the creamed spinach evenly over the filet, leaving a 1-inch border around the edges. Roll up the filet and tie with kitchen twine at 1-inch intervals. Rub the filet with the olive oil and season with salt and pepper. Roast for 30 to 35 minutes, until medium-rare within and an instant-read thermometer inserted in the center registers 120°. Transfer to a cutting board and let rest for 10 minutes. Slice ½ inch thick and serve warm. —*Kay Chun*

MAKE AHEAD The creamed spinach can be refrigerated for 2 days; bring to room temperature before using.

WINE Peppery Rioja Reserva: 2010 Remelluri.

Spiced Grilled T-Bone Steaks

Total **30 min**; Serves **2 to 4**

A good T-bone steak doesn't need much, but to give it a little boost, F&W's Justin Chapple rubs it with a mixture of brown sugar, coriander, cumin, paprika and salt for even more flavor.

- Two 1½-inch-thick T-bone steaks (2½ lbs.)
- Smoky Spiced Sugar Rub (p. 374)
- Extra-virgin olive oil, for brushing
- Flaky sea salt and cracked pepper, for sprinkling

Sprinkle the steaks generously all over with the rub and let stand for 15 minutes. Light a grill and oil the grate. Grill the steaks over moderately high heat, turning once, until lightly charred, about 4 minutes per side for medium-rare. Let rest on a carving board for 5 minutes. Sprinkle with salt and pepper and serve. —*Justin Chapple*

WINE Robust Napa Cabernet Sauvignon: 2014 Textbook.

Steak with Arabic Sauces

Total **45 min**; Serves **4**

At Restaurante El Churrasco in Córdoba, Spain, they serve both salsa verde and salsa roja in small containers alongside juicy grilled steak. The salsa verde is bright and tangy, while the salsa roja is smoky and garlicky. They're both delicious.

SALSA VERDE

- 2 cups packed parsley leaves
- 4 peperoncini, stemmed
- 1 garlic clove
- 1 tsp. dried oregano
- ¾ cup extra-virgin olive oil
  - Kosher salt

SALSA ROJA

- 1 cup extra-virgin olive oil
- 7 garlic cloves, finely grated
- 1 tsp. pimentón de la Vera (smoked sweet Spanish paprika)
- ½ tsp. ground cumin
- ½ tsp. cayenne
  - Kosher salt

STEAK

- Two 1½-inch-thick T-bone steaks (2½ lbs.)
- Kosher salt and pepper
- Oil, for brushing

1. Make the salsa verde In a food processor, combine the parsley, peperoncini, garlic and oregano and pulse until very finely chopped; scrape down the side of the bowl as needed. With the machine on, gradually add the olive oil until incorporated. Scrape into a medium bowl and season with salt.

2. Make the salsa roja In a medium bowl, whisk the olive oil with the garlic, pimentón, cumin and cayenne and season generously with salt.

3. Grill the steaks Season the steaks generously with salt and pepper and let stand for 15 minutes. Light a grill and oil the grate. Grill the steaks over moderately high heat, turning occasionally, until lightly charred, about 4 minutes per side for medium-rare. Let rest on a carving board for 5 minutes, then carve off the bone and serve with the sauces. —*José Andrés*

MAKE AHEAD The salsas can be refrigerated separately overnight. Bring to room temperature before serving.

WINE Peppery Bierzo red: 2015 Armas de Guerra Mencía.

Porterhouse Steak

Active **15 min**; Total **45 min plus overnight salting**; Serves **4 to 6**

For a perfectly tender and crusty steak, brothers Michael and Bryan Voltaggio salt the meat up to 12 hours before and let it sit uncovered in the refrigerator. This step seasons the meat to its core and pulls out moisture for a better sear.

- **One 36-oz. porterhouse steak, cut 2 inches thick**
- **Kosher salt and freshly ground black pepper**
- 1 **Tbsp. unsalted butter**

1. Set a rack in a rimmed baking sheet. Season the steak with 1 tablespoon of salt and transfer to the rack. Refrigerate, uncovered, overnight. Let the steak come to room temperature 30 minutes before cooking.

2. Preheat the oven to 400°. Heat a large cast-iron skillet until very hot, about 5 minutes. Pat the steak dry with paper towels and season with salt and pepper. Cook the steak over moderate heat until browned and crusty, about 3 minutes. Add the butter, turn the meat and transfer the skillet to the oven. Roast until an instant-read thermometer inserted in the thickest part registers 120° for medium-rare, 12 to 15 minutes. Transfer the steak to a work surface and let rest for 10 minutes before serving. —*Bryan Voltaggio and Michael Voltaggio*

SERVE WITH Green Peppercorn Jus, Curry-Mustard Mayonnaise and House Steak Sauce (recipes follow).

WINE Robust, structured Napa Cabernet: 2014 Buehler Papa's Knoll Cabernet Sauvignon.

CURRY-MUSTARD MAYONNAISE

Total **5 min**; Makes **about 1½ cups**

"I'm a mustard fiend," says chef Bryan Voltaggio. At his DC-area restaurant Voltaggio Brothers Steak House, Bryan and his brother, Michael, serve every steak with a tray of sauces for dipping. "You will want to lather this simple sauce on everything."

- 1 **cup mayonnaise**
- ½ **cup Dijon mustard**
- 2 **Tbsp. yellow mustard**
- 2 **tsp. soy sauce**
- 2 **tsp. curry powder**

In a medium bowl, whisk together all of the ingredients until smooth. —*BV and MV*

MAKE AHEAD The mayo can be refrigerated for up to 1 week.

GREEN PEPPERCORN JUS

Total **25 min**; Makes **1½ cups**

- 4 **Tbsp. unsalted butter**
- 1 **shallot, finely chopped**
- ⅓ **cup drained brined green peppercorns**
- ¼ **cup Cognac**
- ½ **cup beef stock or low-sodium broth**
- 1 **cup heavy cream**
- 2 **Tbsp. whole-grain mustard**
- 1 **Tbsp. tamari**
- 2 **Tbsp. minced chives**
- **Kosher salt and pepper**

In a medium saucepan, melt the butter. Add the shallot and cook over moderate heat, stirring occasionally, until softened, 2 to 3 minutes. Add the peppercorns and Cognac and cook until the liquid is reduced by half, 2 to 3 minutes. Add the beef stock and cook until reduced by half, about 5 minutes. Whisk in the cream, mustard and tamari and simmer until the sauce is thickened and reduced by one-third, about 3 minutes more. Stir in the chives, season with salt and pepper and serve immediately. —*BV and MV*

MAKE AHEAD The peppercorn jus can be refrigerated overnight. Reheat gently and stir in the chives just before serving.

HOUSE STEAK SAUCE

Active **30 min**; Total **1 hr 30 min plus cooling**; Makes **1½ cups**

- 3 **Tbsp. extra-virgin olive oil**
- 1 **onion, finely chopped**
- 2 **garlic cloves, finely chopped**
- 2 **Tbsp. raisins**
- 1 **Tbsp. gochujang (Korean red pepper paste)**
- ¾ **tsp. smoked paprika**
- ½ **tsp. black peppercorns**
- ⅛ **tsp. celery seeds**
- 2 **Tbsp. fresh orange juice**
- ⅓ **cup balsamic vinegar**
- ¼ **cup Worcestershire sauce**
- 3 **Tbsp. ketchup**
- 2 **Tbsp. Dijon mustard**
- 2 **Tbsp. soy sauce**
- 1 **Tbsp. light brown sugar**
- **Kosher salt**

1. In a medium saucepan, heat the olive oil. Add the onion, garlic and raisins and cook over moderate heat, stirring occasionally, until the onion is softened, 6 to 8 minutes. Add the gochujang, paprika, peppercorns and celery seeds and cook, stirring, until the gochujang deepens in color, about 1 minute. Add the orange juice and scrape up any browned bits from the bottom of the pan. Add all of the remaining ingredients, except the salt, along with ¾ cup of water and simmer over moderate heat, stirring occasionally, until thickened slightly, about 30 minutes. Season with salt and scrape the sauce into a blender; let cool slightly. Wipe out the saucepan.

2. Puree the steak sauce until very smooth, about 2 minutes. Pass it through a fine sieve set over the saucepan, pressing on the solids. Simmer the steak sauce over moderately low heat, stirring occasionally, until thickened, about 30 minutes. Let cool to room temperature before serving. —*BV and MV*

MAKE AHEAD The steak sauce can be refrigerated for up to 1 week.

Skirt Steak Sizzle with Carrots and Arugula

⏲ Total **30 min**; Serves **4**

Steak fajitas are common in the Baja region of Mexico. Here, F&W's Justin Chapple makes his with smoky paprika and fragrant coriander, as well as an abundance of vegetables.

- 1 lb. skirt steak, cut into 4 pieces
- 3 Tbsp. extra-virgin olive oil, plus more for brushing
- 1 Tbsp. crushed coriander seeds
- 1 Tbsp. smoked sweet paprika
- 1½ tsp. finely grated lime zest
  Kosher salt and pepper
- 1 red onion, halved and sliced lengthwise ¼ inch thick
- 3 multicolored carrots, thinly sliced on the bias
- 1 jalapeño—halved, seeded and cut into julienne
- 6 garlic cloves, thickly sliced
  One 6-oz. bunch of arugula (not baby), trimmed and coarsely chopped
- 2 Tbsp. fresh lime juice, plus wedges for serving
  Warm tortillas, for serving

1. Brush the steaks with olive oil and season with the coriander, smoked paprika, lime zest, salt and pepper. Refrigerate for 15 minutes.

2. Preheat a large cast-iron skillet or griddle over high heat until smoking. Add 2 tablespoons of the olive oil and the steaks and cook over high heat, turning once, until charred on the outside and medium-rare within, about 4 minutes total; do not wipe out the skillet. Transfer the steaks to a carving board and let rest for 10 minutes, then thinly slice against the grain.

3. Meanwhile, in the same skillet or on the griddle, heat the remaining 1 tablespoon of olive oil. Add the onion, carrots, jalapeño and garlic and cook over high heat, stirring, until softened, about 5 minutes. Stir in the arugula and lime juice and cook until sizzling, about 1 minute. Top with the sliced steak and serve with warm tortillas and lime wedges. —*Justin Chapple*

WINE Spicy, blackberry-rich Shiraz: 2015 Oxford Landing.

Skirt Steak with Charred-Okra and Plum Salad

Active **45 min**; Total **2 hr 45 min**
Serves **6**

"I love okra, but pretty much only when it's charred," says *Top Chef* winner Brooke Williamson. "It enhances the flavor of the vegetable, without giving you that unpleasant sliminess." Williamson tosses the okra with sweet plums and crisp jicama to make a bright salad that's great served with sliced skirt steak or tossed all together.

STEAK

- ¼ cup soy sauce
- 2 Tbsp. Worcestershire sauce
- 2 Tbsp. whole-grain mustard
- 2 Tbsp. canola oil
- 1½ Tbsp. packed light brown sugar
- 2 tsp. crushed red pepper
- 4 garlic cloves, minced
- 2¼ lbs. skirt steak, cut into 6 pieces
  Kosher salt and pepper

SALAD

- ½ lb. medium okra, halved lengthwise
- 1 Tbsp. canola oil
  Kosher salt and pepper
- 2 Tbsp. fresh lime juice
- 2 Tbsp. extra-virgin olive oil
- 1 medium shallot, minced
- 4 plums—halved, pitted and cut into ½-inch-thick wedges
- 1 cup peeled and diced jicama (5 oz.)
- ½ cup lightly packed inner celery leaves
- 1 serrano chile—stemmed, seeded and thinly sliced

1. Marinate the steak In a large bowl, whisk all of the ingredients through the garlic until smooth. Put the steak in a large resealable plastic bag and pour in the marinade. Seal the bag and refrigerate for at least 2 hours or up to 8 hours.

2. Light a grill or preheat a grill pan. Remove the steak from the marinade and season lightly with salt and pepper. Grill over high heat, turning once, until lightly charred outside and medium-rare within, 5 to 6 minutes. Transfer to a carving board and let rest. Leave the grill on.

3. Meanwhile, make the salad In a large bowl, toss the okra with the canola oil and season with salt and pepper. Grill cut side down over high heat until charred, 3 to 5 minutes. Transfer to a plate and let cool slightly. In a serving bowl, whisk the lime juice with the olive oil and shallot and season with salt and pepper. Add the plums, jicama, celery leaves, serrano and charred okra and toss well. Season with salt and pepper. Carve the steak against the grain and serve with the salad. —*Brooke Williamson*

WINE Spicy Zinfandel: 2014 Bedrock Wine Co. Old Vine.

Skirt Steak Tips from the Pros

MARINATE IT "I love skirt steak. I like it marinated with something that's salty and sweet, then charred." —*Jamie Bissonnette, Toro, NYC and Boston*

COOK IT COLD "Meat right from the fridge is easier to move in the skillet and stays juicier." —*Alex Guarnaschelli, Butter, NYC*

KNOW WHEN IT'S DONE "For the most tender texture, cook skirt steak, a flavorful and inexpensive cut, to medium-rare." —*Brooke Williamson, Hudson House, Redondo Beach*

Skirt Steak Sizzle with
Carrots and Arugula

Beef-and-Celery Yakitori

Sourdough Tortillas with Charred Steak and Scallion Salsa

Active **1 hr 15 min**; Total **4 hr 35 min**
Serves **6 to 8**

- 1 cup buttermilk
- ¾ cup water
- 1 Tbsp. sugar
- 2½ oz. fresh sourdough starter (see Note)
- 2 tsp. active dry yeast
- 3¾ cups bread flour, plus more for dusting
- Kosher salt and pepper
- Canola oil, for greasing
- 12 large scallions
- ½ cup fresh lime juice
- 1 serrano chile—stemmed, seeded and minced
- 2 lbs. skirt steak, cut into 5-inch lengths

1. In a small saucepan, heat the buttermilk, water and sugar until an instant-read thermometer registers 95°. Transfer to the bowl of a stand mixer and whisk in the sourdough starter and yeast. Let stand until foamy, about 20 minutes. Attach the dough hook. Add the 3¾ cups of bread flour and mix on low speed until smooth, about 7 minutes. Add 2½ teaspoons of salt and mix on low speed until incorporated, about 3 minutes. Transfer the dough to a large greased bowl, cover with plastic wrap and let rise in a warm place until doubled in bulk, about 45 minutes.

2. Cut the dough into 20 pieces. Gently shape into balls and transfer to 2 large greased baking sheets. Very loosely cover the dough with plastic wrap. Let stand in a warm place until doubled in bulk, about 2 hours.

3. Heat a cast-iron griddle or large skillet over moderately high heat. On a lightly floured work surface, dust 1 ball of dough with flour and roll ⅛ inch thick. Griddle the tortilla, turning once, until browned in spots and pliable, about 30 seconds per side. Wrap the tortilla in a towel and repeat with the remaining balls of dough.

4. Light a grill or preheat a grill pan. Grill the scallions over moderately high heat, turning, until lightly charred, 3 minutes total. Transfer to a work surface to cool, then cut into ½-inch pieces. In a medium bowl, mix the scallions with the lime juice and serrano and season with salt. Leave the grill on.

5. Season the steak with salt and pepper. Grill over moderately high heat, turning once, until lightly charred outside and medium-rare within, about 6 minutes total. Transfer to a carving board and let rest for 5 minutes, then carve against the grain. Serve the steak in the tortillas with the scallion salsa. —*Val M. Cantu*

NOTE Fresh sourdough starter kits are available at kingarthurflour.com. Follow the feeding instructions before using.

MAKE AHEAD The tortillas can be stored in an airtight container overnight.

BEER Dark Mexican lager: Negra Modelo.

Beef-and-Celery Yakitori

Total **30 min**; Serves **4**

- ¼ cup low-sodium soy sauce
- ¼ cup unseasoned rice vinegar
- 2 Tbsp. packed light brown sugar
- 2 tsp. finely grated peeled fresh ginger
- 2 lbs. boneless rib eye steak (1½ inches thick), cut into 2-inch pieces
- 3 large celery ribs, cut into 1½-inch lengths
- 6 to 8 long skewers, soaked in water if wooden
- Canola oil, for brushing
- Kosher salt and pepper

1. In a small saucepan, whisk the soy sauce with the vinegar, sugar and ginger. Bring to a boil over moderately high heat, stirring to dissolve the sugar. Keep warm.

2. Light a grill or preheat a grill pan. Thread the rib eye and celery onto the skewers, alternating them. Brush with canola oil and season with salt and pepper. Grill over moderately high heat, turning occasionally, until lightly charred and the steak is medium-rare to medium, about 10 minutes. Transfer the skewers to a platter and serve with the warm sauce. —*Justin Chapple*

MAKE AHEAD The soy-ginger sauce can be refrigerated for up to 3 days. Bring to room temperature before using.

WINE Oregon Gamay: 2015 Bow & Arrow Willamette Valley.

Vinegar-Marinated Beef Yakitori

Active **20 min**; Total **40 min**
Serves **4**

For her addictive short rib and shiitake skewers, F&W's Laura Rege does a very quick and simple marinade of mirin, vinegar, sake, soy sauce and brown sugar, which imparts a fantastic sweet and salty flavor to the dish.

- ½ cup mirin
- ½ cup unseasoned rice vinegar
- ¼ cup sake or sherry
- 2 Tbsp. light brown sugar
- 2 Tbsp. soy sauce
- 1½ lbs. boneless short ribs—sliced ½ inch thick, then cut into 2-inch pieces (have your butcher do this)
- 10 scallions, white and light green parts sliced crosswise into thirds
- 20 bamboo skewers, soaked in water
- ¾ lb. shiitake mushrooms, stemmed
- Rice bran oil, for brushing
- Kosher salt and pepper
- Togarashi, for serving

1. In a large bowl, whisk the mirin, vinegar, sake, brown sugar and soy sauce. Toss in the short ribs along with the scallions and mushrooms. Cover and refrigerate for 20 minutes.

2. Alternately thread the beef and scallions onto half of the skewers. Thread the mushrooms on the remaining skewers. Brush with rice bran oil. Season with salt and pepper.

3. Preheat a grill pan. Grill the beef and mushroom skewers over moderately high heat until the meat is medium-rare and the mushrooms are tender, about 2 minutes per side. Transfer the skewers to a platter, sprinkle with togarashi and serve. —*Laura Rege*

WINE Aromatic French red: 2015 Michel Gahier Le Clousot Arbois Trousseau.

Texas Chile Short Rib Tacos

Active **30 min**; Total **3 hr 30 min**; Serves **6**

To round out the tang and heat from the tomatoes and chiles in this intensely flavored sauce, brothers and cookbook co-authors Matt and Ted Lee add a little semisweet chocolate. "It's mellow and sweet," says Ted. "The chocolate puts everything in balance."

3½ lbs. English-cut beef short ribs
    Kosher salt and pepper

3 large onions, quartered lengthwise

8 skin-on garlic cloves, lightly crushed

3 Tbsp. plus 1 tsp. peanut or canola oil

3 ancho chiles, stemmed and seeded

3 pasilla chiles, stemmed and seeded

2 cups beef stock or low-sodium broth
    One 28-oz. can chopped tomatoes

3 Tbsp. semisweet chocolate chips
    Warm small corn tortillas, sliced avocado, sliced radishes, sliced pickled jalapeños, crumbled Cotija or ricotta salata cheese, cilantro leaves and lime wedges, for serving

1. Season the short ribs with 2 teaspoons of salt, then cover and refrigerate for at least 1 hour or up to 1 day.

2. Preheat the broiler and position a rack 4 to 6 inches from the heat. On a large rimmed baking sheet, toss the onions and garlic with 1 teaspoon of the oil and season with salt and pepper. Broil for 10 to 12 minutes, until the onions and garlic are charred in spots. Let cool, then discard the garlic skins. Reduce the oven temperature to 325°.

3. In a large enameled cast-iron casserole, heat 1 tablespoon of the oil until shimmering. Add the ancho and pasilla chiles and toast over moderate heat, turning occasionally, until they are fragrant and pliable, about 2 minutes. Add the beef stock, remove from the heat, cover and let stand until the chiles are softened, about 5 minutes. In a blender, working in 2 batches, puree the chopped tomatoes with the chocolate chips, onions, garlic and the chiles and their soaking liquid until smooth; season with salt and pepper. Wipe out the casserole.

4. Pat the short ribs dry with paper towels. In the casserole, heat the remaining 2 tablespoons of oil until shimmering. Add half of the ribs and cook over moderately high heat, turning once, until browned, about 8 minutes. Transfer to a plate and repeat with the remaining short ribs. Add the sauce and return the first batch of short ribs and their juices to the casserole. Bring to a simmer, cover and braise in the oven for about 2 hours, until the short ribs are very tender.

5. Transfer the ribs to a plate and let cool slightly, then skim the fat from the surface of the sauce. Shred the meat into bite-size pieces and discard the bones. Return the meat to the sauce and cook over moderately low heat until heated through. Serve the short ribs in warm corn tortillas and garnish with sliced avocado, radishes, pickled jalapeños, crumbled cheese, cilantro leaves and lime wedges. —*Matt Lee and Ted Lee*

MAKE AHEAD The short ribs can be refrigerated in their sauce for up to 3 days. Reheat gently before serving.

BEER Malty, lightly hoppy amber lager: Live Oak Brewing Company Big Bark.

Prime Rib with Sour Cherry Conserva, Truffle and Chocolate

Active **1 hr 15 min**; Total **5 hr 15 min plus overnight salting**; Serves **12 to 14**

Chef Angie Mar of New York City's The Beatrice Inn is a master with meat, like this enormous, decadent and completely fabulous dry-aged beef rib roast. Mar's trick is to take the meat out of the oven for 30 minutes during its overall cooking time, which creates evenly cooked and perfectly juicy meat throughout the roast.

> **One 14-lb. 50-day dry-aged prime rib roast, rib bones frenched (see Note)**
> **Kosher salt and pepper**
>
> **2 bunches of long rosemary sprigs**
>
> **1 lb. sour cherries, pitted**
>
> **½ cup sugar**
>   **Softened beurre de baratte or other European-style butter, finely grated bitter chocolate (80%) and shaved summer truffle, such as Périgord, for serving**

1. Put the prime rib roast on a large rimmed baking sheet and generously season all over with salt. Refrigerate uncovered overnight. Let the roast stand at room temperature for 2 hours before cooking.

2. Preheat the oven to 475°. Set a rack in a large roasting pan and lay the rosemary sprigs across the rack. Season the roast all over with salt and set it on the rosemary, fat side up. Roast for 30 minutes, until browned. Reduce the oven temperature to 275° and roast for 40 minutes longer, until an instant-read thermometer inserted in the center registers about 65°. Remove from the oven and let stand for 30 minutes. Return the roast to the oven and roast until an instant-read thermometer inserted in the center registers 125°, 40 minutes to 1 hour. Remove from the oven and let rest for 30 minutes.

3. Meanwhile, in a large saucepan, combine the cherries with the sugar and a pinch of salt and cook over moderately high heat, stirring occasionally, until the cherries start to break down and are coated in syrup, about 15 minutes. Season with salt and pepper. Keep warm over very low heat.

4. Transfer the roast to a very large carving board. Carve between the bones. Spread the steaks with some softened butter and top with the warm cherry conserva, finely grated chocolate and shaved truffle. Serve. —*Angie Mar*

NOTE The 50-day dry-aged rib roast is available at select butcher shops and from lafrieda.com.

WINE Full-bodied, luscious Cabernet Sauvignon: 2013 Le Dix de Los Vascos.

Prime Rib with
Sour Cherry
Conserva, Truffle
and Chocolate

Brisket with
Sweet-and-Sour
Onions

Brisket with Sweet-and-Sour Onions

Active **20 min**; Total **5 hr**; Serves **10**

This brisket recipe is from Jessamyn Rodriguez, the founder and CEO of Hot Bread Kitchen, the New York–based social enterprise that helps immigrant women and others launch careers and food businesses. She calls the brisket her "crowning glory," and says the secret is cooking it low and slow.

One 5-lb. brisket, preferably first cut

Kosher salt and pepper

4 onions, sliced into ¼-inch-thick rings

¼ cup ketchup

2 Tbsp. tomato paste

1 Tbsp. soy sauce

1 Tbsp. dark brown sugar

4 garlic cloves, minced

Small cilantro sprigs, for garnish

1. Preheat the oven to 300°. Season the brisket generously with salt and pepper. In a large enameled cast-iron casserole, spread the onions in a single layer and lay the brisket on top. In a small bowl, whisk the ketchup with the tomato paste, soy sauce, brown sugar and garlic. Spread the sauce all over the brisket.

2. Cover the casserole and transfer to the oven. Braise the brisket for about 3 hours, until the meat is very tender. Uncover and continue cooking for 1 hour, until the sauce has thickened. Let the brisket cool slightly in the sauce for 30 minutes.

3. Transfer the brisket to a work surface and slice across the grain. Arrange the slices on a platter and spoon some of the sauce over the top. Garnish with cilantro and serve with the remaining sauce on the side. —*Jessamyn Rodriguez*

MAKE AHEAD The brisket can be refrigerated in its sauce for up to 5 days.

WINE Robust Zinfandel: 2015 Cline Ancient Vines.

Beef Rib Roast

📷 PAGE 180

Active **35 min**; Total **5 hr plus overnight salting**; Serves **6 to 8**

1 bunch of thyme sprigs

One 6½-lb. prime rib roast with 4 ribs—hinged, frenched and tied

¼ cup kosher salt, plus more for seasoning

1 Tbsp. unsalted butter, cut into small cubes

2 medium shallots, minced

2 Tbsp. drained capers

1 Tbsp. Cognac

2 cups beef stock or low-sodium broth

3 Tbsp. heavy cream

Pepper

1. Wedge the thyme sprigs into the hinge between the bones and meat of the rib roast. Season the roast all over with the ¼ cup of salt and place bone side down on a plate; refrigerate uncovered overnight.

2. Set the roast in a roasting pan and let stand at room temperature for 2 hours. Preheat the oven to 225°. Cook the roast until an instant-read thermometer inserted in the thickest part registers 90°, about 2 hours. Remove the pan from the oven and increase the oven temperature to 500°. Once the oven is at 500°, return the roast to the oven and cook until golden brown and 110° to 115° for rare, 15 to 30 minutes. (Alternatively, you can let the roast rest at room temperature for 2 hours before roasting at 500°; it will take 30 to 40 minutes to reach 110°.) Transfer the roast to a carving board. Dot with the butter, tent with foil and let stand for 30 minutes.

3. Meanwhile, set the roasting pan over 2 burners over moderately high heat. Add the shallots and cook, stirring, for 1 minute. Add the capers and cook, stirring, for 30 seconds. Add the Cognac, then the beef stock. Bring to a boil and cook for 5 minutes. Stir in the cream, season with salt and pepper and pour the gravy into a pitcher or gravy boat. Discard the string and thyme sprigs from the roast, carve the meat and serve. —*Jocelyn Guest*

WINE Structured, curranty Australian Cabernet Sauvignon: 2014 Wynns Black Label.

Beef Rib Roast Know-How

ON BUYING A prime rib roast is typically made up of about seven rib chops. To ensure the most uniform results when cooking this special-occasion meat, buy the lean end of the rib roast, which is about four ribs. It's not as fatty as the chuck end, but it's a more reliable cut to prepare for a big holiday feast.

ON PREPPING It's worth having your butcher hinge the roast, which entails removing the bones from the meat, then tying those bones back on. This creates the juiciest meat and helps the meat cook most evenly. Plus, after it's cooked, you can squirrel away the bones in the kitchen to save them for yourself! Pro tip: Salt the heck out of the roast at least a few hours ahead of time.

ON COOKING You can always cook the meat to 90° a few hours ahead. Then, flash-broil it to 110° to 115°, let it rest and serve. The meat gets brown and crusty, and stays perfectly rare in the center. To serve, remove the hinged bones, then use the whole length of a long, sharp knife to slice the meat. Do. Not. Saw.
—*Jocelyn Guest, White Gold Butchers*

Corned Beef with Pickled Cabbage and Potato Salad

Active **45 min**; Total **3 hr 15 min**
Serves **6**

>   One 5-lb. corned beef with seasoning packet
>
>   Two 12-oz. bottles pale ale
>
> 1 large onion, quartered
>
> 6 garlic cloves, crushed
>
> 2 bay leaves
>
> 1½ lbs. baby red potatoes, halved if small or quartered if large
>
> 3 cups distilled white vinegar
>
> 2 Tbsp. mustard seeds
>
> 2 Tbsp. sugar
>
> 1 Tbsp. kosher salt
>
> 1½ lbs. green cabbage, cored and sliced ½ inch thick
>
> 1 cup chopped parsley
>
> 2 Tbsp. each whole-grain mustard and Dijon mustard, combined

1. In a large pot, combine the corned beef and its seasonings with the beer, onion, garlic, bay leaves and 12 cups of water and bring to a boil over high heat. Cover and simmer over low heat until the beef is tender, about 2 hours and 30 minutes.

2. Meanwhile, in a medium saucepan, combine the potatoes with the vinegar, mustard seeds, sugar, salt and 3 cups of water and bring to a boil. Simmer over moderate heat until the potatoes are tender, 12 to 15 minutes. Transfer to a large heatproof bowl and let cool completely in the liquid. Stir in the cabbage and refrigerate for 1 hour, stirring occasionally. Drain well, transfer to a serving bowl and stir in the parsley.

3. Transfer the corned beef to a carving board and let rest for 15 minutes, then slice against the grain. Serve alongside the salad, passing the mixed mustards at the table. —*Justin Chapple*

MAKE AHEAD The sliced corned beef can be refrigerated in the cooking liquid for up to 3 days.

WINE Robust California Merlot: 2013 Duckhorn Napa Valley.

Rare Roast Beef with Pickled Green Tomatoes

Active **30 min**; Total **3 hr plus overnight curing**; Serves **6**

Chef Chris Behr's technique, featured in his cookbook *Carne*, yields a perfectly medium-rare roast beef that he thinly slices and serves at room temperature. The flavorful oil from the pickles doubles as a finishing sauce.

>   One 3½-lb. beef eye of round roast, trimmed and tied
>
>   Kosher salt
>
> 3 unripe medium green tomatoes (2½ lbs.), cored and sliced ¼ inch thick
>
> 3 cups white wine or apple cider vinegar
>
> 1 Tbsp. sugar
>
> 1¼ cups extra-virgin olive oil
>
> 6 garlic cloves, thinly sliced
>
> ⅓ cup mint leaves, torn
>
> 1 tsp. crushed red pepper
>
> 2 Tbsp. canola oil
>
>   Flaky sea salt, for serving

1. Season the beef with kosher salt and transfer to a large plate. Refrigerate, uncovered, for at least 12 hours or up to 24 hours. Bring to room temperature before cooking.

2. Meanwhile, in a large colander, toss the tomatoes with 1 teaspoon of kosher salt and let stand for 30 minutes. In a medium saucepan, bring the vinegar, sugar, 1 tablespoon of kosher salt and 3 cups of water to a boil, stirring to dissolve. Add half of the tomatoes and simmer over moderately low heat until they start to soften, about 3 minutes. Using a slotted spoon, spread them on a large rimmed baking sheet to cool. Repeat with the remaining tomatoes. Discard the brine; wipe out the saucepan.

3. In the medium saucepan, heat the olive oil. Add the garlic and cook over moderate heat until fragrant but not browned, about 1 minute. Remove from the heat. In a large bowl or two 1-quart heatproof jars, layer the tomatoes with the olive oil, garlic, mint and crushed red pepper. Let cool completely, then refrigerate. Bring to room temperature before serving.

4. Preheat the oven to 225°. Pat the beef dry with paper towels. In a large skillet, heat the canola oil. Cook the beef over moderate heat, turning, until browned all over, about 8 minutes. Set a rack in a small roasting pan and place the beef on it. Transfer to the oven and roast for 1½ to 2 hours, until an instant-read thermometer inserted into the center of the meat registers 120° for medium-rare. Transfer the beef to a cutting board and tent with foil. Let rest for 30 minutes.

5. Discard the string and thinly slice the roast beef against the grain; transfer to a platter. Drizzle with some of the tomato oil and sprinkle with flaky sea salt. Serve the beef warm or at room temperature with the pickled green tomatoes. —*Chris Behr*

MAKE AHEAD The pickles can be refrigerated for up to 1 week.

WINE Medium-bodied, herbal Sicilian red: 2015 Valle dell'Acate Il Frappato.

Leslie Bruni's Meatloaf

Active **30 min**; Total **1 hr 50 min**
Serves **6**

"This meatloaf is pure nostalgia," says journalist Frank Bruni of his mother's recipe. A flavorful tomato sauce makes the meat extra tender, and a little brown sugar gives it a delicious, mild sweetness.

> Nonstick cooking spray, for greasing
> 1 Tbsp. unsalted butter
> 1 medium onion, minced
> 1 cup plain tomato sauce
> 1½ Tbsp. distilled white vinegar
> 1½ Tbsp. brown sugar
> 1 Tbsp. Dijon mustard
> 1½ tsp. Worcestershire sauce
> 3 slices white sandwich bread, crusts removed and bread torn
> ½ cup whole milk
> 1½ lbs. ground beef chuck
> ½ cup fine breadcrumbs
> 2 large eggs, lightly beaten
> 2 tsp. kosher salt
> ½ tsp. pepper

1. Preheat the oven to 350°. Line a 9-by-13-inch baking pan with foil; lightly grease. In a medium skillet, melt the butter. Add the onion and cook over moderate heat, stirring occasionally, until softened, 8 minutes.

2. In a small bowl, whisk the tomato sauce with the vinegar, brown sugar, mustard and Worcestershire. In another small bowl, dip the bread in the milk, then gently squeeze out the liquid. Transfer the bread to a large bowl and discard the milk. Add the onion, ground beef, breadcrumbs, eggs, salt, pepper and ¼ cup of the tomato sauce and mix until just combined; transfer to the pan.

3. Firmly pat the meat mixture into a 9-by-5-inch loaf; spread the remaining sauce over the top. Bake for 1 hour and 10 minutes, until an instant-read thermometer inserted in the center registers 160°. Let rest for 10 minutes; serve. —*Frank Bruni*

MAKE AHEAD The meatloaf can be refrigerated for up to 3 days. Reheat gently before serving.

Square Meatballs with Pomodoro Sauce

Total **1 hr**; Serves **4**

For a better sear, chef Stefan Bowers of Battalion in San Antonio, Texas, presses his meatball mixture into a rectangle and then cuts it into squares instead of rolling into balls.

SAUCE

> ¼ cup extra-virgin olive oil
> ¼ small onion, finely chopped
> 4 garlic cloves, minced
> ½ tsp. crushed red pepper
> 4 basil sprigs, plus chopped leaves for garnish
> One 15-oz. can crushed tomatoes
> 1 tsp. sugar
> 1 tsp. red wine vinegar
> Kosher salt

MEATBALLS

> 1½ lbs. ground beef
> 1½ lbs. ground pork
> 1¾ cups shredded Parmigiano-Reggiano cheese, plus more for garnish
> 1 cup shredded Asiago cheese
> 1 cup shredded mozzarella
> ½ onion, finely chopped
> 4 garlic cloves, minced
> ½ cup dried breadcrumbs
> 2 large eggs
> ½ cup packed finely chopped parsley
> 1 Tbsp. finely chopped oregano
> Juice and zest of 1 lemon
> 1 Tbsp. kosher salt
> Black pepper
> 2 Tbsp. extra-virgin olive oil

1. Make the sauce In a medium saucepan, heat the olive oil. Add the onion and cook over moderate heat, stirring occasionally, until tender, about 5 minutes. Add the garlic and cook, stirring, until fragrant, about 1 minute. Add the crushed red pepper, basil sprigs, tomatoes and sugar and simmer until thickened slightly, about 15 minutes. Add the vinegar and season with salt. Keep warm.

2. Make the meatballs Line a 9-by-13-inch rimmed baking sheet with parchment paper. In a large bowl, combine all of the ingredients except the olive oil. Scrape the meat onto the prepared baking sheet and press into a 9-by-13-inch rectangle. Refrigerate until chilled, at least 20 minutes.

3. Unmold and cut the meat into 2-by-2-inch squares. In a large nonstick pan, heat the olive oil. Cook the meatballs over moderate heat, turning once, until they are a deep brown and just cooked through, about 10 minutes.

4. To serve, spoon the pomodoro sauce into shallow bowls. Top with meatballs and garnish with chopped basil and more Parmesan. —*Stefan Bowers*

Autumn Grilling Pointers

Don't pack up your grill tools when summer barbecue season is over. Here are tips from three wood-fired-cooking stars.

KNOW YOUR INGREDIENTS
"Summer is about quick grilling, but fall foods like a longer process," says Lee Desrosiers, the chef at Achilles Heel in Brooklyn, New York. He especially likes to slow-roast in-season squash and cabbage.

PAY ATTENTION TO THE FIRE
NYC chef Norberto Piattoni of Metta grew up grilling every Sunday with family in Argentina–no matter the weather. So he knows about adjusting for the seasons. "When it's cooler outside, you will need to compensate with more heat, so turn up the fire and monitor closely," he says.

MAKE USE OF THE COALS
Those glowing embers are perfect for low-and-slow cooking, notes Garett McMahan, the chef behind Celestine in Brooklyn. "Peel a whole onion and leave it in the smoldering coals for hours," he says. "You get an amazing bittersweet flavor."

Spiced Harissa Ragù
with Tahini Yogurt

Spiced Harissa Ragù with Tahini Yogurt

Active **30 min**; Total **2 hr 30 min**
Serves **6 to 8**

With warm spices, fiery harissa and chopped pistachios, this meaty ragù from Tel Aviv chef Salah Kurdi is solidly Middle Eastern. Don't let that stop you from ladling it over gnocchi or layering it into baked pasta.

- ¼ cup vegetable oil
- 3 large onions, finely chopped
  Kosher salt and pepper
- 1 lb. ground beef
- 1 lb. ground lamb
- 10 garlic cloves, finely chopped
- 1 cup shelled pistachios, coarsely chopped, plus more for garnish
- 1 Tbsp. harissa
- 2½ tsp. ground cumin
- 1½ tsp. hot paprika
- 1 tsp. ground coriander
- ½ tsp. ground turmeric
- ½ tsp. ground cinnamon
- ½ tsp. ground cardamom
- ¼ tsp. ground ginger
- ⅛ tsp. ground cloves
- 1 cup whole-milk yogurt
- ¼ cup tahini
  Roasted cherry tomatoes and warm pita, for serving

1. In a large saucepan, heat the oil until shimmering. Add the onions and a generous pinch of salt and cook over moderate heat, stirring occasionally, until lightly browned, about 12 minutes. Add the beef, lamb and garlic and cook, breaking up the meat with a wooden spoon, until the meat is cooked through, 8 to 10 minutes. Stir in the 1 cup of pistachios, the harissa, cumin, paprika, coriander, turmeric, cinnamon, cardamom, ginger, cloves and a generous pinch each of salt and pepper. Cover and simmer over low heat, stirring occasionally, until the meat and pistachios are very tender, about 2 hours.

2. In a medium bowl, whisk the yogurt with the tahini; season with salt and pepper. Swipe some of the yogurt into shallow bowls. Top with the ragù, garnish with pistachios and serve with roasted tomatoes and pita. —*Salah Kurdi*

Fried Green Tomato Double Cheeseburgers

Total **1 hr**; Serves **4**

SAUCE

- ¼ cup mayonnaise
- 1½ Tbsp. Sriracha
- 1 Tbsp. ketchup
- ½ tsp. Worcestershire sauce
- ¼ tsp. garlic powder

SLAW

- ¼ cup apple cider vinegar
- 1 small garlic clove, finely grated
- ½ celery rib, finely grated
- 1 Tbsp. toasted sesame seeds
- 1 tsp. sugar
- 1 tsp. Asian fish sauce
- ½ tsp. Dijon mustard
  Kosher salt and pepper
- ½ lb. iceberg lettuce, finely shredded (4 cups)

FRIED GREEN TOMATO

- ½ cup all-purpose flour
- 1 cup panko
  Kosher salt and pepper
- ½ cup buttermilk
- 1 large egg
- ⅓ cup canola oil
- 1 large unripe green tomato, cut into 4 thick slices

BURGERS

- 1½ lbs. ground chuck, 20% fat
  Kosher salt and pepper
- 1 Tbsp. canola oil
- 8 slices of American cheese
- 4 sesame seed buns, split and toasted

1. Make the sauce In a small bowl, whisk together all of the ingredients until smooth.

2. Make the slaw In a medium bowl, whisk the vinegar with the garlic, celery, sesame seeds, sugar, fish sauce and mustard. Season with salt and pepper. Just before serving, toss with the lettuce.

3. Prepare the green tomato Spread the flour and panko in separate shallow bowls and season each with salt and pepper. In another shallow bowl, whisk the buttermilk and egg and season with salt and pepper. In a large nonstick skillet, heat the oil. Dredge the tomato slices in the flour, shaking off the excess. Dip in the buttermilk-egg mixture, then dredge in the panko. Fry the tomato slices over moderate heat, turning once, until golden and crisp, about 3 minutes. Transfer to a paper towel–lined plate to drain, then season with salt.

4. Make the burgers Form the beef into eight ⅛-inch-thick patties and season with salt and pepper. In a large cast-iron skillet set on the grate of a preheated grill or on the stovetop, heat the oil. Working in 2 batches, cook the burgers over moderate heat until browned on the bottom, about 2 minutes. Flip, top each with a slice of cheese and cook, covered, until the burgers are browned and the cheese is melted, about 1 minute longer. Transfer to a work surface and repeat with the remaining 4 patties and cheese slices.

5. Spread the sauce on the cut sides of the buns. Place a burger on each bottom bun. Top with a fried green tomato slice, another burger and the slaw. Close the burgers and serve. —*Edward Lee*

F&W's Ultimate Burger

Active **25 min**; Total **50 min**
Makes **8 burgers**

Superstar butcher Pat LaFrieda of LaFrieda Meat Purveyors worked with us to create the most delectable homemade burger blend, combining five cuts of meat into the juiciest, beefiest and most consistently delicious burger you'll ever have.

- 1 **lb. beef chuck, sliced ¾ inch wide**
- ¾ **lb. boneless beef short ribs, sliced ¾ inch wide**
- ½ **lb. flatiron steak, sliced ¾ inch wide**
- ½ **lb. hanger steak, sliced ¾ inch wide**
- ½ **lb. beef brisket, sliced ¾ inch wide**
  Kosher salt
- 8 **hamburger buns, split**
  Ketchup, mustard, torn lettuce and sliced tomatoes, for serving

1. Freeze the meat in a single layer on a parchment-lined baking sheet until firm, 30 minutes.

2. In a grinder fitted with a chilled medium plate, gradually add the meat slices and grind at medium-high speed into a chilled bowl; do not force it. Working quickly, gradually regrind the ground meat, pushing gently only if necessary.

3. Light a grill or preheat a grill pan. Form the meat into eight ¾-inch-thick patties. Generously season with salt. Grill over high heat until browned outside and medium-rare within, 3 to 4 minutes per side. Serve the burgers in buns with ketchup, mustard, lettuce and tomato. —*Justin Chapple*

WINE Spicy Zinfandel: 2015 Seghesio Sonoma County.

Pimento Cheeseburgers with Bacon Jam

⏲ Total **45 min**; Serves **4**

BACON JAM

- ¼ **lb. slab bacon, finely diced (⅓ cup)**
- ½ **small onion, finely chopped**
- 2 **Tbsp. brewed coffee**
- 1½ **Tbsp. soy sauce**
- 1 **Tbsp. apple cider vinegar**
- 1 **Tbsp. brown sugar**
- 1 **Tbsp. granulated sugar**
  Kosher salt and pepper

PIMENTO CHEESE

- 6 **oz. sharp cheddar cheese, shredded (1½ cups)**
- 1 **oz. cream cheese (2 Tbsp.), at room temperature**
- ⅓ **cup mayonnaise**
- ¼ **cup drained and chopped jarred pimentos**
- 1 **small garlic clove, finely grated**
- 1 **Tbsp. gochujang (Korean red pepper paste)**
- ¼ **tsp. Worcestershire sauce**
- ¼ **tsp. pepper**

BURGERS

- 1½ **lbs. ground chuck, preferably 20% fat**
  Kosher salt and pepper
- 1 **Tbsp. canola oil**
- 4 **potato rolls, split and toasted**
  Sliced dill pickles and thinly sliced scallions, for serving

1. Make the bacon jam In a medium skillet, cook the bacon over moderate heat, stirring occasionally, until crisp, about 5 minutes. Transfer to a paper towel–lined plate to drain. Drain all but 1 tablespoon of the bacon fat from the skillet. Add the onion and cook over moderate heat, stirring occasionally, until softened, about 4 minutes. Return the bacon to the skillet along with the coffee, soy sauce, vinegar and both sugars. Cook over moderate heat, stirring, until the liquid is reduced and the jam is thick and glossy, about 5 minutes. Season with salt and pepper. Scrape the bacon jam into a small bowl and let cool to room temperature.

2. Meanwhile, make the pimento cheese In a medium bowl, combine all of the ingredients.

3. Make the burgers Form the beef into four ¾-inch-thick patties and season with salt and pepper. In a large cast-iron skillet set on the grate of a preheated grill or on the stovetop, heat the oil. Cook the burgers over moderate heat until browned on the bottom, about 3 minutes. Flip and cook, covered, until browned and medium-rare, about 3 minutes. Transfer to a work surface and let rest for 5 minutes.

4. Place a burger on each roll bottom. Top with some of the pimento cheese, bacon jam, sliced pickles and scallions. Close the burgers and serve. —*Edward Lee*

MAKE AHEAD The spreads can be refrigerated for up to 3 days.

Hot Dogs with Grilled Pickle Relish

Total **25 min** plus cooling
Makes **2 cups relish**

- 4 **dill pickles, sliced lengthwise into ¼-inch-thick slabs**
- 2 **Tbsp. canola oil**
- 1 **cup finely chopped white onion**
  Kosher salt
- ½ **cup distilled white vinegar**
- 2 **Tbsp. sugar**
- 1 **Tbsp. yellow mustard seeds**
- 2 **Tbsp. finely chopped parsley**
- 8 **all-beef hot dogs**
- 8 **hot dog buns, split and toasted**

1. Light a grill or preheat a grill pan. Grill the pickle slices over high heat, turning once, until lightly charred on both sides, 3 to 5 minutes. Transfer to a work surface to cool, then finely chop.

2. In a medium saucepan, heat the oil. Add the onion and a generous pinch of salt. Cook over moderate heat, stirring occasionally, until softened, 5 minutes. Add the vinegar, sugar and mustard seeds and simmer for 5 minutes. Remove from the heat and stir in the pickles; let cool completely. Fold in the parsley and season with salt.

3. Relight your grill or heat the grill pan. Grill the hot dogs over moderate heat, turning occasionally, until cooked through, about 5 minutes. Serve the hot dogs in the buns with the relish. —*Justin Chapple*

F&W's Ultimate Burger

Humm Dogs

Humm Dogs

Total **1 hr 15 min** plus overnight
pickling; Serves **8**

This crazy-luxurious and addictively delicious hot dog is a signature of star chef
Daniel Humm of New York City's Eleven
Madison Park and Made Nice. It's all-beef,
deep-fried and bacon-wrapped, piled into
a bun with truffle mayo, Gruyère cheese
and a bright and crunchy relish made with
mustard seeds, celery and celery root.

RELISH

- ½ cup plus 1 Tbsp. white balsamic
  vinegar
- ¼ cup sugar
- 1½ Tbsp. kosher salt, plus more
  for seasoning
- ¼ cup yellow mustard seeds
- ½ cup finely diced peeled celery root
- ¼ cup finely diced celery
- ¼ cup finely diced half-sour pickle

TRUFFLE MAYONNAISE

- 1 large egg yolk
- 1 Tbsp. fresh lemon juice
- 1 tsp. Dijon mustard
- 1 tsp. kosher salt
- ½ cup canola oil
- 1 Tbsp. minced fresh black truffle
  or 1½ tsp. white truffle oil

HOT DOGS

- 8 all-beef hot dogs
- 8 thin slices of bacon
  Canola oil, for frying
- 8 split-top hot dog buns
- 8 slices of Gruyère, halved
  Inner celery leaves,
  for garnish

1. Make the relish In a small saucepan,
combine ½ cup of the vinegar with the
sugar, ¼ cup of water and the 1½ tablespoons of salt and bring to a boil, stirring
to dissolve the sugar and salt. Add the
mustard seeds and let cool completely.
Transfer to a bowl, cover and refrigerate
overnight. Drain before using.

2. In a medium bowl, mix the celery root,
celery and half-sour pickle with 3 tablespoons of the drained mustard seeds and
the remaining 1 tablespoon of vinegar. Season the relish with salt. Save the remaining
mustard seeds for another use.

3. Make the mayonnaise In a mini food
processor, puree the egg yolk with the
lemon juice, mustard and salt until smooth.
With the machine on, very gradually add the
canola oil until emulsified and the mayonnaise is thick. Scrape into a small bowl and
stir in the truffle.

4. Make the hot dogs Preheat the oven
to 350°. Pat the hot dogs and bacon dry
with paper towels. Wrap each dog with a
slice of bacon in a spiral; secure the bacon
with toothpicks.

5. In a large saucepan, heat 3 inches of
canola oil to 350°. Fry the hot dogs over
moderately high heat, turning occasionally, until browned and the bacon is crisp,
about 3 minutes. Transfer to paper towels
to drain. Discard the toothpicks.

6. Arrange the buns cut side up on a large
rimmed baking sheet. Spread the inside
of each bun with some of the truffle mayonnaise and fill with a hot dog and a slice
of Gruyère. Bake for about 5 minutes, until
the cheese is melted. Top with some of
the relish and garnish with celery leaves.
Serve right away. —*Daniel Humm*

MAKE AHEAD The celery relish and the
truffle mayonnaise can be refrigerated
separately overnight.

WINE Juicy sparkling rosé: NV Juvé y
Camps Pinot Noir Brut Rosé.

Lamb Burgers with Onion
Soup Aioli

Active **30 min**; Total **1 hr**
Serves **4**

Instead of putting caramelized onions
on these tasty lamb burgers, F&W's Justin
Chapple whisks onion soup mix into mayonnaise for a playful and delicious spread.

- ½ cup mayonnaise
- 1 Tbsp. prepared onion soup mix,
  such as Lipton
- 1 tsp. fresh lemon juice
- 2 Persian cucumbers, very thinly
  sliced lengthwise
- 1 tsp. sugar
  Kosher salt and pepper
- 1½ lbs. ground lamb
- 4 hamburger buns, split and toasted
  Halved and seeded piquillo peppers
  and baby arugula, for serving

1. In a bowl, whisk the mayonnaise, onion
soup mix and lemon juice. Cover and
refrigerate for at least 30 minutes.

2. Meanwhile, in a medium bowl, toss the
cucumbers with the sugar and ½ teaspoon
of salt and let stand until pliable, about
20 minutes.

3. Light a grill or preheat a grill pan. Form
the lamb into 4 patties, about ½ inch thick.
Using your thumb, make an impression
in the center of each patty. Season with
salt and pepper. Grill over moderate heat,
turning once, until nearly cooked through,
about 6 minutes total.

4. Spread the aioli on the bun bottoms
and top with the burgers, cucumbers,
peppers and arugula. Close and serve.
—*Justin Chapple*

MAKE AHEAD The aioli can be refrigerated
for up to 3 days. Stir well before using.

WINE Spicy, intense southern French red:
2016 Saint Cosme Côtes du Rhône.

Beef-and-Lamb Kibbeh

Active **2 hr**; Total **2 hr 30 min**
Makes **24**

A Middle Eastern favorite in Israel year-round, fried kibbeh are especially popular around Hanukkah. TV chef Andrew Zimmern wraps a fine bulgur–ground lamb "dough" around a spiced, ground-beef filling sweetened with dried fruit plumped. For dipping, he offers an herb-packed yogurt sauce seasoned with tart sumac.

YOGURT SAUCE

- 1 cup whole-milk Greek yogurt
- 2 Tbsp. fresh lime juice
- 1 garlic clove, finely grated
- 1 Tbsp. finely chopped dill
- 1 Tbsp. finely chopped mint
- 1 Tbsp. finely chopped cilantro
  Kosher salt
  Extra-virgin olive oil and sumac, for garnish

FILLING

- ⅓ cup pine nuts
- ½ cup apple juice
- ¼ cup finely chopped dried apricots
- 3 Tbsp. dried currants
- 2 Tbsp. vegetable oil
- ½ cup finely chopped shallots
- 10 oz. ground beef
- 2 Tbsp. sumac
- 1 Tbsp. dried mint
- ¼ tsp. ground cinnamon
- ¼ tsp. ground allspice
- ¼ tsp. freshly ground white pepper
- ¼ tsp. cayenne
  Kosher salt
- 3 Tbsp. finely chopped parsley

SHELLS

- 3 cardamom pods
- 2 dried chiles, stemmed
  One 1-inch cinnamon stick, broken
- ½ tsp. whole allspice
- ½ tsp. whole black peppercorns
- 1 cup fine bulgur
- 1 lb. ground lamb
- 1 small onion, finely chopped
  Kosher salt
  Vegetable oil, for frying

1. Make the yogurt sauce In a medium bowl, combine the yogurt with the lime juice, garlic, dill, mint and cilantro and season with salt. Refrigerate until ready to serve.

2. Make the filling In a medium skillet, cook the pine nuts over moderate heat, stirring constantly, until golden, about 4 minutes. Transfer to a plate.

3. In a microwavable bowl, heat the apple juice at high power for 1 minute. Add the apricots and currants and cover with plastic wrap. Let stand for 30 minutes; drain.

4. Meanwhile, in a medium skillet, heat the oil. Add the shallots and cook over moderate heat, stirring, until caramelized, about 3 minutes. Add the beef and cook, stirring to break it up, until no trace of pink remains, about 5 minutes. Stir in the sumac, mint, cinnamon, allspice, white pepper and cayenne and season with salt. Stir in the dried fruit, toasted pine nuts and parsley and remove from the heat.

5. Make the shells In a small skillet, combine the cardamom with the chiles, cinnamon stick, allspice and peppercorns. Toast over moderate heat until lightly golden and fragrant, about 3 minutes. Grind to a fine powder.

6. In a large bowl, cover the bulgur with water and let stand for 2 minutes. Drain in a sieve and rinse in cold water until the water is clear. Return to the bowl, cover with fresh water and let soak for 20 minutes. Drain, transfer to cheesecloth and squeeze dry. In the same bowl, combine the bulgur with the lamb, onion and ground spices and season with salt. Knead the mixture like bread dough until smooth, about 5 minutes. Refrigerate until cold, about 30 minutes.

7. Line a baking sheet with wax paper. Using moistened hands, roll 2 tablespoons of the bulgur mixture at a time into balls and set on the prepared baking sheet. Using your forefinger and thumb, indent a ball to form a pocket, then gently hollow out into a 3-inch-long, ¼-inch-thick oval shell. Cradling the shell in one hand so the walls don't collapse, spoon a heaping tablespoon of the beef filling into the pocket. Pinch to seal and shape the kibbeh into a 3-inch torpedo. Return to the prepared baking sheet. Repeat with the remaining bulgur and filling. Freeze until firm, about 15 minutes.

8. Line a metal rack with paper towels. In a medium saucepan, heat 2 inches of oil over moderate heat to 375°. Fry the kibbeh, without crowding, until dark brown, about 3 minutes. Using a slotted spoon, transfer them as they're done to the prepared rack; season with salt. Garnish the yogurt sauce with olive oil and sumac and serve with the kibbeh. —Andrew Zimmern

MAKE AHEAD The fried kibbeh can be refrigerated for up to 2 days and reheated in a 400° oven for about 10 minutes.

Slow-Cooked Lamb Neck Roti

Active **1 hr**; Total **3 hr**; Serves **6**

LAMB

- **3** Tbsp. canola oil
- **5** lbs. bone-in lamb necks
  Kosher salt and pepper
- **2** large white onions, chopped
- **3** medium carrots, chopped
- **3** celery ribs, chopped
- **8** garlic cloves
- **2** Tbsp. thyme leaves
- **3** bay leaves
- **¼** cup tomato paste
- **¼** cup sherry vinegar

PEPPER PASTE

- **8** dried guajillo chiles (about 2 oz.), stemmed and seeded
- **2** Tbsp. caraway seeds
- **1** Tbsp. coriander seeds
- **1** Tbsp. cumin seeds
- **2** garlic cloves
- **2** Tbsp. canola oil
- **2** Tbsp. hot sauce
- **½** Tbsp. Sriracha
- **½** tsp. red wine vinegar

ROTI ASSEMBLY

- **1** cup whole-milk Greek-style yogurt
- **1½** tsp. lemon zest plus 1 Tbsp. fresh lemon juice
  Kosher salt
  Warm roti paratha bread, mint leaves, dill sprigs, thinly sliced cucumber, thinly sliced white onion and cracked pepper, for serving

1. Make the lamb Preheat the oven to 325°. In a large enameled cast-iron casserole, heat the oil. Season the lamb with salt and pepper. In 3 batches, brown the lamb over moderately high heat, turning once, about 10 minutes per batch. Transfer to a plate. Add the onions, carrots, celery, garlic, thyme and bay leaves and cook over moderate heat, stirring occasionally, until the vegetables are softened and golden, about 15 minutes. Add the tomato paste and cook, stirring, until it begins to darken, about 1 minute. Add the sherry vinegar and cook, scraping up any browned bits. Return the lamb to the casserole along with 6 cups of water and bring to a simmer. Cover and braise in the oven for about 2 hours, or until the meat is very tender. Uncover and let cool for 30 minutes.

2. Transfer the lamb to a large rimmed baking sheet. Strain the braising liquid through a sieve into a medium saucepan, pressing on the solids; discard the solids. Skim off the fat. Boil the liquid over moderately high heat until thickened and reduced to 2 cups, about 25 minutes.

3. Meanwhile, make the pepper paste In a medium bowl, cover the chiles with boiling water and let stand until softened, about 30 minutes. Drain, reserving ½ cup of the soaking liquid. In a medium skillet, toast the caraway, coriander and cumin seeds over moderately low heat until fragrant, about 2 minutes; let cool. In a spice grinder, grind the seeds to a powder. In a blender, puree the ground seeds with the chiles, garlic, oil, hot sauce, Sriracha and vinegar, adding the soaking liquid a tablespoon at a time as needed, until smooth.

4. Whisk ½ cup of the pepper paste into the reduced braising liquid. Shred the lamb necks, discarding the bones and cartilage. Add to the braising liquid; season with salt.

5. Assemble the roti In a medium bowl, mix the yogurt with the lemon zest and juice. Season with salt. Pile the lamb on the warm roti. Drizzle with the lemon yogurt and top with mint, dill, cucumber, onion and cracked pepper; serve. —*Mason Hereford*

WINE Robust California Syrah: 2015 Melville Estate.

Lamb Fillets with Favas and Spring Vegetables

⏱ Total **40 min**; Serves **4**

- **1** lb. shelled fava beans or 2 cups thawed frozen beans
  Kosher salt and pepper
  Four 6- to 7-oz. trimmed boneless lamb sirloin fillets (also called chump chops)
- **2** Tbsp. extra-virgin olive oil
- **3** Tbsp. unsalted butter
- **½** lb. carrots, thinly sliced into coins
- **2** Tbsp. chicken stock or low-sodium broth
  One 10-oz. package thawed frozen peas
- **3** Tbsp. chopped mint, plus whole leaves for garnish

1. In a medium saucepan of boiling water, blanch the fava beans until barely tender, about 2 minutes; reserve 1 cup of the cooking water. Drain and cool under cold running water, then peel the beans. Set aside ⅓ cup for garnish. Transfer the remaining beans to a food processor. Add ½ cup of the reserved cooking water and puree until smooth, adding more water as necessary to reach a smooth consistency. Season with salt and pepper. Scrape the fava puree into a small bowl and keep warm.

2. Preheat the oven to 350°. Season the lamb with salt and pepper. In a large ovenproof skillet, heat the olive oil with 1 tablespoon of butter. Add the lamb and cook, turning once, until browned, 2 to 3 minutes per side. Transfer the skillet to the oven and cook the lamb for about 5 minutes longer, until a thermometer inserted in the thickest part registers 125° for mediumrare. Transfer the lamb to a work surface and let stand for 5 minutes.

3. Meanwhile, in a medium saucepan, heat the remaining 2 tablespoons of butter until the foam subsides. Add the carrots and chicken stock and cook over moderate heat, stirring occasionally, until the carrots begin to soften, 3 to 5 minutes. Add the peas and cook until just warmed through, about 3 minutes. Remove the saucepan from the heat, stir in the chopped mint and season with salt and pepper. Spoon any lamb juices from the skillet into the peas.

4. Spoon the fava puree onto 4 plates. Thinly slice the lamb across the grain and transfer to the plates along with the carrots and peas in their sauce. Top with the reserved fava beans and mint leaves and serve. —*James Golding*

WINE Rich, berry-scented rosé sparkling wine: 2013 Hush Heath Balfour Brut Rosé.

Lamb Chops with Burnt-Bread Salsa Verde

Lamb Chops with Burnt-Bread Salsa Verde

◔ Total **35 min**; Serves **4**

To make bright and tangy salsa verde even more delicious, F&W's Justin Chapple adds a slice of burned bread, which deepens and intensifies the flavors.

One ½-inch-thick slice (2 oz.) of rustic boule or other hearty bread

¾ cup extra-virgin olive oil, plus more for brushing

1 cup lightly packed parsley

1 cup lightly packed arugula

2 Tbsp. fresh lemon juice

1 Tbsp. drained capers

½ tsp. crushed red pepper

Kosher salt and black pepper

16 lamb rib chops

1. Light a grill or preheat a grill pan. Brush the bread with olive oil and grill over high heat, turning occasionally, until burned, about 4 to 5 minutes. Let cool, then tear into small pieces. Transfer to a food processor and pulse into fine crumbs. Add the parsley, arugula, lemon juice, capers, crushed red pepper and 2 tablespoons of water and pulse to a paste. With the machine on, gradually add the ¾ cup of olive oil until incorporated. Transfer the salsa to a bowl; season generously with salt and black pepper.

2. Light a grill or preheat a grill pan. Season the lamb chops with salt and black pepper. Grill over high heat, turning once, until lightly charred and medium-rare, about 6 minutes total. Transfer to a platter and serve with the salsa verde. —*Justin Chapple*

SERVE WITH Grilled zucchini and yellow summer squash.

MAKE AHEAD The burnt bread salsa verde can be refrigerated overnight. Bring to room temperature before serving.

WINE Spicy, dark-fruited Syrah from Washington state: 2014 Charles Smith Boom Boom.

Lamb Blade Chops with Cherry and Pickled Fennel Couscous

Active **45 min**; Total **1 hr**; Serves **4**

Lamb blade chops are our new favorite cut: They cook quickly and are inexpensive and very flavorful. Instead of marinating his lamb, chef Joshua McFadden of Ava Gene's in Portland, Oregon, tops them with an herby coriander dressing as soon as they come off the grill.

1 cup Israeli couscous

1 tsp. finely grated lemon zest plus 2 Tbsp. fresh lemon juice

¼ cup plus 2 Tbsp. extra-virgin olive oil

10 oz. sweet cherries (2 cups), pitted and halved

2 cups drained Pickled Fennel (recipe follows)

3 scallions, thinly sliced

½ cup lightly packed mint leaves

½ cup roasted unsalted almonds (3 oz.), chopped

Kosher salt and black pepper

1 Tbsp. finely chopped oregano

2 tsp. crushed coriander seeds

2 tsp. minced garlic

½ tsp. crushed red pepper

Canola oil, for brushing

Four 10-oz. lamb blade chops

1. In a medium saucepan of salted boiling water, cook the couscous until al dente. Drain well and transfer to a large bowl. Stir in the lemon juice and 2 tablespoons of the olive oil. Let cool completely, then stir in the cherries, pickled fennel, scallions, mint and almonds. Season with salt and black pepper.

2. Meanwhile, in a small bowl, whisk the remaining ¼ cup of olive oil with the oregano, coriander, garlic, crushed red pepper and lemon zest. Season with salt and black pepper.

3. Light a grill and oil the grate. Season the lamb with salt and pepper. Grill over moderately high heat, turning once, until lightly charred and medium within, 3 to 4 minutes per side.

4. Pile the couscous on a platter and arrange the lamb chops on top. Brush the dressing on the chops and serve right away. —*Joshua McFadden*

WINE Cherry-scented Rioja Reserva: 2012 Torre de Oña.

PICKLED FENNEL

Active **30 min**; Total **4 hr 30 min** Makes **1 qt**

McFadden pickles fennel in early summer, at its peak, and then uses it in everything from grain salads to sandwiches piled high with salumi.

1½ cups hot water

½ cup unseasoned rice vinegar

⅓ cup sugar

1 Tbsp. white wine vinegar

1½ Tbsp. kosher salt

2 small fennel bulbs, halved and very thinly sliced lengthwise through the core on a mandoline

5 garlic cloves, crushed

2 rosemary sprigs

2 small dried hot chiles, such as árbol

In a 1-quart jar with a tight-fitting lid, shake the water, rice vinegar, sugar, white wine vinegar and salt until the sugar and salt dissolve. Pack the fennel, garlic, rosemary and chiles into the jar, cover and refrigerate for at least 4 hours. Drain the pickles before serving. —*JM*

MAKE AHEAD The picled fennel in its brine can be refrigerated for up to 3 weeks.

Grilled Lamb Chops and Peppers

⏱ Total **25 min**; Serves **8**

A hardwood charcoal fire imparts excellent smoky flavor to grilled lamb chops and bell peppers.

- **1 lb. mixed bell peppers**
- **Kosher salt and pepper**
- **Three 8-bone racks of lamb (not frenched), cut into chops**
- **Extra-virgin olive oil, for drizzling**

1. Light a hardwood charcoal fire. Grill the bell peppers, turning occasionally, until charred all over, about 10 minutes. Transfer to a bowl, cover tightly with plastic wrap and let steam for 15 minutes. Peel and seed the bell peppers, then cut into thin strips and season with salt and pepper.

2. Meanwhile, season the lamb chops with salt and pepper and grill over high heat, turning once or twice, until nicely charred outside and medium-rare within, about 6 minutes total. Transfer the chops to a platter and let rest for 5 minutes. Transfer the bell peppers to the platter and drizzle with olive oil. Serve. —*Álavaro Palacios*

WINE Subtle, raspberry-scented Rioja: 2015 Palacios Remondo La Montesa.

Petite Leg of Lamb with Pickled Rhubarb Salsa

Active **40 min**; Total **2 hr 45 min**; Serves **6**

F&W's Justin Chapple loves leg of lamb, but it's sometimes such a commitment to make a whole one. Here, he opts to roast a petite leg, which is the shank end with the hip bone removed. It's ideal for a small group.

SALSA
- **1 cup apple cider vinegar**
- **3 Tbsp. sugar**
- **1 Tbsp. kosher salt**
- **½ lb. rhubarb, cut into ⅓-inch pieces**
- **2 Tbsp. minced red onion**
- **¼ cup finely chopped parsley**

LAMB
- **¼ cup extra-virgin olive oil**
- **¼ cup minced garlic**
- **2 Tbsp. finely chopped thyme**
- **1 Tbsp. crushed fennel seeds**
- **1 Tbsp. kosher salt**
- **2 tsp. pepper**
- **One 4½-lb. semi-boneless leg of lamb (shank end; hip bone removed)**

1. Make the salsa In a medium saucepan, combine the cider vinegar with the sugar, salt and 1 cup of water and bring to a boil. Remove from the heat and add the rhubarb and onion. Let cool completely, then transfer to a medium bowl and refrigerate for 1 hour. Drain well, return to the bowl and stir in the parsley.

2. Meanwhile, make the lamb Preheat the oven to 400° and set a rack on a baking sheet. In a small bowl, whisk the olive oil with the garlic, thyme, fennel seeds, salt and pepper. Using a paring knife, poke holes all over the lamb. Rub the garlic mixture all over the lamb and transfer it to the rack.

3. Roast the lamb for about 1 hour and 20 minutes, until an instant-read thermometer inserted in the thickest part registers 135°. Transfer the lamb to a carving board and let rest for 30 minutes. Carve the lamb and serve with the salsa. —*Justin Chapple*

MAKE AHEAD The pickled rhubarb salsa can be refrigerated for up to 2 days. Stir in the parsley before serving.

WINE Spicy red from the Rhône Valley: 2015 Château de Saint Cosme Gigondas.

Roast Leg of Lamb

Active **20 min**; Total **2 hr 30 min** Serves **6 to 8**

Chef April Bloomfield of New York City's The Spotted Pig believes that a great leg of lamb doesn't need much fuss. Here she rubs it with a simple garlic-and-rosemary paste before roasting until it's juicy and delicious.

- **One 4½-lb. leg of lamb, tied**
- **3 garlic cloves**
- **½ cup rosemary needles, chopped**
- **3 Tbsp. extra-virgin olive oil**
- **Kosher salt and pepper**

1. Let the lamb stand at room temperature for 1 hour. Preheat the oven to 400°. Using the back of a knife, smash the garlic to a paste. Scrape into a small bowl and whisk in the rosemary and olive oil. Season the lamb generously with salt and pepper and rub the paste all over the lamb. Transfer to a shallow roasting pan.

2. Roast the lamb for about 1 hour and 15 minutes, until an instant-read thermometer inserted in the thickest part registers 130°. Transfer the lamb to a carving board and let rest for 15 minutes. Carve the lamb and serve. —*April Bloomfield*

WINE Gamey, intense Rhône red: 2014 J.L. Chave Offerus Saint-Joseph.

Leg of Lamb Know-How

ON BUYING Leg of lamb is typically sold from either the shank, which is the lower part of the leg, or the sirloin end, from the knee to the hip. The shank is leaner, flavorful and pretty to present, whereas the sirloin is more fatty and rich. If you buy the sirloin, have your butcher remove the hip bone to make it easier to cook and carve.

ON PREPPING Have your butcher tie the leg, which allows the meat to cook more evenly. Season the lamb generously with salt, ideally at least an hour before you cook it.

ON COOKING Instead of watching a clock, use a probe thermometer inserted in the thickest part of the meat and cook the lamb 5 degrees below the goal temperature. Let the meat rest for 15 minutes to allow the juices to "reintroduce" themselves. To serve, use a sharp knife and slice against the grain. —*April Bloomfield, White Gold Butchers*

Petite Leg of Lamb with Pickled
Rhubarb Salsa

Herb-Crusted
Rack of Lamb

Herb-Crusted Rack of Lamb

Total **1 hr**; Serves **10 to 12**

To make the most of tasty lamb chops, cookbook author Ayesha Curry spreads the racks with mustard and honey, then coats them with herb-packed breadcrumbs. The result is juicy chops with a fantastic crust.

¼ cup extra-virgin olive oil

2 racks of lamb, frenched (2 lbs. each)

Kosher salt and pepper

2 Tbsp. whole-grain mustard

1 tsp. honey

¾ cup plain dry breadcrumbs

2 Tbsp. finely chopped parsley

1 Tbsp. finely chopped mint leaves

1 Tbsp. finely chopped rosemary

1 tsp. finely grated lemon zest

1 lb. cherry tomatoes, preferably on the vine

1. Preheat the oven to 400°. Preheat a large cast-iron skillet, then heat 1 tablespoon of the olive oil in it. Season the lamb all over with salt and pepper. In batches if necessary, add the lamb racks to the skillet, fat side down, and cook over moderately high heat until browned, about 3 minutes. Turn the lamb fat side up and cook for 2 minutes longer. Transfer the lamb fat side up to a large rimmed baking sheet.

2. In a small bowl, mix the mustard with the honey. In another small bowl, mix the breadcrumbs with the parsley, mint, rosemary, lemon zest, the remaining 3 tablespoons of olive oil and a generous pinch each of salt and pepper. Brush the lamb with the honey mustard and coat with the breadcrumb mixture, pressing to help it adhere.

3. Roast the lamb for 15 minutes. Scatter the tomatoes around it and roast for 20 to 25 minutes longer, until an instant-read thermometer inserted in the center of the meat registers 130° for medium-rare. Transfer the lamb to a carving board and let rest for 10 minutes. Cut the racks into chops and serve with the tomatoes. —*Ayesha Curry*

WINE Full-bodied Napa Valley Cabernet: 2014 Beaulieu Vineyard Rutherford.

Rabo de Toro

Active **1 hr 35 min**; Total **5 hr plus overnight sitting**; Serves **6**

This lusty braised-oxtails dish is common in Córdoba, Spain. The meaty oxtails are simmered in a mix of tomatoes, red wine and sherry until they're wonderfully tender and flavorful.

4 lbs. oxtails, cut into 1-inch pieces

Kosher salt

2 Tbsp. extra-virgin olive oil

2 large Spanish onions, chopped

4 Roma tomatoes, chopped

4 celery ribs, chopped, plus leaves for garnish

1 large carrot, chopped

1 head of garlic, cloves crushed

1 bottle medium-bodied red wine, such as Rioja

2 cups oloroso sherry

1 bay leaf

1 Tbsp. black peppercorns

Bread, for serving

1. Preheat the oven to 300°. Season the oxtails with salt. In a large enameled cast-iron casserole, heat the olive oil over moderately high heat. Working in 3 batches, brown the oxtails for 7 to 10 minutes, turning occasionally. Transfer to a large plate. Remove all but 2 tablespoons of fat from the casserole. Add the onions, tomatoes, celery, carrot and garlic and cook over moderately high heat until just starting to brown, about 15 minutes. Stir in the wine and sherry, bring to a boil and cook for 10 minutes. Return the oxtails to the casserole. Add 8 cups of water along with the bay leaf and peppercorns. Bring to a boil, then cover and transfer to the oven. Braise, stirring the oxtails a few times, until very tender, about 3½ hours. Let cool, then cover and refrigerate overnight. Skim the fat from the top of the stew.

2. Gently reheat the stew over moderate heat. Transfer the oxtails to a large plate. Strain the sauce into a large bowl, pressing on the solids. Discard the solids. Return the sauce to the casserole and bring to a boil, then simmer for about 10 minutes, until slightly thickened. Season with salt. Return the oxtails to the sauce and simmer until warm. Transfer the oxtails and sauce to bowls, garnish with celery leaves and serve with bread. —*José Andrés*

WINE Robust, dark-fruited Monastrell blend: 2013 Casa Castillo Las Gravas.

3 Uses for Leftover Lamb

SALAD Toss baby arugula with chopped basil and thyme, chilled slices of lamb, crumbled goat cheese and toasted pecans. Dress with a raspberry vinaigrette.

TACOS Fill flour tortillas with thinly sliced lamb, fresh mint, grilled onions and feta cheese. Fold the tortillas over, brush with olive oil and grill on both sides until the tacos are crispy and the cheese has melted.

PASTA Dice leftover lamb and add it to a luscious tomato sauce to serve over penne.

VEGETABLES
& TOFU

Vermouth-Braised
Shallots (p. 221)
OPPOSITE Roasted
Carrots with Labneh,
Urfa, Pickled Shallots
and Lime (p. 218)

Celery Root, Apple and Fennel Slaw

Total **45 min**; Serves **8**

Kansas City, Missouri chefs Colby and Megan Garrelts serve this sweet and crunchy slaw as an accompaniment to their rich and meaty chili (p. 174), but it also would be excellent alongside barbecued meat and chicken.

- 1 **lb. celery root, peeled and julienned, preferably on a mandoline**
- ½ **cup sugar**
- 1 **tsp. kosher salt, plus more for seasoning**
- ¼ **cup extra-virgin olive oil**
- 2 **Tbsp. apple cider vinegar**
- 1 **Tbsp. Dijon mustard**
- 1 **Tbsp. capers, chopped**
- 1 **Tbsp. drained prepared horseradish**
- 2 **Braeburn or Lady apples, cored and julienned, preferably on a mandoline**
- 5 **celery ribs, thinly sliced, plus ½ cup lightly packed celery leaves**
- 1 **small fennel bulb—halved, cored and julienned, preferably on a mandoline**
- ½ **cup lightly packed parsley leaves**
- 2 **Tbsp. finely chopped oregano**
  Pepper

1. In a large bowl, toss the celery root with the sugar and 1 teaspoon of salt; let stand for 15 minutes. Drain the celery root well in a colander and squeeze out some of the excess liquid. Wipe out the bowl.

2. In the same bowl, whisk the olive oil with the vinegar, Dijon, capers and horseradish. Add the celery root, apples, celery ribs and leaves, fennel, parsley and oregano; toss well. Season with salt and pepper and toss again. Serve right away.
—*Colby and Megan Garrelts*

Avocado-and-Cabbage Slaw

Total **30 min**; Serves **6**

This slaw evokes the crunch and tang of *chaat*, the iconic Indian snack. "There's nothing Indian about it, yet it's entirely Indian," says New Dehli chef Suvir Saran.

- 3 **Tbsp. fresh lime juice**
- 2 **Tbsp. honey**
- 1 **Tbsp. finely grated peeled fresh ginger**
- 2 **tsp. Sriracha**
- 2 **tsp. soy sauce**
- 2 **tsp. Asian fish sauce**
- 1 **tsp. white wine vinegar**
- ¾ **tsp. chaat masala (see box, p. 231)**
- ¼ **tsp. ground cumin**
  Kosher salt and pepper
- 1 **lb. green and/or red cabbage, cored and finely shredded**
- 6 **scallions, light green and white parts only, thinly sliced**
- 1 **pint cherry or grape tomatoes, halved**
- ½ **cup cilantro leaves, finely chopped**
- ¼ **cup mint leaves, finely chopped**
- 2 **Hass avocados—peeled, pitted and diced, plus avocado slices for serving**
- 1 **cup roasted salted cashews, chopped, plus more for garnish**
  Microgreens, for garnish

In a large bowl, whisk the lime juice with the honey, ginger, Sriracha, soy sauce, fish sauce, vinegar, chaat masala and cumin until combined. Season with salt and pepper. Add the cabbage, scallions, tomatoes, cilantro, mint, diced avocados and the 1 cup of chopped cashews and toss to coat. Garnish with avocado slices, more chopped cashews and microgreens; serve.
—*Suvir Saran*

MAKE AHEAD The dressing can be refrigerated overnight.

Glazed Pickled Red Cabbage

Active **20 min**; Total **5 hr 40 min**; Serves **8**

This recipe is a riff on traditional Danish red cabbage, a very popular dish eaten throughout the year, especially at Christmas. It's a lovely balance of sweet and tangy, with some richness from the addition of duck fat.

- 1 **cup apple cider vinegar**
- 1 **cup pomegranate or maple syrup**
- 3 **whole allspice berries**
- 2 **whole cloves**
- 2 **bay leaves**
  One 3-inch cinnamon stick
- 1 **tsp. coriander seeds**
  One 2½-lb. head of red cabbage— outer leaves discarded, cabbage cored and sliced ⅛ inch thick
- ¼ **cup duck fat or schmaltz**
  Kosher salt and pepper

1. In a medium saucepan, combine 2 cups of water with the vinegar and pomegranate syrup and bring to a boil over moderately high heat. Remove from the heat and add the allspice, cloves, bay leaves, cinnamon stick and coriander seeds and let stand for 1 hour. Set a fine sieve over a medium bowl and strain the vinegar mixture. Discard the solids.

2. Bring a large pot of water to a boil, add the cabbage and cook over moderately high heat for 20 minutes, until just tender. Drain and return to the pot. Pour the vinegar mixture over the cabbage and toss to coat. Cover the pot with a lid and let the cabbage marinate at room temperature for 2 hours.

3. Place the pot with the cabbage over moderately high heat and add the duck fat. Bring to a boil. Cover the surface of the cabbage with a round of parchment paper and cook over low heat until the cabbage is very soft, 1½ hours. Transfer to a bowl, season with salt and pepper and serve.
—*Nadine Levy Redzepi*

MAKE AHEAD The finished cabbage can be refrigerated for up to 2 days.

Avocado-and-Cabbage Slaw

Sautéed Cabbage
with Cumin Seeds
and Turmeric

Sautéed Cabbage with Cumin Seeds and Turmeric

Total **25 min**; Serves **6**

Cabbage is one of the best vegetables to keep on hand because it stays fresh for weeks in the refrigerator and can be eaten in so many different ways—raw, steamed, roasted, grilled or, as here, stir-fried.

- **2 Tbsp. extra-virgin olive oil**
- **1½ tsp. cumin seeds**
- **3 lbs. green cabbage, cored and thinly shredded**
- **1½ tsp. turmeric**
- **1½ tsp. kosher salt**

In a large saucepan, heat the olive oil over moderate heat. Stir in the cumin seeds and cook until fragrant, about 30 seconds. Add the cabbage, turmeric and salt and cook, stirring occasionally, until the cabbage is softened and browned in spots, 15 to 20 minutes. Serve hot. —*Julia Turshen*

SERVE WITH Brown rice, yogurt and chutney, or with roast chicken.

MAKE AHEAD The cabbage can be refrigerated for up to 2 days. Reheat gently before serving.

Roasted Brussels Sprouts with Peanuts and Fish Sauce

Active **10 min**; Total **35 min**; Serves **4**

Cookbook author Julia Turshen says that having peanuts and fish sauce in the cupboard means that she can quickly turn simple roasted brussels sprouts into this crunchy, nutty, umami-rich dish.

- **1½ lbs. brussels sprouts, trimmed and halved**
- **3 Tbsp. extra-virgin olive oil**
  Kosher salt
- **1 Tbsp. Asian fish sauce**
- **1 Tbsp. unseasoned rice vinegar**
  Chopped roasted unsalted peanuts, for garnish

1. Preheat the oven to 425°. On a large rimmed baking sheet, toss the brussels sprouts with 2 tablespoons of the olive oil and season with salt. Spread in an even layer and roast for about 25 minutes, stirring occasionally, until softened and browned.

2. In a small bowl, whisk the remaining 1 tablespoon of olive oil with the fish sauce and vinegar. Drizzle the sauce over the warm brussels sprouts. Transfer to a platter, sprinkle with chopped peanuts and serve. —*Julia Turshen*

SERVE WITH Brown rice and fried eggs.

Whole-Roasted Kohlrabi

Active **20 min**; Total **2 hr 15 min**
Serves **4 to 6**

Kohlrabi is a cruciferous vegetable. Tel Aviv chef Asaf Doktor's slow-roasted, unctuous version gets great flavor from a jalapeño-sesame-feta topper.

- **8 medium kohlrabi (3 lbs.)**
  Extra-virgin olive oil, for drizzling
  Kosher salt and pepper
- **4 oz. feta cheese, crumbled (1 cup)**
- **2 jalapeños—halved lengthwise, seeded and very thinly sliced crosswise**
- **2 Tbsp. thyme leaves**
  Toasted sesame seeds, for garnish

1. Preheat the oven to 450°. On a large rimmed baking sheet, drizzle the kohlrabi with olive oil and season with salt and pepper. Roast for about 1½ hours, until charred on the outside and tender within. Let cool slightly, then peel.

2. Arrange the kohlrabi on a platter. Generously drizzle with olive oil and season with salt and pepper. Sprinkle with the feta, jalapeños, thyme and sesame seeds and serve. —*Asaf Doktor*

Basic Roasted Carrots

Total **20 min**; Serves **4**

To achieve good caramelization on carrots, sauté them before finishing in the oven.

- **2 tsp. unsalted butter**
- **2 tsp. extra-virgin olive oil**
- **1 lb. medium carrots with green tops, scrubbed well, greens reserved for another use**
- **¾ tsp. kosher salt**
- **½ tsp. pepper**

Preheat the oven to 375°. In a large heat-proof skillet, melt the butter with the olive oil over moderately high heat. Add the carrots, salt and pepper and cook, turning occasionally, until browned all over, 3 to 4 minutes. Transfer the skillet to the oven and roast the carrots for 6 to 8 minutes, until they are just tender but still crisp in the center. Transfer to a plate and serve. —*Hugh Acheson*

Maple–Cider Vinegar Roasted Carrots

Total **30 min**; Serves **4**

- **2 tsp. unsalted butter**
- **2 tsp. extra-virgin olive oil**
- **1 lb. medium carrots with green tops, scrubbed well, 2 Tbsp. of the greens chopped and reserved for garnish**
- **¾ tsp. kosher salt**
- **½ tsp. pepper**
- **2 Tbsp. apple cider vinegar**
- **2 Tbsp. pure maple syrup**
- **¼ cup chopped roasted cashews**

Preheat the oven to 375°. In a large heat-proof skillet, melt the butter in the olive oil over moderately high heat. Add the carrots, salt and pepper and cook, turning occasionally, until browned all over, 3 to 4 minutes. Remove the skillet from the heat and add the vinegar and maple syrup. Shake the skillet to coat the carrots. Transfer to the oven and roast for 6 to 8 minutes, until the carrots are just tender but still crisp in the center. Transfer to a platter, top with the cashews and carrot greens and serve. —*Hugh Acheson*

Roasted Carrots with Labneh, Urfa, Pickled Shallots and Lime

📷 PAGE 212

⏱ Total **30 min**; Serves **4**

Tangy labneh is an excellent match with the sweet roasted carrots in this great recipe from chef Hugh Acheson. It's worth making the quick pickled shallots, too.

- **2 tsp. unsalted butter**
- **2 tsp. extra-virgin olive oil**
- **1 lb. medium carrots with green tops, scrubbed well, greens reserved for another use**
- **¾ tsp. kosher salt**
- **½ tsp. pepper**
- **1 tsp. Urfa biber (see Note)**
- **¼ cup Pickled Shallots (recipe follows)**
- **½ lime**
- **½ cup labneh (about 3 oz.)**

1. Preheat the oven to 375°. In a large heat-proof skillet, melt the butter in the olive oil over moderately high heat. Add the carrots, salt and pepper and cook, turning occasionally, until browned all over, 3 to 4 minutes. Transfer the skillet to the oven and roast the carrots for 6 to 8 minutes, until they are just tender but still crisp in the center.

2. Transfer the carrots to a platter and sprinkle with the Urfa. Scatter the pickled shallots on top, squeeze the lime over the carrots and serve with the lebneh on the side. —*Hugh Acheson*

NOTE Urfa biber (commonly referred to as Urfa pepper) is a Turkish chile that's distinctive for its dark burgundy color, irregularly sized flakes and intriguing salty-sweet-smoky-sour flavor. It's available at laboiteny.com or amazon.com.

Pickled Shallots

Total **10 min plus 4 hr marinating**
Makes **1 cup**

These pickled shallots, which are tasty in salads and sandwiches, take only minutes to make and can keep in the fridge for days.

- **1 cup apple cider vinegar**
- **1 Tbsp. kosher salt**
- **1 Tbsp. sugar**
- **4 large shallots (about ½ lb.), thinly sliced crosswise into rings**

In a small saucepan, combine the vinegar, salt and sugar with ½ cup of water and simmer over moderate heat until the sugar dissolves. Put the shallots in a small bowl or pint-size jar and pour the vinegar mixture on top. Cover and refrigerate for at least 4 hours before using. —*Hugh Acheson*

MAKE AHEAD The shallots can be refrigerated in the pickling liquid for up to 2 weeks

Maple-Roasted Radishes

⏱ Total **20 min**; Serves **6**

- **1 bunch of small radishes with greens (½ lb.)**
- **1 bunch of small breakfast radishes with greens (½ lb.)**
- **3 Tbsp. extra-virgin olive oil**
- **1 Tbsp. pure maple syrup**
- **Gray sea salt and pepper**
- **Dukka, for sprinkling**

Preheat the oven to 400°. On a large rimmed baking sheet, toss the radishes with the olive oil and maple syrup. Season with salt. Spread in a single layer and bake until crisp-tender, about 10 minutes. Sprinkle with more salt, pepper and dukka and serve. —*Angèle Ferreux-Maeght*

NOTE Dukka, an Egyptian spice blend, is available at kalustyans.com.

Roasted Vegetables with Smashed-Walnut Vinaigrette

Active **20 min**; Total **1 hr 15 min**; Serves **10**

- **1 lb. medium brussels sprouts, halved**
- **One 2-lb. head of cauliflower, cored and cut into florets**
- **1½ lbs. multicolored carrots, sliced lengthwise into 4- to 5-inch pieces**
- **½ cup plus 6 Tbsp. extra-virgin olive oil**
- **Kosher salt and pepper**
- **¼ cup sherry vinegar**
- **1 Tbsp. maple syrup**
- **2 tsp. Dijon mustard**
- **½ cup whole walnuts, toasted and smashed**
- **2 Tbsp. chopped parsley, plus more for garnish**
- **1 Tbsp. grated orange zest, plus more for garnish**

1. Preheat the oven to 425° with racks positioned in the upper and lower thirds. Spread the brussels sprouts, cauliflower and carrots on 3 separate rimmed baking sheets. Toss the vegetables on each sheet with 2 tablespoons of the oil. Season with salt and pepper.

2. Roast the brussels sprouts until tender, about 20 minutes. Tent with foil and keep warm. Roast the cauliflower and carrots until golden and tender, about 30 minutes. Let cool slightly, then transfer the vegetables to bowls.

3. Meanwhile, in a medium bowl, whisk the vinegar with the maple syrup and Dijon. While whisking constantly, slowly drizzle in the remaining ½ cup of olive oil until incorporated. Scrape the smashed walnuts into the bowl, then stir in the 2 tablespoons of parsley and the 1 tablespoon of orange zest and season with salt. Drizzle the vinaigrette over the roasted vegetables, garnish with more parsley and orange zest and serve. —*Laura Rege*

Roasted Vegetables
with Smashed-Walnut
Vinaigrette

Roasted Veggie Burgers with Carrot Ketchup

Total **1 hr**; Serves **4**

- 1 medium eggplant, cut into eight ½-inch-thick slices
- ½ cup extra-virgin olive oil
- 1 medium zucchini, sliced on a mandoline ⅛ inch thick
  Kosher salt and pepper
- 1 large red beet, peeled and sliced on a mandoline ⅛ inch thick
- 1 medium sweet potato, peeled and sliced on a mandoline ⅛ inch thick
- 4 medium carrots, thinly sliced
- ½ small onion, finely chopped
- 2 dried apricots, chopped
- 2 garlic cloves, chopped
- ¼ cup dry white wine
- 3 Tbsp. apple cider vinegar
- 1 Tbsp. Asian fish sauce
- 1½ tsp. Worcestershire sauce
- ½ tsp. soy sauce
- ½ tsp. ground ginger
- ¼ tsp. ground fennel
- 8 slices of Muenster cheese
- 4 poppy seed buns, split and toasted
  Red-leaf romaine lettuce leaves or mixed baby greens and sliced dill pickles, for serving

1. Preheat the oven to 400° and line 2 large rimmed baking sheets with foil. On opposite ends of 1 baking sheet, separately toss the eggplant with 3 tablespoons of the olive oil and the zucchini with 1 tablespoon of the olive oil. Season the eggplant and zucchini with salt and pepper and spread each vegetable in a single layer. On opposite ends of the second baking sheet, separately toss the beet and the sweet potato each with 1 tablespoon of the olive oil. Season with salt and pepper and spread in a single layer. Roast all of the vegetables until tender, about 10 minutes for the zucchini and about 25 minutes for the remaining vegetables; rotate the baking sheets halfway through baking. Let the vegetables cool slightly. Keep the oven on.

2. Meanwhile, in a medium saucepan, heat the remaining 2 tablespoons of olive oil. Add the carrots, onion, apricots and garlic and cook over moderate heat, stirring occasionally, until just softened, about 5 minutes. Add the wine and ¾ cup of water and simmer over moderately low heat until the carrots are very tender, 15 minutes. Remove from the heat and stir in the vinegar, fish sauce, Worcestershire, soy sauce, ground ginger and fennel. Scrape into a blender and let cool slightly. Puree until very smooth, adding water 1 tablespoon at a time to loosen the sauce, if necessary. Season the carrot ketchup with salt and pepper.

3. On a large rimmed baking sheet lined with foil, make 4 stacks of 2 eggplant slices. Top each with 1 cheese slice, 4 to 6 slices each of the sweet potato and beet, the remaining cheese and 4 to 6 zucchini slices. Transfer to the oven and bake for 5 minutes, until the cheese is melted and the veggie burgers are heated through.

4. Place the burgers on the bottom buns and top with lettuce and pickles. Spread the carrot ketchup on the top buns, close the burgers and serve. —*Edward Lee*

MAKE AHEAD The carrot ketchup can be refrigerated for up to 3 days

Roasted Onion and Shallot Tarts

Active **1 hr**; Total **2 hr 30 min**; Serves **6**

These tarts are best made with patience. Dane Allchorne, the chef at The Milk House in Kent, England, says that slow-cooking the onions and shallots allows them to melt down in a way that's almost caramel-like.

PASTRY

- 2 cups all-purpose flour, plus more for dusting
- ¾ tsp. kosher salt
- 1½ sticks chilled unsalted butter, diced
- 1 large egg
- 1 Tbsp. ice water

FILLING AND TOPPING

- 3 Tbsp. unsalted butter
- 3 large onions (2½ lbs.), halved lengthwise and thinly sliced crosswise
- 12 medium shallots, sliced
- 1 Tbsp. chopped thyme leaves
- 1 tsp. brown sugar
  Kosher salt and pepper
- ⅔ cup panko
- ⅓ cup finely grated Parmigiano-Reggiano
- ¼ cup pine nuts, lightly toasted
- 3 Tbsp. extra-virgin olive oil

1. Make the pastry In a food processor, pulse the 2 cups of flour and the salt to combine. Add the butter and pulse until the mixture resembles coarse meal. In a small bowl, whisk the egg and ice water; drizzle into the food processor and pulse just until a rough dough forms. Scrape onto a lightly floured work surface, gather up any crumbs and knead gently just until the dough comes together. Pat into 2 equal disks, wrap in plastic and refrigerate until firm, about 1 hour.

2. On a lightly floured surface, using a lightly floured rolling pin, roll out 1 piece of dough to a 14-inch square, about ⅛ inch thick. Using a knife, cut out three 7-inch rounds. Ease each round into a 4-inch tart pan with a removable bottom, then trim the overhang and prick the dough all over with a fork. Repeat with the remaining piece of dough. Freeze until firm, about 15 minutes.

3. Preheat the oven to 375°. Arrange the tart shells on a large rimmed baking sheet. Line the shells with parchment paper and fill with pie weights or dried beans. Bake for about 20 minutes, until the edges are lightly golden. Remove the paper and weights and let cool to warm, about 30 minutes.

4. Meanwhile, make the filling In a large skillet, melt the butter. Add the onions and shallots and cook over moderate heat, stirring occasionally, until softened and golden brown, 35 to 40 minutes. Stir in the thyme and brown sugar and season with salt and pepper. Let cool.

5. In a food processor, pulse the panko, cheese and pine nuts until coarsely ground. Drizzle in the olive oil and pulse to form fine crumbs. Transfer the mixture to a small skillet and toast over moderate heat, stirring frequently, until golden, about 4 minutes.

6. Spoon the onion-shallot mixture into the tart shells. Sprinkle the tops with 2 tablespoons of the toasted crumbs. Bake until the edges of the pastry are golden and the crumbs are deep golden, about 20 minutes. Let cool on a rack for 10 minutes, then unmold the tarts and let cool to warm, about 10 minutes. Serve. —*Dane Allchorne*

SERVE WITH A green salad.

MAKE AHEAD The onion tarts can be refrigerated overnight. Reheat in a low oven to serve.

WINE Citrusy, focused sparkling wine: 2013 Hattingley Valley Classic Reserve.

Vermouth-Braised Shallots

PAGE 213
Active **30 min**; Total **1 hr**; Serves **8**

For easy peeling, first blanch the shallots in simmering water and then trim the ends.

16 large shallots (2 lbs.)
Kosher salt and pepper
½ stick unsalted butter, cubed
1 cup dry vermouth
2 tsp. white wine vinegar
¼ cup heavy cream

1. Preheat the oven to 325°. In a medium saucepan, cover the shallots with water and bring to a boil. Add a pinch of salt, reduce the heat to moderately low and simmer for 10 minutes. Drain the shallots and let cool slightly. Trim off the root and top ends and remove the skins.

2. In a large skillet, melt the butter. Add the shallots, season with salt and pepper and cook over moderate heat, stirring occasionally, until browned, 3 to 5 minutes. Add the vermouth and bring to a boil. Cook over moderate heat until the liquid is reduced by half, about 3 minutes. Remove the skillet from the heat and stir in the vinegar. Transfer the shallots and any liquid to a 1½-quart baking dish. Cover with foil and bake for 30 minutes, until the shallots are very tender. Transfer 3 tablespoons of the sauce to a small bowl and whisk in the cream. Stir the mixture back into the shallots and season with salt and pepper; serve. —*Eli Dahlin*

MAKE AHEAD The roasted shallots (without the cream) can be refrigerated overnight. Reheat, covered, in a low oven.

Seared Fennel and Tomatoes with Mustard Vinaigrette

Total **30 min**; Serves **8**

At La Granja resort in Ibiza, Spain, the cooking is all about the gorgeous vegetables overflowing from the property's garden. In September, when produce is at its peak, the resort's chef, José Catrimán, says to treat it simply. Here he gives fennel and plump tomatoes a quick char and a drizzle of vinaigrette for a no-fuss side dish that is ready in 30 minutes.

2 Tbsp. Dijon mustard
2 Tbsp. red wine vinegar
½ cup plus 6 Tbsp. extra-virgin olive oil
Kosher salt and pepper
4 large Roma tomatoes (1 lb.), halved lengthwise
3 fennel bulbs (1 lb.)—trimmed and sliced ½ inch thick lengthwise through the core, small fronds reserved for garnish
Tarragon leaves, for garnish

1. In a small bowl, whisk the mustard with the vinegar. While whisking constantly, drizzle in ½ cup of the olive oil until emulsified. Season with salt and pepper.

2. Heat a griddle or large cast-iron skillet. Brush the tomatoes and fennel all over with the remaining 6 tablespoons of olive oil and season with salt and pepper. Working in batches, cook the tomatoes cut side down until lightly charred, about 3 minutes. Transfer to a platter charred side up. Working in batches, cook the fennel, turning once, until just tender and lightly charred, about 6 minutes. Transfer to the platter with the tomatoes. Drizzle the vegetables with the vinaigrette and garnish with the reserved fennel fronds and tarragon. Serve warm or at room temperature. —*José Catrimán*

Parsnip Mash with Fried Brussels Sprout Leaves

Total **40 min**; Serves **6 to 8**

Mashed parsnips might be even better than mashed potatoes. They have the same creamy, luscious texture and a distinctly nutty, slightly sweet flavor. Topped with crispy brussels sprout leaves, this dish is irresistible.

2 lbs. parsnips, peeled and cut into ½-inch pieces
4 cups whole milk
1 stick unsalted butter
1 cup heavy cream
Kosher salt and black pepper
1 lb. brussels sprouts, leaves removed, cores reserved for another use
1 Tbsp. extra-virgin olive oil
Flaky sea salt and crushed red pepper, for serving

1. In a medium saucepan, combine the parsnips and milk. Bring to a boil over moderately high heat, then simmer over moderately low heat until the parsnips are tender, about 30 minutes. Drain the parsnips.

2. Set a food mill over the saucepan and pass the parsnips through it. Alternatively, mash the parsnips with a masher. Add the butter and cream and cook over low heat, stirring, until the butter is melted and fully combined. Season the mash with kosher salt and black pepper.

3. Meanwhile, preheat the oven to 375°. On a rimmed baking sheet, toss the brussels sprout leaves with the olive oil. Roast for about 15 minutes, stirring a few times, until golden and crisp.

4. Spoon the parsnip puree into a serving bowl and top with the brussels sprout leaves. Sprinkle with flaky sea salt and crushed red pepper and serve. —*Jocelyn Guest*

MAKE AHEAD The parsnip puree can be refrigerated overnight. Reheat over low heat and add additional heavy cream to thin out, if necessary.

Fried Zucchini Chips

Fried Zucchini Chips

Active **25 min**; Total **1 hr 25 min**; Serves **4**

It's hard to stop snacking on these addictive chips, which get a sprinkle of sweet and tangy balsamic just before serving.

- **2 small zucchini, very thinly sliced on a mandoline**
- **Kosher salt**
- **Cold-pressed grapeseed oil, for frying**
- **4 garlic cloves, thinly sliced**
- **¾ cup all-purpose flour**
- **Flaky sea salt**
- **2 Tbsp. aged balsamic vinegar**
- **⅓ cup packed small basil leaves**
- **⅓ cup packed mint leaves**

1. Set a colander over a large bowl. Toss the zucchini with 1 tablespoon of kosher salt and transfer to the colander. Let stand for 1 hour. Using your hands, squeeze the zucchini, a small handful at a time, to remove any remaining liquid.

2. Set a wire rack over a rimmed baking sheet. Heat ¼ inch of grapeseed oil in a large, heavy-bottomed skillet until shimmering. Fry the garlic over moderate heat until light golden, about 1 minute. Using a slotted spoon, transfer the garlic to the wire rack.

3. Spread the flour in a shallow bowl. Working in batches, dredge the zucchini in the flour and shake off the excess. Fry over moderate heat until golden and crisp, turning once, 1 to 2 minutes per batch. Using a slotted spoon, transfer the zucchini to the wire rack with the garlic. Season with flaky sea salt and let cool. Drizzle the zucchini and garlic with the balsamic vinegar, transfer to a serving bowl, toss with the basil and mint and serve. —*Laura Rege*

WINE Citrusy sparkling wine: NV Gloria Ferrer Sonoma Brut.

Delicata Squash with Labneh and Pomegranate Seeds

Active **20 min**; Total **1 hr**; Serves **10**

- **3 pounds Delicata squash (3 to 4 squash), halved lengthwise, seeded and cut into 2-inch pieces**
- **¼ cup extra-virgin olive oil, plus more for drizzling**
- **½ teaspoon crushed red pepper**
- **Kosher salt and black pepper**
- **1 ½ cups labneh**
- **1 cup pomegranate seeds**

1. Preheat the oven to 400°. On a large rimmed baking sheet, toss the squash with the ¼ cup of olive oil and the crushed red pepper. Season generously with salt and pepper and toss again. Roast for about 30 minutes, until browned in spots and just tender. Let cool to room temperature, about 30 minutes.

2. In a medium bowl, mix the labneh with a generous pinch each of salt and pepper. Spread the labneh on a large serving platter. Mound the squash on the labneh and scatter the pomegranate seeds on top. Drizzle with olive oil and serve. —*Justin Chapple*

Winter Squash and Savoy Cabbage Gratin with Garlic Crema

Active **30 min**; Total **1 hr 30 min**; Serves **6 to 8**

San Francisco chef Matthew Accarrino of SPQR looks to cornstarch to thicken the creamy milk-based roasted-garlic sauce here. This fantastic dish is rich but healthy.

- **10 garlic cloves**
- **¾ cup extra virgin olive oil, plus more for greasing**
- **¼ cup hazelnuts**
- **One 2-lb. butternut squash—peeled, halved lengthwise, seeded and cut into ½-inch-thick slices**
- **One 1-lb. Delicata squash—halved lengthwise, seeded and cut into ½-inch-thick slices**
- **Kosher salt and pepper**
- **1 lb. Savoy cabbage, cored and cut into 2-inch pieces (about 16 cups)**
- **2 cups low-fat milk**
- **2 Tbsp. cornstarch whisked with ¼ cup water**
- **4 oz. mild white cheddar or Fontina cheese, shredded**
- **3 Tbsp. chopped parsley**
- **1½ Tbsp. chopped fresh sage**

1. Preheat the oven to 375°. In a small saucepan or skillet, cook the garlic with ½ cup of the olive oil over moderately low heat until the garlic is softened, about 15 minutes. Transfer the garlic to a small bowl and mash to a paste. Reserve the oil for another use.

2. Spread the hazelnuts in a pie plate and toast for about 12 minutes, until fragrant. Transfer to a clean kitchen towel and let cool slightly, then rub together to remove the skins. Coarsely chop the hazelnuts.

3. On a large rimmed baking sheet, toss the squash with 2 tablespoons of olive oil; season with salt and pepper. Arrange in a layer and bake for about 30 minutes, until softened and golden. Leave the oven on.

4. Meanwhile, lightly grease eight 8-ounce ramekins or gratin dishes with olive oil and arrange on a large rimmed baking sheet. In a large saucepan, heat the remaining 2 tablespoons of olive oil. Add the cabbage, season with salt and cook over moderate heat, stirring occasionally, until wilted, 10 to 12 minutes. Transfer the cabbage to the prepared ramekins and top with the roasted squash.

5. In a medium saucepan, heat the milk with the mashed garlic over moderate heat until it just comes to a boil. Add the cornstarch slurry, whisking until thickened, about 1 minute. Whisk in the cheese and herbs and season with salt and pepper. Pour the sauce evenly into the ramekins. Bake in the center of the oven for about 30 minutes, until bubbling.

6. Turn the broiler to high. Transfer the baking sheet with the ramekins to the top rack of the oven and broil 6 inches from the heat source for about 2 minutes, until the squash is browned in spots. Sprinkle with the chopped hazelnuts and serve. —*Matthew Accarrino*

NOTE The gratin can also be baked in a 3-quart shallow baking dish.

MAKE AHEAD The assembled unbaked gratins can be refrigerated overnight; bring to room temperature before baking.

WINE Creamy California Chardonnay: 2014 Sbragia Home Ranch.

Summer Squash Gratin

Active **1 hr**; Total **1 hr 30 min**; Serves **4**

¼ cup extra-virgin olive oil

3 small leeks (½ lb.), white and tender green parts thinly sliced into rounds

¼ cup dry white wine

3 medium zucchini, cut lengthwise into ⅛-inch-thick slices, preferably on a mandoline

3 medium yellow summer squash, cut lengthwise into ⅛-inch-thick slices, preferably on a mandoline

Kosher salt and pepper

1 cup finely shredded Gruyère cheese (about 2 oz.)

1 plum tomato, very thinly sliced crosswise

Flaky sea salt and crusty bread, for serving

1. Preheat the oven to 425°. In a large skillet, heat 1 tablespoon of the oil over moderately high heat. Add the leeks and cook, stirring occasionally, until softened, about 3 minutes. Add the wine and cook until evaporated, about 2 minutes. Spread in a 9-inch round baking dish.

2. Meanwhile, on 2 large baking sheets, spread the zucchini and yellow squash and brush with the remaining 3 tablespoons of oil; season with kosher salt and pepper. Sprinkle with the cheese and let sit until slightly softened, about 5 minutes.

3. Tightly roll 1 piece of zucchini and set it on the leeks in the center of the dish. Working outward from that center slice, continue rolling and coiling additional pieces of zucchini and yellow squash until you reach the edge of the baking dish. Season the tomato slices with kosher salt and pepper, then tuck in intervals between the zucchini and squash. Scrape any cheese off the baking sheets and sprinkle on top.

4. Bake for 30 minutes, until the zucchini and squash are tender and browned in spots. Sprinkle with sea salt. Let cool slightly, then serve with crusty bread.
—*Laura Rege*

WINE Citrusy Chardonnay: 2015 La Crema Sonoma Coast.

Savory Plum Tarts with Arugula Salad

Active **1 hr**; Total **3 hr**; Serves **4**

Angie Mar of NYC's Beatrice Inn uses beef suet in the crust for her sweet-savory plum tarts. It adds rich flavor as well as structure and flakiness to the pastry.

CRUST

2½ cups all-purpose flour, plus more for dusting

2 Tbsp. sugar

1 Tbsp. finely chopped rosemary

2 tsp. kosher salt

1 stick unsalted butter, cubed and chilled

½ cup beef suet, chopped (see Note)

½ cup plus 2 Tbsp. ice water

FILLING

6 black plums (2¼ lbs.)—halved, pitted and cut into 1-inch wedges

3 Tbsp. sugar

1 Tbsp. thyme leaves

1½ tsp. ground cinnamon

1½ tsp. kosher salt

¼ tsp. freshly grated nutmeg

½ tsp. freshly ground black pepper

1 large egg beaten with 1 tsp. water

SALAD

6 cups baby arugula

2 cups parsley leaves

½ cup shaved Parmigiano-Reggiano cheese

2 Tbsp. fresh lemon juice

2 Tbsp. extra-virgin olive oil

Flaky sea salt

1. Make the crust In a food processor, pulse the 2½ cups of flour with the sugar, rosemary and kosher salt. Add the chilled butter and beef suet and pulse until the mixture resembles coarse meal. Drizzle the ice water over the top and pulse until the dough just starts to come together. Scrape the dough out onto a work surface, gather up any crumbs and knead until the dough is just smooth. Cut the dough into 4 pieces and pat into disks. Wrap the disks in plastic and refrigerate until well chilled, about 1 hour.

2. Preheat the oven to 400°. Line 2 large rimmed baking sheets with parchment paper. On a lightly floured work surface, roll out each disk of dough to an 8-inch round. Transfer the rounds to the prepared baking sheets and dust with flour; refrigerate for 15 minutes.

3. Make the filling In a large bowl, toss the plums, sugar, thyme, cinnamon, kosher salt, nutmeg and pepper. Spoon the plums and some juices into the center of the pastry rounds, leaving a 2-inch border. Fold the pastry up and over the plums and brush the rims with the egg wash. Bake the tarts for 40 to 45 minutes, until the crusts are browned and the plums are just tender; rotate the pans halfway through baking. Let cool slightly.

4. Make the salad In a large bowl, toss the arugula with the parsley, Parmigiano, lemon juice and olive oil. Season the salad with flaky sea salt. Transfer the tarts to plates and pile the salad alongside. Serve.
—*Angie Mar*

NOTE Beef suet is the fat that encases the kidneys. Look for it in the supermarket freezer aisle or at your local butcher shop.

MAKE AHEAD The tarts can be tented with foil and stored at room temperature overnight. Warm in a 400° oven for about 10 minutes before serving.

WINE Juicy California rosé: 2016 Red Car Rosé of Pinot Noir.

Summer Squash Gratin

Giant Summer
Tomato Tart

Giant Summer Tomato Tart

Active **15 min**; Total **1 hr 10 min**
Serves **8 to 10**

In the height of summer, when tomatoes are at their most delicious, F&W's Laura Rege showcases them in this simple, fresh tart. She layers and bakes phyllo with breadcrumbs to create an extra-crispy base, then spreads the crust with a mix of mayo and cream cheese before topping the tart with colorful, juicy, glorious tomatoes.

- **6** Tbsp. extra-virgin olive oil, plus more for drizzling
- **8** sheets of phyllo dough, thawed
- **½** cup fine dry breadcrumbs
- **8** oz. cream cheese
- **¼** cup mayonnaise
- **1½** lbs. mixed heirloom tomatoes, thinly sliced
  Flaky sea salt and pepper
  Basil leaves, for garnish

1. Preheat the oven to 375°. Brush a large rimmed baking sheet with 2 teaspoons of the olive oil. Lay 1 sheet of the phyllo dough on the baking sheet; keep the rest covered with damp paper towels. Brush the phyllo with 2 teaspoons of olive oil and sprinkle all over with 1 tablespoon of the breadcrumbs. Repeat the layering with the remaining phyllo, olive oil and breadcrumbs.

2. Bake the crust for about 25 minutes, until golden and crisp; rotate the baking sheet halfway through cooking. Let cool completely.

3. In a food processor, pulse the cream cheese with the mayonnaise until smooth. Spread the cream cheese mixture in the center of the tart, leaving a ½-inch border all around. Arrange the tomato slices on top and sprinkle with flaky sea salt and pepper. Drizzle lightly with olive oil and garnish with basil leaves. Cut into squares and serve. —*Laura Rege*

WINE Crisp Provençal rosé: 2016 Domaines Ott by.Ott.

Lemony Seared Endives

Total **30 min**; Serves **8**

- **4½** Tbsp. extra-virgin olive oil, plus more for drizzling
- **8** large Belgian endives, halved lengthwise
  Kosher salt
- **1** Tbsp. finely grated lemon zest plus 1 Tbsp. fresh lemon juice
  Flaky sea salt, for sprinkling

In a large skillet, heat 1½ tablespoons of the olive oil until shimmering. Add one-third of the halved endives; season with kosher salt. Cook over moderately high heat, turning once, until browned and starting to soften, about 3 minutes; transfer to a platter. Repeat in 2 more batches with the remaining olive oil and endives. Top with the lemon zest and juice, drizzle with more olive oil and sprinkle with sea salt. Serve immediately. —*Eli Dahlin*

Grilled Endives with Sun-Dried Tomato Relish

Total **15 min**; Serves **8**

- **½** cup drained oil-packed sun-dried tomatoes (4 oz.), chopped
- **½** cup torn kalamata olives
- **¼** cup extra-virgin olive oil, plus more for brushing
  One 3-inch strip of lemon zest, julienned
- **1** tsp. chopped thyme leaves, plus small sprigs for garnish
- **8** endives (1¾ lbs.), halved lengthwise
  Kosher salt and pepper
  Sage leaves, for garnish

1. In a small bowl, mix the sun-dried tomatoes with the olives, the ¼ cup of olive oil, the lemon zest and the chopped thyme.

2. Light a grill or preheat a grill pan and oil the grate. Brush the endives with olive oil and season with salt and pepper. Grill over moderately high heat, turning once, until crisp-tender and lightly charred, about 5 minutes. Transfer the endives cut side up to a platter and spoon the sun-dried tomato relish on top. Garnish with thyme sprigs and sage leaves and serve. —*José Catrimán*

Basic Sautéed Greens

Total **15 min**; Serves **4**

When it comes to cooking greens, we have more kinds to choose from than ever.

- **2** Tbsp. grapeseed or peanut oil
- **1** lb. Swiss chard or beet greens, stems and inner ribs removed and thinly sliced, leaves coarsely chopped
  Kosher salt
- **1** tsp. unsalted butter

In a large pot, heat the oil over moderately high heat until shimmering. Add the greens, stems and ½ teaspoon of salt and cook undisturbed for 20 seconds (the greens will brown a bit), then continue to cook, tossing occasionally with tongs, until wilted and just tender, about 3 minutes. Let stand off the heat for 30 seconds, then add the butter and toss until melted. Season with salt and serve. —*Hugh Acheson*

ARUGULA VARIATION Cook for 30 seconds, then pull off the heat.

BOK CHOY VARIATION Same method and timing as basic greens. Cut the upper greens into bite-size pieces and finely chop the core bulb. Finish with toasted sesame oil and soy sauce.

BROCCOLI LEAVES VARIATION Same method and timing as basic greens. Finish with chopped capers, anchovies and crushed red pepper.

RADISH GREENS VARIATION Same method as basic greens, but cook for just 2 minutes. Toss with raw radish, diced tofu and Basic Vinaigrette (p. 34).

SPINACH VARIATION Same as arugula variation.

SWEET POTATO GREENS VARIATION Cook for 1 minute, then let rest for 30 seconds. Finish with a touch of mirin, soy sauce and some torn nori.

TATSOI VARIATION Same as arugula method.

TURNIP GREENS VARIATION Cook at slightly lower heat than basic greens. Add more butter at the end and a squeeze of lemon.

TUSCAN KALE VARIATION Same method and timing as basic greens. Finish with a squeeze of lemon and some crushed almonds.

Silky Spinach with Fresh Cheese

Active **1 hr 15 min**; Total **2 hr 30 min**
Serves **8 to 10**

10   cups whole milk

3½ cups heavy cream

⅔   cup distilled white vinegar

½   cup ghee (see box, p. 231)
     Kosher salt and white pepper

1   large onion, finely chopped (2 cups)
     One 5-inch piece of ginger, peeled
     and grated (2 Tbsp.)

3   garlic cloves, minced

2   tsp. cumin seeds, ground

2   tsp. ground turmeric

2   tsp. ground coriander

½   tsp. chili powder

¼   tsp. cayenne
     Three 10-oz. packages thawed
     frozen chopped spinach,
     squeezed dry

1   large tomato, chopped

1. In the sink, line a large colander with
4 layers of moistened cheesecloth, leaving
2 inches of overhang. In a very large saucepan, bring the milk and 2 cups of the cream
to a simmer over moderate heat, stirring
occasionally, about 20 minutes. Reduce
the heat to low and slowly add the vinegar,
stirring constantly, then cook until the milk
separates into fluffy curds and watery
whey, about 2 minutes. Pour into the colander and let drain for 1 hour.

2. Gather the corners of the cheesecloth
and twist the curds into a ball, squeezing
out as much liquid as possible. Tie the
cheesecloth, then transfer the curds to
a work surface with the twisted end to the
side. Set a cutting board on top and weigh
it down with heavy skillets or large cans.
Let the curds stand until firm and dry,
about 15 minutes. Remove the cheesecloth
and cut the cheese into 1-inch pieces.

3. In a large nonstick skillet, heat ¼ cup
of the ghee until shimmering. Season the
cheese with salt and add half of it to the
skillet. Cook over moderate heat, turning
often, until the cheese is golden on all
sides, 6 to 8 minutes. Using a slotted
spoon, transfer to a plate. Repeat with
the remaining cheese.

4. Add the remaining ¼ cup of ghee and
the onion to the skillet and cook over moderate heat, stirring occasionally, until the
onion is lightly browned, about 10 minutes.
Add the ginger, garlic, cumin, turmeric,
coriander, chili powder and cayenne and
cook, stirring, for 2 minutes. Add the spinach and tomato and cook, stirring, until
warm, about 2 minutes. Stir in the remaining 1½ cups of cream and 1 cup of water
and cook, stirring, until most of the liquid is
evaporated, about 5 minutes. Fold in the
cheese, season with salt and white pepper
and serve. —*Andrew Zimmern*

VARIATION Swap the frozen spinach
for a mix of fresh stemmed kale, amaranth
and watercress.

MAKE AHEAD The precooked cheese can
be refrigerated for up to 3 days.

Creamed Spinach

Total **30 min**; Serves **8**

Cognac and Pernod add complex flavor
to this steakhouse staple.

2   cups chicken stock or low-sodium
     broth
     Three 8-oz. bags baby spinach

½   stick unsalted butter

2   large shallots, minced

3   large garlic cloves, finely grated

2   Tbsp. Cognac

1   Tbsp. Pernod

1   cup heavy cream

2   thyme sprigs
     Freshly grated nutmeg
     Kosher salt and white pepper

1. In a large pot, bring the chicken stock
to a boil over moderately high heat. Add
the spinach, cover and cook for 1 minute.
Toss the spinach with tongs, cover and
cook for 1 minute longer, until just wilted.
Drain the spinach and let cool, then
squeeze out as much liquid as possible.

2. In a large, shallow pot, cook the butter,
shallots and garlic over moderate heat,
stirring occasionally, until soft and translucent but not browned, about 5 minutes.
Remove the pot from the heat and add the
Cognac and Pernod. Carefully tilt the pan
over the burner to ignite the alcohol; cook
until the flames subside. (Alternatively,
remove the pan from the heat and ignite

with a long match, then return to the heat.)
Stir in the drained spinach, cream and
thyme. Bring to a boil and cook, stirring,
until thickened, about 2 minutes. Discard
the thyme sprigs. Season with a pinch of
nutmeg, salt and white pepper and transfer
to a bowl. Serve the creamed spinach hot.
—*Erika Nakamura*

MAKE AHEAD The creamed spinach can be
refrigerated overnight.

Catalan-Style Spinach

Total **30 min**; Serves **8**

In this very simple dish from Spanish
winemaker Álvaro Palacios, curly spinach
is cooked just enough to retain its great
flavor when mixed with sautéed garlic,
toasted pine nuts and plump raisins.

½   cup raisins

½   cup pine nuts
     Four 10-oz. bags stemmed
     curly spinach

¼   cup extra-virgin olive oil

4   large garlic cloves, very finely
     chopped
     Kosher salt and pepper

1. In a small bowl, cover the raisins with
warm water and let stand until plumped,
about 10 minutes; drain well. Meanwhile,
in a medium skillet, toast the pine nuts
over moderate heat, tossing, until lightly
browned, about 5 minutes. Transfer to
a plate.

2. In a large saucepan, bring ½ cup of
water to a boil. Add half the spinach in large
handfuls, letting each batch wilt slightly
before adding more. Cook over moderately
high heat, stirring, until just wilted, about
5 minutes. Transfer to a colander to drain.
Repeat with another ½ cup of water and
the remaining spinach.

3. In the large saucepan, heat the olive oil
until shimmering. Add the garlic and cook
over moderately high heat, stirring, until
fragrant and lightly browned, about 3 minutes. Stir in the spinach, raisins, pine nuts
and a generous pinch of salt. Cook, stirring
occasionally, until the spinach is hot, about
5 minutes. Season with salt and pepper
and serve. —*Álvaro Palacios*

Silky Spinach with
Fresh Cheese

Charred Shishito Peppers
with Furikake

Mustard Greens Saag Paneer

Total **50 min**; Serves **4**

"Saag paneer is usually cooked for hours," says chef Anita Jaisinghani of New York City's Pondicheri. "I cook my greens quickly, so they retain their flavor and that vivid green color."

- ¼ cup ghee (see box)
- 1 medium yellow onion, chopped
  Kosher salt and pepper
- 3 garlic cloves, minced
- 2 serrano chiles—stemmed, seeded and minced
- 2½ Tbsp. peeled fresh ginger, minced
- 2 Tbsp. dried fenugreek leaves (see box)
- 2 lbs. leafy spinach, stemmed and chopped
- 8 oz. mustard greens, stemmed and chopped
- 2 tsp. garam masala (see box)
- ¾ cup heavy cream, plus warmed cream for serving
- 1 lb. paneer or halloumi cheese, cut into 1-inch pieces
  Steamed basmati rice, for serving

1. In a large saucepan, heat 3 tablespoons of the ghee. Add the onion, season with salt and pepper and cook over moderately low heat, stirring occasionally, until soft and golden brown, about 20 minutes. Add the garlic, chiles, ginger and fenugreek leaves and cook over moderate heat, stirring occasionally, until softened, about 5 minutes. In 3 batches, add the spinach and mustard greens, letting each batch wilt before adding more. Stir in the garam masala and season with salt and pepper. Scrape the greens into a medium bowl and let cool slightly. Wipe out the saucepan.

2. In a food processor, pulse half of the greens with half of the heavy cream until finely chopped. Return to the saucepan and repeat with the remaining greens and cream. Keep the saag warm over very low heat, stirring occasionally.

3. In a medium nonstick skillet, heat ½ tablespoon of the ghee until shimmering. Add half of the paneer and cook over moderate heat, turning once, until golden brown, about 5 minutes; drain. Repeat with the remaining ghee and paneer. Fold the paneer into the saag and cook over

low heat until warmed through, 2 to 3 minutes; season with salt. Transfer to a bowl and drizzle with warm cream. Serve with basmati rice. —*Anita Jaisinghani*

Charred Coconut Green Beans

Active **25 min**; Total **1 hr 10 min**; Serves **4**

To get a perfect char on these fresh-tasting green beans from San Francisco chef Rupam Bhagat, make sure they are dried before adding them to the hot skillet.

- 1 cup unsweetened flaked coconut
- ½ jalapeño—stemmed, seeded and minced
- 2½ Tbsp. full-fat Greek yogurt
- 1½ tsp. finely chopped peeled fresh ginger
- 2 Tbsp. plus 2 tsp. vegetable oil
- 2 fresh curry leaves (see box), chopped
- ½ tsp. brown mustard seeds
  Kosher salt and pepper
- 1 lb. green beans, trimmed
- 2 Tbsp. chopped cilantro

1. In a medium bowl, cover the coconut with water and let stand at room temperature until softened, 45 minutes. Drain and transfer to a food processor. Add the jalapeño, yogurt and ginger and pulse until a coarse paste forms.

2. In a small skillet, heat 2 teaspoons of the oil. Add the curry leaves and mustard seeds and cook over moderate heat, stirring frequently, until the seeds start to pop, about 30 seconds. Transfer to the food processor with the coconut mixture and pulse until just combined. Season with salt and pepper.

3. In a large cast-iron skillet, heat 1 tablespoon of the oil. Add half of the green beans, season with salt and pepper and cook over high heat, stirring occasionally, until tender and lightly charred, 2 to 3 minutes. Transfer to a large bowl. Repeat with the remaining oil and green beans. Toss the charred beans with the coconut mixture and cilantro, transfer to a platter and serve. —*Rupam Bhagat*

Charred Shishito Peppers with Furikake

Total **15 min**; Serves **4**

Atlanta chef Ryan Smith makes his own version of the Japanese spice blend furikake. A store-bought blend works well too. Look for one without wasabi, as that can be a bit intense on these shishitos.

- 2 tsp. grapeseed or canola oil
- 1 lb. shishito peppers
- 1 Tbsp. furikake (see Note), plus more for garnish
- 1 Tbsp. fresh lime juice
- 1 tsp. shoyu or other soy sauce
  Flaky sea salt
  Lime wedges, for serving

1. In a large cast-iron skillet, heat 1 teaspoon of the grapeseed oil. Add half of the peppers and cook over moderately high heat, turning occasionally, until charred and tender, about 4 minutes. Transfer to a large bowl. Repeat with the remaining oil and peppers.

2. Add the 1 tablespoon of furikake, the lime juice and shoyu to the shishitos and toss to combine; season with flaky sea salt. Transfer to a platter; garnish with more furikake. Serve immediately with lime wedges. —*Ryan Smith*

NOTE Furikake is available at Asian markets and many Whole Foods stores.

Indian Staples

CHAAT MASALA A tart spice blend of dry mango powder, salt, pepper, cumin, dried chiles, and asafoetida.

FRESH CURRY LEAVES These dark-green leaves impart a citrusy flavor to dishes.

FENUGREEK LEAVES The tiny dried leaves have a subtle flavor reminiscent of fennel or celery.

GARAM MASALA Every family has a different recipe for this spice mix, which can include pepper, cloves, star anise, black cardamom, and more.

GHEE A type of clarified butter.
—*Chitra Agrawal, brooklyndelhi.com*

Chiles Rellenos

Total **1 hr**; Serves **8**

Whisking egg whites and then adding the yolks and whisking again creates a fluffy yet sturdy batter for these wonderful fried cheese-and-rice-stuffed chiles. The pleasant heat of the poblanos is amped up with the bittersweet spiciness of the charred-vegetable salsa.

- **8** poblano chiles (1½ lbs.)
- **2** medium tomatoes, cored
- **2** dried árbol chiles (½ oz.), stemmed
- **1** serrano chile, stemmed
- **½** jalapeño, stemmed
- **1** large garlic clove, peeled
  Kosher salt
- **½** cup long-grain rice
- **1** cup shredded Monterey Jack cheese (3 oz.)
- **½** cup crumbled Cotija or feta cheese (2.2 oz.)
- **4** large egg whites
- **2** large egg yolks
  Grapeseed oil, for frying
- **½** cup all-purpose flour

1. Preheat the broiler and position a rack 2 inches from the heat. Spread the poblanos on a baking sheet and broil, turning occasionally, until blistered and blackened, about 15 minutes. Transfer to a large bowl, cover with plastic wrap and let stand for 15 minutes. Wipe off the baking sheet. Peel the poblanos and discard the skins. Make |a 2-inch slit lengthwise in each poblano; do not remove the seeds or core.

2. Meanwhile, spread the tomatoes, árbol chiles, serrano, jalapeño and garlic on the same baking sheet. Broil, turning the vegetables occasionally, until blistered and blackened, 2 to 4 minutes for the árbol chiles; 8 to 10 minutes for the serrano, jalapeño and garlic; and 15 to 20 minutes for the tomatoes. Transfer the vegetables as they're done to a food processor and let cool. Pulse a few times until combined but still chunky. Scrape the salsa into a medium bowl and season with salt.

3. In a small saucepan, combine the rice with ⅔ cup of water and bring to a boil. Add a generous pinch of salt. Cover and cook over low heat until the water is absorbed and the rice is tender, about 15 minutes. Remove the pan from the heat. Fluff the rice with a fork and fold in the Monterey Jack and Cotija cheeses. Using a small spoon, stuff the poblanos with the rice mixture.

4. In a stand mixer fitted with the whisk, beat the egg whites at high speed until soft peaks form, about 1 minute. Add the yolks and beat at high speed until the mixture doubles in size, about 5 minutes.

5. Set a wire rack on a baking sheet. In a large cast-iron skillet, heat ¼ inch of oil until shimmering. Spread the flour in a shallow bowl. In batches of 2, dredge the poblanos in the flour and shake off the excess. Dip in the whipped eggs and fry over moderately high heat, turning once, until golden brown, 3 to 5 minutes. Transfer to the rack and season with salt. Serve immediately with the salsa.
—*Lorena Herrera*

MAKE AHEAD The salsa can be refrigerated for up to 1 week. The rice stuffing can be refrigerated overnight.

WINE Rich Chardonnay: 2014 Mi Sueño Los Carneros.

Eggplant Mash-Up

Active **30 min**; Total **2 hr**; Serves **6 to 8**

- **2** large eggplants (2 lbs. total), cut into 1-inch-thick rounds
  Sea salt and pepper
- **¼** cup extra-virgin olive oil
- **1** medium shallot, minced
- **3** garlic cloves, minced
- **1½** Tbsp. Madras curry powder
- **1½** tsp. dried oregano
- **1** tsp. ground cumin
- **3** cups thinly sliced Savoy cabbage (9 oz.)
- **1** pint multicolored cherry tomatoes, halved
- **1** red bell pepper, diced
- **⅓** cup chopped parsley, plus leaves for garnish
- **¼** small red onion, minced
- **¼** cup chopped mint, plus leaves for garnish
- **¼** cup chopped cilantro, plus sprigs for garnish
- **2** Tbsp. fresh lime juice

1. Arrange the eggplant rounds in a single layer on a wire rack set on a rimmed baking sheet. Sprinkle with salt, cover with a second baking sheet and let stand for 1 hour. Pat dry.

2. Light a grill or preheat the broiler. Season the eggplant with salt; brush with 2 tablespoons of the oil. Grill over moderate heat, turning once, until tender, 8 to 10 minutes. Transfer to the rack to cool. Cut into 1-inch pieces.

3. Meanwhile, in a medium saucepan, heat the remaining 2 tablespoons of oil. Add the shallot, garlic, curry powder, oregano and cumin and cook over moderate heat, stirring, until softened, about 2 minutes. Add the cabbage and cook until softened, 3 minutes.

4. In a bowl, combine the eggplant, cabbage, tomatoes, bell pepper, parsley, onion, mint, cilantro and lime juice; season with salt and pepper. Top with parsley and mint leaves and cilantro sprigs and serve.
—*Andrew Zimmern*

Baharat-Spiced Eggplant
with Hazelnuts, Cherries
and Tarragon

Berenjenas con Miel (Fried Eggplant with Honey)

Active **25 min**; Total **2 hr 45 min**; Serves **6**

Fried eggplant and honey is a combination served across the Andalusia region of Spain, especially in Córdoba. This version is the one chef José Andrés serves at Jaleo in Washington, DC.

- **4** Japanese eggplants (1½ lbs. total), trimmed and cut crosswise on the bias ¼ inch thick
- **2** Tbsp. kosher salt
- **2½** cups whole milk
  Canola oil, for frying
- **1** cup all-purpose flour
  Sea salt
- **3** Tbsp. honey
  Finely grated lemon zest, for garnish

1. Place the eggplant in a single layer on a rack set over a large rimmed baking sheet and season with the kosher salt. Top with another baking sheet and press firmly. Let stand for 20 minutes. Press again to help release the juices from the eggplant. Transfer the slices to a large bowl and cover with the milk. Cover and refrigerate for at least 2 hours or overnight.

2. In a large enameled cast-iron casserole, heat 1 inch of oil to 350°. In a shallow bowl, spread the flour. Remove the eggplant from the milk, shaking off any excess liquid. Dredge in the flour and shake off the excess. Working in batches, fry the eggplant, turning a few times, until golden brown, about 3 minutes. Transfer the eggplant to a paper towel–lined baking sheet and immediately season with sea salt.

3. Transfer the eggplant to a serving platter, drizzle with the honey and garnish generously with lemon zest. Sprinkle with more sea salt and serve immediately.
—*José Andrés*

WINE Fruity Spanish rosé: 2016 Los Dos.

Baharat-Spiced Eggplant with Hazelnuts, Cherries and Tarragon

Total **1 hr** plus overnight brining
Serves **4**

EGGPLANT

- **1½** cups kosher salt
- **1** cup sugar
- **4** Chinese eggplants, cut crosswise into 3-inch pieces

ONIONS

- **3** cipollini onions, peeled and thinly sliced crosswise
- **½** cup distilled white vinegar
- **1** Tbsp. kosher salt
- **2** tsp. sugar

BAHARAT SPICE MIXTURE

- **1** Tbsp. whole allspice berries
- **2** tsp. coriander seeds
- **1** tsp. cumin seeds
- **¾** tsp. whole cloves
  One ½-inch piece of cinnamon stick
- **¼** tsp. black peppercorns
- **11** cardamom pods—smashed and seeded (¼ tsp. seeds), pods discarded

ASSEMBLY

- **2** Tbsp. extra-virgin olive oil
- **½** garlic clove
- **2** cups Rainier cherries, halved and pitted
- **1** Tbsp. sugar
- **1** Tbsp. fresh lemon juice
  Kosher salt
  Canola oil, for frying
- **¼** cup hazelnuts, toasted, plus grated hazelnuts for serving
- **¼** cup parsley leaves
- **2** Tbsp. tarragon leaves
- **1** cup lebneh
  Finely grated lemon zest, for serving

1. Brine the eggplant In a large bowl, mix 8 cups of warm water with the salt and sugar, stirring to dissolve. Cut a ⅛-inch-deep slit lengthwise down one side of each eggplant piece; do not cut in half. Add the eggplant to the brine and cover with a plate to submerge. Cover with plastic wrap and refrigerate for at least 3 hours or, preferably, overnight. Drain well and discard the brine.

2. Meanwhile, prepare the onions In a small bowl, soak the onions in ice water for 15 minutes. Drain. In the same bowl, mix ½ cup of warm water with the vinegar, salt and sugar, stirring to dissolve the salt and sugar. Add the soaked onions. Cover and refrigerate for at least 3 hours or overnight.

3. Make the spice mixture In a small, dry skillet, toast all of the spices over moderately high heat until fragrant, about 2 minutes. Transfer to a spice grinder and let cool, then grind to a powder.

4. Finish and assemble the dish In a small skillet, cook the olive oil and garlic over moderately high heat, stirring occasionally, until the oil is hot and fragrant, about 3 minutes. Remove the skillet from the heat and let the garlic oil cool. Meanwhile, in a medium bowl, toss the cherries with the sugar, lemon juice and a pinch of salt.

5. In a large cast-iron skillet, heat 2 inches of canola oil to 325°. Add the drained eggplant and fry in batches, turning occasionally, until the eggplant is completely tender, about 5 minutes per batch. Using a slotted spoon, transfer the eggplant to a paper towel–lined baking sheet to drain. When cool enough to handle, open up the eggplant pieces along the cut side so that they are flattened but still intact. Sprinkle the eggplant all over with the spice mixture and season all over with salt.

6. Carefully pour off all but 1 tablespoon of the hot canola oil from the skillet. Heat the skillet over moderately high heat and cook half of the eggplant, turning once, until golden brown, about 4 minutes. Transfer to a plate and brush with the garlic oil. Repeat with the remaining eggplant.

7. Just before serving, drain the onions. Transfer to a bowl and toss with the toasted hazelnuts, parsley and tarragon. Spread the lebneh on 4 plates and top with the eggplant, cherries and the onion-herb mixture. Top with grated lemon zest and grated hazelnuts and serve. —*Sara Kramer and Sarah Hymanson*

MAKE AHEAD The spice mixture can be stored in an airtight container for up to 2 weeks.

WINE Smoky Lebanese white: 2014 Chateau Musar Jeune.

Spicy Eggplant Gratin

Active **30 min**; Total **2 hr**; Serves **6**

For this lighter take on eggplant parmesan, chef Chris Behr roasts the vegetable instead of breading and frying it.

- **3 lbs. eggplant, cut into 1-inch pieces**
- **½ cup plus 3 Tbsp. extra-virgin olive oil**
- **Kosher salt and black pepper**
- **1 medium yellow onion, finely chopped**
- **3 garlic cloves, chopped**
- **1 tsp. crushed red pepper**
- **30 basil leaves**
- **Two 28-oz. cans whole peeled tomatoes, crushed**
- **6 oz. smoked scamorza or mozzarella cheese, cubed (1½ cups)**
- **3 oz. Parmigiano-Reggiano cheese, finely grated (1 cup)**
- **Crusty bread, for serving**

1. Position racks in the upper and lower thirds of the oven and preheat to 375°. Line 2 large rimmed baking sheets with foil. Divide the eggplant between the prepared baking sheets and toss each sheet with 2 tablespoons of the olive oil. Season with salt and black pepper and spread out in a single layer. Bake for 45 minutes, until golden brown; rotate the baking sheets halfway through baking. Keep the oven on.

2. Meanwhile, heat ¼ cup of the olive oil in a large enameled cast-iron casserole. Add the onion, season with salt and cook over moderately low heat, stirring occasionally, until softened, 8 minutes. Add the garlic, crushed red pepper and 5 of the basil leaves and cook, stirring, until the garlic is softened and fragrant, 1 minute. Add the tomatoes and simmer, stirring occasionally, until the sauce is thickened, about 45 minutes. Let cool slightly, then transfer to a food processor and pulse until almost smooth; season with salt. You should have about 6 cups of tomato sauce.

3. Spread 1 cup of the sauce in the bottom of a 2½-quart shallow baking dish. Top with half of the eggplant and the remaining basil leaves. Drizzle with 1 tablespoon of the olive oil. Spread 2 cups of the sauce on top and sprinkle with half of each cheese. Drizzle with 1 tablespoon of the olive oil. Top with the remaining eggplant, sauce, scamorza and 1 tablespoon of olive oil.

4. Bake the gratin in the upper third of the oven for about 30 minutes, until bubbling. Remove from the oven and preheat the broiler to high. Sprinkle the remaining ½ cup of Parmesan over the top and broil for 3 minutes, until golden brown. Let cool for 10 minutes before serving. —*Chris Behr*

MAKE AHEAD The gratin can be assembled through Step 3 and refrigerated overnight. Bring to room temperature before baking.

WINE Smoky, full-bodied Sicilian Nero d'Avola: 2015 Cusumano.

Grilled Corn with Nasturtium Emulsion and Flowers

:) Total **30 min**; Serves **6**

Jay Blackinton, the chef at Hagstone's Wood Oven on Orcas Island, Washington, emulsifies fresh nasturtium leaves from his garden with mustard, apple cider vinegar and grapeseed oil to form a bright-tasting spread for grilled sweet corn. For a striking presentation, he sprinkles it with herbs and edible flowers.

- **4 oz. nasturtium or hydroponic watercress leaves**
- **2 Tbsp. Dijon mustard**
- **2 Tbsp. apple cider vinegar**
- **½ cup grapeseed oil**
- **Kosher salt**
- **6 ears of corn, husked**
- **Melted unsalted butter, for brushing**
- **Edible flowers and herb leaves, for decorating**

1. In a food processor or blender, combine the nasturtium leaves, Dijon, vinegar and 1 tablespoon of water; puree until a paste forms. With the machine on, gradually add the oil; puree until thick and smooth. Scrape into a small bowl and season the emulsion with salt.

2. Light a grill or preheat a grill pan. Brush the corn with melted butter and season with salt. Grill over high heat, turning occasionally, until lightly charred, about 5 minutes. Spread the nasturtium emulsion on the corn and decorate with edible flowers and herb leaves. Serve. —*Jay Blackinton*

Smoked Tofu–Stuffed Vegetables

Active **25 min**; Total **50 min**; Serves **6**

In place of a more traditional veal, pork or beef filling, Parisian chef Angèle Ferreux-Maeght stuffs the vegetables in this Provençal-inspired recipe with firm smoked tofu and plenty of fresh herbs and garlic. The smokiness of the tofu and the savory miso give this dish a hearty quality.

- **⅓ cup extra-virgin olive oil, plus more for greasing**
- **¾ lb. smoked tofu, finely chopped**
- **1 medium yellow onion, finely chopped, plus 3 small yellow onions**
- **2 garlic cloves, minced**
- **1 cup packed parsley leaves, chopped**
- **½ cup packed mint leaves, chopped**
- **5 scallions, thinly sliced**
- **3 Tbsp. white miso**
- **1 Tbsp. capers, chopped**
- **Fine gray sea salt**
- **6 firm-ripe small heirloom tomatoes**
- **3 small zucchini**

1. Preheat the oven to 400°. In a large skillet, heat the ⅓ cup of olive oil. Add the tofu, chopped onion and the garlic and cook over moderately high heat, stirring occasionally, until lightly browned, about 8 minutes. Scrape into a medium bowl and stir in the parsley, mint, scallions, miso and capers. Season with salt.

2. Trim as little as possible from the bottom of the vegetables so they sit flat. Cut off the top ¼ inch of the small onions and tomatoes. Lay the zucchini flat and trim ¼ inch lengthwise off the top. Set the vegetable tops aside. Using a small spoon, scoop out the insides of the vegetables, leaving ¼-inch-thick walls.

3. Brush a large rimmed baking sheet with olive oil and arrange the vegetables on the baking sheet. Spoon the filling into the vegetables and cover with the tops. Bake until the vegetables are tender and the filling is hot, 20 to 22 minutes for the tomatoes and 25 to 30 minutes for the onions and zucchini. Transfer to a platter and serve. —*Angèle Ferreux-Maeght*

MAKE AHEAD The tofu filling can be refrigerated overnight.

Spicy Eggplant Gratin

POTATOES, GRAINS & BEANS

Herb-Scented Mashed
Potatoes (p. 244)
OPPOSITE Hobo
Pack Bibimbap
(p. 255)

Caramel Potatoes

Active **30 min**; Total **1 hr**; Serves **8**

Danish home cook Nadine Levy Redzepi (whose husband is famed Noma chef René) serves these classic sticky-sweet caramelized potatoes as part of a holiday meal that includes roast goose, pork belly and red cabbage. A good hit of crunchy salt is perfect here.

4¼ lbs. small, waxy potatoes, such as creamers, peeled

2¼ cups sugar

1 stick unsalted butter, cut into 6 pieces

Kosher salt

1. In a large saucepan, cover the potatoes with 2 inches of water and bring to a boil. Cook over moderate heat, partially covered, until the potatoes are just barely tender, 12 to 14 minutes. Drain the potatoes. Clean and dry the saucepan.

2. Add ½ cup of the sugar to the cleaned saucepan and cook over moderate heat, swirling the pan occasionally, until the sugar has melted, about 4 minutes. Continue adding the sugar in ½-cup increments, melting each addition before adding the next, until all the sugar has melted to a light amber color. Reduce the heat to low and stir in the butter, 1 piece at a time.

3. Return the potatoes to the saucepan. The melted sugar will firm up; gently stir until the caramel is smooth again. Simmer over low heat, stirring occasionally, until the potatoes are coated in caramel (a layer of caramel will remain in the bottom of the pan), about 20 minutes more. Season the potatoes with salt. Using a slotted spoon, transfer the potatoes to a bowl and serve. *—Nadine Levy Redzepi*

MAKE AHEAD The potatoes can be prepared through Step 1 and refrigerated overnight.

Potato Pancakes

Active **40 min**; Total **1 hr 10 min**; Serves **8**

TV chef Andrew Zimmern's killer potato pancakes get great texture from mixing cooked mashed Yukon Golds with raw shredded russet potatoes before frying. Toppings like smoked fish, crème fraîche and fresh dill are crucial to the full latke experience.

1¼ lbs. Yukon Gold potatoes, peeled and cubed

Kosher salt

1½ lbs. russet potatoes

1 large onion, grated

2 large eggs, lightly beaten

½ cup matzo meal

½ tsp. freshly ground white pepper

Vegetable oil, for frying

Applesauce, crème fraîche, smoked fish and dill sprigs, for serving

1. In a medium saucepan, cover the Yukon Golds with cold water, season generously with salt and bring to a boil. Cook until tender, about 15 minutes. Drain and pass through a ricer into a large bowl.

2. Peel the russets. Shred them on the large holes of a box grater into a colander. Rinse under cold water, then pat dry with a clean kitchen towel. Add half to the riced potatoes.

3. In a food processor, pulse the remaining shredded potatoes with the onion until pasty, about 20 times. Transfer to a sieve and press dry. Add to the riced potatoes. Stir in the eggs, matzo meal, pepper and 2 teaspoons of salt.

4. Line a baking sheet with paper towels. In a large, heavy skillet, heat ¼ inch of oil over moderate heat to 350°. Working in batches, spoon 2 tablespoons of the batter into the oil for each pancake and press to flatten. Fry, turning once, until golden and crisp on both sides, about 7 minutes. Transfer to the prepared baking sheet and sprinkle lightly with salt. Serve with applesauce, crème fraîche, smoked fish and dill. *—Andrew Zimmern*

MAKE AHEAD The latkes can be refrigerated overnight. Reheat in a 375° oven for 5 minutes.

WINE Rich Israeli Chardonnay: 2014 Barkan Classic.

Patatas Bravas

Total **30 min**; Serves **8**

These crispy fried potatoes are a staple at Spanish tapas bars. They're supremely delicious topped with a sweet "ketchup" made from fresh tomatoes and a hit of hot sauce.

1¼ lbs. medium tomatoes, cored and scored on the bottom with an X

2 Tbsp. extra-virgin olive oil, plus more for frying

2 tsp. sugar

Kosher salt

½ tsp. Louisiana-style hot sauce

2 lbs. russet potatoes—peeled, cut into 1-inch pieces and patted dry

½ cup mayonnaise mixed with 1 Tbsp. water

1. In a medium saucepan of boiling water, blanch the tomatoes just until the skins wrinkle, about 30 seconds. Drain well, then peel and finely chop. In the saucepan, heat the 2 tablespoons of olive oil until shimmering. Add the tomatoes, sugar and 1 teaspoon of salt. Cook over moderate heat, stirring occasionally, until thick, 10 to 12 minutes. Stir in the hot sauce and let cool completely.

2. In a large saucepan, heat 2 inches of olive oil to 360°. Add the potatoes and fry at 300°, stirring occasionally, until tender and golden, about 15 minutes. Using a slotted spoon, transfer the potatoes to paper towels and season with salt.

3. Pile the potatoes in a serving bowl. Top with some of the salsa brava and mayonnaise and serve the rest on the side. *—Álvaro Palacios*

MAKE AHEAD The salsa brava can be refrigerated for up to 3 days. Bring to room temperature before serving.

Caramel Potatoes

Haricots Verts and
Potato Salad with Pesto

Classic Potato Salad with Crunchy Trout Roe

⏱ Total **45 min**; Serves **6 to 8**

This potato salad gets its creamy texture from olive oil and eggs, and tons of flavor from the tuna and salty trout roe.

- **3** large russet potatoes, peeled
- **3** large carrots, halved crosswise
- **1** cup frozen peas
- **5** large eggs
- **½** cup extra-virgin olive oil, plus more for drizzling
- **1** Tbsp. fresh lemon juice
  Kosher salt
- **10** oz. good-quality oil-packed tuna
- **4** oz. trout roe

1. In a medium saucepan, cover the potatoes and carrots with cold water. Bring to a boil over high heat, then simmer over moderately low heat until the carrots are tender, about 10 minutes. Using tongs, transfer the carrots to a plate to cool. Continue to simmer the potatoes until tender, about 20 minutes longer; add the peas for the last 30 seconds of cooking. Drain and let the potatoes stand until cool enough to handle, about 10 minutes. Cut the potatoes and carrots into 1-inch pieces.

2. Meanwhile, in another medium saucepan, cover 4 of the eggs with cold water and bring to a boil. Cover the saucepan, remove from the heat and let stand for 8 minutes. Drain and cool the eggs under cold running water. Peel the eggs, then cut them into bite-size pieces.

3. In a large bowl, using a hand mixer, beat the remaining egg with 1 tablespoon of the olive oil, the lemon juice and ½ teaspoon of salt until combined. Slowly beat in the remaining 7 tablespoons of olive oil at high speed until emulsified. Gently stir in the potatoes, carrots and peas and season with salt. Fold in the tuna and the chopped eggs. Transfer the salad to a serving dish. Drizzle with olive oil, top with the trout roe and serve. —*José Andrés*

Haricots Verts and Potato Salad with Pesto

⏱ Total **35 min**; Serves **6**

- **3** cups packed basil leaves
- **10** sage leaves
- **2** small rosemary sprigs
- **1** bay leaf, preferably fresh
- **4** black peppercorns
- **1½** lbs. haricots verts, trimmed and halved crosswise
- **1½** lbs. small fingerling or new potatoes
- **1** large garlic clove
- **¼** cup pine nuts (1½ oz.)
- **2** oz. finely grated Grana Padano cheese (¾ cup), plus more for serving
- **1** oz. finely grated Pecorino Siciliano or Pecorino Romano cheese (⅓ cup)
- **½** cup plus 2 Tbsp. extra-virgin olive oil, plus more for drizzling
  Kosher salt and pepper
- **½** cup roasted unsalted almonds (2 oz.), chopped

1. Fill a large bowl with ice water. In a large saucepan of salted boiling water, blanch the basil until just wilted, about 10 seconds. Using a slotted spoon, transfer to the ice water to cool. Remove the basil and pat dry with paper towels. Keep the water boiling.

2. In a small square of cheesecloth, tie the sage, rosemary, bay leaf and peppercorns into a bundle. Add the herb bundle and haricots verts to the saucepan and cook until crisp-tender, 3 to 4 minutes. Using a slotted spoon, transfer the haricots verts to the ice water to cool. Do not remove the herb bundle. Add the potatoes to the saucepan and cook over moderate heat until just tender when pierced with a fork, 10 to 12 minutes. Drain and transfer to the ice water with the haricots verts. Let cool completely, then drain the vegetables and pat dry. Cut the potatoes in half or, if large, slice ¼ inch thick. Transfer the vegetables to a large serving bowl. Discard the herb bundle.

3. Meanwhile, in a food processor, pulse the garlic until finely chopped. Add the blanched basil, the pine nuts and cheeses and pulse until finely chopped. With the machine on, drizzle in the olive oil until incorporated. Season with salt and pepper.

4. In the large serving bowl, toss the vegetables with the almonds and ½ cup of the pesto. Season with salt and pepper. Drizzle with more olive oil and serve, passing the remaining pesto at the table. —*Chris Behr*

Grilled Baby Potato Salad

Active **30 min**; Total **1 hr**; Serves **8**

Charring the spuds lends this mayo-free salad smoky notes.

- **3** lbs. baby potatoes
  Kosher salt and pepper
- **1** small red onion, sliced
- **½** cup Champagne vinegar
- **¼** cup extra-virgin olive oil, plus more for brushing
- **1** cup lightly packed parsley, chopped
- **2** cups kettle-cooked salt-and-vinegar chips, coarsely crushed

1. In a large saucepan, cover the potatoes with water and bring to a boil. Add a generous pinch of salt and cook over moderately high heat until tender, about 20 minutes. Drain and spread on a baking sheet to cool, then cut in half.

2. Meanwhile, in a large bowl, mix the red onion with the Champagne vinegar and let stand for 10 minutes.

3. Light a grill and oil the grate. Grill the potatoes cut side down over moderately high heat until lightly charred, about 5 minutes. Transfer to the bowl with the onion. Add the ¼ cup of olive oil and mix well. Let cool completely. Stir in the parsley and season with salt and pepper. Top with the chips; serve. —*Justin Chapple*

Herb-Scented Mashed Potatoes

📷 PAGE 239

Active **30 min**; Total **1 hr**; Serves **10**

The secret to these buttery and fragrant mashed potatoes is a ricer, which creates the perfect fluffy texture.

1¼ cups heavy cream

1¼ cups whole milk

2 sticks unsalted butter, plus melted butter for brushing

Two 4-inch rosemary sprigs

2 sage sprigs

2 garlic cloves, crushed

5 lbs. baking potatoes, peeled and cut into 2-inch pieces

Kosher salt and pepper

1. In a medium saucepan, combine the cream, milk and the 2 sticks of butter with the rosemary, sage and garlic and bring just to a simmer. Remove from the heat and let steep for 15 minutes, then discard the rosemary, sage and garlic.

2. Meanwhile, in a large pot, cover the potatoes with water and bring to a boil. Add a generous pinch of salt and simmer over moderate heat until tender, about 20 minutes. Drain well, then pass the potatoes through a ricer into the pot. Fold in the cream mixture and season generously with salt and pepper.

3. Light the broiler and position the rack 8 inches from the heat. Scrape the potatoes into a 12-inch round flameproof pan or baking dish (2 inches deep) and, using a spoon, decoratively swirl the top. Gently brush with melted butter. Broil for about 8 minutes, until the top is browned in spots. Serve hot. —*Justin Chapple*

MAKE AHEAD The mashed potatoes can be prepared through Step 2 and refrigerated overnight. Reheat gently before scraping into the baking dish and broiling.

Spice-Rubbed Roasted Potatoes

Active **20 min**; Total **1 hr 15 min**
Serves **10 to 12**

TV cook Ayesha Curry uses a colorful mix of potatoes in her pan-roast, which also includes sweet shallots and lots of delicious garlic. She gives the dish fantastic flavor with spicy harissa seasoning as well as a fragrant hit of cumin.

2 lbs. sweet potatoes, peeled and cut into 2-inch pieces

2 lbs. baking potatoes, scrubbed and cut into 2-inch pieces

2 lbs. red or purple potatoes, scrubbed and cut into 2-inch pieces

8 medium shallots, halved lengthwise

16 garlic cloves, halved if large

½ cup extra-virgin olive oil

¼ cup harissa seasoning

1 Tbsp. ground cumin

Kosher salt and pepper

1. Preheat the oven to 425°. In a large bowl, toss all of the potatoes with the shallots, garlic, olive oil, harissa seasoning and cumin. Season generously with salt and pepper and toss again.

2. Spread the potatoes on 2 large rimmed baking sheets. Roast in the upper and lower thirds of the oven for 40 to 45 minutes, until tender and lightly browned; rotate the pans halfway through roasting. Let stand for 10 minutes before serving. —*Ayesha Curry*

Currywurst Poutine

Active **30 min**; Total **1 hr**; Serves **6**

Currywurst is a traditional German dish of bratwurst served with curry ketchup and a side of fries. Here, F&W's Justin Chapple turns that into a variation on poutine, the Canadian combo of French fries, cheese curds and gravy. In his version, crispy fries are piled with creamy cheese sauce, juicy bratwurst and curry ketchup.

One 28- to 32-oz. package frozen steak fries

2 Tbsp. extra-virgin olive oil

¾ lb. bratwurst, cut into ½-inch dice

1 cup minced red onion, plus more for serving

2 Tbsp. all-purpose flour

2 cups whole milk

½ lb. Emmental cheese, shredded (2 cups)

Kosher salt and pepper

Chopped parsley and curry ketchup (see Note), for serving

1. Preheat the oven to 450°. Spread the fries on a large rimmed baking sheet. Bake for about 20 minutes, until crisp.

2. Meanwhile, in a medium saucepan, heat the oil. Add the bratwurst and cook over moderately high heat, stirring, until browned in spots, 5 minutes. Using a slotted spoon, transfer to a bowl. Add the 1 cup of onion to the saucepan and cook, stirring, until softened. Stir in the flour to coat. Gradually stir in the milk and bring to a boil. Simmer over moderately low heat until slightly thickened, about 7 minutes. Remove from the heat. Stir in 1 cup of the cheese. Season with salt and pepper.

3. Mound the fries in the middle of the baking sheet and spoon the sauce on top. Scatter the bratwurst and the remaining cheese on top. Bake for 7 minutes, until the cheese is melted. Sprinkle with red onion and parsley. Drizzle with curry ketchup and serve right away. —*Justin Chapple*

NOTE Curry ketchup is a combination of ketchup and curry powder. Look for it at most supermarkets.

Spice-Rubbed
Roasted Potatoes

Chickpeas and Kale in
Spicy Pomodoro Sauce

Chickpeas and Kale in Spicy Pomodoro Sauce

Active **20 min**; Total **45 min**; Serves **4**

Chef Missy Robbins of Brooklyn's Lilia restaurant swaps chickpeas for pasta in her riff on spicy pomodoro. She finishes the dish with a shower of fresh herbs and salty pecorino cheese.

- **½ cup extra-virgin olive oil**
- **5 garlic cloves, thinly sliced**
- **One 28-oz. can whole peeled Italian tomatoes, crushed by hand**
- **1½ tsp. fennel seeds**
- **1 tsp. crushed red pepper**
- **Kosher salt**
- **One 8-oz. bunch of Tuscan kale, stemmed and chopped**
- **Two 15-oz. cans chickpeas, rinsed and drained**
- **Torn basil and marjoram leaves, for garnish**
- **Finely grated Pecorino Romano, for serving**

1. In a large saucepan, heat the olive oil over low heat. Add the garlic and cook, stirring occasionally, until very fragrant but not browned, about 5 minutes. Add the tomatoes, fennel seeds, crushed red pepper and a generous pinch of salt. Cook over moderately low heat, stirring occasionally, until the tomatoes break down and the sauce is thickened, about 25 minutes.

2. Stir the kale into the sauce and cook over moderately low heat, stirring occasionally, until wilted, about 3 minutes. Stir in the chickpeas and cook until heated through, about 3 minutes. Season with salt. Spoon into bowls and garnish with torn basil and marjoram leaves. Top with finely grated pecorino and serve hot. —*Missy Robbins*

WINE Ripe, fruity Puglian red: 2015 Tormaresca Calafuria.

Summer Bean Salad with Potlikker Vinaigrette

Active **1 hr 30 min**; Total **3 hr**; Serves **8 to 10**

Potlikker, as it's called in the South, is the savory, starchy, über-flavorful liquid left over after cooking beans or greens. Here, it is whisked into a vinaigrette, but you can also use it in soups or pasta sauces.

- **2 qts. chicken stock or low-sodium broth**
- **⅓ cup plus ¼ cup extra-virgin olive oil, plus more for brushing**
- **Kosher salt and black pepper**
- **One 2-oz. piece of country ham (optional)**
- **½ tsp. crushed red pepper**
- **1 lb. thawed frozen lima beans**
- **5 ears of corn, shucked**
- **1 lb. haricots verts, trimmed and halved crosswise**
- **3 lbs. fresh fava beans, shelled (3½ cups)**
- **¼ cup Champagne vinegar**
- **4 radishes, cut into thin wedges**
- **2 large heirloom tomatoes, chopped**
- **¼ cup packed chopped dill**
- **¼ cup packed chopped parsley leaves**

1. In a large pot, combine the stock with ⅓ cup of the olive oil, 1 tablespoon of salt and 1 teaspoon of black pepper. Add the ham, if using, and the crushed red pepper and bring to a boil. Reduce the heat to moderately low and simmer for 15 minutes. Add the lima beans, remove from the heat and let cool in the cooking liquid for 1 hour. Set a fine sieve over a large bowl and strain the beans; discard the ham. Transfer the beans to a serving bowl. Reserve ¾ cup of the cooking liquid. Save the remaining liquid for another use.

2. Meanwhile, light a grill and oil the grate. Brush the corn with olive oil and season with salt and black pepper. Grill the corn over moderate heat, turning, until lightly charred, about 8 minutes. Transfer to a work surface and let cool slightly, then cut the kernels from the cob. Add the corn to the bowl with the lima beans.

3. Set up an ice bath. In a large pot of salted boiling water, blanch the haricots verts until crisp-tender, 3 minutes. Using a slotted spoon, transfer them to the ice bath to cool, then pat dry and add to the bowl with the lima beans and corn.

4. Return the water in the pot to a boil and blanch the fava beans until tender, 2 minutes. Drain and transfer to the ice bath to cool. Drain. Squeeze the favas from their skins and add to the bowl with the other vegetables; discard the skins.

5. In a medium bowl, whisk the remaining ¼ cup of olive oil with the vinegar and the reserved ¾ cup of cooking liquid. Season the vinaigrette with salt and black pepper. Gently fold the radishes, tomatoes, dill, parsley and vinaigrette into the vegetables and season with salt and black pepper; serve. —*Joe Kindred*

WINE Crisp Txakoli rosé from Spain: 2016 Ameztoi Rubentis.

Hearty Mexican Cranberry Beans

📷 PAGE 254

Active **15 min**; Total **2 hr 20 min**; Serves **8**

A crunchy topping of diced onions, tomato, jalapeño and tons of cilantro wakes up this no-soak, creamy pot o' beans.

- **1 lb. dried cranberry or pinto beans, rinsed**
- **1 small white onion, halved, plus more, diced, for garnish**
- **2 garlic cloves**
- **Kosher salt**
- **Diced tomato, chopped cilantro and thinly sliced jalapeño, for garnish**

In a large pot, combine the beans with enough water to cover by 4 inches. Add the halved onion and the garlic and bring to a boil over moderately high heat. Reduce the heat to low and simmer until the beans are very tender, about 2 hours. If the beans are soupy, strain them and reserve the cooking liquid for another use. Discard the onion and garlic and season the beans generously with salt. Ladle into bowls, garnish with diced onion, tomato, cilantro and jalapeño and serve. —*Lorena Herrera*

MAKE AHEAD The cooked beans can be refrigerated in the cooking liquid for up to 2 days before reheating and garnishing.

Spring Chickpea Salad with Avocado Hummus

⏱ Total **40 min**; Serves **4 to 6**

HUMMUS

- 2 avocados, halved and pitted
- Two 15-oz. cans chickpeas, rinsed and drained
- 1 shallot, finely chopped
- 2 bunches of parsley, stems and leaves
- Juice of 2 lemons, plus more as needed
- Kosher salt

SALAD

- Two 15-oz. cans chickpeas, rinsed and drained
- 2 cups Taggiasca olives, pitted and torn
- 2 cups Castelvetrano olives, pitted and torn
- 1 canned chipotle chile in adobo, finely chopped
- ½ cup basil leaves, finely chopped
- 1 shallot, finely chopped
- 1 preserved lemon, skin only, julienned
- 2 tsp. aged balsamic vinegar
- 1 tsp. chopped rosemary
- Kosher salt
- Baguette croutons and Thai basil and parsley leaves, for garnish

1. Make the hummus In a large bowl, combine the avocados, chickpeas, shallot, parsley and lemon juice. Working in 2-cup batches, transfer to a food processor and puree with ⅓ cup of water until smooth. Scrape into a medium bowl and season with salt and lemon juice. Press a piece of plastic wrap against the surface of the hummus and refrigerate until chilled, about 30 minutes.

2. Meanwhile, make the salad In a large bowl, combine all of the ingredients except the salt and garnishes. Season with salt.

3. Spread the hummus in the bottom of shallow bowls. Top with the salad and garnish with croutons, Thai basil and parsley; serve. —*Anthony Sasso*

Warm Lentil and Root Vegetable Salad with Coconut Tzatziki

Active **30 min**; Total **1 hr 15 min**
Serves **4 to 6**

LENTILS

- 1 cup French green lentils, picked over
- Fine Himalayan pink salt and pepper
- 1½ lbs. medium multicolored carrots, cut on the bias into 2-inch pieces
- 1½ lbs. medium parsnips, halved lengthwise and cut into 2-inch pieces
- 2¼ tsp. ground cumin
- 2¼ tsp. ground coriander
- ½ tsp. ancho chile powder
- ½ cup plus 2 Tbsp. extra-virgin olive oil
- ⅓ cup fresh lemon juice
- ¾ cup chopped mint, plus torn leaves for garnish
- ¾ cup chopped cilantro, plus leaves for garnish

TZATZIKI

- 1 cup coconut milk yogurt
- ¼ cup finely diced seeded cucumber
- 1 Tbsp. extra-virgin olive oil
- 1 Tbsp. fresh lemon juice
- 1 tsp. finely chopped dill
- 1 tsp. finely chopped chives
- 1 garlic clove, minced
- Fine Himalayan pink salt and pepper

1. Make the lentils In a large saucepan, cover the lentils with 2 inches of water and bring to a boil. Simmer over moderate heat until just tender, 20 minutes. Remove from the heat, add a generous pinch of salt and let stand for 5 minutes; drain. Spread on a rimmed baking sheet and let cool slightly.

2. Meanwhile, preheat the oven to 400°. On a large rimmed baking sheet, toss the carrots and parsnips with the cumin, coriander, chile powder and ¼ cup of the olive oil. Season generously with salt and pepper. Roast the vegetables until tender and browned in spots, 20 to 25 minutes.

3. In a large bowl, toss the lentils with the warm roasted vegetables, the lemon juice and the remaining ¼ cup plus 2 tablespoons of olive oil. Fold in the chopped mint and cilantro and season the salad with salt and pepper. Transfer to a platter and garnish with mint and cilantro leaves.

4. Make the tzatziki In a small bowl, whisk all of the ingredients together and season with salt and pepper. Serve alongside the warm lentil salad. —*Whitney Tingle and Danielle DuBoise*

Seafood Paella

Active **45 min**; Total **1 hr 15 min**
Serves **6 to 8**

- 4 cups chicken stock or low-sodium broth
- 2 cups fish stock or clam broth
- ¼ tsp. saffron threads, crumbled
- ¼ cup extra-virgin olive oil
- ½ cup finely chopped onion
- 3 garlic cloves, minced
- ½ tsp. smoked paprika
- 2¼ cups Bomba or arborio rice
- One 12-oz. package cooked chorizo, sausages halved lengthwise and crosswise
- 8 large head-on shrimp
- 1 lb. littleneck clams and cockles, scrubbed
- ½ lb. mussels, scrubbed
- ¼ cup thawed frozen peas
- Chopped parsley, for garnish

1. In a medium saucepan, combine the chicken stock with the fish stock and crumbled saffron and bring to a simmer.

2. Meanwhile, in a 15-inch paella pan or large enameled cast-iron casserole, heat the olive oil. Add the onion and cook over moderate heat, stirring occasionally, until softened, about 5 minutes. Add the garlic and paprika and cook until fragrant, about 2 minutes. Add the rice and cook, stirring, until it is evenly coated in the oil, 1 minute. Add the hot broth and stir the rice once to evenly spread it in the pan. Cook over moderate heat, without stirring but rotating the pan for even cooking, until half of the liquid is absorbed, about 15 minutes. Reduce the heat to low. Nestle the chorizo and shrimp into the rice. Add the clams, cockles and mussels hinge side down and cook, turning the shrimp halfway through, until the shrimp and shellfish are cooked through and all of the liquid is absorbed, about 20 minutes. Scatter the peas on top and let stand for 5 minutes. Garnish with parsley and serve. —*Kay Chun*

Seafood Paella

Taiwanese Congee
with Sweet Potato

Italian Rice Salad with Soppressata and Caciocavallo

⏱ Total **30 min;** Serves **6**

Rice salad is a classic Italian snack eaten with an aperitivo. Here, chef Chris Behr of Rome's Sustainable Food Project elevates the standard happy hour dish with fresh herbs, crunchy fennel and soppressata for a light lunch. An Aperol spritz is still a must.

1½ **cups arborio rice (10 oz.)**

1½ **cups fresh or thawed frozen peas**

 3 **Tbsp. white wine vinegar, plus more for drizzling (optional)**

 2 **cups loosely packed shaved caciocavallo or aged provolone cheese (5 oz.)**

 4 **oz. thinly sliced soppressata, sliced into ½-inch strips**

 1 **cup pitted green olives, such as Cerignola or Castelvetrano, halved**

 1 **medium fennel bulb—halved lengthwise, cored and very thinly sliced on a mandoline, plus ⅓ cup small fronds for garnish**

 4 **scallions, white and light green parts only, thinly sliced**

⅓ **cup parsley leaves**

⅓ **cup extra-virgin olive oil**

 Kosher salt and pepper

1. In a medium saucepan of salted boiling water, cook the rice over moderate heat until al dente, about 15 minutes. Just before draining, add the peas and cook for 1 minute. Drain the rice and peas well and spread in an even layer on a large rimmed baking sheet. Drizzle the 3 tablespoons of vinegar, if using, over the rice and peas and let cool slightly, about 15 minutes.

2. In a large bowl, toss the rice and peas with the cheese, soppressata, olives, sliced fennel, scallions and parsley. Drizzle with the olive oil and more vinegar, if desired. Season with salt and pepper and toss to combine. Garnish with the fennel fronds and serve. —*Chris Behr*

WINE Fruity Sicilian rosé: 2016 Tasca d'Almerita Le Rose di Regaleali.

Taiwanese Congee with Sweet Potato

Total **1 hr;** Serves **4**

Congee, the popular rice porridge that's eaten throughout Asia, is simple to make for a soothing meal any time of day. In Taiwan, cooks top it with sweet potato.

 1 **cup short-grain rice, rinsed and drained**

 One 3-inch piece of peeled fresh ginger, thinly sliced, plus 1 Tbsp. minced ginger

1½ **lbs. mixed sweet potatoes, peeled and cut into 2-inch pieces**

 Kosher salt

 5 **Tbsp. canola oil**

½ **cup thinly sliced scallions**

1. In a large, heavy-bottomed saucepan, combine the rice, sliced ginger and 12 cups of water and bring to a simmer. Cook over moderately low heat, stirring occasionally, until it starts to look creamy, about 30 minutes. Add the sweet potatoes and cook, stirring occasionally, until the rice and potatoes are tender and the porridge is thick, about 15 minutes longer. Season with salt.

2. Meanwhile, in a small bowl, combine the oil with the scallions and minced ginger and season with salt.

3. Divide the congee among bowls and drizzle with the scallion-ginger oil. —*Kay Chun*

MAKE AHEAD The congee and the scallion-ginger oil can be refrigerated separately overnight. Reheat the congee slowly, adding more water if too thick.

Charcuterie Fried Rice

⏱ Total **40 min;** Serves **4**

This Chinese-Italian fried rice mash-up combines salami and mortadella with more traditional ingredients like ginger, soy sauce and scallions.

¼ **cup canola oil**

 4 **large eggs, beaten**

 Kosher salt and pepper

 4 **oz. spicy salami, cut into ¼-inch dice**

 4 **oz. mortadella with pistachios, cut into ¼-inch dice**

¼ **cup minced ginger**

 6 **garlic cloves, minced**

 6 **cups steamed white rice, cooled**

 3 **Tbsp. low-sodium soy sauce**

 3 **Tbsp. fresh lime juice**

 1 **cup chopped cilantro**

 3 **scallions, thinly sliced**

 Sambal oelek, for serving

1. In a large nonstick skillet, heat 1 tablespoon of the oil until shimmering. Add the eggs and a generous pinch of salt and cook over moderate heat until set on the bottom, about 2 minutes. Fold the omelet over itself and cook until just golden and set, about 2 minutes more. Using a slotted spatula, transfer to a work surface to cool slightly, then coarsely chop.

2. Heat the remaining 3 tablespoons of oil in the skillet. Add the salami and mortadella and stir-fry over moderately high heat until lightly browned and barely rendered, about 3 minutes. Add the ginger and garlic and stir-fry until fragrant and softened, about 2 minutes. Add the rice and stir-fry until hot, about 3 minutes. Stir in the soy sauce and lime juice, then fold in the eggs, cilantro and scallions. Season with salt and pepper. Serve with sambal oelek. —*Justin Chapple*

WINE Italian rosé: 2016 La Valentina Cerasuolo d'Abruzzo.

Bacon, Egg and Shrimp Fried Rice

Total **30 min**; Serves **4**

Athens, Georgia, chef Hugh Acheson's shrimp fried rice also includes bits of crispy bacon and irresistible bites of fresh tatsoi. It's a perfect meal in a bowl.

- ¼ lb. bacon, chopped
- 2 Tbsp. canola oil
- ½ lb. medium shrimp, shelled and deveined
- 6 scallions, white parts minced, green parts thinly sliced on the bias
- 2 garlic cloves, minced
  Jasmine Rice (recipe at far right) or 3 cups cooked white rice, cooled
- 2 large eggs, beaten
- ½ cup thawed frozen English peas
- 3 Tbsp. unseasoned rice vinegar
- 1 tsp. toasted sesame oil
- 2 cups sliced tatsoi or leaf spinach
  Kosher salt

1. In a large nonstick skillet, cook the bacon in the canola oil over moderate heat, stirring occasionally, until browned and crisp, about 8 minutes. Using a slotted spoon, transfer to a paper towel–lined plate to drain. Do not wipe out the skillet.

2. Heat the fat in the skillet until shimmering. Add the shrimp and cook over moderately high heat, turning once, until just cooked through, about 3 minutes. Transfer to a plate.

3. Add the scallion whites and garlic to the skillet and stir-fry over moderately high heat until softened, 1 to 2 minutes. Add the rice and stir-fry until hot, about 3 minutes. Using a wooden spoon, make a well in the center of the rice. Add the eggs to the well and cook, slowly stirring them into the rice, until just set, 1 to 2 minutes. Add the bacon, shrimp, peas, vinegar and sesame oil and stir-fry until hot, 2 minutes. Stir in the tatsoi until just wilted. Season the rice with salt. Garnish with the scallion greens. —Hugh Acheson

New Mexican Rice

Active **30 min**; Total **1 hr**; Serves **4**

For this tangy and fragrant rice, chef Hugh Acheson makes sofrito, a classic blend of onion, peppers and garlic. He adds even more flavor to the dish with tomatillos, tomatoes and cumin.

- 1 Tbsp. extra-virgin olive oil
- 1 small onion, finely chopped
- 1 tomatillo—husked, rinsed and finely chopped
- 1 garlic clove, minced
  Kosher salt
- 1½ tsp. ground cumin
  One 15-oz. can diced tomatoes
- ¼ cup (2 oz.) canned diced green Hatch chiles
- ¼ cup Basic Chicken Stock (p. 68) or low-sodium broth
  Jasmine Rice (recipe follows) or 3 cups warm cooked white rice
  Chopped cilantro, for garnish

1. In a large, deep skillet, heat the olive oil until shimmering. Add the onion, tomatillo, garlic and a generous pinch of salt. Cook over moderate heat, stirring occasionally, until softened and just starting to brown, about 7 minutes. Stir in the cumin and cook until fragrant, about 1 minute. Add the tomatoes, chiles and stock and bring to a boil. Simmer over moderate heat, stirring occasionally, until the liquid is reduced by half, about 20 minutes. Transfer the sofrito to a blender or food processor and let cool slightly, then puree until smooth.

2. Wipe out the skillet and cook the sofrito in it over moderate heat, stirring, until hot, about 5 minutes. Gradually fold in the rice and cook just until it is hot and coated in the sofrito, about 5 minutes. Season with salt, garnish with cilantro and serve. —Hugh Acheson

MAKE AHEAD The sofrito can be refrigerated in an airtight container for up to 10 days.

Jasmine Rice

Active **5 min**; Total **30 min**; Serves **4**

- 1 cup jasmine rice
- ½ tsp. kosher salt

In a medium saucepan, combine the rice and salt with 1½ cups of water and bring to a boil. Stir once, cover and simmer over low heat until the rice is tender and the water is absorbed, about 15 minutes. Remove from the heat and let steam for 10 minutes, then fluff with a fork and serve. —Hugh Acheson

Fragrant Rice with Pepitas and Dates

Active **15 min**; Total **50 min**; Serves **10 to 12**

This aromatic rice from cookbook author and TV cook Ayesha Curry is nicely spiced and just a bit sweet, with a pleasant crunch from pepitas (hulled pumpkin seeds).

- 3 cups basmati rice, rinsed well and drained
- 8 Medjool dates, pitted and diced (4 oz.)
- ½ tsp. ground allspice
- ½ tsp. ground cardamom
  Kosher salt
- 3 Tbsp. unsalted butter
- ½ cup pepitas, toasted
  Parsley leaves, for garnish

In a large saucepan, combine the rice, dates, allspice, cardamom and 2 teaspoons of salt. Add 4½ cups of water and bring to a boil. Stir once, then cover and simmer over low heat until the water is absorbed and the rice is tender, about 20 minutes. Scatter the butter on top of the rice, cover and remove from the heat. Let steam for 5 minutes. Fluff with a fork and season with salt. Transfer to a serving bowl, sprinkle with the pepitas and parsley and serve hot or at room temperature. —Ayesha Curry

MAKE AHEAD The rice can be tented with foil and kept at room temperature for 2 hours.

Hearty Mexican Cranberry Beans
(p. 247), Spanish Rice

Hobo Pack Bibimbap

📷 PAGE 238

Total **50 min;** Serves **4**

Korean bibimbap is a no-brainer for a hobo pack—the rice gets so nice and crispy during grilling.

- **4 tsp. canola oil**
- **½ lb. ground pork**
- **1 Tbsp. minced fresh ginger**
- **1 scallion, minced**
- **1 Tbsp. unseasoned rice vinegar**
- **1 Tbsp. soy sauce**
- **½ tsp. toasted sesame oil**
  Kosher salt and pepper
- **6 cups prepared sushi rice**
- **2 cups baby spinach, chopped**
- **4 large eggs**
- **1 cup julienned carrots**
  Sliced cucumber, gochujang and toasted sesame seeds, for serving

1. Light a grill. Arrange four 18-inch sheets of heavy-duty foil on a work surface. Put a 14-inch sheet of nonstick foil on each sheet and drizzle 1 teaspoon of canola oil in the center of each.

2. In a bowl, mix the pork, ginger, scallion, vinegar, soy sauce, sesame oil and a generous pinch each of salt and pepper.

3. Mound the rice in the center of the foil sheets and, using damp hands, press into ¾-inch-thick rounds. Top each mound with one-fourth of the spinach, then crack an egg on top of each mound. Crumble one-fourth of the pork around each mound, then pile the carrots alongside; season with salt and pepper. Bring 2 sides of the foil up over the filling to form a seam across the top, leaving space for the egg. Fold the remaining 2 sides to seal.

4. Slide the foil packets onto the grill and cook over medium heat until the rice is crisp on the bottom and the egg whites are firm but the yolks are runny, 8 to 12 minutes; open once to check the eggs. Open the packets and, using a thin spatula, slide the bibimbaps onto 4 plates. Serve with cucumber, gochujang and sesame seeds. —*Justin Chapple*

MAKE AHEAD The uncooked packets can be refrigerated for a few hours.

Spanish Rice

Active **15 min;** Total **50 min;** Serves **8**

Think paella without the animal protein. Tomatoes pureed with onion, garlic and stock give this rice pilaf subtle flavor. It's a perfect side for spicy dishes like Chiles Rellenos (p. 232) and Pork Tamales (165).

- **2 medium tomatoes, chopped**
- **1 medium onion, coarsely chopped**
- **2 garlic cloves**
  Kosher salt and pepper
- **⅓ cup grapeseed oil**
- **2 cups long-grain white rice**
- **1 cup chicken stock or low-sodium broth**

1. In a blender or food processor, puree the tomatoes with the onion, garlic and 1 teaspoon of salt until smooth.

2. In a large saucepan, heat the oil. Add the rice and cook over moderate heat, stirring, until lightly toasted, about 5 minutes. Pour in the tomato mixture and stock and bring to a boil. Cover and cook over low heat until the liquid has evaporated and the rice is tender, about 20 minutes. Remove the pan from the heat and let stand, covered, for 15 minutes. Fluff with a fork, season with salt and pepper and serve. —*Lorena Herrera*

MAKE AHEAD The cooked rice can stand, covered, for up to 30 minutes.

Herbed Rice (Sabzi Polo)

Active **1 hr 10 min;** Total **2 hr 30 min** Serves **8 to 10**

Sabzi polo is a staple on the Persian New Year's table. It's made with basmati rice and layers of fresh herbs, but what is most coveted is the *tahdig*—the crunchy crust that forms on the bottom of the pot. To make *polo* perfectly, rinse the rice several times in fresh water; this helps the grains stay separate while they cook.

- **2 cups basmati rice**
  Kosher salt
- **2½ cups minced cilantro**
- **2½ cups minced parsley**
- **2 cups minced chives or scallions**
- **1 cup minced dill**
- **¼ cup minced garlic**
- **¼ cup canola oil**
- **3 Tbsp. whole-milk yogurt**
- **1 large egg yolk**
- **¼ cup Brewed Saffron (p. 352), plus more for drizzling**
- **¼ cup boiling water**
- **3 Tbsp. unsalted butter, thinly sliced**

1. In a large bowl, cover the rice with cold water. Using your hand, agitate the rice to release the starch, then carefully pour off the water. Rinse the rice 5 to 7 more times, until the water runs clear. Cover the rice with water, add 2 teaspoons of salt and let soak for 30 minutes, then drain.

2. Fill a 5-quart nonstick Dutch oven half full with water, bring to a boil and add 2 tablespoons of salt. Add the rice and boil over high heat until it is al dente and just starts to soften; this can take from 3 to 8 minutes, depending on your rice (do not overcook it). Let stand for 2 minutes, then drain well. Wipe out the pot.

3. In a medium bowl, mix the cilantro, parsley, chives and dill with the garlic. Put the oil in the bottom of the Dutch oven. In a small bowl, whisk the yogurt with the egg yolk and 2 tablespoons of the brewed saffron and drizzle over the oil in the pot. Gently scatter one-quarter of the rice into the pot (you want it to stay fluffy) and season with salt. Sprinkle with one-third of the herb mixture. Repeat the layering with the remaining rice and herb mixture, ending with a layer of rice.

4. Cover the pot and set it over moderately high heat until it starts to steam, about 5 minutes. Uncover the rice and drizzle with the remaining 2 tablespoons of brewed saffron and ¼ cup of boiling water. Scatter the butter slices on top. Cover the pot with parchment paper, then cover tightly with the lid. Cook on a heat diffuser (if you have one) over moderately low heat until the rice is tender and very fragrant, about 45 minutes.

5. Discard the parchment. Carefully invert the rice onto a large platter. Using a spoon or spatula, crack the crust (*tahdig*) and spread the pieces apart. Drizzle the rice with a little brewed saffron and serve warm. —*Mahin Gilanpour Motamed*

Noodle Rice (Reshteh Polo)

Active **1 hr 10 min**; Total **2 hr 30 min**
Serves **8 to 10**

- 1½ **cups basmati rice**
  Kosher salt
- ½ **lb. linguine fini, broken into thirds**
- ⅓ **cup canola oil**
- ¼ **cup Brewed Saffron (p. 352), plus more for serving**
- 2 **tsp. ground coriander**
- ½ **tsp. ground cardamom**
- ¼ **cup boiling water**
- 8 **Tbsp. unsalted butter, thinly sliced**
- ½ **lb. dried Tunisian dates, pitted**
- 1 **cup golden raisins, rinsed and drained**
- ½ **cup fresh clementine juice**
- ½ **cup unsalted pistachios, slivered**
  Gold leaf and dried rose petals, for garnish (optional)

1. In a large bowl, cover the rice with cold water. Using your hand, agitate the rice to release the starch, then carefully pour off the water. Rinse the rice 5 to 7 more times, until the water runs clear. Cover the rice with water, add 2 teaspoons of salt and soak for 30 minutes; drain.

2. Meanwhile, preheat the oven to 350°. Spread the linguine on a large rimmed baking sheet and toast for 8 to 10 minutes, until well browned. Let cool.

3. Fill a 5-quart nonstick Dutch oven half full with water, bring to a boil and add 2 tablespoons of salt. Add the noodles and boil over high heat until barely softened, about 2 minutes. Add the rice to the Dutch oven and boil until it is al dente and just starts to soften; this can take from 3 to 8 minutes, depending on your rice (do not overcook it). Drain well.

4. Put the oil and ¼ cup of water in the bottom of the Dutch oven. Drizzle 2 tablespoons of the brewed saffron on top. Gently scatter one-quarter of the noodle rice into the pot (you want it to stay fluffy) and season with salt. Sprinkle with one-third of the coriander and cardamom. Repeat with the remaining noodle rice, coriander and cardamom, ending with a layer of noodle rice.

5. Cover the pot and set it over moderately high heat until it starts to steam, about 5 minutes. Uncover the noodle rice and drizzle with the remaining 2 tablespoons of brewed saffron and ¼ cup of boiling water. Scatter 6 tablespoons of the butter on top. Cover the pot with parchment paper, then cover tightly with the lid. Cook on a heat diffuser (if you have one) over moderately low heat until tender and very fragrant, about 45 minutes.

6. Meanwhile, in a large nonstick skillet, melt the remaining 2 tablespoons of butter over moderate heat. Add the dates, raisins, clementine juice and a generous pinch of salt and cook, stirring, until the fruit is softened and plumped, about 5 minutes. Keep warm.

7. Spoon the noodle rice onto a platter. Invert the crust onto a work surface and, using a spatula, crack it into pieces. Drizzle the rice with brewed saffron and pour the dates and raisins on top. Serve with the crust. Garnish with the slivered pistachios and gold leaf and rose petals, if using.
—*Mahin Gilanpour Motamed*

Coconut Rice

Active **20 min**; Total **1 hr**; Serves **6 to 8**

- 1 **cup shredded unsweetened coconut**
- 3 **Tbsp. unsalted butter**
- 1½ **cups basmati rice**
- 1 **small onion, finely chopped**
- 3 **Tbsp. raisins**
- 3 **Tbsp. raw cashews**
  Kosher salt
- 1½ **tsp. ground coriander**
- 1 **tsp. sugar**
- 3 **cardamom pods**
- 1 **Scotch Bonnet or habanero chile, cut in half lengthwise**
- 1 **cinnamon stick**
- 2 **cups whole milk**
- 1 **bay leaf**

1. Preheat the oven to 350°. Spread the coconut in a pie plate and bake for 6 to 8 minutes, until lightly browned.

2. In a large saucepan, melt the butter over moderate heat. Add the rice, toasted coconut, onion, raisins, cashews, 2 teaspoons of salt, the coriander, sugar, cardamom, chile and cinnamon stick and cook, stirring often, until the rice is lightly toasted, about 5 minutes. Add the milk, 1¼ cups of water and the bay leaf and bring to a boil. Cover and cook over moderately low heat until the rice is tender and the water is absorbed, about 20 minutes. Remove from the heat and let stand for 15 minutes. Fluff the rice with a fork; discard the cinnamon stick and bay leaf. Season with salt and serve.
—*Andrew Zimmern*

Quinoa Pilaf with Dried Apricots

Active **15 min**; Total **1 hr**; Serves **4 to 6**

This fluffy, Moroccan-inspired quinoa dish is the perfect accompaniment for roasted meats, grilled vegetables or rich, spiced stews.

- 2 **Tbsp. extra-virgin olive oil**
- 1 **medium onion, finely chopped**
  Fine Himalayan pink salt
- 1½ **cups quinoa**
- ⅓ **cup dried apricots, finely chopped**
- 4 **green cardamom pods, cracked**
- 4 **saffron threads**
- ¼ **tsp. ground turmeric**
- ⅓ **cup roasted, salted shelled pistachios, chopped**

In a medium saucepan, heat the olive oil. Add the onion and a generous pinch of salt and cook over moderate heat, stirring occasionally, until softened and just starting to brown, about 7 minutes. Add the quinoa, apricots, cardamom, saffron and turmeric and cook, stirring, until fragrant, about 2 minutes. Add 3 cups of water and bring to a boil. Cover and simmer over low heat until the water is absorbed and the quinoa is tender, about 20 minutes. Remove from the heat and let steam, covered, for 20 minutes, then discard the cardamom pods and fluff the quinoa with a fork. Fold in the pistachios and season with salt; serve.
—*Whitney Tingle and Danielle DuBoise*

MAKE AHEAD The quinoa pilaf can be refrigerated overnight. Serve warm or at room temperature.

Red Quinoa Tabbouleh

Active **30 min**; Total **1 hr 45 min**; Serves **8**

- 2 cups red quinoa, rinsed and drained
  One ½-inch piece of ginger
- 1 tsp. ras el hanout (see Note)
  Kosher salt and pepper
- ½ cup extra-virgin olive oil
- 1 tsp. honey
- ½ tsp. finely grated lemon zest, plus 3 Tbsp. fresh lemon juice
- 1 red apple, such as Fuji, cored and finely chopped
- 1 English cucumber, peeled and finely chopped
- 1 red bell pepper—stemmed, seeded and finely chopped
- 1 cup grape or cherry tomatoes, halved, plus more for garnish
- ½ cup chopped mint leaves
  Lemon wedges, for serving

1. In a medium saucepan, combine the quinoa with the ginger, ras el hanout, ½ teaspoon of salt and 3 cups of water and bring to a boil. Cover and simmer over low heat until the water is absorbed and the quinoa is tender, about 15 minutes. Fluff with a fork and let cool slightly; discard the ginger. Cover and refrigerate for 1 hour.

2. In a large bowl, whisk the olive oil with the honey and the lemon zest and juice. Season with salt and pepper. Add the quinoa, apple, cucumber, bell pepper, 1 cup of tomatoes and the mint leaves. Season with salt and pepper. Garnish with more halved tomatoes and serve with lemon wedges. —*José Catrimán*

NOTE Ras el hanout, a North African spice mix, is available at specialty food stores and from kalustyans.com

MAKE AHEAD The cooked quinoa can be refrigerated overnight.

Quinoa Meatballs with Tomato Sauce and Tuscan Kale

Active **1 hr 15 min**; Total **1 hr 45 min**
Serves **6**

PILAF

- 1½ Tbsp. extra-virgin olive oil
- ½ onion, finely chopped
- 1 cup quinoa, rinsed and drained
- 2 Tbsp. dry white wine
- 1 tsp. kosher salt
- 2 Tbsp. each finely chopped basil, parsley, scallion and dill

QUINOA MEATBALLS

- Baking spray
- 2 large eggs
- ½ Tbsp. whole milk
- ½ Tbsp. extra-virgin olive oil
- 1 cup plus 2 Tbsp. fine dried breadcrumbs
- 1 cup finely grated Parmigiano-Reggiano, plus more for garnish
- ¼ cup fine semolina
- 2 tsp. onion powder
- 1 tsp. garlic powder
- ½ tsp. kosher salt
- ½ tsp. pepper

TOMATO SAUCE

- 2 Tbsp. extra-virgin olive oil
- ½ onion, finely chopped
- 5 garlic cloves, minced
- ¾ cup dry white wine
  One 28-oz. can whole tomatoes in juice (preferably San Marzano), tomatoes chopped and juices reserved
  Pinch each of dried oregano and crushed red pepper
- 3 Tbsp. chopped basil, plus more for garnish
  Kosher salt and black pepper
- 1 small bunch of Tuscan kale (8 oz.), stemmed and chopped

1. Make the pilaf In a medium saucepan, heat the olive oil. Add the onion and cook over moderate heat until softened, about 8 minutes. Add the quinoa and cook, stirring, until toasted, about 2 minutes. Add 2 cups of water along with the wine and salt and bring to a boil. Cover and simmer over low heat until the quinoa is tender and the water is absorbed, about 20 minutes.

Spread the quinoa onto a large rimmed baking sheet to cool, then transfer to a medium bowl and stir in the herbs. Set aside 1 cup of the quinoa pilaf.

2. Make the quinoa meatballs Preheat the oven to 375°. Line a large rimmed baking sheet with foil and coat with baking spray. In a medium bowl, beat the eggs with the milk, olive oil and ⅔ cup of water. Add the reserved 1 cup of quinoa pilaf along with the breadcrumbs, the 1 cup of Parmigiano, the semolina, onion powder, garlic powder, salt and pepper and mix well. Form the mixture into twenty-six 1½-inch meatballs, using about 1 tablespoon of the mixture for each. Transfer to the baking sheet. Bake the meatballs for 10 to 12 minutes, until browned on the bottoms, then turn and bake for 10 to 12 minutes longer, until browned all over.

3. Make the tomato sauce Meanwhile, in a medium enameled cast-iron casserole, heat the olive oil over moderate heat. Add the onion and garlic and cook until softened, about 6 minutes. Add the wine and tomato juices and cook until the liquid is reduced by one-third, about 8 minutes. Add the chopped tomatoes, oregano and crushed red pepper and simmer over moderately low heat for 20 minutes. Stir in the 3 tablespoons of chopped basil and season with salt and black pepper. Add the kale, cover and cook over moderately low heat until it begins to wilt, about 5 minutes. Add the meatballs to the casserole and simmer until the kale is tender and the meatballs are heated through, 10 to 15 minutes.

4. Spoon the quinoa pilaf into shallow bowls and top with the meatballs and sauce. Garnish with chopped basil and grated Parmigiano and serve. —*Matthew Accarrino*

WINE Medium-bodied, herbal Chianti: 2014 Badia a Coltibuono Cetamura.

Quinoa Egg Bowl with Pecorino

⏱ Total **30 min**; Serves **4**

Cookbook author Melissa Clark takes inspiration from Caesar salad in this quinoa bowl, which includes a soft runny egg and a lemony, cheese-spiked dressing. It's one of the best grain bowls we've ever had.

- **2** Tbsp. fresh lemon juice
- **3** garlic cloves, minced
  Kosher salt and coarsely ground black pepper
- **¾** cup extra-virgin olive oil
- **3** oz. Pecorino Toscano or Manchego cheese, coarsely shredded, plus more for garnish
- **1½** cups quinoa, rinsed and drained well
  One 1-lb. bunch of mustard greens, Swiss chard or kale, stems and ribs removed, leaves chopped
- **½** lb. sugar snap peas, trimmed
  4 soft-cooked eggs, peeled and sliced
  Sliced radishes, for garnish

1. In a medium bowl, whisk the lemon juice, garlic and ¾ teaspoon salt. Whisk in the olive oil and 3 ounces of shredded cheese.

2. Bring a pot of salted water to a boil; whisk in the quinoa and boil until tender, 12 to 15 minutes. Drain and keep warm.

3. Meanwhile, set a steamer basket in a saucepan with 1 inch of water and bring to a boil. Add the greens, cover and steam until crisp-tender, 5 minutes. Transfer to a bowl. Add the sugar snap peas to the steamer and cook, covered, until crisp-tender, about 2 minutes. Transfer to the bowl with the greens.

4. Divide the warm quinoa among bowls. Arrange the greens, snap peas and eggs on top. Drizzle each bowl with the dressing, garnish with cheese, pepper and radishes and serve. —*Melissa Clark*

Farro-and-Sausage Parmigiano

Active **30 min**; Total **3 hr**; Serves **4 to 6**

- **3** Tbsp. extra-virgin olive oil
- **1** yellow onion, chopped
  Kosher salt and black pepper
- **1** lb. hot or sweet Italian sausage, casings removed
- **3** garlic cloves, minced
- **1** tsp. dried oregano
- **1** tsp. crushed red pepper
- **½** tsp. fennel seeds, crushed
- **1** Tbsp. white wine vinegar
- **1½** cups (9 oz.) farro
  One 28-oz. can crushed fire-roasted tomatoes
- **2** scallions, thinly sliced
- **1½** cups panko
- **½** cup chopped parsley
- **1** tsp. grated lemon zest
- **2** Tbsp. minced fresh oregano
- **¾** cup freshly grated Parmigiano-Reggiano cheese
- **6** oz. lightly salted fresh mozzarella, thinly sliced

1. In a large skillet, heat 1 tablespoon of the olive oil. Add the onion, season with salt and cook over moderately high heat, stirring occasionally, until softened, 3 minutes. Add the sausage and cook, breaking it up, until cooked through, about 7 minutes. Add two-thirds of the garlic, the dried oregano, crushed red pepper and fennel seeds. Cook until fragrant, 1 minute. Stir in the vinegar, then scrape into a 6-quart slow cooker. Add the farro, crushed tomatoes and 2½ cups of water. Season with salt and black pepper. Cover and cook on high until the farro is tender, 2½ hours. Stir in the scallions.

2. Meanwhile, in a medium skillet, heat the remaining 2 tablespoons of olive oil. Add the panko and cook over moderately high heat, stirring, until golden brown, about 3 minutes. Add the parsley, lemon zest, fresh oregano and the remaining garlic. Cook, stirring, until the garlic is tender, 1 minute. Season with salt. Transfer to a plate.

3. Preheat the broiler and position a rack 6 inches from the heat. Scrape the farro mixture into a 3-quart oval baking dish or 4 small baking dishes. Sprinkle with the grated Parmesan and top with the mozzarella. Broil until the cheese is melted and starting to brown, about 5 minutes; rotate the baking dish halfway through broiling. Transfer to a rack and let stand for 10 minutes. Sprinkle with the panko and serve. —*Sarah DiGregorio*

MAKE AHEAD The cooled panko can be kept in an airtight container at room temperature overnight.

WINE Ripe, intense Primitivo from Puglia: 2014 Cantele.

Tabbouleh with Pine Nuts and Almonds

Active **40 min**; Total **1 hr 20 min**
Serves **4 to 6**

At Magdalena restaurant in Migdal, Israel, Yousef Hanna's nutty twist on the classic salad is mainly herbs and vegetables with a smattering of fine bulgur.

- **½** cup fine bulgur
  Boiling water
- **½** cup pine nuts
- **½** cup raw almonds
- **3** medium tomatoes—halved, seeded and finely diced
- **8** cups lightly packed parsley leaves, finely chopped (from ½ lb. parsley)
- **1** cup packed mint leaves, finely chopped
- **1** cup thinly sliced scallions
- **½** cup extra-virgin olive oil
- **¼** cup plus 2 Tbsp. fresh lemon juice
- **1** tsp. ground cumin
  Kosher salt

1. In a large heatproof bowl, cover the bulgur with at least 2 inches of boiling water. Cover and let stand until tender, about 30 minutes. Drain well.

2. Meanwhile, preheat the oven to 375°. On a rimmed baking sheet, toast the pine nuts and almonds for about 8 minutes, until lightly browned. Let cool. Finely chop the almonds.

3. In a large bowl, toss the bulgur with the tomatoes, parsley, mint, scallions, olive oil, lemon juice, cumin, pine nuts and almonds. Season the tabbouleh with salt and serve. —*Yousef Hanna*

Farro-and-Sausage
Parmigiano

BREADS, PIZZAS & SANDWICHES

Loaves of Tartine
Manufactory's
country bread
OPPOSITE Spiced-
Lamb Pizza (p. 272).

Buttermilk Biscuits with Salty Sorghum Butter

Active **30 min;** Total **50 min;** Makes **10**

For his ultralight biscuits, North Carolina chef Joe Kindred sifts the flour before measuring it out. He recommends using a soft flour like White Lily for a finer, more delicate crumb.

BISCUITS

5½ cups sifted White Lily brand all-purpose flour (see Note) or **5 cups** sifted all-purpose flour, plus more for dusting

1 Tbsp. plus **2 tsp.** baking powder

1 Tbsp. kosher salt

2 sticks unsalted butter, cubed and chilled

1½ cups cold buttermilk

SORGHUM BUTTER

1 stick unsalted butter, softened

½ tsp. flaky sea salt, plus more for garnish

1 Tbsp. sorghum syrup (see Note)

1. Make the biscuits Preheat the oven to 500°. In a large bowl, whisk the sifted flour with the baking powder and salt. Add the butter and, using your fingers, pinch it into the flour, making thin flakes. Refrigerate for 20 minutes.

2. Lightly dust a work surface with flour. Make a well in the center of the dry ingredients and add the buttermilk. Using a rubber spatula and working from the edge of the bowl, fold the dry ingredients into the buttermilk. Turn the dough out onto the floured surface and gather into a round. Fold the dough in half, then flatten into a 1½-inch-thick round. Repeat this process |9 more times.

3. Using a floured 2½-inch round or square biscuit cutter, stamp out the biscuits as closely together as possible. Gently press the scraps together and stamp out more biscuits. Arrange the biscuits on a large baking sheet about ½ inch apart and bake for 12 to 15 minutes, until risen and golden brown; rotate the baking sheet halfway through baking.

4. Meanwhile, make the sorghum butter In a stand mixer fitted with the paddle, beat the softened butter with the ½ teaspoon of sea salt at high speed until fluffy, about 1 minute. With the machine on, drizzle in the sorghum syrup until incorporated. Scrape the sorghum butter into small ramekins and garnish with more sea salt. Serve with the warm biscuits. —*Joe Kindred*

NOTE White Lily flour and sorghum syrup are available at some specialty food shops and on amazon.com.

MAKE AHEAD The sorghum butter can be refrigerated for up to 1 week.

Scallion-Corn Muffins

⏱ Active **20 min;** Total **45 min;** Makes **24**

Kansas City, Missouri, chefs Colby and Megan Garrelts say that if you can measure and stir, then you can make a mean cornbread. These moist muffins get fantastic flavor from corn kernels and scallions.

1¾ cups fine cornmeal

1¼ cups all-purpose flour

¾ cup sugar

1½ Tbsp. baking powder

2 tsp. kosher salt

2 large eggs

1½ cups whole milk

1 stick unsalted butter, melted

1 cup fresh or thawed frozen corn kernels

¼ cup finely chopped scallions

1. Preheat the oven to 350°. Grease the cups of two 12-cup muffin pans with non-stick cooking spray.

2. In a large bowl, whisk the cornmeal with the flour, sugar, baking powder and salt. In a medium bowl, beat the eggs with the milk and butter until smooth. Stir the wet ingredients into the dry until combined, then fold in the corn kernels and scallions.

3. Spoon the batter into the prepared muffin cups. Bake for about 15 minutes, until a toothpick inserted in the center of a muffin comes out clean. Let the muffins cool in the pan for 10 minutes before serving. —*Colby and Megan Garrelts*

MAKE AHEAD The corn muffins can be stored in an airtight container overnight. Warm in a low oven before serving.

Pull-Apart Rolls

Active **30 min;** Total **3 hr 30 min** Makes **14**

These insanely tasty, pillow-like rolls get their great golden color from the addition of butter and eggs.

1 stick unsalted butter, melted and cooled, plus softened butter for brushing

1 package active dry yeast

¼ cup lukewarm water (100° to 110°)

¼ cup sugar

1 cup whole milk, warmed

2 large eggs, at room temperature

4 cups all-purpose flour, plus more for dusting

2½ tsp. kosher salt

1. Brush a large bowl with butter. In the bowl of a stand mixer fitted with the paddle, combine the yeast with the water and a pinch of the sugar and let stand until foamy, about 10 minutes. Add the milk, melted butter, eggs and the remaining sugar and mix until combined. Switch to the dough hook and add the flour and salt. Knead at low speed until a smooth ball forms, about 2 minutes. Scrape the dough into the prepared bowl. Cover with plastic wrap and let stand in a warm place until doubled in bulk, about 1½ hours.

2. Preheat the oven to 350°. Grease a 9-by-13-inch baking dish. Turn the dough out onto a lightly floured surface and form into a ball. Cut in half, then slice each half into 7 wedges and arrange them top side up in the prepared baking dish. Cover with plastic wrap and let stand in a warm place until doubled in volume, about 30 minutes.

3. Bake the rolls for 20 to 25 minutes, until golden. Serve warm or at room temperature. —*Laura Rege*

MAKE AHEAD The baked rolls can be covered in plastic wrap and stored overnight at room temperature. Reheat the rolls before serving.

DIY Garlic Knots

*At Gristmill in Brooklyn, dough wunderkind **Jake Novick-Finder** has a devoted following for his reinvention of the beloved pizza shop snack. Made with fresh, locally milled flour (which is more nutrient-dense) and whole-grain spelt flour, his garlic knots are chewier and more flavorful than your standard knots. He finishes them with a liberal sprinkling of toppings.*

Spelt Garlic Knots

Active **1 hr 45 min**; Total **5 hr 40 min**
Makes **16**

Novick-Finder prefers a combination of all-purpose and spelt flours for these crusty garlic knots. "The high-protein content of spelt flour gives this dough extra energy," he says. "That energy imparts structure, a perfect chew and a poofy interior after it's baked."

- ¼ cup extra-virgin olive oil
- 2 tsp. active dry yeast
- 2 cups all-purpose flour, plus more for dusting
- 2 cups spelt flour, such as Farmer Ground (see Note)
- 1 Tbsp. kosher salt

1. In the bowl of a stand mixer fitted with the dough hook, mix the olive oil and yeast with 1¼ cups of water. Let stand until foamy, about 5 minutes. Add both flours and mix on low speed until the dough comes together, about 5 minutes. The dough should be smooth but not sticky; add 1 tablespoon of water if it is too dry. Let rest for 15 minutes.

2. Add the salt and mix on medium-low speed until the dough is stiff and springs back when you touch it, 10 to 15 minutes. Shape into a ball and transfer to a large bowl. Cover the bowl with a damp kitchen towel and let stand in a warm place until the dough is doubled in bulk, about 1 hour.

3. Turn the dough out onto a very lightly floured work surface. Gently stretch it into a square and fold each of the 4 sides into the center. Flip the dough seam side down and return to the bowl. Cover with the damp towel and let rise in a warm place until the dough is doubled in bulk and springs back slowly after you touch it, about 1 hour.

4. Line 2 large rimmed baking sheets with parchment paper. Turn the dough out onto a lightly floured work surface and, using a large knife or a bench scraper, cut it into 16 equal portions. Gently roll each piece of dough into a ball and carefully transfer to the prepared baking sheets. Loosely cover with damp kitchen towels and let stand in a warm place for 30 minutes.

5. Invert 1 ball of dough onto an unfloured work surface so it is sticky side up. Using your pointer fingers, press the outside edges of the dough together to seal the sticky side. Using your palm, flatten the dough, then turn it so the longer side is facing you. Working from the opposite side, fold the dough over itself 3 or 4 times to form a tight log. Roll the log into a 12-inch rope, then tie into a loose knot with 2 long tails. Transfer the knot to the baking sheet and repeat with the remaining balls of dough.

6. Carefully slide each baking sheet into a clean, unscented 13-gallon plastic kitchen bag and tie the bags closed; leave air in the bags to prevent the plastic from touching the dough. Let the knots rise in a warm place until the dough is puffed and springs back slowly after you touch it, about 1 hour. Toppings and baking instructions are at right.

NOTE Farmer Ground spelt flour can be found at Whole Foods, but any local, finely ground spelt flour will work here.

STEP-BY-STEP GARLIC KNOT LESSON

PINCH THE DOUGH With the sticky side up, press the outside edges of the ball together to seal.

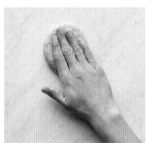

FLATTEN Press down on the dough with your palm and rotate the oval so the long side faces you.

FORM A LOG Working from the opposite side, fold the dough over itself 3 or 4 times to form a tight log.

ROLL IT OUT Using both hands and working from the center of the log to the ends, roll into a 12-inch rope.

TOPPINGS

Classic Garlic Knots
Active 15 min; Total 1 hr 30 min
Makes 16

Preheat the oven to 425°. In a medium saucepan, melt 2 sticks **unsalted butter** in 1 cup **extra-virgin olive oil**. Add 20 cloves (about 1 head) coarsely chopped **garlic** and cook over low heat, stirring occasionally, until the garlic is very soft and golden, about 45 minutes. Keep warm over very low heat. Gently brush the knots with the garlic butter, leaving the garlic pieces behind, and sprinkle with **flaky sea salt**. Bake the garlic knots for about 20 minutes, until puffed and browned. Drizzle with more **garlic butter** and sprinkle with finely chopped **parsley**. Serve warm.

Cacio e Pepe Knots
Active 10 min; Total 35 min; Makes 16

Preheat the oven to 425°. Brush the knots with **garlic butter** (recipe above), leaving the garlic pieces behind, and top with freshly grated **Parmigiano-Reggiano**, freshly ground **black pepper** and **flaky sea salt**. Bake the knots for about 20 minutes, until puffed and browned. Drizzle with more **garlic butter** and garnish with more **Parmigiano-Reggiano** and **pepper**. Serve warm.

Cacio e Pepe Knots

Classic Garlic Knots

Everything Knots
Active 10 min; Total 35 min; Makes 16

Preheat the oven to 425°. In a small bowl, mix 2 Tbsp. each **poppy seeds** and **sesame seeds**. Brush the knots with **garlic butter** (recipe above left), leaving the garlic pieces behind, and sprinkle with the seeds. Bake the knots for about 20 minutes, until puffed and browned. Drizzle with more **garlic butter** and sprinkle with 2 Tbsp. **dried onion flakes**. Serve warm.

TIE A KNOT Tie the rope into a loose knot with 2 long tails. Transfer to a baking sheet; repeat.

LET RISE Slide the baking sheets into 2 very large plastic bags. Fill with air and tie. Proof for 1 hour.

ADD TOPPINGS Brush the knots with butter and add toppings.

Garlic Bread Rolls

Active **2 hr 15 min**; Total **3 hr 15 min plus overnight chilling**; Makes **24**

ROLLS

- **1 cup whole milk, at room temperature**
- **1 large egg, beaten**
- **1 envelope active dry yeast**
- **4 cups plus 3 Tbsp. all-purpose flour, plus more for dusting**
- **1 Tbsp. plus 1 tsp. kosher salt**
- **1 Tbsp. plus 2 tsp. sugar**
- **9 Tbsp. unsalted butter, cubed and softened**

GARLIC BUTTER

- **5½ sticks unsalted butter**
- **⅔ cup finely chopped garlic (from 2 large heads)**
- **1½ cups finely grated Parmigiano-Reggiano cheese**
- **2 Tbsp. kosher salt**
- **2 tsp. pepper**

TOPPING

- **½ cup plus 2 Tbsp. all-purpose flour**
- **½ cup plus 2 Tbsp. finely grated Parmigiano-Reggiano cheese**
- **1 tsp. kosher salt**
- **5 Tbsp. unsalted butter, melted**

1. Prepare the rolls In the bowl of a stand mixer, combine the milk, egg and yeast and let stand until foamy, about 5 minutes. Attach the dough hook and beat at low speed until combined. Add the flour, salt and sugar and beat at medium speed until combined, about 2 minutes. With the mixer on medium speed, gradually add the butter and mix until the dough is smooth. Transfer to a parchment paper–lined baking sheet, cover with plastic wrap and flatten with your palms. Refrigerate the dough overnight.

2. Meanwhile, make the garlic butter In a medium saucepan, melt 1½ sticks of butter over moderately low heat. Add the garlic and cook, stirring frequently, until soft and lightly browned, about 12 minutes. Transfer to a food processor and let cool slightly, then puree until smooth. Let cool.

3. In a stand mixer fitted with the paddle, beat the remaining 4 sticks of butter with the cheese, salt and pepper until smooth. With the mixer on low, gradually add the cooled garlic butter and beat until smooth. Scrape the mixture into a pastry bag fitted with a ¼-inch round tip.

4. Line a large baking sheet with parchment paper. On a lightly floured work surface, roll out the dough to a 9-by-12-inch rectangle. Using a large knife, cut the dough into three 4-by-9-inch strips. Arrange 1 strip of dough so that the long side is facing you. Pipe a strip of the garlic butter lengthwise onto the top half, then fold the top edge over the butter to the center, pressing to seal. Pipe another strip of the garlic butter along the seam. Fold the bottom edge of the dough over the butter, pinching to seal. Cut the stuffed dough into 8 pieces and arrange seam side down and ½ inch apart on the prepared baking sheet. Repeat with the remaining 2 strips of dough and the garlic butter to form a total of 24 garlic bread rolls. Cover loosely with a large sheet of greased plastic wrap and let rise in a warm place until doubled in bulk, about 2 hours. Reserve the remaining garlic butter.

5. Meanwhile, make the topping In a stand mixer fitted with the paddle, beat the flour with the cheese and salt until mixed. With the machine on low, gradually beat in the melted butter until evenly moistened and crumbly.

6. Preheat the oven to 375°. In a small saucepan, melt the reserved garlic butter over low heat. Brush the rolls with the melted garlic butter and sprinkle with the topping. Bake for about 40 minutes, until golden and puffed. Serve warm.
—*Daniel Humm*

Easy Seeded Rye Bread

Active **20 min**; Total **8 hr plus overnight chilling**; Makes **two 9-inch loaves**

- **3 cups rye flour, preferably organic**
- **2 cups whole-wheat flour**
- **1¾ cups cracked rye**
- **1½ cups flaxseeds**
- **1 cup roasted salted sunflower seeds**
- **¾ cup toasted sesame seeds**
- **2½ cups cold water**
- **1 cup buttermilk**
- **⅔ cup dubbel-style Belgian beer, such as Chimay Première**
- **1 Tbsp. flaky sea salt**
- **1½ tsp. active dry yeast**
- **Canola oil or nonstick cooking spray, for greasing**

1. In a large bowl, whisk both flours with the cracked rye and the flax, sunflower and sesame seeds.

2. In the bowl of a stand mixer fitted with the dough hook, mix the water with the buttermilk, beer, salt and yeast at low speed until combined. Add the dry ingredients and mix at medium-low speed until incorporated and the dough is the consistency of a thick cake batter, about 10 minutes.

3. Lightly grease two 9-by-4-inch loaf pans and divide the dough between the pans; smooth the top of the dough with a spatula. Each loaf pan will have about 2½ pounds of dough. Cover loosely with plastic wrap and refrigerate overnight, at least 12 hours or up to 6 days.

4. Remove the loaf pans from the refrigerator and let stand at room temperature in a warm place until an instant-read thermometer inserted in the center of the dough reads 73°, about 3 hours. Preheat the oven to 350°. Unwrap the dough and bake for 2 hours, until the crust is a deep brown and an instant-read thermometer inserted in the center reads 200°.

5. Transfer the loaf pans to a wire rack and let cool for 30 minutes. Carefully remove the bread from the pans and let cool completely, about 2 hours. —*Claus Meyer*

NOTE Cracked rye can be found at some health food stores and on amazon.com.

MAKE AHEAD Bread wrapped in foil can be kept at room temperature for up to 1 week.

Coconut Curry Cornbread Stuffing

Active **40 min**; Total **3 hr**; Serves **10 to 12**

Cookbook author Ayesha Curry includes chunks of sourdough bread to add some nice chew to this sweet cornbread stuffing.

CORNBREAD

  Coconut oil, for greasing

2 cups fine yellow cornmeal

2 cups all-purpose flour

½ cup sugar

2 Tbsp. baking powder

2 tsp. kosher salt

2 large eggs

2 cups unsweetened coconut milk

⅔ cup vegetable oil

STUFFING

2 cups vegetable stock or low-sodium broth

1 large onion, chopped (2 cups)

3 celery ribs, chopped (1½ cups)

  Coconut oil, for greasing

2 large eggs

¾ cup unsweetened coconut milk

½ stick unsalted butter, melted

1 tsp. Madras curry powder

  Kosher salt and pepper

4 oz. crustless sourdough bread, cubed (2½ cups)

1. Make the cornbread Preheat the oven to 400°. Grease a large cast-iron skillet with coconut oil. In a large bowl, whisk the cornmeal with the flour, sugar, baking powder and salt. In a medium bowl, beat the eggs with the coconut milk and vegetable oil. Stir the wet ingredients into the dry until combined. Scrape the batter into the prepared skillet and smooth the top.

2. Bake the cornbread for 20 to 25 minutes, until lightly browned and a toothpick inserted in the center comes out clean. Let cool completely, then cut into 1-inch pieces.

3. Make the stuffing In a medium saucepan, combine the vegetable stock with the onion and celery and bring to a boil. Simmer over moderate heat until the vegetables are tender, 10 minutes. Let cool.

4. Grease a 9-by-13-inch baking dish with coconut oil. In a large bowl, beat the eggs with the coconut milk, melted butter, curry powder, 2 teaspoons of salt and 1 teaspoon

of pepper. Add the cornbread and sourdough and mix well. Stir in the cooled stock and vegetables, then scrape the mixture into the prepared baking dish.

5. Bake the stuffing for about 40 minutes, until set and the top is lightly browned. Let stand for 10 minutes; serve. —*Ayesha Curry*

NOTE Curry often serves the stuffing with a quick chili butter. Mix 3 sticks softened butter with 3 tablespoons chili powder and 1 teaspoon ground cumin; season with salt.

MAKE AHEAD The unbaked stuffing can be refrigerated overnight. Bring to room temperature before baking.

Sourdough Stuffing with Sausage, Red Onion and Kale

Active **1 hr**; Total **2 hr 20 min**; Serves **10**

½ stick unsalted butter, cubed, plus more for greasing

1 lb. sweet Italian sausage, casings removed and meat crumbled

2 medium red onions, cut into 1-inch wedges through the core

¼ cup extra-virgin olive oil

  Kosher salt and black pepper

1 lb. curly kale, leaves torn

4 large eggs

2½ cups chicken stock or low-sodium broth

1¼ lbs. sourdough bread, torn into 2-inch pieces

½ cup chopped parsley

1 Tbsp. thyme leaves

1 tsp. crushed red pepper

1. Preheat the oven to 375°. Butter a 9-by-13-inch baking dish. On a large rimmed baking sheet, toss the sausage, onions and oil and season with salt and black pepper. Roast for about 20 minutes, until browned and softened. Scatter the kale on top of the sausage and onions and roast for about 5 minutes, until just wilted. Transfer one-fourth of the mixture to a plate and reserve. Let cool slightly.

2. In a large bowl, beat the eggs with the chicken stock. Add the bread, the ½ stick of butter, the parsley, thyme, crushed red pepper, 1½ teaspoons of salt and 1 teaspoon of black pepper; mix well. Fold in the three-fourths of sausage-kale mixture, then scrape into the prepared baking dish.

Decoratively scatter the reserved sausage-kale mixture on top, gently pressing it into the stuffing. Cover the baking dish tightly with foil.

3. Bake the stuffing for 30 minutes, until hot. Uncover and bake 30 minutes longer, until lightly browned. Let stand for 10 minutes before serving. —*Justin Chapple*

MAKE AHEAD The recipe can be prepared through Step 2 and refrigerated overnight. Bring to room temperature before baking.

Mushroom, Sourdough and Poblano Stuffing

Active **30 min**; Total **2 hr 30 min**; Serves **10**

The trick to make-ahead stuffing is adding a little stock before reheating it.

  Unsalted butter, for greasing

1 lb. oyster mushrooms, torn into bite-size pieces

3 large poblano peppers, stemmed and sliced

2 medium red onions, cut into 1-inch wedges through the core

¼ cup extra-virgin olive oil

  Kosher salt and black pepper

4 large eggs

2½ cups chicken stock or low-sodium broth

1 lb. sourdough bread, cut or torn into bite-size pieces

1. Preheat the oven to 375°. Butter a 9-by-13-inch baking dish. On two large rimmed baking sheets, toss the mushrooms with the poblanos, red onions and the olive oil. Season with salt and pepper and toss again. Roast for about 25 to 30 minutes, until lightly browned and tender. Let cool.

2. In a large bowl, beat the eggs with 2½ cups of the chicken stock, 1½ teaspoons salt and ¾ teaspoon pepper. Add the bread and vegetables and mix well. Scrape into the prepared baking dish, cover tightly with foil and let stand at room temperature for 1 hour.

3. Bake the stuffing for 30 minutes, until hot. Uncover and bake for 20 to 25 minutes longer, until lightly browned. Let stand for 10 minutes before serving. —*Justin Chapple*

Bacon-Chile Naan

Active **1 hr 40 min**; Total **5 hr**; Makes **9**

 1 **cup plus 2 Tbsp. whole milk**
 3 **cups all-purpose flour**
2½ **tsp. baking powder**
1½ **tsp. kosher salt**
 1 **large egg, beaten**
    Canola oil
 1 **lb. bacon**
 7 **oz. mild white cheddar, shredded (2 cups)**
 1 **Tbsp. crushed red pepper**
    Melted butter

1. In a small saucepan, warm the milk over low heat until it registers 110° on an instant-read thermometer, 3 to 5 minutes. In a stand mixer fitted with the dough hook, mix the flour with the baking powder and salt. Whisk the egg into the warm milk and add to the mixer bowl. Mix at medium speed until the dough pulls away from the side of the bowl, 3 minutes. Transfer to a work surface and knead into a ball. Rub the dough with oil and transfer to an oiled bowl. Cover with plastic wrap and let rest at least 4 hours, or refrigerate overnight.

2. Preheat the oven to 375°. Arrange the bacon on a rack over a baking sheet. Bake for 25 minutes, until browned and crisp. Drain on paper towels and let cool. Finely chop and transfer to a medium bowl. Stir in the cheese and red pepper. Increase the oven temperature to 500° and set 2 large cast-iron skillets on the center rack.

3. Meanwhile, divide the dough into nine 3-ounce balls and cover with a damp kitchen towel. On a lightly floured work surface, use your fingertips to press 1 ball of dough into a 5-inch round, leaving it thicker in the center (it should look like a filled ravioli). Press a scant ¼ cup of the bacon-cheddar filling into the center of the dough, then pull the edges over the filling to form a ball; press the seams to seal. Place the ball seam side down and flatten gently with your palm. Using a lightly floured rolling pin, roll out the ball to a 6-inch round. Repeat with remaining dough and filling.

4. Working in batches, bake the naan in the hot skillets until puffed and golden, 5 to 7 minutes per batch. Brush with melted butter and serve warm. —*Vikram Sunderam*

Persian Flatbread (Nan-e Barbari)

⟳ Active **15 min**; Total **40 min**; Serves **8**

Store-bought pizza dough makes quick work of this Persian flatbread, traditionally baked in a *tanoor*. The trick is to gently stretch the dough to form the oblong shape, then use the side of your hand to press deep channels into it before brushing with yogurt for an extra-crunchy crust.

¼ **cup whole-milk yogurt**
¼ **cup water**
   Two 1-lb. balls of pizza dough
   Nigella seeds, sesame seeds and flaky sea salt (optional), for sprinkling

1. Preheat the oven to 450°. In a small bowl, whisk the yogurt with the water.

2. On a large rimmed baking sheet, stretch and press 1 ball of the dough to a 14-by-5-inch rectangle. Using your fingers, press 5 to 6 deep lengthwise channels into the dough (slight tearing is okay). Brush the surface with some of the yogurt mixture and sprinkle with nigella and sesame seeds; season with salt, if using. Repeat on another baking sheet with the other ball of dough.

3. Bake the flatbreads for 20 to 25 minutes, until browned; rotate halfway through. Serve. —*Mahin Gilanpour Motamed*

SERVE WITH Sabzi khordan, an appetizer platter of fresh herbs, vegetables, nuts and feta cheese that's served at most Persian meals.

Pizza Dough

Active **30 min**; Total **6 hr 30 min**
Makes **two 12-oz. balls of pizza dough**

 1 **cup lukewarm water**
 ½ **tsp. active dry yeast**
2¾ **cups 0 flour (see Note)**
 1 **Tbsp. extra-virgin olive oil, plus more for greasing**
1¼ **tsp. kosher salt**

1. In a large bowl, whisk the water with the yeast and let stand until foamy, about 5 minutes. Add the flour, olive oil and salt and stir until a dough forms. Scrape onto a work surface and knead until smooth, about 5 minutes. Transfer to a large greased bowl. Cover with plastic and let stand in a warm place for 1 hour.

2. Cut the dough in half and form into 2 balls. Transfer the balls to 2 large greased bowls. Cover with plastic and let stand in a warm place until doubled in bulk, about 5 hours. Punch down the dough before using. —*Daniele Uditi*

NOTE "Tipo 0" is the Italian designation for finely ground, high-protein flour; all-purpose flour can be substituted.

MAKE AHEAD The dough can be refrigerated overnight or frozen for up to 1 month. Let the dough come to room temperature before using.

Grilled Lemon Pizzas

Total **1 hr**; Makes **two 12-inch pizzas**

All you need to turn out beautifully charred pies is a gas or charcoal grill, a batch of dough and toppings. Place the crust on the grate, then, in the last minutes of cooking, flip it and add the remaining ingredients.

    Extra-virgin olive oil, for brushing and drizzling
 2 **lemons, thinly sliced**
    Pizza Dough (recipe at left)
1½ **lbs. fresh mozzarella, torn**
 4 **oz. goat cheese**
¼ **cup toasted pine nuts**
    Flaky sea salt and pepper
    Torn basil, for garnish

1. Light a grill and oil the grate. Grill the lemon slices over moderately high heat until lightly charred on both sides, 3 to 5 minutes. Transfer to a plate.

2. On a lightly oiled large baking sheet, stretch 1 ball of pizza dough to a 12-inch oval or round and brush with olive oil. Grill the dough over moderate heat until lightly charred on the bottom, 2 to 3 minutes. Flip the crust and scatter half each of the mozzarella and lemon slices on top. Close the grill and cook until the cheese is melted and the crust is firm, 3 to 5 minutes. Transfer to a large board and top with half each of the goat cheese and pine nuts. Season with salt and pepper. Garnish with torn basil and a drizzle of olive oil.

3. Repeat with the remaining dough, mozzarella, lemon slices, goat cheese, pine nuts, seasoning and garnishes. Cut the pizzas into wedges and serve. —*Daniele Uditi*

WINE Bright rosé: 2016 Domaine de Cala.

Bacon-Chile Naan

Hummus and
Salad Pizza

Hummus and Salad Pizza

⟳ Active **30 min**; Total **45 min**
Makes **one 12-inch pizza**

This fun dish was inspired by the spring greens pie chef Eric Korsh serves at NYC's North End Grill. We spread plain hummus on the warm pizza crust, but anything spreadable will work, from fresh ricotta or tangy yogurt to smoky baba ghanoush.

- 1 **lb. pizza dough**
  Extra-virgin olive oil, for brushing and drizzling
- 1 **cup mesclun greens**
- 1 **cup parsley leaves**
- 1 **cup mint leaves**
- 1 **cup snipped pea shoots, sunflower sprouts or purslane**
- 2 **Tbsp. fresh lemon juice**
- 1 **cup prepared hummus, at room temperature**
  Flaky sea salt and pepper
  Shredded ricotta salata, for serving

1. Preheat the oven to 450° for at least 30 minutes. On a large rimmed baking sheet, stretch and pull the dough to a 14-inch-long oval and brush with olive oil. Bake for about 15 minutes, until the crust is puffed and browned.

2. In a bowl, toss the mesclun with the parsley, mint, pea shoots and lemon juice. Spread the hummus on the hot crust. Pile the salad on the pizza and season with flaky sea salt and pepper. Drizzle with olive oil and top with shredded ricotta salata. Cut into wedges and serve right away.
—*Justin Chapple*

WINE Light-bodied, lemony white: 2015 Hugues de Beaulieu Picpoul de Pinet.

Grilled Asparagus Pizzas with Gremolata

Total **1 hr**; Makes **two 12-inch pizzas**

The heat of the grill can wilt the freshest toppings, so L.A. chef Daniele Uditi spoons something bright—a blend of fresh herbs, crushed red pepper and garlic—over the pizza once it comes off the grate.

- ½ **cup extra-virgin olive oil, plus more for brushing**
- ½ **cup chopped parsley**
- 2 **tsp. chopped oregano**
- 1½ **tsp. grated lemon zest plus 3 Tbsp. fresh lemon juice**
- 1 **garlic clove, minced**
- ¼ **tsp. crushed red pepper**
  Kosher salt and black pepper
- 1 **lb. thin asparagus, trimmed**
  Pizza Dough (p. 268)
- 1½ **lbs. fresh mozzarella, torn**

1. In a small bowl, whisk the ½ cup of olive oil with the parsley, oregano, lemon zest and juice, the garlic and crushed red pepper. Season the gremolata with salt and black pepper.

2. Light a grill and oil the grate. Brush the asparagus with olive oil and season with salt and black pepper. Grill over moderately high heat, turning, until lightly charred, 3 to 5 minutes. Transfer to a carving board and let cool; cut into 2-inch lengths.

3. On a lightly oiled large baking sheet, stretch 1 ball of pizza dough to a 12-inch oval or round and brush with olive oil. Grill the dough over moderate heat until lightly charred on the bottom, 2 to 3 minutes. Flip the crust and scatter half each of the mozzarella and asparagus on top. Close the grill and cook until the cheese is melted and the crust is firm, 3 to 5 minutes. Transfer to a large board. Repeat with the remaining dough, mozzarella and asparagus. Drizzle the pizzas with the gremolata, cut into wedges and serve. —*Daniele Uditi*

WINE Citrusy Sauvignon Blanc: 2016 Villa Maria Private Bin.

Summer Margherita Pizzas

Total **1 hr**; Makes **two 12-inch pizzas**

The tomatoes go on after the pizza cooks with mozzarella, so you get both oozy cheese and fresh, sun-ripened flavor.

- 1 **Tbsp. extra-virgin olive oil, plus more for brushing**
- 2 **large tomatoes, sliced**
- 1 **small garlic clove, minced**
  Kosher salt and pepper
  Pizza Dough (p. 268)
- 1½ **lbs. fresh mozzarella, torn**
  Torn basil, for garnish

1. Light a grill and oil the grate. Spread the tomato slices on a platter and top with the 1 tablespoon of olive oil and the garlic. Season generously with salt and pepper.

2. On a lightly oiled large baking sheet, stretch 1 ball of pizza dough to a 12-inch oval or round and brush with olive oil. Grill the dough over moderate heat until lightly charred on the bottom, 2 to 3 minutes. Flip the crust and scatter half of the mozzarella on top. Close the grill and cook until the cheese is melted and the crust is firm, 3 to 5 minutes. Transfer to a large board and top with half of the tomatoes. Sprinkle with salt and pepper. Garnish with torn basil.

3. Repeat with the remaining dough, mozzarella, tomatoes, seasoning and basil. Cut the pizzas into wedges and serve.
—*Daniele Uditi*

WINE Juicy Australian Grenache: 2015 Sucette.

Smoked Whitefish Pizza with Seeded Crust

⏱ Total **45 min**; Makes **one 12-inch pizza**

- 2 tsp. caraway seeds
- 2 tsp. sesame seeds
- 2 tsp. poppy seeds
- 1 tsp. garlic powder
- 1 tsp. onion powder
- 1 tsp. flaky sea salt
- ⅓ cup thinly sliced celery
- ¼ cup mayonnaise
- ¼ cup sour cream
- ¼ cup finely chopped chives, plus more for garnish
- 2 cups flaked skinless, boneless smoked whitefish (10 oz.)
   Kosher salt and pepper
- 1 lb. pizza dough
   Semolina flour, for dusting
- ½ cup mascarpone, at room temperature
- 2 Tbsp. capers, patted dry
- 1 large egg beaten with 2 Tbsp. milk
   Extra-virgin olive oil, small dill sprigs and lemon wedges, for serving

1. Preheat the oven to 450°. Place a pizza stone on the lower rack and heat for at least 30 minutes. In a small bowl, mix the caraway, sesame and poppy seeds, the garlic and onion powders and the sea salt. In a medium bowl, mix the celery, mayonnaise, sour cream and the ¼ cup of chives. Fold in the whitefish and season with kosher salt and pepper.

2. Stretch the pizza dough to a 12-inch round and transfer to a flour-dusted pizza peel. Spread the mascarpone all over the dough, leaving a ½-inch border, dollop with the whitefish salad, and top with capers.

3. Carefully slide the pizza onto the hot stone and bake for 6 minutes, until the crust is puffed and just starting to brown. Using tongs, return the pizza to the peel. Brush the crust with the egg wash and sprinkle generously with the seed mixture. Slide the pizza back onto the stone and bake for 5 to 8 minutes longer, until the crust is browned and the bottom is crisp. Drizzle with olive oil, top with chives and dill sprigs and serve with lemon wedges. —Michael Scelfo

Spiced-Lamb Pizzas

📷 PAGE 260

Active **1 hr**; Total **1 hr plus 24 hr rising**
Makes **six 8-inch pies**

DOUGH

- 1 Tbsp. extra-virgin olive oil, plus more for brushing
- 2 tsp. finely crumbled fresh yeast
- 1½ tsp. sugar
- 3 cups bread flour, plus more for dusting
- 1½ tsp. kosher salt

SAUCE

- ¼ cup extra-virgin olive oil
- 2 garlic cloves, minced
- 2 Tbsp. finely chopped jalapeño
   One 28-oz. can crushed tomatoes
- 1½ tsp. sugar
   Four 4-inch basil sprigs
   Kosher salt and pepper

TOPPINGS

- 2 Tbsp. extra-virgin olive oil
- 1 medium onion, finely chopped (1½ cups)
- 1 Tbsp. baharat spice (see Note)
- 1 Tbsp. finely chopped garlic
- 1 lb. ground lamb
   Kosher salt and pepper
- 6 medium tomatoes (1¼ lbs.)—halved, seeded and cut into ¼-inch dice
- ¼ cup chopped mint, plus leaves for garnish
- 1 Tbsp. fresh lemon juice

1. Make the dough Brush a large bowl with olive oil. In the bowl of a stand mixer, whisk 1¼ cups of water with the yeast and sugar and let stand until foamy, about 5 minutes. Add the 3 cups of flour, the salt and the 1 tablespoon of olive oil. Attach the paddle to the mixer and beat at medium-low speed until a dough forms. Switch to the dough hook and knead at medium speed until the dough is smooth, about 5 minutes. Transfer the dough to the prepared bowl, cover with plastic wrap and let rise in the refrigerator until doubled in bulk, 24 to 48 hours. Let the dough rest at room temperature for 1 hour before baking.

2. Meanwhile, make the sauce In a medium saucepan, heat the olive oil. Add the garlic and jalapeño and cook over moderately low heat, stirring occasionally, until softened, 2 to 3 minutes. Add the crushed tomatoes, sugar and ½ cup of water and simmer over moderately low heat, stirring occasionally, until thickened, about 25 minutes. Strain the sauce through a sieve, pressing on the solids; discard the solids. Return the sauce to the pan, add the basil and simmer over moderate heat for 10 minutes. Discard the basil; season with salt and pepper.

3. Prepare the toppings In a large skillet, heat the olive oil. Add the onion and cook over moderate heat, stirring occasionally, until lightly browned, 8 to 10 minutes. Stir in the baharat and 2 teaspoons of the garlic and cook, stirring, until softened, about 2 minutes. Add the lamb and cook, breaking up the meat with a spoon, until no pink remains, about 6 minutes. Using a slotted spoon, transfer to a paper towel–lined plate, then transfer to a medium bowl. Season with salt and pepper.

4. In a medium bowl, toss the diced tomatoes with the chopped mint, lemon juice and remaining 1 teaspoon of garlic. Season with salt and pepper.

5. Put a pizza stone in the oven and preheat to 500°, at least 30 minutes. Cut the dough into 6 pieces and roll them into balls. On a lightly floured work surface, dust the balls with flour and let rest for 10 minutes. Work with 1 piece of dough at a time: On a floured inverted baking sheet, stretch a ball of dough into an 8-inch round. Spread 2 tablespoons of the sauce on the dough, leaving a ½-inch border. Top with a scant ⅔ cup of the lamb mixture.

6. Carefully slide the pie onto the pizza stone and bake for 6 to 7 minutes, until the edges of the crust are golden and crisp. Transfer to a plate. Repeat with the remaining dough, sauce and lamb. Top the pies with some of the tomato salad. Garnish with mint leaves and serve. —Tomer Agay

NOTE Baharat spice blend commonly includes black pepper, cumin and cinnamon, and is available at kalustyans.com.

MAKE AHEAD The tomato sauce and lamb topping can be refrigerated for 2 days.

WINE Robust Israeli red blend: 2014 Psâgot Sinai.

Buckwheat Flatbreads

Active **30 min**; Total **2 hr 45 min plus cooling**; Makes **32 small flatbreads**

These chewy buckwheat flatbreads from Sakara Life, a plant-based meal delivery company, are a hearty, healthy vehicle for a variety of toppings.

- ⅔ cup lukewarm water
- 1 Tbsp. coconut sugar
- ¾ tsp. active dry yeast
- 1½ tsp. extra-virgin olive oil, plus more for greasing
- ⅔ cup brown rice flour (see Note)
- ½ cup buckwheat flour (see Note)
- 2 Tbsp. tapioca starch (see Note)
- 2 Tbsp. finely chopped walnuts
- 1 Tbsp. flaxseeds
- ½ tsp. fine Himalayan pink salt
- ¼ tsp. baking powder

1. In a small bowl, whisk the lukewarm water with the coconut sugar, yeast and the 1½ teaspoons of olive oil. Let stand until foamy, about 5 minutes.

2. In a stand mixer fitted with the paddle attachment, mix both flours with the tapioca starch, walnuts, flaxseeds, salt and baking powder. Add the wet ingredients and mix on low speed until just combined. Cover the bowl with a kitchen towel and let stand at room temperature for 2 hours.

3. Preheat the oven to 375°. Grease a large sheet of parchment paper with olive oil. Scrape the dough onto the parchment and, using a generously greased rolling pin, roll out the dough to a 12-by-16½-inch rectangle, ¹⁄₁₆ inch thick. Slide the parchment onto a large rimmed baking sheet and cut the dough into 2-by-3-inch rectangles. You will have about 32 pieces. Bake for 12 to 15 minutes, until the flatbreads are set and starting to crisp around the edges. Let cool. —*Whitney Tingle and Danielle DuBoise*

NOTE Brown rice flour, buckwheat flour and tapioca starch can be found at Whole Foods and on amazon.com.

MAKE AHEAD The flatbreads can be stored at room temperature for up to 5 days.

Roasted Cauliflower Flatbreads with Celery Root Puree

Active **30 min**; Total **1 hr 15 min** Serves **4 to 6**

PUREE

- One 1-lb. celery root, peeled and cut into 1-inch pieces
- ¼ cup extra-virgin olive oil
- ¼ cup fresh lemon juice
- 1 tsp. chopped thyme leaves
- Fine Himalayan pink salt

TOPPINGS

- One 1½-lb. head of purple cauliflower, cored and cut into 1-inch florets
- 2 Tbsp. extra-virgin olive oil, plus more for drizzling
- Fine Himalayan pink salt
- Buckwheat Flatbreads (recipe at left) or rye crackers, for serving
- Mixed microgreens and hulled hemp seeds, for garnish

1. Make the puree In a large saucepan of salted boiling water, cook the celery root until tender, about 15 minutes. Drain and transfer to a large bowl. Using a potato masher, mash the celery root with the olive oil, lemon juice and thyme until almost smooth; season with salt.

2. Meanwhile, make the toppings Preheat the oven to 400°. On a large rimmed baking sheet, toss the cauliflower with the 2 tablespoons of olive oil and season with salt. Roast for 20 to 25 minutes, until tender and browned in spots.

3. Spread the puree on the buckwheat flatbreads and top with the cauliflower. Garnish with microgreens and hulled hemp seeds. Drizzle the flatbreads with olive oil, season with salt and serve. —*Whitney Tingle and Danielle DuBoise*

WINE Lightly herbal Italian white: 2014 Poggio al Tesoro Solosole Vermentino.

Mushroom Flatbreads with Winter Pesto

Active **20 min**; Total **1 hr**; Serves **4 to 6**

PESTO

- ¼ cup hazelnuts
- 1½ cups lightly packed basil leaves
- ¼ cup lightly packed baby arugula
- 1 Tbsp. finely chopped sage
- 1 Tbsp. nutritional yeast (see Note)
- 1 tsp. minced rosemary
- 1½ tsp. apple cider vinegar
- 1½ tsp. fresh lemon juice
- ½ cup extra-virgin olive oil
- Fine Himalayan pink salt and pepper

TOPPINGS

- ½ lb. chanterelle or black trumpet mushrooms, cut into 1-inch pieces
- 2 Tbsp. extra-virgin olive oil, plus more for drizzling
- Fine Himalayan pink salt and pepper
- 1 Thai bird chile, minced
- One 8-oz. head of radicchio—halved, cored and cut into 1-inch wedges
- 2 Tbsp. balsamic vinegar
- 2 Tbsp. honey, preferably liquid raw
- Buckwheat Flatbreads (recipe at left) or rye crackers, for serving

1. Make the pesto Preheat the oven to 375°. Spread the hazelnuts in a pie plate and roast for 8 to 10 minutes, until golden and fragrant. Let cool slightly, then rub them together in a kitchen towel to remove the skins. Leave the oven on.

2. In a food processor, pulse the hazelnuts with the basil, arugula, sage, nutritional yeast, rosemary, vinegar and lemon juice until a coarse puree forms. With the machine on, gradually add the olive oil until incorporated. Season with salt and pepper.

3. Make the toppings On a large rimmed baking sheet, toss the mushrooms with the 2 tablespoons of olive oil and season with salt and pepper. Roast for about 20 minutes, until the mushrooms are tender and browned. Stir in the chile.

4. Meanwhile, arrange the radicchio on a rimmed baking sheet. In a small bowl, whisk the vinegar with the honey until smooth. Drizzle over the radicchio and season with salt and pepper. Roast for about 15 minutes, until wilted and browned in spots.

5. Spread the pesto on the buckwheat flatbreads and top with the radicchio and mushrooms. Drizzle with olive oil, season with salt and serve.
—Whitney Tingle and Danielle DuBoise

NOTE Nutritional yeast, a nutty-tasting vegan seasoning, can be found at Whole Foods and on amazon.com

MAKE AHEAD The pesto can be refrigerated overnight. Bring to room temperature to serve.

WINE Light, fruity California Pinot Noir: 2014 Mark West.

Moroccan Flatbreads with Roasted Tomatoes

Active **25 min;** Total **1 hr;** Serves **4 to 6**

CARROT PUREE

- **1½ lbs. carrots, cut into ½-inch pieces**
- **6 garlic cloves**
- **¾ cup extra-virgin olive oil**
- **1½ Tbsp. Madras curry powder**
- **1 Tbsp. ground turmeric**
- **Fine Himalayan pink salt**

TOPPINGS

- **4 plum tomatoes, quartered lengthwise and cored**
- **2 Tbsp. extra-virgin olive oil, plus more for drizzling**
- **1 Tbsp. honey, preferably liquid raw (see Note)**
- **1 Tbsp. ground coriander**
- **Fine Himalayan pink salt**
- **Buckwheat Flatbreads (recipe opposite page) or rye crackers, for serving**
- **Chopped shelled, salted and roasted pistachios, for garnish**

1. Make the puree Preheat the oven to 400°. In a large bowl, toss the carrots with the garlic, olive oil, curry powder and turmeric and season with salt. Transfer to a large rimmed baking sheet and roast for about 30 minutes, until the carrots are very tender. Scrape into a food processor, let cool slightly, and puree until smooth; season with salt.

2. Meanwhile, make the toppings On a large rimmed baking sheet, toss the tomatoes with the 2 tablespoons of olive oil, the honey and coriander; season with salt. Roast for about 20 minutes, until the tomatoes are softened and lightly browned in spots. Let cool completely.

3. Spread the carrot puree on the buckwheat flatbreads and top with the roasted tomatoes. Garnish with pistachios, drizzle with olive oil and season with salt; serve.
—Whitney Tingle and Danielle DuBoise

NOTE Raw, unprocessed honey can be found at most health food stores.

MAKE AHEAD The carrot puree and roasted tomatoes can be refrigerated separately overnight. Bring to room temperature to serve.

WINE Crisp French rosé: 2015 Château d'Aqueria Tavel.

5 Ways to Hack a Wine List

Gone are the days of simply going with the house red or white. Here are some tips on how to order more wisely.

SEEK OUT A GRAPE YOU DON'T RECOGNIZE "Oftentimes, the most unusual wine is the somm's pet favorite and a good value," Bianca Bosker says.

AVOID THE "GIMME WINE" Beware: That Chianti or Chardonnay usually commands a premium price. "This is instantly recognizable and makes people go, 'Give it to me. I don't care what it costs,'"Bosker says.

LOOK FOR REPETITION If you see three Chenin Blancs, it's no mistake. "When you figure out the somm's 'thing,' order that thing."

DON'T FALL FOR THE SECOND-LEAST-EXPENSIVE WINE Instead, speak up about your budget and what you like. "A good somm can steer you in the right direction."

CONSIDER WHAT'S MISSING If you don't see Bordeaux on the menu, don't ask for it. "The sommelier wants you to try something new!"
— Bianca Bosker, author of Cork Dork

Grilled Strawberry-Avocado
Toasts with Burrata

Grilled Strawberry-Avocado Toasts with Burrata

Total **45 min**; Serves **4**

Meet your new favorite avocado toast. Serve as a light lunch (knife and fork encouraged) or cut into thick slices for poolside hors d'oeuvres. Good balsamic vinegar is key here.

- 6 **scallions**
- 2 **cups strawberries, hulled and quartered**
- 1 **Hass avocado—peeled, pitted and cut into 1-inch pieces**
- 2 **Tbsp. fresh lemon juice**
- ¼ **tsp. crushed red pepper**

  Kosher salt and black pepper

  Four 1-inch-thick slices of rustic bread

  Extra-virgin olive oil, for brushing and drizzling
- 1 **garlic clove**
- 8 **oz. burrata, cut into bite-size pieces**

  Balsamic vinegar, for drizzling

  Flaky sea salt and torn basil, for garnish

1. Light a grill. Grill the scallions over high heat, turning once, until lightly charred, 3 minutes. Transfer to a work surface and let cool, then cut into 1-inch lengths. Leave the grill on.

2. In a medium bowl, mix the scallions with the strawberries, avocado, lemon juice and crushed red pepper. Season with kosher salt and black pepper and let stand at room temperature for 15 minutes.

3. Meanwhile, brush the bread with olive oil and grill over high heat, turning once, until lightly charred, about 3 minutes. Transfer to a platter and rub with the garlic clove. Top with the burrata and the strawberry salad. Drizzle with olive oil and balsamic vinegar. Garnish with flaky sea salt and torn basil; serve. —*Joshua McFadden*

Green Potato Smørrebrød

Active **40 min**; Total **1 hr 30 min plus overnight pickling**; Serves **4**

- 1 **cup apple cider vinegar**
- ¾ **cup sugar**
- ½ **lb. pearl onions, peeled (see Note)**

  Kosher salt and pepper
- 6 **oz. fingerling potatoes**

  Five 3-inch strips of lemon zest
- 3 **dill stems**
- ¼ **tsp. black peppercorns**
- ½ **cup mayonnaise**
- 2 **Tbsp. finely chopped dill, plus small sprigs for garnish**
- 1 **tsp. Dijon mustard**
- 1 **tsp. white wine vinegar**

  Unsalted European-style butter, softened, for spreading
- 4 **slices of dense rye bread**

  Very thinly sliced shallot and small potato chips, for garnish

1. In a medium saucepan, combine the apple cider vinegar with the sugar and 1 cup of water and bring to a boil. Add the pearl onions and a pinch of salt. Transfer to a heatproof jar and let cool completely. Refrigerate overnight.

2. In a medium saucepan, cover the potatoes, lemon zest, dill stems and peppercorns with water and bring to a boil. Add a generous pinch of salt and simmer until just tender, about 20 minutes. Remove from the heat and let the potatoes cool in the cooking liquid, about 30 minutes. Drain well and discard the aromatics. Cut the potatoes into ¼-inch-thick slices.

3. In a small bowl, whisk the mayonnaise with the chopped dill, mustard and white wine vinegar. Season with salt.

4. Cut 4 of the pickled pearl onions in half and separate the layers. Reserve the remaining onions for another use. Spread butter on the rye bread and arrange the potato slices on top. Dollop the dill mayonnaise on the potatoes and season with salt and pepper. Garnish with the pickled onion petals, shallot, dill sprigs and potato chips; serve immediately. —*Claus Meyer*

NOTE Thawed frozen pearl onions can also be used for this recipe.

WINE Tart Spanish white: 2015 Martínsancho Rueda.

Smoked Salmon Smørrebrød

Total **30 min**; Serves **4**

This gorgeous open-face rye sandwich from chef Claus Meyer of the Great Northern Food Hall in New York City's Grand Central Terminal makes for the perfect light lunch or, when cut into smaller squares, an impressive hors d'oeuvre.

- ½ **fennel bulb—halved lengthwise, cored and very thinly sliced**
- ½ **Granny Smith apple, cored and very thinly sliced**
- 3 **tsp. fresh lemon juice**
- 3 **Tbsp. crème fraîche**
- 1½ **Tbsp. skyr (Icelandic yogurt) or Greek yogurt**
- 1 **Tbsp. finely grated fresh horseradish**

  Pinch of sugar

  Kosher salt

  Unsalted European-style butter, softened, for spreading
- 4 **slices of dense rye bread**
- ½ **lb. sliced smoked salmon**

  Small dill sprigs and flaky sea salt, for garnish

1. Fill a medium bowl with ice water. Add the sliced fennel and apple and let sit until crisp, about 10 minutes. Drain well and pat dry. In a medium bowl, toss the fennel and apple with 1 teaspoon of the lemon juice.

2. Meanwhile, in a small bowl, mix the crème fraîche with the skyr, horseradish, sugar and the remaining 2 teaspoons of lemon juice. Season the horseradish crème with salt.

3. Spread butter on the rye bread and arrange the smoked salmon on top. Dollop the horseradish crème on the salmon, then top with the fennel-apple salad. Garnish with dill and sprinkle with flaky sea salt; serve. —*Claus Meyer*

MAKE AHEAD The horseradish crème can be refrigerated overnight.

WINE Citrusy Sauvignon Blanc: 2015 Villa Maria Private Bin.

Crab Tartines

Total **30 min**; Serves **4**

Chef Sam Goinsalvos's genius twist to these simple open-face sandwiches: homemade black rice crispies on top.

Canola oil, for frying

¼ **cup forbidden black rice**

½ **cup mayonnaise**

¼ **cup Dijon mustard**

1½ **Tbsp. fresh lemon juice**

½ **tsp. Old Bay Seasoning**

1 **lb. jumbo lump crabmeat, picked over**

¼ **cup finely chopped chives**

Kosher salt and pepper

4 **slices rustic rye bread**

Microgreens, for garnish

1. In a medium saucepan, heat ½ inch of canola oil to 350°. Fry the rice until puffed, 1 minute. Using a fine sieve, transfer the crispy rice to paper towels.

2. In a large bowl, whisk the mayonnaise with the mustard, lemon juice and Old Bay. Fold in the crab and chives. Season with salt and pepper. Serve the crab mixture on the bread with the crisped rice, garnished with microgreens. —*Sam Goinsalvos*

WINE Citrusy New Zealand Sauvignon Blanc: 2016 Dog Point.

Rye Tartines with Chicken and Pickled Celery

Active **45 min**; Total **1 hr 15 min plus 4 hr pickling**; Serves **4**

PICKLED CELERY

1 **cup apple cider vinegar**

½ **cup water**

1 **Tbsp. kosher salt**

1 **Tbsp. sugar**

1 **cup thinly sliced peeled celery (2 to 3 ribs)**

TARTINES

4 **Tbsp. unsalted butter, cubed**

4 **slices rye bread**

½ **cup whole-milk Greek yogurt**

½ **English cucumber, sliced ¼ inch thick**

Kosher salt

2 **cups shredded Best-Ever Roast Chicken (p. 146) or rotisserie chicken**

Small dill sprigs, for garnish

1. Make the pickled celery In a small saucepan, combine the vinegar, water, salt and sugar and bring to a boil, stirring to dissolve the salt and sugar. Let cool completely, then transfer to a medium bowl. Add the celery, cover and refrigerate for at least 4 hours or overnight. Drain before using.

2. Make the tartines In a large skillet or on a griddle, melt half of the butter. Add the bread and cook over moderate heat until golden on the bottom, about 2 minutes. Flip the bread, add the remaining butter and cook until the bread is toasted, 1 to 2 minutes more. Transfer to a work surface.

3. Spread the yogurt on the toasts. Top with the sliced cucumber and season with salt. Top the tartines with the chicken and half of the drained pickled celery; reserve the remaining celery for another use. Garnish with small dill sprigs and serve right away. —*Hugh Acheson*

MAKE AHEAD The pickled celery can be refrigerated in the pickling liquid for up to 1 week.

WINE Fruity, dry Oregon sparkling wine: 2013 Argyle Brut.

Knife-and-Fork Grilled Cheese with Honey

Total **30 min**; Serves **4**

San Francisco chef Chris Cosentino proves here that you can elevate the humble grilled cheese sandwich into something magical with just a few tweaks. His buttery, crisp version is filled with luscious Taleggio cheese, then topped with honey, flaky salt and coarsely ground black pepper. It's so simple, but also jaw-droppingly good.

Softened unsalted butter, for spreading

Eight ½-inch-thick slices of sourdough boule

1 **lb. Taleggio cheese, rind removed and cheese sliced**

Honey (preferably bitter), for drizzling

Flaky sea salt and coarsely ground black pepper

1. Preheat a large griddle or very large skillet over moderate heat. Spread butter on one side of each slice of bread and arrange them buttered side down on a work surface. Top 4 bread slices with the cheese. Close the sandwiches, pressing lightly to flatten.

2. Cook the sandwiches over moderate heat, turning once, until golden on the outside and the cheese is melted, 3 to 4 minutes per side. Transfer the sandwiches to plates. Drizzle with honey and season with salt and pepper. Serve right away. —*Chris Cosentino*

WINE Tart Italian rosé from Piedmont: 2015 Cantalupo Il Mimo.

Mushroom Frankies with
Cilantro Chutney

Chile Grilled Cheese Sandwiches

Active **45 min**; Total **1 hr 15 min**; Serves **4**

- ½ tsp. coriander seeds
- ½ tsp. mustard seeds
- 1 Tbsp. canola oil
- 1 small onion, minced
- Kosher salt and black pepper
- ¼ cup white wine vinegar
- 1 Tbsp. sugar
- 1 Tbsp. plus 2 tsp. minced peeled fresh ginger
- 2 ripe mangoes, chopped
- ¼ tsp. crushed red pepper
- 1½ cups shredded Monterey Jack cheese
- 1½ cups shredded sharp white cheddar cheese
- 1 jalapeño, minced
- 2 Tbsp. minced cilantro
- Eight ½-inch-thick slices of sourdough boule
- 3 Tbsp. unsalted butter, melted

1. In a medium saucepan, toast the seeds over moderate heat for 2 minutes, then coarsely crush them.

2. In the same saucepan, heat the oil. Add the onion, season with salt and cook over moderate heat, stirring occasionally, until softened, 5 minutes. Add the vinegar, sugar and 1 tablespoon of the ginger and cook, stirring occasionally, until the vinegar is slightly reduced, 2 minutes. Add the mangoes, crushed seeds and crushed red pepper and cook over moderately high heat, stirring, until the mixture resembles jam, 5 minutes. Scrape the chutney into a small bowl and let cool. Season with salt.

3. Heat a griddle over moderately low heat. In a large bowl, toss both cheeses with the jalapeño, cilantro and remaining 2 teaspoons of ginger. Season with salt and black pepper.

4. Brush 1 side of each bread slice with butter. Arrange 4 slices buttered side down on the griddle. Top each with one-fourth of the cheese mixture and 3 tablespoons of the chutney. Close the sandwiches and cook until golden, 3 minutes per side. Let rest for 2 minutes, then cut in half and serve. —*Gail Simmons*

MAKE AHEAD The chutney can be refrigerated for up to 5 days.

Mushroom Frankies with Cilantro Chutney

Total **1 hr 45 min**; Serves **6**

This popular Mumbai wrap is similar to a kathi roll, but the roti is griddled with a little beaten egg so that it can stand up to a rich, saucy filling. Instead of the usual chicken tikka masala, chef Anita Jaisinghani of New York City's Pondicheri stuffs hers with mushrooms, sweet potato and fresh cilantro.

CHUTNEY

- 1 cup full-fat yogurt
- ½ Granny Smith apple, cored and thinly sliced
- ½ cup roasted unsalted peanuts
- 1 serrano chile—stemmed, seeded and chopped
- 2 Tbsp. fresh lemon juice
- 2 cups chopped cilantro leaves and tender stems
- Kosher salt

FRANKIES

- 1 small sweet potato, peeled and cut into ½-inch dice
- ¼ cup plus 1 Tbsp. canola oil or ghee (see box, p. 231)
- 1 tsp. cumin seeds
- 1 medium yellow onion, thinly sliced
- 2 tsp. minced garlic
- 1 lb. mixed mushrooms, sliced ¼ inch thick
- 1 Tbsp. finely grated peeled fresh ginger
- 1 tsp. garam masala (see box, p. 231)
- 1 tsp. chili powder
- ½ tsp. ground turmeric
- ½ cup unsweetened coconut milk
- ⅓ cup chopped cilantro, plus small sprigs for assembling
- Kosher salt and pepper
- 3 large eggs
- Six 8-inch roti or flour tortillas
- 2 cups finely shredded green cabbage

1. Make the chutney In a blender, puree the yogurt with the apple, peanuts, serrano and lemon juice until smooth. Add the cilantro and pulse until just combined; season with salt. Refrigerate until ready to use.

2. Make the frankies In a medium saucepan of salted boiling water, cook the sweet potato until tender, about 10 minutes. Drain well and pat dry with paper towels.

3. In a large nonstick skillet, heat ¼ cup of the oil. Add the cumin and cook over moderate heat, stirring, until fragrant, about 1 minute. Add the onion and cook, stirring occasionally, until softened, about 5 minutes. Stir in the garlic and cook until fragrant, 30 seconds. Add the mushrooms and cook, stirring occasionally, until tender and almost all of the liquid has evaporated, 8 to 10 minutes. Stir in the sweet potato, ginger, garam masala, chili powder and turmeric. Add the coconut milk and cook until hot, 2 to 3 minutes. Stir in the chopped cilantro and season with salt. Scrape the mushroom filling into a large bowl and keep warm. Clean the skillet.

4. In a medium bowl, whisk the eggs and season with salt and pepper. In the skillet, heat ½ teaspoon of the oil. Arrange 1 roti in the skillet and drizzle one-sixth of the beaten egg (about 2 tablespoons) over it. Flip and cook the roti over moderate heat until the egg sets, 1 minute. Transfer to a plate and tent with foil. Repeat with the remaining oil, roti and eggs.

5. Arrange each roti egg side up on a platter or plates and top with some of the mushroom filling. Drizzle with some of the chutney and finish with the shredded cabbage and cilantro sprigs. Roll up the roti and serve, passing more chutney on the side. —*Anita Jaisinghani*

MAKE AHEAD The mushroom filling and chutney can be refrigerated separately overnight. Gently reheat the filling before proceeding.

WINE Earthy Oregon Pinot Noir: 2014 Argyle Willamette Valley.

Butter-Poached Lobster Rolls with Spicy Sauce

Total **1 hr 15 min**; Serves **4**

Star chef Geoffrey Zakarian makes the most decadent lobster rolls. First he boils the lobsters, then he poaches the meat in butter. To balance all of that richness, he tops the rolls with a spicy mustard mayo.

Three 1½-lb. lobsters

3 **sticks cold unsalted butter, cubed, plus softened butter for brushing**

Kosher salt and pepper

2 Tbsp. mayonnaise

1 Tbsp. Dijon mustard

1 tsp. mustard powder

1 Tbsp. plus 1 tsp. fresh lemon juice

4 brioche hot dog rolls, split and toasted

8 small Bibb lettuce leaves

Snipped chives, for garnish

Lemon wedges, for serving

1. Set up a very large ice bath. In a large pot of boiling water, cook the lobsters until they turn bright red but are not cooked through, about 6 minutes. Drain well and transfer to the ice bath to cool. Drain well.

2. Twist the bodies from the lobster tails. Using scissors, cut along the underside of the shells and remove the meat. Halve the tails lengthwise and discard the dark intestines. Crack the claws and knuckles and remove the meat. Cut all the lobster meat into chunks and transfer to a bowl.

3. In a medium saucepan, melt 1 stick of the butter with 2 tablespoons of water over moderate heat. Transfer the mixture to a blender. With the machine on, gradually add the remaining cold butter until emulsified. Return the butter to the saucepan and warm over medium heat, then season generously with salt and pepper. Add the lobster meat and cook over moderately low heat, stirring occasionally, until just cooked through, about 5 minutes.

4. Meanwhile, in a small bowl, whisk the mayonnaise with the Dijon, mustard powder, 1 teaspoon of the lemon juice and 1½ teaspoons of water. Season the mustard-mayo sauce with salt and pepper.

5. Using a slotted spoon, transfer the lobster to a medium bowl. Stir in the remaining 1 tablespoon of lemon juice and season with salt and pepper.

6. Brush the toasted rolls with softened butter and fill with the lettuce leaves and the warm lobster. Garnish with snipped chives, drizzle with the mustard-mayo sauce and serve right away with lemon wedges. —*Geoffrey Zakarian*

WINE Full-bodied, creamy Chardonnay: 2014 Frank Family Vineyards Carneros.

Crispy Grouper Sandwiches with Green Tomato–Cucumber Relish

Active **35 min**; Total **50 min**; Makes **4**

"Every seafood joint along the Gulf Coast has its own version of the grouper sandwich," says chef John Besh. For his take, the crispy fish is topped with a tangy relish and a charred-jalapeño ranch dressing. If you plan to cook your catch, he says, keep the fish on ice for a day before preparing it: "This will allow the flesh to rest and become a bit less firm and much more tender and flaky."

2 jalapeños

¼ cup buttermilk

¼ cup mayonnaise

2 Tbsp. sour cream

½ tsp. garlic powder

½ tsp. onion powder

½ tsp. celery salt

½ tsp. fresh lemon juice

Hot sauce

Kosher salt and pepper

½ cup plus 1 Tbsp. extra-virgin olive oil

2 tsp. sherry vinegar

½ cucumber, peeled and cut into ¼-inch pieces (¾ cup)

1 small ripe green tomato, cut into ¼-inch pieces (¾ cup)

1 Tbsp. packed chopped dill

1¼ cups panko

½ cup milk

1 large egg

¼ cup all-purpose flour

Four 4-oz. grouper fillets (about 1 inch thick)

4 brioche buns, split and toasted

1. Roast the jalapeños directly over a gas flame or under the broiler, turning, until charred all over, 2 to 3 minutes. Transfer to a bowl, cover tightly with plastic wrap and let cool. Peel, stem and seed the jalapeños, then finely chop.

2. In a medium bowl, whisk the buttermilk with the mayonnaise, sour cream, garlic and onion powders, celery salt, lemon juice and a dash of hot sauce. Whisk in the chiles and season the jalapeño-ranch dressing with salt and pepper.

3. In another medium bowl, whisk 1 tablespoon of the olive oil with the vinegar. Add the cucumber, tomato and dill and toss to combine. Season with salt.

4. In a mini food processor, pulse the panko until finely ground. Spread in a shallow bowl. In a second shallow bowl, whisk the milk with the egg. In a third shallow bowl, spread the flour. Season the fish with salt and pepper, then dredge in the flour and shake off the excess. Dip the fish in the milk-egg mixture, then dredge gently in the panko.

5. In a large, deep skillet or saucepan, heat the remaining ½ cup of olive oil. Fry the fish over moderately high heat, turning once, until golden brown, about 10 minutes. Transfer to a paper towel–lined plate to drain and season with salt.

6. Spread some of the ranch dressing on the bottom buns. Top with a piece of fish and the green tomato–cucumber relish. Drizzle with more dressing, close the sandwiches and serve, passing any remaining ranch dressing at the table. —*John Besh*

MAKE AHEAD The jalapeño-ranch dressing can be refrigerated for up to 1 week.

WINE Juicy Spanish rosado: 2016 Bodegas Faustino VII.

Crispy Grouper Sandwiches with
Green Tomato–Cucumber Relish

Fried Green Tomato
and Okra Po'boys
with Smoked-Fish
Vinaigrette

Fried Green Tomato and Okra Po'boys with Smoked-Fish Vinaigrette

Total **1 hr**; Serves **4**

To add surprising flavor to these po'boys, F&W's Justin Chapple makes a delicious fish vinaigrette with smoked whitefish.

- ¼ lb. smoked whitefish
- 3 Tbsp. extra-virgin olive oil
- 2 Tbsp. Champagne vinegar
- 2 Tbsp. minced chives, plus snipped for garnish
- Kosher salt and pepper
- 1½ cups all-purpose flour
- 1½ cups fine cornmeal
- 2 large eggs
- 2 unripe green tomatoes, sliced ¼ inch thick
- 12 small okra (4 oz.)
- Canola oil, for frying
- 4 hoagie rolls, tops split and toasted
- Lettuce, pickled red onion and hot sauce, for serving

1. In a food processor, puree the smoked fish, olive oil and vinegar with 2 tablespoons of water until smooth. Scrape into a bowl, stir in the 2 Tbsp. chives and season with salt and pepper.

2. Put the flour and cornmeal in 2 separate shallow bowls and season with salt and pepper. In another bowl, beat the eggs and season with salt and pepper.

3. Dip the tomato slices in the flour, then in the egg, then in the cornmeal, pressing to help it adhere. Transfer the slices to a wax paper–lined baking sheet. Dip the okra in the flour, then in the egg, then in the cornmeal, pressing to help it adhere. Transfer the okra to the baking sheet.

4. In a very large skillet, heat ¼ inch of canola oil until shimmering. In batches, fry the tomatoes and okra over moderately high heat until crisp, 3 minutes for the okra and 5 minutes for the tomatoes. Transfer to paper towels to drain.

5. Spread the vinaigrette in the rolls and fill with lettuce, the fried green tomatoes and okra, and pickled onion. Top with chives and serve with hot sauce. —*Justin Chapple*

BEER Smoky dark lager: Shiner Bock.

Fried Chicken Sandwiches with Hot Sauce Aioli

Total **1 hr 30 min** plus 6 hr marinating
Serves **4**

This meal-in-a-bun hits all the pleasure buttons: It's crisp, spicy, rich, tart, sweet and juicy. The tender chicken is topped with a crunchy, tangy slaw and spicy aioli. It's messy and delicious and completely addictive.

MARINADE

- 1 cup buttermilk
- 1 Tbsp. fresh lime juice
- 2 thyme sprigs
- 1 garlic clove, minced
- 1 bay leaf
- ½ tsp. sugar
- Cayenne, kosher salt and pepper
- Two 4- to 5-oz. chicken cutlets, cut in half and lightly pounded

SLAW

- 2 Tbsp. buttermilk
- 2 Tbsp. mayonnaise
- 1 Tbsp. minced parsley
- 1 tsp. ranch dressing powder, such as Hidden Valley Ranch
- ½ tsp. fresh lime juice
- 4 cups shredded cabbage
- 1 medium kohlrabi, peeled and julienned
- 1 Granny Smith apple, peeled and julienned
- Kosher salt and pepper

AIOLI

- ¼ cup mayonnaise
- 1 Tbsp. hot sauce, preferably Cholula, plus more for drizzling
- ¼ tsp. grated lime zest plus 2 tsp. fresh lime juice
- ½ garlic clove, finely grated
- Kosher salt and pepper

SANDWICHES

- 2 cups all-purpose flour
- 2 tsp. kosher salt
- Canola oil, for frying
- 4 sesame seed burger buns, split and toasted
- Pickled jalapeños, for serving

1. Marinate the chicken In a large bowl, mix the buttermilk with the lime juice, thyme, garlic, bay leaf and sugar. Season with cayenne, salt and pepper. Stir in the chicken, cover and refrigerate for 6 hours.

2. Meanwhile, make the slaw In a large bowl, whisk the buttermilk with the mayonnaise, parsley, ranch powder and lime juice. Toss in the cabbage, kohlrabi and apple. Season with salt and pepper. Refrigerate.

3. Make the aioli In a small bowl, whisk the mayonnaise with the 1 tablespoon of hot sauce, the lime zest and juice and the garlic. Season with salt and pepper. Refrigerate for 15 minutes.

4. Make the sandwiches Using tongs, transfer the chicken to a baking sheet. In a shallow bowl, whisk the flour with the salt. Dredge the chicken in the flour. Dip the coated chicken back in the marinade, dredge again in the flour, then return to the sheet.

5. In a large saucepan, heat 1 inch of oil to 350°. Fry the chicken, turning occasionally, until golden, about 6 minutes. Using tongs, transfer the fried chicken to paper towels.

6. Lightly drizzle some aioli on the bun bottoms. Top with the chicken cutlets, slaw and pickled jalapeños. Drizzle with more aioli and hot sauce, close the sandwiches and serve. —*Larry McGuire and Tom Moorman*

WINE Fruity Chilean rosé: 2016 Montes Cherub Rosé of Syrah.

Feta-Brined Chicken Sandwiches

Active **30 min**; Total **1 hr**; Serves **4**

The secret to these incredibly flavorful chicken cutlets is a quick marinade in feta brine before grilling. F&W's Justin Chapple then whips the feta cheese with lemon juice and olive oil to use as a spread for these excellent sandwiches.

½ **lb. feta cheese, crumbled, plus ¾ cup of the brine**

1 **Tbsp. Louisiana-style hot sauce, preferably Tabasco**

Four 4-oz. chicken cutlets

1 **Tbsp. fresh lemon juice**

⅓ **cup extra-virgin olive oil, plus more for brushing**

Kosher salt and pepper

Four 6-inch ciabatta rolls, split and toasted

Arugula (not baby), sliced cucumber, red onion and seeded piquillo peppers, for serving

1. In a large resealable plastic bag, mix the feta brine and hot sauce. Add the chicken cutlets, seal the bag and turn to coat. Refrigerate for 30 minutes.

2. Meanwhile, in a food processor, pulse the feta cheese and lemon juice. Slowly blend in the ⅓ cup of oil until smooth. Season with salt and pepper.

3. Preheat a grill pan. Remove the chicken from the brine and pat dry; discard the brine. Brush with oil and season with salt and pepper. Grill the cutlets over moderately high heat, turning once, until cooked through, about 5 minutes total.

4. Spread the rolls with some of the feta. Top with the chicken, arugula, cucumber, onion and peppers and serve.
—*Justin Chapple*

WINE Floral Chenin Blanc from California: 2014 Lang & Reed.

WLTs (Wurst, Lettuce and Tomato Sandwiches)

Total **30 min**; Serves **4**

1 **Tbsp. extra-virgin olive oil**

½ **lb. bratwurst, cut into 4-inch lengths and thinly sliced lengthwise into slabs**

Mayonnaise, for spreading

8 **slices of multigrain sandwich bread, lightly toasted**

2 **medium tomatoes, sliced**

2 **Persian cucumbers, thinly sliced on the bias**

Kosher salt and pepper

Baby lettuce leaves, for serving

1. In a large nonstick skillet, heat the olive oil. Add the bratwurst and cook over moderately high heat, turning once, until browned and sizzling, about 5 minutes.

2. Spread mayonnaise on each slice of toast. Arrange the tomato and cucumber slices on 4 slices of the toast and season with salt and pepper. Top with the hot bratwurst and lettuce. Close the sandwiches and serve. —*Justin Chapple*

WINE Juicy, lively Pinot Noir rosé: 2016 Toad Hollow Eye of the Toad.

Empanada Gallega with Tuna

Active **50 min**; Total **3 hr 30 min**
Serves **8 to 10**

⅓ **cup extra-virgin olive oil, plus more for greasing**

1 **large white onion, quartered lengthwise and very thinly sliced crosswise**

2 **medium green bell peppers— stemmed, seeded and very thinly sliced into strips**

2 **large garlic cloves, very thinly sliced**

Kosher salt and pepper

Large pinch of saffron, finely ground in a mortar

¼ **cup boiling water**

2 **medium tomatoes, halved crosswise**

2 **roasted red bell peppers, drained well and very thinly sliced**

1 **tsp. sweet paprika**

Two 6-oz. jars oil-packed tuna, preferably ventresca (from the belly), drained well and flaked

½ **cup pitted green Spanish olives, sliced**

½ **cup finely chopped flat-leaf parsley**

1 **Tbsp. fresh lemon juice**

Two 13.8-oz. cans pizza crust, such as Pillsbury

1 large egg beaten with 1 Tbsp. water

1. In a large skillet, heat the ⅓ cup of olive oil until shimmering. Add the onion and cook over moderate heat, stirring occasionally, until just starting to soften, about 5 minutes. Add the green bell peppers, garlic and a generous pinch of salt. Cover and cook over moderately low heat, stirring occasionally, until very soft, about 25 minutes; add a bit of water if the pan is too dry.

2. Meanwhile, in a small heatproof bowl, mix the saffron with the boiling water until dissolved. Let stand until cooled, about 10 minutes. Grate the tomato halves on the large holes of a box grater set in a bowl until only the skins remain; discard the skins.

3. Add the roasted red peppers, grated tomatoes, brewed saffron and the paprika to the skillet and cook over moderate heat, stirring occasionally, until the mixture is very thick, about 10 minutes. Scrape the mixture into a colander and let drain for 10 minutes.

4. In a large bowl, combine the pepper mixture with the tuna, olives, parsley and lemon juice and season with salt and pepper. Let the filling cool completely, about 45 minutes.

5. Preheat the oven to 425°. Grease a large rimmed baking sheet. Unroll 1 of the pizza crusts on the prepared baking sheet. Spoon the cooled filling evenly on the dough, leaving a 1-inch border. Unroll the remaining pizza crust and lay it on top of the filling; crimp the edges to seal. Brush the empanada with the egg wash and, using a paring knife, cut a few slits in the top. Bake for 13 to 15 minutes, until puffed and browned. Slide onto a rack to cool completely, about 1 hour. Cut into squares and serve. —*Anya von Bremzen*

MAKE AHEAD The empanada can be kept at room temperature for a few hours before serving.

WINE Stony, lemon-scented white blend from Galicia: 2016 Terras Gauda O Rosal.

Empanada Gallega with Tuna

BREAKFAST & BRUNCH

Tater Tot Waffles
(p. 303)
OPPOSITE Swedish
Pancakes with
Lingonberry
Compote (p. 300)

Fried Eggs with Jamón and Caviar

⏱ Total **30 min**; Serves **4**

This recipe is inspired by chef José Andrés's two favorite places to eat fried eggs in Andalusia, Spain: Mesón Riofrío, where they're served with a generous scoop of caviar, and Venta El Toro, a small bar behind the hills of Vejer de la Frontera, where Maruja Gallardo fries eggs and potatoes in olive oil until both are soft and creamy, then crowns them with a few slices of *jamón ibérico*. If you're feeling especially flush, Andrés says, you can go *mar y montaña*—surf and turf—with a little bit of each.

Extra-virgin olive oil, for frying

4 **large Yukon Gold potatoes, peeled and cut into ¼-inch-thick fries**

Kosher salt

8 **large eggs**

8 **slices of jamón ibérico or serrano ham**

2 **oz. caviar (optional), preferably from a sustainable producer**

1. Preheat the oven to 275°. Set a rack in a large baking sheet. In a large cast-iron skillet, heat ¾ inch of olive oil to 300°. Working in 2 batches, fry the potatoes until golden brown and lightly crisp on the outside, about 7 minutes. Transfer the potatoes to the rack to drain and immediately season with kosher salt. Keep warm in the oven.

2. Carefully transfer 1 cup of the hot olive oil from the cast-iron skillet to a large nonstick skillet. Crack 4 of the eggs into the skillet and gently fry over moderately low heat until the whites are set and the yolks are slightly runny, about 5 minutes. Transfer to a plate. Repeat with the remaining 4 eggs.

3. Divide the fries among 4 plates. Top each plate with 2 fried eggs, 2 slices of ham and a spoonful of caviar, if desired, and serve immediately. —*José Andrés*

WINE Earthy, toasty Cava: 2013 Juvé y Camps Reserva de la Familia.

Golden Steak and Eggs

⏱ Total **40 min**; Serves **4**

L.A. chef Marcel Vigneron loves using healthy turmeric in both its fresh and powdered forms. Here, he seasons a flat-iron steak with it, then fries eggs with fresh turmeric, lending the dish a peppery flavor and bright orange hue.

One 1-lb. flatiron steak

Kosher salt and pepper

2 **tsp. turmeric powder**

¼ **cup coconut oil**

12 **cups baby spinach (7½ oz.)**

1 **Tbsp. finely grated peeled fresh horseradish**

1 **Tbsp. finely grated peeled fresh turmeric**

4 **large eggs**

4 **slices wheat bread, toasted**

1. Preheat the oven to 450°. Season the steak with salt and pepper, then rub all over with the turmeric powder. In a large ovenproof skillet, heat 1 tablespoon of the coconut oil over moderately high heat. Add the steak and cook, turning once, until lightly charred on both sides and medium-rare within, about 4 minutes per side. Transfer the steak to a carving board and let rest for 10 minutes. Wipe out the skillet.

2. Meanwhile, in a large saucepan, heat 1 tablespoon of the coconut oil over moderately high heat. Add the spinach and a pinch of salt and cook, stirring, until just wilted, about 3 minutes. Stir in the horseradish and season with salt. Keep warm.

3. In the large ovenproof skillet, heat the remaining 2 tablespoons of coconut oil over moderate heat. Stir in the fresh turmeric until the sizzling subsides and the oil is golden. Crack the eggs into the skillet and fry until the whites are almost set, about 2 minutes. Transfer the skillet to the oven and bake for about 3 minutes, until the whites are set but the yolks are runny.

4. Thinly slice the steak against the grain. Pile the spinach on the toasts and top with the steak. Carefully invert the fried eggs onto the steak and serve. —*Marcel Vigneron*

Eggs Benedict Salad

⏱ Total **30 min**; Serves **4**

2 **English muffins, split and torn into bite-size pieces**

8 **large eggs**

¼ **cup yogurt**

3 **Tbsp. extra-virgin olive oil**

1½ **Tbsp. Dijon mustard**

⅛ **tsp. finely grated lemon zest plus 1½ Tbsp. fresh lemon juice**

Kosher salt and pepper

5 **oz. mixed baby greens**

½ **head of radicchio, torn into bite-size pieces**

4 **oz. thinly sliced ham, torn into bite-size pieces**

⅓ **cup snipped chives**

1. Preheat the oven to 350°. Spread the English muffins on a baking sheet and toast for about 7 minutes, until golden. Let cool.

2. Meanwhile, bring a large, deep skillet of water to a simmer. One at a time, crack the eggs into a small bowl, then gently slide them into the skillet. Poach over moderately low heat until the whites are set and the yolks are runny, 4 to 5 minutes. Using a slotted spoon, transfer the poached eggs to a plate.

3. In a large bowl, whisk the yogurt with the olive oil, mustard, lemon zest and lemon juice. Season the dressing with salt and pepper. Add the mixed greens, radicchio, ham, chives and croutons and toss to coat. Transfer to plates and top with the poached eggs. Sprinkle with pepper and serve right away. —*Justin Chapple*

Golden Steak and Eggs

Za'atar Baked Eggs

Green Eggs with Whipped Goat Cheese and Grilled Kale

Total **1 hr 15 min**; Serves **4**

- 8 oz. curly kale, stems discarded and leaves torn
- 4 oz. arugula
- ¾ cup plus 1 Tbsp. grapeseed oil
- ½ lb. fresh goat cheese
   Kosher salt
- 4 large eggs
   Apple cider vinegar, for spritzing (optional)
   Flaky sea salt, for garnish

1. Preheat the oven to 325°. Spread half the kale on a large rimmed baking sheet and bake for about 20 minutes, until dried. Let cool, then transfer to a food processor and grind into a powder. Sift the kale powder into a medium bowl.

2. Meanwhile, set up an ice bath in a medium bowl. In a medium saucepan of salted boiling water, blanch the arugula until tender, 2 to 3 minutes. Using a slotted spoon, transfer to the ice bath to cool. Drain well, then squeeze out the excess water and transfer to a blender. Add ¾ cup of the grapeseed oil and puree until very smooth, about 2 minutes. Strain the arugula oil through a cheesecloth-lined fine sieve into a small bowl, pressing on the solids. Discard teh solids.

3. In a food processor, puree the goat cheese until just smooth. Add ¼ cup of the arugula oil and puree until light and very smooth. Scrape the goat cheese into a medium bowl and season with kosher salt.

4. Set up another ice bath. Bring a medium saucepan of water to a boil. Using a slotted spoon, carefully lower the eggs into the water and simmer for 5 minutes and 30 seconds. Using a slotted spoon, transfer the eggs to the ice bath to cool completely. Carefully peel the eggs. Keep the water in the saucepan hot.

5. Light a grill or preheat a grill pan. In a medium bowl, toss the remaining kale with the remaining 1 tablespoon of grapeseed oil and season with kosher salt. Grill over high heat, turning occasionally, until lightly charred, 3 to 5 minutes. Transfer to a plate and use a spray bottle to spritz lightly with apple cider vinegar, if desired.

6. Decoratively spoon the whipped goat cheese into the center of 4 plates and arrange the grilled kale around it. Using a slotted spoon, carefully lower the peeled eggs into the saucepan of hot water and warm for 1 minute, then transfer them to a paper towel–lined plate to drain slightly. Coat the eggs in the kale powder and place them on the goat cheese mounds. Sprinkle with flaky sea salt and dust with more kale powder. Serve right away. —Jay Blackinton

MAKE AHEAD The kale powder can be stored in an airtight container for up to 2 weeks.

WINE Lemony French Sauvignon Blanc from Gascony: 2015 Domaine du Tariquet.

Rolled Japanese Omelet

Total **15 min**; Serves **2**

This delicate omelet, called *tamagoyaki,* consists of thin layers of cooked egg that are rolled and sliced. Flavored with mirin, a rice wine vinegar, it has a mild, lightly sweet flavor ideal for breakfast.

- 5 large eggs
- 1 Tbsp. mirin
- ½ tsp. low-sodium soy sauce
- ½ tsp. kosher salt
   Canola oil, for brushing

1. In a medium bowl, whisk the eggs with the mirin, soy sauce and salt.

2. Brush a 10-inch nonstick skillet with oil. Add one-third of the eggs and swirl the skillet to evenly coat. Cook over moderate heat until the egg is almost set, about 1 minute. Using a spatula, roll up the omelet and push it to the side of the skillet. Brush the skillet with more oil, then add another one-third of the eggs, lifting the rolled omelet so the uncooked egg flows underneath it. Cook until the egg is almost set, about 1 minute. Roll up the first omelet in the cooked egg, forming a second layer; push to the side of the skillet. Repeat this process one more time with more oil and the remaining eggs. Turn out the omelet onto a work surface and slice 1 inch thick. Serve warm. —Kay Chun

Za'atar Baked Eggs

Total **30 min**; Serves **4**

- 3 Tbsp. extra-virgin olive oil, plus more for drizzling
- 1 medium yellow onion, thinly sliced
   Kosher salt and pepper
- 2 pints cherry tomatoes
- 2 red bell peppers, chopped
- ¼ cup plus 2 tsp. finely chopped parsley, plus more for garnish
- 2 tsp. za'atar, plus more for garnish
- 4 large eggs
- 1 cup plain yogurt
- ½ cup finely chopped seeded English cucumber
- 1 Tbsp. fresh lemon juice, plus more for drizzling
- ½ tsp. sumac
- 2 tsp. finely chopped mint

1. Preheat the oven to 375°. In a large ovenproof skillet, heat the 3 tablespoons of olive oil until shimmering. Add the onion, season with salt and pepper and cook over moderate heat, stirring occasionally, until softened, about 5 minutes. Add the tomatoes and cook, stirring occasionally, until some of them burst, 5 to 7 minutes. Add the bell peppers and cook, stirring occasionally, until the peppers are softened and all of the tomatoes have burst, about 10 minutes. Remove from the heat and stir in ¼ cup of the parsley and 1½ teaspoons of the za'atar. Season the tomato sauce with salt and pepper.

2. Using a spoon, make 4 wells in the tomato sauce, then crack an egg into each one; season with salt and pepper. Transfer the skillet to the oven and bake for 10 to 12 minutes, until the egg whites are just set and the yolks are still runny.

3. Meanwhile, in a small bowl, mix the yogurt with the cucumber, the 1 tablespoon of lemon juice, the sumac, mint and the remaining 2 teaspoons of parsley and ½ teaspoon of za'atar. Season with salt and garnish with za'atar. Drizzle the eggs with olive oil and garnish with parsley. Drizzle the tomato sauce with lemon juice. Serve with the cucumber yogurt. —Gail Simmons

Rye and Crème Fraîche Strata with Smoked Salmon

Active **25 min**; Total **2 hr 25 min**
Serves **6 to 8**

- 8 oz. crème fraîche
- 6 large eggs, at room temperature
- 2½ cups half-and-half
- 2 tsp. kosher salt
- 1 tsp. pepper
- 1 lb. rustic rye bread with crust, cut into 1-inch pieces
- 4 scallions, thinly sliced,
- ¼ cup capers, plus more for garnish
  Thinly sliced smoked salmon and sliced red onion, for serving

1. In a large bowl, whisk the crème fraîche with the eggs, half-and-half, salt and pepper. Add the bread, scallions and the ¼ cup of capers and mix well. Scrape into a 9-by-13-inch baking dish, cover with plastic wrap and let soak for 1 hour.

2. Preheat the oven to 375°. Bake the strata for 45 to 50 minutes, until puffed and the top is golden. Let stand for 10 minutes. Scatter some salmon on top and garnish with red onion and capers. Serve, passing more salmon at the table.
—*Justin Chapple*

MAKE AHEAD The unbaked strata can be covered and refrigerated overnight. Bring to room temperature before baking.

Green Hatch Chile Shakshuka

Active **15 min**; Total **30 min**; Serves **2**

Serve this vibrant shakshuka over thick slices of toasted bread to sop up the sauce.

- 1½ cups stemmed, seeded and chopped hatch chiles or jalapeños
- 2 tomatillos, husks removed
- 3 garlic cloves
- ¼ cup chopped cilantro, plus small sprigs for garnish
- ¼ cup extra-virgin olive oil
- 1 Tbsp. finely chopped onion
- 1 Tbsp. distilled white vinegar
- 1 tsp. dried Mexican oregano
- ½ tsp. ground cumin
- ½ tsp. ancho chile powder
  Kosher salt
- 4 large eggs
  Toasted rustic bread, for serving

1. Preheat the oven to 400°. In a food processor, pulse all of the ingredients except for the eggs and bread until finely chopped. Season the sauce with salt.

2. In an ovenproof 8-inch skillet, heat the sauce over low heat until warm, about 5 minutes. Using a large spoon, make 4 indentations in the sauce and crack an egg into each. Cover with a large sheet of aluminum foil and transfer to the oven. Bake for 10 to 12 minutes, until the egg whites are just set and the yolks are still runny. Garnish with cilantro sprigs and serve immediately, with toasted bread.
—*Aneesha Hargrave*

Spinach Shakshuka

Total **45 min**; Serves **2**

Portland chef Jenn Louis makes her shakshuka with a mix of Malabar spinach and tomatillos, jalapeños, cilantro and spices. The result is a bright, tangy and spicy brunch dish that's ideal with toasty challah.

- 1 lb. tomatillos, husks removed, halved
- 4 oz. Malabar spinach (see Note), large-leaf spinach or Swiss chard, ribs and leaves coarsely chopped (about 8 cups)
- 1 cup cilantro, plus sprigs for garnish
- 1 jalapeño, stemmed and cut into thirds
- 3 Tbsp. extra-virgin olive oil
- 1 small onion, minced
- 2 garlic cloves, minced
- ½ tsp. each ground cumin, coriander, caraway and turmeric
  Fine sea salt
- 4 large eggs
- ½ cup crumbled feta cheese (2 oz.)

1. In a food processor, finely chop the tomatillos, spinach, 1 cup of cilantro and the jalapeño (do not puree). In a medium skillet, heat the olive oil over moderate heat. Add the onion, garlic and spices and cook, stirring, until softened, about 6 minutes. Add the tomatillo mixture and cook until thickened, 15 to 20 minutes. Season with salt.

2. Using a large spoon, make 4 indentations in the sauce and crack an egg into each. Cover the skillet and cook over moderate heat until the egg whites are just set and the yolks are still runny, about 6 minutes. Sprinkle the feta on top, garnish with cilantro sprigs and serve.
—*Jenn Louis*

NOTE Malabar spinach has thick, juicy leaves and a citrusy flavor. Find it at local markets.

WINE Italian Sauvignon Blanc: 2015 Russiz Superiore.

Asparagus-and-Zucchini Frittata

Active **20 min**; Total **45 min**; Serves **6**

- 2 medium zucchini, halved lengthwise and sliced crosswise ¼ inch thick
- 6 oz. asparagus—trimmed, stems sliced ¼ inch thick on the diagonal and tips left whole
- 8 large eggs
  Kosher salt and pepper
- ¾ cup fresh ricotta cheese (6 oz.)
- 1 Tbsp. extra-virgin olive oil
- 6 zucchini blossoms—stems and pistils removed, blossoms halved, for garnish (optional)

1. Preheat the oven to 325°. In a medium saucepan of salted boiling water, blanch the zucchini and asparagus for 1 minute, then drain well and pat dry.

2. In a large bowl, beat the eggs with ½ teaspoon of salt and ¼ teaspoon of pepper. Stir in the vegetables. In a bowl, season the ricotta with salt and pepper.

3. In a 12-inch ovenproof nonstick skillet, heat the oil. Add the egg-vegetable mixture and cook over moderately low heat, stirring occasionally, until starting to set at the edge, 3 minutes. Dot the ricotta on top and garnish with the zucchini blossoms, if using. Transfer the skillet to the oven and bake for 20 to 25 minutes, until the frittata is just set. Let cool slightly, transfer to a platter, cut into wedges and serve.
—*Chris Behr*

SERVE WITH Sliced salumi, pecorino cheese drizzled with honey, dried or fresh fruit, and crusty bread.

WINE Round, peach-scented Sicilian white blend: 2015 Donnafugata Anthìlia.

Persian Frittata (Kuku Sibzamini)

Active **30 min**; Total **1 hr 30 min**
Serves **6 to 8**

Kuku is great eaten warm or cold. Shredded carrots, onion, zucchini and potato give it excellent texture—light and airy but deeply satisfying—while saffron adds a distinct Persian flavor. The key to making it right is squeezing just enough liquid out of the shredded vegetables so they stay moist but don't make the *kuku* too wet. A deep nonstick skillet is also essential.

- ¾ **lb. zucchini, partially peeled lengthwise**
- ¾ **lb. Yukon Gold potatoes, peeled**
- ½ **lb. carrots, peeled**
- 1 **medium yellow onion**
  Kosher salt
- 5 **large eggs, beaten**
- 3 **Tbsp. finely chopped cilantro**
- 1 **Tbsp. Brewed Saffron (p. 352)**
- ¾ **tsp. freshly ground black pepper**
- ¼ **cup canola oil**

1. Working over a colander set in a large bowl, shred the zucchini, potatoes, carrots and onion on the medium holes of a box grater. Add 2 teaspoons of salt to the vegetables and toss to coat. Let stand for 15 minutes, then squeeze to release some of the excess water. Transfer the vegetables to another bowl. Stir in the eggs, cilantro, brewed saffron and pepper.

2. In a deep 9- to 10-inch nonstick skillet, heat the oil until shimmering. Add the vegetable mixture and cook over moderately low heat until lightly browned on the bottom and nearly set, about 20 minutes. Blot dry with paper towels. Carefully invert the *kuku* onto a plate, then slide it back into the skillet. Cook over low heat until lightly browned on the bottom and set, 18 to 20 minutes.

3. Invert the *kuku* onto a paper towel–lined plate and blot dry with paper towels, then invert onto a platter. Let stand for 5 minutes before serving. —*Mahin Gilanpour Motamed*

MAKE AHEAD The *kuku* can be refrigerated overnight.

Ricotta and Scallion Egg Pie

Active **40 min**; Total **4 hr 45 min**
Serves **8 to 10**

Ricotta makes this variation on vegetable quiche, from Hollywood chef Roxana Jullapat, extra-moist and light. You'll want to hang on to her winner of a piecrust recipe, made with butter and cream cheese—it's flaky, golden and crisp.

PIECRUST

- 1¾ **cups all-purpose flour, plus more for dusting**
- ½ **tsp. kosher salt**
- 1½ **sticks unsalted butter, cubed and chilled**
- 6 **oz. cream cheese, cubed and chilled**
- 2 **Tbsp. ice water**

FILLING

- 10 **scallions, trimmed**
- 1 **Tbsp. extra-virgin olive oil**
- ½ **tsp. thyme leaves**
  Kosher salt and pepper
- 6 **large eggs**
- 1¼ **cups heavy cream**
- 1 **cup whole milk**
- 1 **cup loosely packed baby spinach leaves**
- 1 **cup grated Gruyère**
- 1 **cup ricotta**

1. Make the piecrust In a large bowl, whisk the 1¾ cups of flour with the salt. Using a pastry blender or your fingers, cut the butter and cream cheese into the flour until pea-size. Add the ice water and gently knead just until the dough comes together. Press into a disk, wrap in plastic and refrigerate until firm, at least 30 minutes.

2. On a lightly floured surface, roll out the dough to a 14-inch round. Ease into a 10-inch cast-iron skillet and trim the overhang to ½ inch. Fold the edge of the dough in over itself and, if desired, crimp it. Wrap in plastic and refrigerate for at least 30 minutes.

3. Preheat the oven to 350°. Line the piecrust with parchment paper and fill with pie weights or dried beans. Blind bake for about 1 hour, until the crust is set and lightly browned. Remove the weights and parchment paper, transfer the skillet to a wire rack and let cool completely. Leave the oven on.

4. Make the filling On a rimmed baking sheet, toss the scallions with the olive oil and thyme. Season with salt and pepper. Roast for 10 minutes, until tender. Let cool. Reserve 3 whole scallions. Coarsely chop the remaining scallions.

5. Reduce the oven temperature to 325°. In a large bowl, whisk the eggs with the cream, milk and 2 teaspoons of salt. Stir in the chopped scallions, the spinach, Gruyère and ricotta. Pour the custard into the piecrust and arrange the reserved whole scallions on top. Bake for 45 to 55 minutes, rotating halfway through, until the filling is puffed and lightly browned. Transfer to a rack and let cool for at least 20 minutes. Serve the pie warm or at room temperature.

VARIATION In summer, sub in young stinging nettles (before they flower) for the spinach. Remember to wear gloves when handling raw nettles.

WINE Crisp California sparkling wine: NV Schramsberg Mirabelle Brut Rosé.

Vegetable Tortilla

Active **45 min**; Total **2 hr 45 min**
Serves **6 to 8**

The key to this Spanish tortilla is cooking it on the stovetop the entire time, which creates a lovely custard-like texture.

- 1 **Yukon Gold potato**
- **Kosher salt and pepper**
- **Pinch of saffron, finely ground in a mortar**
- 2 **Tbsp. boiling water**
- ½ **cup extra-virgin olive oil**
- 1 **small onion, quartered lengthwise and very thinly sliced**
- 1 **medium zucchini, thinly sliced**
- 1 **small red bell pepper—stemmed, seeded and thinly sliced**
- 1 **cup packed baby spinach, sliced**
- 6 **large eggs**
- ¼ **cup mayonnaise**
- 1 **small garlic clove, grated**

1. In a medium saucepan, cover the potato with water and bring to a boil. Add a generous pinch of salt and simmer over moderate heat until the potato is tender, 20 to 25 minutes. Drain and let cool completely, then peel and cut into ⅓-inch pieces.

2. Meanwhile, in a small heatproof bowl, mix the saffron with the boiling water until dissolved; let cool.

3. In a deep 8-inch nonstick skillet, heat ¼ cup of the olive oil until shimmering. Add the onion and a generous pinch of salt and cook over moderately high heat, stirring occasionally, until just softened, about 3 minutes. Add the zucchini, bell pepper and a generous pinch of salt and cook, stirring occasionally, until tender, about 5 minutes. Add the potato and cook until coated and hot, 2 to 3 minutes. Stir in the spinach until just wilted. Season generously with salt and pepper. Transfer the vegetables to a colander to drain and cool completely, about 30 minutes.

4. In a large bowl, beat the eggs with the brewed saffron and a pinch of salt. Fold in the vegetables; let stand for 10 minutes.

5. In a large skillet, heat 1 tablespoon of olive oil until almost smoking. Add the egg mixture and cook over moderately high heat, shaking the pan and stirring quickly with a spatula, until some of the egg starts to set, 1 to 2 minutes. Smooth the top, then cook over moderately low heat until the tortilla is mostly set but the top is slightly wet, about 7 minutes; gently lift the sides of the tortilla with a spatula while tilting the skillet to spread the egg around.

6. Remove the skillet from the heat. Put a large, flat heatproof plate on top of the skillet, then carefully invert the tortilla onto the plate. Slide the tortilla back into the skillet and cook over moderately low heat until set, about 5 minutes longer. Slide the tortilla onto a serving board or platter and blot dry with paper towels. Let cool completely, about 45 minutes.

7. Meanwhile, in a small bowl, whisk the mayonnaise with the garlic and the remaining 3 tablespoons of olive oil. Season with salt. Cut the tortilla into wedges and serve with the garlic mayonnaise.
—*Anya von Bremzen*

MAKE AHEAD The tortilla can be wrapped in plastic and refrigerated overnight. Bring to room temperature before serving.

Avocado Halves with Flaxseed Furikake

Total **15 min**; Serves **1**

- 2 **sheets of toasted nori, torn into small pieces**
- 2 **Tbsp. bonito flakes**
- 2 **Tbsp. flaxseeds**
- 2 **Tbsp. toasted sesame seeds**
- 1¼ **tsp. kosher salt**
- ½ **tsp. sugar**
- 1 **Hass avocado, halved and pitted**
- **Extra-virgin olive oil, for drizzling**

1. In a spice grinder or mini food processor, pulse the nori and bonito until finely chopped. Transfer to a small bowl. Add the flaxseeds to the grinder and pulse until very finely crushed. Transfer to the bowl. Stir in the sesame seeds, salt and sugar.

2. Drizzle the avocado halves with olive oil, sprinkle with some of the flaxseed furikake and serve. —*Justin Chapple*

MAKE AHEAD The furikake can be stored in an airtight container for up to 3 weeks.

Coffee Granola

Active **15 min**; Total **45 min plus cooling**
Makes **11 cups (2¾ pounds)**

Ari Taymor, the chef at Alma restaurant in Los Angeles, finds most granola too sweet, so he adds coffee to make his version more savory and nutty-tasting. It also adds a caffeine jolt for a morning boost.

- 1½ **lbs. rolled oats (7½ cups)**
- ½ **cup finely ground coffee**
- ½ **cup granulated sugar**
- ⅓ **cup packed light brown sugar**
- ⅓ **cup all-purpose flour**
- ¼ **cup rye flour**
- ½ **tsp. kosher salt**
- 2 **sticks unsalted butter, frozen**
- ¾ **cup dark porter**
- ¼ **cup unsulfured molasses**

1. Preheat the oven to 350°. Line 2 large rimmed baking sheets with parchment paper. In a large bowl, toss the rolled oats with the coffee, both sugars, both flours and the salt. Using a box grater, shred the frozen butter into the bowl, then toss to mix. Stir in the porter and molasses until evenly coated. Spread the mixture on the prepared baking sheets.

2. Bake the granola for about 30 minutes, stirring every 8 to 10 minutes, until golden and nearly crisp. Let cool completely, stirring occasionally. —*Ari Taymor*

SERVE WITH Yogurt and fruit.

MAKE AHEAD The granola can be stored in an airtight container for up to 3 weeks.

Vegetable Tortilla

Breakfast Popcorn
and Milk

Almond Oats with Muesli and Skyr

Active **1 hr**; Total **1 hr 30 min plus 2 days soaking**; Serves **4**

This is a clever mash-up of a few breakfast staples: oatmeal, muesli and yogurt.

- **1½ cups whole blanched almonds, plus more for serving**
- **6 tsp. birch syrup (see Note)**
- **1 dried apricot seed (see Note)**
- **Kosher salt**
- **3 Medjool dates, pitted**
- **½ vanilla bean, split**
- **2½ cups old-fashioned oats**
- **½ cup steel-cut oats**
- **1½ tsp. golden flaxseeds**
- **1 cup skyr yogurt**
- **4 tsp. dried melilot (see Note)**
- **1 Tbsp. unsalted butter, melted**
- **¾ cup whole almonds**
- **1 tsp. Demerara sugar**
- **½ cup fresh red or black currants or gooseberries, plus more for serving**

1. In a medium bowl, combine the 1½ cups of blanched almonds with 2 teaspoons of the birch syrup, the apricot seed and a large pinch of salt. Add 3 cups of water. Cover and refrigerate overnight.

2. Line a fine sieve with cheesecloth and set it over a medium bowl. Transfer the almond mixture to a blender. Puree on high speed until very smooth, about 5 minutes. Strain the nut milk into the bowl, pressing on the solids; you should have 2 cups of milk. Discard the solids.

3. Line the sieve again with cheesecloth and set it over a large bowl. Return the nut milk to the blender and add the dates, vanilla bean and ½ teaspoon of salt. Puree on high speed until smooth, about 1 minute. Strain the nut milk into the bowl. Stir in 1 cup of the old-fashioned oats along with the steel-cut oats and flaxseeds. Cover and refrigerate the oats overnight.

4. Line a large rimmed baking sheet with parchment paper. Using a small offset spatula, spread the skyr on the baking sheet until about ⅛ inch thick. Place four 4-inch round ring molds over the yogurt. Cover with plastic wrap and freeze until firm, at least 1 hour.

5. Preheat the oven to 275°. In a medium bowl, combine the remaining 1½ cups of old-fashioned oats with the melilot, melted butter, ½ teaspoon salt and the remaining 4 teaspoons of birch syrup. Spread in an even layer on a large rimmed baking sheet. Bake the muesli for about 40 minutes, stirring every 15 minutes or so, until light golden brown. Let cool.

6. Increase the oven temperature to 300°. Spread the almonds in a pie plate and toast for 20 minutes, until browned. Transfer to a food processor and let cool completely. Add the sugar and ½ teaspoon salt and process until a paste forms.

7. Spoon the almond butter into 4 bowls (they will need to be at least 5 inches round at the top) and top with the ½ cup of currants, the overnight oats and the muesli. Using a Microplane, grate some blanched almonds over the muesli. Using an offset spatula, remove the skyr in the ring molds and gently press the rounds out of the molds. Place on top of the bowls, garnish with more currants and serve immediately. —*Jordan Kahn*

NOTE Birch syrup, dried apricot seeds and melilot (also known as sweet clover) can all be purchased on amazon.com. If birch syrup is not available, you can substitute maple syrup.

MAKE AHEAD The muesli can be stored in an airtight container for up to a week.

Breakfast Popcorn and Milk

Total **25 min**; Serves **4**

- **2 Tbsp. good-quality pork lard**
- **¼ cup popping corn**
- **Kosher salt**
- **Whole milk, pure maple syrup, diced apple, fresh berries, cinnamon and toasted nuts, for serving**

1. In a large saucepan, combine the lard and popping corn. Cover and cook over moderately high heat until the corn starts to pop. Continue cooking, shaking the pan occasionally, until the corn stops popping, 3 to 5 minutes. Remove from the heat, season with salt and let cool.

2. Transfer the popped corn to bowls. Serve with milk, maple syrup, apple, berries, cinnamon and toasted nuts. —*Kristin Kimball*

Farro Breakfast Porridge with Raspberries

Total **30 min**; Serves **4**

Missy Robbins, the chef at Lilia in Brooklyn, mixes up her morning breakfast routine with farro porridge, which she tops with a superspeedy and delicious (not to mention healthy) sauce made with frozen raspberries and honey.

- **2 Tbsp. unsalted butter**
- **1½ cups pearled farro**
- **3½ cups boiling water, plus more if needed**
- **1 cup frozen raspberries**
- **2 Tbsp. honey**
- **½ cup fat-free Greek-style yogurt**
- **½ tsp. ground cinnamon**
- **Kosher salt**
- **Chopped unsalted pistachios, for garnish**

1. In a medium saucepan, melt the butter over moderate heat. Add the farro and cook, stirring, until toasted, about 2 minutes. Gradually stir in the boiling water, ½ cup at a time, stirring in more as the water is almost absorbed but the farro is still soupy, 10 to 15 minutes total. Cover the saucepan and simmer over moderately low heat until the farro is al dente, about 15 minutes.

2. Meanwhile, in a small saucepan, cook the raspberries over moderately low heat until they just begin to break down, about 3 minutes. Stir in the honey.

3. Stir the yogurt and cinnamon into the farro and season with salt. (If a looser porridge is preferred, stir in more boiling water, a tablespoon at a time.) Spoon the porridge into bowls, top with the raspberry sauce and pistachios and serve. —*Missy Robbins*

Swedish Pancakes with Lingonberry Compote

📷 PAGE 289

Total **1 hr**; Makes **8**

Bizarre Foods host Andrew Zimmern prefers Sweden's thin, wheaty pannkakor to fluffy American pancakes. Like crêpes, they can tilt savory or sweet.

COMPOTE

- **4 cups fresh or frozen lingonberries (see Note)**
- **1 cup sugar**
- **½ cup verjus**
- **¼ tsp. pure vanilla extract**
- **2 star anise pods**

PANCAKES

- **½ cup slivered almonds**
- **1¼ cups whole-wheat flour**
- **1 tsp. kosher salt**
- **2 cups whole milk**
- **½ cup heavy cream**
- **2 large eggs**
- **4½ Tbsp. unsalted butter**
- **½ cup clotted cream, crème fraîche or whipped cream**

1. Make the compote In a medium saucepan, combine the berries with the sugar, verjus, vanilla and star anise and cook over moderate heat, stirring occasionally and scraping down the side of the pan, until the juices have thickened, about 30 minutes. Let cool completely, then discard the star anise.

2. Make the pancakes Preheat the oven to 350°. Spread the almonds on a rimmed baking sheet and bake for 15 minutes, until lightly toasted. Reduce the oven temperature to 200°.

3. In a medium bowl, whisk the flour and salt. In a large bowl, whisk the milk and cream with the eggs until smooth. Gradually whisk the flour mixture into the milk mixture until fully incorporated; the batter will be very thin.

4. Line a baking sheet with parchment paper. Heat a large cast-iron skillet over moderate heat. Add 1 tablespoon of the butter and cook until it starts to brown, about 2 minutes; swirl the skillet. Add ½ cup of the batter and tilt the skillet to distribute the batter evenly. Cook until bubbles appear and the top looks dry, 2 to

4 minutes. Flip and cook until the pancake is lightly browned on the bottom, about 2 minutes. Transfer to the prepared baking sheet and keep warm in the oven. Repeat with the remaining batter, melting ½ tablespoon of the butter in the skillet between cooking each pancake and stacking the pancakes in the oven as they're made.

5. Fold each pancake in half, then in half again to form a triangle. Top with the clotted cream, compote and toasted almonds and serve. —*Andrew Zimmern*

NOTE Frozen lingonberries are available at nwwildfoods.com. Alternatively, you can substitute raspberries and reduce the cooking time to 20 minutes.

MAKE AHEAD The pancakes can be wrapped in plastic and refrigerated for up to 3 days; reheat in the microwave. The lingonberry compote can be refrigerated for up to 1 week.

Chorizo Molletes with Roasted Salsa and Pickled Onion

Active **1 hr 15 min;** Total **4 hr;** Serves **4**

Molletes (a type of open-face sandwich) are a breakfast staple in Toluca, Mexico.

PICKLED ONION

- **½ cup red wine vinegar**
- **¼ cup fresh lime juice**
- **1 Tbsp. kosher salt**
- **1 Tbsp. sugar**
- **1 medium red onion, halved and thinly sliced**

SALSA

- **2 plum tomatoes, cored and halved**
- **1 medium white onion, quartered**
- **4 garlic cloves**
- **4 dried guajillo chiles, stemmed and seeded**
  Boiling water
- **3 small chipotle chiles in adobo**
- **2 epazote sprigs, stemmed (optional)**
  Kosher salt

BEANS

- **One 15-oz. can black beans, rinsed and drained**
- **1 shallot, halved**
- **1 garlic clove, lightly crushed**
  Kosher salt

SANDWICHES

- **1 lb. fresh chorizo, casings removed**
- **1 Tbsp. extra-virgin olive oil**
- **4 bolillos or ciabatta rolls, split and lightly toasted**
- **½ lb. Oaxaca cheese, shredded (2 cups)**
  Micro cilantro or cilantro leaves, for garnish

1. Pickle the onion In a medium bowl, whisk the vinegar with the lime juice, salt and sugar until the salt and sugar dissolve. Add the onion and refrigerate until bright pink and crisp, about 2 hours.

2. Make the salsa Preheat the oven to 400°. On a large rimmed baking sheet, roast the tomatoes, onion and garlic until softened and lightly charred, about 30 minutes. Let cool.

3. Meanwhile, in a medium bowl, cover the guajillos with boiling water and let stand until softened, about 15 minutes. Drain well and transfer to a blender. Add the tomatoes, onion, garlic, chipotles and epazote leaves, if using, and pulse until a chunky salsa forms. Transfer to a medium bowl and season generously with salt. Let cool completely.

4. Meanwhile, prepare the beans In a small saucepan, combine the beans, shallot, garlic and a generous pinch of salt. Add 2 cups of water and bring to a boil, then simmer over moderately low heat for 15 minutes. Drain, reserving 3 tablespoons of the cooking water; discard the shallot and garlic. In a food processor, combine the beans with the reserved cooking water and pulse until a chunky puree forms. Season the puree generously with salt.

5. Make the sandwiches Preheat the oven to 350°. In a large skillet, cook the chorizo in the olive oil over moderately high heat, breaking it up with a wooden spoon, until browned and cooked through, about 7 minutes.

6. Arrange the rolls cut side up on a large rimmed baking sheet. Spread each piece with some of the pureed beans and top with the chorizo and cheese. Bake for about 10 minutes, until the cheese is melted.

Spoon some of the salsa on top and garnish with some of the drained pickled onions and micro cilantro. Serve right away, passing more salsa at the table. —*Rico Torres and Diego Galicia*

MAKE AHEAD The pickled red onions and salsa can be refrigerated separately for up to 1 week.

WINE Spicy, lightly peppery Ribera del Duero red: 2013 Bodegas Áster Crianza.

Vietnamese Fried Eggs

Active **30 min**; Total **1 hr**; Serves **4**

- ½ large fennel bulb, cored and very thinly sliced on a mandoline, fronds reserved
- ½ cup fresh lime juice
- ¼ cup Asian fish sauce
- ¼ cup sugar
- ⅓ cup minced scallion
- 1 Tbsp. toasted and ground sesame seeds
- 1 Thai red chile, minced
- 1 large garlic clove, minced
- 1 Tbsp. peanut oil, plus more for frying
- 4 large eggs
- 2 cups lightly packed cilantro leaves
- 2 cups lightly packed mint leaves
- 1 small orange bell pepper, julienned
- ½ English cucumber—halved lengthwise, seeded and julienned
- 2 Tbsp. unseasoned rice vinegar
  Crispy Shallots (p. 106), for serving

1. Fill a medium bowl with ice and water. Add the fennel bulb and let stand until crisp, about 20 minutes. Drain well and pat dry.

2. Meanwhile, in another medium bowl, whisk the lime juice with the fish sauce, sugar and ¼ cup of water until the sugar is dissolved. Whisk in the scallion, sesame seeds, chile and garlic.

3. In a large saucepan, heat 1 inch of oil to 375°. One at a time, crack the eggs into a small heatproof bowl and very carefully slide them into the hot oil. Fry until the whites are just firm but the yolks are runny, 30 seconds to 1 minute. Using a slotted spoon, transfer the eggs to a plate and gently blot with paper towels.

4. In a large bowl, toss the sliced fennel with the cilantro, mint, bell pepper, cucumber, rice vinegar, fennel fronds and the 1 tablespoon of oil.

5. Spoon the lime sauce into bowls. Top with the eggs and salad, garnish with the shallots and serve right away. —*Andrew Zimmern*

MAKE AHEAD The lime sauce can be refrigerated overnight. Bring to room temperature before using.

Cambodian Breakfast Noodles

Active **45 min**; Total **2 hr 45 min**
Serves **4**

Chef Erik Bruner-Yank includes this brothy breakfast noodle dish on his menu at The Line Hotel in Washington, DC. Why soup in the morning? "In Cambodia," he says, "the day starts so much earlier—Phnom Penh is fully vibrant by 6 a.m., so you need something hearty."

- 1 rack baby back ribs (1½ lbs.), rack cut in half
- 1 Granny Smith apple, cored and cut into 1-inch pieces
- 2 small heads of garlic, cloves peeled and crushed
- 4 oz. fresh ginger, peeled and coarsely chopped
- 1 medium onion, chopped
- ⅓ cup Asian fish sauce
- 2 tsp. instant dashi powder
- 1 tsp. Chinese five-spice powder
- 8 oz. thin rice noodles
  Boiling water
- 6 oz. Broccolini or Chinese broccoli, trimmed and cut into 1½-inch pieces
  Thinly sliced scallions and jalapeño, for serving
  Mint, basil and cilantro leaves, for serving

1. In a large pot, cover the ribs, apple, garlic, ginger and onion with 3 quarts of water and bring to a boil over high heat, then simmer over moderately low heat until the ribs are very tender and the liquid is reduced by half, about 2 hours. Transfer the ribs to a work surface and let cool slightly, then cut the rack into individual ribs.

2. Strain the broth through a fine-mesh sieve into a heatproof bowl, discarding the solids. You should have 6 cups of broth; add water if needed. Return the broth to the pot and stir in the fish sauce, dashi and five-spice powder. Bring to a simmer over moderately high heat, then keep warm over very low heat.

3. Meanwhile, in a large baking dish, cover the noodles with boiling water and let stand until softened, about 20 minutes. Drain well.

4. In a large saucepan of salted boiling water, blanch the Broccolini until crisp-tender, about 2 minutes. Drain well and gently pat dry.

5. Transfer the noodles to 4 bowls and ladle the broth over them. Top with the ribs and Broccolini. Serve with thinly sliced scallions and jalapeño, as well as mint, basil and cilantro leaves. —*Erik Bruner-Yang*

MAKE AHEAD The ribs in the broth can be refrigerated for up to 2 days.

Tater Tot Waffles with
Prosciutto and Mustard

Tater Tot Waffles

⏱ Total **40 min;** Makes **four 8-inch waffles**

Jen Pelka of The Riddler Champagne bar in San Francisco makes supercrunchy and delicious waffles using Tater Tots, then tops them with everything from poached eggs and truffles to smoked salmon and caviar.

Nonstick cooking spray

8 **cups thawed frozen Tater Tots (32 oz.)**

Flaky sea salt

Heat an 8-inch waffle iron; preheat the oven to 200°. Grease the waffle iron with nonstick spray. Spread 2 cups of the tots on it; sprinkle with salt. Close and cook on medium high until nearly crisp, about 5 minutes. Open the waffle iron and fill in any holes in the waffle with more tots, then close and cook until golden and crispy, 2 to 3 minutes. Transfer to a baking sheet; keep warm in the oven. Repeat with the remaining tots. Serve. —*Jen Pelka*

Tater Tot Waffles with Prosciutto and Mustard

📷 PAGE 289

⏱ Total **40 min;** Makes **four 8-inch waffles**

Nonstick cooking spray

8 **cups thawed frozen Tater Tots (32 ounces)**

Flaky sea salt

¼ **cup crème fraîche**

2 **Tbsp. whole-grain mustard**

2 **cups baby arugula**

1 **tsp. fresh lemon juice**

1 **tsp. extra-virgin olive oil**

12 **thin slices of prosciutto**

Thinly sliced cornichons, for garnish

1. Heat an 8-inch waffle iron; preheat the oven to 200°. Grease the waffle iron with nonstick spray. Spread 2 cups of the tots on it; sprinkle with salt. Close and cook on medium high until nearly crisp, about 5 minutes. Open the waffle iron and fill in any holes in the waffle with more tots, then close and cook until golden and crispy, 2 to 3 minutes. Transfer to a baking sheet; keep warm in the oven. Repeat with the remaining tots.

2. Meanwhile, in a bowl, mix the crème fraîche and mustard. In another bowl, toss the arugula with the lemon juice and olive oil. Top each warm waffle with 1½ tablespoons of the mustard crème fraîche, 3 slices of prosciutto and ½ cup of the dressed arugula. Garnish with cornichons and serve. —*Jen Pelka*

Tater Tot Waffles with Smoked Salmon and Caviar

📷 PAGE 289

⏱ Total **40 min;** Makes **four 8-inch waffles**

Nonstick cooking spray

8 **cups thawed frozen Tater Tots (32 ounces)**

Flaky sea salt

6 **tablespoons crème fraîche**

12 **thin slices of smoked salmon**

Dill sprigs, caviar and fresh lemon juice, for serving

1. Heat an 8-inch waffle iron; preheat the oven to 200°. Grease the waffle iron with nonstick spray. Spread 2 cups of the tots on it; sprinkle with salt. Close and cook on medium high until nearly crisp, about 5 minutes. Open the waffle iron and fill in any holes in the waffle with more tots, then close and cook until golden and crispy, 2 to 3 minutes. Transfer to a baking sheet; keep warm in the oven. Repeat with the remaining tots.

2. Top each warm waffle with 1½ table-spoons of crème fraîche, 3 slices of smoked salmon, a few small sprigs of dill, a dollop of caviar and a squeeze of lemon juice. Serve immediately. —*Jen Pelka*

Tater Tot Waffles with Truffled Eggs

⏱ Total **40 min;** Makes **four 8-inch waffles**

Nonstick cooking spray

8 **cups thawed frozen Tater Tots (32 ounces)**

Flaky sea salt

4 **large eggs**

Shaved black truffle, for garnish

1. Heat an 8-inch waffle iron; preheat the oven to 200°. Grease the waffle iron with nonstick spray. Spread 2 cups of the tots on it; sprinkle with salt. Close and cook on medium high until nearly crisp, about 5 minutes. Open the waffle iron and fill in any holes in the waffle with more tots, then close and cook until golden and crispy, 2 to 3 minutes. Transfer to a baking sheet; keep warm in the oven. Repeat with the remaining tots.

2. Meanwhile, bring a large, deep skillet of water to a simmer. Crack the eggs into the skillet and simmer over moderately low heat until the whites are set and the yolks are runny, about 4 minutes. Using a slotted spoon, transfer the poached eggs to a plate; blot dry with paper towels and season with salt. Top each warm waffle with a poached egg and shaved truffle and serve. —*Jen Pelka*

Beaten Biscuit Breakfast Sandwich with Tomato Jam

Total **1 hr**; Serves **4**

Chef Marcus Samuelsson makes incredible biscuits, adding a little bit of nutty brown butter to amp up the flavor. He serves them warm, spread with tangy-sweet tomato jam, fried ham and perfectly scrambled eggs with cheddar cheese.

BISCUITS

- **6** Tbsp. unsalted butter, 4 Tbsp. frozen and cubed
- **1** cup all-purpose flour
- **1½** tsp. baking powder
- **½** tsp. kosher salt
- **⅛** tsp. baking soda
- **½** cup buttermilk

FILLING

- **4** oz. sliced country ham
- **1** Tbsp. unsalted butter
- **8** large eggs, beaten
- **½** cup sharp cheddar
  Kosher salt and pepper
  Tomato Jam (recipe follows), for serving

1. Make the biscuits Preheat the oven to 375°. In a small skillet, cook the 2 tablespoons of nonfrozen butter over moderate heat, stirring, until the milk solids turn brown, 3 to 5 minutes. Transfer to a bowl.

2. In a large bowl, whisk the flour with the baking powder, salt and baking soda. Using your fingers, work the frozen butter into the flour until the mixture resembles coarse meal. Stir in the buttermilk and 2 teaspoons of the browned butter until the dough comes together. Transfer to a lightly floured work surface and press or roll into a ³/₄-inch-thick round. Using a 3-inch round cutter, stamp out 4 biscuits. Gently press the scraps together to form 1 more biscuit.

3. Arrange the biscuits on a large baking sheet and brush the tops with the remaining brown butter. Bake for about 20 minutes, until golden on the outside and cooked through. Let cool slightly.

4. Meanwhile, prepare the filling In a large nonstick skillet, cook the ham over moderately high heat, turning, until browned, about 3 minutes. Transfer to a plate. In the skillet, melt the butter. Add the eggs and cook over moderate heat, stirring gently, until the eggs are just set, about 5 minutes. Stir in the cheese and season the eggs with salt and pepper.

5. Split 4 of the biscuits and spread with the tomato jam. Fill with the ham and eggs. Close and serve, saving the remaining biscuit for snacking. —*Marcus Samuelsson*

MAKE AHEAD The biscuits can be stored in an airtight container overnight. Rewarm gently before serving.

TOMATO JAM

Total **40 min plus cooling**; Makes **2 cups**

- **¼** cup dried currants
- **¼** cup apple cider vinegar
- **2** Tbsp. canola oil
- **½** cup very thinly sliced shallots
- **¼** cup very thinly sliced garlic
- **¼** cup very thinly sliced peeled fresh ginger
- **1** Tbsp. tomato paste
- **2** cups tomato puree
- **1** cup diced fresh tomatoes
- **2** Tbsp. dark brown sugar
- **1** Tbsp. finely chopped fresh curry leaves (see Note)
- **1½** tsp. crumbled fenugreek leaves (see Note)
  Kosher salt and pepper

1. In a small bowl, cover the currants with the vinegar and let stand until plumped, about 10 minutes.

2. Meanwhile, in a medium saucepan, heat the oil until shimmering. Add the shallots, garlic and ginger and cook over moderate heat, stirring occasionally, until softened and just starting to brown, about 5 minutes. Add the tomato paste and cook, stirring, until the vegetables are evenly coated, about 1 minute. Add the tomato puree, diced tomatoes, sugar, currants and vinegar and bring to a boil over high heat. Simmer over moderate heat, stirring frequently, until thickened, about 20 minutes. Stir in the chopped curry leaves and crumbled fenugreek leaves and let cool. Season the tomato jam with salt and pepper. —*MS*

NOTE Fresh curry leaves and dried fenugreek leaves are available at Indian markets and on amazon.com.

MAKE AHEAD The tomato jam can be refrigerated for up to 1 week.

Double-Lemon Scones

Active **25 min**; Total **1 hr 35 min**
Makes **8**

Lemon–poppy seed cake meets scones in this delightful recipe from F&W's Justin Chapple.

- **2¼** cups all-purpose flour, plus more for dusting
- **¼** cup granulated sugar
- **1** Tbsp. baking powder
- **2** Tbsp. finely grated lemon zest plus ¼ cup fresh lemon juice
- **1** tsp. kosher salt
- **1** Tbsp. poppy seeds
- **1** stick unsalted butter, cut into cubes and chilled
- **1** cup heavy cream, plus more for brushing
- **1** cup confectioners' sugar

1. Preheat the oven to 375°. Line a large baking sheet with parchment paper. In a food processor, pulse the 2¼ cups of flour with the granulated sugar, baking powder, lemon zest, salt and 2 teaspoons of the poppy seeds. Add the butter and pulse until it resembles coarse meal. Add the 1 cup of heavy cream and pulse until evenly moistened.

2. Transfer the dough to a lightly floured surface, gather any crumbs and knead a couple of times until the dough just comes together. Using a lightly floured rolling pin, roll the dough into a 9-by-6-inch rectangle. Using a large knife, cut the dough into 8 scones. Transfer the scones to the prepared baking sheet and brush with heavy cream. Bake in the lower third of the oven for about 25 minutes, until firm and lightly golden. Let the scones cool.

3. In a medium bowl, whisk the confectioners' sugar with the lemon juice and the remaining 1 teaspoon of poppy seeds. Brush the scones with the glaze and let stand until set, about 15 minutes. —*Justin Chapple*

MAKE AHEAD The scones can be stored in an airtight container for up to 2 days.

Smashed-Banana Bread

White Chocolate–Walnut Muffins

Active **25 min**; Total **50 min plus cooling**
Makes **12**

When white chocolate is baked into a muffin, little bits of it get irresistibly toasty and caramelized.

- 1¼ **cups walnuts (4.75 oz.)**
- 1½ **cups all-purpose flour**
- 1¼ **tsp. kosher salt**
- ½ **tsp. baking powder**
- ¼ **tsp. baking soda**
- 1 **stick unsalted butter, softened**
- ⅔ **cup sugar, plus more for sprinkling**
- 1 **large egg, at room temperature**
- ¾ **cup sour cream, at room temperature**
- 1 **tsp. pure vanilla extract**
- 6 **oz. Valrhona Ivoire white chocolate, chopped**

1. Preheat the oven to 350°. Line a 12-cup muffin pan with liners. Spread the walnuts on a baking sheet and toast for 7 minutes, until lightly browned. Let cool, then coarsely chop.

2. In a medium bowl, whisk the flour, salt, baking powder and baking soda. In a stand mixer fitted with the paddle, beat the butter with the ⅔ cup of sugar at medium speed until fluffy, about 2 minutes. Beat in the egg, then beat in the sour cream and vanilla. Scrape down the side of the bowl, then beat in the dry ingredients until just incorporated. At low speed, beat in three-fourths each of the chocolate and walnuts until mixed.

3. Spoon the batter into the prepared muffin cups, then scatter the remaining chocolate and walnuts on top, pressing them slightly into the batter. Sprinkle with sugar and bake for 25 minutes, until a toothpick inserted in the center comes out clean. Let the muffins cool slightly, then transfer to a rack to cool. —*Justin Chapple*

Sticky Coconut-Rice Bread

Active **30 min**; Total **2 hr**;
Makes **one 10-inch round bread**

Bibingka is a traditional Filipino coconut-rice bread made with sweet rice flour, shredded coconut and coconut milk.

BIBINGKA

- **Banana leaves, rinsed and patted dry (see Note)**
- 1 **lb. sweet rice flour, such as Blue Star Mochiko (3½ cups)**
- ½ **cup unsweetened shredded coconut**
- 1 **tsp. baking powder**
- ¼ **tsp. kosher salt**
- 1 **stick unsalted butter, softened**
- 2 **cups sugar**
- 4 **large eggs**
- **One 14-oz. can unsweetened coconut milk**
- 1 **cup sour cream**
- 1 **tsp. pure vanilla extract**
- **Sweetened shredded coconut, for garnish**

BUTTER

- 1 **stick unsalted butter, softened**
- ¼ **cup pure maple syrup, at room temperature**
- 1 **tsp. black pepper**
- ½ **tsp. kosher salt**

1. Make the bibingka Preheat the oven to 350°. Line a 10-inch cast-iron skillet with banana leaves. In a medium bowl, whisk the rice flour, unsweetened coconut, baking powder and salt. In a stand mixer fitted with the paddle, beat the butter, sugar and eggs on medium speed until fluffy, 1 to 2 minutes. Beat in the coconut milk, sour cream and vanilla until incorporated. On low speed, beat in the dry ingredients until just incorporated. Scrape the batter into the prepared skillet.

2. Bake the bread for about 1 hour, until the edge is lightly browned and the center is just set. Garnish with sweetened shredded coconut and let cool for 30 minutes.

3. Meanwhile, make the butter In a small bowl, using a fork, blend the butter with the maple syrup, pepper and salt. Serve the bread with the maple butter. —*Dale Talde*

NOTE Frozen banana leaves are available at large supermarkets and templeofthai.com.

Smashed-Banana Bread

Active **30 min**; Total **2 hr 10 min plus cooling**; Makes **one 9-inch loaf**

- ½ **cup pecans, chopped**
- 1½ **cups all-purpose flour**
- ¾ **tsp. baking powder**
- ¾ **tsp. baking soda**
- ¾ **tsp. fine sea salt**
- 2 **large eggs**
- 1½ **cups smashed very ripe banana**
- ¼ **cup plus 2 Tbsp. sour cream**
- 1 **tsp. pure vanilla extract**
- ¾ **tsp. banana liqueur or dark rum**
- 5 **Tbsp. unsalted butter, softened, plus more for serving**
- 1 **cup granulated sugar**
- **Confectioners' sugar, for dusting**

1. Preheat the oven to 350°. Grease a 9-by-5-inch metal loaf pan with nonstick spray and line the bottom with parchment paper, allowing 2 inches of overhang on the 2 long sides. Spread the pecans on a baking sheet and toast for about 7 minutes, until lightly browned and fragrant. Let cool.

2. In a medium bowl, whisk the flour with the baking powder, baking soda and salt. In another bowl, beat the eggs with the banana, sour cream, vanilla and banana liqueur until combined.

3. In a stand mixer fitted with the paddle or using a hand mixer, beat the 5 tablespoons of butter with the granulated sugar at medium speed until fluffy, about 2 minutes. At low speed, gradually beat in the wet ingredients until incorporated, then beat in the dry ingredients until just combined; fold in the toasted pecans.

4. Scrape the batter into the prepared pan and bake in the center of the oven for about 1 hour and 30 minutes, until a toothpick inserted into the center of the loaf comes out clean. Transfer the pan to a rack and let cool for 45 minutes, then turn the bread out onto the rack and let cool completely. Dust the top with confectioners' sugar, cut into slices and serve with softened butter. —*Gilda Bain-Pew*

MAKE AHEAD The bread can be wrapped in plastic and refrigerated for up to 1 week.

PIES, TARTS & FRUIT DESSERTS

Raw Berry Tart
with Coconut
Cream (p. 316)
OPPOSITE
Berry Vinegar Tart
(p. 316)

Cumin-and-Jaggery-Glazed Apple Pie

Active **1 hr**; Total **3 hr 15 min plus cooling**
Makes **one 9-inch pie**

CRUST

- **3 cups all-purpose flour, plus more for dusting**
- **1½ tsp. kosher salt**
- **½ tsp. baking powder**
- **2 sticks plus 2 Tbsp. unsalted butter, cubed and chilled**
- **7 oz. cream cheese, cubed and chilled**
- **¼ cup ice water**

FILLING

- **6 Granny Smith apples—peeled, cored and cut into 1-inch-thick wedges**
- **½ cup finely grated jaggery (see Note)**
- **2 Tbsp. all-purpose flour**
- **1 tsp. ground cinnamon**
- **½ tsp. cumin seeds**

GLAZE

- **4 Tbsp. unsalted butter**
- **1 tsp. cumin seeds**
- **⅓ cup finely grated jaggery**

1. Make the crust In a food processor, pulse the 3 cups of flour with the salt and baking powder until combined. Add the butter and cream cheese and pulse to form coarse crumbs. With the machine on, drizzle in the ice water until the dough starts to come together. Transfer to a work surface, gather any crumbs and press into a ball. Divide the dough into 2 equal pieces and pat into disks. Wrap in plastic and refrigerate until firm, 1 hour.

2. Make the filling Preheat the oven to 350°. In a large bowl, combine all of the ingredients.

3. On a lightly floured work surface and using a lightly floured rolling pin, roll out each piece of dough to a 14-inch round, about ⅛ inch thick. Ease 1 dough round into a 9-inch cast-iron skillet or deep-dish pie plate. Scrape the filling into the skillet and top with the second dough round. Press the edges of the dough together, then trim the overhang to about 1 inch, fold it under itself and crimp decoratively. Cut 4 slits in the top of the pie and bake for about 1 hour and 15 minutes, until golden brown. Transfer to a rack and let cool completely.

4. Meanwhile, make the glaze In a small saucepan, melt the butter. Add the cumin and cook over moderately low heat, stirring, until fragrant, about 1 minute. Add the jaggery and 2 tablespoons of water and cook until the jaggery dissolves and the mixture is slightly thickened, 2 to 3 minutes. Brush some of the glaze over the pie and serve, passing the remaining glaze at the table. —*Asha Gomez*

NOTE Jaggery is an unrefined sweetener made with solidified sugar cane juice, which tastes like a mild molasses.

Stone Fruit and Hibiscus Pie

Active **2 hr**; Total **4 hr plus cooling**
Makes **one 9-inch pie**

- **3 cups all-purpose flour, plus more for dusting**
- **1 cup plus 2 tsp. granulated sugar, plus more for sprinkling**
- **Kosher salt**
- **2 sticks plus 2 Tbsp. unsalted butter, cubed and chilled**
- **⅓ cup ice water**
- **3 Tbsp. hibiscus tea leaves (from 5 tea bags)**
- **1 vanilla bean, split lengthwise and seeds scraped**
- **3 plums (about 1 lb.)—peeled, pitted and cut into ½-inch-thick wedges**
- **3 nectarines (about 1 lb.)—peeled, pitted and cut into ½-inch-thick wedges**
- **3 peaches (about 1 lb.)—peeled, pitted and cut into ½-inch-thick wedges**
- **¼ cup fresh lemon juice**
- **2 Tbsp. quick-cooking tapioca**
- **1 Tbsp. honey**
- **1 Tbsp. orange liqueur, such as Grand Marnier**
- **¼ cup light brown sugar**
- **1 tsp. finely grated peeled fresh ginger**
- **1 large egg beaten with 1 tsp. kosher salt**
- **Vanilla ice cream, for serving**

1. In a food processor, pulse 2¾ cups of the flour with 2 teaspoons of the granulated sugar and ½ teaspoon of salt. Add 2 sticks of the butter and pulse until the mixture resembles coarse meal, with some pea-size pieces remaining. Add the ice water, 1 tablespoon at a time, and pulse just until the

dough comes together. Turn the dough out onto a work surface and press into 2 equal disks. Wrap in plastic and refrigerate until firm, at least 1 hour.

2. Line a large rimmed baking sheet with parchment paper. On a lightly floured work surface, roll out each disk of dough to a 12-inch round. Ease one of the rounds into a 9-inch metal pie plate and trim the overhang to 1 inch. Wrap the crust in plastic and refrigerate for 1 hour. Transfer the other dough round to the prepared baking sheet. Using a pastry or pizza cutter and a ruler as a guide, cut ten 1-inch strips. Wrap the baking sheet in plastic and refrigerate for 1 hour.

3. Meanwhile, in a food processor, pulse the remaining 1 cup of granulated sugar with the hibiscus tea leaves and vanilla bean seeds until the tea is finely chopped. Transfer to a large bowl and toss with all of the stone fruit. Cover and refrigerate for 1 hour.

4. Preheat the oven to 425°. In a medium bowl, whisk the lemon juice with the tapioca, honey and orange liqueur. Gently fold the mixture into the fruit along with the brown sugar, ginger and the remaining ¼ cup of flour until incorporated.

5. Using a slotted spoon, transfer the fruit to the chilled pie shell and carefully pour the juices over the pie until the liquid reaches the rim. Scatter the remaining 2 tablespoons of butter over the fruit. Arrange the dough strips across the pie in a lattice pattern, pressing them into the crust and trimming the overhang to ½ inch. Fold the overhanging dough over itself and crimp decoratively. Brush the egg wash all over the crust. Sprinkle with more granulated sugar.

6. Line a rimmed baking sheet with foil and set the pie on it. Bake for 20 minutes. Reduce the oven temperature to 375° and bake for about 55 minutes more, until the filling is bubbling and the crust is deep golden; rotate the pie twice during baking. Transfer to a rack and let cool completely. Serve with vanilla ice cream. —*Joe Kindred*

MAKE AHEAD The pie can be made up to 2 days ahead and kept at room temperature.

Stone Fruit and
Hibiscus Pie

Sweet Potato and
Coffee Cream Pie

Sweet Potato and Coffee Cream Pie

Active **1 hr 25 min**; Total **9 hr**; Serves **8 to 10**

Want some coffee with that slice? At Angela Pinkerton's counter-style pie and sandwich shop, Theorita, in San Francisco, the caffeine's built in. Espresso flavors the cookie crust and the whipped pastry cream atop an orange-infused sweet potato filling.

COOKIE SHELL

¾ **cup all-purpose flour**

2½ **tsp. espresso powder**

¼ **tsp. baking soda**

Kosher salt

5 **Tbsp. unsalted butter, softened, plus 6 Tbsp. melted and cooled**

¼ **cup plus 2 Tbsp. granulated sugar**

¼ **cup packed light brown sugar**

1 **large egg**

1 **cup shelled pecans**

1 **Tbsp. finely grated orange zest**

FILLINGS

3 **large sweet potatoes**

⅓ **cup honey**

1 **Tbsp. fresh orange juice**

2½ **cups whole milk**

¾ **cup roasted coffee beans**

6 **tsp. powdered gelatin (from 2 envelopes)**

⅔ **cup granulated sugar**

1 **large egg plus 2 large egg yolks**

2½ **tsp. espresso powder**

¼ **cup cornstarch**

5 **Tbsp. unsalted butter, softened**

1 **cup heavy cream**

Julienned candied citrus peel (see Note), for garnish

1. Make the cookie shell Preheat the oven to 325°. Line a baking sheet with parchment paper. In a medium bowl, whisk the flour with the espresso powder, baking soda and ½ teaspoon of salt. In a stand mixer fitted with the paddle, beat the softened butter with ¼ cup of the granulated sugar and the brown sugar at medium-high speed until light and fluffy, about 2 minutes. Beat in the egg. At low speed, beat in the dry ingredients until combined.

2. Scrape the soft dough into the center of the prepared baking sheet. Top with another sheet of parchment paper and roll into a thin sheet. Refrigerate until firm, about 15 minutes. Remove the top paper and bake for about 15 minutes, until golden. Transfer to a rack and let cool completely.

3. Increase the oven temperature to 350°. Break the cookie into pieces and transfer to a food processor. Add the pecans, the remaining 2 tablespoons of granulated sugar, the orange zest and ¼ teaspoon of salt and pulse until fine crumbs form. Add the melted butter and pulse to incorporate. Press the crumbs evenly over the bottom and up the side of a 9-inch metal pie plate. Bake for about 20 minutes, until fragrant and browned. Transfer to a rack and let cool completely.

4. Make the fillings Increase the oven temperature to 400°. Prick the sweet potatoes with a fork, wrap each in foil and transfer to a baking sheet. Roast for about 1 hour, until tender. Let cool slightly.

5. Split the sweet potatoes lengthwise and scrape the flesh into a medium saucepan. Add the honey and cook over moderate heat, stirring often, until thickened to a paste, about 20 minutes. In a food processor, blend the sweet potatoes with the orange juice until smooth. Spread in the cookie shell and refrigerate until cold, 1 hour.

6. Meanwhile, in a medium saucepan, bring 2 cups of the milk to a bare simmer over moderate heat. Remove from the heat and add the coffee beans. Let stand for 30 minutes. Strain; discard the coffee beans. In the same pan, bring the coffee milk to a bare simmer over moderate heat.

7. In a small bowl, whisk the gelatin with the remaining ½ cup of milk. In a large heatproof bowl, whisk the granulated sugar with the whole egg, egg yolks, espresso powder and cornstarch. Gradually whisk in half of the hot coffee milk. Scrape the mixture into the same saucepan and bring to a boil over moderate heat, stirring constantly. Cook, whisking constantly, until the pastry cream is thickened, about 2 minutes. Remove the saucepan from the heat and whisk in the gelatin and softened butter.

8. Scrape the pastry cream into the bowl of a stand mixer. Press plastic wrap directly on the surface and refrigerate until chilled, at least 4 hours.

9. In the stand mixer fitted with the paddle, beat the pastry cream at medium-high speed until smooth. Switch to the whisk and whip in the heavy cream until fluffy and stiff peaks form, about 1 minute. Mound the pastry cream over the sweet potatoes and smooth the top. Refrigerate until cold, at least 4 hours or overnight. Garnish the pie with candied citrus peel and serve cold. —*Angela Pinkerton*

NOTE Excellent small-batch candied citrus peel is available from junetaylorjams.com.

Stone Fruit Crisp

Active **15 min**; Total **1 hr**; Serves **4 to 6**

This rustic, supersimple crisp can be assembled in less than 15 minutes. Slivered almonds give the crumb topping an extra-toasty crunch.

¾ **cup packed light brown sugar**

½ **cup all-purpose flour**

½ **tsp. kosher salt**

1 **stick cold unsalted butter, cubed**

¾ **cup slivered almonds**

2 **lbs. firm ripe peaches, nectarines, plums or apricots—halved, pitted and cut into ½-inch wedges**

1 **Tbsp. granulated sugar**

1. Preheat the oven to 350°. In a large bowl, mix the brown sugar with the flour and salt. Add the butter and, using your fingers, work it into the dry ingredients until the mixture resembles coarse meal. Mix in the almonds.

2. Spread the fruit in a 1½-quart baking dish. Sprinkle with the granulated sugar, then scatter the crumble on top. Bake for 35 to 40 minutes, until the fruit is bubbling and the topping is golden brown. Let cool for 15 minutes before serving.
—*Chantal Dussouchaud*

Apple-Pomegranate Cobbler

Active **30 min**; Total **2 hr**; Serves **8 to 10**

This juicy and bright apple cobbler is just the right amount of sweet, with an irresistibly tender and crunchy crust on top.

- 2 cups pomegranate juice
- 6 Granny Smith apples (3 lbs.)— peeled, halved, cored and sliced ½ inch thick
- 1 cup sugar, plus more for sprinkling
- 2¼ cups all-purpose flour
- Kosher salt
- 2 tsp. baking powder
- 1 stick cold unsalted butter, cut into small pieces
- 1 cup cold heavy cream, plus more for brushing
- Pomegranate seeds and vanilla ice cream, for serving

1. Preheat the oven to 375°. Place an 8-by-8-inch glass baking dish on a foil-lined rimmed baking sheet. In a small saucepan, bring the pomegranate juice to a boil over moderately high heat until reduced to ⅓ cup, about 15 minutes. Pour the juice into a large bowl and fold in the apples, ¾ cup of the sugar, ¼ cup of the flour and ½ teaspoon of salt. Scrape the mixture into the baking dish.

2. In another large bowl, whisk the remaining 2 cups of flour with the remaining ¼ cup of sugar, the baking powder and ½ teaspoon of salt. Add the butter and, using a pastry cutter or 2 knives, cut the butter into the dry ingredients until the mixture resembles very coarse crumbs, with some pieces the size of small peas. Gently stir in the 1 cup of cream just to combine.

3. Gather the topping into small clumps and scatter over the apple filling. Brush the topping with cream and sprinkle generously with sugar. Bake the cobbler for 60 to 70 minutes, or until the filling is bubbling and the topping is golden. Tent with foil if the crust browns too quickly. Let cool for 20 minutes. Serve sprinkled with pomegranate seeds and topped with vanilla ice cream. —*Laura Rege*

VARIATION To bake the cobbler in individual portions, spoon the batter into 4 miniature skillets (2-cup capacity). Bake for 50 minutes.

Butterscotch Pudding Pie

Active **1 hr 15 min**; Total **5 hr 50 min**
Makes **one 9-inch pie**

PIECRUST

- ½ cup plus 1 Tbsp. chopped pecans
- 1¼ cups all-purpose flour
- ½ tsp. kosher salt
- 6 Tbsp. unsalted butter, cubed and chilled
- ¼ cup ice water

FILLING

- 1¾ cups whole milk
- 1½ cups heavy cream
- 6 Tbsp. unsalted butter, cubed
- 1 cup packed dark brown sugar
- 2 large eggs
- 3 Tbsp. cornstarch
- ¾ tsp. kosher salt
- 2 Tbsp. Scotch whisky
- 2 tsp. pure vanilla extract
- Turbinado sugar, for garnish

1. Make the piecrust Preheat the oven to 350°. Spread the pecans on a baking sheet and toast for about 8 minutes, until fragrant and lightly browned. Let cool.

2. In a food processor, pulse ½ cup of the pecans until finely ground. Add the flour and salt and pulse to mix. Add the butter and pulse until pea-size pieces form. Add the ice water and pulse until a dough starts to come together. Transfer the dough to a 9-inch round fluted tart pan with a removable bottom and press it evenly over the bottom and up the side. Prick the piecrust all over with a fork, then freeze it for 30 minutes.

3. Preheat the oven to 375°. Put the piecrust on a large baking sheet and bake for about 35 minutes, until the edge is lightly browned and the crust is firm. Let cool completely.

4. Meanwhile, make the filling In a small saucepan, bring the milk and ½ cup of the cream to a simmer over moderate heat. Remove from the heat. In a medium saucepan, melt the butter over moderately high heat. Add the brown sugar and cook, whisking constantly, until the mixture is bubbling and smooth, about 2 minutes. Remove from the heat and gradually whisk in the milk mixture.

5. In a medium bowl, beat the eggs with the cornstarch and salt. Very gradually whisk in ½ cup of the milk mixture. Scrape the mixture into the medium saucepan and cook over moderate heat, stirring constantly, until very thick, about 7 minutes. Strain the pudding into a medium bowl and stir in the Scotch and vanilla. Let cool slightly, then press a piece of plastic directly on the surface and refrigerate until well chilled, at least 4 hours or overnight.

6. Scrape the butterscotch filling into the piecrust and smooth the top. In a large bowl, using a hand mixer, beat the remaining 1 cup of cream until stiff peaks form. Mound the whipped cream on the pie and garnish with turbinado sugar and the remaining 1 tablespoon of pecans. Cut the pie into wedges and serve.
—*Gail Simmons*

NOTE Use the bottom of a metal measuring cup to help press the dough into an even layer in the tart pan.

MAKE AHEAD The pie can be refrigerated overnight.

MoKan Nut Pie

Active **1 hr**; Total **9 hr 30 min**
Makes **one 9-inch pie**

CRUST

- 1¼ cups all-purpose flour, plus more for dusting
- 1½ tsp. sugar
- ½ tsp. kosher salt
- 4 Tbsp. unsalted butter, cubed and frozen
- 4 Tbsp. rendered pork lard, cubed and frozen
- ⅓ cup ice water

FILLING

- 1½ cups pecans, chopped
- 1½ cups walnuts, chopped
- 1 stick plus 2 Tbsp. unsalted butter, cubed
- 6 large eggs, at room temperature
- 1 cup sugar
- 1 cup cane syrup, preferably Steen's, or dark corn syrup
- 2½ Tbsp. bourbon
- 2 tsp. kosher salt
- 1 tsp. pure vanilla extract
- Unsweetened whipped cream, for serving

1. Make the crust In a food processor, pulse the 1¼ cups of flour with the sugar and salt until combined. Add the butter and lard and pulse until the mixture resembles coarse meal. Drizzle the ice water on top and pulse until the dough just comes together. Turn the dough out onto a work surface, gather any crumbs and pat into a disk. Wrap in plastic and refrigerate until well chilled, about 4 hours or overnight.

2. On a lightly floured work surface, roll out the dough to a 13-inch round. Ease the dough into a 9-inch deep-dish pie plate. Fold the overhang under itself and crimp decoratively. Freeze the crust until well chilled, at least 1 hour.

3. Preheat the oven to 375° and put the crust on a large rimmed baking sheet. Line the crust with parchment paper and fill with pie weights or dried beans. Bake for about 20 minutes, until the crust is just set. Remove the parchment and weights. Bake for about 15 minutes longer, until just starting to brown. Let cool completely.

4. Make the filling Preheat the oven to 350°. Spread the pecans and walnuts on a large rimmed baking sheet. Toast in the oven for 8 to 10 minutes, until fragrant and lightly browned. Let cool.

5. In a medium skillet, cook the butter over moderately low heat, stirring occasionally, until foamy, about 5 minutes. Continue to cook, stirring frequently, until the milk solids turn brown and the butter smells nutty, about 4 minutes longer. Strain the brown butter through a fine sieve into a heatproof bowl. Let cool to room temperature.

6. In a large bowl, beat the eggs with the cooled brown butter, sugar, cane syrup, bourbon, salt and vanilla until smooth. Stir in the pecans and walnuts.

7. Pour the filling into the cooled crust. Bake for about 45 minutes, until the filling is nearly set. Transfer the pie to a rack and let cool completely, about 4 hours. Cut into wedges and serve with unsweetened whipped cream. —*Megan Garrelts*

MAKE AHEAD The pie can be covered and kept at room temperature for 3 days.

Bittersweet Chocolate Tarts

Active **45 min**; Total **4 hr 45 min**; Serves **6**

You will need six 4-inch tart pans with removable bottoms to make these rich and chocolaty tarts.

PASTRY

- **3 cups pastry flour, plus more for dusting**
- **1 cup confectioners' sugar**
- **1 tsp. fine sea salt**
- **½ vanilla bean, split lengthwise and seeds scraped**
- **2 sticks chilled unsalted butter, diced**
- **¾ cup chilled heavy cream**

CARAMEL

- **1 cup superfine sugar**
- **2 Tbsp. water**
- **½ cup heavy cream**

CHOCOLATE FILLING

- **6½ oz. bittersweet chocolate (70% cocoa), chopped**
- **4 large egg whites, at room temperature**
- **Fine sea salt**
- **½ cup chilled heavy cream**
- **Cocoa powder, preferably black, for dusting**
- **Crème fraîche and turbinado sugar, for serving**

1. Make the pastry In a food processor, pulse the 3 cups of flour, the confectioners' sugar, salt and vanilla seeds until combined. Add the butter and pulse until the mixture resembles coarse meal. Drizzle in the cream and pulse just until a dough starts to form. Scrape onto a lightly floured work surface, gather up any crumbs and knead gently just until the dough comes together. Pat into 2 equal disks, wrap in plastic and refrigerate until firm, about 1 hour.

2. Between 2 sheets of plastic wrap, roll out 1 piece of dough to a 14-inch square, about ⅛ inch thick. Using a knife, cut out three 7-inch rounds. Ease each round into a 4-inch tart pan with a removable bottom, then trim the overhang and prick the dough all over with a fork. Repeat with the remaining piece of dough. Freeze until firm, about 15 minutes.

3. Preheat the oven to 350°. Line the tart shells with parchment paper and fill with pie weights or dried beans. Set the shells on a large rimmed baking sheet. Bake for 20 minutes, until the edges are lightly golden. Remove the paper and weights and bake for 15 to 20 minutes longer, until the shells are golden. Transfer to a rack and let cool completely.

4. Meanwhile, make the caramel In a medium saucepan, gently stir the superfine sugar with the water. Using a wet pastry brush, wash down the side of the saucepan to remove any sugar crystals. Cook over moderately high heat until a medium-amber caramel forms, about 8 minutes. Remove from the heat and slowly add the cream (the mixture will bubble vigorously). Return to the heat and cook for 1 minute, stirring the caramel until smooth. Transfer to a bowl and let cool, then cover and refrigerate until cold and firm, about 2 hours.

5. Make the filling Put the chocolate in a heatproof medium bowl and set it over a saucepan of barely simmering water. Melt the chocolate, stirring occasionally, until smooth. Remove from the heat and let cool. In the bowl of a stand mixer fitted with the whisk, beat the egg whites with a pinch of salt at medium-high speed until stiff peaks form, about 2 minutes. Fold one-third of the beaten whites into the cooled chocolate to lighten it, then fold in the remaining whites until combined. In a clean bowl, beat the heavy cream to soft peaks. Gently fold the chocolate mixture into the whipped cream until combined. Spoon the chocolate cream into the pastry shells and smooth the tops. Chill until firm, about 1 hour.

6. Preheat the oven to 350°. Just before serving, remove the tarts from the pans and arrange on a baking sheet. Heat for 2 to 3 minutes, until the chocolate begins to melt and the tops appear shiny. Dust the tarts liberally with cocoa powder, then transfer to plates. Put a spoonful of crème fraîche on each plate and sprinkle with turbinado sugar. Scoop some caramel alongside and serve. —*Stephen Harris*

MAKE AHEAD The finished tarts (without the cocoa) can be refrigerated overnight. Bring to room temperature for 30 minutes before heating. The caramel can be refrigerated for up to 1 week.

Berry Vinegar Tart

📷 PAGE 308

Active **30 min**; Total **3 hr**; Serves **8**

12 whole graham crackers

1¼ cups plus 1 Tbsp. sugar
      Kosher salt

5 Tbsp. unsalted butter, melted

8 large egg yolks

½ cup blackberry vinegar

2 Tbsp. cornstarch

6 oz. raspberries (1¾ cups),
      plus more for garnish

1 Tbsp. virgin coconut oil

¾ cup heavy cream

1. Preheat the oven to 350°. In a food processor, pulse the graham crackers with ¼ cup of the sugar and ¼ teaspoon of salt until fine crumbs form. Add the butter and pulse until incorporated. Press the crumbs evenly over the bottom and up the sides of a 13-by-4-inch fluted tart pan with a removable bottom. Bake the crust for about 12 minutes, until fragrant and browned. Transfer to a rack and let cool completely.

2. Set a fine sieve over a medium bowl. In a medium saucepan, whisk the egg yolks with 1 cup of the sugar until well blended. Whisk in the vinegar, cornstarch and ½ teaspoon of salt and cook over moderate heat, whisking, until the mixture just starts to bubble, about 5 minutes. Add the raspberries and return to a simmer. Simmer over moderate heat, whisking, until the berries are broken down and the filling is very thick, about 5 minutes longer.

3. Remove the saucepan from the heat and whisk in the coconut oil. Strain the custard through the fine sieve, pressing on the solids; there should be just over 1 cup of custard. Pour the custard into the crust, cover with plastic wrap and refrigerate until cold, at least 2 hours.

4. Transfer the tart to a platter. In a large bowl, whisk the cream with the remaining 1 tablespoon of sugar until medium peaks form. Dollop the whipped cream on top of the tart, garnish with berries and serve. —*Laura Rege*

Raw Berry Tart with Coconut Cream

📷 PAGE 309

Active **30 min**; Total **3 hr 30 min**
Serves **8 to 10**

This nutty tart, made with almond flour and hazelnuts, is the perfect dessert for a late-summer dinner party because there's no oven required. Sweet, gooey dates hold the crust together, and the entire dish can be prepared a day in advance and pulled out of the fridge right before you eat.

¾ lb. Medjool dates

2 cups hazelnuts (½ lb.)

¼ cup almond flour
      Grey sea salt

½ cup coconut oil, melted and cooled

1½ cups (12 oz.) unsweetened
      coconut cream (see Note)

2 Tbsp. agar flakes (see Note)

¼ cup confectioners' sugar, plus
      more for dusting

12 oz. blackberries and/or raspberries
      Microbasil (optional), for garnish

1. In a medium bowl, cover the dates with water and let soak for 2 hours; drain. Pit the dates.

2. Line a baking sheet with parchment paper. In a food processor, pulse the hazelnuts until coarsely chopped. Add the dates, almond flour, a pinch of salt and 6 tablespoons of the coconut oil and pulse until the dough just comes together. Turn the dough out onto the prepared baking sheet. Top with a sheet of parchment paper and press the dough into a 10-inch round, about ¼ inch thick. Freeze the crust until firm, at least 1 hour.

3. Meanwhile, in a medium saucepan, bring the coconut cream and agar to a simmer, whisking to dissolve the agar. Remove from the heat and whisk in the ¼ cup of confectioners' sugar and the remaining 2 tablespoons of coconut oil. Scrape into a large bowl, cover and refrigerate until chilled and firm, at least 1 hour.

4. Carefully transfer the tart shell to a platter and peel off the top sheet of parchment paper. Using a hand mixer, beat the coconut cream mixture at high speed until smooth and fluffy, about 5 minutes. Spread it all over the tart shell, leaving

a ¼-inch border, and top with the berries. Loosely cover the tart and refrigerate for 30 minutes. Dust with confectioners' sugar and garnish with microbasil, if desired. Serve cold. —*Angèle Ferreux-Maeght*

NOTE Coconut cream and agar, a natural thickener, are available at Whole Foods and on amazon.com.

MAKE AHEAD The tart can be refrigerated overnight.

White Wine–Baked Apples

Active **15 min**; Total **1 hr 15 min**; Serves **8**

The key to these simple baked apples from Spanish winemaker Álvaro Palacios is using a drinking wine, like white Rioja.

8 baking apples, such as Golden
      Delicious, cored

4 Tbsp. unsalted butter

1 cup dry white Rioja wine, such
      as Plácet Valtomelloso

16 tsp. sugar

1. Preheat the oven to 400°. Arrange the apples in a small roasting pan and add ¼ cup of water. Fill each apple cavity with ½ tablespoon of butter. Drizzle with the wine and sprinkle each with 2 teaspoons of sugar.

2. Cover the apples loosely with foil and bake for 45 minutes, until barely tender. Uncover and bake for 15 to 25 minutes longer, until the apples are tender but still hold their shape. Serve with the pan juices. —*Álvaro Palacios*

Red Wine–Macerated Peaches

Active **15 min**; Total **4 hr 15 min**; Serves **8**

These wine-macerated peaches are delicious on their own or with vanilla ice cream. Bonus: You can drink the tasty macerating liquid or use it to make an excellent sangria.

One 750-ml bottle red Rioja
      wine, such as La Vendimia

3 Tbsp. sugar

One 3-inch cinnamon stick

2 lbs. peaches, peeled and diced

In a large bowl, mix the wine, sugar and cinnamon stick. Add the peaches, cover and chill for 4 hours or overnight. Serve chilled. —*Álvaro Palacios*

Red Wine–Macerated Peaches

Summer Pavlova with
Fresh and Grilled Berries

Smoky Pineapple

Total **2 hr**; Serves **8**

Slow-grilling whole pineapples concentrates their natural sugar and gives them a really intense flavor. It's a clean, sweet way to end a meal.

- **2 whole pineapples**
  Black sea salt, lime wedges and Korean chile powder, for serving

Set up a grill for indirect cooking and heat to 300°. Grill the pineapples, turning occasionally, until lightly browned and slightly softened, 2 to 3 hours. Transfer to a carving board and let cool slightly, then quarter each pineapple lengthwise through the leaves. Sprinkle with black sea salt and serve with lime wedges dipped in chile powder. —*Rocky Barnette*

Pomegranate Gelée (Jeleh-ye Anar)

Active **15 min**; Total **4 hr 20 min**
Serves **8**

This simple and delicious gelée is made with just two ingredients: pomegranate juice and gelatin. If you like it sweeter, add sugar to the saucepan at the beginning of Step 2.

- **6 cups pomegranate juice**
- **3 envelopes unflavored gelatin**
  Pomegranate seeds and pistachios, for garnish

1. Pour 1 cup of the pomegranate juice into a small bowl. Sprinkle the gelatin on top and let stand until the gelatin is evenly moistened, about 3 minutes.

2. In a medium saucepan, bring 2 cups of the pomegranate juice just to a boil over moderately high heat. Whisk in the dissolved gelatin mixture and simmer over moderate heat until completely dissolved, about 1 minute. Stir in the remaining 3 cups of pomegranate juice and let cool slightly. Pour the mixture into 8 glasses and refrigerate until set, about 4 hours or overnight. Garnish with pomegranate seeds and pistachios before serving. —*Mahin Gilanpour Motamed*

MAKE AHEAD The pomegranate gelée can be refrigerated for up to 3 days.

Summer Pavlova with Fresh and Grilled Berries

Active **1 hr**; Total **4 hr 30 min**
Serves **8 to 10**

Grilling berries in a foil packet makes a fruity sauce for summer meringue.

- **6 large egg whites**
- **⅛ tsp. cream of tartar**
  Kosher salt
- **1½ cups plus 2 Tbsp. sugar**
- **½ tsp. pure vanilla extract**
- **1 lb. strawberries, hulled and halved, or quartered if large**
- **1 lb. raspberries**
- **1 Tbsp. fresh lemon juice**
- **2 cups heavy cream**
- **¼ cup raspberry preserves**

1. Preheat the oven to 225°. Line a large baking sheet with parchment paper. In the bowl of a stand mixer fitted with the whisk, beat the egg whites with the cream of tartar and ½ teaspoon of salt at high speed until foamy, 2 minutes. At medium speed, gradually beat in 1½ cups of the sugar, then beat at high speed until stiff peaks form, about 8 minutes. Beat in the vanilla.

2. Using a large spoon, dollop the meringue onto the prepared sheet and spread into a 12-inch oval. Bake the meringue for about 1 hour and 45 minutes, until crisp but still chewy on the inside. Turn the oven off and let the meringue rest in the oven for 1 hour. Transfer the baking sheet to a rack and let the meringue cool completely, about 1 hour and 30 minutes.

3. Light a grill or preheat a grill pan. Layer 2 large sheets of heavy-duty foil. On the foil, toss half each of the strawberries and raspberries with the lemon juice and the remaining 2 tablespoons of sugar. Fold the foil over the berries and seal the packet. Grill over high heat until juicy, about 8 minutes. Transfer to a medium bowl and let cool completely.

4. In a stand mixer fitted with the whisk, beat the heavy cream with the raspberry preserves until stiff peaks form. Spoon the raspberry whipped cream onto the cooled meringue. Spoon the grilled berries onto the whipped cream, then scatter the remaining fresh strawberries and raspberries on top. Serve. —*Justin Chapple*

MAKE AHEAD The meringue can be stored in an airtight container overnight.

Cherry Clafoutis with Malted Whipped Cream

Total **1 hr**; Serves **6**

- **2 Tbsp. unsalted butter, cubed, plus more for greasing**
- **1¼ lbs. sweet cherries (4 cups), pitted**
- **1¼ cups half-and-half**
- **3 large eggs**
- **½ cup all-purpose flour**
- **¼ cup granulated sugar**
  Kosher salt
- **1 cup heavy cream**
- **1 Tbsp. malt powder**
- **2 tsp. confectioners' sugar**
- **¼ tsp. pure vanilla extract**

1. Preheat the oven to 350° and butter a 12-inch gratin or shallow baking dish. Spread the cherries in a single layer in the prepared gratin dish.

2. In a blender, puree the half-and-half, eggs, flour, granulated sugar and a generous pinch of salt until smooth. Pour the batter over the cherries, then scatter the cubed butter on top.

3. Bake the clafoutis for about 35 minutes, until puffed and a toothpick inserted in the center comes out clean.

4. In a large bowl, using a hand mixer, beat the heavy cream, malt powder, confectioners' sugar, vanilla and ¼ teaspoon of salt until stiff peaks form. Serve the clafoutis warm or at room temperature with the malted whipped cream. —*Joshua McFadden*

Strawberry Baked Alaska

Active **1 hr 30 min**; Total **11 hr**; Makes **8**

Chef Andrea Reusing of The Durham in North Carolina makes every part of these lovely basked Alaskas from scratch—even the graham crackers for the base. But you can use store-bought grahams. And if making homemade ice cream isn't your thing, sub in a good prepared brand.

ICE CREAM

- **1½ cups** buttermilk
- **½ cup** granulated sugar
- **1 cup** heavy cream
- **½ cup** crème fraîche
- **⅓ cup** strawberry syrup made with real strawberries
- **¼ tsp.** kosher salt

BERRIES

- **1 lb.** strawberries, quartered
- **2 Tbsp.** granulated sugar
- **1 Tbsp.** fresh lemon juice

CRUST

- **9 whole** graham crackers, half finely crushed and half coarsely crushed
- **7 Tbsp.** unsalted butter, melted
- **¼ cup** packed light brown sugar
- **½ tsp.** kosher salt

MERINGUE

- **½ cup** granulated sugar
- **3 large** egg whites
- **¼ tsp.** cream of tartar
- Pinch of kosher salt

1. Prepare the ice cream In a large bowl, whisk the buttermilk with the granulated sugar until the sugar is dissolved. Whisk in the heavy cream, crème fraîche, strawberry syrup and salt. Refrigerate the ice cream base until it is well chilled, about 2 hours.

2. Meanwhile, marinate the berries In a medium bowl, toss the quartered strawberries with the granulated sugar and lemon juice and let stand at room temperature for 1 hour, stirring the strawberries occasionally. Finely chop ½ cup of the strawberries and refrigerate the rest.

3. Make the crust In a medium bowl, mix the finely crushed and coarsely crushed graham cracker crumbs with the butter, brown sugar and salt until evenly moistened.

4. Line eight 4- to 6-ounce ramekins with small pieces of plastic wrap, allowing 1 inch of overhang all around. Pour the ice cream base into an ice cream maker; freeze according to the manufacturer's instructions. Fold in the finely chopped strawberries, then spoon the ice cream into the ramekins. Sprinkle the crumbs on top of each ramekin, pressing to adhere. Wrap the overhanging plastic over the crust, then freeze until very firm, at least 6 hours.

5. Prepare the meringue In a saucepan, combine the granulated sugar and ¼ cup of water. Bring to a boil, then cook over moderate heat until the syrup registers 240° on a candy thermometer, about 10 minutes. Meanwhile, in the bowl of a stand mixer fitted with the whisk, beat the egg whites, cream of tartar and salt at medium-high speed until soft peaks form. At medium speed, carefully beat in the hot sugar syrup until incorporated. Increase the speed to high and beat until the meringue is stiff, glossy and firm, 3 to 5 minutes.

6. Use the plastic wrap to lift the ice cream cakes out of the ramekins; invert onto a platter. Using a small offset spatula and working quickly, spread the meringue all over the cakes. Freeze until firm, 1 hour.

7. Using a pastry torch, toast the meringue until browned in spots. Serve with the macerated strawberries. —*Andrea Reusing*

MAKE AHEAD The recipe can be prepared through Step 6 and frozen for up to 3 days.

---

3 Strawberry and Cream Desserts

Some things are classics for a reason. These quick riffs on the same theme ensure you'll never grow tired of it.

STRAWBERRIES IN PROSECCO WITH VANILLA ICE CREAM In a bowl, toss 2½ lbs. sliced strawberries with ¼ cup sugar and let stand until the sugar is dissolved, about 30 minutes. Spoon the berries and any syrup into glasses and top with chilled Prosecco and a scoop of ice cream.
–*Ethan Stowell, Tavolàta, Seattle*

STRAWBERRY-AND-CREAM MILK SHAKES In a blender, puree 1 pint softened ice cream and ½ cup whole milk until smooth. Pour into 4 glasses. Rinse out the blender. Add 1 lb. hulled and quartered strawberries and 2 tsp. finely grated lemon zest and puree. Top the milk shakes with strawberry puree and serve.
–*Kay Chun, NYC recipe developer*

STRAWBERRY ICE CREAM SAUCE In a medium saucepan, combine 2 lbs. hulled and quartered strawberries, 2 cups sugar, ½ tsp. finely grated lemon zest and the seeds of 1 vanilla bean and bring to a boil. Reduce the heat to moderate and simmer, stirring, until thickened, 10 minutes. Let cool; refrigerate until ready to use. Serve over ice cream.
–*Annabelle Topacio and Ian Flores, Mr. and Mrs. Miscellaneous, San Francisco*

Strawberry
Baked Alaska

Strawberry-Mango Paletas

Active **30 min**; Total **5 hr 30 min**
Makes **8 ice pops**

When she's crafting new paletas for her NYC-based Mexican-sweets shop, La Newyorkina, Fany Gerson's rule of thumb is this: If the colors of her ingredients go together, the flavors will, too. These red-and-orange-hued ice pops are perfect to make in May, when juicy strawberries are at their peak.

1¼ cups chopped strawberries (5 oz.)
½ cup granulated sugar
3 Tbsp. fresh lime juice
½ tsp. kosher salt
2 ripe medium mangoes (about 2 lbs.)—peeled, pitted and chopped

1. In a small saucepan, toss the strawberries with ¼ cup of the sugar and let stand at room temperature for 15 minutes. Add ¼ cup of water and bring to a simmer over moderate heat. Cook the strawberries until thickened slightly, about 5 minutes. Remove from the heat and stir in 1 tablespoon of the lime juice and ¼ teaspoon of the salt. Let cool completely, about 45 minutes.

2. Meanwhile, in a blender, puree the mangoes with the remaining ¼ cup of sugar, 2 tablespoons of lime juice and ¼ teaspoon of salt until smooth. Scrape into a medium bowl and clean the blender.

3. In the blender, puree the strawberry mixture until smooth.

4. Spoon 2 tablespoons of the mango puree into the bottom of eight 3-ounce ice pop molds. Add 2 tablespoons of the strawberry puree to each mold, then top with the remaining mango puree, leaving ½ inch between the filling and the top of the mold. Using a small knife, gently swirl the mango and strawberry layers together. Insert wooden ice pop sticks and freeze until solid, at least 4 hours and preferably overnight. Dip the molds in hot water for a few seconds, then unmold the paletas and serve right away. —*Fany Gerson*

MAKE AHEAD The paletas can be covered and frozen in a single layer for up to 1 week.

Creamy Avocado Paletas

Active **30 min**; Total **5 hr 30 min**
Makes **8 ice pops**

These tangy, luxurious ice pops are completely dairy-free: Avocado and coconut milk give them a super-velvety texture. The pops are incredible as is or dipped in melted chocolate and coated with toasted coconut, as here.

3 Hass avocados—halved, pitted and peeled
1 cup unsweetened coconut milk
½ cup sugar
¼ cup fresh lime juice
1 Tbsp. honey
1 tsp. kosher salt
½ cup sweetened shredded coconut
4 oz. bittersweet chocolate, finely chopped
2 Tbsp. coconut oil

1. In a blender, puree the avocados with the coconut milk, sugar, lime juice, honey and salt until smooth. Divide the mixture among eight 3-ounce ice pop molds, leaving ½ inch between the filling and the top of the mold. Insert wooden ice pop sticks and freeze until solid, at least 4 hours and preferably overnight.

2. Preheat the oven to 350°. Spread the coconut in a pie plate and bake until lightly browned, about 12 minutes. Let cool completely.

3. In a medium microwave-safe bowl, melt the chocolate with the coconut oil at high power in 20-second intervals, stirring between bursts. Let stand at room temperature until cooled, about 20 minutes.

4. Set a wire cooling rack on a rimmed baking sheet. Dip the molds in hot water for a few seconds, then unmold the paletas. Dip in the melted chocolate and sprinkle with toasted coconut. Transfer to the cooling rack and repeat with the remaining paletas. Return to the freezer for at least 30 minutes before serving. —*Fany Gerson*

MAKE AHEAD The chocolate shell can be stored in an airtight container at room temperature for up to 2 days, and the paletas can be covered and frozen in a single layer for up to 1 week.

Pineapple Paletas with Chiles

Active **20 min**; Total **5 hr 30 min**
Makes **8 ice pops**

In Mexico, sweet fruit and spicy chiles go hand in hand. These beautiful ice pops are a nod to the traditional Mexican snack of mango dusted with chili powder.

¼ cup plus 3 Tbsp. sugar
½ tsp. kosher salt
One 3-lb. pineapple—peeled, cored and finely chopped (4 cups)
2 Tbsp. fresh lime juice
1 small serrano chile or jalapeño, stemmed and thinly sliced

1. In a small saucepan, bring the sugar and ½ cup of water to a boil, stirring to dissolve the sugar. Transfer 2 tablespoons of the syrup to a medium bowl, then scrape the remaining syrup into a blender. Let cool to room temperature, about 45 minutes. Add the salt and 1 cup of the pineapple to the blender and puree until smooth. Strain through a fine sieve set over a medium bowl, pressing on the solids. Stir the lime juice into the pineapple syrup.

2. Meanwhile, toss the chile and the 3 remaining cups of pineapple with the reserved 2 tablespoons of syrup.

3. Divide the pineapple-chile mixture among eight 3-ounce ice pop molds and top with the pineapple syrup, leaving ½ inch between the filling and the top of the mold. Freeze until slightly frozen and slushy, about 45 minutes. Insert wooden ice pop sticks and freeze until solid, at least 4 hours longer and preferably overnight. Dip the molds in hot water for a few seconds, then unmold the paletas and serve right away. —*Fany Gerson*

MAKE AHEAD The paletas can be covered and frozen in a single layer for up to 1 week.

Strawberry-Mango Paletas

CAKES,
COOKIES
& MORE

Rum-Caramel Bread
Pudding (p. 352)
OPPOSITE Moody
Tongue's Chocolate
Cake (p. 329)

Lemon Loaf Cakes with Poached Rhubarb

Active **40 min**; Total **3 hr**
Makes **four 5-by-3-inch loaves**

Co-chefs Umber Ahmad and Shelly Acuña Barbera of New York City's Mah-Ze-Dahr Bakery serve these moist cakes with juicy, sweet poached rhubarb. It's the quintessential spring dessert, but you can omit the rhubarb and serve the cake on its own or with lightly sweetened whipped cream.

CAKES

Nonstick baking spray
2 cups all-purpose flour
2 tsp. baking powder
1 tsp. kosher salt
3 medium lemons
12 Tbsp. unsalted butter, softened
1½ cups sugar
4 large eggs
1 tsp. pure vanilla extract
¾ cup plus 2 Tbsp. crème fraîche

POACHED RHUBARB

2 cups sugar
1 vanilla bean, split lengthwise, seeds scraped
Three 4-inch strips of orange zest, removed with a vegetable peeler
1¼ lbs. rhubarb (about 4 large stalks), halved lengthwise and cut into ½-inch pieces

1. Make the cakes Preheat the oven to 350°. Grease four 5-by-3-inch loaf pans with baking spray and line the bottom of each pan with parchment paper.

2. In a medium bowl, whisk the flour with the baking powder and salt. Using a Microplane, finely grate the zest of the 3 lemons; you should have about 2 tablespoons. Using a sharp knife, cut the skin and white pith from the lemons. Working over a fine strainer set over a bowl, cut between the membranes to release the lemon sections into the strainer. Discard the seeds and cut the sections into ½-inch pieces. Return the chopped sections to the strainer.

3. In a stand mixer fitted with the paddle, beat the butter with the sugar and lemon zest at medium speed until light and fluffy, about 4 minutes. Add the eggs one at a time, beating well after each addition and scraping down the bowl as needed. Beat in the vanilla. At low speed, beat in the dry ingredients and the crème fraîche in 2 alternating additions, scraping down the bowl as needed, just until combined. Using a rubber spatula, fold in the chopped lemon sections. Divide the batter among the 4 loaf pans and smooth the surface of each.

4. Bake for about 45 minutes, until a skewer inserted in the center of a cake comes out clean; shift the pans from front to back halfway through baking. Transfer to a rack and let cool completely, about 1 hour. Invert the loaves and peel off the parchment paper. Transfer to a platter.

5. Meanwhile, make the rhubarb In a medium saucepan, combine the sugar with the vanilla bean and seeds, orange zest and 2 cups of water. Bring to a simmer over moderate heat, whisking occasionally to help the sugar dissolve. Add the rhubarb and poach until just tender, about 6 minutes. Transfer to a bowl and let cool, about 30 minutes. Discard the vanilla bean and orange zest.

6. Serve the cakes with the poached rhubarb and syrup. —*Umber Ahmad and Shelly Acuña Barbera*

NOTE The lemon loaves can also be baked in one 9-by-5-inch loaf pan. Bake at 350° for 55 minutes, tenting the loaf with foil after the first 30 minutes to prevent the top from getting too dark.

MAKE AHEAD The loaves can be wrapped in foil and kept at room temperature for up to 2 days. The poached rhubarb and syrup can be refrigerated for 4 days.

Chocolate, Cinnamon and Almond Loaf Cake

Active **20 min**; Total **2 hr**; Serves **8 to 10**

This low-sugar chocolate loaf cake is richly flavored and deliciously moist.

Baking spray, for greasing
2½ cups superfine almond meal
½ cup unsweetened Dutch-process cocoa, sifted
2 tsp. baking powder
½ tsp. kosher salt
2½ tsp. ground cinnamon
6 large eggs, separated
1 cup coconut palm sugar
½ stick unsalted butter, melted and cooled slightly
½ cup cooled brewed coffee
2 tsp. pure vanilla extract
1 cup heavy cream

1. Preheat the oven to 350°. Grease a 9-by-5-inch loaf pan with baking spray and line it with parchment paper, allowing 2 inches of overhang on the short sides.

2. In a medium bowl, whisk the almond meal with the cocoa powder, baking powder, salt and 1½ teaspoons of the cinnamon. In a large bowl, whisk the egg yolks with the coconut sugar, melted butter, coffee and vanilla. Stir the dry ingredients into the wet ingredients until the batter is smooth.

3. In a stand mixer fitted with the whisk, beat the egg whites at medium-high speed until stiff peaks form, 1 to 2 minutes. Fold one-third of the beaten egg whites into the batter to lighten it, then fold in the remaining egg whites until no streaks remain.

4. Scrape the batter into the prepared pan and bake for 45 to 50 minutes, until a toothpick inserted in the center comes out with a few crumbs attached. Transfer to a rack to cool for 20 minutes, then unmold and let cool completely.

5. Meanwhile, in a medium bowl, beat the heavy cream with the remaining 1 teaspoon of cinnamon until soft peaks form. Cut the cake into slices and serve with a dollop of the cinnamon cream. —*Julia Turshen*

MAKE AHEAD The cake can be stored in an airtight container overnight.

Lemon Loaf Cakes
with Poached Rhubarb

Chocolate Torta Soffice

Chocolate Torta Soffice

Active **40 min**; Total **3 hr**
Makes **one 8-inch cake**

- 1 **stick salted butter, cubed and softened, plus more for greasing**
- ½ **cup plus 2 Tbsp. unsweetened cocoa powder, plus more for dusting**
- 1⅔ **cups all-purpose flour**
- 2 **tsp. baking powder**
- 5 **large eggs, separated**
- 1¼ **cups granulated sugar**
- ½ **cup plus 2 Tbsp. whole milk**
- ¾ **cup mascarpone**
- ¾ **cup heavy cream**
  Confectioners' sugar, for dusting
  Chopped roasted unsalted pistachios, for garnish

1. Preheat the oven to 375°. Butter an 8-inch round cake pan and line with parchment paper. Butter the paper and dust the pan with cocoa powder, tapping out the excess. In a fine sieve set over a medium bowl, sift the ½ cup plus 2 tablespoons of cocoa powder with the flour and baking powder.

2. In a stand mixer fitted with the whisk, beat the egg yolks at medium-high speed until thickened slightly, about 2 minutes. Beat in 1 cup of the granulated sugar, ¼ cup at a time, beating well after each addition, then beat until the mixture is very thick and pale yellow, about 3 minutes longer.

3. Beat in the cubed butter at medium speed, a few pieces at a time, beating well after each addition, then beat until the mixture is fluffy, about 2 minutes longer. Reduce the speed to low and mix in the dry ingredients in 2 additions, alternating with the milk, until smooth. Scrape the batter into a large bowl. Clean the mixing bowl and whisk.

4. In the stand mixer fitted with the whisk, beat the egg whites at medium speed until thick and foamy, about 2 minutes. Gradually beat in 3 tablespoons of the granulated sugar, beating well after each addition. Beat until the whites are thick and glossy, about 1 minute longer. Using a rubber spatula, mix one-third of the egg whites into the batter until smooth, then gently fold in the remaining egg whites until no streaks remain. Clean the mixing bowl and whisk.

5. Scrape the batter into the prepared cake pan. Bake for about 45 minutes, until the edge of the torta is firm and a toothpick inserted in the center of the cake comes out slightly wet. The torta will continue to set as it cools. Transfer the pan to a rack to cool for 30 minutes, then turn out the torta onto the rack, peel off the parchment and turn the cake so it's flat side down. Let cool completely, about 1 hour.

6. Just before serving, in the stand mixer fitted with the whisk, beat the mascarpone with the cream and the remaining 1 tablespoon of granulated sugar at medium-high speed until soft peaks form. Dust the torta with confectioners' sugar and serve with the whipped mascarpone and pistachios. —*Chris Behr*

Moody Tongue's Chocolate Cake

📷 PAGE 324

Active **2 hr 35 min**; Total **5 hr 15 min**
Makes **one 10-inch layer cake**

CHOCOLATE CAKES

- 1 **cup canola oil, plus more for greasing**
- 3½ **cups all-purpose flour**
- 4 **cups granulated sugar**
- 1½ **cups Dutch-process cocoa**
- 4 **tsp. baking soda**
- 2 **tsp. baking powder**
- 2 **tsp. kosher salt**
- 2 **cups buttermilk**
- 4 **large eggs**
- 2 **tsp. pure vanilla extract**
- 1 **cup hot coffee mixed with 1 cup hot water**

GERMAN CHOCOLATE FILLING

- 1 **cup evaporated milk**
- 1 **cup granulated sugar**
- 1 **stick unsalted butter**
- 3 **large egg yolks**
- 1 **tsp. kosher salt**
- 1½ **cups shredded sweetened coconut**
- 1 **cup toasted pecans, coarsely chopped**
- 2 **tsp. pure vanilla extract**

CHEESECAKES

- **Nonstick cooking spray**
- 4 **whole graham crackers, crushed**
- ⅓ **cup mini pretzels**

- ⅓ **cup chocolate cereal, such as Annie's Cocoa Bunnies or Cocoa Puffs**
- ½ **stick unsalted butter, melted**
- 1 **lb. cream cheese, at room temperature**
- ⅔ **cup granulated sugar**
- 2 **large eggs**
- 1 **Tbsp. espresso powder**
- 1 **tsp. pure vanilla extract**

BUTTERCREAM

- 2 **cups confectioners' sugar**
- ½ **cup Dutch-process cocoa**
- ½ **tsp. kosher salt**
- 6 **large egg whites**
- 1½ **cups granulated sugar**
- 1 **Tbsp. pure vanilla extract**
- 4 **sticks unsalted butter, softened and cut into cubes**
- ¾ **cup vegetable shortening**

GANACHE

- 2 **cups heavy cream**
- 3 **Tbsp. light corn syrup**
- 3 **Tbsp. unsalted butter**
- 1 **lb. chopped dark chocolate (2¾ cups)**

1. Make the chocolate cakes Preheat the oven to 350°. Grease two 10-inch round cake pans, line with parchment and grease the parchment. In the bowl of a stand mixer, whisk the flour, sugar, cocoa powder, baking soda, baking powder and salt. In a large bowl, whisk the buttermilk with the 1 cup of oil, the eggs and vanilla. At low speed, using the paddle, beat the buttermilk mixture into the dry ingredients. Add the hot coffee and beat until just combined.

2. Pour the batter into the prepared pans and bake for 35 to 45 minutes, until a toothpick inserted in the center comes out clean. Transfer the cakes to a rack to cool for 15 minutes, then turn them out onto the rack, peel off the parchment and let cool completely. Wrap in plastic and refrigerate.

3. Make the German chocolate filling In a medium saucepan, cook the evaporated milk, sugar, butter, egg yolks and salt over moderate heat, stirring, until the mixture comes to a boil and thickens, 8 to 10 minutes. Remove from the heat and stir in the coconut, pecans and vanilla. Scrape the filling into a bowl. Refrigerate until cold.

(continued)

(continued)

4. Make the cheesecakes Preheat the oven to 350°. Spray two 10-inch round cake pans with cooking spray, line with parchment and spray the parchment. In a food processor, pulse the graham crackers, pretzels and chocolate cereal until fine crumbs form. Add the melted butter and pulse to combine. Press the crumbs evenly over the bottom of one of the cake pans to form a very thin crust. Bake the crust for 5 minutes, until fragrant and browned. Transfer to a rack and let cool completely.

5. Reduce the oven temperature to 300°. In the bowl of a stand mixer fitted with the paddle, beat the cream cheese with the sugar at medium-high speed until light and fluffy, about 2 minutes. Add the eggs, espresso powder and vanilla and beat until combined. Divide the batter between the prepared pans (one with the crust, one without) and spread the batter evenly. Bake for about 15 minutes, until the cheesecake is set. Transfer to a rack to cool for 30 minutes, then wrap the pans in plastic and refrigerate until completely cooled.

6. Make the buttercream In a medium bowl, whisk the confectioners' sugar, cocoa powder and salt. In a double boiler, whisk the egg whites with the granulated sugar over simmering water until the sugar has dissolved, about 2 minutes. Pour the egg whites into the bowl of a stand mixer fitted with the whisk and beat at high speed until stiff, glossy and cool, about 5 to 7 minutes. At medium speed, whisk in the cocoa mixture until combined, then add the vanilla. Using the paddle attachment, beat in the butter and shortening, adding a few tablespoons of each at a time, until the buttercream is fluffy and firm, about 5 minutes.

7. Assemble the cake Using a serrated knife, trim the domed tops of the chocolate cakes to flatten them; reserve the scraps for another use. Cut each chocolate cake horizontally into 2 even layers.

8. Place a small spoonful of buttercream in the center of a large, flat plate. Invert the crusted cheesecake onto another plate and remove the parchment, then turn it crust side down and center it on top of the buttercream. Spread 1½ cups of the buttercream on top of the cheesecake and top with 1 layer of chocolate cake. Spread half of the German chocolate filling on top of the chocolate cake and top with the second layer of chocolate cake. Spread ½ cup of the buttercream over the chocolate cake (a very thin layer) and top with the crustless cheesecake. Remove the parchment from the cheesecake. Spread 1½ cups of the buttercream over the cheesecake and top with the third layer of chocolate cake. Spread the remaining German chocolate filling over the chocolate cake and cover with the remaining fourth layer of cake. Spread the remaining buttercream all over the cake using an offset spatula, to ensure that the top and side are smooth and even. Freeze the cake for 20 minutes.

9. Make the ganache In a small saucepan, bring the cream, corn syrup and butter to a boil. Remove the saucepan from the heat. Add the chocolate and whisk until it's melted and the mixture is smooth. The ganache should be warm to the touch but not hot. If the ganache is too cold, microwave in 20-second increments.

10. Set a cooling rack over a rimmed baking sheet. Very carefully transfer the cake from the plate to the rack. Starting at the center and working outward in circles, slowly pour the ganache over the cake until you reach the edge, letting the ganache drip over the side to enrobe the cake. Let set for a few minutes, then very carefully transfer the cake to a platter. Refrigerate until ready to serve, at least 30 minutes. If cold, let the cake come to room temperature before serving. —*Shannon Morrison*

MAKE AHEAD The chocolate cakes, cheesecakes and German chocolate filling can be refrigerated for up to 2 days. The finished cake can be refrigerated for up to 1 week.

Persian Love Cake

Total **1 hr;** Makes **one 8-inch cake**

"This enchanting cake reminds me of a Persian garden in the late spring, adorned with the floral scent of rosewater and citrus, and decorated with bright green pistachios," says cookbook author and blogger Yasmin Khan. "The oil in the ground almond base ensures a moist, densely textured cake that will keep well for a couple of days, covered in foil—if it is not devoured in one sitting. A sprinkling of dried rose petals looks ever so pretty for special occasions, but don't worry if you can't get hold of any. It's still a cake to win hearts."

CAKE

- 1¾ **sticks unsalted butter, plus more for greasing**
- ⅔ **cup plus 2 Tbsp. superfine sugar**
- 4 **large eggs**
- 12 **cardamom pods**
- ¾ **cup all-purpose flour, sifted**
- 2¾ **cups almond flour**
  Zest of 1 lemon plus ¼ cup fresh lemon juice
- 1½ **Tbsp. rosewater**
- 1 **tsp. baking powder**
  Pinch of fine sea salt

ICING

- 1¼ **cups confectioners' sugar**
- 1 **Tbsp. fresh lemon juice**
  Chopped pistachios and dried rose petals (optional), for garnish

1. Make the cake Preheat the oven to 320°. Grease an 8-inch springform pan and line it with parchment paper.

2. In a large bowl and using a hand mixer, beat the butter and ⅔ cup of the sugar until fluffy, then beat in the eggs one at a time until incorporated.

3. In a mortar and using a pestle, crack the cardamom pods to release the seeds. Discard the pods and grind the seeds to a fine powder. Beat the powder into the batter along with the all-purpose flour, almond flour, lemon zest, 3 tablespoons of the lemon juice, 1 tablespoon of the rosewater, the baking powder and salt until smooth. Pour the batter into the prepared pan and bake until the cake is set and a toothpick inserted in the middle comes out clean, about 45 minutes. Transfer the pan to a rack and let cool slightly.

4. Meanwhile, in a small saucepan, bring the remaining 2 tablespoons of sugar, 1 tablespoon of lemon juice and ½ tablespoon of rosewater to a simmer, stirring to dissolve the sugar. Poke holes all over the cake and pour the warm syrup over the cake. Let the cake cool completely, then remove from the pan and transfer to a cake platter.

5. Make the icing In a medium bowl, whisk the confectioners' sugar, lemon juice and 2 teaspoons of cold water until smooth. Spoon the icing over the cake and garnish with pistachios and rose petals, if using; serve. —*Yasmin Khan*

NOTE For a high-quality, pure rosewater, look for Sadaf brand, available at kalustyans.com.

Three-Layer Thanksgiving Cake

Active **35 min**; Total **2 hr**; Serves **10**

CAKES

1½ **sticks unsalted butter, melted and cooled, plus softened butter for greasing**

2¼ **cups plus 1 Tbsp. all-purpose flour**

1⅛ **tsp. baking soda**

¾ **tsp. baking powder**

¾ **tsp. kosher salt**

1¼ **cups granulated sugar**

1 **cup buttermilk, at room temperature**

3 **large eggs, at room temperature**

⅓ **cup pure pumpkin puree**

1¼ **tsp. pumpkin pie spice**

1¼ **cups fresh or frozen cranberries, thawed and drained if frozen**

⅓ **cup stone-ground yellow cornmeal**

1¼ **cups candied pecans, roughly chopped**

FROSTING

1¼ **lbs. cream cheese, softened**

2½ **sticks unsalted butter, softened**

5 **cups confectioners' sugar**

Kosher salt

1. Make the cakes Preheat the oven to 350° with racks positioned in the upper and lower thirds. Butter three 9-by-9-inch metal cake pans and line them with parchment paper; allow 2 inches of overhang on 2 sides. Butter the paper.

2. In a medium bowl, whisk 2¼ cups of the flour with the baking soda, baking powder and salt. In a large bowl, whisk the melted butter with the granulated sugar, buttermilk and eggs until well combined. Whisk in the dry ingredients until just combined.

3. Divide the batter among 3 medium bowls (1½ cups per bowl). Whisk the pumpkin puree, pumpkin pie spice and the remaining 1 tablespoon of flour into one of the bowls, then scrape the batter into one of the prepared pans. Fold the cranberries and cornmeal into another bowl and scrape into a second prepared pan. Fold the pecans into the final bowl and scrape the batter into the last prepared pan.

4. Transfer all 3 pans to the oven and bake the cakes for about 15 minutes, rotating halfway through, until a toothpick inserted in the center of each cake comes out clean. Let the cakes cool in the pans for 15 minutes, then invert onto a rack to cool completely. Peel off the parchment paper.

5. Meanwhile, make the frosting In the bowl of a stand mixer fitted with the paddle, beat the cream cheese, butter, confectioners' sugar and a pinch of salt at medium speed until smooth.

6. Place the pecan layer on a platter. Scrape ¾ cup of the frosting on top and spread to the edge. Top with the cranberry layer; scrape another ¾ cup of the frosting on top and spread to the edge. Top with the pumpkin layer. Spread a thin layer of frosting all over the cake and refrigerate until set, 15 minutes. Spread the remaining frosting all over the cake. Refrigerate until firm, at least 30 minutes, before serving. —*Laura Rege*

MAKE AHEAD The layer cake can be refrigerated for up to 3 days.

Cake Frosting Pointers

While sometimes frosting a cake can look intimidating, we learned some tricks from NYC vegan bakery Sweets by Chloe.

LEVEL YOUR CAKE The most important thing is to level your cake first. Make sure it's completely cool before you cut it—if the cake is warm, it will become a crumbly disaster.

PIPE Piping bags make the whole frosting process easier. Pipe the frosting on the top of the first cake layer in big circles before stacking the next layer. To frost the sides smoothly, it is usually good practice to first put down a thin layer, called a crumb coat, to lock in the loose crumbs. Chill the cake before adding another, thicker layer of frosting.

Boston Cream Pie

Boston Cream Pie

Active **1 hr**; Total **6 hr**; Serves **12**

Pastry chef Stella Parks makes the very best Boston cream pie, with an addictively light and delicately sweet pastry cream filling and a great sponge cake. She tops it with just enough silky chocolate ganache and serves it cold.

PUDDING

- 1½ **cups whole milk**
- 1 **cup heavy cream**
- 1 **vanilla bean, split lengthwise and seeds scraped**
- 4 **large egg whites**
- 1 **cup sugar**
- ¼ **cup cornstarch**
- ½ **tsp. kosher salt**
- 2 **Tbsp. unsalted butter**
- 1 **tsp. pure vanilla extract**
- ⅛ **tsp. almond extract (optional)**

CAKE AND TOPPING

- **Nonstick baking spray**
- 2 **cups bleached cake flour**
- 2 **tsp. baking powder**
- 12 **large egg yolks, at room temperature**
- 1⅓ **cups sugar**
- 1 **Tbsp. pure vanilla extract**
- ¼ **tsp. kosher salt**
- ¼ **tsp. freshly grated nutmeg**
- 1 **cup whole milk, at room temperature**
- 4 **Tbsp. unsalted butter, melted**
- ⅓ **cup heavy cream**
- 2½ **oz. dark chocolate (62%), roughly chopped (½ cup)**

1. Make the pudding In a medium saucepan, combine the whole milk and heavy cream with the vanilla bean (not the seeds) and bring to a simmer over moderately low heat, about 2 minutes. Remove from the heat, cover and let the milk steep for 30 minutes.

2. In a large bowl, whisk the egg whites with the sugar, cornstarch, salt and the vanilla seeds until smooth.

3. Return the milk mixture to a simmer over moderately low heat; discard the vanilla bean. Ladle ½ cup of the hot milk into the egg white mixture, whisking to combine. Continue adding the milk, ½ cup at a time, until fully incorporated. Scrape the mixture back into the saucepan, add the butter and cook, whisking gently over moderately low heat, until the pudding begins to thicken, about 4 minutes. Strain the pudding through a fine sieve set over a medium bowl. Stir in the vanilla and almond extract (if using) and let stand for 5 minutes. Press a sheet of plastic wrap directly onto the surface of the pudding and refrigerate until cold, about 3 hours.

4. Meanwhile, make the cake Preheat the oven to 350°. Spray two 8-inch round cake pans and line with parchment paper. Spray the paper.

5. Sift the cake flour into a medium bowl and whisk in the baking powder. In a stand mixer fitted with the whisk, beat the egg yolks, sugar, vanilla, salt and nutmeg at medium speed until thick and doubled in volume, about 6 minutes. Reduce the speed to medium-low and beat in the milk and melted butter, then gently whisk in the dry ingredients until combined.

6. Scrape the batter into the prepared pans and bake for about 30 minutes, until a toothpick inserted in the center of each cake comes out clean. Transfer to a rack to cool for 10 minutes, then invert onto the rack and leave the pans on top of the cakes to trap the steam. Let cool to room temperature, about 1 hour. Remove the pans and discard the paper.

7. Fold a 26-inch-long sheet of foil in thirds lengthwise to create a 4-inch-wide band. Using a serrated knife, trim the domed crust from the tops of the cakes. Set 1 cake layer cut side up on a platter. Wrap the foil around the cake to form a collar and secure it with tape. Stir the chilled pudding until smooth, then spread it on top of the cake, keeping the foil collar secure. Top with the second cake layer. Cover the cake with plastic wrap and refrigerate until cold, at least 2 hours or up to 12 hours.

8. In a small saucepan, bring the heavy cream just to a simmer over moderate heat, about 2 minutes. Remove from the heat and whisk in the dark chocolate until smooth. Scrape the ganache into a glass measuring cup and refrigerate until thickened but still warm, about 15 minutes.

9. Remove the plastic wrap and the foil collar from the cake. Stir the ganache until smooth and pour it directly onto the center of the cake. Using the back of a spoon, spread the ganache toward the edge to let it drip down in a few places over the side. Serve. —*Stella Parks*

MAKE AHEAD The cake can be refrigerated overnight. Serve chilled.

The Easiest Way to Line a Round Cake Pan

If you want a level cake that doesn't stick to the pan, then you need to line the pan with parchment paper. To make sure you cut the perfect size every time, follow these simple steps.

STEP 1 Fold a 12-inch square of parchment paper in half to create a rectangle. Fold it in half again to create a square. With the folded edges on the left and bottom, bring the bottom right corner up to meet the left edge, making a triangle; fold the same way again (bring the right folded edge up to meet the left edge).

STEP 2 Hold the sharpest point of the triangle in the center of an inverted round cake pan. Using scissors, cut the paper where it lines up with the edge of the pan.

STEP 3 Unfold the parchment and line your cake pan perfectly.

Tres Leches Cake

Active **50 min**; Total **4 hr 50 min**; Serves **12**

 Unsalted butter, softened,
 for brushing

6 large eggs, separated

1 cup granulated sugar

1 cup all-purpose flour

1 cup coconut flakes (1½ oz.)

1 can (14 oz.) sweetened
 condensed milk

1 cup evaporated milk

¾ cup whole milk

2 Tbsp. dark rum

1½ tsp. pure vanilla extract

1 cup heavy cream

1 Tbsp. confectioners' sugar

 Ground cinnamon, for dusting

1. Preheat the oven to 350°. Brush a 9-by-13-inch baking dish with butter. In a stand mixer fitted with the paddle, beat the egg yolks with the granulated sugar at high speed until light and fluffy, about 5 minutes. Scrape into a large bowl. Clean the mixer bowl.

2. In the stand mixer fitted with the whisk, beat the egg whites at high speed until medium peaks form, about 1 minute. Using a rubber spatula, stir a large scoop of the egg whites into the egg yolk mixture to lighten it. Gently fold the remaining whites into the egg yolk mixture until no white streaks remain.

3. Sift the flour over the egg mixture, then gently fold together until just combined. Scrape the batter into the prepared baking dish and smooth the top. Bake for about 15 minutes, until springy and light golden. Let cool. Leave the oven on.

4. Meanwhile, spread the coconut on a small rimmed baking sheet and toast in the oven, stirring halfway through, for about 5 minutes, until golden. Let cool.

5. Using a bamboo skewer or a fork, poke holes all over the cooled cake. In a medium bowl, whisk the condensed milk with the evaporated milk, whole milk, rum and vanilla. Pour the milk mixture evenly over the cake. Cover the baking dish with plastic wrap and refrigerate until the cake is evenly moist, at least 3 hours.

6. In a medium bowl, whisk the cream with the confectioners' sugar until medium peaks form. Dollop the whipped cream on the cake and spread it in an even layer. Sprinkle the toasted coconut over the top. Dust the cake with cinnamon and cut into squares. Serve, spooning some of the milk mixture from the baking dish onto each plate. —*Lorena Herrera*

MAKE AHEAD The coconut flakes can be toasted and stored at room temperature for up to 3 days. The cake can soak in the refrigerator overnight.

Honey Cake with Citrus Frosting

Active **1 hr**; Total **4 hr**; Makes **one 8-inch cake**

HONEY CAKE

 Nonstick baking spray

1¾ cups all-purpose flour

1¾ tsp. ground cinnamon

½ tsp. baking powder

½ tsp. baking soda

¼ tsp. each kosher salt, ground
 cloves and allspice

⅛ tsp. ground ginger

½ cup vegetable oil

½ cup honey

2 large eggs, at room temperature

½ cup granulated sugar

½ cup packed dark brown sugar

½ cup plus 2 Tbsp. hot brewed coffee

2 Tbsp. fresh orange juice

½ tsp. vanilla paste

CITRUS FROSTING

1 cup granulated sugar

¼ cup plus 1 Tbsp. all-purpose flour

1 cup whole milk

2 sticks unsalted butter, softened

1 tsp. finely grated orange zest

1 tsp. pure vanilla extract

¼ tsp. kosher salt

 Candied orange slices (see Note),
 for garnish

1. Make the cake Preheat the oven to 350°. Grease an 8-inch springform pan with baking spray and line the bottom with parchment paper. Wrap the outside of the pan with foil and set on a rimmed baking sheet.

2. In a bowl, whisk the flour, cinnamon, baking powder, baking soda, salt, cloves, allspice and ginger. In another bowl, whisk the oil and honey. In a stand mixer fitted with the whisk, beat the eggs with both sugars at medium-high speed until thick and nearly doubled in volume, 4 minutes. Slowly beat in the oil-honey mixture until just combined, about 1 minute. (The batter will look broken but will emulsify.) In a measuring cup, combine the coffee, orange juice and vanilla paste. At low speed, beat the dry ingredients and the coffee mixture into the batter in 3 alternating additions, until just combined.

3. Scrape the batter into the prepared pan. Bake for about 55 minutes, until a toothpick inserted in the center comes out clean. Transfer the cake to a rack and let cool for 1 hour. Run a knife around the edge of the cake and remove the springform ring. Invert the cake and remove the springform bottom. Discard the parchment. Let the cake cool completely, about 45 minutes, then transfer to a large plate.

4. Meanwhile, make the frosting In a small saucepan, whisk ½ cup of the granulated sugar with the flour, then whisk in the milk. Bring to a boil over moderately low heat, whisking constantly, about 10 minutes. Scrape into a heatproof bowl and press a sheet of plastic wrap directly onto the surface. Let cool for 1 hour.

5. In a stand mixer fitted with the paddle, beat the butter with the remaining ½ cup of granulated sugar and the orange zest at medium speed until fluffy and smooth, about 5 minutes. Beat in the cooled flour mixture, 1 tablespoon at a time, beating well after each addition. Beat in the vanilla and salt and continue beating until smooth, about 2 minutes.

6. Spread a thin layer of frosting all over the cake and refrigerate until set, about 15 minutes. Spread the remaining frosting over the top and side of the cake. Refrigerate until the frosting is just firm, about 30 minutes. Top with candied orange slices before serving. —*Umber Ahmad and Shelly Acuña Barbera*

NOTE To make the candied orange slices, bring 1½ cups water and ½ cup sugar to a boil. Add 1 navel orange (sliced ¼ inch thick) and simmer for 30 minutes. Transfer the slices to a rack to cool.

Honey Cake with
Citrus Frosting

Strawberry-Honey
Cake with Sour
Whipped Cream

Strawberry-Honey Cake with Sour Whipped Cream

Active **30 min**; Total **3 hr plus overnight macerating**; Serves **8**

Don't be shy when poking the holes: The more there are, the more the syrup will penetrate every last bite.

CAKE

- **1 lb. strawberries, hulled and quartered, plus more for serving**
- **1¼ cups sugar**
- **1½ sticks unsalted butter, at room temperature, plus more for greasing**
- **2⅓ cups all-purpose flour, plus more for dusting**
- **1 tsp. baking powder**
- **½ tsp. baking soda**
- **1 tsp. kosher salt**
- **3 large egg yolks, at room temperature**
- **2 large eggs, at room temperature**
- **⅓ cup sour cream**
- **1 tsp. fresh lemon juice**
- **1 tsp. pure vanilla extract**

TOPPINGS

- **¾ cup wildflower or clover honey**
- **1 Tbsp. unsalted butter**
- **1 cup heavy cream**
- **1 cup sour cream**

1. Make the cake In a medium bowl, mix the 1 pound of strawberries with ¼ cup of the sugar. Cover and refrigerate overnight. Strain the berries through a fine sieve set over a small bowl. Reserve the syrup for serving. In a food processor, pulse the macerated strawberries until finely chopped.

2. Preheat the oven to 325°. Generously butter a 12-cup Bundt pan and dust with flour, tapping out the excess. In a medium bowl, whisk the 2⅓ cups of flour with the baking powder, baking soda and salt. In a stand mixer fitted with the paddle, beat the 1½ sticks of butter with the remaining 1 cup of sugar at medium speed until light and fluffy, about 3 minutes. Reduce the speed to low and beat in the egg yolks and eggs one at time until just incorporated; scrape down the side of the bowl. At low speed, beat in the sour cream, lemon juice and vanilla. Beat in the dry ingredients until just combined, then beat in the chopped strawberries. Scrape the batter into the prepared Bundt pan and bake for 50 to 55 minutes, until a toothpick inserted into the cake comes out with a few moist crumbs. Transfer to a rack and let cool in the pan for 20 minutes. Line a large rimmed baking sheet with parchment paper. Invert the cake onto the cooling rack, then set the rack on the baking sheet.

3. Meanwhile, make the toppings In a small saucepan, bring the honey, butter and ¼ cup of water to a boil over moderate heat, stirring until the honey is dissolved, about 3 minutes. Using a wooden skewer, gently poke holes all over the cake. Slowly pour the honey syrup over the top, letting it get absorbed before adding more. Let the cake cool completely.

4. In a stand mixer fitted with the whisk, beat the heavy cream and sour cream until soft peaks form. Slice the cake and serve with the whipped cream, reserved syrup and more fresh strawberries. —*Eli Dahlin*

MAKE AHEAD The cake can be prepared through Step 2 and loosely wrapped in foil. Store at room temperature overnight.

Devil's Food Snacking Cake

Active **30 min**; Total **3 hr 15 min**
Makes **one 9-by-13-inch cake**

CAKE

- **Nonstick baking spray**
- **2¼ cups all-purpose flour**
- **1⅛ tsp. baking soda**
- **¾ tsp. kosher salt**
- **¾ cup unsweetened Dutch-process cocoa powder**
- **1 Tbsp. instant coffee**
- **1½ cups boiling water**
- **1 cup packed dark brown sugar**
- **¾ cup buttermilk**
- **2½ tsp. pure vanilla extract**
- **12 Tbsp. salted butter, softened**
- **1¾ cups granulated sugar**
- **3 large eggs, at room temperature**

GANACHE FROSTING

- **8 oz. bittersweet chocolate, finely chopped**
- **1 cup heavy cream**
- **1½ Tbsp. light corn syrup**
- **Crispy chocolate pearls, for topping (optional; see Note)**

1. Make the cake Preheat the oven to 350°. Grease a 9-by-13-inch baking pan with baking spray and line the bottom with parchment paper.

2. In a medium bowl, whisk the flour with the baking soda and salt. In a large heatproof bowl, whisk the cocoa powder with the instant coffee, then whisk in 1½ cups of boiling water. Stir in the brown sugar and buttermilk until no lumps remain. Let cool for 5 minutes, then stir in the vanilla.

3. In a stand mixer fitted with the paddle, beat the butter at medium-high speed until lightened, about 1 minute. Beat in the granulated sugar in 3 additions, beating well after each one, until light and fluffy, about 5 minutes. Add the eggs one at a time, beating well after each addition. At low speed, beat in the dry ingredients and the cocoa mixture in 3 alternating additions, scraping down the side and bottom of the bowl as necessary, until just combined.

4. Scrape the batter into the prepared pan. Bake for about 35 minutes, until a toothpick inserted in the center comes out clean; rotate the pan halfway through baking. Transfer the cake to a rack and let cool for 1 hour. Run a knife around the edge of the pan, then invert the cake and remove the parchment. Let cool completely, about 30 minutes.

5. Meanwhile, make the frosting Put the chocolate in the bowl of a stand mixer. In a small saucepan, bring the cream and corn syrup to a simmer. Pour the hot cream over the chocolate; let stand for 2 minutes, then whisk until smooth. Let the ganache cool until barely warm, 45 minutes. In the stand mixer fitted with the whisk, beat the ganache at medium-high speed until light and spreadable, about 2 minutes.

6. Spread the ganache frosting over the top of the cake, top with pearls (if using) and serve. —*Umber Ahmad and Shelly Acuña Barbera*

NOTE Chocolate pearls are available at specialty food shops and amazon.com.

Chewy Black Licorice Chocolate Brownies

Active **30 min** Total **1 hr 10 min plus cooling**
Makes **12**

This deeply dark-chocolaty brownie from *Top Chef* judge Gail Simmons has a sophisticated touch of salt, plus notes of molasses and anise from black licorice. The combo makes a brilliant treat that is irresistibly chewy and not too sweet.

1½ **sticks unsalted butter, melted, plus more for brushing**

1 **cup all-purpose flour**

½ **cup unsweetened cocoa powder**

2 **Tbsp. licorice root powder (see Note)**

2 **tsp. ground anise seeds**

½ **tsp. kosher salt**

1 **cup granulated sugar**

1 **cup packed brown sugar**

3 **large eggs**

1 **tsp. pure vanilla extract**

2 **oz. bittersweet chocolate, chopped**

½ **cup chopped soft black licorice chews (3 oz.)**

1. Preheat the oven to 350°. Line a 9-inch-square baking pan with paper or foil, leaving 2 inches of overhang on 2 sides. Brush the paper with butter.

2. In a medium bowl, whisk the flour with the cocoa powder, licorice root powder, anise and salt. In a large bowl, whisk the melted butter with both sugars, then whisk in the eggs and vanilla. Stir in the dry ingredients, then three-fourths of the chocolate and licorice chews. Scrape the batter into the prepared pan and smooth the top. Gently press the remaining chocolate and licorice chews into the batter.

3. Bake the brownies for about 40 minutes, until a toothpick inserted in the center comes out clean, with a few moist crumbs attached. Let the brownies cool completely, then lift them out of the pan using the paper. Cut the brownies into 12 rectangles and serve. —*Gail Simmons*

NOTE Licorice root powder is available from kalustyans.com.

MAKE AHEAD The brownies can be stored in an airtight container for up to 5 days.

Chocolate Espresso Pie Bars

Active **45 min;** Total **3 hr 45 min**
Makes **48**

CRUST

4 **sticks unsalted butter, melted, plus more for brushing**

4½ **cups all-purpose flour**

¾ **cup packed light brown sugar**

¾ **tsp. kosher salt**

FILLING

3 **sticks unsalted butter, cut into large dice**

1 **cup dark chocolate chips**

1 **Tbsp. pure vanilla extract**

3 **cups granulated sugar**

1 **Tbsp. instant espresso powder**

1 **tsp. ground cinnamon**

½ **tsp. kosher salt**

6 **large eggs**

Confectioners' sugar, for dusting

1. Make the crust Preheat the oven to 350°. Brush a large rimmed baking sheet with melted butter. Line the baking sheet with parchment paper, leaving a 1-inch overhang.

2. In a large bowl, using your fingers, combine the flour with the brown sugar and salt. Drizzle in the 4 sticks of melted butter and stir with a fork until a lumpy dough forms. Press the dough evenly over the bottom and up the sides of the prepared baking sheet. Refrigerate until firm, about 15 minutes.

3. Line the pie shell with parchment paper and fill to the top with pie weights or dried beans. Bake in the center of the oven for about 20 minutes, until lightly browned. Remove the pie weights and parchment paper. Transfer the crust to a wire rack to cool, about 1 hour.

4. Meanwhile, make the filling Reduce the oven temperature to 325°. In a heat-proof medium bowl set over a saucepan of simmering water, melt the diced butter with the chocolate chips, stirring occasionally, until smooth, about 3 minutes. Stir in the vanilla and remove the bowl from the heat. Whisk in the granulated sugar, espresso, cinnamon and salt until blended. Whisk in the eggs one at a time. Pour the filling into the cooled crust. Bake for about 45 minutes, until the center is set and the top begins to crack. Transfer the pie to a wire rack to cool completely, about 2 hours.

5. Cut the pie into 2-inch-square bars. Dust the top with confectioners' sugar and serve. —*Cheryl Day*

MAKE AHEAD The pie bars can be stored in an airtight container for up to 2 days.

Salty-Sweet Chocolate Pretzel Bars

Active **40 min;** Total **1 hr plus cooling**
Makes **12**

14 **oz. graham crackers (28 whole crackers), finely ground**

1½ **sticks unsalted butter, melted**

3 **Tbsp. sugar**

Pinch of kosher salt

One 14-oz. can sweetened condensed milk

One 10-oz. bag bittersweet chocolate chips

6 **oz. thin hard pretzels (4 cups), broken**

Flaky sea salt, for sprinkling

1. Preheat the oven to 350°. Line a 9-inch-square baking pan with foil, allowing 2 inches of overhang on 2 sides. In a medium bowl, using a fork, mix the graham cracker crumbs with the butter, sugar and kosher salt until evenly moistened. Press the crumbs evenly into the bottom of the prepared pan.

2. In a medium saucepan, combine the condensed milk with the chocolate chips and cook over low heat, stirring, until melted and smooth, about 5 minutes.

3. Scrape the mixture onto the crust and smooth the top. Scatter the pretzels evenly on top, gently pressing them into the chocolate. Sprinkle with flaky sea salt and bake for 15 to 20 minutes, until the edges are set. Let cool completely, then refrigerate until chilled, about 45 minutes. Unmold and cut into bars. —*Justin Chapple*

MAKE AHEAD The bars can be stored in an airtight container for up to 3 days.

Chewy Black Licorice
Chocolate Brownies

Chocolate Pretzels
with Sea Salt

Chocolate Pretzels with Sea Salt

Active **1 hr 10 min**; Total **2 hr**; Makes **36**

In star chef Daniel Humm's clever (and gluten-free!) version of this salty-sweet snack, ground pretzels and white chocolate get piped into a pretzel shape and chilled before being dipped in dark chocolate.

- **12** oz. gluten-free salted pretzels, such as Glutino
- **1** lb. white chocolate, finely chopped
- **12** oz. dark chocolate (72% cacao)
  Flaky sea salt, for garnish

1. In a food processor, pulse the pretzels into a fine powder. Sift through a medium sieve into a bowl.

2. In a large microwave-safe bowl, melt the white chocolate at high power in 20-second increments, stirring after each, until smooth. Stir in the pretzel powder until evenly moistened. Let cool slightly, then scrape into a pastry bag fitted with a ⅓-inch round tip.

3. Line 3 large baking sheets with parchment paper. Using a 3-inch round cutter and a permanent marker, trace 12 circles onto each sheet of parchment. Flip the paper so the ink is on the bottom. Using the circles as a guide, pipe pretzels onto the parchment. Refrigerate until set, about 30 minutes.

4. Meanwhile, in another microwave-safe bowl, melt the dark chocolate at high power in 20-second increments, stirring after each, until smooth. Let cool slightly.

5. Using 2 forks or tweezers and working with 1 pretzel at a time, coat the chilled pretzels in the melted dark chocolate and return to the baking sheet; immediately garnish with flaky sea salt. Let stand at room temperature until the dark chocolate is set, about 20 minutes. Serve. —*Daniel Humm*

MAKE AHEAD The pretzels can be stored l;jk oin an airtight container for up to 1 week.

Chocolate-Cardamom Cookies

Active **20 min**; Total **1 hr 15 min plus overnight chilling**; Makes **24**

Despite their healthy ingredients, these gluten- and dairy-free chocolate chip |cookies are superdecadent. Almond flour gives them a nutty, crumbly texture and almond butter keeps them wonderfully moist.

- **4** cups almond flour
- **2** tsp. baking powder
- **1** tsp. ground cardamom
- **1** tsp. fine Himalayan pink salt
- **2** cups roasted salted almond butter (18 oz.)
- **1½** cups honey, preferably liquid raw (see Note)
- **1** tsp. pure vanilla extract
- **6** oz. dark chocolate, chopped

1. In a stand mixer fitted with the paddle, mix the almond flour with the baking powder, cardamom and salt at low speed until combined. At medium speed, beat in the almond butter, honey and vanilla until smooth. Add the chocolate chunks and beat until just incorporated. Cover the bowl with plastic wrap and refrigerate overnight.

2. Preheat the oven to 350° and arrange racks in the upper and lower thirds of the oven. Line 2 large baking sheets with parchment paper. Scoop ¼-cup mounds of the dough onto the prepared baking sheets and flatten into ½-inch-thick disks. Bake the cookies for about 15 minutes, until they are lightly browned and firm around the edges; shift the baking sheets from front to back and top to bottom halfway through baking. Let cool completely before serving. —*Whitney Tingle and Danielle DuBoise*

NOTE Raw, unprocessed honey can be found at most health food stores and on amazon.com.

MAKE AHEAD The cookies can be stored in an airtight container at room temperature for up to 3 days.

Peppermint Sandwich Cookies

Active **50 min**; Total **3 hr**; Makes **32**

- **2** cups all-purpose flour
- **6** Tbsp. unsweetened cocoa powder
- **½** tsp. baking soda
- **1** tsp. kosher salt
- **3** sticks unsalted butter, softened
- **¾** cup packed light brown sugar
- **8** oz. dark chocolate, finely chopped (1¾ cups)
- **1** tsp. pure vanilla extract
- **1¼** cups confectioners' sugar
- **½** tsp. pure peppermint extract

1. In a large bowl, whisk the flour with the cocoa powder, baking soda and salt. In a stand mixer fitted with the paddle, beat 2 sticks of the butter with the brown sugar at medium-high speed until fluffy, about 3 minutes. Beat in the dry ingredients at low speed until just combined. Stir in the chocolate and vanilla. Divide the dough in half and press into disks. Wrap in plastic and refrigerate for 1 hour.

2. Preheat the oven to 375°. Line 3 baking sheets with parchment paper. Roll out the dough into ¼-inch-thick rounds. Using a 2-inch round cookie cutter, cut out cookies. Transfer to the prepared baking sheets, spacing them 1 inch apart. Bake for 6 minutes. Transfer the baking sheets to wire racks and let cool completely.

3. Meanwhile, in the stand mixer fitted with the paddle, beat the remaining 1 stick of butter with the confectioners' sugar and peppermint extract at medium-high speed until white and fluffy, about 3 minutes. Spoon a heaping teaspoon of the filling onto the flat sides of half of the cookies. Sandwich with the remaining cookies and serve. —*Josh Graves*

MAKE AHEAD The cookies can be refrigerated in an airtight container for up to 3 days.

Chocolate Peppermint Marshmallow Cookies

Active **1 hr 15 min**; Total **3 hr 30 min**
Makes **48**

"Mallomars are my absolute favorite," says L.A. pastry chef Della Gossett. "In my variation, the crunch of peppermint candies balances the pillowy marshmallow."

MARSHMALLOWS

Nonstick cooking spray
¼ cup powdered gelatin
2 large egg whites, at room temperature
2¼ cups sugar
1 Tbsp. light corn syrup
2 tsp. pure vanilla extract
1 cup crushed peppermint candies (10 oz.), plus more for sprinkling
8 to 12 drops of red food coloring

COOKIES

1¼ cups bread flour
1 cup pastry flour
½ tsp. kosher salt
2 sticks unsalted butter, at room temperature
1 cup sugar
½ vanilla bean, split lengthwise and seeds scraped
1 large egg
1 large egg yolk
2 tsp. pure vanilla extract
Neutral oil, such as grapeseed, for brushing

GLAZE

28 oz. dark chocolate (65% to 70% cocoa), chopped
4 oz. cocoa butter

1. Make the marshmallows Coat a 13-by-18-inch rimmed baking sheet with cooking spray. Line with parchment paper and coat with cooking spray. In a small microwavable bowl, whisk the gelatin with ¾ cup of water. Microwave on high in 10-second increments, stirring after each one, until the gelatin is just melted, about 50 seconds.

2. In a stand mixer fitted with the whisk, beat the egg whites at medium-low speed until very foamy. Meanwhile, in a medium saucepan, combine the sugar with the corn syrup and 1 cup of water and bring to a boil, stirring occasionally. Cook over moderate heat, without stirring, until the sugar syrup registers 260° on a candy thermometer, about 10 minutes. Remove the pan from the heat and carefully stir in the gelatin until melted.

3. Carefully drizzle the hot syrup into the egg whites down the side of the bowl, beating at medium speed. Add the vanilla and beat at high speed until thick and glossy, about 10 minutes. Using a rubber spatula, fold in the 1 cup of peppermint candies. Sprinkle in the food coloring, then quickly scrape the marshmallow mixture onto the prepared baking sheet, swirling the food coloring, and smooth the surface. Let stand at room temperature until set, at least 2 hours or overnight.

4. Meanwhile, make the cookies In a medium bowl, whisk the bread flour with the pastry flour and salt. In a stand mixer fitted with the paddle, beat the butter with the sugar and vanilla bean seeds at medium speed until fluffy, about 5 minutes. Beat in the egg, egg yolk and vanilla. Beat in the dry ingredients at low speed until just combined. Divide the dough in half and press into disks. Wrap in plastic and refrigerate until firm, at least 1 hour or overnight.

5. On a lightly floured sheet of parchment paper, roll out 1 disk of dough into a rectangle, ¼ inch thick. Transfer on the parchment paper to a baking sheet and refrigerate until firm, about 30 minutes. Repeat with the second disk of dough.

6. Preheat the oven to 325°. Using a square cookie cutter or a knife, cut 2-inch squares from the dough and arrange on the baking sheets 1 inch apart. Reroll the scraps and cut more squares. Bake the cookies for 10 to 12 minutes, until golden brown. Transfer the baking sheets to wire racks and let the cookies cool.

7. Lightly brush the cookie cutter or a knife with oil, repeating as needed. Cut out forty-eight 2-inch marshmallows. Place 1 marshmallow on top of each cookie and transfer to baking sheets. Freeze until cold, at least 15 minutes.

8. Make the glaze In a large microwavable bowl, combine the chocolate with the cocoa butter. Microwave on high in 20-second increments, stirring after each, until the mixture is melted and smooth.

9. Coat 2 rimmed baking sheets with cooking spray. Line with parchment paper and coat with cooking spray. Using a fork, dip each cookie in the glaze, then set on a prepared baking sheet and sprinkle with some peppermint candy. Refrigerate until set, at least 15 minutes, and serve cold. —*Della Gossett*

MAKE AHEAD The cookies can be refrigerated in an airtight container for 4 days.

Einkorn Shortbreads

Active **25 min**; Total **2 hr 25 min**; Makes **20**

These unique cookies from Roxana Jullapat, chef-owner of L.A.'s Friends & Family, get nutty, caramel-like notes from the wheatlike grain einkorn.

6 Tbsp. confectioners' sugar
⅓ cup dark brown sugar
2 sticks unsalted butter, cubed, at room temperature
1¼ cups whole-grain einkorn flour (see Note)
1 cup all-purpose flour
1¾ tsp. kosher salt

1. Preheat the oven to 300°. In a food processor, pulse the confectioners' sugar with the brown sugar until combined. Add the butter and pulse to combine. Add the einkorn flour, all-purpose flour and salt and pulse until the dough comes together. Divide in half and press into disks. Wrap in plastic and refrigerate for 30 minutes.

2. Roll out each disk of dough between 2 sheets of parchment paper into a ¼-inch-thick round. Peel off the top layer of parchment. Using a 2½-inch round cookie cutter, stamp out cookies and transfer to 2 baking sheets, spaced ½ inch apart. Using a small star-shaped cookie cutter, stamp out a star in the upper right corner of each cookie. Transfer the stars to a separate baking sheet. Reroll the scraps and cut out more cookies.

3. Bake the cookies and stars until deep golden brown, 25 to 30 minutes for the cookies and 10 to 12 minutes for the stars. Transfer the baking sheets to wire racks and let cool completely. —*Roxana Jullapat*

NOTE Einkorn flour is available from jovialfoods.com.

MAKE AHEAD The cookies can be stored in an airtight container for up to 3 days.

Einkorn
Shortbreads,
(p. 342)

Chocolate
Peppermint
Marshmallow
Cookies, (p. 342)

Key Lime
Macarons,
(p. 344)

Christmas Morning
Biscotti, (p. 349)

Spiced
Italian Pecan
Meringues,
(p. 344)

Spiced Italian Pecan Meringues

📷 PAGE 343

Active **15 min**; Total **2 hr**; Makes **about 18**

"Don't judge the taste of these cookies by the crags and cracks," says sous-chef Merrin Mae Gray of L.A.'s Rossoblu. (Their Italian name is *brutti ma buoni*, "ugly but good.") The pecans and grappa add an unexpected elegance, and the crisp outsides and chewy centers make them seriously addictive.

- ¾ cup shelled pecans
- 3 large egg whites
- ¾ cup sugar
- 1½ tsp. grappa
- ¼ tsp. ground cinnamon
- ⅛ tsp. ground nutmeg
- ⅛ tsp. ground cloves

1. Preheat the oven to 300°. Spread the pecans on a small rimmed baking sheet and toast, tossing them halfway through, for about 20 minutes, until browned. Transfer to a work surface and let cool, then coarsely chop.

2. Line 2 rimmed baking sheets with parchment paper. In a stand mixer fitted with the whisk, beat the egg whites at medium-high speed until foamy, about 30 seconds. Beat in the sugar 1 tablespoon at a time until the whites are stiff and glossy, 5 to 7 minutes. Beat in the grappa, cinnamon, nutmeg and cloves. Using a rubber spatula, gently fold in the chopped pecans.

3. Spoon heaping tablespoons of the meringue onto the prepared baking sheets, spaced 1 inch apart. Bake for 15 minutes. Reduce the oven temperature to 200° and bake for 1 hour and 15 minutes, until the meringues are firm on the outside but still chewy in the center. Transfer the baking sheets to wire racks and let cool completely. —*Merrin Mae Gray*

MAKE AHEAD The meringues can be stored in an airtight container for up to 1 week.

Key Lime Macarons

📷 PAGE 343

Active **1 hr**; Total **3 hr**; Makes **70**

These tangy, one-bite sandwiched meringues from Uyen Nguyen, the executive pastry chef at Manhattan Beach Post in L.A., get a surprise pop of flavor courtesy of fennel seeds.

FILLING

- 3 large eggs
- ½ tsp. powdered gelatin
- ¾ cup fresh Key lime juice
- ¾ cup granulated sugar
- 1½ sticks unsalted butter, cubed and chilled

MACARON SHELLS

- 2 cups almond flour
- 1⅔ cups confectioners' sugar
- 5 large egg whites, at room temperature
- 2 tsp. finely grated lime zest
- 30 drops of green food coloring or 5 drops of green food gel
- 1 cup granulated sugar
- 1½ tsp. fennel seeds

1. Make the filling In a medium bowl, beat the eggs to mix. In a small bowl, whisk the gelatin with 1 tablespoon of water. In a medium saucepan, combine the Key lime juice with the granulated sugar and bring to a boil over moderately high heat, stirring occasionally. Slowly pour the juice mixture into the eggs, whisking constantly. Scrape the egg mixture back into the pan and cook over moderate heat, stirring, until bubbles appear and the mixture thickens, about 3 minutes. Add the gelatin mixture and stir until melted.

2. Set a fine sieve over a small heatproof bowl. Strain the custard into the bowl; discard the solids. Gradually whisk the butter into the custard until it is fully incorporated. Cover with plastic and refrigerate until cold, at least 2 hours. Spoon the custard into a small pastry bag fitted with a ¼-inch tip or use a sturdy, resealable plastic bag and snip off a corner.

3. Make the macaron shells Line 4 or 5 baking sheets with silicon mats or parchment paper. In a medium bowl, sift the almond flour with the confectioners' sugar. Stir in half of the egg whites, the lime zest and food coloring until a smooth paste forms; the color should be a shade or two darker than the final desired color.

4. In a small saucepan, combine the granulated sugar with ¼ cup of water and bring to a boil, stirring occasionally. Cook over moderate heat, without stirring, until the sugar syrup reaches 240° on a candy thermometer, about 5 minutes.

5. Meanwhile, in a stand mixer fitted with the whisk, beat the remaining egg whites at medium speed until medium peaks form, about 4 minutes. Carefully drizzle in the hot syrup at medium speed. Increase the speed to high and beat the meringue until stiff and glossy, about 5 minutes.

6. Stir one-third of the meringue into the almond mixture. Using a rubber spatula, fold in the remaining meringue, then cut through it, pressing it against the side of the bowl to slightly deflate to a thick, lavalike consistency.

7. Transfer the meringue to a pastry bag fitted with a plain ½-inch tip; pipe onto the prepared baking sheets in 1-inch mounds, 1 inch apart. Tap the sheets on the counter and top each macaron shell with a few fennel seeds. Let dry until a skin forms, 1 to 3 hours.

8. Preheat the oven to 350°. Bake the meringues for 9 to 12 minutes, until crisp on the outside and slightly chewy on the inside. Transfer the baking sheets to wire racks and let cool completely. Using a thin metal spatula, peel the meringues off the baking sheets. Pipe the custard onto the flat sides of half the meringues. Top with the remaining meringues. —*Uyen Nguyen*

MAKE AHEAD The macarons can be refrigerated in an airtight container for up to 5 days.

Raspberry Linzer Bars

Active **25 min**; Total **3 hr plus overnight chilling**; Makes **24**

These linzer bars from Della Gossett, the executive pastry chef at Spago in L.A., are a sturdier version of her Austrian-born boss Wolfgang Puck's adored but delicate cookies. "I added rye flour for an earthy taste," she says, "and I turned them into bars so they hold up for a cookie swap."

- 1½ **cups all-purpose flour**
- ¾ **cup rye flour**
- 6 **Tbsp. hazelnut flour**
- 1½ **tsp. baking powder**
- 1 **tsp. ground cinnamon**
- ¾ **tsp. kosher salt**
- 2 **sticks unsalted butter, at room temperature**
- 1½ **cups granulated sugar**
- 4 **tsp. grated lemon zest**
- 1 **tsp. pure vanilla extract**
- 3 **large egg yolks**
  Nonstick cooking spray
- 1¼ **cups raspberry jam**
  Confectioners' sugar, for dusting

1. In a medium bowl, whisk the 3 flours with the baking powder, cinnamon and salt. In a stand mixer fitted with the paddle, beat the butter with the granulated sugar, lemon zest and vanilla at medium speed until smooth, about 5 minutes. Beat in the egg yolks one at a time, scraping down the side of the bowl, until incorporated. Beat in the dry ingredients at low speed until the dough just comes together. Press one-third of the dough and two-thirds of the dough into 2 disks and wrap in plastic. Refrigerate overnight until firm.

2. Preheat the oven to 350°. Coat a 9-by-13-inch metal baking pan with cooking spray. Line with parchment paper, leaving a 2-inch overhang on the 2 long sides, and coat with cooking spray. Using the large holes of a box grater, shred the larger disk of dough evenly in the pan.

3. Spread the jam over the shredded dough, leaving a ½-inch border. Shred the smaller disk over the jam. Bake, rotating the pan halfway through, for 35 to 45 minutes, until the top is deep golden brown. Transfer to a wire rack and let cool. Refrigerate in the pan until firm, at least 2 hours.

4. Using the paper, transfer the pastry to a work surface. Dust with confectioners' sugar, cut into 2-inch bars and serve cold or at room temperature. —*Della Gossett*

MAKE AHEAD The bars can be stored in an airtight container for up to 4 days.

Matcha Tea Marshmallow Crispy Treats

Active **15 min**; Total **1 hr 15 min**; Makes **15**

Ted Hopson is generally not a cookie fan, but he loves Rice Krispies Treats. "And I especially like this nontraditional combo of tannic, floral green tea and subtly sweet white chocolate," says the executive chef and co-owner of The Bellwether in L.A.

- 5 **Tbsp. unsalted butter, sliced, plus more at room temperature for brushing**
- 1 **lb. marshmallows**
- 8½ **cups crisped rice cereal (8 oz.), preferably Rice Krispies**
- 1 **cup white chocolate chips (6 oz.)**
- 1 **tsp. flaky sea salt**
- 2 **Tbsp. matcha tea powder**

1. Brush a 9-by-13-inch baking dish with butter. In a large pot, melt the 5 tablespoons of butter over moderate heat. Add the marshmallows and cook, stirring with a wooden spoon, until completely melted, about 3 minutes. Remove the pot from the heat, add the cereal and stir to coat. Let the mixture stand until cool to the touch, about 2 minutes.

2. Working quickly, fold in the white chocolate and salt until just combined. Scrape the mixture into the prepared baking dish and press into an even layer. Let stand at room temperature until cool, about 45 minutes. Using a sieve, dust with the matcha powder. Cut into 3-inch squares and serve. —*Ted Hopson*

MAKE AHEAD The treats can be stored in an airtight container for up to 2 days.

Sweet Tea Madeleines

Active **25 min**; Total **55 min plus cooling** Makes **22**

- 6 **Tbsp. unsalted butter, melted and cooled, plus more for greasing**
- ⅔ **cup all-purpose flour**
- ½ **tsp. baking powder**
- ⅓ **cup granulated sugar**
- 4 **tsp. crushed black tea leaves (from 4 tea bags)**
- 1 **vanilla bean, split lengthwise and seeds scraped**
- 2 **large eggs**
- 1 **Tbsp. honey**
- ½ **tsp. kosher salt**
- 1 **Tbsp. whole milk at room temperature**
  Confectioners' sugar, for dusting

1. Preheat the oven to 400° and position racks in the upper and lower thirds. Grease 22 madeleine molds and set on 2 large rimmed baking sheets.

2. In a medium bowl, whisk the flour with the baking powder. In a food processor, pulse the granulated sugar with the black tea leaves and vanilla bean seeds until the tea leaves are finely chopped. Scrape into a large bowl and whisk in the eggs, honey and salt until smooth. Whisk in the dry ingredients until just combined. Stir in the milk and the 6 tablespoons of melted butter until incorporated.

3. Spoon heaping tablespoons of the batter into the prepared madeleine molds, filling them three-quarters of the way to the top. Transfer to the refrigerator and chill until cold, about 20 minutes.

4. Bake the madeleines for about 10 minutes, until the edges are golden brown and the cakes spring back when lightly pressed; rotate the baking sheets from front to back and top to bottom halfway through baking. Let cool slightly in the molds, then loosen with the tip of a small knife and transfer to a baking rack to cool completely. Dust with confectioners' sugar before serving. —*Joe Kindred*

MAKE AHEAD The madeleines can be stored in an airtight container at room temperature overnight.

Ricotta Cookies with Sour Cream Glaze

Active **25 min**; Total **1 hr**; Makes **about 18**

Cookbook author and TV host Valerie Bertinelli enjoys these tender, buttery cookies with a cup of coffee in the afternoon or an after-dinner espresso.

RICOTTA COOKIES

- 2 **cups all-purpose flour**
- ½ **tsp. baking soda**
- ½ **tsp. kosher salt**
- 2 **sticks unsalted butter, softened**
- 1 **cup granulated sugar**
- 8 **oz. ricotta cheese (about 1 cup)**
- 1 **tsp. grated lemon zest (from 1 lemon)**
- 1 **tsp. pure vanilla extract**
- 2 **large eggs**

SOUR CREAM GLAZE

- 1½ **cups confectioners' sugar**
- ¼ **cup sour cream**
- 2 **Tbsp. unsalted butter, melted**
- ½ **tsp. pure vanilla extract**
- ½ **cup sliced almonds, toasted**

1. Make the ricotta cookies Preheat the oven to 350°. In a medium bowl, whisk together the flour, baking soda and salt. In a large bowl, beat the butter and granulated sugar with a hand mixer at medium speed until light and fluffy, 2 to 3 minutes. Beat in the ricotta, lemon zest and vanilla. Add the eggs one at a time, beating until blended after each addition. Gradually add the flour mixture, beating at low speed until blended. Drop the dough by tablespoonfuls 2 inches apart onto large baking sheets lined with parchment paper.

2. Bake until the cookies are set and golden around the edges, rotating the pans as needed, about 12 minutes. Cool the cookies on the pans for 5 minutes, then transfer to wire racks and let cool completely, about 20 minutes.

3. Make the sour cream glaze In a medium bowl, whisk together the confectioners' sugar, sour cream, butter and vanilla until smooth. Spread evenly over the cooled cookies; sprinkle with the toasted almonds. —*Valerie Bertinelli*

Molasses Thumbprints with Cajeta

Active **55 min**; Total **3 hr**; Makes **about 36**

"The cajeta filling for these cookies was a natural twist at a Mexican restaurant," says pastry chef Ivan Arturo Marquez of Broken Spanish in L.A. "I also like the play of the sweet goat-milk caramel, slightly bitter molasses and sharp candied ginger."

CAJETA

- 4 **cups goat milk**
- 1 **cup granulated sugar**
- 1 **tsp. finely grated lemon zest**
- ½ **tsp. baking soda**
- ½ **vanilla bean, split lengthwise and seeds scraped**

COOKIES

- 1½ **cups all-purpose flour**
- 1 **Tbsp. cornstarch**
- 1½ **tsp. ground ginger**
- 1 **tsp. ground cinnamon**
- 1 **tsp. ground cloves**
- ¾ **tsp. baking soda**
- 6 **Tbsp. unsalted butter, at room temperature**
- ½ **cup light brown sugar**
- ¼ **cup unsulfured molasses**
- 1 **large egg**
- ½ **tsp. pure vanilla paste**
- ½ **cup finely chopped candied ginger (2½ oz.)**
- ½ **cup turbinado sugar**

1. Make the cajeta In a medium saucepan, combine the goat milk with the granulated sugar and lemon zest and bring to a simmer over moderate heat. Remove the pan from the heat and whisk in the baking soda and the vanilla bean seeds. Return the pan to moderately low heat and simmer, whisking occasionally, until the caramel is amber and the consistency of condensed milk, about 1 hour and 30 minutes. Set a fine sieve over a small heatproof bowl. Strain the caramel into the bowl; discard the solids. Let cool slightly. Cover with plastic wrap and refrigerate until firm and cold, at least 1 hour.

2. Meanwhile, make the cookies In a medium bowl, whisk the flour with the cornstarch, ground ginger, cinnamon, cloves and baking soda. In a stand mixer fitted with the paddle, beat the butter with the brown sugar at medium speed until light and fluffy, about 2 minutes. Add the molasses and beat until incorporated. Add the egg and vanilla paste and beat until smooth. Beat in the dry ingredients at low speed until just combined. Stir in the candied ginger. Cover the bowl with plastic wrap and refrigerate until cold, at least 1 hour.

3. Preheat the oven to 325°. Line 2 baking sheets with parchment paper. Spread the turbinado sugar in a shallow bowl. Roll tablespoons of dough into balls, then coat in the turbinado sugar; transfer to the prepared baking sheets, spaced 1 inch apart. Freeze for 15 minutes.

4. Bake the cookies, rotating the baking sheets halfway through, for about 10 minutes, until crisp on the outside but still tender on the inside. Remove the baking sheets from the oven. Using the back of a ½-teaspoon measuring spoon, make an indentation in the center of each warm cookie. Transfer the baking sheets to wire racks and let cool completely.

5. Fill each cookie with about ½ teaspoon of the cold caramel and refrigerate just until set, about 30 minutes.
—*Ivan Arturo Marquez*

MAKE AHEAD The caramel can be refrigerated in an airtight container for up to a week. The cookies can be refrigerated for up to 3 days.

Molasses Thumbprints
with Cajeta

Persian Rice Cookies (Nan-e Berenji)

Active **30 min;** Total **2 hr 40 min;** Makes **40**

A thimble is the perfect tool for pressing the traditional Persian design into these cookies.

2¼ cups rice flour

1 Tbsp. cornstarch

1 cup clarified butter (see Note)

1 cup confectioners' sugar

3 large egg yolks

¼ cup pure rosewater, preferably Sadaf brand (see Note)

Poppy seeds, for sprinkling

1. Sift the rice flour with the cornstarch into a medium bowl. In a stand mixer fitted with the paddle, beat the clarified butter with the confectioners' sugar at medium speed until smooth, about 1 minute. At low speed, beat in the egg yolks one at a time, then gradually add the rosewater until incorporated. Add the dry ingredients and beat at low speed until smooth. Scrape the dough into a medium bowl, press a piece of plastic wrap directly on the surface and refrigerate until just firm, about 1 hour.

2. Preheat the oven to 350°. Line 3 large baking sheets with parchment paper. Scoop tablespoon-size mounds of the cookie dough onto the baking sheets. Roll the mounds into balls, then gently press them ½ inch thick. Using the wide end of a thimble, gently press 3 slightly overlapping rings onto each round. Sprinkle the center of each cookie with poppy seeds.

3. Bake the cookies for about 18 minutes, until they are firm and just starting to color on the bottom. Let cool completely, about 45 minutes. Using a thin metal spatula, transfer the cookies to a platter and serve.
—*Mahin Gilanpour Motamed*

NOTE To make clarified butter, melt 1 pound of butter over low heat. Remove from the heat and skim off the foam. Using a ladle, remove the clear melted butter, leaving the milky white solids behind; discard the solids. Refrigerate the clarified butter until solidified but not hard, about 30 minutes. Using a high-quality, pure rosewater is essential here. Look for Sadaf brand, available at kalustyans.com.

MAKE AHEAD The cookies can be stored in an airtight container for up to 3 days.

St. Nicholas Day Letters

Active **50 min;** Total **3 hr 15 min;** Makes **16**

L.A. chef David LeFevre twists his flaky, buttery almond cream–filled cookies into the letter S in honor of his sister, Suzanne, but they can be adapted to make any letter. Whatever the shape, a hit of fleur de sel just before baking kicks up the flavor.

1½ cups all-purpose flour

2 sticks unsalted butter, cubed and chilled

½ cup ice water

4 oz. almond paste

1 large egg white

⅓ cup granulated sugar

2 Tbsp. light brown sugar

½ tsp. pure vanilla extract

¼ tsp. ground cardamom

1 large egg

2 Tbsp. whole milk

Fleur de sel, for sprinkling

1. In a food processor, pulse the flour with the butter until the mixture resembles coarse meal. Add the ice water and pulse just until the dough comes together. Divide in half and press into disks. Wrap in plastic and refrigerate until firm, at least 1 hour or overnight.

2. Meanwhile, in a stand mixer fitted with the paddle, beat the almond paste with the egg white, both sugars, vanilla and cardamom at medium speed until smooth, about 4 minutes. Spoon the spiced almond paste into a pastry bag fitted with a ½-inch tip or use a sturdy, resealable plastic bag and snip off a corner.

3. Line 2 baking sheets with parchment paper. In a small bowl, lightly beat the egg with the milk. On a lightly floured surface, roll out 1 disk of dough into a 14-by-8-inch rectangle. Cut the dough crosswise into eight 1¾-inch strips.

4. Pipe a line of almond paste down the center of each strip. Brush one side of each strip with the beaten egg. Roll one side over the filling and pinch the seam closed. Transfer the logs to one of the prepared baking sheets seam side down. Form each log into an S shape. Repeat with the remaining disk of dough, almond paste and beaten egg. Freeze the cookies until firm, about 1 hour.

5. Preheat the oven to 375°. Brush the cookies with the remaining beaten egg and sprinkle with fleur de sel. Bake for 20 to 25 minutes, until golden. Transfer the cookies to a wire rack and let cool slightly. Serve warm or at room temperature.
—*David LeFevre*

MAKE AHEAD The cookies can be stored in an airtight container for up to 3 days.

Walnut Crescents

Active **30 min;** Total **50 min**
Makes **about 3½ dozen cookies**

2 cups walnuts

2 cups all-purpose flour

¼ tsp. fine sea salt

2 sticks salted butter, at room temperature

½ cup granulated sugar

1 vanilla bean, split lengthwise and seeds scraped

Confectioners' sugar, for dusting

1. Preheat the oven to 350°. Line 2 large rimmed baking sheets with parchment paper. In a food processor, pulse the walnuts with ½ cup of the flour until the walnuts are powdery, about 4 pulses. Add the remaining 1½ cups of flour and the salt and pulse to combine.

2. In a stand mixer fitted with the paddle, beat the butter, granulated sugar and vanilla bean seeds at moderately high speed until pale and light, about 2 minutes. Reduce the speed to low and gradually add the flour mixture until the dough comes together.

3. Roll tablespoons of the dough into balls on the prepared baking sheets. Using your hands, roll the balls of dough into 2-inch ropes. Taper the ends slightly and form the ropes into crescents. Bake the crescents for about 19 minutes, rotating the baking sheets halfway through, until the cookies are lightly browned around the edges. Transfer the baking sheets to a wire rack and let cool. Dust the crescents with confectioners' sugar before serving.
—*Nadine Levy Redzepi*

MAKE AHEAD The cookies can be stored in an airtight container for up to 5 days.

Christmas-Morning Biscotti

📷 PAGE 343

Active **25 min**; Total **1 hr 45 min**; Makes **24**

L.A. sous-chef Merrin Mae Gray is Filipina, not Italian, but she really connects with Italy's soulful food: "These biscotti spiced with cocoa nibs and anise seeds are my Italian interpretation of *biskotso*, a twice-baked cookie I grew up eating with hot chocolate."

Nonstick cooking spray

1¾ **cups all-purpose flour**

1 **tsp. baking powder**

½ **tsp. baking soda**

Kosher salt

5 **Tbsp. unsalted butter, softened**

⅔ **cup sugar**

3 **large eggs**

1 **Tbsp. plus 1 tsp. anisette liqueur**

¼ **cup cocoa nibs**

1½ **tsp. whole anise seeds**

1. Preheat the oven to 325°. Coat a baking sheet with cooking spray. Line with parchment paper; coat with cooking spray.

2. In a medium bowl, whisk the flour with the baking powder, baking soda and a pinch of salt. In a stand mixer fitted with the paddle, beat the butter with the sugar at medium-high speed until fluffy, about 3 minutes. Beat in 2 of the eggs one at a time. Beat in 1 tablespoon of the anisette. Beat in the dry ingredients at low speed until just combined. Mix in the cocoa nibs and anise seeds.

3. On the prepared baking sheet, using lightly floured fingers, shape the dough into a slightly flattened 12-inch log ¾ inch thick. In a small bowl, lightly whisk the remaining egg with the remaining 1 teaspoon of anisette. Brush the log with the egg mixture. Bake for 20 minutes, until pale golden. Transfer the baking sheet to a wire rack and let the log cool slightly.

4. Using a serrated knife, cut the log into diagonal, ½-inch-thick slices. Arrange on the baking sheet; bake, flipping halfway through, for about 10 minutes, until toasted. Transfer the baking sheet to a wire rack; let the biscotti cool.
—*Merrin Mae Gray*

MAKE AHEAD The biscotti can be stored in an airtight container for up to 1 week.

Tofu Doughnuts with Mezcal Condensed Milk

Active **40 min**; Total **1 hr 15 min**; Makes **16**

Austin chef Yoshi Okai's crisp fried doughnuts have an appealing chew, almost like mochi. He says, "At Nishiki Market in Kyoto, Japan, there is a tofu shop where they've been making tofu for over 50 years and tofu doughnuts for 25 to 30 years. I was a teenager when I ate them, and I re-created the recipe later because I was kind of homesick. I don't have a recipe for them from Nishiki, but I made them from memory, and I think they came out pretty good."

4 **oz. silken tofu, drained**

2 **tsp. sugar**

¾ **cup all-purpose flour**

1 **tsp. baking powder**

½ **tsp. kosher salt**

1 **Tbsp. mezcal**

⅓ **cup sweetened condensed milk**

Canola oil, for frying

1 **medium orange—peeled, supremed and cut into ½-inch pieces**

4 **tsp. extra-virgin olive oil**

Shichimi togarashi, for garnish

1. In a medium bowl, vigorously whisk the silken tofu with the sugar until smooth. Using a wooden spoon, stir in the flour, baking powder and salt until combined. Form the dough into 16 balls and transfer to a parchment paper–lined plate; freeze for 30 minutes.

2. Meanwhile, in a small saucepan, simmer the mezcal over moderate heat for about 3 minutes to burn off the alcohol. Whisk in the sweetened condensed milk and cook, stirring, until the mezcal sauce is hot and smooth. Let cool.

3. In a large saucepan, heat 1 inch of canola oil to 365°. Add half of the tofu balls and fry over moderately high heat, turning occasionally, until puffed and browned, about 6 minutes. Using a slotted spoon, transfer to paper towels to drain. Repeat with the remaining tofu balls.

4. Spoon 4 small dollops of the mezcal sauce onto each of 4 plates. Place a warm tofu doughnut on each dollop, then top with the orange pieces. Drizzle each plate with 1 teaspoon of olive oil and garnish with shichimi togarashi. Serve. —*Yoshi Okai*

MAKE AHEAD The uncooked tofu balls can be frozen overnight. Let stand for 15 minutes before frying. The mezcal sauce can be refrigerated for up to 1 week. Bring to room temperature before using.

Baking Wisdom

Christina Tosi, founder of the Milk Bar empire, wants to help amateur bakers "demystify the illusion that baking is a perfect pursuit." She does, however, have one crucial secret weapon that she uses in her desserts: "Start by using really great butter. Don't skimp on the butter. I like unsalted European-style butter. Really good butter kind of heals all in the flavor department."

Hanukkah Doughnuts

Hanukkah Doughnuts

Active **30 min**; Total **4 hr 30 min**; Makes **24**

Hebrew for "doughnuts," sufganiyot are the most popular Hanukkah food in Israel. Bakeries and markets start frying them weeks before the actual holiday and keep going until the week after. With TV chef Andrew Zimmern's recipe, you can prepare them year-round.

- ¾ **cup whole milk**
- 1 **Tbsp. active dry yeast**
- 3 **cups plus 1 Tbsp. all-purpose flour**
- ⅓ **cup superfine sugar**
- 6 **Tbsp. unsalted butter, at room temperature, diced**
- 1 **large egg**
- 4 **tsp. Armagnac or apple brandy**
- 1 **tsp. pure vanilla extract**
- ½ **tsp. kosher salt**
- 5 **cups canola oil, plus more for brushing**
- 1 **cup granulated sugar**
- 1 **Tbsp. ground cinnamon**
- 3 **cups strawberry jam**

1. In a small microwavable bowl, warm the milk at high power to 110°, 1 minute. Sprinkle the yeast over the milk and let stand until foamy, about 10 minutes.

2. In a stand mixer fitted with the dough hook, combine the flour with the superfine sugar. Add the milk mixture, the butter, egg, Armagnac, vanilla and salt. Knead at low speed, scraping down the side of the bowl, until the dough starts to come together, about 4 minutes. Increase the speed to medium and knead until the dough is soft and pulls away from the bowl, about 10 minutes.

3. Lightly brush a large bowl with oil. Place the dough in the bowl, cover with plastic wrap and let stand in a warm spot until doubled in bulk, about 2 hours. Lightly brush 2 rimmed baking sheets with oil. Punch down the dough and cut in half. Roll each half into a 12-inch log. Cut each log into 12 equal pieces, roll into balls and arrange on the prepared baking sheets, about 3 inches apart. Cover with plastic wrap and let stand until doubled in bulk, about 1½ hours.

4. In a medium bowl, combine the granulated sugar with the cinnamon.

5. In a large saucepan, heat the 5 cups of oil over moderate heat to 325°. Working in batches, fry the doughnuts, turning once, until golden, about 2 minutes per side. Using a slotted spoon, transfer the doughnuts as they're done to the cinnamon sugar and toss to coat. Let cool on a rack, about 15 minutes.

6. Spoon the jam into a pastry bag or small resealable plastic bag with 1 corner snipped. Pipe about 2 tablespoons of jam into 2 opposite ends of each doughnut and serve as soon as possible.
—*Andrew Zimmern*

MAKE AHEAD The doughnuts can be stored in an airtight container overnight.

Almond Rice Pudding with Sweet Cherry Sauce and Caramel Cream

Active **50 min**; Total **2 hr plus overnight chilling**; Serves **8**

A tangy-sweet cherry sauce and a dollop of caramel cream top this irresistible rice pudding from cookbook author Nadine Levy Redzepi.

- 1 **cup arborio rice**
- 5 **cups whole milk**
- 2 **vanilla beans—split lengthwise, seeds scraped and pods reserved**
- 1½ **cups plus 6 Tbsp. sugar**
- **Kosher salt**
- 2 **cups natural sweet cherry juice**
- 1 **tsp. cornstarch**
- ½ **lb. pitted fresh or thawed frozen sweet cherries**
- ¼ **cup boiling water**
- 2¼ **cups heavy cream**
- 1¼ **cups whole blanched almonds (7 oz.)**

1. Bring 1¼ cups of water to a boil in a medium saucepan. Add the rice and cook, stirring, for 3 minutes. Stir in the milk and one of the vanilla bean pods and its seeds and bring to a boil. Cover and cook over low heat, stirring occasionally, until the liquid is absorbed and the rice is tender, 35 to 40 minutes. Remove the saucepan from the heat. Immediately stir in 6 tablespoons of the sugar and 2 pinches of salt. Let cool, then discard the vanilla bean pod. Cover the rice pudding and refrigerate overnight.

2. In a medium saucepan, combine ¼ cup of the cherry juice with ½ cup of the sugar and the remaining vanilla bean pod and its seeds and bring to a boil over high heat. In a small bowl, whisk the remaining 1¾ cups of cherry juice with the cornstarch and pour into the saucepan. Continue to cook over high heat, whisking, until the sauce turns clear, about 4 minutes. Discard the vanilla bean pod. Stir in the cherries and keep the sauce warm.

3. In another medium saucepan, cook the remaining 1 cup of sugar over moderate heat, stirring, until a golden caramel forms, about 9 minutes; brush down the side of the pan with a wet pastry brush if crystals form. While whisking, slowly and carefully pour the boiling water into the caramel. Remove the pan from the heat and let cool.

4. In a medium bowl, using a hand mixer, beat 1¼ cups of the cream until soft peaks form. Using a spatula, fold the caramel into the whipped cream.

5. Stir the almonds into the chilled rice pudding. In a medium bowl, using a hand mixer, beat the remaining 1 cup of cream until firm peaks form, about 3 minutes. Fold the cream into the pudding and serve with the cherry and caramel sauces.
—*Nadine Levy Redzepi*

MAKE AHEAD The recipe can be prepared through Step 2 and refrigerated overnight.

Saffron Rice Pudding (Sholeh Zard)

Active **1 hr**; Total **3 hr 30 min** plus overnight soaking; Serves **8**

- 1 **cup jasmine rice**
- 1 **tsp. kosher salt**
- 1½ **cups sugar**
- 6 **Tbsp. Brewed Saffron (recipe follows)**
- 3 **Tbsp. unsalted butter**
- 3 **green cardamom pods, lightly cracked**
- 2 **Tbsp. pure rosewater, preferably Sadaf brand (see Note on p. 348)**
- **Ground cinnamon and slivered almonds, for garnish**

1. In a large bowl, cover the rice with water. Using your hand, agitate the rice to release the starch, then carefully pour off the water. Rinse the rice 5 to 7 more times, until the water runs clear. Cover the rice with water and refrigerate overnight. Drain, then coarsely crumble with your hands.

2. In a large nonstick saucepan, combine the crumbled rice with 9 cups of water and the salt and bring to a boil. Simmer over moderately low heat, stirring frequently, until the rice is softened, about 30 minutes.

3. Stir the sugar, brewed saffron, butter and cardamom into the rice. Cover and simmer over moderately low heat, stirring occasionally, until the rice breaks down and the pudding is the texture of loose porridge, 20 to 30 minutes; discard the cardamom pods. Stir in the rosewater. Spoon the pudding into 8 glasses and let cool slightly. Cover the glasses with plastic and refrigerate until thickened, about 1 hour.

4. Decorate the puddings with cinnamon and slivered almonds. Let stand at room temperature for 25 minutes before serving. —*Mahin Gilanpour Motamed*

BREWED SAFFRON

Active **5 min**; Total **15 min** plus cooling Makes **1½ cups**

- 1 **Tbsp. lightly packed saffron threads**
- 1½ **cups boiling water**

In a mortar, using a pestle, finely grind the saffron. In a heatproof jar, mix the finely ground saffron with the boiling water. Let stand until cool, then refrigerate for up to 1 week. —*MGM*

Rum-Caramel Bread Pudding with No-Churn Pumpkin Ice Cream and Candied Pepitas

📷 PAGE 325

Active **45 min**; Total **2 hr 40 min** Serves **10 to 12**

CARAMEL

- 1½ **cups sugar**
- 1½ **tsp. fresh lemon juice**
- 1 **vanilla bean, split lengthwise and seeds scraped**
- ¾ **cup heavy cream**
- 3 **Tbsp. cold unsalted butter, cubed**
- **Pinch of kosher salt**
- 3 **Tbsp. dark rum**

BREAD PUDDING

- **Unsalted butter, for greasing**
- 2 **cups whole milk**
- 2 **Tbsp. light brown sugar**
- 2 **cinnamon sticks**
- 2 **tsp. pure vanilla extract**
- **Pinch of salt**
- 4 **large eggs**
- **Two 14-oz. brioche loaves, torn into 2-inch pieces**
- **No-Churn Pumpkin Ice Cream and Candied Pepitas (recipes follow), for serving**

1. Make the caramel In a medium saucepan, mix the sugar, ¼ cup of water, the lemon juice and vanilla bean and seeds. Cook over moderately high heat until the sugar is dissolved. Using a wet pastry brush, wash down any crystals from the side of the pan. Continue to cook, gently swirling the pan occasionally, until an amber caramel forms, about 10 minutes.

2. Remove the pan from the heat and carefully whisk in the cream, butter and salt until smooth; the caramel will bubble up. Transfer to a bowl and let cool to warm, about 1 hour. Discard the vanilla pod, then stir in the rum.

3. Make the bread pudding Preheat the oven to 400°. Butter a 9-by-13-inch baking dish. In a small saucepan, combine the milk, brown sugar, cinnamon sticks, vanilla and salt. Bring just to a boil, then remove from the heat and let steep for 10 minutes; discard the cinnamon sticks.

4. In a large bowl, beat the eggs. Add the brioche and steeped milk and mix well. Scrape the mixture into the prepared baking dish and drizzle 1 cup of the warm caramel on top. Bake for 25 to 30 minutes, until puffed and the top is golden. Serve warm with No-Churn Pumpkin Ice Cream, Candied Pepitas and the remaining caramel. —*Ayesha Curry*

NO-CHURN PUMPKIN ICE CREAM

Total **30 min** plus overnight freezing; Serves **10 to 12**

- 1 **cup heavy cream**
- **One 14-oz. can sweetened condensed milk**
- ¾ **cup pure pumpkin puree**
- 1 **tsp. pure vanilla extract**
- ½ **tsp. ground cinnamon**
- **Kosher salt**

1. In a large chilled bowl, beat the heavy cream until stiff peaks form. In another large bowl, whisk the condensed milk with the pumpkin puree, vanilla, cinnamon and a pinch of salt. Fold one-third of the whipped cream into the pumpkin mixture to lighten it, then gently fold in the rest until no streaks remain.

2. Scrape the ice cream into a chilled 9-by-5-inch loaf pan. Press a piece of plastic wrap directly on the surface and freeze overnight before serving.

MAKE AHEAD The ice cream can be frozen for up to 3 days.

CANDIED PEPITAS

Total **20 min**; Makes **1 cup**

- 1 **cup pepitas**
- 2 **Tbsp. sugar**
- ¼ **tsp. freshly grated nutmeg**
- ¼ **tsp. ground cinnamon**
- ⅛ **tsp. cayenne**
- **Pinch of kosher salt**

In a large skillet, mix the pepitas with the sugar, nutmeg, cinnamon, cayenne and salt. Cook over moderate heat, stirring and tossing occasionally, until the pepitas are lightly browned and coated in a very light caramel, about 7 minutes. Transfer to a plate to cool completely before serving.

Saffron Rice Pudding
(Sholeh Zard)

Milk Chocolate–
Peanut Custards

Rhubarb Panna Cottas

Active **45 min;** Total **5 hr 30 min;** Serves **6**

1½ lbs. rhubarb stalks, chopped
  (½ inch)

½ cup plus ⅓ cup sugar
  Canola oil, for greasing

4 tsp. unflavored powdered gelatin

4 cups heavy cream

2 vanilla beans, split lengthwise
  and seeds scraped

3 Tbsp. chunky ginger preserves or
  chopped stem ginger in syrup

1 Tbsp. finely grated lemon zest
  plus 3 Tbsp. fresh lemon juice

2 Tbsp. chopped mint leaves

1. In a medium saucepan, combine half of the chopped rhubarb with ½ cup of the sugar and ¾ cup of water. Simmer over moderate heat until the syrup is deep pink, about 15 minutes. Remove from the heat and let steep for 1 hour. Strain the syrup through a fine sieve into a small bowl, pressing on the solids, then return the syrup to the saucepan. Discard the solids.

2. Lightly grease six 6-ounce ramekins. Fill a large bowl with ice water. In a small bowl, sprinkle the gelatin over ½ cup of the cream and let stand until softened, 5 to 10 minutes.

3. Add the remaining 3½ cups of cream and the vanilla seeds to the rhubarb syrup and bring to a simmer over moderately low heat; do not boil. Stir the softened gelatin into the saucepan until dissolved. Transfer the mixture to a medium bowl and set the bowl in the ice bath, stirring occasionally, until the custard is cool and begins to thicken, 15 to 20 minutes. Pour the mixture into the prepared ramekins and refrigerate until set, at least 4 hours.

4. Meanwhile, in a small saucepan, combine the remaining chopped rhubarb with the remaining ⅓ cup of sugar. Add ¾ cup of water, the ginger preserves, lemon zest and lemon juice. Cook over moderate heat, stirring, until the rhubarb is just softened, about 5 minutes; strain the syrup and reserve the poached rhubarb and ginger for garnish. Return the syrup to the saucepan and boil over moderately high heat until thickened and reduced by half, about 10 minutes. Transfer to a bowl; let cool. Stir in the mint.

5. Run a knife around the inside of each ramekin. Invert each panna cotta onto a plate. Spoon some poached rhubarb and ginger around each panna cotta, drizzle with the syrup and serve. —*Dane Allchorne*

MAKE AHEAD The panna cottas can be refrigerated for up to 2 days.

Milk Chocolate–Peanut Custards

Active **15 min;** Total **1 hr 15 min;** Serves **4**

San Francisco chef Matthew Accarrino of SPQR is a firm believer in making desserts nutritious. He uses pureed peanuts to thicken this rich chocolate custard and add a good amount of protein and fiber.

½ cup low-fat chocolate milk

⅓ cup heavy cream

⅔ cup roasted unsalted peanuts

3 oz. silken tofu

6½ oz. milk chocolate, chopped

1 Tbsp. light agave or corn syrup

¼ tsp. kosher salt
  Fat-free Greek-style vanilla yogurt,
  chocolate granola, unsweetened
  cocoa powder and coarse sea salt,
  for serving

1. In a small saucepan, combine the chocolate milk, cream and peanuts and cook over moderately low heat until it just comes to a boil. Transfer to a blender. Add the tofu, milk chocolate, agave syrup and kosher salt and blend at high speed until smooth, about 2 minutes (the mixture will be slightly grainy). Divide the custard into four 8-ounce ramekins or small dessert bowls. Refrigerate until set, 1 to 2 hours.

2. Serve the custards topped with vanilla yogurt, granola, a dusting of cocoa powder and a pinch of coarse sea salt.
—*Matthew Accarrino*

Cheese Flans

Active **35 min;** Total **4 hr;** Serves **8**

2 cups sugar

8 oz. cream cheese

½ cup ricotta cheese

4 large eggs

2 large egg yolks

1½ cups whole milk

1 cup heavy cream

1½ tsp. pure vanilla extract
  Pinch of kosher salt
  Boiling water

1. In a medium saucepan, stir 1 cup of the sugar with 3 tablespoons of water. Bring to a boil over moderate heat. Cook, swirling the pan occasionally, until an amber caramel forms, 6 to 8 minutes. Working quickly, pour the caramel into eight 8-ounce ceramic ramekins, swirling to coat the bottoms.

2. Preheat the oven to 325°. Line a small roasting pan with a double layer of paper towels and set the ramekins on the towels. In a large bowl, using a hand mixer, beat both cheeses with the remaining 1 cup of sugar at medium-high speed until very smooth, 1 to 2 minutes. Beat in the whole eggs and yolks one at a time until incorporated, then beat in the milk, heavy cream, vanilla and salt. Pour the custard into the prepared ramekins. Add enough boiling water to the roasting pan to reach halfway up the sides of the ramekins.

3. Loosely tent the pan with foil and bake the flans for about 50 minutes, until just set but still jiggly in the center. Using tongs, carefully transfer the ramekins to a rack and let the flans cool completely. Cover the ramekins with plastic and refrigerate for at least 2 hours or overnight.

4. Run a thin knife around each flan. Invert a plate over each ramekin, then turn the flan out onto the plate, shaking the ramekin gently if necessary. Serve immediately.
—*Anya von Bremzen*

WINE Nutty oloroso sherry: El Maestro Sierra 15 Años.

Goat Milk–and–Corn Panna Cotta with Blackberries

Active **1 hr 15 min**; Total **5 hr 35 min**
Serves **6**

- 5 ears of corn, preferably white, shucked
- 1 cup whole goat milk
- 1 cup heavy cream
- ¼ cup honey
- 1 tsp. vanilla bean paste
- 3 thyme sprigs, plus 1 tsp. thyme leaves
-   Kosher salt
- 1 envelope unflavored gelatin (2¼ tsp.)
-   Nonstick cooking spray
- 1 pint blackberries, halved
- 2 Tbsp. sugar
- ¼ tsp. finely grated lemon zest plus 1 Tbsp. fresh lemon juice
-   Caramel corn, for garnish

1. Cut the kernels off the corncobs and transfer to a blender; reserve 3 of the cobs. Puree the kernels until smooth, 1 to 2 minutes. Strain the puree through a fine sieve set over a medium bowl, pressing on the solids; discard the solids. You should have about 1 cup of corn juice.

2. In a medium saucepan, whisk the corn juice with the goat milk, heavy cream, honey, vanilla bean paste, thyme sprigs and ¼ teaspoon of salt. Add the reserved corncobs and bring to a simmer over low heat. Remove from the heat and let steep for 10 minutes, then discard the corncobs and strain the panna cotta base through a fine sieve set over a medium bowl.

3. In a small bowl, sprinkle the gelatin over 3 tablespoons of water and let stand until softened, about 3 minutes. Whisk the gelatin mixture into the strained panna cotta base until dissolved, then strain again through a fine sieve set over a large measuring cup with a spout.

4. Lightly grease six 6-ounce ramekins with nonstick spray and set them on a rimmed baking sheet. Fill the ramekins with the panna cotta base, cover and refrigerate until set, at least 4 hours or overnight.

5. In a medium bowl, toss the blackberries with the sugar, lemon zest and juice, the thyme leaves and a pinch of salt. Let stand until juicy, about 1 hour.

6. Run a knife around the panna cottas and invert onto plates. Top with the blackberries and caramel corn; serve immediately. —*Brooke Williamson*

Vanilla Cupcake Ice Cream Sandwiches

Active **45 min**; Total **3 hr 45 min**; Makes **6**

- 1½ cups all-purpose flour
- 1½ tsp. baking powder
- ¼ tsp. kosher salt
- ⅔ cup whole milk
- 1½ tsp. pure vanilla extract
- 1 stick unsalted butter, at room temperature
- ¾ cup sugar
- 2 large eggs, at room temperature
- 1 pint pistachio ice cream or sorbet, slightly softened

1. Preheat the oven to 325°. Line a 12-cup muffin pan with paper liners. In a medium bowl, whisk the flour with the baking powder and salt. In a small bowl, whisk the milk with the vanilla.

2. In a stand mixer fitted with the paddle, beat the butter with the sugar at medium-high speed, scraping down the bowl once or twice, until light and fluffy, about 2 minutes. At medium-low speed, beat in the eggs one at a time until incorporated. At low speed, beat in the dry ingredients and the milk mixture in 3 alternating additions until smooth. Spoon about ¼ cup of the batter into each prepared cup.

3. Bake the cupcakes for 25 to 30 minutes, until a toothpick inserted in the centers comes out clean. Let cool in the pan for 5 minutes, then cool completely on a wire rack, about 1 hour.

4. Working with 1 cupcake at a time, peel off the liner. Turn the cupcake top side down in the palm of one hand, cover with the other hand and gently twist off the cake top. Reserve the cupcake bottom for another use. Arrange the top smooth side down on a platter. Repeat with the remaining cupcakes. Freeze the tops for 1 hour.

5. Spread ¼ cup of the ice cream onto each of 6 cupcake tops. Close the sandwiches with the remaining cupcake tops and gently press together. Freeze for 30 minutes before serving. —*Candace Nelson*

Neapolitan Tacos

Active **40 min**; Total **50 min**
Serves **20**

PIZZELLES

- ⅔ cup all-purpose flour
- 6 Tbsp. granulated sugar
- 2 Tbsp. Dutch-process cocoa
- 2 Tbsp. baking powder
- ¼ tsp. kosher salt
- 4 Tbsp. unsalted butter, melted
- ¼ cup whole milk
- 1 large egg

FILLING

- 2½ cups chopped fresh strawberries (about 14 oz.)
- 2 Tbsp. granulated sugar
- 1½ Tbsp. chopped fresh mint
- 7½ cups vanilla ice cream

1. Make the pizzelles Preheat a pizzelle maker according to the manufacturer's instructions. In a medium bowl, whisk together the flour, sugar, cocoa, baking powder and salt. In a small bowl, whisk together the melted butter, milk and egg; add to the flour mixture and whisk until blended and smooth.

2. Coat the pizzelle maker with cooking spray. Spoon 1 tablespoon of the batter in the hot pizzelle maker; cook until set and slightly darker in color, 45 to 50 seconds. Use a small offset spatula to remove the pizzelle and immediately drape it over the handle of a wooden spoon (about ¾ inch to 1 inch in diameter) to form a taco shape; let stand until completely cool, about 3 minutes. Transfer to a wire rack and repeat with remaining batter.

3. Make the filling In a medium bowl, combine the strawberries, sugar and mint; let stand for about 10 minutes, stirring occasionally to dissolve the sugar.

4. Spoon 3 small scoops of the vanilla ice cream (about 2 tablespoons per scoop) into each pizzelle taco; top each with about 1½ tablespoons of the strawberry mixture. —*Valerie Bertinelli*

MAKE AHEAD The pizzelle shells can be refrigerated in an airtight container for up to 1 week

Goat Milk–and–Corn Panna
Cotta with Blackberries

Rosewater-and-Saffron
Ice Cream (Bastani Irani)

Peaches and Cream Ice Cream Cake

Active **50 min**; Total **3 hr plus overnight freezing**; Serves **8 to 10**

In a riff on traditional ice cream cake, F&W's Laura Rege spreads ice cream in between and all around the tender cake layers, omitting any use of frosting in the recipe.

- **1 stick unsalted butter, at room temperature, plus more for greasing**
- **1½ cups all-purpose flour**
- **1½ tsp. baking powder**
- **½ tsp. baking soda**
- **Kosher salt**
- **2 cups plus 1 Tbsp. sugar**
- **½ vanilla bean, split lengthwise and seeds scraped**
- **2 large eggs**
- **⅔ cup buttermilk**
- **3 lbs. firm ripe peaches—2 lbs. peeled and cut into 1-inch chunks, 1 lb. sliced into thin wedges**
- **5 pints vanilla ice cream, softened slightly**
- **¼ cup heavy cream**

1. Preheat the oven to 350°. Butter a 9-inch round springform pan and line the bottom with parchment paper. Butter the parchment. In a medium bowl, whisk the flour with the baking powder, baking soda and ¼ teaspoon of salt. In the bowl of a stand mixer fitted with the paddle, beat the stick of butter with 1 cup of the sugar and the vanilla seeds at medium-high speed until light and fluffy, about 4 minutes. Beat in the eggs one at a time. At low speed, alternately beat in the dry ingredients and buttermilk until just combined.

2. Scrape the batter into the prepared pan and bake for about 35 minutes, until a toothpick inserted in the center comes out clean. Let the cake cool on a wire rack for 30 minutes, then remove the ring and let cool completely.

3. Meanwhile, in a medium saucepan, combine the peach chunks with 1 cup of the sugar and a large pinch of salt. Bring to a boil, stirring until the sugar is dissolved, then simmer over moderate heat, stirring occasionally, until the fruit is broken down and the sugar is just beginning to caramelize, about 20 minutes. Let the jam cool.

4. Using a serrated knife, trim the cake to form a 7-inch round, then trim the domed top to flatten it; reserve the scraps for another use. Discard the parchment. Cut the cake horizontally into 2 even layers and place them side by side on a baking sheet. Spread the peach jam evenly on top of both cakes. Freeze until the jam is firm, about 15 minutes.

5. Place a clean 9-inch springform pan on a rimmed baking sheet. Place one of the cake rounds in the center of the springform pan. Spread 2½ pints of the ice cream over the jam and around the side of the cake, filling the space between the cake and the pan. Level the ice cream with an offset spatula. Freeze until the ice cream is firm, about 20 minutes.

6. Place the second cake layer on top of the first. Spread the remaining 2½ pints of ice cream over the jam and around the side of the cake, as with the first layer. Level the ice cream with the offset spatula; the ice cream should be flush with the top of the springform pan. Cover and freeze overnight.

7. Rub a hot, wet towel around the outside of the pan to loosen the cake. Remove the ring and transfer the cake to a platter. Return the cake to the freezer.

8. In the bowl of a stand mixer fitted with the whisk, beat the heavy cream with the remaining 1 tablespoon of sugar until firm peaks form. Spread the whipped cream on top of the cake and arrange the peach wedges in a decorative pattern on top. Freeze the cake for 20 minutes before serving. —*Laura Rege*

MAKE AHEAD The cake can be prepared through Step 6, wrapped in plastic and frozen for up to 1 week.

Rosewater-and-Saffron Ice Cream (Bastani Irani)

Active **45 min**; Total **9 hr 15 min** Makes **about 1 qt**

In Iran, this ice cream is sold sandwiched between two wafers, but it's equally delicious on its own. We decorate it with fragrant dried Mohammadi roses from the Isfahan province of Iran.

- **6 large egg yolks**
- **1½ cups heavy cream**
- **1½ cups whole milk**
- **¾ cup sugar**
- **½ tsp. kosher salt**
- **½ tsp. saffron, finely ground**
- **¼ cup pure rosewater, preferably Sadaf brand (see Note on p. 348)**
- **½ tsp. pure vanilla extract**
- **Dried roses, for garnish**

1. Set a medium bowl in a large bowl of ice water. In another medium bowl, beat the egg yolks until pale, 1 to 2 minutes.

2. In a medium saucepan, whisk the cream with the milk, sugar, salt and saffron. Bring to a simmer over moderate heat, whisking, until the sugar is completely dissolved. Very gradually whisk half of the hot cream mixture into the beaten egg yolks in a thin stream, then whisk this mixture back into the saucepan. Cook over moderately low heat, stirring constantly with a wooden spoon, until the custard is thick enough to lightly coat the back of the spoon, about 12 minutes; don't let it boil.

3. Strain the custard through a fine-mesh sieve into the bowl set in the ice water. Let the custard cool completely, stirring occasionally. Stir in the rosewater and vanilla extract. Press a piece of plastic wrap directly on the custard and refrigerate until well chilled, at least 4 hours.

4. Pour the custard base into an ice cream maker and freeze according to the manufacturer's instructions. Transfer the ice cream to a chilled 9-by-4-inch metal loaf pan, cover and freeze until firm, at least 4 hours.

5. Serve the ice cream in bowls, garnished with dried roses.
—*Mahin Gilanpour Motamed*

SNACKS, CONDIMENTS & SAUCES

Grandfather's
Pickles (p. 375)
OPPOSITE Cheesy
Nachos with Fried
Eggs and Giardiniera
(p. 365)

Mexican Corn Popcorn

📷 PAGE 366

⏱ Total **30 min**; Serves **6**

Jen Pelka, of The Riddler Champagne bar in San Francisco, offers flavored popcorns to snack on while drinking Champagne.

- **½ cup white cheese powder, such as King Arthur Vermont Cheese Powder (see Note)**
- **2 Tbsp. kosher salt**
- **1 tsp. chipotle chile powder**
- **1 tsp. crushed dried cilantro**
- **½ tsp. ground dried lime zest or 1 tsp. finely grated lime zest**
- **¼ tsp. cayenne**
- **⅓ cup canola oil**
- **¾ cup popping corn**
- **4 Tbsp. unsalted butter, melted**

1. In a bowl, mix the cheese powder, salt, chile powder, cilantro, zest and cayenne.

2. In a large saucepan, combine the oil and popping corn. Cover and cook over moderately high heat until it starts to pop. Shake the pan and cook, shaking occasionally, until the corn stops popping, 3 to 5 minutes. Transfer to a large bowl, add the melted butter and toss to coat. Add the cheese mixture and toss again. Serve. —*Jen Pelka*

NOTE King Arthur Vermont Cheese Powder is available at kingarthurflour.com.

Everything-Bagel Popcorn

📷 PAGE 366

⏱ Total **25 min**; Serves **6**

- **2 tsp. caraway seeds**
- **2 Tbsp. flaky sea salt**
- **1 tsp. black sesame seeds**
- **1 tsp. white sesame seeds**
- **2 tsp. granulated garlic**
- **2 tsp. granulated onion**
- **⅓ cup canola oil**
- **¾ cup popping corn**
- **4 Tbsp. unsalted butter, melted**

1. In a small skillet, toast the caraway seeds over moderate heat, shaking the pan, until fragrant, about 1 minute. Transfer to a mortar. Add the salt and, using a pestle, coarsely crush the seeds and salt. Transfer to a small bowl.

2. In the skillet, toast the black and white sesame seeds over moderate heat, shaking the pan, until fragrant and the white seeds are golden, about 2 minutes. Transfer to the small bowl and stir in the granulated garlic and onion.

3. In a large saucepan, combine the oil and popping corn. Cover and cook over moderately high heat until the corn starts to pop. Continue cooking, shaking the pan occasionally, until the corn stops popping, 3 to 5 minutes. Transfer to a large bowl, add the melted butter and toss to coat. Add the everything-bagel spices and toss again. Serve. —*Jen Pelka*

MAKE AHEAD The popcorn can be stored in an airtight container overnight.

Spiced Candied Almonds

Active **25 min**; Total **45 min** plus cooling
Makes **2 cups**

Inspired by the candied nuts sold at carts throughout New York City, these not-too-sweet toasted almonds have a great crackly shell.

- **2 cups raw almonds**
- **¼ cup light corn syrup**
- **2 tsp. kosher salt**
- **1 tsp. sweet pimentón de la Vera**
- **½ tsp. piment d'Espelette**

1. Preheat the oven to 325° and line a large rimmed baking sheet with parchment paper. Lightly coat a large bowl and 2 large spoons with nonstick spray. Spread the almonds on the baking sheet and bake for about 10 minutes, until golden. Transfer to the prepared bowl. Leave the oven on.

2. In a small saucepan, combine the corn syrup with the salt, pimentón de la Vera, piment d'Espelette and 1 tablespoon of water. Cook over moderate heat, stirring occasionally, until hot and thin, 3 to 5 minutes. Immediately drizzle the hot syrup over the almonds and, using the greased spoons, toss to coat.

3. Spread the almonds on the parchment paper–lined baking sheet; bake for 10 minutes, until coated in a sticky glaze; stir the almonds twice during baking. Return the nuts to the greased bowl and let cool, stirring occasionally to separate them. —*Daniel Humm*

Mixed Nuts with Crispy Herbs and Garlic

⏱ Total **30 min**; Makes **about 4 cups**

For the most addictive snack, F&W's Justin Chapple crisps garlic, sage and rosemary in oil, then uses that fragrant oil to coat a mix of pecans, cashews, pistachios and almonds.

- **1 cup raw pecans**
- **1 cup raw cashews**
- **Extra-virgin olive oil, for frying**
- **6 large garlic cloves, very thinly sliced**
- **6 large rosemary sprigs (6 inches each), stemmed**
- **½ cup lightly packed sage leaves**
- **1 cup unsalted shelled pistachios**
- **1 cup roasted unsalted marcona almonds**
- **Kosher salt and pepper**

1. Preheat the oven to 350°. Spread the pecans and cashews on a rimmed baking sheet and toast for 8 to 10 minutes, until fragrant and the cashews are golden. Let cool.

2. Meanwhile, in a large skillet, heat ¼ inch of olive oil until shimmering. Add the garlic and cook over moderate heat, stirring, until golden and crisp, about 5 minutes. Using a slotted spoon, transfer the crispy garlic to paper towels to drain. Carefully add the rosemary and sage to the skillet and cook until the sizzling slows and the herbs are crisp, about 30 seconds. Using a slotted spoon, transfer to paper towels to drain.

3. Pour off all but 2 tablespoons of the garlic-herb oil from the skillet. Add the toasted nuts along with the pistachios and almonds and cook over moderate heat, tossing and stirring frequently, until the nuts are warm and coated in the oil, 1 to 2 minutes. Season generously with salt and pepper, then fold in the crispy garlic and herbs. Transfer to a medium bowl and serve warm or at room temperature. —*Justin Chapple*

MAKE AHEAD The mixed nuts can be stored in an airtight container at room temperature for up to 5 days.

Mixed Nuts with Crispy
Herbs and Garlic

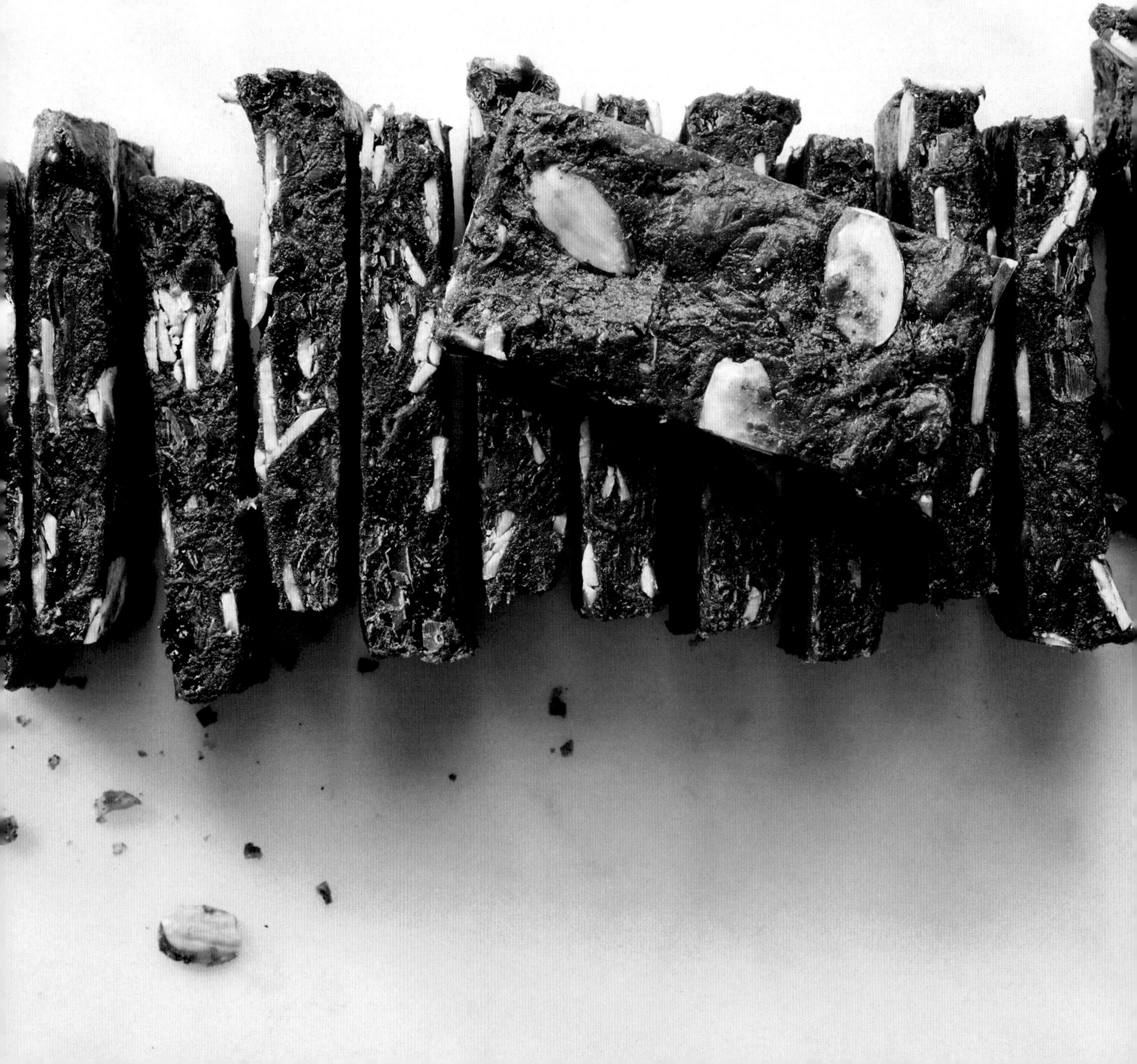

Tobacco Onions

Active **25 min**; Total **2 hr 30 min**
Serves **4 to 6**

The name of this old English dish came about because people used to think these crispy fried onions tossed with paprika and celery salt looked like shaved tobacco.

- **3 large white onions (2 lbs.), halved lengthwise and very thinly sliced crosswise**
- **2 cups whole milk**
- **2 cups all-purpose flour**
- **¼ cup plus 2 Tbsp. smoked paprika**
- **2½ Tbsp. celery salt**
- **2½ qts. canola or vegetable oil**
- **Kosher salt**

1. In a large bowl, combine the onions with the milk and stir to coat. Cover and refrigerate for 2 hours.

2. In a medium bowl, whisk the flour with the paprika and celery salt. Drain the onions very well in a colander, then set the colander over a large bowl. Sprinkle the flour mixture over the onions and toss with your hands to evenly coat. Shake well to remove any excess flour.

3. In a large saucepan, heat the oil to 350°. In about 5 batches, fry the onions over moderate heat until golden brown, about 2 minutes per batch. Using a slotted spoon, transfer the onions to paper towels to drain; season lightly with salt. Return the oil to 350° between batches. Serve hot.
—*James Golding*

Cheesy Nachos with Fried Eggs and Giardiniera

📷 PAGE 360

🕐 Total **30 min**; Serves **6**

- **3 Tbsp. extra-virgin olive oil, plus more for brushing**
- **12 oz. sweet Italian sausage, casings removed**
- **One 13-oz. bag thick-cut tortilla chips**
- **1½ lbs. Monterey Jack, coarsely shredded (6 cups)**
- **One 15-oz. can black beans, rinsed and drained**
- **1½ cups chopped mixed drained giardiniera**
- **1½ cups chopped mixed pickled sweet and hot peppers, such as peperoncini and Peppadew**
- **6 large eggs**
- **Kosher salt**
- **Chopped cilantro, for garnish**
- **Hot sauce and sour cream, for serving**

1. Preheat the oven to 400°. In a medium skillet, heat 1 tablespoon of the olive oil. Add the sausage and cook over moderate heat, breaking it up with a wooden spoon, until just cooked through, about 6 minutes. Transfer to a plate.

2. Brush a large rimmed baking sheet with olive oil. Spread half of the tortilla chips on the sheet and top with half each of the cheese, beans, giardiniera, pickled peppers and sausage. Repeat the layering with the remaining tortillas chips, cheese, beans, giardiniera, pickled peppers and sausage. Bake for 12 to 15 minutes, until the cheese is melted.

3. Meanwhile, in a large nonstick skillet, heat 1 tablespoon of the olive oil. Crack 3 eggs into the skillet. Season with salt and cook over moderately high heat until the whites are firm and the yolks are runny, 3 to 5 minutes. Using a spatula, transfer to a plate. Repeat with the remaining 1 tablespoon of olive oil and 3 eggs.

4. Top the nachos with the fried eggs. Garnish with cilantro and serve with hot sauce and sour cream. —*Justin Chapple*

BEER Lightly hoppy pale ale: Deschutes Mirror Pond.

Clean Bars

Active **30 min**; Total **2 hr 30 min**
Makes **about 18**

San Francisco chef Chris Cosentino is an avid cyclist. He developed these clean bars to take on the road: They have minimal ingredients but pack a ton of flavor. His secret ingredient is coffee salt, which gives a jolt of energy while also replenishing sodium levels.

- **Nonstick spray, for greasing**
- **½ cup sliced almonds**
- **1 lb. Medjool dates, split and pitted**
- **Two 3.5-oz. dark chocolate bars (72%), coarsely chopped**
- **¾ cup raisins**
- **1½ Tbsp. Bitterman's Espresso Salt (see Note)**
- **1 Tbsp. extra-virgin olive oil**

1. Preheat the oven to 350°. Grease the bottom and sides of a 9-inch-square baking pan with nonstick spray. Line the pan with parchment paper, allowing a 2-inch overhang on 2 sides.

2. Spread the almonds in a pie plate and bake in the oven for about 5 minutes, until lightly toasted. Let cool completely.

3. In a stand mixer fitted with the paddle, beat the dates with the chocolate at medium speed until the dates are pasty and the chocolate is evenly distributed, about 1 minute. At low speed, beat in the toasted almonds, raisins, coffee salt and olive oil until well mixed, about 5 minutes; scrape down the side of the bowl as needed.

4. Transfer the mixture to the prepared pan, top with a lightly greased sheet of parchment paper and pack in an even layer. Refrigerate until well chilled, about 2 hours. Cut into 18 bars and serve chilled.
—*Chris Cosentino*

NOTE Bitterman's Espresso Salt is available at themeadow.com. You can also substitute 1 tablespoon of flaky sea salt mixed with 1½ teaspoons of instant espresso powder.

MAKE AHEAD The bars can be refrigerated in an airtight container for up to 1 week.

Red, White and Black
Gunpowders (p. 374-375)
OPPOSITE Mexican
Corn Popcorn and
Everything-Bagel
Popcorn (p. 362)

Grass-Fed Beef Jerky

Active **45 min;** Total **6 hr 45 min plus 3 with marinating;** Makes **1 lb.**

Seamus Mullen of NYC's Tertulia restaurant makes his delightful beef jerky with grass-fed flank steak. He seasons it with Bragg Liquid Aminos (similar to tamari) as well as ginger, garlic, maple and smoky chipotle. It holds up well in the fridge, making it perfect for snacking.

½ **cup Bragg Liquid Aminos sauce (see Note)**

2 **Tbsp. finely grated peeled fresh ginger**

2 **Tbsp. finely grated garlic**

1 **Tbsp. pure maple syrup**

1 **Tbsp. adobo sauce (from a can of chipotles in adobo)**

1 **Tbsp. coarsely ground black pepper**

1 **tsp. fine sea salt**

2 **lbs. grass-fed flank steak, frozen for 45 minutes, then sliced ⅛ inch thick against the grain**

1. In a large resealable plastic bag, whisk together everything except the flank steak. Add the steak, seal the bag and turn to coat. Refrigerate for at least 3 hours or up to 6 hours.

2. Preheat the oven to 165° or the lowest possible setting. Set a rack on each of 3 large rimmed baking sheets. Remove the beef from the marinade and spread the slices on the racks, leaving ¼ inch between the slices. Bake for about 6 hours, or until the jerky is dried but still chewy; flip the slices halfway through baking. Let cool on the racks before serving. —*Seamus Mullen*

NOTE Bragg Liquid Aminos is a gluten-free, soybean-based sauce that's often used in place of soy sauce and tamari. It's available on amazon.com.

MAKE AHEAD The beef jerky can be refrigerated for 2 weeks.

Cranberry Sauce with Cointreau and Star Anise

Active **15 min;** Total **40 min plus chilling** Makes **5 cups**

Food Network star Ayesha Curry adds Cointreau and orange zest to her cranberry sauce to infuse it with big, boozy citrus flavor.

Two 12-oz. bags fresh or frozen cranberries

2 **cups sugar**

1½ **cups water**

¼ **cup Cointreau**

Two ½-inch-wide strips of orange zest, preferably blood orange

6 **whole star anise, wrapped in damp cheesecloth and tied**

1½ **tsp. ground cinnamon**

Pinch of kosher salt

In a large saucepan, combine all the ingredients and bring to a boil. Simmer over moderately low heat, stirring frequently, until the cranberries burst and the sauce is jamlike, 20 to 25 minutes. Transfer to a bowl and discard the star anise sachet and zest. Let cool completely, then refrigerate until chilled. —*Ayesha Curry*

Roasted Cranberry-Grape Sauce

Active **5 min;** Total **1 hr;** Serves **10**

1 **lb. seedless red grapes, stemmed**

Two 10-oz. bags fresh or thawed frozen cranberries (5 cups)

⅔ **cup sugar**

6 **thyme sprigs**

2 **tsp. finely grated lemon zest plus 1 Tbsp. fresh lemon juice**

Pinch of kosher salt

Preheat the oven to 425°. On a parchment paper–lined baking sheet, toss the grapes with the cranberries, sugar, thyme, lemon zest, lemon juice and salt. Roast, stirring halfway through, until the cranberries and grapes just start to burst, 20 minutes. Let cool before serving. —*Laura Rege*

Homemade Applesauce with Chinese Five-Spice

Active **30 min;** Total **2 hr;** Serves **8**

Chinese five-spice is a bold and fragrant mix of five or more spices. Here, Erika Nakamura uses six.

3 **allspice berries**

3 **whole cloves**

½ **Tbsp. fennel seeds**

1 **tsp. whole black peppercorns**

½ **cinnamon stick**

1 **star anise**

6 **Granny Smith apples—peeled, cored and thinly sliced**

6 **McIntosh apples—peeled, cored and thinly sliced**

7 **Tbsp. fresh lemon juice**

2 **Tbsp. light brown sugar**

2 **Tbsp. unsalted butter**

Flaky sea salt

1. Preheat the oven to 350°. Wrap the allspice, cloves, fennel seed, black peppercorns, cinnamon stick and star anise in a small piece of cheesecloth. Using twine, tie the cheesecloth into a bundle.

2. In a large bowl, toss the apples with 6 tablespoons of the lemon juice and the brown sugar. In a large Dutch oven, melt the butter. Add the apples and cook over moderately high heat, stirring occasionally, until they begin to let off moisture, about 5 minutes. Put the spice bundle in the pot, cover and transfer to the oven. Bake for about 1 hour and 30 minutes, until the apples have softened.

3. Discard the spice bundle. Add the remaining 1 tablespoon of lemon juice to the apples, season with sea salt and stir until a chunky sauce forms. Scrape the applesauce into a bowl and serve warm or cover and refrigerate until chilled.

MAKE AHEAD The applesauce can be refrigerated in an airtight container for up to 5 days.

Roasted Cranberry-
Grape Sauce

Guajillo Mayonnaise, Green Cocktail Sauce, Apple-Cucumber Mignonette

Yogurt-and-Cucumber Salad (Mast-o Khiar)

Total **15 min**; Serves **8**

Mast-o Khiar is a refreshing Persian yogurt salad made with cucumbers, dill, garlic and shallot. It can be served alongside everything from flatbread to meats and fish.

- **2 cups Greek yogurt**
- **4 small Persian cucumbers, finely diced**
- **½ cup finely chopped dill**
- **1 small shallot, minced**
- **1 small garlic clove, minced**
- **Kosher salt and pepper**
- **Dried mint and rose petals, for garnish**

In a medium bowl, stir the yogurt with the cucumbers, dill, shallot and garlic; season with salt and pepper. Transfer to a serving bowl and garnish with dried mint and rose petals. —*Mahin Gilanpour Motamed*

Guajillo Mayonnaise

Active **15 min**; Total **45 min**
Makes **1½ cups**

- **½ cup extra-virgin olive oil**
- **2 guajillo chiles—stemmed, seeded and chopped**
- **1 cup mayonnaise**
- **Kosher salt and pepper**

1. In a medium skillet, heat the olive oil until shimmering. Add the chiles and fry over moderate heat, stirring, until fragrant and the color deepens, about 30 seconds. Remove from the heat; let cool completely.

2. In a food processor, combine the chiles and oil with the mayonnaise and puree until nearly smooth. Scrape into a bowl and season with salt and pepper. —*Justin Chapple*

MAKE AHEAD The Guajillo Mayonnaise can be refrigerated in an airtight container for up to 2 weeks.

SERVE WITH Chilled cooked lobster tails and shrimp.

Green Cocktail Sauce

Total **40 min**; Makes **2 cups**

Elevate a shellfish platter with this easy and addictive sauce.

- **1 lb. tomatillos—husked, rinsed and quartered**
- **1 cup lightly packed cilantro**
- **2 Tbsp. drained prepared horseradish**
- **1 Tbsp. green hot sauce**
- **Kosher salt and pepper**

In a food processor, combine everything except the salt and pepper. Puree until nearly smooth. Scrape into a bowl and season with salt and pepper. Cover and refrigerate until chilled, about 30 minutes. —*Justin Chapple*

MAKE AHEAD The sauce can be refrigerated in an airtight container for up to 1 week.

SERVE WITH Shucked oysters and chilled cooked lobster tails and shrimp.

Apple-Cucumber Mignonette

Total **40 min**; Makes **1½ cups**

- **¾ cup Champagne vinegar**
- **¼ Pink Lady or Honeycrisp apple, cored and minced**
- **1 Persian cucumber, minced**
- **2 Tbsp. minced chives**
- **1 tsp. coarsely ground white pepper**
- **Kosher salt**

In a medium bowl, whisk together everything except the salt. Season the mignonette with salt, cover and refrigerate until chilled, about 30 minutes. —*Justin Chapple*

MAKE AHEAD The mignonette can be refrigerated for up to 3 days.

SERVE WITH Shucked oysters and chilled cooked lobster tails and shrimp.

Party-Throwing Commandments

Rico Gagliano and Brendan Francis Newnam, hosts of The Dinner Party Download podcast and authors of *Brunch Is Hell*, lay down a few rules for entertaining.

FLOWERS MAKE A GREAT CENTERPIECE...BEFORE DINNER. "They not only give off scents that can conflict with food, but they block sight lines and make everyone feel like they're talking to plants. That worked out for Moses but will drive your guests insane."

APPETIZERS ARE PREVENTATIVE CARE. "Without snacks to graze on, your hungry dinner party guest could have one martini and promptly become drunk and prone to looking up exes on Facebook."

ASK ABOUT ALLERGIES. "You may be right to suspect that the self-diagnosed "celiac" at your dinner party is a fad dieter. But don't find out you're wrong by sneaking in wheat and making them pop like a balloon."

MIX UP THE GUEST LIST. "The most interesting gatherings are ones where some of the guests are people you don't 1,000 percent agree with."

THE IDEAL DINNER PARTY IS A MUSICAL DICTATORSHIP. "Be vigilant! Otherwise you'll find your stereo hijacked by guests who insist that everybody just has to hear this one song."

EMBRACE THE PDPDP (Post-Dinner-Party Dance Party). "As we get older, opportunities to dance dwindle. But the tail end of a dinner party is the perfect time to dance: Everyone is friends and everyone is loose."

SAVE THE DISHES FOR THE MORNING. "Just be sure to soak pots with egg or strands of pasta grafted onto them—or you'll need a pickax to get that off tomorrow."

Basic Tomato Sauce

Active **15 min**; Total **1 hr**; Makes **3 cups**

Georgia chef Hugh Acheson uses a little grated carrot to offset the acidity in his tomato sauce.

- **2 Tbsp. extra-virgin olive oil**
- **1 small white onion, finely chopped**
- **1 medium carrot, grated**
- **One 28-oz. can whole plum tomatoes in juice, coarsely pureed**
- **Kosher salt**
- **1 Tbsp. unsalted butter**
- **2 tsp. fresh oregano, finely chopped**

In a medium saucepan, heat the olive oil over moderate heat until shimmering. Add the onion and cook, stirring, until softened, about 8 minutes. Stir in the carrot, then add the tomatoes and season with salt. Simmer over moderately low heat, stirring occasionally, until the sauce has thickened, about 40 minutes. Remove from the heat and stir in the butter and oregano. —*Hugh Acheson*

MAKE AHEAD The tomato sauce can be refrigerated for up to 1 week.

Romesco Sauce

Active **45 min**; Total **1 hr 15 min**
Makes **2½ cups**

- **4 dried Nora or ancho chiles (¾ oz.), stemmed and seeded**
- **4 sun-dried tomatoes**
- **2 plum tomatoes**
- **¼ cup plus 2 Tbsp. extra-virgin olive oil**
- **Two ½-inch-thick slices of baguette**
- **6 large garlic cloves, halved lengthwise**
- **½ cup blanched almonds**
- **¼ cup blanched hazelnuts**
- **1 roasted red bell pepper, seeded and chopped**
- **1 tsp. sweet paprika**
- **2 Tbsp. sherry vinegar**
- **2 Tbsp. minced parsley**
- **Kosher salt and pepper**

1. In a medium saucepan, bring 1½ cups of water to a boil. Remove from the heat and add the chiles and sun-dried tomatoes. Let stand until softened, about 1 hour. Drain, reserving the soaking liquid.

2. Meanwhile, roast the plum tomatoes directly over a flame or under the broiler until lightly charred in spots and the skin is blistered. Let cool, then peel and coarsely chop.

3. In a medium skillet, heat ¼ cup of the olive oil until almost smoking. Add the bread and garlic and cook over moderately high heat, turning occasionally, until browned all over, 2 to 3 minutes. Using tongs, transfer to a plate. Add the almonds and hazelnuts to the skillet and cook over moderate heat, stirring, until browned, about 3 minutes. Using a slotted spoon, transfer to the plate. Reserve the garlic oil.

4. In a food processor, pulse the bread, garlic and nuts until very finely chopped. Add the drained chiles and sun-dried tomatoes, the roasted tomatoes and bell pepper and the paprika; puree until smooth. With the machine on, gradually add the vinegar, ⅓ cup of the chile soaking liquid, 1 tablespoon of the garlic oil and the remaining 2 tablespoons of olive oil. Transfer to a medium bowl. Stir in the parsley and season generously with salt and pepper. —*Anya von Bremzen*

SERVE WITH Grilled vegetables, bread, fish or steak.

Salsa Picante

Total **10 min**; Makes **2 cups**

This nutty and toasty dried-chile salsa can gussy up fried eggs, soup, Hearty Mexican Cranberry Beans (p. 247), braised vegetables, meat—and even guacamole!

- **1 cup grapeseed oil**
- **15 dried chiles de árbol (4 oz.), stemmed**
- **15 dried puya chiles (1 oz.), stemmed**
- **15 dried japones chiles (½ oz.), stemmed**
- **10 dried cascabel chiles (2 oz.), stemmed**
- **6 garlic cloves**
- **Kosher salt**

In a large skillet, heat ¼ cup of the oil. Add all of the chiles and cook over moderate heat, stirring often, until fragrant and toasted, about 4 minutes. Scrape into a food processor and add the garlic and remaining ¾ cup of oil. Pulse until finely chopped. Season with salt. —*Lorena Herrera*

MAKE AHEAD The salsa can be refrigerated.

Minty Salsa Verde

Total **15 min**; Serves **6 to 8**

- **3 salt-packed anchovies—rinsed, soaked and filleted**
- **1 Tbsp. capers**
- **½ small garlic clove**
- **¼ cup plus 2 Tbsp. extra-virgin olive oil**
- **3 Tbsp. red wine vinegar**
- **1 Tbsp. Dijon mustard**
- **2 cups packed mint leaves**
- **1½ cups packed parsley leaves**
- **Flaky sea salt and pepper**

In a food processor, pulse the anchovies with the capers and garlic until a fine paste forms. Add the olive oil, vinegar and mustard and pulse to combine. Add the herbs and pulse until finely chopped. Scrape the mixture into a small bowl. Season with salt and pepper and serve. —*April Bloomfield*

MAKE AHEAD The salsa verde can be refrigerated overnight.

Romesco Sauce

Baltimore-Style Rub

⏱ Total **10 min**; Makes **about ⅓ cup**

This homemade version of Old Bay is equally spicy and zippy, but it's far less salty.

- 2 Tbsp. celery seeds
- 2 Tbsp. mustard seeds
- 1½ Tbsp. paprika
- 1 Tbsp. kosher salt
- 1 tsp. black pepper
- ½ tsp. crushed red pepper
- ½ tsp. ground ginger
- 1 bay leaf, crushed

In a spice grinder, combine all of the ingredients and pulse until finely ground. Transfer to a small bowl. —*Justin Chapple*

MAKE AHEAD The rub can be stored in an airtight container for up to 3 months.

USE ON Fish, shellfish, chicken and pork.

Dried-Herb Rub

⏱ Total **5 min**; Makes **about ½ cup**

A hit of lemon zest and four kinds of herbs are the ideal combination for a bright spice rub like this one; a good dose of crushed red pepper gives it some great heat as well.

- 2 Tbsp. dried oregano, rubbed
- 2 Tbsp. dried parsley, rubbed
- 2 Tbsp. dried basil, rubbed
- 1 Tbsp. finely chopped thyme
- 1 tsp. finely grated lemon zest
- 1 tsp. crushed red pepper

In a small bowl, whisk all of the ingredients until combined. —*Justin Chapple*

MAKE AHEAD The rub can be stored in an airtight container for up to 3 months.

USE ON Fish, shellfish, chicken and pork.

Smoky Spiced Sugar Rub

⏱ Total **5 min**; Makes **about ½ cup**

Sweet and lightly spiced, this rub is perfect on steaks and also delicious on pork and lamb.

- ½ cup packed light brown sugar
- 1 Tbsp. ground coriander
- 1 Tbsp. kosher salt
- 2 tsp. ground cumin
- 2 tsp. smoked paprika

In a small bowl, whisk all of the ingredients until well combined. —*Justin Chapple*

MAKE AHEAD The rub can be stored in an airtight container for up to 3 months.

USE ON Beef, lamb, chicken and pork.

Pineapple-Soy Marinade

⏱ Total **15 min**; Makes **about 2½ cups**

- 2 cups pineapple juice
- ¼ cup soy sauce
- 2 Tbsp. distilled white vinegar
- 2 Tbsp. canola oil
- 2 garlic cloves, finely grated
- 1 tsp. kosher salt
- 1 tsp. pepper

In a medium bowl, whisk all of the ingredients until combined. —*Justin Chapple*

USE ON Beef, pork, chicken, swordfish and salmon.

Tomato-Fennel Marinade

⏱ Total **15 min**; Makes **1½ cups**

Fresh tomatoes and tomato paste combine to make an ultra-tomatoey marinade. It's great on seafood and chicken.

- 1 lb. ripe tomatoes, halved
- ¼ cup extra-virgin olive oil
- ¼ cup tomato paste
- 1 Tbsp. ground fennel
- 1 tsp. black pepper
- 2 garlic cloves, finely grated

Working over a medium bowl, grate the tomatoes on a box grater until only the skins are left in your hand; discard the skins. Whisk in the olive oil, tomato paste, fennel, pepper and garlic. —*Justin Chapple*

USE ON Shrimp, fish and pork.

Gin-and-Lemon Marinade

⏱ Total **10 min**; Makes **1½ cups**

A dream on chicken and pork, this boozy marinade is also terrific on shrimp for a quick 15-minute marinade.

- ¾ cup gin
- ¼ cup plus 2 Tbsp. honey
- 3 garlic cloves, crushed
- 1½ Tbsp. chopped thyme
- 1 lemon, thinly sliced

In a small bowl, mix all of the ingredients except the lemon slices. Once combined, add the lemon slices. —*Justin Chapple*

USE ON Shrimp, chicken and pork.

Black Gunpowder

📷 PAGE 367

⏱ Total **20 min**; Makes **about 1 cup**

At Tiffin Asha, in Portland, Oregon, chef Elizabeth Golay makes a trio of south Indian dried chutneys known as gunpowders, or *pudi*. This mild black seeded one is delicious over rice.

- ½ cup black sesame seeds
- 2 Tbsp. whole urad dal (see Note)
- ½ tsp. black peppercorns
- ½ tsp. brown mustard seeds
- ½ tsp. cumin seeds
- ½ tsp. nigella seeds
- 1 Tbsp. poppy seeds
- 1 tsp. kosher salt

1. In a medium skillet, toast the sesame seeds over moderately low heat, stirring occasionally, until fragrant, about 2 minutes. Transfer to a small bowl.

2. In the skillet, toast the dal over moderate heat, shaking the pan, until lightly browned, 2 minutes. Add the peppercorns and the mustard, cumin and nigella seeds and toast until the seeds start to pop, 2 minutes. Add the poppy seeds and toast for 30 seconds. Transfer the contents of the skillet to a food processor, add the salt and pulse until finely ground. Add the sesame seeds and pulse until incorporated. Store in an airtight container in the refrigerator until ready to use. —*Elizabeth Golay*

NOTE Urad dal is a tiny, skin-on black lentil. Find it at kalustyans.com and amazon.com.

White Gunpowder

📷 PAGE 367

⏲ Total **20 min**; Makes **1¼ cup**

This nutty, almost cheesy blend of three kinds of dal is fantastic tossed with popcorn.

- ½ **cup chana dal (see Note)**
- ¼ **cup toor dal**
- ¼ **cup whole urad dal**
- 4 **dried chiles de árbol**
- 1 **tsp. cumin seeds**
- ¼ **tsp. asafetida**
- 1 **tsp. untoasted sesame oil**
- 20 **fresh curry leaves**
- 2 **teaspoons kosher salt**

1. In a large skillet, toast the chana dal over moderate heat, stirring occasionally, until golden brown and fragrant, about 5 minutes; scrape into a medium bowl. In the skillet, toast the toor dal and urad dal over moderate heat, stirring occasionally, until golden brown and fragrant, about 5 minutes; transfer to the bowl. Toast the chiles, cumin seeds and asafetida over moderate heat, stirring occasionally, until fragrant, about 1 minute; transfer to the bowl.

2. In the skillet, heat the sesame oil. Cook the curry leaves over low heat, stirring, until they are crispy and start to pop, about 1 minute. Transfer to the bowl and let cool completely.

3. In a mini food processor, pulse the gunpowder until finely ground; season with salt. Store in an airtight container until ready to use. —*Elizabeth Golay*

NOTES Chana dal is a mildly sweet split yellow lentil. You can find it on kalustyans. com and amazon.com.

MAKE AHEAD The white gunpowder can be refrigerated for up to 3 months.

Red Gunpowder

📷 PAGE 367

⏲ Total **20 min**; Makes **1 cup**

Packed with spicy arbol chiles, this fiery blend is made for sprinkling over your morning eggs.

- 1 **oz. chiles de árbol**
- 1 **tsp. toor dal (see Note)**
- 1 **tsp. whole urad dal**
- 1 **tsp. coriander seeds**
- ⅛ **tsp. asafetida**
- ½ **tsp. untoasted sesame oil**
- 10 **fresh curry leaves**
- ¼ **cup roasted unsalted peanuts**
- 1½ **tsp. kosher salt**

1. Preheat the oven to 450°. In a large skillet, toast the chiles over moderately low heat, stirring occasionally, until lightly browned in spots and fragrant, about 5 minutes. Transfer to a medium bowl.

2. In the skillet, toast the toor dal and urad dal over moderately low heat, stirring occasionally, until lightly browned, about 3 minutes. Add the coriander and asafetida and toast, stirring, until very fragrant, about 2 minutes. Transfer to the bowl with the chiles.

3. In the skillet, heat the sesame oil. Add the curry leaves and cook over low heat, stirring, until they become crispy and start to pop, about 1 minute. Transfer the curry leaves to the bowl and let cool completely.

4. In a mini food processor, pulse the cooled dal mixture until finely ground; return to the bowl. In the food processor, pulse the peanuts until finely chopped, then stir them into the dal mixture along with the salt. Store in an airtight container until ready to use. —*Elizabeth Golay*

NOTE Toor dal, also known as arhar dal, is a slightly sweet variety of a yellow split pea. You can find it on kalustyans.com and amazon.com.

MAKE AHEAD The red gunpowder can be refrigerated for up to 3 months.

Pickled Jicama and Shiso

Total **20 min plus 1 hr brining**; Makes **1 qt**

Pickles are a part of many Japanese meals. These take only a few minutes to prep.

- 1 **cup low-sodium soy sauce**
- 6 **Tbsp. distilled white vinegar**
- 6 **Tbsp. unseasoned rice vinegar**
- 3 **garlic cloves, crushed**
- 2 **Tbsp. kosher salt**
- 2 **tsp. sugar**
- ¾ **tsp. crushed red pepper**
- 1 **lb. jicama, peeled and cut into thin wedges**
- 1½ **oz. shiso leaves (60 leaves)**

1. In a medium saucepan, combine all of the ingredients except the jicama and shiso with 2 cups of water and bring to a simmer over moderate heat, stirring to dissolve the sugar. Cool until lukewarm.

2. In a large bowl, combine the jicama and shiso with the brine. Let stand at room temperature for 1 hour and serve, or refrigerate until ready to serve. —*Kay Chun*

MAKE AHEAD The pickles can be refrigerated in the brine for up to 3 days.

Grandfather's Pickles

📷 PAGE 361

Total **10 min plus 2 hr pickling**; Makes **1 qt**

These North Carolina–style pickles don't use sugar and have just one simple step.

- 1 **English cucumber, sliced crosswise ¼ inch thick, preferably on a mandoline**
- ½ **small onion, thinly sliced**
- 1 **oil-packed Calabrian chile, drained and thinly sliced, or ¼ tsp. crushed red pepper**
- ½ **cup apple cider vinegar**
- 2 **Tbsp. kosher salt**

Pack the cucumber, onion and Calabrian chile into a 1-quart jar with a tight-fitting lid. In a medium bowl, whisk the vinegar with the salt and 1 cup of water until the salt dissolves. Pour the brine over the cucumbers, cover and refrigerate for at least 2 hours. Drain the pickles before serving. —*Joe Kindred*

MAKE AHEAD The pickles can be refrigerated in the brine for up to 1 week.

DRINKS

Lavender Gin
Cocktail (p. 382)
OPPOSITE Spicy
Margarita Punch
(p. 381)

Coconut–Sparkling Wine Spritzer

Active: **5 min**; Total **2 hr, including chilling**
Makes **1 drink**

Most grenadine cocktails are sweet color bombs (think: tequila sunrise), but this subtle drink plays up delicate coconut water and a lively spritz.

- **2 thin lime slices**
- **1½ oz. coconut water**
- **½ oz. simple syrup (see Note)**
- **Splash of grenadine**
- **4 oz. chilled sparkling wine, such as Prosecco or Cava**

In a chilled glass, muddle 1 lime slice. Add the coconut water, simple syrup and grenadine. Slowly pour in the sparkling wine and garnish with the remaining lime slice. –*Amanda Crawford*

NOTE To make simple syrup, in a small saucepan, combine ½ cup each of sugar and water. Simmer over high heat, stirring to dissolve the sugar. Let cool completely, then refrigerate until cold. The syrup can be refrigerated for up to 1 month. Makes about 6 ounces.

Rhubarb-Bénédictine Spritzer

Active **10 min**; Total **1 hr plus chilling**
Makes **1 drink**

Homemade rhubarb syrup adds a tangy note to this sprightly drink.

- **1½ lbs. rhubarb, coarsely chopped (4 cups)**
- **1 cup sugar**
- **One 3-inch strip of orange peel**
- **¾ oz. fresh lemon juice**
- **¾ oz. Bénédictine**
- **A few dashes of orange bitters**
- **4 oz. chilled sparkling wine, such as Prosecco or Cava**

1. In a medium saucepan, bring the rhubarb, sugar, orange peel and 1 cup of water to a boil. Simmer over moderately low heat, stirring occasionally, until the rhubarb breaks down, about 15 minutes. Let steep for 30 minutes. Strain through a fine sieve set over a medium bowl, pressing on the solids; discard the solids. Refrigerate the syrup until cold.

2. In a chilled glass, combine ¾ ounce of the rhubarb syrup, the lemon juice, Bénédictine and orange bitters. Top with the sparkling wine and serve immediately. Use the remaining rhubarb syrup to make more cocktails. –*Amanda Crawford*

NOTE A mixture of dry white wine and club soda can replace the sparkling wine.

MAKE AHEAD The rhubarb syrup can be refrigerated for up to 1 week.

Clementine 75

Active **15 min**; Total **1 hr 15 min**
Makes **8 drinks**

This juicy cocktail is a riff on a classic French 75: Instead of using lemon juice, F&W's Justin Chapple swaps in clementine juice. For an excellent mocktail, use apple cider vinegar and seltzer instead of the gin and Champagne.

- **½ cup sugar**
- **One 3-inch piece of fresh ginger, thinly sliced**
- **¼ cup juniper berries, crushed**
- **¼ cup dried cranberries**
- **2 cinnamon sticks**
- **Ice**
- **6 oz. fresh clementine juice**
- **4 oz. gin**
- **Chilled brut Champagne or Prosecco, for topping**

1. In a small saucepan, combine the sugar, ginger, juniper berries, cranberries, cinnamon sticks and ½ cup of water and bring to a boil, stirring to dissolve the sugar. Remove from the heat and let steep for 1 hour. Strain the juniper syrup through a fine sieve into a small bowl, pressing on the solids; discard the solids.

2. Fill a cocktail shaker with ice. Add the clementine juice, gin and the juniper syrup and shake well. Pour into 8 Champagne flutes and top with Champagne.
—*Justin Chapple*

VARIATION For a booze-free version, substitute 4 ounces of apple cider vinegar for the gin and top the cocktails with chilled seltzer instead of Champagne.

MAKE AHEAD The juniper syrup can be refrigerated for up to 2 weeks.

Boozy Watermelon Slushy

Total **10 min plus 4 hr for freezing**
Makes **4 drinks**

- **12 oz. watermelon juice, preferably Wtrmln Wtr brand**
- **4 oz. chilled vodka**
- **2 oz. chilled Aperol**
- **2 oz. chilled fino sherry**
- **¼ oz. fresh lemon juice (from ½ lemon)**
- **2 Tbsp. agave syrup, plus more as needed**
- **3 cups crushed ice**
- **Thin watermelon wedges and black and white sesame seeds, for garnish**

1. Pour the watermelon juice into an ice cube tray and freeze until solid, about 4 hours.

2. In a blender, pulse the watermelon ice cubes with the vodka, Aperol, sherry, lemon juice, agave and crushed ice until smooth. Add more agave if desired. Divide among 4 chilled glasses and garnish with watermelon wedges and sesame seeds. Serve immediately. —*Carlos Yturria*

MAKE AHEAD The watermelon ice cubes can be frozen for up to 1 month.

Watermelon Margranita

Active **30 min**; Total **6 hr 30 min**; Serves **4**

- **4 cups diced seedless watermelon (1 lb.)**
- **3 Tbsp. sugar**
- **2 tsp. fresh lime juice**
- **Pinch of kosher salt**
- **4 oz. very cold tequila**

1. In a blender, combine the watermelon with the sugar, lime juice, salt and ⅓ cup of water. Puree until smooth, about 1 minute. Pour the mixture into an 8-by-8-inch metal or glass baking dish and freeze for 1 hour. Scrape the frozen edges into the center and freeze for about 3 hours longer, scraping hourly, until the granita is icy and flaky. Freeze for at least 2 hours or, preferably, overnight.

2. Scrape half of the granita into 4 small glasses and top with the tequila and the remaining granita. Serve immediately.
—*Laura Rege*

MAKE AHEAD The granita can be frozen for up to 4 days. Fluff before serving.

Rosemary-Ginger Sparkler

Spicy Margarita Punch

📷 PAGE 376

Active **15 min**; Total **1 hr 15 min**; Serves **10**

F&W's Justin Chapple loves making a big bowl of punch with his spicy margaritas.

- **1 English cucumber, thinly sliced, plus more for garnish**
- **1 small jalapeño, thinly sliced, plus more for garnish**
- **¼ cup lightly packed cilantro**
- **¼ cup lightly packed mint**
- **One 750-ml. bottle silver tequila**
- **2 cups fresh lime juice**
- **1 cup light agave nectar**
- **½ cup fresh orange juice**
- **Ice, lime wedges and kosher salt, for serving**

1. In a punch bowl, muddle the cucumber with the jalapeño, cilantro and mint. Add the tequila, lime juice, agave and orange juice and stir well. Refrigerate until well chilled, about 1 hour.

2. Using a fine sieve, remove and discard the solids from the punch. Garnish with more thinly sliced cucumber and jalapeño. Serve ice and lime wedges alongside, as well as salt for rimming glasses. —*Justin Chapple*

MAKE AHEAD The punch can be refrigerated overnight.

Margarita Jellies

Total **15 min plus overnight setting.** Serves **10** Makes **about 9 dozen**

- **6 envelopes of unflavored gelatin**
- **Spicy Margarita Punch (recipe above)**
- **Decorating sugar**

In a large bowl, sprinkle the gelatin evenly over 1 cup of the Spicy Margarita Punch. In a saucepan, bring 1 cup of punch just to a simmer. Whisk in the gelatin mixture until completely dissolved, then return to the large bowl. Whisk in the remaining punch. Pour into a lightly oiled 9-by-13-inch baking dish. Refrigerate overnight. Unmold and cut into 1-inch cubes. Dip in decorating sugar and serve. —*Justin Chapple*

Rosemary-Ginger Sparkler

⏱ Total **5 min**; Makes **1 drink**

This festive drink is a play on a classic Moscow Mule, but in place of the vodka and lime, Whitney Tingle and Danielle DuBoise, creators of the cult plant-based meal delivery service Sakara Life, mix in bourbon and a homemade rosemary-ginger syrup. "We try to live a balanced life," says Danielle. "So on the weekend, we want a cocktail!"

- **Ice**
- **2 oz. bourbon**
- **½ oz. fresh lemon juice**
- **½ oz. Rosemary-Ginger Syrup (recipe follows)**
- **2 oz. chilled ginger beer**
- **1 small rosemary sprig, for garnish**

Fill a rocks glass with ice. Add the bourbon, lemon juice and rosemary-ginger syrup; stir well. Top with ginger beer and stir once. Garnish with the rosemary sprig and serve. —*Whitney Tingle and Danielle DuBoise*

ROSEMARY-GINGER SYRUP

Active **10 min**; Total **55 min plus chilling** Makes **1¼ cups**

- **1 cup sugar**
- **4 oz. fresh ginger, peeled and sliced ¼ inch thick**
- **One 3-inch rosemary sprig**

In a small saucepan, bring the sugar and 1 cup of water to a boil. Add the ginger and rosemary and return to a boil, stirring to dissolve the sugar. Remove from the heat and let cool completely, about 45 minutes. Strain the syrup through a fine sieve set over a small bowl; discard the solids. Refrigerate until chilled. —*Whitney Tingle and Danielle DuBoise*

MAKE AHEAD The syrup can be refrigerated for up to 1 month.

East Jaffa Mule

⏱ Total **10 min**; Makes **1 drink**

- **Crushed ice**
- **1 oz. vodka**
- **1 oz. fig eau de vie, such as Boukha Bokobsa**
- **1 oz. fresh red grapefruit juice**
- **½ oz. ginger simple syrup (see Note)**
- **½ oz. fresh lime juice**
- **½ oz. date syrup or agave nectar**
- **Freshly grated nutmeg, lime wheel and mint sprig, for garnish**

Fill a cocktail shaker with crushed ice. Add the vodka, eau de vie, grapefruit juice, ginger syrup, lime juice and date syrup and shake well. Strain into a crushed-ice-filled Moscow mule mug. Garnish with grated nutmeg, a lime wheel and a mint sprig. Serve right away. —*Yotam Shilo*

NOTE To make ginger simple syrup, simmer 1 cup each of sugar and water with 2 ounces of sliced fresh ginger, stirring, until the sugar dissolves. Let cool completely, then strain. The syrup can be refrigerated for up to 1 month. Makes about 12 ounces.

Epazote Gin Martini

Total **10 min plus 8 hr steeping** Makes **1 drink**

The coupe glass gets rinsed with herbal French Chartreuse before the gin is added.

- **3 cups gin**
- **⅔ cup (1 oz.) dried epazote (see Note)**
- **Green Chartreuse, for rinsing**
- **Ice**
- **2 fresh epazote leaves**

In a 1-quart jar, steep the gin with the dried epazote for 8 hours. Strain into a pitcher. Rinse a chilled coupe glass with Chartreuse, then discard. Fill a cocktail shaker with ice. Add 2½ ounces of the epazote gin and shake well. Strain into the glass. Garnish with the fresh epazote and serve. Use the remaining epazote gin to make more cocktails. —*Rocky Barnette*

NOTE Epazote is a Mexican herb with notes of camphor, mint and citrus. It's available dried at kalustyans.com.

Gin-and-Honey Spritzer

⏱ Active **10 min**; Total **40 min**
Makes **1 drink**

½ cup honey
1½ oz. dry gin, preferably Cardinal
1 oz. soda water
¾ oz. fresh lemon juice
Ice
Thinly sliced English cucumber
and 1 small mint sprig, for garnish

In a small saucepan, bring the honey and ½ cup of water to a simmer, stirring to dissolve the honey. Transfer the honey syrup to a small heatproof jar and refrigerate until cold, about 30 minutes. In a collins glass, mix the gin with the soda water, lemon juice and ½ ounce of the honey syrup. Add ice and garnish with cucumber and mint; serve immediately. Use the remaining honey syrup for more cocktails. —Joe Kindred

MAKE AHEAD The honey syrup can be refrigerated for up to 2 weeks.

Lavender Gin Cocktail

📷 PAGE 377

Active **5 min**; Total **50 min**; Makes **1 drink**

1 cup boiling water
2 Tbsp. dried lavender buds
2 oz. tonic water, preferably
Fever Tree
1 oz. dry gin
1 oz. fresh lime juice plus 1 lime
wedge for garnish
½ oz. agave syrup
Ice
Lavender sprig, for garnish

1. In a small heatproof bowl, pour the boiling water over the dried lavender buds and let steep for 30 minutes. Strain the lavender infusion through a fine sieve set over a small bowl; discard the solids. Cover and refrigerate until cold.

2. In a rocks glass, stir the tonic with the gin, lime juice, agave and ½ ounce of the lavender infusion. Fill the glass with ice, garnish with a lavender sprig and a lime wedge and serve. Use the remaining lavender infusion to make more cocktails. —José Catrimán

MAKE AHEAD The lavender infusion can be refrigerated for up to 1 week.

Salado Verde Cocktail

⏱ Active **15 min**; Total **30 min**
Makes **8 drinks**

1 small cactus pad—thorns removed,
peeled and finely chopped (1 cup;
see Note)
½ cup plus ½ tsp. kosher salt
3½ English cucumbers, peeled and
halved lengthwise
2 serrano chiles, stemmed and seeded
9 oz. mezcal, preferably Yola
4 oz. fresh lime juice (from about
3 limes)
2 oz. dry vermouth
Ice

1. In a shallow bowl, toss the cactus with ½ cup of the salt. Let sit for 5 minutes. Rinse in a fine sieve under running water until the water is clear and the cactus is clean, 3 to 4 minutes.

2. Using an electric juicer, juice the cucumbers and serranos, then strain through a fine sieve set over a medium bowl. Stir in the remaining ½ teaspoon of salt and refrigerate until chilled, about 15 minutes.

3. In a pitcher, combine the cucumber-serrano juice with the mezcal, lime juice and vermouth. Fill 8 rocks glasses with ice and pour in the cocktail. Garnish each drink with 1 tablespoon of the cured cactus; serve immediately. Save the remaining cured cactus for another use. —Laura Rege

NOTE If you cannot find cactus, skip Step 1 and garnish each drink with 1 tablespoon of finely diced English cucumber.

Dreams of July

Total **45 min** plus 1 hr chilling; Serves **20**

8 oz. kumquats or 4 mandarins,
sliced into thin wedges with the peel,
plus halves or slices for garnish
2 cups honey
9 kiwis, peeled and seeded,
plus slices for garnish
20 oz. cachaça
10 oz. limoncello
10 oz. dry vermouth
½ oz. orange bitters
Large ice chunks

1. Set a fine sieve over a heatproof medium bowl. In a medium saucepan, using a wooden spoon, crush the citrus wedges against the side of the pan to release the

oils and juice. Add the honey and 1⅓ cups of cold water and bring to a boil, then simmer over moderately low heat until flavorful and thick, about 30 minutes. Strain the syrup into the bowl; discard the solids. Let cool slightly. Cover with plastic and refrigerate until cold, at least 1 hour.

2. In a blender, puree the kiwis until very smooth. Working in batches, strain through a fine seive into a medium bowl. In a large punch bowl, stir the syrup with the kiwi puree, 2½ cups of cold water and the remaining ingredients. Garnish with kiwi slices and citrus and serve. —Joshua Fossitt

MAKE AHEAD The syrup can be refrigerated for up to 1 week.

Thai Basil, Grapefruit and Chia Tonic

Active **15 min**; Total **2 hr 15 min**; Serves **4**

¾ cup fresh grapefruit juice with pulp
2 Tbsp. pure maple syrup
2 Tbsp. chia seeds
1 Thai basil sprig or 4-inch rosemary
sprig

In a large pitcher, combine the grapefruit juice with the maple syrup, chia seeds, Thai basil and 4 cups of water and stir well. Cover and refrigerate for at least 2 hours. Stir the tonic before serving. —Seamus Mullen

Spicy Agua Fresca

Active **30 min**; Total **2 hr 30 min**; Serves **4**

One 4-lb. pineapple—peeled, cored
and cut into chunks (2¼ lbs.)
One 1-lb. papaya—peeled, seeded
and cut into chunks (10 oz.)
1 serrano chile, stemmed and
quartered
½ cup fresh lemon juice
½ cup fresh orange juice
⅓ cup fresh lime juice
Kosher salt

In a food processor, in batches if necessary, puree the pineapple, papaya and serrano until nearly smooth. Transfer to a large bowl and stir in the lemon, orange and lime juices. Strain the mixture through a fine sieve into a pitcher. Stir in a generous pinch of salt and refrigerate until well chilled, about 2 hours. —Val M. Cantu

Thai Basil, Grapefruit and Chia Tonic

Spiced Pumpkin Lassi

Mock Red Wine

Total **20 min plus overnight chilling**
Serves **4**

2¼ lbs. Granny Smith apples, quartered

¾ lb. beets, scrubbed and quartered

4 oolong tea bags

2 cups boiling water

1. Using an electric juicer, juice the apples and beets into a large bowl or liquid measuring cup; refrigerate overnight.

2. Meanwhile, in a heatproof medium bowl, cover the tea bags with the boiling water and let steep for 5 minutes. Discard the tea bags and let the tea cool completely. Refrigerate until chilled, at least 1 hour.

3. Strain the juice through damp cheesecloth into a large pitcher. Stir in the tea and pour into glasses; serve chilled.
—*Eamon Rockey*

Faux Pastis

Total **15 min plus overnight steeping**
Serves **6**

To start off a meal, Parisian chef and naturopath Angèle Ferreux-Maeght serves this playful infusion. "It's very herbal and smells just like French pastis."

½ cup agave syrup

1½ stalks of lemongrass, thinly sliced (1½ oz.)

One 6-inch piece of licorice root (see Note), halved crosswise

One 3-inch piece of fresh turmeric, thinly sliced

4 star anise pods

5 tsp. fennel seeds

Ice

Lemon wedges, for serving

1. In a medium saucepan, bring 9 cups of water to a boil over high heat. Remove the saucepan from the heat and stir in the agave, lemongrass, licorice root, turmeric, star anise and fennel seeds. Let cool, then cover and refrigerate overnight.

2. Strain the drink through a fine sieve set over a large pitcher, pressing on the solids; discard the solids. Pour into ice-filled glasses and serve with lemon wedges.
—*Angèle Ferreux-Maeght*

NOTE Licorice root is available at most health food stores.

Spiced Pumpkin Lassi

Total **40 min plus chilling;** Makes **4 drinks**

2 Tbsp. vegetable oil

Four 2-inch cinnamon sticks

4 whole star anise

4 cups peeled, ½-inch-diced sugar pumpkin or kabocha squash (1 lb.)

Kosher salt

1½ cups whole milk

2 cups full-fat Greek yogurt

¾ cup sugar

Ground cinnamon, for garnish

1. In a large skillet, heat the oil. Add the cinnamon sticks and star anise and cook over moderate heat until fragrant, 2 to 3 minutes. Add the pumpkin, season with salt and cook, stirring occasionally, until the pumpkin is lightly browned and starting to soften, 10 minutes. Add the milk and simmer until the pumpkin is very soft and the milk has thickened slightly, 10 minutes. Remove the skillet from the heat and let cool briefly; discard the spices.

2. In a blender, puree the pumpkin, milk and ½ teaspoon of salt until smooth. Transfer the blender to the refrigerator and chill until cold, at least 30 minutes.

3. Add the yogurt, sugar and ½ cup of water to the blender and puree until very smooth. For a thinner consistency, blend in more water, ¼ cup at a time. Pour the pumpkin lassi into 4 glasses, sprinkle with ground cinnamon and serve chilled.
—*Rupam Bhagat*

Layered Blackberry-and-Turmeric Lemonade

Active **30 min**; Total **1 hr 30 min**
Makes **4 drinks**

This summery mocktail is a showstopper with its distinct pink and yellow layers.

⅔ cup sugar

½ cup fresh lemon juice, plus lemon wheels for garnish

½ tsp. ground turmeric

1 cup blackberries (4 oz.)

Ice

12 oz. seltzer

Thai basil sprigs with flowers, for garnish (optional)

1. In a small saucepan, bring ⅓ cup of the sugar and ⅓ cup of water to a boil, stirring to dissolve the sugar. Pour the simple syrup into a heatproof 1-quart jar and refrigerate until cold, about 30 minutes. Add the lemon juice, turmeric and 1 cup of water. Cover and shake to combine.

2. Meanwhile, in a small saucepan, gently simmer the blackberries with the remaining ⅓ cup of sugar and ½ cup of water for 10 minutes, pressing on the berries with the back of a spoon to break them up. Strain the syrup through a fine sieve. Cover and refrigerate until cold, 30 minutes.

3. To serve, fill 4 collins glasses with ice. Shake the turmeric lemonade once more and divide among the glasses. Whisk the seltzer into the blackberry syrup and pour over the lemonade. Do not mix. Garnish with lemon wheels and Thai basil, if desired; serve immediately. —*Julia Momose*

NOTE Swap in raspberries or strawberries for the blackberries, or double the recipe for a crowd.

MAKE AHEAD The lemonade and the syrup can be refrigerated separately for 2 weeks.

Iced Tahini Mocha

Total **5 min;** Makes **1 drink**

This clever coffee drink gets a touch of savory complexity from tahini. It can also be served hot in the colder months.

1½ Tbsp. tahini

2 tsp. unsweetened Dutch-process cocoa

2 oz. hot brewed espresso

1 oz. hot water

1 Tbsp. agave nectar

Pinch of kosher salt

Ice

6 oz. whole milk

Toasted sesame seeds, for garnish

In a small measuring cup, whisk the tahini with the cocoa. Whisk in the espresso, hot water, agave and salt until smooth. Fill a tall glass with ice and add the milk. Pour the tahini-espresso mixture on the top and garnish with toasted sesame seeds; serve.
—*Melody Shemtov*

Recipe Index

A

ALMONDS

Almond Oats with Muesli and Skyr, 299

Almond-Poached Chicken Salad, 120, **121**

Baked Kabocha Falafel with Almond Milk Yogurt, 31

Salmon Skewers with Almond Charmoula, 92

Spiced Candied Almonds, 362

Tabbouleh with Pine Nuts and Almonds, 258

Anchovy Fritters, Caesar Salad with, 34, **35**

APPLES

Apple-Cucumber Mignonette, **370,** 371

Apple-Pomegranate Cobbler, 314

Celery Root, Apple and Fennel Slaw, 214

Chilled Tofu with Apple Soy Sauce, **14,** 15

Cumin-and-Jaggery-Glazed Apple Pie, 310

Goose Stuffed with Apples and Armagnac-Soaked Prunes, 156, **157**

Homemade Applesauce with Chinese Five-Spice, 368

Mock Red Wine, 385

Pork-and-Apple Bedfordshire Clangers, **172,** 173

Pork Loin Stuffed with Apples and Pumpkin Seeds, **158,** 162

Saffron Butter–Basted Poussins with Apples (Joojeh ba Sib), 156

White Wine–Baked Apples, 316

APRICOTS

Grilled Eggplant, Apricot and Tomato Salad, 46, **47**

Quinoa Pilaf with Dried Apricots, 256

Artichoke Salad, Shaved, 42

ARUGULA

Arugula-and-Squash Salad, 52

Greens Pasta Salad, 72

Sautéed Arugula, 227

Savory Plum Tarts with Arugula Salad, 224

Skirt Steak Sizzle with Carrots and Arugula, 188, **189**

Spinach-and-Arugula Bruschetta with Dukka, 16

ASPARAGUS

Asparagus-and-Zucchini Frittata, 294

Grilled Asparagus Pizzas with Gremolata, 271

Spring Asparagus Salad with Feta, 48

Thin Spaghetti with Crab and Asparagus, 78

AVOCADOS

Avocado-and-Cabbage Slaw, 214, **215**

Avocado Halves with Flaxseed Furikake, 296

Chilled Avocado Soup with Crab, 59

Creamy Avocado Paletas, 322

Grilled Rockamole, 12

Grilled Strawberry-Avocado Toasts with Burrata, **276, 277**

Persimmon-and-Endive Salad with Honey Vinegar and Avocado Oil Vinaigrette, **32, 42**

Radish-and-Avocado Salad, 49

Spring Chickpea Salad with Avocado Hummus, 248

B

BACON

Bacon-Chile Naan, 268, **269**

Bacon, Egg and Shrimp Fried Rice, 252

Baked Clams with Bacon and Garlic, 114

Clams Carbonara, 79

Grilled Oysters with Bacon Vinaigrette, **116,** 117

Kale Salad with Bacon–Brown Sugar Vinaigrette, 38, **39**

Pancetta-Wrapped Trout with Sage and Lemon, 96

Pimento Cheeseburgers with Bacon Jam, 200

Sheet Pan Chicken with Sourdough and Bacon, **132,** 133

Smoked Gouda Carbonara, **71,** 79

BANANAS

Shrimp with Green Banana Cocktail Sauce, 22, **23**

Smashed-Banana Bread, **306,** 307

Barberries (Mahi-e Fivij), Walnut-Stuffed Fish with, 104

Barley Soup with Herbs and Egg Noodles, Chicken-, 69

BEANS. See also Chickpeas; Green Beans

Fabada (Spanish Bean Stew with Chorizo and Blood Sausage), 177

Harissa White Bean Stew with Turmeric Yogurt, **62,** 63

Hearty Mexican Cranberry Beans, 247, **254**

Lamb Fillets with Favas and Spring Vegetables, 205

Spaghetti with Squash Blossom Butter and Summer Beans, **74,** 75

Summer Bean Salad with Potlikker Vinaigrette, 247

Summer Vegetable Soup, 60, **61**

BEEF. See also Veal

Albóndigas with Mushrooms, **30,** 31

Beef-and-Celery Yakitori, **190, 191**

Beef-and-Lamb Kibbeh, 204

Beef Rib Roast, **180,** 195

Brisket with Sweet-and-Sour Onions, **194,** 195

Corned Beef with Pickled Cabbage and Potato Salad, 196

Creamed Spinach–Stuffed Filet Roast, 186

Cuban Flank Steak, 182

Fried Green Tomato Double Cheeseburgers, 199

F&W's Ultimate Burger, 200, **201**

Gochujang Flank Steak and Korean Pasta Salad, 182

Golden Steak and Eggs, 290, **291**

Grass-Fed Beef Jerky, 368

Grilled and Chilled Beef with Buttermilk-Horseradish Sauce, 185

Juicy Steak-and-Tomato Salad, 185

Leslie Bruni's Meatloaf, 197

Pimento Cheeseburgers with Bacon Jam, 200

Pork-and-Brisket Chili, 174, **175**

Porterhouse Steak, 187

Prime Rib with Sour Cherry Conserva, Truffle and Chocolate, 192, **193**

Rabo de Toro, 211

Rare Roast Beef with Pickled Green Tomatoes, 196

Seaweed Soup, 60

Sirloin, Celery and Cherry Salad, 45

Skirt Steak Sizzle with Carrots and Arugula, 188, **189**

Skirt Steak with Charred-Okra and Plum Salad, 188

Sourdough Tortillas with Charred Steak and Scallion Salsa, 191

Spiced Grilled T-Bone Steaks, 186

Spiced Harissa Ragù with Tahini Yogurt, **198,** 199

Square Meatballs with Pomodoro Sauce, 197

Steak and Brassicas with Red Wine Sauce, 182, **183**

Steak with Arabic Sauces, 186

Texas Chile Short Rib Tacos, 192

Vietnamese Steak au Poivre, **184,** 185

Vinegar-Marinated Beef Yakitori, 191

Page numbers in **bold** indicate photographs.

BEETS
Beet-and-Onion Salad, 51
Beet-and-Quinoa Salad, 52
Beet-and-Vodka-Cured Gravlax, 18
Beet Muhammara, 10
Beet Salad with Shiso, 51
BERRIES. See also specific berries
Berry Vinegar Tart, **308,** 316
Raw Berry Tart with Coconut
Cream, **309,** 316
Summer Pavlova with Fresh and Grilled
Berries, **318,** 319
Bibimbap, Hobo Pack, **238,** 255
BISCUITS
Beaten Biscuit Breakfast Sandwich with
Tomato Jam, 304
Buttermilk Biscuits with Salty Sorghum
Butter, 262
BLACKBERRIES
Layered Blackberry-and-Turmeric
Lemonade, 385
Smoked Ribs with Blackberry-Habanero
BBQ Sauce, 170, **171**
BOK CHOY
Sautéed Bok Choy, 227
Whole Roast Snapper with Sichuan
Butter, 96
Wu-Tang Clams, 117
Bouillabaisse Sauce and Green Olive Tapenade,
Baked Cod Fillet with, 97
BREADS. See also Biscuits; Flatbreads;
Muffins; Pancakes; Toasts; Waffles
Bacon-Chile Naan, 268, **269**
Cacio e Pepe Knots, 265
Classic Garlic Knots, 265
Double-Lemon Scones, 304, **305**
Easy Seeded Rye Bread, 266
Everything Knots, 265
Garlic Bread Rolls, 266
Green Potato Smørrebrød, 277
Herbed Ricotta with Grilled Bread, 15
Pull-Apart Rolls, 262, **263**
Rum-Caramel Bread Pudding with No-Churn
Pumpkin Ice Cream and Candied
Pepitas, **325,** 352
Salmorejo, 56
Smashed-Banana Bread, **306,** 307
Smoked Salmon Smørrebrød, 277
Spelt Garlic Knots, 264
Sticky Coconut-Rice Bread, 307
Broccoli Leaves, Sautéed, 227
BRUSSELS SPROUTS
Caesar Brussels Salad, 40
Kale–and–Brussels Sprout Caesar
Salad, 40
Parsnip Mash with Fried Brussels Sprout
Leaves, 221
Roasted Brussels Sprouts with Peanuts and
Fish Sauce, 217
Buckwheat Flatbreads, 274

BURGERS
Chicken Burgers with Crispy Cheddar
Cheese, 127
Fried Green Tomato Double
Cheeseburgers, 199
F&W's Ultimate Burger, 200, **201**
Kimchi Pork Burgers, 174
Lamb Burgers with Onion Soup Aioli, 203
Pimento Cheeseburgers with
Bacon Jam, 200
Roasted Veggie Burgers with Carrot
Ketchup, 220
BUTTERMILK
Buttermilk-Brined Roast Chicken, 147
Buttermilk-Dressed Spring Greens, 37
Grilled and Chilled Beef with Buttermilk-
Horseradish Sauce, 185
Butterscotch Pudding Pie, 314

C

CABBAGE
Avocado-and-Cabbage Slaw, 214, **215**
Corned Beef with Pickled Cabbage and
Potato Salad, 196
Glazed Pickled Red Cabbage, 214
Sautéed Cabbage with Cumin Seeds and
Turmeric, **216,** 217
Turkey Shwarma with Cabbage
Salad, **154,** 155
Winter Squash and Savoy Cabbage Gratin
with Garlic Crema, 223
CAKES
Boston Cream Pie, **332,** 333
Chocolate, Cinnamon and Almond Loaf
Cake, 326
Chocolate Torta Soffice, **328,** 329
Devil's Food Snacking Cake, 337
Honey Cake with Citrus Frosting, 334, **335**
Lemon Loaf Cakes with Poached
Rhubarb, 326, **327**
Moody Tongue's Chocolate Cake, **324,** 329
Peaches and Cream Ice Cream Cake, 359
Persian Love Cake, 330
Strawberry-Honey Cake with Sour Whipped
Cream, **336,** 337
Three-Layer Thanksgiving Cake, 331
Tres Leches Cake, 334
Cantaloupe Pico de Gallo, 93
Caprese Salad, 46
CARAMEL
Caramel Potatoes, 240, **241**
Molasses Thumbprints with
Cajeta, 346, **347**
Rum-Caramel Bread Pudding with No-Churn
Pumpkin Ice Cream and Candied
Pepitas, **325,** 352
Tres Leches Cake, 334
CARBONARA
Caviar Carbonara, 76, **77**
Clams Carbonara, 79
Smoked Gouda Carbonara, **71,** 79

CARROTS
Basic Roasted Carrots, 217
Maple–Cider Vinegar Roasted Carrots, 217
Mustard-and-Soy Roast Chicken with Carrot
Top Chimichurri, 147
Roasted Carrots with Lebneh, Urfa, Pickled
Shallots and Lime, **212,** 218
Roasted Veggie Burgers with Carrot
Ketchup, 220
Skirt Steak Sizzle with Carrots and
Arugula, 188, **189**
CAULIFLOWER
Roasted Cauliflower Flatbreads with Celery
Root Puree, 274
Roasted Eggplant and Cauliflower Salad with
Tahini Green Goddess Dressing, **44,** 45
CAVIAR
Caviar Carbonara, 76, **77**
Poached Oysters with Pickled Cucumber
and Caviar, 19
CELERY
Beef-and-Celery Yakitori, **190,** 191
Red Chile Pork and Celery Stir-Fry, 163
Rye Tartines with Chicken and Pickled
Celery, 278
Sirloin, Celery and Cherry Salad, 45
Whitefish, Leek and Celery Chowder with
White Beans, 64
CELERY ROOT
Celery Root, Apple and Fennel Slaw, 214
Roasted Cauliflower Flatbreads with Celery
Root Puree, 274
Charcuterie Fried Rice, 251
CHEESE. See also Ricotta
Beefsteak Tomato and Burrata Salad with
Olive Streusel, 46
Caprese Salad, 46
Chicken Burgers with Crispy Cheddar
Cheese, 127
Chicken Parmesan, 126
Chile Grilled Cheese Sandwiches, 281
Chiles Rellenos, 232, **233**
Classic Cheese Fondue, 26
The Crowd-Pleaser Fondue, 26
Farro-and-Sausage Parmigiano, 258, **259**
Four-Cheese Fondue, 25
Giant Chicken Parmesan, 124
Greek Salad of Sorts, 46
Italian Rice Salad with Soppressata and
Caciocavallo, 251
Knife-and-Fork Grilled Cheese with
Honey, 278, **279**
Mac and Cheese with Cracker
Crumble, **84,** 85
Marinated Watermelon with
Whipped Feta, 49
Pork-and-Ricotta-Stuffed Jumbo
Shells, **70,** 82
Silky Spinach with Fresh Cheese, 228, **229**
Smoked Gouda Carbonara, **71,** 79
The Stinker Cheese Fondue, **9,** 27

Summer Margherita Pizzas, 271
Whole-Roasted Kohlrabi, 217

CHERRIES
Almond Rice Pudding with Sweet Cherry Sauce and Caramel Cream, 351
Baharat-Spiced Eggplant with Hazelnuts, Cherries and Tarragon, **234,** 235
Cherry Clafoutis with Malted Whipped Cream, 319
Cherry Gazpacho, 56, **57**
Lamb Blade Chops with Cherry and Pickled Fennel Couscous, 207
Pork Chops with Cherry-Miso Mostarda, 160, **161**
Prime Rib with Sour Cherry Conserva, Truffle and Chocolate, 192, **193**
Sirloin, Celery and Cherry Salad, 45
Sour Cherry–Glazed Ribs, 170

CHICKEN
Almond-Poached Chicken Salad, 120, **121**
Basic Chicken Stock, **66,** 68
Best-Ever Cold Fried Chicken, 140, **141**
Best-Ever Roast Chicken, **144,** 146
Buffalo Chicken Calzones, 148, **149**
Buttermilk-Brined Roast Chicken, 147
Chicken and Pork Paella, 130, **131**
Chicken-Barley Soup with Herbs and Egg Noodles, 69
Chicken Burgers with Crispy Cheddar Cheese, 127
Chicken-Orzo Soup with 10 Vegetables, **67,** 68
Chicken Parmesan, 126
Chicken Potpie, 134, **135**
Chicken Shwarma with Shredded-Lettuce Salad, **122,** 123
Chicken with Charred-Rosemary Vinaigrette, **119,** 129
Chicken with Roasted-Garlic Pan Sauce, 148
Coconut-Curry Chicken Wings, 133
Crispy Chicken Thighs with Green Papaya Salad, 129
Crispy Chicken with Champagne Vinegar Aioli, 126
Easy Braised Chicken with Kimchi, 139
Fennel, Chicken and Potato Salad, 148
Feta-Brined Chicken Sandwiches, 286
Fried Chicken Sandwiches with Hot Sauce Aioli, 285
Fried Tandoori Chicken, 127
Garlic Grilled Chicken, 146
Gas Station Fried Chicken, 143
Giant Chicken Parmesan, 124
Hobo Pack Chicken Fajitas, 124, **125**
Jerk Chicken with Scallion-Pepper Sauce, **142,** 143
Kewpie-Marinated Chicken, 146
Late-Night Fried Chicken, 140
Miso Chicken Ramen, 86
Mustard-and-Soy Roast Chicken with Carrot Top Chimichurri, 147
Pappardelle with Chicken and Pistachio-Mint Pesto, 76

Perfect Slow Cooker Chicken Breasts, 120
Piri Piri Chicken with Crispy Potatoes, 136, **137**
Red-and-Green Chicken, 136
Red Wine BBQ Chicken, **128,** 129
Rye Tartines with Chicken and Pickled Celery, 278
Saffron Chicken Tagine, **138,** 139
Sheet Pan Chicken and Mushrooms with Parsley Sauce, 130
Sheet Pan Chicken with Sourdough and Bacon, **132,** 133
Slow-Roast Chicken with Green Garlic, 147
Smoky Chicken Cutlets with Herb-Roasted Sweet Potatoes, 123
Spicy Coconut Chicken Stew with Corn, 151
Spicy Green Posole, 69
Sticky Baked Chicken Wings, 133
Stracciatella, 68
Torn Chicken with Crispy Rice and Kimchi Vinaigrette, **145,** 146

CHICKPEAS
Chickpeas and Kale in Spicy Pomodoro Sauce, **246,** 247
Spring Chickpea Salad with Avocado Hummus, 248

CHILES
Buttered Pasta with Clams and Green Chiles, 78
Buttery Spiced Peel-and-Eat Shrimp, **108,** 109
Chile-Kale Salad with Fennel, 38
Chiles Rellenos, 232, **233**
Citrus-Chile-Marinated Pork Tenderloin, 162
Green Hatch Chile Shakshuka, 294
Guajillo Mayonnaise, **370,** 371
Hmong Papaya Salad, 45
Pork Tamales, **164,** 165
Red Chile Pork and Celery Stir-Fry, 163
Salsa Picante, 372
Smoked Ribs with Blackberry-Habanero BBQ Sauce, 170, **171**
Spicy Green Posole, 69
Chili, Pork-and-Brisket, 174, **175**
Chips, Fried Zucchini, **222,** 223

CHIVES
Pork-and-Chive Dumplings, 25
Steamed Shrimp Dumplings with Chinese Chives, **21,** 22

CHOCOLATE
Bittersweet Chocolate Tarts, 315
Boston Cream Pie, **332,** 333
Chewy Black Licorice Chocolate Brownies, 338, **339**
Chocolate-Cardamom Cookies, 341
Chocolate, Cinnamon and Almond Loaf Cake, 326
Chocolate Espresso Pie Bars, 338
Chocolate Peppermint Marshmallow Cookies, 342, **343**
Chocolate Pretzels with Sea Salt, **340,** 341

Chocolate Torta Soffice, **328,** 329
Christmas-Morning Biscotti, **343,** 349
Clean Bars, **364,** 365
Devil's Food Snacking Cake, 337
Milk Chocolate–Peanut Custards, **354,** 355
Moody Tongue's Chocolate Cake, **324,** 329
Peppermint Sandwich Cookies, 341
Salty-Sweet Chocolate Pretzel Bars, 338
White Chocolate–Walnut Muffins, 307
Choucroute, Halibut with Beurre Blanc and Daikon, 100
Chowder with White Beans, Whitefish, Leek and Celery, **54,** 64

CHUTNEY
Crispy Squid with Everything Chutney, 19
Mushroom Frankies with Cilantro Chutney, **280,** 281

CLAMS
Baked Clams with Bacon and Garlic, 114
Buttered Pasta with Clams and Green Chiles, 78
Clams Carbonara, 79
Garlicky Littleneck Clams with Fregola, 114, **115**
Wu-Tang Clams, 117

CLEMENTINES
Clementine-and-Garlic Roast Turkey, **118, 150,** 151
Clementine 75, 378, **379**

COCONUT
Charred Coconut Green Beans, 231
Coconut-Curry Chicken Wings, 133
Coconut Curry Cornbread Stuffing, 267
Coconut-Sparkling Wine Spritzer, 378
Coconut Rice, 256
Raw Berry Tart with Coconut Cream, **309,** 316
Shrimp Curry with Coconut, Mustard Seeds and Chiles, 109
Spicy Coconut Chicken Stew with Corn, 151
Spinach-Sprout Salad with Coconut Ranch, 41
Sticky Coconut-Rice Bread, 307
Warm Lentil and Root Vegetable Salad with Coconut Tzatziki, 248
Coffee Granola, 296

CONDIMENTS. See also Dressings & Vinaigrettes; Jams; Marinades; Rubs; Sauces
Black Gunpowder, **367,** 374
Brewed Saffron, 352
Red Gunpowder, **367,** 375
White Gunpowder, **367,** 375
Congee with Sweet Potato, Taiwanese, **250,** 251

COOKIES & BARS
Chewy Black Licorice Chocolate Brownies, 338, **339**
Chocolate-Cardamom Cookies, 341
Chocolate Espresso Pie Bars, 338
Chocolate Peppermint Marshmallow Cookies, 342, **343**

Christmas-Morning Biscotti, **343,** 349

Clean Bars, **364,** 365

Einkorn Shortbreads, 342, **343**

Key Lime Macarons, **343,** 344

Matcha Tea Marshmallow Crispy
Treats, 345

Molasses Thumbprints with
Cajeta, 346, **347**

Peppermint Sandwich Cookies, 341

Persian Rice Cookies (Nan-e Berenji), 348

Raspberry Linzer Bars, 345

Ricotta Cookies with Sour Cream Glaze, 346

Salty-Sweet Chocolate Pretzel Bars, 338

St. Nicholas Day Letters, 348

Sweet Tea Madeleines, 345

Walnut Crescents, 348

CORN

Goat Milk–and–Corn Panna Cotta with
Blackberries, 356, **357**

Green Corn Soup, **58,** 59

Grilled Cobia Salad with Corn and
Watermelon, 49

Grilled Corn with Nasturtium Emulsion and
Flowers, 236

Scallion-Corn Muffins, 262

Couscous, Lamb Blade Chops with Cherry and
Pickled Fennel, 207

CRAB

Chilled Avocado Soup with Crab, 59

Crab and Smoked Salmon Pintxos with
Vanilla Oil, 18

Crab Summer Rolls with Nuoc Cham
Sauce, **8,** 24

Crab Tartines, 278

Deviled Crab Dip, 12

Thin Spaghetti with Crab and Asparagus, 78

Cracklings, Standing Pork Rib Roast
with, **168,** 169

CRANBERRIES

Cranberry Sauce with Cointreau and Star
Anise, 368

Roasted Cranberry-Grape Sauce, 368, **369**

CRUDO

Amberjack Crudo "Tacos," 93

Striped Bass Crudo with Popcorn Crema
and Shishito Vinaigrette, 19, **20**

CUCUMBERS

Apple-Cucumber Mignonette, **370,** 371

Grandfather's Pickles, **361,** 375

Grilled Pepper Salad with Cucumbers, 48

Margarita Jellies, 381

Poached Oysters with Pickled Cucumber
and Caviar, 19

Pork Schnitzel with Cucumber Salad, 163

Salado Verde Cocktail, 382

Spicy Margarita Punch, **376, 380,** 381

Steamed Fish with Spicy Broth and
Cucumber, 97

Yogurt-and-Cucumber Salad (Mast-o
Khiar), 371

CURRY

Curry-Mustard Mayonnaise, 187

Pork-and-Potato Curry, 166, **167**

Shrimp Curry with Coconut, Mustard Seeds
and Chiles, 109

D

DAL

Black Gunpowder, **367,** 374

Red Gunpowder, **367,** 375

White Gunpowder, **367,** 375

**DESSERTS. See also Cakes; Cookies & Bars;
Doughnuts; Meringues; Pies; Puddings;
Tarts**

Apple-Pomegranate Cobbler, 314

Cheese Flans, 355

Cherry Clafoutis with Malted Whipped
Cream, 319

Chocolate Pretzels with Sea Salt, **340,** 341

Chocolate Torta Soffice, **328,** 329

Creamy Avocado Paletas, 322

Goat Milk–and–Corn Panna Cotta with
Blackberries, 356, **357**

Milk Chocolate–Peanut Custards, **354,** 355

Neapolitan Tacos, 356

No-Churn Pumpkin Ice Cream, 352

Pineapple Paletas with Chiles, 322

Pomegranate Gelée (Jeleh-ye Anar), 319

Red Wine–Macerated Peaches, 316, **317**

Rhubarb Panna Cottas, 355

Rosewater-and-Saffron Ice Cream (Bastani
Irani), **358,** 359

Smoky Pineapple, 319

Stone Fruit Crisp, 313

Strawberry Baked Alaska, 320, **321**

Strawberry-Mango Paletas, 322, **323**

Vanilla Cupcake Ice Cream Sandwiches, 356

White Wine–Baked Apples, 316

Dill Sauce, Smoked Salmon Salad with, 37

**DIPS & SPREADS. See also Fondue;
Hummus; Mayonnaise; Salsa**

Beet Muhammara, 10

Deviled Crab Dip, 12

Green Olive Tapenade, 97

Green Tahini, 10

Grilled Rockamole, 12

Herbed Ricotta with Grilled Bread, 15

Herbed Salmon Tartare with Chips, 18

Old Bay Aioli, 64

DOUGHNUTS

Hanukkah Doughnuts, **350,** 351

Tofu Doughnuts with Mezcal Condensed
Milk, 349

**DRESSINGS & VINAIGRETTES. See also
specific salad recipes**

Basic Vinaigrette, 34

Dill Pickle Vinaigrette, 34

French-Style Vinaigrette, 34

Ginger Vinaigrette, 34

Greek Vinaigrette, 34

Kimchi Thousand Island Dressing, 52

Kimchi Vinaigrette, 34

Miso Vinaigrette, 34

Spicy Sesame Vinaigrette, 34

DRINKS

Boozy Watermelon Slushy, 378

Clementine 75, 378, **379**

Coconut-Sparkling Wine Spritzer, 378

Dreams of July, 382

East Jaffa Mule, 381

Epazote Gin Martini, 381

Faux Pastis, 385

Gin-and-Honey Spritzer, 382

Iced Tahini Mocha, 385

Lavender Gin Cocktail, **377,** 382

Layered Blackberry-and-Turmeric
Lemonade, 385

Margarita Jellies, 381

Mock Red Wine, 385

Rhubarb-Bénédictine Spritzer, 378

Rosemary-Ginger Sparkler, 378, **380**

Salado Verde Cocktail, 382

Spiced Pumpkin Lassi, **384,** 385

Spicy Agua Fresca, 382

Spicy Margarita Punch, **376,** 381

Thai Basil, Grapefruit and Chia Tonic, 382

Watermelon Margranita, 378

Duck B'steeya, 155

DUMPLINGS

Pork-and-Chive Dumplings, 25

Steamed Shrimp Dumplings with Chinese
Chives, **21,** 22

E

Eel and Rice Bowl, Japanese-Style, 94

EGGPLANT

Baharat-Spiced Eggplant with Hazelnuts,
Cherries and Tarragon, **234,** 235

Berenjenas con Miel (Fried Eggplant with
Honey), 235

Black Bass with Parsley Sauce, Eggplant,
Freekeh and Chipotles, **102,** 103

Eggplant Mash-Up, 232

Grilled Eggplant, Apricot and Tomato
Salad, 46, **47**

Grilled Sea Bass with Marinated
Eggplant, 104

Roasted Eggplant and Cauliflower Salad with
Tahini Green Goddess Dressing, **44,** 45

Spicy Eggplant Gratin, 236, **237**

EGGS

Asparagus-and-Zucchini Frittata, 294

Bacon, Egg and Shrimp Fried Rice, 252

Brock Eggs, 12

Cheesy Nachos with Fried Eggs and
Giardiniera, **360,** 365

Eggs Benedict Salad, 290

Fried Eggs with Jamón and Caviar, 290

Golden Steak and Eggs, 290, **291**

Green Eggs with Whipped Goat Cheese and Grilled Kale, 293
Persian Frittata (Kuku Sibzamini), 295
Quinoa Egg Bowl with Pecorino, 258
Ricotta and Scallion Egg Pie, 295
Rolled Japanese Omelet, 293
Soba Noodles with Poached Egg, 85
Stracciatella, 68
Tater Tot Waffles with Truffled Eggs, 303
Vietnamese Fried Eggs, 301
Za'atar Baked Eggs, **292**, 293
Empanada Gallega with Tuna, 286, **287**

ENDIVES
Grilled Endives with Sun-Dried Tomato Relish, 227
Lemony Seared Endives, 227
Persimmon-and-Endive Salad with Honey Vinegar and Avocado Oil Vinaigrette, **32**, 42
Escarole Salad, Acorn Squash and, 52, **53**
Escovitch, Snapper, 99
Everything-Bagel Popcorn, 362, **366**
Everything Knots, 265

F

Fajitas, Hobo Pack Chicken, 124, **125**
Falafel with Almond Milk Yogurt, Baked Kabocha, 31

FENNEL
Chile-Kale Salad with Fennel, 38
Fennel, Chicken and Potato Salad, 148
Pickled Fennel, 207
Quick-Pickled Fennel, 27
Seared Fennel and Tomatoes with Mustard Vinaigrette, 221
Tomato-Fennel Marinade, 374
Fig Salad, Chorizo-and-, **50,** 51

FISH. See also Anchovy; Salmon; Trout; Tuna
Amberjack Crudo "Tacos," 93
Arctic Char with Soba and Green Beans, 90, **91**
Baked Cod Fillet with Bouillabaisse Sauce and Green Olive Tapenade, 97
Black Bass with Parsley Sauce, Eggplant, Freekeh and Chipotles, **102**, 103
Brown Butter Sole with Herb Salad, 100
Citrus-Roasted Halibut and Braised Radishes, 100, **101**
Crispy Grouper Sandwiches with Green Tomato–Cucumber Relish, 282, **283**
Crusted Hake with Radishes and Turnips, **98,** 99
Fried Fish in Adobo, 105
Frogmore Stew with Old Bay Aioli, **55,** 64, **65**
Gochujang Cioppino, 110
Grilled Cobia Salad with Corn and Watermelon, 49
Grilled Fish Tacos with Cantaloupe Pico de Gallo, 93

Grilled Sea Bass with Marinated Eggplant, 104
Halibut with Beurre Blanc and Daikon Choucroute, 100
Japanese-Style Eel and Rice Bowl, 94
Salt-Baked Fish, **89,** 103
Seafood Spiedini, 106
Smoked Whitefish Pizza with Seeded Crust, 272, **273**
Snapper Escovitch, 99
Steamed Fish with Spicy Broth and Cucumber, 97
Steamed Grouper with Martini Relish and Sour Orange Sauce, **88,** 105
Striped Bass Crudo with Popcorn Crema and Shishito Vinaigrette, 19, **20**
Turmeric-Marinated Swordfish with Dill and Rice Noodles, 106, **107**
Walnut-Stuffed Fish with Barberries (Mahi-e Fivij), 104
Whitefish, Leek and Celery Chowder with White Beans, **54,** 64
Whole Roast Snapper with Sichuan Butter, 96
Whole Sardines with Parsley, 94, **95**

FLATBREADS
Buckwheat Flatbreads, 274
Moroccan Flatbreads with Roasted Tomatoes, 275
Mushroom Flatbreads with Winter Pesto, 274
Persian Flatbread (Nan-e Barbari), 268
Roasted Cauliflower Flatbreads with Celery Root Puree, 274

FONDUE
Classic Cheese Fondue, 26
The Crowd-Pleaser Fondue, 26
Four-Cheese Fondue, 25
The Stinker Cheese Fondue, **9,** 27

FRITTERS
Caesar Salad with Anchovy Fritters, 34, **35**
Tortillitas de Camarones (Shrimp Fritters), 110

FRUIT. See also specific fruits
Dreams of July, 382
Spicy Agua Fresca, 382
Stone Fruit and Hibiscus Pie, 310, **311**
Stone Fruit Crisp, 313

G

Galette, Winter, 28, **29**
Gazpacho, Cherry, 56, **57**
Ginger Vinaigrette, 34
Gnocchi with Mint–Pine Nut Pesto, Sweet Potato, 81
Goose Stuffed with Apples and Armagnac-Soaked Prunes, 156, **157**

GRAINS. See also Oats; Rice
Einkorn Shortbreads, 342, **343**
Farro-and-Sausage Parmigiano, 258, **259**

Farro Breakfast Porridge with Raspberries, 299
Spelt Garlic Knots, 264
Granola, Coffee, 296
Grapefruit and Chia Tonic, Thai Basil, 382

GRATIN
Spicy Eggplant Gratin, 236, **237**
Summer Squash Gratin, 224, **225**
Winter Squash and Savoy Cabbage Gratin with Garlic Crema, 223

GREEN BEANS
Arctic Char with Soba and Green Beans, 90, **91**
Charred Coconut Green Beans, 231
Haricots Verts and Potato Salad with Pesto, **242**, 243

GREENS. See also Arugula; Cabbage; Endives; Kale; Lettuce; Spinach
Basic Sautéed Greens, 227
Garlicky Spaghetti with Mixed Greens, 72, **73**
Mustard Greens Saag Paneer, 231
Pasta with Sausage and Mustard Greens, **80,** 81
Sautéed Radish Greens, 227
Sautéed Sweet Potato Greens, 227
Sautéed Turnip Greens, 227
Supergreen Gumbo, 60
Grits, Sancerre-Poached Scallops with Soft, **112,** 113
Gumbo, Supergreen, 60

H

HAM. See also Prosciutto
Brock Eggs, 12
Fried Eggs with Jamón and Caviar, 290
Supergreen Gumbo, 60

HARISSA
Harissa White Bean Stew with Turmeric Yogurt, **62,** 63
Spiced Harissa Ragù with Tahini Yogurt, **198,** 199

HERBS. See also specific herbs
Brown Butter Sole with Herb Salad, 100
Dried-Herb Rub, 374
Grilled Romanesco Salad with Charred-Herb Dressing, **36,** 37
Herb-Crusted Rack of Lamb, **210,** 211
Herbed Rice (Sabzi Polo), 255
Herb-Scented Mashed Potatoes, **239,** 244
Late-Night Fried Chicken, 140
Hobo Pack Bibimbap, **238,** 255
Hobo Pack Chicken Fajitas, 124, **125**

HONEY
Berenjenas con Miel (Fried Eggplant with Honey), 235
Gin-and-Honey Spritzer, 382
Honey Cake with Citrus Frosting, 334, **335**
Strawberry-Honey Cake with Sour Whipped Cream, **336,** 337

Hot Dish, Farmhouse Turkey, 152

HOT DOGS

Hot Dogs with Grilled Pickle Relish, 200

Humm Dogs, **202,** 203

Pigs in a Blanket with Black Pepper Pastry, 28

HUMMUS

Hummus and Salad Pizza, **270,** 271

Spring Chickpea Salad with Avocado Hummus, 248

J

JAMS

Pimento Cheeseburgers with Bacon Jam, 200

Tomato Jam, 304

JICAMA

Pickled Jicama and Shiso, 375

Watermelon Slabs with Jicama, 49

K

KALE

Chickpeas and Kale in Spicy Pomodoro Sauce, **246,** 247

Chile-Kale Salad with Fennel, 38

Garlicky Spaghetti with Mixed Greens, 72, **73**

Green Eggs with Whipped Goat Cheese and Grilled Kale, 293

Kale–and–Brussels Sprout Caesar Salad, 40

Kale Salad with Bacon–Brown Sugar Vinaigrette, 38, **39**

Sautéed Tuscan Kale, 227

Savory Kale Salad, 38

Sourdough Stuffing with Sausage, Red Onion, and Kale, 267

Kibbeh, Beef-and-Lamb, 204

KIMCHI

Easy Braised Chicken with Kimchi, 139

Icy-Cold Kimchi Ramen, 86

Kimchi Pork Burgers, 174

Kimchi Thousand Island Dressing, 52

Kimchi Vinaigrette, 34

Torn Chicken with Crispy Rice and Kimchi Vinaigrette, **145,** 146

Kohlrabi, Whole-Roasted, 217

L

Labneh and Pomegranate Seeds, Delicata Squash with, 223

LAMB

Beef-and-Lamb Kibbeh, 204

Grilled Lamb Chops and Peppers, 208

Herb-Crusted Rack of Lamb, **210,** 211

Lamb Blade Chops with Cherry and Pickled Fennel Couscous, 207

Lamb Burgers with Onion Soup Aioli, 203

Lamb Chops with Burnt-Bread Salsa Verde, **206,** 207

Lamb Fillets with Favas and Spring Vegetables, 205

Petite Leg of Lamb with Pickled Rhubarb Salsa, 208, **209**

Roast Leg of Lamb, 208

Slow-Cooked Lamb Neck Roti, 205

Spiced Harissa Ragù with Tahini Yogurt, **198,** 199

Spiced-Lamb Pizzas, **260,** 272

Lavender Gin Cocktail, **377,** 382

Lebneh, Urfa, Pickled Shallots and Lime, Roasted Carrots with, **212,** 218

LEMONS

Double-Lemon Scones, 304, **305**

Gin-and-Lemon Marinade, 374

Grilled Lemon Pizzas, 268

Lemon Loaf Cakes with Poached Rhubarb, 326, **327**

Lemon-Pepper Roast Turkey, 151

Lemony Seared Endives, 227

Pancetta-Wrapped Trout with Sage and Lemon, 96

Perfect Slow Cooker Chicken Breasts, 120

Quick-Brined Roast Salmon with Lemon-Garlic Oil, 93

Lentil and Root Vegetable Salad with Coconut Tzatziki, Warm, 248

LETTUCE

Buttermilk-Dressed Spring Greens, 37

Lettuces with Parmigiano, Radish and Dill Pickle Vinaigrette, 34

Little Gems with Warm Garlic Dressing, 34

Supersimple Green Salad, 40

Winter Salad with Walnut Milk Vinaigrette, 41

LIME

Green Tahini, 10

Key Lime Macarons, **343,** 344

Lingonberry Compote, Swedish Pancakes with, **288,** 300

Lobster Rolls with Spicy Sauce, Butter-Poached, 282

M

Mac and Cheese with Cracker Crumble, **84,** 85

MAPLE SYRUP

Maple–Cider Vinegar Roasted Carrots, 217

Maple-Roasted Radishes, 218

Pecan-and-Maple-Glazed Salmon, 90

MARINADES

Gin-and-Lemon Marinade, 374

Pineapple-Soy Marinade, 374

Tomato-Fennel Marinade, 374

Marshmallow Crispy Treats, Matcha Tea, 345

MAYONNAISE

Crispy Chicken with Champagne Vinegar Aioli, 126

Curry-Mustard Mayonnaise, 187

Fried Chicken Sandwiches with Hot Sauce Aioli, 285

Guajillo Mayonnaise, **370,** 371

Kewpie-Marinated Chicken, 146

Lamb Burgers with Onion Soup Aioli, 203

Old Bay Aioli, 64

MEAT. See BEEF, Lamb; Pork; Veal

MEATBALLS

Albóndigas with Mushrooms, **30,** 31

Hot-and-Sour Meatball Soup, 69

Quinoa Meatballs with Tomato Sauce and Tuscan Kale, 257

Square Meatballs with Pomodoro Sauce, 197

Vietnamese Lemongrass Meatballs, 174

Meatloaf, Leslie Bruni's, 197

MERINGUES

Spiced Italian Pecan Meringues, **343,** 344

Summer Pavlova with Fresh and Grilled Berries, **318,** 319

MINT

Minty Salsa Verde, 372

Pappardelle with Chicken and Pistachio-Mint Pesto, 76

Sweet Potato Gnocchi with Mint–Pine Nut Pesto, 81

MISO

Miso Chicken Ramen, 86

Miso Vinaigrette, 34

Pork Chops with Cherry-Miso Mostarda, 160, **161**

Molasses Thumbprints with Cajeta, 346, **347**

MUFFINS

Scallion-Corn Muffins, 262

White Chocolate–Walnut Muffins, 307

MUSHROOMS

Albóndigas with Mushrooms, **30,** 31

Mushroom Flatbreads with Winter Pesto, 274

Mushroom Frankies with Cilantro Chutney, **280,** 281

Mushroom, Sourdough and Poblano Stuffing, 267

Sheet Pan Chicken and Mushrooms with Parsley Sauce, 130

Spaghetti Pie with Wild Mushrooms and Spinach, 82, **83**

Mussels, Grill-Steamed, 117

MUSTARD

Curry-Mustard Mayonnaise, 187

Mustard-and-Soy Roast Chicken with Carrot Top Chimichurri, 147

Seared Fennel and Tomatoes with Mustard Vinaigrette, 221

Skillet Pork Tenderloin with Mustard and Smoked Paprika, 162

N

Nachos with Fried Eggs and Giardiniera, Cheesy, **360,** 365
Nasturtium Emulsion and Flowers, Grilled Corn with, 236

NOODLES

Arctic Char with Soba and Green Beans, 90, **91**
Buckwheat Soba Tiger Salad, 85
Cambodian Breakfast Noodles, 301
Chicken-Barley Soup with Herbs and Egg Noodles, 69
Curried Noodles with Shrimp, 86, **87**
Icy-Cold Kimchi Ramen, 86
Miso Chicken Ramen, 86
Noodle Rice (Reshteh Polo), 256
Soba Noodles with Poached Egg, 85
Turmeric-Marinated Swordfish with Dill and Rice Noodles, 106, **107**

NUTS. See also specific nuts

Mixed Nuts with Crispy Herbs and Garlic, 362, **363**
MoKan Nut Pie, 314

O

Oats with Muesli and Skyr, Almond, 299
Octopus with Potatoes), Pulpo a la Gallega (Grilled, 111

OIL

Crab and Smoked Salmon Pintxos with Vanilla Oil, 18
Persimmon-and-Endive Salad with Honey Vinegar and Avocado Oil Vinaigrette, **32,** 42
Quick-Brined Roast Salmon with Lemon-Garlic Oil, 93

OKRA

Fried Green Tomato and Okra Po'boys with Smoked-Fish Vinaigrette, **284,** 285
Skirt Steak with Charred-Okra and Plum Salad, 188

OLIVES

Beefsteak Tomato and Burrata Salad with Olive Streusel, 46
Chilled Tomato Soup with Parsley-Olive Salsa, 56
Green Olive Tapenade, 97
Smoked-Trout Crackers with Broken Tapenade, 16, **17**
Steamed Grouper with Martini Relish and Sour Orange Sauce, **88,** 105

ONIONS

Atún Encebollado (Tuna Smothered in Onions), 94
Beet-and-Onion Salad, 51
Braised Veal Shanks, 178
Brisket with Sweet-and-Sour Onions, **194,** 195

Hearty Mexican Cranberry Beans, 247, **254**
Pickled Onions with Trout Roe and Verbena, 13
Rabo de Toro, 211
Roasted Onion and Shallot Tarts, 220
Sourdough Stuffing with Sausage, Red Onion and Kale, 267
Tobacco Onions, 365

ORANGES

Citrus-Chile-Marinated Pork Tenderloin, 162
Steamed Grouper with Martini Relish and Sour Orange Sauce, **88,** 105

OYSTERS

Grilled Oysters with Bacon Vinaigrette, **116,** 117
Poached Oysters with Pickled Cucumber and Caviar, 19

P

PAELLA

Chicken and Pork Paella, 130, **131**
Seafood Paella, 248, **249**

PANCAKES

Potato Pancakes, 240
Swedish Pancakes with Lingonberry Compote, **288,** 300
Papaya Salad, Hmong, 45

PARSLEY

Black Bass with Parsley Sauce, Eggplant, Freekeh and Chipotles, **102,** 103
Chilled Tomato Soup with Parsley-Olive Salsa, 56
Red-and-Green Chicken, 136
Sheet Pan Chicken and Mushrooms with Parsley Sauce, 130
Tabbouleh with Pine Nuts and Almonds, 258
Whole Sardines with Parsley, 94, **95**
Parsnip Mash with Fried Brussels Sprout Leaves, 221

PASTA. See also Couscous; Noodles

Bucatini Amatriciana, 81
Buttered Pasta with Clams and Green Chiles, 78
Caviar Carbonara, 76, **77**
Chicken-Orzo Soup with 10 Vegetables, **67,** 68
Chorizo-Poached Shrimp Pasta, 79
Clams Carbonara, 79
Garlicky Spaghetti with Mixed Greens, 72, **73**
Gochujang Flank Steak and Korean Pasta Salad, 182
Greens Pasta Salad, 72
Mac and Cheese with Cracker Crumble, **84,** 85
Pappardelle with Chicken and Pistachio-Mint Pesto, 76

Pasta with Sausage and Mustard Greens, **80,** 81
Pasta with Scallops, Capers and Grilled Scallions, 113
Pork-and-Ricotta-Stuffed Jumbo Shells, **70,** 82
Rye Capellini with Yeast Butter and Truffles, 75
Smoked Gouda Carbonara, **71,** 79
Spaghetti Pie with Wild Mushrooms and Spinach, 82, **83**
Spaghetti with Squash Blossom Butter and Summer Beans, **74,** 75
Thin Spaghetti with Crab and Asparagus, 78
Vinegar-Glazed Butternut Squash Pasta Salad, 72

PEACHES

Braised Pork Shanks with Grilled Peach Salad, 166
Peaches and Cream Ice Cream Cake, 359
Red Wine–Macerated Peaches, 316, **317**

PEANUTS

Milk Chocolate–Peanut Custards, **354,** 355
Roasted Brussels Sprouts with Peanuts and Fish Sauce, 217

PEAS

Greens Pasta Salad, 72
Snap Pea–Radish Salad with Herbed Yogurt , 51

PECANS

Pecan-and-Maple-Glazed Salmon, 90
Spiced Italian Pecan Meringues, **343,** 344

PEPPERCORNS

Green Peppercorn Jus, 187
Spatchcocked Turkey with Pink Peppercorns and Thyme, 152, **153**
Vietnamese Steak au Poivre, **184,** 185

PEPPERS. See also Chiles

Brat-and-Pepper Tacos, **176,** 177
Charred Shishito Peppers with Furikake, **230,** 231
Grilled Lamb Chops and Peppers, 208
Grilled Pepper Salad with Cucumbers, 48
Snapper Escovitch, 99
Striped Bass Crudo with Popcorn Crema and Shishito Vinaigrette, 19, **20**
Persimmon-and-Endive Salad with Honey Vinegar and Avocado Oil Vinaigrette, **32,** 42

PESTO

Haricots Verts and Potato Salad with Pesto, **242,** 243
Mushroom Flatbreads with Winter Pesto, 274
Pappardelle with Chicken and Pistachio-Mint Pesto, 76
Sweet Potato Gnocchi with Mint–Pine Nut Pesto, 81

PICKLED

Corned Beef with Pickled Cabbage and Potato Salad, 196
Glazed Pickled Red Cabbage, 214
Petite Leg of Lamb with Pickled Rhubarb Salsa, 208, **209**

Pickled Fennel, 207

Pickled Jicama and Shiso, 375

Pickled Onions with Trout Roe and
Verbena, 13

Pickled Shallots, 218

Poached Oysters with Pickled Cucumber
and Caviar, 19

Quick-Pickled Fennel, 27

Rare Roast Beef with Pickled Green
Tomatoes, 196

Rye Tartines with Chicken and Pickled
Celery, 278

PICKLES

Dill Pickle Vinaigrette, 34

Grandfather's Pickles, **361,** 375

Hot Dogs with Grilled Pickle Relish, 200

Pickled Jicama and Shiso, 375

PIES

Butterscotch Pudding Pie, 314

Chicken Potpie, 134, **135**

Cumin-and-Jaggery-Glazed Apple Pie, 310

Duck B'steeya, 155

MoKan Nut Pie, 314

Pork-and-Apple Bedfordshire
Clangers, **172,** 173

Ricotta and Scallion Egg Pie, 295

Spaghetti Pie with Wild Mushrooms and
Spinach, 82, **83**

Stone Fruit and Hibiscus Pie, 310, **311**

Sweet Potato and Coffee Cream
Pie, **312,** 313

Pigs in a Blanket with Black Pepper Pastry, 28

PINEAPPLE

Hawaiian Pork Bowl, 165

Pineapple Paletas with Chiles, 322

Pineapple-Soy Marinade, 374

Smoky Pineapple, 319

PINTXOS

Crab and Smoked Salmon Pintxos with
Vanilla Oil, 18

Potato, Tuna and Pepper Confetti
Pintxos, 16

Piri Piri Chicken with Crispy Potatoes, 136, **137**

PISTACHIOS

Pappardelle with Chicken and Pistachio-
Mint Pesto, 76

Persian Love Cake, 330

PIZZA

Grilled Asparagus Pizzas with
Gremolata, 271

Grilled Lemon Pizzas, 268

Hummus and Salad Pizza, **270,** 271

Pizza Dough, 268

Smoked Whitefish Pizza with Seeded
Crust, 272, **273**

Spiced-Lamb Pizzas, **260,** 272

Summer Margherita Pizzas, 271

PLANTAINS

Tostones, 12

Plum Tarts with Arugula Salad, Savory, 224

POMEGRANATE

Apple-Pomegranate Cobbler, 314

Pomegranate Gelée (Jeleh-ye Anar), 319

Pomegranate Seeds, Delicata Squash with
Labneh and, 223

POPCORN

Breakfast Popcorn and Milk, **298,** 299

Everything-Bagel Popcorn, 362, **366**

Mexican Corn Popcorn, 362, **366**

Striped Bass Crudo with Popcorn Crema
and Shishito Vinaigrette, 19, **20**

PORK. See also Bacon; Ham; Sausages

Albóndigas with Mushrooms, **30,** 31

Bilbro Family Sausage, 177

Braised Pork Shanks with Grilled Peach
Salad, 166

Cambodian Breakfast Noodles, 301

Chicken and Pork Paella, 130, **131**

Citrus-Chile-Marinated Pork Tenderloin, 162

Ham-Brined Pork Chops, 160

Hawaiian Pork Bowl, 165

Hobo Pack Bibimbap, **238,** 255

Hot-and-Sour Meatball Soup, 69

Kimchi Pork Burgers, 174

Million Dollar Stew, 63

Pork-and-Apple Bedfordshire
Clangers, **172,** 173

Pork-and-Brisket Chili, 174, **175**

Pork-and-Chive Dumplings, 25

Pork-and-Potato Curry, 166, **167**

Pork-and-Ricotta-Stuffed Jumbo
Shells, **70,** 82

Pork Belly Porchetta with Truffles, 173

Pork Chops with Cherry-Miso
Mostarda, 160, **161**

Pork Chops with Sunflower Seed
Gremolata, **159,** 160

Pork Loin Stuffed with Apples and Pumpkin
Seeds, **158,** 162

Pork Ribs Vindaloo, 169

Pork Schnitzel with Cucumber Salad, 163

Pork Shoulder Skewers, 169

Pork Tamales, **164,** 165

Red Chile Pork and Celery Stir-Fry, 163

Roast Pork with Fingerlings and Grapes, 163

Skillet Pork Tenderloin with Mustard and
Smoked Paprika, 162

Smoked Ribs with Blackberry-Habanero
BBQ Sauce, 170, **171**

Sour Cherry–Glazed Ribs, 170

Square Meatballs with Pomodoro
Sauce, 197

Standing Pork Rib Roast with
Cracklings, **168,** 169

Vietnamese Lemongrass Meatballs, 174

Porridge with Raspberries, Farro
Breakfast, 299

**POTATOES. See also Sweet Potatoes; Tater
Tots**

Caramel Potatoes, 240, **241**

Classic Potato Salad with Crunchy
Trout Roe, 243

Crispy Potato Tarte Flambée, 25

Currywurst Poutine, 244

Green Potato Smørrebrød, 277

Grilled Baby Potato Salad, 243

Haricots Verts and Potato Salad with
Pesto, **242,** 243

Herb-Scented Mashed Potatoes, **239,** 244

Patatas Bravas, 240

Piri Piri Chicken with Crispy
Potatoes, 136, **137**

Pork-and-Potato Curry, 166, **167**

Potato Pancakes, 240

Potato, Tuna and Pepper Confetti
Pintxos, 16

Pulpo a la Gallega (Grilled Octopus with
Potatoes), 111

Roast Pork with Fingerlings and Grapes, 163

Spice-Rubbed Roasted Potatoes, 244, **245**

Veal Roast with Green Mashed
Potatoes, 178, **179**

Potlikker Vinaigrette, Summer Bean Salad
with, 247

Poussins with Apples (Joojeh ba Sib), Saffron
Butter–Basted, 156

Poutine, Currywurst, 244

PROSCIUTTO

Tater Tot Waffles with Prosciutto and
Mustard, **302,** 303

Tomatillo Toasts with Prosciutto and
Manchego, 15

Prunes, Goose Stuffed with Apples and
Armagnac-Soaked, 156, **157**

PUDDINGS

Almond Rice Pudding with Sweet Cherry
Sauce and Caramel Cream, 351

Rum-Caramel Bread Pudding with No-Churn
Pumpkin Ice Cream and Candied
Pepitas, **325,** 352

Saffron Rice Pudding (Sholeh
Zard), 352, **353**

PUMPKIN

No-Churn Pumpkin Ice Cream, 352

Spiced Pumpkin Lassi, **384,** 385

Three-Layer Thanksgiving Cake, 331

PUMPKIN SEEDS

Candied Pepitas, 355

Fragrant Rice with Pepitas and
Dates, 252, **253**

Pork Loin Stuffed with Apples and Pumpkin
Seeds, **158,** 162

Q

QUAIL

Brock Eggs, 12

QUINOA

Beet-and-Quinoa Salad, 52

Quinoa Egg Bowl with Pecorino, 258

Quinoa Meatballs with Tomato Sauce and
Tuscan Kale, 257

Quinoa Pilaf with Dried Apricots, 256

Red Quinoa Tabbouleh, 257

R

RADISHES

Citrus-Roasted Halibut and Braised Radishes, 100, **101**

Crusted Hake with Radishes and Turnips, **98,** 99

Halibut with Beurre Blanc and Daikon Choucroute, 100

Lettuces with Parmigiano, Radish and Dill Pickle Vinaigrette, 34

Maple-Roasted Radishes, 218

Radish-and-Avocado Salad, 49

Sautéed Radish Greens, 227

Snap Pea–Radish Salad with Herbed Yogurt , 51

Ragù with Tahini Yogurt, Spiced Harissa, **198,** 199

Raspberry Linzer Bars, 345

RHUBARB

Lemon Loaf Cakes with Poached Rhubarb, 326, **327**

Petite Leg of Lamb with Pickled Rhubarb Salsa, 208, **209**

Rhubarb-Bénédictine Spritzer, 378

Rhubarb Panna Cottas, 355

RICE

Almond Rice Pudding with Sweet Cherry Sauce and Caramel Cream, 351

Bacon, Egg and Shrimp Fried Rice, 252

Charcuterie Fried Rice, 251

Coconut Rice, 256

Fragrant Rice with Pepitas and Dates, 252, **253**

Herbed Rice (Sabzi Polo), 255

Hobo Pack Bibimbap, **238,** 255

Italian Rice Salad with Soppressata and Caciocavallo, 251

Japanese-Style Eel and Rice Bowl, 94

Jasmine Rice, 252

New Mexican Rice, 252

Noodle Rice (Reshteh Polo), 256

Persian Rice Cookies (Nan-e Berenji), 348

Saffron Rice Pudding (Sholeh Zard), 352, **353**

Spanish Rice, 255

Torn Chicken with Crispy Rice and Kimchi Vinaigrette, **145,** 146

RICOTTA

Cheese Flans, 355

Herbed Ricotta with Grilled Bread, 15

Pork-and-Ricotta-Stuffed Jumbo Shells, **70,** 82

Ricotta and Scallion Egg Pie, 295

Ricotta Cookies with Sour Cream Glaze, 346

Winter Galette, 28, **29**

ROSEMARY

Chicken with Charred-Rosemary Vinaigrette, **119,** 129

Roast Leg of Lamb, 208

Rosemary-Ginger Sparkler, 378, **380**

Rosemary-Ginger Syrup, 378

Rosewater-and-Saffron Ice Cream (Bastani Irani), **358,** 359

Roti, Slow-Cooked Lamb Neck, 205

RUBS

Baltimore-Style Rub, 374

Dried-Herb Rub, 374

Pure Magic Dry Rub, 170

Smoky Spiced Sugar Rub, 374

S

Saag Paneer, Mustard Greens, 231

Saffron, Brewed, 352

SALADS. See also Slaws

Acorn Squash and Escarole Salad, 52, **53**

Almond-Poached Chicken Salad, 120, **121**

Arugula-and-Squash Salad, 52

Beefsteak Tomato and Burrata Salad with Olive Streusel, 46

Beet-and-Onion Salad, 51

Beet-and-Quinoa Salad, 52

Beet Salad with Shiso, 51

Braised Pork Shanks with Grilled Peach Salad, 166

Brown Butter Sole with Herb Salad, 100

Buckwheat Soba Tiger Salad, 85

Buttermilk-Dressed Spring Greens, 37

Caesar Brussels Salad, 40

Caesar Salad with Anchovy Fritters, 34, **35**

Caprese Salad, 46

Chicken Shwarma with Shredded-Lettuce Salad, **122,** 123

Chile-Kale Salad with Fennel, 38

Chorizo-and-Fig Salad, **50,** 51

Classic Potato Salad with Crunchy Trout Roe, 243

Corned Beef with Pickled Cabbage and Potato Salad, 196

Crispy Chicken Thighs with Green Papaya Salad, 129

Eggs Benedict Salad, 290

Fennel, Chicken and Potato Salad, 148

Gochujang Flank Steak and Korean Pasta Salad, 182

Greek Salad of Sorts, 46

Greens Pasta Salad, 72

Grilled Baby Potato Salad, 243

Grilled Cobia Salad with Corn and Watermelon, 49

Grilled Eggplant, Apricot and Tomato Salad, 46, **47**

Grilled Pepper Salad with Cucumbers, 48

Grilled Romanesco Salad with Charred-Herb Dressing, **36,** 37

Haricots Verts and Potato Salad with Pesto, **242,** 243

Hmong Papaya Salad, 45

Italian Rice Salad with Soppressata and Caciocavallo, 251

Juicy Steak-and-Tomato Salad, 185

Kale–and–Brussels Sprout Caesar Salad, 40

Kale Salad with Bacon–Brown Sugar Vinaigrette, 38, **39**

Lettuces with Parmigiano, Radish and Dill Pickle Vinaigrette, 34

Little Gems with Warm Garlic Dressing, 34

Marinated Watermelon with Whipped Feta, 49

Persimmon-and-Endive Salad with Honey Vinegar and Avocado Oil Vinaigrette, **32,** 42

Pork Schnitzel with Cucumber Salad, 163

Radish-and-Avocado Salad, 49

Roasted Eggplant and Cauliflower Salad with Tahini Green Goddess Dressing, **44,** 45

Savory Kale Salad, 38

Savory Plum Tarts with Arugula Salad, 224

Shaved Artichoke Salad, 42

Sirloin, Celery and Cherry Salad, 45

Skirt Steak with Charred-Okra and Plum Salad, 188

Smoked Salmon Salad with Dill Sauce, 37

Snap Pea–Radish Salad with Herbed Yogurt , 51

Spinach-Sprout Salad with Coconut Ranch, 41

Spring Asparagus Salad with Feta, 48

Spring Chickpea Salad with Avocado Hummus, 248

Squid Salad with Herbed Breadcrumbs, 111

Summer Bean Salad with Potlikker Vinaigrette, 247

Sunflower Sprout and Herb Salad with Pomegranate Dressing, 41

Supersimple Green Salad, 40

Tabbouleh with Pine Nuts and Almonds, 258

Tomatoes with Bagna Cauda and Chinese Sausage, 48

Turkey Shwarma with Cabbage Salad, **154,** 155

Vinegar-Glazed Butternut Squash Pasta Salad, 72

Warm Lentil and Root Vegetable Salad with Coconut Tzatziki, 248

Warm Spinach and Sunchoke Salad, 42, **43**

Watermelon Slabs with Jicama, 49

Winter Salad with Walnut Milk Vinaigrette, 41

Yogurt-and-Cucumber Salad (Mast-o Khiar), 371

SALMON

Beet-and-Vodka-Cured Gravlax, 18

Charmoula-Spiced Salmon with Za'atar Vegetables, 92

Crab and Smoked Salmon Pintxos with Vanilla Oil, 18

Crispy Salmon and Wilted Chard, 90

Herbed Salmon Tartare with Chips, 18

Pecan-and-Maple-Glazed Salmon, 90

Quick-Brined Roast Salmon with Lemon-Garlic Oil, 93

Rye and Crème Fraîche Strata with Smoked Salmon, 294

Salmon Skewers with Almond Charmoula, 92

Smoked Salmon Salad with Dill Sauce, 37

Smoked Salmon Smørrebrød, 277

Tater Tot Waffles with Smoked Salmon and Caviar, 303

Salmorejo, 56

SALSA

Cantaloupe Pico de Gallo, 93

Chilled Tomato Soup with Parsley-Olive Salsa, 56

Chorizo Molletes with Roasted Salsa and Pickled Onion, 300

Lamb Chops with Burnt-Bread Salsa Verde, **206,** 207

Minty Salsa Verde, 372

Petite Leg of Lamb with Pickled Rhubarb Salsa, 208, **209**

Salsa Picante, 372

Sourdough Tortillas with Charred Steak and Scallion Salsa, 191

Salt-Baked Fish, **89,** 103

SANDWICHES. See also Burgers

Beaten Biscuit Breakfast Sandwich with Tomato Jam, 304

Buffalo Chicken Calzones, 148, **149**

Butter-Poached Lobster Rolls with Spicy Sauce, 282

Chicken Shwarma with Shredded-Lettuce Salad, **122,** 123

Chile Grilled Cheese Sandwiches, 281

Chorizo Molletes with Roasted Salsa and Pickled Onion, 300

Crab Tartines, 278

Crispy Grouper Sandwiches with Green Tomato–Cucumber Relish, 282, **283**

Empanada Gallega with Tuna, 286, **287**

Feta-Brined Chicken Sandwiches, 286

Fried Chicken Sandwiches with Hot Sauce Aioli, 285

Fried Green Tomato and Okra Po'boys with Smoked-Fish Vinaigrette, **284,** 285

Knife-and-Fork Grilled Cheese with Honey, 278, **279**

Mushroom Frankies with Cilantro Chutney, **280,** 281

Rye Tartines with Chicken and Pickled Celery, 278

Turkey Shwarma with Cabbage Salad, **154,** 155

WLTs (Wurst, Lettuce and Tomato Sandwiches), 286

Sardines with Parsley, Whole, 94, **95**

Sashimi, Local Scallop, 111

SAUCES. See also Dips & Spreads; Salsa

Apple-Cucumber Mignonette, **370,** 371

Basic Tomato Sauce, 372

Cranberry Sauce with Cointreau and Star Anise, 368

Green Cocktail Sauce, **370,** 371

Green Peppercorn Jus, 187

Homemade Applesauce with Chinese Five-Spice, 368

House Steak Sauce, 187

Roasted Cranberry-Grape Sauce, 368, **369**

Romesco Sauce, 372, **373**

SAUSAGES

Bilbro Family Sausage, 177

Brat-and-Pepper Tacos, **176,** 177

Chorizo-and-Fig Salad, **50,** 51

Chorizo Molletes with Roasted Salsa and Pickled Onion, 300

Chorizo-Poached Shrimp Pasta, 79

Currywurst Poutine, 244

Fabada (Spanish Bean Stew with Chorizo and Blood Sausage), 177

Farro-and-Sausage Parmigiano, 258, **259**

Pasta with Sausage and Mustard Greens, **80,** 81

Sourdough Stuffing with Sausage, Red Onion and Kale, 267

Tomatoes with Bagna Cauda and Chinese Sausage, 48

WLTs (Wurst, Lettuce and Tomato Sandwiches), 286

Wu-Tang Clams, 117

SCALLIONS

Jerk Chicken with Scallion-Pepper Sauce, **142,** 143

Pasta with Scallops, Capers and Grilled Scallions, 113

Ricotta and Scallion Egg Pie, 295

Scallion-Corn Muffins, 262

SCALLOPS

Grilled Scallops on the Shell, 113

Local Scallop Sashimi, 111

Pasta with Scallops, Capers and Grilled Scallions, 113

Sancerre-Poached Scallops with Soft Grits, **112,** 113

SEAFOOD. See also Fish; Shellfish

Seafood Paella, 248, **249**

Seafood Spiedini, 106

SEAWEED

Avocado Halves with Flaxseed Furikake, 296

Classic Shoyu Musubi, 24

Seaweed Soup, 60

SESAME SEEDS

Black Gunpowder, **367,** 374

Spicy Sesame Vinaigrette, 34

SHAKSHUKA

Green Hatch Chile Shakshuka, 294

Spinach Shakshuka, 294

SHALLOTS

Crispy Shallots, 106

Pickled Shallots, 218

Roasted Onion and Shallot Tarts, 220

Vermouth-Braised Shallots, **213,** 221

SHELLFISH. See also Clams; Crab; Oysters; Scallops; Shrimp; Squid

Butter-Poached Lobster Rolls with Spicy Sauce, 282

Frogmore Stew with Old Bay Aioli, **55,** 64, **65**

Gochujang Cioppino, 110

Pulpo a la Gallega (Grilled Octopus with Potatoes), 111

Shiso, Beet Salad with, 51

Shoyu Musubi, Classic, 24

SHRIMP

Bacon, Egg and Shrimp Fried Rice, 252

Buttery Spiced Peel-and-Eat Shrimp, **108,** 109

Chorizo-Poached Shrimp Pasta, 79

Curried Noodles with Shrimp, 86, **87**

Gambas al Ajillo (Garlic Shrimp), 110

Hot-and-Sour Meatball Soup, 69

Shrimp Curry with Coconut, Mustard Seeds and Chiles, 109

Shrimp with Green Banana Cocktail Sauce, 22, **23**

Steamed Shrimp Dumplings with Chinese Chives, **21,** 22

Tortillitas de Camarones (Shrimp Fritters), 110

SLAWS

Avocado-and-Cabbage Slaw, 214, **215**

Celery Root, Apple and Fennel Slaw, 214

SNACKS

Cheesy Nachos with Fried Eggs and Giardiniera, **360,** 365

Clean Bars, **364,** 365

Everything-Bagel Popcorn, 362, **366**

Grass-Fed Beef Jerky, 368

Margarita Jellies, 381

Mexican Corn Popcorn, 362, **366**

Mixed Nuts with Crispy Herbs and Garlic, 362, **363**

Spiced Candied Almonds, 362

Tobacco Onions, 365

Sorbet, Green Zebra Tomatoes with Tomato-Dashi, 15

Sorghum Butter, Buttermilk Biscuits with Salty, 262

SOUPS. See also Stews

Basic Chicken Stock, **66,** 68

Cherry Gazpacho, 56, **57**

Chicken-Barley Soup with Herbs and Egg Noodles, 69

Chicken-Orzo Soup with 10 Vegetables, **67,** 68

Chilled Avocado Soup with Crab, 59

Chilled Tomato Soup with Parsley-Olive Salsa, 56

Chilled Watercress Soup with Crème Fraîche and Za'atar, 59

Green Corn Soup, **58,** 59

Hot-and-Sour Meatball Soup, 69

Salmorejo, 56

Seaweed Soup, 60

Steamed Fish with Spicy Broth and Cucumber, 97

Stracciatella, 68

Summer Vegetable Soup, 60, **61**

Whitefish, Leek and Celery Chowder with White Beans, **54,** 64

SPINACH
Catalan-Style Spinach, 228
Creamed Spinach, 228
Creamed Spinach–Stuffed Filet Roast, 186
Sautéed Spinach, 227
Silky Spinach with Fresh Cheese, 228, **229**
Spinach-and-Arugula Bruschetta with Dukka, 16
Spinach Shakshuka, 294
Spinach-Sprout Salad with Coconut Ranch, 41
Warm Spinach and Sunchoke Salad, 42, **43**

SPROUTS
Spinach-Sprout Salad with Coconut Ranch, 41
Sunflower Sprout and Herb Salad with Pomegranate Dressing, 41

SQUASH. See also Zucchini
Acorn Squash and Escarole Salad, 52, **53**
Amberjack Crudo "Tacos," 93
Arugula-and-Squash Salad, 52
Baked Kabocha Falafel with Almond Milk Yogurt, 31
Delicata Squash with Labneh and Pomegranate Seeds, 223
Spaghetti with Squash Blossom Butter and Summer Beans, **74,** 75
Summer Squash Gratin, 224, **225**
Vinegar-Glazed Butternut Squash Pasta Salad, 72
Winter Squash and Savoy Cabbage Gratin with Garlic Crema, 223

SQUID
Crispy Squid with Everything Chutney, 19
Squid Salad with Herbed Breadcrumbs, 111

STARTERS. See also Dips & Spreads; Fondue; Toasts
Albóndigas with Mushrooms, **30,** 31
Baked Kabocha Falafel with Almond Milk Yogurt, 31
Beet-and-Vodka-Cured Gravlax, 18
Brock Eggs, 12
Chilled Tofu with Apple Soy Sauce, **14,** 15
Classic Shoyu Musubi, 24
Crab and Smoked Salmon Pintxos with Vanilla Oil, 18
Crab Summer Rolls with Nuoc Cham Sauce, **8,** 24
Crispy Potato Tarte Flambée, 25
Crispy Squid with Everything Chutney, 19
Green Zebra Tomatoes with Tomato-Dashi Sorbet, 15
Pickled Onions with Trout Roe and Verbena, 13
Pigs in a Blanket with Black Pepper Pastry, 28
Poached Oysters with Pickled Cucumber and Caviar, 19

Pork-and-Chive Dumplings, 25
Potato, Tuna and Pepper Confetti Pintxos, 16
Quick-Pickled Fennel, 27
Shrimp with Green Banana Cocktail Sauce, 22, **23**
Smoked-Trout Crackers with Broken Tapenade, 16, **17**
Spinach-and-Arugula Bruschetta with Dukka, 16
Steamed Shrimp Dumplings with Chinese Chives, **21,** 22
Striped Bass Crudo with Popcorn Crema and Shishito Vinaigrette, 19, **20**
Summer Vegetable Tower, 10, **11**
Tostones, 12
Winter Galette, 28, **29**

STEWS
Fabada (Spanish Bean Stew with Chorizo and Blood Sausage), 177
Frogmore Stew with Old Bay Aioli, **55,** 64, **65**
Gochujang Cioppino, 110
Harissa White Bean Stew with Turmeric Yogurt, **62,** 63
Million Dollar Stew, 63
Saffron Chicken Tagine, **138,** 139
Spicy Coconut Chicken Stew with Corn, 151
Spicy Green Posole, 69
Stock, Basic Chicken, **66,** 68
Stracciatella, 68
Strata with Smoked Salmon, Rye and Crème Fraîche, 294

STRAWBERRIES
Grilled Strawberry-Avocado Toasts with Burrata, **276,** 277
Strawberry Baked Alaska, 320, **321**
Strawberry-Honey Cake with Sour Whipped Cream, **336,** 337
Strawberry-Mango Paletas, 322, **323**

STUFFINGS
Coconut Curry Cornbread Stuffing, 267
Mushroom, Sourdough and Poblano Stuffing, 267
Sourdough Stuffing with Sausage, Red Onion and Kale, 267
Summer Rolls with Nuoc Cham Sauce, Crab, **8,** 24
Sunchoke Salad, Warm Spinach and, 42, **43**
Sunflower Seed Gremolata, Pork Chops with, **159,** 160

SWEET POTATOES
Crispy Potato Tarte Flambée, 25
Sautéed Sweet Potato Greens, 227
Smoky Chicken Cutlets with Herb-Roasted Sweet Potatoes, 123
Spice-Rubbed Roasted Potatoes, 244, **245**
Sweet Potato and Coffee Cream Pie, **312,** 313
Sweet Potato Gnocchi with Mint–Pine Nut Pesto, 81

Taiwanese Congee with Sweet Potato, **250,** 251

SWISS CHARD
Crispy Salmon and Wilted Chard, 90
Syrup, Rosemary-Ginger, 378

T

Tabbouleh, Red Quinoa, 257

TACOS
Amberjack Crudo "Tacos," 93
Brat-and-Pepper Tacos, **176,** 177
Grilled Fish Tacos with Cantaloupe Pico de Gallo, 93
Neapolitan Tacos, 356
Texas Chile Short Rib Tacos, 192

TAHINI
Green Tahini, 10
Iced Tahini Mocha, 385
Roasted Eggplant and Cauliflower Salad with Tahini Green Goddess Dressing, **44,** 45
Spiced Harissa Ragù with Tahini Yogurt, **198,** 199
Tamales, Pork, **164,** 165
Tandoori Chicken, Fried, 127

TAPENADE
Green Olive Tapenade, 97
Smoked-Trout Crackers with Broken Tapenade, 16, **17**

TARTS
Berry Vinegar Tart, **308,** 316
Bittersweet Chocolate Tarts, 315
Crispy Potato Tarte Flambée, 25
Giant Summer Tomato Tart, **226,** 227
Raw Berry Tart with Coconut Cream, **309,** 316
Roasted Onion and Shallot Tarts, 220
Savory Plum Tarts with Arugula Salad, 224

TATER TOTS
Tater Tot Waffles, **289,** 303
Tater Tot Waffles with Prosciutto and Mustard, **302,** 303
Tater Tot Waffles with Smoked Salmon and Caviar, 303
Tater Tot Waffles with Truffled Eggs, 303
Tatsoi, Sautéed, 227
Thanksgiving Cake, Three-Layer, 331

TOASTS
Grilled Strawberry-Avocado Toasts with Burrata, **276,** 277
Tomatillo Toasts with Prosciutto and Manchego, 15

TOFU
Chilled Tofu with Apple Soy Sauce, **14,** 15
Smoked Tofu–Stuffed Vegetables, 236
Tofu Doughnuts with Mezcal Condensed Milk, 349

TOMATILLOS
Green Cocktail Sauce, **370,** 371
Spicy Green Posole, 69

Tomatillo Toasts with Prosciutto and Manchego, 15

TOMATOES

Basic Tomato Sauce, 372

Beefsteak Tomato and Burrata Salad with Olive Streusel, 46

Bucatini Amatriciana, 81

Chilled Tomato Soup with Parsley-Olive Salsa, 56

Crispy Grouper Sandwiches with Green Tomato–Cucumber Relish, 282, **283**

Eggplant Mash-Up, 232

Fried Green Tomato and Okra Po'boys with Smoked-Fish Vinaigrette, **284,** 285

Fried Green Tomato Double Cheeseburgers, 199

Giant Summer Tomato Tart, **226,** 227

Green Zebra Tomatoes with Tomato-Dashi Sorbet, 15

Grilled Endives with Sun-Dried Tomato Relish, 227

Grill-Steamed Mussels, 117

Juicy Steak-and-Tomato Salad, 185

Moroccan Flatbreads with Roasted Tomatoes, 275

Patatas Bravas, 240

Quinoa Meatballs with Tomato Sauce and Tuscan Kale, 257

Rare Roast Beef with Pickled Green Tomatoes, 196

Salmorejo, 56

Seared Fennel and Tomatoes with Mustard Vinaigrette, 221

Spanish Rice, 255

Tomatoes with Bagna Cauda and Chinese Sausage, 48

Tomato-Fennel Marinade, 374

Tomato Jam, 304

TORTILLAS. See also Tacos

Sourdough Tortillas with Charred Steak and Scallion Salsa, 191

Vegetable Tortilla, 296, **297**

Tortillitas de Camarones (Shrimp Fritters), 110

Tostones, 12

TROUT

Classic Potato Salad with Crunchy Trout Roe, 243

Pancetta-Wrapped Trout with Sage and Lemon, 96

Pickled Onions with Trout Roe and Verbena, 13

Smoked-Trout Crackers with Broken Tapenade, 16, **17**

TRUFFLES

Pork Belly Porchetta with Truffles, 173

Rye Capellini with Yeast Butter and Truffles, 75

TUNA

Atún Encebollado (Tuna Smothered in Onions), 94

Empanada Gallega with Tuna, 286, **287**

Potato, Tuna and Pepper Confetti Pintxos, 16

TURKEY

Clementine-and-Garlic Roast Turkey, **118, 150,** 151

Farmhouse Turkey Hot Dish, 152

Lemon-Pepper Roast Turkey, 151

Spatchcocked Turkey with Pink Peppercorns and Thyme, 152, **153**

Turkey Shwarma with Cabbage Salad, **154, 155**

TURMERIC

Sautéed Cabbage with Cumin Seeds and Turmeric, **216,** 217

Turmeric-Marinated Swordfish with Dill and Rice Noodles, 106, **107**

Turnips, Crusted Hake with Radishes and, **98,** 99

V

Vanilla Cupcake Ice Cream Sandwiches, 356

VEAL

Braised Veal Shanks, 178

Veal Roast with Green Mashed Potatoes, 178, **179**

VEGETABLES. See also specific vegetables

Basic Chicken Stock, **66,** 68

Buckwheat Soba Tiger Salad, 85

Charmoula-Spiced Salmon with Za'atar Vegetables, 92

Chicken-Orzo Soup with 10 Vegetables, **67,** 68

Chicken Potpie, 134, **135**

Frogmore Stew with Old Bay Aioli, **55,** 64, **65**

Greek Salad of Sorts, 46

Grilled Romanesco Salad with Charred-Herb Dressing, **36,** 37

Lamb Fillets with Favas and Spring Vegetables, 205

Persian Frittata (Kuku Sibzamini), 295

Roasted Vegetables with Smashed-Walnut Vinaigrette, 218, **219**

Roasted Veggie Burgers with Carrot Ketchup, 220

Saffron Chicken Tagine, **138,** 139

Smoked Tofu–Stuffed Vegetables, 236

Steak and Brassicas with Red Wine Sauce, 182, **183**

Summer Vegetable Soup, 60, **61**

Summer Vegetable Tower, 10, **11**

Supergreen Gumbo, 60

Vegetable Tortilla, 296, **297**

Warm Lentil and Root Vegetable Salad with Coconut Tzatziki, 248

Winter Galette, 28, **29**

Za'atar Baked Eggs, **292,** 293

Verbena, Pickled Onions with Trout Roe and, 13

Vindaloo, Pork Ribs, 169

W

WAFFLES

Tater Tot Waffles, **289,** 303

Tater Tot Waffles with Prosciutto and Mustard, **302,** 303

Tater Tot Waffles with Smoked Salmon and Caviar, 303

Tater Tot Waffles with Truffled Eggs, 303

WALNUTS

Roasted Vegetables with Smashed-Walnut Vinaigrette, 218, **219**

Walnut Crescents, 348

Walnut-Stuffed Fish with Barberries (Mahi-e Fivij), 104

White Chocolate–Walnut Muffins, 307

Winter Salad with Walnut Milk Vinaigrette, 41

Watercress Soup with Crème Fraîche and Za'atar, Chilled, 59

WATERMELON

Boozy Watermelon Slushy, 378

Marinated Watermelon with Whipped Feta, 49

Watermelon Margranita, 378

Watermelon Slabs with Jicama, 49

Y

YAKITORI

Beef-and-Celery Yakitori, **190,** 191

Vinegar-Marinated Beef Yakitori, 191

YOGURT

Baked Kabocha Falafel with Almond Milk Yogurt, 31

Harissa White Bean Stew with Turmeric Yogurt, **62,** 63

Snap Pea–Radish Salad with Herbed Yogurt, 51

Spiced Harissa Ragù with Tahini Yogurt, **198,** 199

Warm Lentil and Root Vegetable Salad with Coconut Tzatziki, 248

Yogurt-and-Cucumber Salad (Mast-o Khiar), 371

Z

ZUCCHINI

Asparagus-and-Zucchini Frittata, 294

Fried Zucchini Chips, **222,** 223

Summer Squash Gratin, 224, **225**

Contributors

MATTHEW ACCARRINO, an F&W Best New Chef 2014, is the chef of SPQR in San Francisco.

HUGH ACHESON, an F&W Chef-in-Residence, is the chef and owner of Five & Ten and The National in Athens, Georgia, and Empire State South and Spiller Park Coffee in Atlanta.

MEIR ADONI is the chef of Lumina and Blue Sky restaurants in Tel Aviv and Nur in New York City.

TOMER AGAY is chef at Santa Katarina in Tel Aviv.

UMBER AHMAD and **SHELLY ACUÑA BARBERA** are co-chefs and partners of Mah-Ze-Dahr Bakery in New York City.

DANE ALLCHORNE is the chef at The Milk House in Kent, England.

JOSÉ ANDRÉS, an F&W Chef-in-Residence, is the chef and owner of Jaleo in Washington, DC and other restaurants in cities worldwide, including Las Vegas, Los Angeles, Miami Beach, Mexico City and Dorado, Puerto Rico.

AISHA PEW and her mother **GILDA BAIN-PEW** and partner Cole own Dovecote Café a coffee shop in Baltimore.

ROCKY BARNETTE is the chef and co-owner, with his wife **VIRGINIA LEBERMANN,** of Capri and the Thunderbird in Marfa, Texas

GREG BAXTROM is the chef at Olmsted in Brooklyn, New York.

CHRIS BEHR is the chef of the American Academy in Rome's Sustainable Food Project

JOHN BESH, an F&W Best New Chef alum, is the chef and owner of the Besh Restaurant Group, which includes August and Domenica in New Orleans and Lüke in San Antonio.

VALERIE BERTINELLI is an actress and host of the Food Network show *Valerie's Home Cooking* and co-host of *Kids Baking Championship*. She is the author of *Valerie's Home Cooking*.

RUPAM BHAGAT is the chef of Indian soul food truck and restaurant Dum in San Francisco.

RICHARD BLAIS is the chef and co-owner of Juniper & Ivy in San Diego and a judge on *Top Chef*. He is the author of *So Good*.

JAY BLACKINTON, an F&W Best New Chef 2017, is chef at Hogstone's Wood Oven on Orcas Island, Washington.

APRIL BLOOMFIELD, an F&W Chef-in-Residence and Best New Chef 2007, is the chef and co-owner of several New York City restaurants, including The Spotted Pig, The Breslin and White Gold, and Tosca Cafe in San Francisco. She is the author of *A Girl and Her Pig*.

MATT BOLUS is chef at 404 Kitchen in Nashville.

STEFAN BOWERS is chef at Feast in San Antonio.

ANDREW BROCHU is the chef at Roister, an Alinea Group restaurant, in Chicago.

BRUCE BROMBERG and **ERIC BROMBERG** are the owners of Blue Ribbon Restaurants.

ERIK BRUNER-YANG is chef at Spoken English and Maketto in Washington, DC.

FRANK BRUNI is a bestselling author and the op-ed columnist for the *New York Times*. He is the co-author of *A Meatloaf in Every Oven*.

GIANCARLO CLADESI and **KATIE CALDESI** are the chefs of Caffè Caldesi in London and the authors of *Around The World in 120 Salads*.

VAL M. CANTU, an F&W Best New Chef 2017, is chef at Californios San Francisco in the Bay Area.

FLOYD CARDOZ is the chef at Paowalla in New York City and Bombay Canteen in Bombay, India. He is the author of *Flavorwalla*.

JOSÉ CATRIMÁN is chef at La Granja on Ibiza.

JUSTIN CHAPPLE, F&W's culinary director, is the talent behind the Mad Genius Tips videos and the author of *Mad Genius Tips*.

PETER CHO, an F&W Best New Chef 2017, is chef at Han Oak in Portland, Oregon.

KAY CHUN is a former F&W Test Kitchen editor.

MELISSA CLARK is a staff food writer for the *New York Times* and the author of dozens of cookbooks, including *Dinner* and *Dinner in an Instant*.

TOM COLICCHIO is chef and owner of Temple Court, Craft, and Riverpark in New York City and restaurants in Los Angeles and Las Vegas. He is head judge on *Top Chef*.

NINA COMPTON, an F&W Best New Chef 2017, is the chef and co-owner of Compère Lapin in New Orleans.

CHRIS COSENTINO is chef and co-owner of Cockscomb in San Francisco. He is a *Top Chef Masters* winner and the author of *Offal Good*.

AMANDA CRAWFORD is wine director of Pizzana in Los Angeles.

AYESHA CURRY is the host of the Food Network show *Ayesha's Home Kitchen*. She is the author of *The Seasoned Life*.

ELI DAHLIN is a chef in Portland, Oregon. He was formerly at Dame.

OSAMA DALAL is the chef at Maiar in Tel Aviv

CHERYL DAY is the co-founder of Back in the Day Bakery in Savannah, Georgia.

SARAH DIGREGORIO is a food writer and the author of *Adventures in Slow Cooking*.

ASAF DOKTOR is the chef at Dok in Tel Aviv.

CHANTAL DUSSOUCHAUD is a French-born architectural designer and founder of Atelier de Chantal, a home accessories company.

EMILY FIFFER and **HEATHER SPERLING** are co-owners of Botanica, a restaurant, market and magazine in Los Angeles.

ANGÈLE FERREUX-MAEGHT is chef and owner of La Guinguette d'Angèle in Paris, France.

JOSHUA FOSSITT is a bartender at Bad Hunter in Chicago.

BOBBY FLAY is the chef and owner of five restaurants, including Gato and Bar Americain in NYC. He is the host of many popular Food Network shows.

COLBY GARRELTS, an F&W Best New Chef 2005, is the chef and co-owner, with pastry chef **MEGAN GARRELTS,** of Bluestem in Kansas City, Missouri, and Rye in Leawood, Kansas.

FANY GERSON is the pastry chef behind the La Newyorkina in New York City.

SAM GOINSALVOS is the chef at Henry's in Berkeley, California and was opening chef at Tartine Manufactory in San Francisco.

ELIZABETH GOLAY is the chef and co-owner of Tiffin Asha in Portland, Oregon.

JAMES GOLDING is the chef-director of The Pig in Brockenhurst, England.

ASHA GOMEZ is founder of DYAD Tea and Spice and the author of *My Two Souths*.

DELLA GOSSETT is the head of the pastry kitchen at Spago Beverly Hills.

JOSHUA GRAVES is the pastry chef at Rose Cafe in Venice.

MERRIN MAE GRAY is the sous-chef at Rossoblu in Los Angeles.

JOCELYN GUEST is a butcher and co-owner of White Gold Butchers in New York City.

YOUSEF HANNA MAGDALENA is the chef at Migdal in Israel.

ANEESHA HARGRAVE is the chef for the New York-based salad chain Chop't Creative Salads.

STEPHEN HARRIS is chef and owner of The Sportsman in Kent, England.

LORENA HERRERA and her husband Rolando Herrera own Mi Sueño Winery in Napa, California.

MASON HEREFORD is the chef at Turkey and the Wolf in New Orleans.

KATIANNA HONG is the chef at The Charter Oak in St. Helena, Napa Valley.

TED HOPSON is the chef and co-owner of The Bellwether in Studio City.

MICHAEL HUDMAN and **ANDY TICER,** F&W Best New Chefs 2013, are co-owners of five New Orleans restaurants, including Andrew Michael Italian Kitchen and Josephine Estelle.

DANIEL HUMM is the chef and co-owner of Eleven Madison Park, Made Nice and The NoMad restaurant, all in New York City.

SAM JACOBSON is the owner of the Stargazy bakeshop in Philadelphia.

ANITA JAISINGHANI is the chef at Pondichericafe in New York City.

MATT JENNINGS is chef at Townsman in Boston.

ROXANA JULLAPAT is chef of Friends & Family in Los Angeles.

JORDAN KAHN, an F&W Best New Chef 2017, is the chef of Destroyer, Los Angeles.

YASMIN KHAN is the author of *Saffron Tales*.

NICK KIM and **JIMMY LAU** are the chefs and owners of Shuko in New York City.

SOHUI KIM is the chef and co-owner of The Good Fork and Insa in Brooklyn and author of *The Good Fork Cookbook.*

KRISTIN KIMBALL is a writer and co-founder of Essex Farm, a CSA in New York.

JOE KINDRED is the chef and co-owner of Kindred in Davidson, North Carolina.

SARA KRAMER and **SARAH HYMANSON** are F&W Best New Chefs 2017 and co-chefs of Kismet in Los Angeles.

SALAH KURDI is chef of Al Ashi in Tel Aviv.

EDWARD LEE is chef and owner of several restaurants, including 610 Magnolia and Whisky Dry in Louisville, Kentucky and Succotash in Washington, DC.

MATT LEE and his brother **TED LEE** are food and travel journalists and cookbook authors.

DAVID LEFEVRE is a Los Angeles chef, who owns The Arthur J, Fishing with Dynamite and Manhattan Beach Post.

JENN LOUIS, an F&W Best New Chef 2012, is chef at Lincoln in Portland, Oregon.

AMANDA MACK is the chef at Dovecote Café in Baltimore.

LACHLAN MACKINNON-PATTERSON, an F&W Best New Chef 2005, is the chef and owner of Tavernetta in Denver

ANGIE MAR, an F&W Best New Chef 2017, is the chef and owner of The Beatrice Inn in Manhattan.

IVAN ARTURO MARQUEZ is the pastry chef of Broken Spanish in Los Angeles. Joshua McFadden is the chef and partner at Ava Gene's and partner at Tusk, both in Portland, Oregon. He is the author of *Six Seasons.*

LARRY MCGUIRE and **TOM MOORMAN** are partners of McGuire Moorman Hospitality in Austin, whose restaurants include Elizabeth Street Café, June's, Perla's and Lamberts.

MANISH MEHROTRA is the chef of Indian Accent in New York City.

JEHANGIR MEHTA is the chef of Graffiti Earth in Manhattan.

GEORGE MENDES, an F&W Best New Chef 2011, is the chef and owner of Aldea, Lupulo and Bica in New York City and the author of *My Portugal: Recipes and Stories.*

CLAUS MEYER co-founded Noma in Copenhagen and is founder of Gustu in La Paz, Bolivia. He opened the Great Northern Food Hall, Agern and Meyer's Bageri in New York City. He is also author of *Meyer's Bakery.*

AMY MILLS and her father champion pitmaster **MIKE MILLS** are authors of *Peace, Love, and Barbecue* and *Praise the Lard.*

JULIA MOMOSE is a bartender and partner at Kumiko in Chicago.

HAROLD MOORE is chef and owner of Harold's Meat + Three and Greenwich Grille in Manhattan.

SHANNON MORRISON is the pastry chef at Moody Tongue in Chicago.

MAHIN GILANPOUR MOTAMED is a Persian cook and mother of F&W's Nilou Motamed.

SEAMUS MULLEN is the chef and owner of Tertulia and El Colmado, both in New York City, and the author of *Hero Food.*

ERIKA NAKAMURA is a butcher and co-owner of White Gold Butchers in New York City.

CANDACE NELSON is founder and pastry chef of Sprinkles Cupcakes.

UYEN NGUYEN is the the executive pastry chef at Manhattan Beach Post in Los Angeles.

YOSHI OKAI, an F&W Best New Chef 2017, is chef at Otoko in Austin.

ERIN O'SHEA is chef of the Rooster Soup Co. in Philadelphia.

CHRIS PAINTER is chef at Wm. Mulherin's Sons in Philadelphia.

ÁLVARO PALACIOS is one of Spain's most influential winemakers with vineyards in the Priorat, Bierzo and Rioja regions of Spain.

JEN PELKA is the owner of The Riddler, a champagne bar in San Francisco.

STELLA PARKS, an F&W Best New Pastry Chef 2012, is the author of *Bravetart.*

SHAWN PHAM is chef of Simbal in Los Angeles.

ANGELA PINKERTON is owner of pie and sandwich shop Theorita in San Francisco.

MICHAEL PSILAKIS is chef and owner of MP Taverna, Fishtag, and Kefi in New York City. He is the author of *Live to Eat.*

MAK KWAI PUI and **LEUNG FAI KEUNG** are chefs and founders of Tim Ho Wan restaurants.

NADINE LEVY REDZEPI, is the author of *Downtime: Deliciousness at Home* and has worked with her husband, René Redzepi, at the restaurant Noma in Copenhagen.

LAURA REGE is a former F&W test kitchen senior editor.

ANDREA REUSING is chef and owner of Lantern in Chapel Hill, North Carolina. She is the author of *Cooking in the Moment.*

EVAN RICH and his wife **SARAH RICH** are chefs and owners of The Rich Table in San Francisco.

MISSY ROBBINS, an F&W Best New Chef 2010, is the chef and co-owner of Lilia in Brooklyn.

ALLISON ROBICELLI is a baker, entrepreneur, and author. She lives in Baltimore.

EAMON ROCKEY, formerly of Betony in New York City, is founder of Rockey's Milk Punch.

JESSAMYN RODRIGUEZ is founder of the nonprofit Hot Bread Kitchen, which provides food industry training for the low-income immigrant community in New York City.

DANIEL ROSE is the chef and co-owner of Le Coucou in New York City and La Bourse et la Vie and Chez la Vieille in Paris.

MARCUS SAMUELSSON is the chef and owner of twelve restaurants, including Red Rooster in New York City and Marcus B&P in New Jersey.

NOAH SANDOVAL, an F&W Best New Chef 2017, is the chef and co-owner of Oriole in Chicago.

SUVIR SARAN is the chef at Unico Taco in Long Island City, New York.

ANTHONY SASSO is the chef at La Sirena in New York City.

MICHAEL SCHLOW, an F&W Best New Chef alum, is a chef and restaurateur with 11 restaurants, including Tico in Boston and Washington, DC and Casolare in Washington, DC.

MICHAEL SCELFO is the chef and owner of Alden & Harlow and Waypoint, both in Cambridge, Massachusetts.

MELODY SHEMTOV is co-owner of Butcher & Bee and The Daily in Charleston, South Carolina.

CHRIS SHEPHERD, an F&W Best New Chef 2013, is chef and owner of Underbelly in Houston.

YOTAM SHILO is the mixologist behind Double Standard and Spicehaus in Tel Aviv.

GAIL SIMMONS is a judge on Bravo's *Top Chef* and author of *Bringing It Home.*

RYAN SMITH is chef at Atlanta's Staplehouse.

SAM SMITH is chef and partner at Tusk in Portland, Oregon.

VIKRAM SUNDERAM is the chef behind Rasika in Washington, DC.

DALE TALDE is chef and partner in Massoni and Rice & Gold in Manhattan and Talde in Brooklyn and New Jersey.

ARI TAYMOR, an F&W Best New Chef 2014, is the chef at Alma in Los Angeles.

LIZ THORPE is the author of *The Book of Cheese.*

WHITNEY TINGLE and **DANIELLE DUBOISE** are co-founders of Sakara Life.

RICO TORRES and **DIEGO GALICIA,** F&W Best New Chef 2017, are chefs and owners of Mixtli in San Antonio.

JULIA TURSHEN is the author of *Small Victories.*

DANIELE UDITI is chef and owner of Pizzana in Los Angeles.

MARCEL VIGNERON is the chef at Wolf in L.A.

BRYAN VOLTAGGIO is the chef and owner of six restaurants including VOLT in Frederick, Maryland and Range in Washington, DC.

MICHAEL VOLTAGGIO is the chef and owner of Los Angeles' ink.well and partner with his brother Bryan in Voltaggio Brothers Steak House at in Oxon Hill, Maryland.

ANYA VON BREMZEN is a food writer and the author of *The New Spanish Table* and *Paladares.*

LEVON WALLACE is the chef at 21c Museum Hotel in Nashville.

JARED WENTWORTH is the chef of Chicago's Longman & Eagle.

JONATHAN WHITENER is the chef at Here's Looking at You Los Angeles.

KEVIN WILLMANN is the chef of Farmhaus in St. Louis, Missouri.

BROOKE WILLIAMSON, winner of *Top Chef* Season 14, is the chef and co-owner of four Southern California restaurants.

LAURIE WOOLEVER is a food writer and the co-author of Anthony Bourdain's *Appetites.*

CARLOS YTURRIA is beverage director at Treasury in San Francisco.

DAN ZOARETZ is chef at Dalida Bar in Tel Aviv.

GEOFFREY ZAKARIAN is chef and partner at The Lambs Club and The National in New York City and Greenwich, Connecticut.and Point Royal in Hollywood, Florida. He is a judge on Food Network's *Chopped* and co-host of *The Kitchen.*

ANDREW ZIMMERN, an F&W Chef-in-Residence, is a chef, writer and teacher. He is the host and creator of the Travel Channel's *Bizarre Foods* series.

Measurement Guide

basic measurements

GALLON	QUART	PINT	CUP	OUNCE	TBSP	TSP	DROPS
1 gal	4 qt	8 pt	16 c	128 fl oz			
½ gal	2 qt	4 pt	8 c	64 fl oz			
¼ gal	1 qt	2 pt	4 c	32 fl oz			
	½ qt	1 pt	2 c	16 fl oz			
	¼ qt	½ pt	1 c	8 fl oz	16 Tbsp		
			⅞ c	7 fl oz	14 Tbsp		
			¾ c	6 fl oz	12 Tbsp		
			⅔ c	5⅓ fl oz	10⅔ Tbsp		
			⅝ c	5 fl oz	10 Tbsp		
			½ c	4 fl oz	8 Tbsp		
			⅜ c	3 fl oz	6 Tbsp		
			⅓ c	2⅔ fl oz	5⅓ Tbsp	16 tsp	
			¼ c	2 fl oz	4 Tbsp	12 tsp	
			⅛ c	1 fl oz	2 Tbsp	6 tsp	
				½ fl oz	1 Tbsp	3 tsp	
					½ Tbsp	1½ tsp	
						1 tsp	60 drops
						½ tsp	30 drops

us to metric conversions

The conversions shown here are approximations. For more precise conversions, use the formulas to the right.

VOLUME			WEIGHT			TEMPERATURE			CONVERSION FORMULAS
1 tsp	=	5 mL	1 oz	=	28 g	475°F	=	246°C	tsp × 4.929 = mL
1 Tbsp	=	15 mL	¼ lb (4 oz)	=	113 g	450°F	=	232°C	Tbsp × 14.787 = mL
1 fl oz	=	30 mL	½ lb (8 oz)	=	227 g	425°F	=	218°C	fl oz × 29.574 = mL
¼ c	=	59 mL	¾ lb (12 oz)	=	340 g	400°F	=	204°C	c × 236.588 = mL
½ c	=	118 mL	1 lb (16 oz)	=	½ kg	375°F	=	191°C	pt × 0.473 = L
¾ c	=	177 mL				350°F	=	177°C	qt × 0.946 = L
1 c	=	237 mL	**LENGTH**			325°F	=	163°C	oz × 28.35 = g
1 pt	=	½ L	1 in	=	2.5 cm	300°F	=	149°C	lb × 0.453 = kg
1 qt	=	1 L	5 in	=	12.7 cm	275°F	=	135°C	in × 2.54 = cm
1 gal	=	4.4 L	9 in	=	23 cm	250°F	=	121°C	(°F − 32) × 0.556 = °C